THE
URGE

THE REVERENTIAL
LIFE

THE NOTEBOOKS OF PAUL BRUNTON
(VOLUME 12)

THE RELIGIOUS URGE

THE REVERENTIAL LIFE

PAUL BRUNTON
(1898–1981)

An in-depth study of
categories seventeen and eighteen
from the notebooks

Published for the
PAUL BRUNTON PHILOSOPHIC FOUNDATION
by Larson Publications

International Standard Book Number (cloth) 0-943914-36-1
International Standard Book Number (paper) 0-943914-37-X
International Standard Book Number (series, cloth) 0-943914-17-5
International Standard Book Number (series, paper) 0-943914-23-X
Library of Congress Catalog Card Number: 87-83595

Manufactured in the United States of America

Published for the
Paul Brunton Philosophic Foundation
by
Larson Publications
4936 Route 414
Burdett, New York 14818

2   4   6   8   10   9   7   5   3

The works of Paul Brunton

A Search in Secret India
The Secret Path
A Search in Secret Egypt
A Message from Arunachala
A Hermit in the Himalayas
The Quest of the Overself
The Inner Reality
(*also titled* Discover Yourself)
Indian Philosophy and Modern Culture
The Hidden Teaching Beyond Yoga
The Wisdom of the Overself
The Spiritual Crisis of Man

Published posthumously

Essays on the Quest

The Notebooks of Paul Brunton

volume 1: Perspectives
volume 2: The Quest
volume 3: Practices for the Quest
               Relax and Retreat
volume 4: Meditation
               The Body
volume 5: Emotions and Ethics
               The Intellect
volume 6: The Ego
               From Birth to Rebirth
volume 7: Healing of the Self
               The Negatives
volume 8: Reflections on My
                  Life and Writings
volume 9: Human Experience
               The Arts in Culture
volume 10: The Orient

(continued next page)

CONTENTS

EDITORS' INTRODUCTION

This twelfth volume in *The Notebooks of Paul Brunton* emphasizes the importance of veneration for the source of Life at all levels of human development. It focuses in detail on *The Religious Urge* and *The Reverential Life*, categories seventeen and eighteen (of twenty-eight) in the personal notebooks Dr. Paul Brunton reserved for posthumous publication.

With broad tolerance and critical insight, *The Religious Urge* speaks directly to the individuating modern mentality. It welcomes the diversity in religion and acknowledges, with profound gratitude, the invaluable services of inspired spiritual teachers throughout the world's history and in the contemporary scene; but at the same time it fully sympathizes with those for whom institutional religion has become an oppressive cause of fruitless conflict. It will be useful to those struggling to re-establish reliable religious values, to those struggling for freedom from religious systems that have become stifling, to those who overvalue religion, and to those who undervalue it.

This section distinguishes the heart's ineradicable religious instinct from traditional religious forms, and clarifies the services and disservices of institutional religion. It stresses that fulfilling the religious instinct is an essential step toward the attainment of wholeness, and that this step may or may not involve the rituals and teachings of an established religious organization.

As throughout his writings, P.B. here discusses religion as the most elementary of three levels of spiritual development, succeeded in turn by the practice of mysticism and by the study and practice of mystical philosophy. A key point of this section, however, is that we should not take "most elementary" to mean "least important." Rather, we should see a complete activation and integration of the religious instinct as our *most fundamental* resource when exploring the nature of self and world. A proper integration of this instinct, in its mature form, is essential to the establishing of a correct relationship between the ego and the divine individuality.

A final introductory remark on this section concerns the fifth chapter. Readers for whom this volume is a first contact with P.B.'s writing should not be misled by the fact that most of the paras on specific religions address Christianity. While this chapter does indeed seem to be intended primarily for an audience whose religious experience has been with and through Christianity, material on a variety of other religions runs throughout *The Notebooks*. (See especially volume ten, *The Orient*.)

Part 2, *The Reverential Life*, focuses on the development of our relationship to the divine through the feeling function. It gives an individualized, practical approach to honest communion with the Sacred through intelligent prayer, rational devotion, and informed, mature humility. A wonderful resource of aspirations, devotions, and practical techniques for reducing the ego's obstructive arrogance, it is first a section to be drawn upon for inspiration and only secondarily a text to be studied.

In preparing these paras for publication, we questioned whether an intellectually contrived structure would help or interfere with material intended to evoke the feeling of reverence. At times it seemed that a thoroughly random arrangement—without a breakdown into major themes like surrender, devotion, prayer, or grace—was most desirable. But later, as the material became more familiar, the need to distinguish true reverence from false, the need to focus eventually on understanding certain practices in order to do them more effectively, became clear.

Because this section addresses primarily the feelings, however, we suggest that the reader begin by reading randomly until a para catches the attention; then pause, let the idea or suggestion sink in. Continue reading in this fashion: as moods of reverence, aspiration, humility, and reflection evoke the deeper spiritual feelings within your heart, carry those feelings into your meditation period. Done regularly and over a period of time, this kind of reading will unfold the depth and power of the insight behind these paras—will enrich not only meditations but also daily living.

The feeling function, by its own nature, learns in a cyclic rather than linear fashion. Only through creative repetition are the feelings transformed from the level of unreflective emotions to that of the subtlest sensitivity to Spirit. The way we learn to appreciate music, or a particular piece of music, illustrates this principle. For this reason, frequent small and inspiring doses of the material in this section should prove very helpful to the quester's daily practice. As the material becomes more familiar and certain questions naturally arise, or if there is a desire to concentrate on a specific practice—of prayer or devotion or humility or surrender—then the organization of the paras into specialized groups will be helpful.

One theme that emerges throughout this material is the need to understand the simultaneous presence of two points of view within each human being—the ego's and the higher self's. What role, for example, does self-effort have in evoking Grace? Can the ego really teach itself humility? Can it really surrender without the help of Grace? En route to developing a standpoint that serves both these perspectives, P.B. addresses each of these themes from a mystical viewpoint in the earlier chapters, and then from the viewpoint of philosophy in the final chapter on Grace. The double standpoint is developed further in categories nineteen and twenty and will be discussed more in the introduction to volume thirteen.

Editorial conventions with regard to quantity and structuring of material, spelling, capitalization, and other copy-editing practices for this volume are the same as have been outlined in earlier introductions. As in earlier volumes, (P) at the end of a para indicates that the para also appears in *Perspectives*, volume one of *The Notebooks* series. Once again we have many friends at Wisdom's Goldenrod and the Paul Brunton Philosophic Foundation to thank for this volume's being ready for press. We would also like to thank, on behalf of the foundation, the still growing number of readers throughout the world whose additional financial support is helping to make it possible for these books to be published at their current rate. Further information about publication schedules and related activities can be obtained from the

Paul Brunton Philosophic Foundation
P.O. Box 89
Hector, NY 14841

Part 1:

The Religious Urge

The essence of religion does not consist in dogma and ritual but in faith in a higher power, worship of that higher power, and moral purification to come closer to it.

One of the Commandments warns men not to take the name of God in vain. The simple and obvious and usually accepted meaning of this is not to utter the word "God" without seriousness and reverence. But the truer meaning is not to talk of religion—and especially of attending places of religious worship—while avoiding the effort involved in seeking a truly religious experience.

1

ORIGIN, PURPOSE OF RELIGIONS

Introductory

Religion should provide a passage along the journey to reality and not a prison for the aspiring soul.

2

Although religion is only the beginning of the quest—the first form which a recognition of the existence of a higher power takes—it would be an error to believe that it is only for the simpler types of person, that worship of this power, that the attitude of reverential devotion which it engenders, is not for more developed and also more educated minds. It is for all.

3

It would be a mistake to believe that because his search will lead him beyond religion, therefore religion is to be thrown aside. It would be more than a mistake: it would imperil his whole quest.

4

Men seek for God because they cannot help themselves. They endure tribulations and make sacrifices in this search because they love God. And the source of this driving urge lies in the tremendous contradiction between what they pathetically are and what they intuitively feel they ought to be.

5

The strength of religion does not come from the strength of popular ignorance or popular superstition. It comes from the innate need of every human creature to worship its source. The religious instinct cannot be killed.

6

Whether in the mosques of Islam or the tabernacles of Israel, the instinct which makes man acknowledge that there *is* some Power behind it all is an authentic instinct.

7

The external observances and visible signs of a formal religion are its least valuable features. More important is the living impulse which gave it birth. It must be sought in the heart's most delicate intuitions and the mind's deepest place, not in the symbolic theatrical shows.

8

The quality of religious veneration is needed by all, from the child in school to the philosopher in the world.

9

Just as the human embryo is nourished and kept alive in complete dependence upon the mother inside whose body it is carried, its consciousness being in dreamless slumber like a hibernating animal, so the human adult is in reality just as dependent for his own existence on the Overself. His spiritual yearnings are a kind of nostalgia for the direct, free, unimpeded-by-the-ego consciousness of that dependence, which is blessfully similar to the embryo's. The womb is a great symbol in several ways.

10

A quester necessarily becomes a pilgrim seeking his destination in a Holy City. He may be a metaphysician or mystic, a profound thinker or connoisseur of Orientalisms, but he may not leave out the simple humble reverences of religious feeling.(P)

11

A human being without the feeling of reverence for the higher power is an uncompleted being.

12

Religiosity as a quality is to be practised rather than religion as a creed, dogma, or sect.

13

It is essential that the religious man should believe in the existence of this power beyond himself, that he should seek to establish some kind of communion with it, and that he should practise virtue and abstain from injuring others.

14

The longing for a worthier kind of life, the aspiration for some sort of linkage or communion with Divine Power, is a sign of the transition from a purely animal consciousness to the animal-human phase of today. To be destitute of these urges quite entirely is uncommon. In the rotation of body-mind cycles—Shakespeare's "seven ages of man"—they appear or vanish briefly or durably in most persons. But because suppressions exist, substitutes often replace them.

15

Too many millions stop with their religion as a cult of worship, and do not go on to extend it into being a way of life also.

16

One day the modern world will wake up to the fact that the four fundamental tenets which the inspired religious prophets taught the old world are as literally true as that two times two is four. That there is an indefinable Power—God—which was never born and will never die. That evil-doing brings a punitive result. That man is called to practise regularly the moral duty of self-control and the spiritual duty of prayer or meditation. The prophets may have erred in some of their other teachings; they may have introduced personal opinion or inherited suggestion or imagined heavens: but they generally agreed on these four things. Why? Because these truths have always been present, outside human opinion, suggestion, or imagination, inherent in Life itself.

17

One who gives the first dynamic impulse to a spiritualizing movement inevitably creates a religion if the emotions of the masses are touched, a metaphysic if the intellect of the elite is touched, a mysticism if the intuition of individuals is touched.

18

We are like flowers torn from our natural soil and suffering the misery of separation. Our fervid mystical yearnings represent the recognition of our need to reunite with our Source.

19

If he were not *already* rooted in spiritual being—yes, here and now!— he would not be able to feel the longing to find that being.

20

All things and all creatures are within the World-Mind, draw their current of life and intelligence from this source. This is why, *in the end*, they come to feel nostalgic for it; this is why religions arise and mystics seek.

21

It is this absence of Spiritual consciousness from man which, when his experience of taking on body after body is sufficiently ripe, drives him to seek its presence.

22

Until the heart is deeply touched, religion remains a mere external form with little value to the individual and less to society.

23

Religion's value arises from its function of morally regulating the common people, teaching them elementary spiritual truths, and repeatedly reminding them of the higher purpose of their life on earth.

24

The first purpose of religion is an individual one. It is to inculcate belief in a higher power and an immaterial reality—God. The second purpose is a social one. It is to teach a code of morals to govern human relations.

25

We must face facts as they are, not as they are imagined to be, and the fact remains that the only kind of religion with which millions of its myriad adherents are acquainted is the kind which takes puerile rituals for communions with the Absolute, and degenerate priests for true vessels of It.

26

To know why he is here and what he has to do is the destiny of every man. Religion should keep pace with his mental growth and feed him this knowledge as his capacity for blind faith decreases. Where it does not do so, he either remains religious in name only and not in reality or turns away altogether from it to destructive atheistic and totalitarian movements.

27

The Light of the Overself impinging on the intellect from behind, or from a realized man, impels it to move upward. This creates a response that appears as a restless mental state, an obscure longing to know what is beyond itself, a blind aspiration. It does not know the real origin of this impulse.

28

In its original purity, before men got hold of it and turned it into organizations and institutions, a religion was a faith beyond such things, in spirit born of felt experience, or an experience born of faith.

29

The religious feeling itself is irradicable but it may get covered up by materialistic feelings or thickly overgrown by animalistic ones.

30

The spiritual instinct may appear to be totally dormant in a man but it is never killed. In another birth, and after other experiences, it will return.

31

What is true in the old religions that have vanished and in the existing ones that have survived can never become outdated, outworn. Even when the religion itself passes on, the truth in it stays among us, reincarnated into a new form, perhaps.

32

The need for religion is a need that most men have for holding on to something higher than themselves.

33

Why did the aspiration toward a higher kind of life appear in human beings? Why does the instinct to worship get felt? Why do men seek the truth about their inner being? Because their Source draws them secretly and presses them outwardly.

34

It is an urge which is felt more often than it is understood.

35

The urge to know our deeper being and the aspiration towards the Perfect lead to one and the same result, for God—perfect being—is within ourselves.

36

Religious fervour is needed but it ought not to lapse into religious fanaticism.

37

True religion would not suffer if a little intelligence were mixed with it.

38

Despite the imperfections and impostures which religions have sometimes practised, despite the superstitions which have been mingled sometimes with their official teachings, there still remains a large residue of basic truth.

39

Multitudes believe they can live without religion, which is possible, and without God, which is not. The very mind which makes this assertion and thinks it has turned its back on such a superstition as God is itself a projection from God.

40

All such turning to religion and mysticism is really due to a sense of nostalgia, a yearning for our true Home.

41

A religious revelation is also a carrier of good news, the gospel that there *is* a higher power, that we are all in relation with it, and that because of this relationship we can have access to truth, goodness, beauty, reality, and peace.

42

The reference of religion is to the unknown. Its means of reference is the incomprehensible.

43

We are moving towards a more reasonable presentation of religion and mysticism, not towards the extinction of both. Yet at times the latter possibility has seemed very real. There has been a passage in several lands from decaying religion to dynamic atheism. It is a change that is inevitable. Out of its present evil there will eventually come forth future good. If the guardians of religion have the foresight and courage to handle this transition by self-reform and self-purification they might avoid its horrors and evils. Alas! history does not support such a likelihood.

44

A groping for his godly source is instinctive in man, although it may take camouflaged forms such as absurd superstition or truth-seeking rationalism.

45

Religion includes all religions. It is a feeling rather than a form of ecclesiasticism.

46

We may accept the fact that great contributions to human welfare have been made by traditional religion while denying its claim to represent the highest truth.

47

The race has not evolved out of true religious ideas because it has not even practised them yet.

On evaluating religion

48

Those who try to make a religion out of ethics alone miss the point. They are well-intentioned but are mixing up two things which belong to different levels.

49

Those foolish men who would remove all ecclesiasticism and priesthood, all rite and dogma, do not understand in what danger they put mankind. For along with the abuses and impostures, the untruths and intolerances which have gathered around these things, there have also been precious moral guidance and precepts, valuable spiritual testimonies and reminders, benevolent philanthropies of a personal and corporate kind. This is the legacy handed down by every religion, every Church. Ought this too to be attacked and destroyed? Is it not better to purify the religion, to reform the Church, than totally to throw it to the dogs?

50

We can get a just view of religion only by placing its defects in parallel with its merits. To get at the truth about religion, and by "religion" is meant here not any particular one but the entire cluster of authentic sacred revelations throughout the world, it is quite insufficient to consider it only in decay and corruption. We must also consider its early purity and original concepts. It is quite unfair to examine only the superstitions that degrade it. We must also examine the truths that inspire it. A balanced view would recognize that underneath all its evils which atheists point out, religion holds much that is good and beneficent.

51

What is it that leads humans to seek satisfaction in religion or in mysticism? The materialists may tell us that biological or personal frustration drives many spinster women to do so, that decaying intellect drives many ageing men to do so, that the natural need of consolation drives many widows and widowers to do so. Marxists call the idea of God "the opium of the masses." That there is some basis of truth in all these criticisms must be admitted, but that there is an immeasurably broader basis of truth in the time-old declaration that man is really related to God and must fulfil the responsibilities of such a relation must be more emphatically affirmed.

52

After we have made our worst criticism of religion we have still to recognize the fact that a world left without any religion at all is a world left in grave peril. For the vacuum left by the disappearance of an outworn religion must be filled with something else. If it should be atheistic immorality, then the belief that evil-doing, selfish aggression, and injury to others are justifiable and unpunished will be rampant.

53

The shameful facts in the history of religious organizations should not be allowed to obscure the basic need of religion itself, nor to detract from the greatness of religious ideals.

54

It is only when religion divides people into hostile hating groups—those who belong to a particular denomination and those who do not—or when it keeps them from becoming acquainted with mystical and philosophic truths, that it becomes a failure, in the first case, and a traitor to itself, in the second one.

55

The history of religion is too often a history of bigotry and fanaticism. But it also shines with the record of divinely inspired, reverence-deserving men and women.

56

Without falling into harsh stricture or bitter criticism, without minimizing the unquestioned services of religion to humanity, it is still needful to be guarded against its disservices.

57

He may consider someone else's religious belief to be idiotic, but this does not mean that he should therefore be disrespectful to it. Men come to God eventually through curious ways and through various ways. Their starting points may be completely different, but their lines of movement will necessarily converge upon the same point.

58

For the karma yogi, all his activity takes on something of the nature of a ritual. Even where religions have become empty, hollow, and hypocritical, we need not be too eager to welcome their destruction. For even then they preserve a teaching, a message, a memory, and a tradition of a holier and better time in that religion's history.

59

The right answer to these questions can never be got so long as the origin, nature, place, and purpose of religion remain misunderstood by its leaders no less than by its adherents. It is this misunderstanding which accounts for its contemporary failures and historic deficiencies. The proponents of religion exaggerate its consolations and services, while the opponents exaggerate its persecutions and crimes. In the upper ground above both, we may hope to discover a truer view, for every institution can be properly appraised only by justly noting *both* its merits and demerits. We may meditate on these questions and unfold a profounder analysis not only if we collect and collate the primitive cultures in a spirit of critical pitying superiority, but also if we listen in tentative, intellectual sympathy to what these cultures have to tell us about themselves. Then only may we learn that modern critics who concentrate only on the fabular side of religion are ill-balanced judges: its significance will be found to be much larger than that.

60

It is ironical indeed that although so much of religion is mere superstitious nonsense, the portion that remains is tremendously worthwhile to humanity.

61

It is needful to weigh the services of religion against its disservices. Nor will it be useful to over-emphasize what it once was historically, whether good or evil. We must consider what it is now, in our own time.

62

The absence of such virtues as kindliness, justice, and sincerity in human relations is testimony to the absence of true religion.

63

The ecclesiastical structure and sacerdotal services of a church are useful to those who believe in them. Those who lack this faith should be tolerant, and not seek to destroy things which still help others. They have their place. The error starts when they are given the *only* place, or when the emphasis is so heavy upon the *outer* forms that the greater need of correcting and shaping the character is missed.

64

Perhaps Emerson was premature when he wrote, "The day of formal religion is past."

Prophets and Messengers

65

While the force of inward attraction and the working of evolution through outward experience are the best guarantees of the triumph of ideals, man is not left to these vast impersonal processes alone, without visible help and visible guidance. Prophets, teachers, sages, and saints appear at his side from time to time, like beacons in the darkness.

66

It was not fear of human ghosts which gave birth to early religions, as so many anthropologists believe, but faith in the Holy Ghost. It was not negative emotion that first gave moral guidance and spiritual hope and cosmic meaning to our race, but positive revelation.

67

Buried underneath the contemporary form of every religion there exists the original and authentic gospel, that which was transmitted by its Seer to his living followers, but which is too subtle or too spiritual for his present-day ones. The truths of religion and the intuitions of mysticism have nothing at all to fear from reason, but the superstitions of religion and the simulations of mysticism may well shrink from the cold contact.

68

The religious teachers of mankind are forced to make concessions to the mental aridity and the emotional coarseness of their followers. They have secrets which they are unable to share with those who lack the power to comprehend such secrets. They have touched levels of consciousness unknown to, and unknowable by, the earthly, the gross, and the complacently self-centered.

69

If a man asks himself the question, "How did I first come to think of the soul?" he will probably have to answer, "Its existence was suggested to me by others." From where did they in their turn get the idea? At some point in the line it must have originally come from a prophet, seer, or mystic.

70

Religion has taken sublime forms but it has also taken grotesque ones. The first happens when men let themselves be led aright by inspired far-seeing prophets; the other happens when they let themselves be misled by blind ones.

71

It is the great individual, and not the great institutions which come after him, who most advances mankind's spiritual progress. .

72

Countless men—both laymen and clergymen—have sought to deceive God at some time by their hypocrisy, but God has never yet deceived a single man. The promises given through every inspired prophet have always been fulfilled. If any think otherwise, it is because the prophet's own mind transmitted the message faultily, or because those who sought fulfilment failed themselves to live and think according to that pattern of a higher life which was a prerequisite condition to it.

73

Mystical experience will not be nullified and philosophical truth will not be falsified even if it could be conclusively proved that men like Jesus and Krishna were mythological constructions of the human mind and never had any historical existence. Nevertheless, we insist that they did once live in a fleshly garb, whatever fancies and fairy tales may have been embroidered around their stories by unphilosophical devotees or priestly cunning in later times. Scientific criticism may easily dispose of these fancies and tales, but it cannot so easily dispose of the fact that only a Jesus-like mind or a Krishna-like character could have invented their existence and forged their teachings—which amounts to much the same as the actual existence of Jesus or Krishna themselves. Their wisdom comes from a source that transcends the common reach.

74

If Jesus and Gautama never existed, some other men with the same deep insights must have existed to have voiced such thoughts and conveyed such inspirations. If the traditions concerning them are scanty, uncertain, and mixed with fable, this need not diminish the belief in their actual existence on the part of any just-minded person. And whatever he may think of the Churches which claim to represent them, of their contradictory teachings and all-too-human history, he ought to give his unhesitating admiration and reverence to this pair of Lights, who themselves gave three-quarters of the human race such sorely needed ideals.

75

The Incarnation-myth, which rests on the possibility of a being who is half-God and half-man, covers a partial truth. The real nature of such a being differs from the ordinary in this, that although still human, he has incarnated on this earth from a higher sphere or a more advanced planet. And he has made this great sacrifice—nearly as great indeed as a human entity's voluntary and altruistic incarnation among a group of gorillas would be—to guide, uplift, and spiritualize his less-grown fellows at a grave crisis of their existence.

76

The philosophical teaching is that the return of every prophet is an inward event and not a physical one. The common people, with their more materialist and less subtle apprehension, expect to see his body again. The initiates expect only to find his mental presence in themselves.(P)

77

If Jesus could have met Buddha, the differences in their teaching would not have prevented their delighted recognition of one another for what each was.

78

Jesus called men to life more abundant, Buddha called them to cessation of desire, Krishna to a training of the thoughts and feelings, Confucius to proper courteous and moral behaviour, while Lao Tzu gently reminded them of their higher allegiance.

79

It is quite proper to give homage and show esteem to a great soul. But it is quite another thing to deify him, to worship him, to forget utterly that he is still a human being, with human fallibility and imperfection.

80

The prophets of God are the servants of God. To deify them is to destroy this truth about their relationship. Such a false attitude must lead to false situations, priestly innovations, sectarianism and intolerance.

81

A prophet is primarily one who brings a *revelation* to mankind, who gives out what has been given to him from on high, not reasoned out by him from available facts.

82

By measuring the degree of enlightenment attained by a prophet we are able to measure the extent of reliance to be placed upon his revelation.

83

Whatever there is of abiding truth in these revelations comes from the prophet's Overself, the rest from the man's own opinion.

84

If the inspiration is received from a superhuman source, its expression goes out as a human activity. This puts all statements about God within the limitations and under the colouring of human beings: that is to say, all religions are imperfect, may at some points be at fault, or even in error. The truly educated man can only accept them as such, if he is to continue as a religious person also. Otherwise he must keep to himself and silently adore the godlike in his own heart.

85

There is room for both—a divine revelation from a personal God and a teaching from an inspired man.

86

Most professors cannot light the mystical fire, but a prophet may. For where they are served only by intellect, he is served by intuition.

87

Only after severe investigation or after severe calamity do men awaken to the dismal fact that their spiritual guides are unreliable, their religious beliefs invalid, their clichés of prayer naïve and useless. Whichever way leads them to be confronted by these unpleasant realities, they cannot go on living in doubt and discouragement for the rest of their years. So they either cast the subject of religion out of their minds altogether or, in the efflux of time, search for a more reliable guide, a better set of beliefs, and a more effective form of worship. But because the ignorant masses are incapable of finding this for themselves, someone must arise as a prophet to guide, teach and help them. He may be quite minor and quite local but if he shows them the next step ahead, he is to that extent a messenger of God.

88

Because in the past it was invariably men who appeared as prophets or founded religions while women became their followers, since the nineteenth century we have witnessed the beginnings of a reversal of this situation. That became evident when a number of minor sects arose in England, all started by women, and when Mrs. Eddy, in America, founded Christian Science, a religion to which many men have attached themselves.

89

Christ and Krishna were actualities in their lifetimes and became felt Presences after their deaths. But with time they were only symbols to remember for most people. Today they can still be found by penetrating heart and mind deeply enough. Its reality is then drawn from their own Overself.

90

When the *Koran* was imparted to Muhammed and the *Upanishads* to the

Rishees of those early times, something more than a momentary glimpse was experienced by the recipients. They were destined to play a historic role in the spiritual education of sections of mankind.

91

All religions are the outgrowth of various men's different statements about their glimpse, discovery, realization, or messenger-ship.

92

Buddha swore an oath under the sacred banyan tree, where he came to know himself, that he would not pass from our sphere of evolution until he had been reborn again and again, to help laggard humanity reach what he himself had reached. So Jesus keeps ever in inner contact with those who need him—and that means millions. He is not dead, cannot die. And the love which brought him here from afar keeps him here.

93

There are two kinds of religious founders—the Prophets and the Messengers. Jesus was a Prophet but Muhammed was a Messenger.

94

He who descends into the crowd to serve some amongst it, and to help many more to come in the generations after it, may know in advance that the crowd will persecute or kill him and yet not falter from making his appearance. If he thought only of his body and not of his purpose, or even more of the one than the other, he would surely desist from such a dangerous mission.

95

If he strives to make the public movement his own in the sense that a man strives to make his own career, he is working for the ego rather than mankind, he is serving professional ambition rather than spiritual aspiration.

96

Jesus and Gautama did not speak to mankind from different levels of being. They spoke from different levels of intellect. Their realization of the truth was one and the same. For there is only one truth. But they could only communicate it to others according to the intellectual equipment, degree, and background of its receivers.

97

Men and women were being enlightened before Gautama arose and after Jesus went. And they are being enlightened today as they will still be in ages yet unborn. Inspired teachers may come and go but the Soul in every man is eternal.

98

The mesmerized members of long-established Churches do not know, cannot comprehend, and will not be persuaded that a man can write revelation even in our own times, that the history of human inspiration has not come to an end. It is true to say that men who could report to us some news of celestial import were always rare and that they are just as rare, even rarer, today. But it is not true to assert that they became long ago extinct. If that were so, if life today, this very moment, did not still hold its possibility of delivering its divine message to some listening mind, then it would be worthless and meaningless. God would be absent from this world, the soul eviscerated from man's Being.

99

That one man could pay by his own suffering for the wrong-doing of all men is not only illogical and unfair but also impossible. It would be a claim that guilt is transferable. Such a transfer is morally wrong and karmically impossible. This is the answer to those in the West who put forward the tenet of the vicarious suffering of Jesus as the price of God's forgiveness of man, as well as to those in India who assert that substitutionary suffering of Ramana Maharshi and Ramakrishna is the result of lifting the burden of karma off their disciples' shoulders.

100

When established religions no longer reflect the pure light which their prophet originally received and radiated to his followers, and reflect only its discolourations by men's own mental creations, then the operation of the cyclic law of evolution begins to bring new prophets into incarnation. They will either purify the old corrupted religions or else establish new ones.

101

There is a wide difference in the styles of two men who meant so much to aspirants. Consider the style of Jesus' sayings and contrast it with Gautama's. The first moves directly to the idea in a pithy, if poetic, announcement, and then leaves it almost immediately. The second seeks to persuade, circles round and round it, and leaves only after its meaning is abundantly clear, only after its logic is sufficiently acceptable. That each man puts a value upon style cannot be gainsaid.

102

Had any sage who later became known as the begetter of a great religion been born in another land at another time, we may be sure that his doctrine would have been different, that both the extent and content of his teaching would have been adjusted to the altered circumstances. For he would not have revealed too much, and thus sailed over people's heads, nor spoken metaphysically where they could comprehend only physically at the most.

103

The sage who ventures forth into public with a message to deliver or a work to perform must shape both message and work to suit the circumstances that surround him.

104

Unless the message is couched in terms with which his contemporaries are familiar they cannot understand it. The prophet who is wise will adjust himself to this fact.

105

Fifteenth-century Kabir, who as a young disciple sometimes taught his own guru, said: "The saints and prophets are all dead. Only the Everliving God lives forever"—which is a hint on what to worship.

106

Why was mention of Jesus' name omitted by all contemporary historians, which could not have been the case if he had secured a really wide following? Why did the Buddha, when speaking of the Messianic teacher Metteya who would come in the far-off future, say: "He shall gather round him a following of brethren that numbers many thousands, just as I have gathered round me a following of brethren that numbers many hundreds"? How relatively disproportionate were such hundreds when compared with the millions of his contemporaries!

107

Who that reads these divine proclamations of a Jesus, these inexorably logical analyses of a Gautama, can fail to recognize that he is in the presence of uncompromising sincerity and unbending truth?

108

Old or new religions which have been established and organized soon lose much of their moral force, to the extent that their teachings become stale through excessive repetition and their tenets become meaningless through constant familiarity. This is why they must produce inspired preachers among themselves or, failing to do so, give way to inspired prophets who can restate the Message in fresh terms.

109

No one has been in the past the only recipient of divine illumination, and no one is so today.

110

Buddha knew, Jesus knew, that what was true for himself was true for all other men.

111

Revelation must precede redemption.

112

It is to be expected that primitive people in most parts of the world are more easily impressed by rituals and ceremonials than educated intellectuals are. They will more readily follow a religious preacher if he shows miracles. Whatever he then tells or teaches them receives assent and evokes faith more quickly. Even the masses of the modern industrialized world, fractionally educated as they mostly are, will to a lesser extent show the same psychological reaction. Even if he only promises a miracle but never shows one, a following will still gather around him and linger on for years, sometimes even imagining that something magical has happened: it will not be long before their invention will pass into history for the benefit of later generations! Philosophers, not desiring to impress anyone nor to acquire a following, do not generally attempt to produce a miracle, even if they might have developed some unusual powers.

113

Not a single word was ever written by Jesus. And yet others collected his spoken words and wrote them down for us. The same is true of Gautama the Buddha.

114

He "inquired of the Lord and was given the answer that any man who forbids the use of meat is not ordained of the Lord." This happened when he, the founder of a religion, was asked by a follower to adopt vegetarianism. So is human opinion delivered as God's command and human activity taken for divine working.

115

A contemporary prophet, Antonio di Nunzio, wrote: "We are only advocates of our Father, God."

116

Is it not worth noting that among those who left their spiritual mark on mankind it is the young rebels who are foremost? Both Buddha and Jesus broke with their traditions.

117

He feels sincerely that he has been entrusted with a revelation, that he has a message to deliver which is valuable and important to thousands of people, and that the task of delivering it is an exalted service, a holy privilege that needs no other reward than the moral satisfaction it brings him. Nor will it make any difference if there be only one man to listen to him during his own lifetime. The need to bear witness has become a matter of inexorable conscience. The result of bearing witness, whether it be worldly honour or worldly persecution, is a matter to which his ego has become emotionally indifferent.

118
Jesus and Buddha tried to purify great religions from the selfishness and sinfulness and commercialism which had destroyed so much of their value to humanity.

119
The message which a prophet gives to his own generation will usually hold elements of value to those of all other generations.

120
Wisdom did not stop appearing among men with any particular century for the simple reason that men did not stop appearing. Nor was it confined to any particular land. Despite that, it is correct to say there were certain great periods when it flourished most and widest. These can be found across the world and across time.

121
It might be too much to ask for an angelic or other transcendental contact, but something visible in space and present in time, some human being who is aware of his link with divinity, would—if he were to make himself known, or to be discovered—be one of the rarest of persons.

122
We do right to turn worthy traits of the character or mystical grades of the achievement of such a man into an ideal to follow. But we do wrong to turn his whole personality into an idol to worship.

123
To mistake the bearer of God's message for God is to fall into idolatry.

124
Such a man, although not a God, is still superior to all other men. For he was born to serve the highest purpose and fulfil the divinest mission.

125
It would be a mistake in philosophy or mysticism to glorify men instead of truths, but it would not be so in religion.

Purpose of popular (mass) religion

126
Those whose feeling is moved and whose mind is impressed by the beauty, antiquity, mystery, and dignity of religious ceremonial must find here their proper path.

127
Religion is the earliest, the easiest, the least-demanding response of the masses to the inner call.

128

Where there is no particular yearning for truth, no particular willingness to work on oneself, to practise discipline, and especially to learn to stand aside from the ego—which refers to the multitude of people—religion provides ideas and goals that can more easily be accepted and followed.

129

All popular religions are intended to help the larger number of people who are not ready for the deeper truth of mysticism, let alone the still deeper truths of Philosophy.

130

Those who do violence to their reason by finally accepting the dogmas of a religious authority because they have become intellectually tired, unable to arrive at firm conclusions, do so because they feel the need of some Power to lean against, to depend on, to check the activity of their own brain. This authority provides what they need, if only because it claims to represent the Higher Power.

131

Religions offer a medium for reaching the masses, who might otherwise be left by the wayside—untutored in higher values, unaware of the idea of God, the very basis of their being, unable to draw on it as the associated source of peace, comfort, healing, and hope.

132

The millions who are wrapped up from the first moment of awakening until sleepfall in their small affairs, who do not know any kind of life other than the personal ego's, need help as well as the questers. It is religion's business to give this help.

133

Most people, and certainly most uneducated people, have not developed the capacity for metaphysical thought or psychic exploration. They cannot mentally deal with invisible realities. They need the simplicities and personalizations of religion, its forms which can be seen or touched or pictured rather than abstract principles, its music which can be heard, and its rites which can be shared. They are necessarily concerned with the little matters of domestic and working life, not with the larger issues requiring leisure, interest, patience, and aspiration beyond the personal self.

134

Philosophy agrees that the bulk of mankind must be furnished with a religion and that religious doctrine must be simplified for their benefit into a few comprehensible dogmas. It is consequently a necessity for human nature at its present evolutionary stage that organized religions should take on a dogmatic character and a creedal form.

135

Whereas philosophy can be brought only to the few qualified to receive it, religion can be brought to a whole people—nay, to the whole of mankind.

136

Sacrament and symbol, rite and image belong to forms of worship intended chiefly for the populace, being outward and touchable.

137

Sorrow-laden men and disappointed women are as much entitled to the services of philosophy as those who are happier and more successful. But religion is more suited to afford them emotional solace, just as they are more likely to seek it in religion.

138

They are too much absorbed by the toil for existence and by the few pleasures that enable them to relax from this toil, to trouble themselves about the higher meaning of that existence. Nor do they possess the means—intuitional or intellectual—of solving the problems connected with the search for such a meaning.

139

Those who can give complete faith to childish dogmas, who can thrust all reason aside and throw themselves blindfolded into the arms of the religious organization sponsoring such dogmas, may certainly find a full peace of mind by doing so. They are persons who have either too little intellect or too much.

140

The masses would not listen to the truth because they could not comprehend the truth. It is practical wisdom to let them keep their myth.

141

The subtle metaphysical truths may be unintelligible to untutored minds whereas the simple religious ones may gain quick belief.

142

It is inevitable too that the poorer and unsuccessful classes should need and seek the consolations of religion much more than the wealthy or successful ones. Despite all the truth and nonsense talked about this matter, it is a fact that the latter are more contented than the former. Their spiritual yearnings are less urgent and less strong, whereas the others have to find internal or over-worldly compensations for their external and this-worldly frustrations.

143

The general mass of people cannot help but stop short of the more developed forms which spiritual seeking takes. Their inward receptivity and outward circumstances usually fix limits for them. Orthodox religion operates within these limits.

144

It is better that people should take a few steps along the Quest than none at all, better that they should rise to their higher manhood than remain in its animal phase only. Therefore mass religion—popular religion—was first created. It was better to have churches and priests so as to remind the people periodically of their religion than none at all; it was better that some priests should be allowed to marry, and others should undertake not to marry, so that both kinds could be helped. All these stages are merely provisional, for the time being, and as the lay folk and the priests progress, they can undertake further commitments.

145

Most of the religious lawgivers—but not all—were also social hygienists, like Moses and Manu. For the multitude, born to be followers, such instruction by advanced individuals was necessary.

146

The poor, having little, come to religion for relief from their burdensome lives; the rich, having satiated themselves, come to it out of curiosity about its mystery.

147

Religion must be simple in form and doctrine because it has to appeal to the unthinking masses. Alone, it is not enough to guarantee the advancement of man. It needs psychology also.

148

If men feel the need of formal religion let them have it. Let them have their churches and temples, attend their masses or mutter their creeds. But let them also be told of what is beyond these things.

149

The popular religion is usually an adjustment to the popular mentality. It is not for searchers after absolute truth. The planet is not peopled by the few searchers but by the multitude.

150

The religious viewpoint is excellent for those who cannot rise to a higher one. Like love and art it provides them with one of their supreme emotional experiences. It brings them a faith in God, hope for and love among themselves. The moral restraints which religion provides for the masses are its practical contribution to social and individual welfare, while its provision of ethical standards to limit the baser actions of men would alone justify its existence. So far as any religion succeeds in imposing moral restraint upon millions of ignorant and simple people and prevents wholesale crime among them, it succeeds in justifying its existence. But of course that is not the primary purpose of religion. It is only one-third part of that primary purpose. Therefore, we may accept the fact that great contributions to human welfare have been made by traditional religion while denying its claims to act as sole intermediary with God, as well as its exaggerated promises and apparently profound assertions which turn out to be the wildest guesses. Asseveration is hardly a suitable substitute for proof.

151

The assertion that religion has failed was often heard in World War I and sometimes heard in World War II. But the fact is that real religion has never failed and never could fail. What have failed are the false ideas and foolish dogmas, the caricatures of God that have got mixed up with what is true in religion. And not less than these, the ecclesiastical hierarchies themselves have failed, sacrificing the proper mission of religion for the selfish preservation of their institution, privilege, power, and income.

152

Until about the turn of the previous century, the truth about religion was never published frankly and plainly. This was because those who wrote about it were either one-sidedly biased in its favour and so refused to see the undesirable aspects, or else they were hostile in their personal standpoint which stopped them from mentioning the deeper merits. Those who really knew what religion was in theory and practice, what were its goods and bads, kept silent. This was because they did not wish to disturb the established faith of the simple masses or else because the latter, being uneducated, were unprepared to receive subtleties which required sufficient mental development to comprehend.(P)

153

Is it strange or is it reasonable that among every people on this planet the idea of this higher power has existed in every epoch? Whence did this idea come? To answer that priests implanted it in simple mentalities for their own selfish benefit does not answer the question but only puts it farther back. Who implanted it into the minds of the priests? No—it is one of those concepts which are absolutely necessary to human existence, whether it takes the most superstitious form or the most developed one. Its absences have always been temporary because their causes can only be temporary.

154

Judge the degree of a faith by its power to make men sacrifice their attachments, whether to things or habits—which is the same as its power to make them sacrifice themselves.

155

Behind the cruellest persecutions of misguided religious organizations and the worst impostures of faithless ones, there hides that which transcends all rituals, dogmas, priests, morality, persecution, and impostures. There is something higher than man in this cosmos. Religion is historically the most widespread way in which he marks his relation to this higher Power.

156

Whether it be a religion of impressive ceremonial and organized priesthood, or one of utter simplicity and without intermediaries, it will serve men only to the extent that it helps each individual follower to come closer to the Overself.

157

The following of moral principles is evidence of having reached a higher evolutionary stage than that of worshipping human leaders. Yet neither faith alone nor morality alone can constitute a religion. It is not enough to believe sincerely in the existence of a higher power. It is not enough to practise righteousness. The two must combine and co-operate if man is to live what may truly be called a religious life. For he is here both to exalt his consciousness above material things and to abase the selfishness of his conduct. A religion which does not inspire him to follow this twofold aim is only a half-religion. This is why a merely ethical humanitarianism can never by itself take the place of any divinely inspired religion.

158

Sceptics, whose spiritual intuition lies dormant, whose religious veneration remains inactivated, are sometimes willing to concede that religious ethics may keep mankind's wickedness within certain bounds, preventing it from being worse than it is, and may be useful for social purposes by providing charities, medical service, educational help. In short, they make religion's purpose more concerned with the community than with the individual. But this is quite imperceptive. It misses the central message of every scripture, that man must establish some sort of a connection with his Maker, be it the blindest faith or the most mystical communion. His is the responsibility to do so; it is a personal matter: for even if he attends church, participates in sacraments, listens to sermons, or accepts an imposed dogma, he has unwittingly given his own sanction to the transaction, pronounced his own judgement upon it. The accepted morality or service merely follows from this.

159

Some kind of worthy religious belief is indispensable to the true well-being of a nation. Without it existence is still possible, but it will be an existence morally flawed to an extent that will in the end, through vice, crime, and selfishness, endanger the nation.

160

The rigours of ego-crushing must be mitigated, the truths of mentalism must be diluted, if the multitude is to be reached. This is why popular religions are born.

161

The multitude need to be consoled and comforted: they need celestial messages of hope, the promise of help. The bare truth is too harsh on the ego, too impersonal to be welcome.

162

In days of anguish men turn to something, someone, some belief, or some idea to help endure them.

163

In the moment of his greatest trial, in the hour of his greatest danger, man looks to the Infinite for his last resource as a babe looks to its mother.

164

We have only to read recent or distant history to see how foolish it would be to expect the average person to accept the ethical ideals of philosophy, let alone live up to them. This is why some sort of accommodation must be made towards his moral limitations by giving him a code which he can accept and to some extent try to live up to. Here is the usefulness of popular religions which do contain such codes.

165

If everything was not told to the masses, it was largely because everything would not be acceptable to the masses, or "the simple ones," as Origen, a Church Father himself, called them. Or it was too metaphysical for them, as the history of Alexandria, with its violent riots against the schools of Philosophy, showed. Origen staunchly included reincarnation and meatless diet in his teachings there, but how far has either of these two been taken hold of by the masses then or since?

166

For most people the history of our time has put a strain upon belief—not the belief that a higher power exists, but that it protects man against his own viciousness. It helps a little at weakening moments to turn to the seers, prophets, and illumined poets to regain some strength.

167

There are many people to whom the ceremonies, the Masses, and the symbols of their religion mean life itself. By these things they are sustained to bear the troubles of human existence or are inspired to rise above them.

168

Religious beliefs, metaphysical conclusions, and mystical experiences are good and necessary in themselves; but they are more valuable still as vehicles to instigate, in those who accept them, the practice of noble virtues.

169

The sincere acceptance of any religious or mystical belief is really one response to the human need of security. Such belief offers inner security, however vaguely, as a bank balance offers outer security, for it puts the believer into favourable relation with the all-pervading mind and force behind the Universe's life and consequently behind his personal life too.

170

The first social utility of religion is to curb the passions and instincts, the hatreds and greeds of the multitude.

171

Even the worship of an imagined God is not all waste of energy. The good in it develops the worshipper himself even when no useful result is directly developed in his life outside.

172

It is not a Church's business to meddle in politics. That is the business of other kinds of organizations which desire to make social reforms or economic changes or administrative betterments. A Church has to try to change men because that is where the roots of such troubles lie.

173

If no truth at all is given the masses, they are left defenseless as soon as any great calamity falls upon them and they dare not think about it.

174

Those malefactors who cannot be deterred from evil-doing by awe of the law and its penalties might yet be put in awe of the invisible powers and their post-mortem penalties. This was in the mind of those who in classical Greek and Roman times formulated worship of the gods. This was their pragmatic and practical conclusion whether they themselves personally believed or disbelieved in the gods' existence at all. Their inheritors among statesmen, priests, and leaders supported popular religion as good for the masses, even when their own education made them sceptical of it.

175

Such people could not be at home in philosophy and would soon find that it is not what they want at all. It is better that they should not experience the discomfort of trying to be. The consolations of religion will help them more.

176

Religion carries with it certain commandments and injunctions of a moral nature. Whoever accepts a particular religion theoretically accepts these obligations with it.

177

The moral restraints which religion imposes upon its believers are a social necessity. Religion cannot be injured without injuring those restraints. But when it is no longer able to impose them, it loses much of its social value.

178

After many years of propaganda work in Europe, Miss Lounsberry, Secretary of the "Friends of Buddhism Society" of Paris, had ruefully to confess (in the *Maha Bodhi* Journal in the middle of World War II): "How can we help now, how can we bring the truth forcibly to bear on men's minds? Surely not by just saying there is no God and no Soul? For God in the West means many things, among others an inherent justice, which is to us Buddhists—Karma." This confession based on experience justifies our own attitude that religion is needed in the sense that belief in a higher Being is needed.

179

Much as we may deplore the weaknesses and failures of religion, we have to admit that without it men abolish all ethical standards and begin to act like wild beasts.

180

Without the religious faith in a higher power, without the religious organizations, buildings, and bibles which keep up and channel this faith, the mass of people might have fallen into a dense materialism devoid of any moral content.

181

Let us be perfectly clear on the matter when its critics say that Christianity (or, equally, Buddhism or Hinduism) has failed. This noble teaching has never failed anyone who has tried to live up to it, but the organizations and institutions which have taken advantage of its name too often, only to betray it, have failed.

On diversity in religion

182

Truth needs to be expressed again and again, each time differently, because it must be expressed each time in the idiom of its period.

183

In its present half-developed state, human nature would soon turn universal religion into an instrument of tyrannous repression of all ideas not held by it and into an agency for totalitarian persecution of all exponents of such ideas. The healthy, free competition of sects and creeds tends to prevent this and to compel tolerance.

184

There is a teaching to meet the need of each type of mind. Because there is such a variety of types in the world, there is room for a variety of teachings. But this said, and in practising our tolerance, we need not blind ourselves to the fact that just as there is a progression of levels of quality among these minds, so there is among the teachings.

185

The differences between men will not vanish, although they may alter as time slowly alters the men themselves. Not only are no two individuals alike but they will never become alike. What is true of their bodies is also true of their minds. All attempts to bring about a uniformity of ideas, a sameness in thinking, in character, and in behaviour, are doomed to fail in the end. Such oneness, whether coerced or suggestioned, would be artificial and unnatural, boring and undesirable.

186

The unequal development of human minds and the wide variation in human temperaments render it as undesirable as it is impossible to impose a single universal religion upon all mankind to the exclusion of all others or to unify all these varieties of belief.

187

A contemporary Indian master, Sitaramdas Omkarnath, was invited to become one of the leaders in a movement organized to unify different religions and establish co-operation among them. In his reply he wrote: "I cannot even believe that a co-ordination of the sects may ever be practicable. The sacred texts differ and the views of their writers clash. They all contributed to the good of the world, but each in his own way. I do not understand how these vast and numerous differences may be reconciled. . . . My rules come from God. Will it be possible for me to conform to rules framed by you and your associates in the proposal for unification? This is of secondary value. What is wanted is direct vision of God."

188

There is no single approach which is the only true one, the only true religion. God is waiting at the end of all roads. But some suit us better than others.

189

Each man is strongly influenced by his inborn tendencies and past experiences, including pre-reincarnational ones, to remain in, or attach himself to, some particular form of spiritual approach. It will be one most suited to his moral, intellectual, and intuitive levels *at the time*.

190

So long as there is variety among human minds and feelings, so long will there be variety among human views. Groups, parties, sects, factions, and schisms will continue to appear in religion as in politics. Given enough time this is unavoidable but not reprehensible. If in one sense it hinders a beginner's search for truth and ideals, in another sense it helps by offering more choices.

191

There are no lost souls, no individuals doomed to everlasting perdition. Nor are there saved souls, a favoured group of God's elect. There are only ignorant or well-informed individuals, immature or mature beings, unevolved or evolved persons.

192

Salvation is for all, the atheist and the devotee, the wicked and good, the ignorant and learned, the indifferent and earnest. It is only the time of its realization that is far off or near at hand but realization itself is certain. "Let no one of Thy boundless Grace despair"—thus Abu Said, an eleventh-century Persian mystic of high degree, holds out the prayerful hope to all men of their impending or eventual liberation. The New Testament parallels the *Bhagavad Gita's* promise of ultimate salvation for all, sinners and good alike. It says: "God willeth that all men should be saved and come to the knowledge of the truth."—1 Tim. 2:4.

193

A religion which would gather into itself the common truths of all existing religions would be an artificial one. It might satisfy the academic intellects. It could not satisfy the intuitive hearts. Religion is real only when it is the spontaneous flowering of one man's communion with the Divine. All attempts to invent a synthetic universal religion based on doctrines common to the existing principal ones are merely academic and bound to end in sterile futility, if not failure. For every religion worth the name must issue forth from one man, one inspired prophet, who gives it life, spirit, reality.

194

We do not say that one faith is as good as another. We acknowledge that divisions in doctrine are significant of grades in development.

195

That form of religion which will suit one temperament will not necessarily suit another. What would benefit one man might not benefit another. There is no universal religion which could profitably be adopted by
everyone. The belief that a single religious form will suit all the different
peoples throughout the world is naïve and just the kind of mechanical
doctrine likely to spring up in the minds of materialistic believers. Each
type will have to find the form suited to its own special temperament and
special mentality. Each will and ought to continue following the different
spiritual path dictated by its particular evolutionary grade. All this said,
there exist certain fundamental principles which are common to all the
varying forms of religion. There still remains a certain minimum foundation upon which all these different forms rest because they have to fit both
human needs and divine revelations.

196

Several years ago my much esteemed friend, Sir Francis Younghusband,
asked me to join the Council of the World Congress of Faiths. I reluctantly
refused to do so, because although I sympathized greatly with his noble
motives in forming the Congress I could not help regarding such well-
intentioned efforts as being unlikely to lead to any practical result. Tolerance between the members of different faiths is something greatly needed
in the world today as much as it ever has been. However, I believe it is a
purely personal matter which can only come with the development of
individual character and not by any organized efforts as such. I am disin-
clined to give active support to the World Congress of Faiths and the
Fellowship of Faiths partly because it will never be more than a drop in the
ocean, so far as effectiveness is concerned, and partly because the old
religions have had their chance and decayed. A mere mixture of such
decaying religions will not renew their vitality or render them more serviceable to mankind. It is wiser for me to devote energies to a *new* faith,
which will have the vigour of youthfulness and *do* something, than to
support a stew of stale faiths.

197

Not only are there intellectual differences between people; there are also
emotional and even aesthetic differences. Most are natural, some are developed. The preferences for bare cold services in one group are caused by
personality traits as much as the preferences for ritualistic incense-filled
services in another group. Why not accept their existence as we accept
other divergences, other variations in nature or life? Why use them as
reasons for contention and competition instead of friendship and co-operation?

198

Wherever we look in the four kingdoms of Nature, we find that she is perpetually striving to achieve diversity. She rejects and abhors a monotonous uniformity. And if we restrict our gaze to the human kingdom, we find that the differences in thought and the divergencies in feeling are the expressions not only of variations in evolutionary growth, but also of this innate striving of Nature herself.

We live in a world where every entity is formed as an individual one. Each is unique. If people have different ideas about the same thing, this is the inevitable result of the differences in their own capacities and perceptions. Why, then, should they not be themselves and therefore different?

It is useless to regret the unavoidable, to pine for the unattainable, and to strive for the undesirable. We should not waste time seeking for unity of thought or creating unity of outlook. These aims are unfeasible; these endeavours are impracticable. Even amongst the very proponents of unity, unity—whether of association or doctrine—has been non-existent. During the course of their short history, they have periodically separated themselves into factions under rival leaders. The ladder of incarnated life stretches all the way through progressively different levels of intelligence and character. It is to be expected, therefore, that there should be inequality, disagreement, and disunity. Men can arrive at the same views when they arrive at the same standpoint, when they all attain an identical level. But this is prevented from happening by the ever-active operations of re-embodiment which, by the special influences brought to bear upon particular groups and by evolution, which admits new entrants to the human kingdom and lets out old inhabitants, differentiate their various evolutionary stages, environments and conditions. A monotonous uniformity of thought and solidarity of aspiration—could they ever be obtained— would be signs of totalitarian compulsion, intellectual paralysis, or moral inactivity. They would not be a social advance, but a social calamity. What is the use of pursuing such an artificial ideal?

It is impossible for all the men and women in the world to think and feel alike. What is repugnantly intricate to one is fascinating and intriguing to another. Consequently it is impossible to persuade them to accept a single ideal, a single religion, a single metaphysic, or a single form of mysticism. This planet is not a nursing ground for the mass production of souls. Each human being represents a divine thought and is consequently working out a divine end. He may be a mere thought of God, but he is nevertheless an important thought to God. We are individuals and have each an individual purpose to fulfil even though the One abides in us all. It is better to be more realistic and less ambitious than to play Don Quixote and tilt at windmills.

199

The existence of so many sects, religions, creeds, and churches is to be traced not only to historical causes—such as rebellion against corruption—but also to psychological ones. Each corresponds to the moral level, mental quality, and intuitive refinement of its members generally.

200

Each man will understand religion in his own way, according to the grade of his intelligence and character. The more ways of approaching God that there are to be found among us, the more opportunity will there be for us to make this approach. A single way might suit one type, but will not suit others. With the offerings of several ways, these too are served. Let us therefore welcome variety and not try to destroy it.

201

The fact that so many different religious sects exist all around us indicates that where choice is free and personal, not reached under social pressure or by family tradition, response to truth shapes itself according to the capacity-level.

202

Salvation is as open to those who adhere to some church or sect as it is to those of no church at all.

203

A single teaching could suit persons at widely different degrees of advancement only by lowering its quality to suit the lowest degree. But it would then no longer be itself.

204

The anti-materialistic teaching will find more response if it suits the needs of the country, the people, and the epoch in which he lives.

205

A union of many religions is a naïve idea, but a tolerant attitude among many religions is an excellent one.

206

The different religions expressed different kinds of temperaments, and different sects within a single religion express different mentalities.

207

The Qualities of a man's character are much more important than the tenets of his formal creed.

208

The protagonists of a world federation of faiths or of a reunion of all Christian sects or of a federation of all rival theosophical societies do not grasp the fact that a marriage of two or more half-corpses cannot produce a living body.

209

The capacity to receive truth is variable from person to person; it is not present equally in all.

On choosing one's religion

210

In this area of religious belief there is, for most people with faith, mere obedience to tradition. Either they do what is correctly anticipated from them, or they do some original thinking for themselves. Thus their religious outlook depends either on surrender to circumstances and environment or on their intellectual capacity. The first group seeks comfort and ease; the second has begun, but only begun, the search for truth.

211

Real thought is rare. How few follow a religion because they have chosen it after independent investigation and reflection, how many slavishly refuse to examine it impartially only because it happens to be popular at the time and in the place where they are born or live! As if popularity were a test of truth!

212

Formal religion does not give enough satisfaction to large numbers of people. Yet open atheism leaves them without hope, in despair at the futility of individual life. Then there are large numbers of others who, unquestioning and complacent, do not trouble their heads beyond their personal and family selfish interests, who observe the forms of their inherited religion in a superficial conventional way and are inwardly unaffected by them.

213

I know that most men depend—and must depend—upon some religious revelation to which they were introduced by their family. In this way a higher faith was ready to hand from birth. But he who awakens to a still higher need, his *own* revelation, has the right to seek for it.

214

Most people have had no revelation, no vision, no soul-shaking inner experience. They must perforce accept the word of someone who has. But unless they are content to remain in the religious denomination acquired by heredity, not by the search for truth, they will be confronted by the difficulty of how to choose among teachers, preachers, and prophets who all contradict one another.

215

There is something radically wrong in rating men quantitatively instead of qualitatively. There is something grotesque in the spectacle of ill-informed conclusions and impulsive judgements on an equality with the broad-based conclusions and well-matured judgements of a trained intelligence and disciplined character. Therefore I do not believe in the fetish of counting the number of followers of a doctrine, and using its largeness as an indicator of its truth.

216

People who belong by birth or choice to any particular cult, religion, or group usually believe that theirs is the highest in theory and the best in practice. This belief usually becomes a mechanical one, so that mere membership in the organization tends to make for less endeavour to find God than if they were thrown on their own individual resources.

217

The irony is that in religion most people distrust the new, and underestimate the unorganized. They feel that in the old, the traditional, and the established religious group they can take hold of what is solid and firm, reliable and safe.

218

Although huge established organizations command respect and claim authority in religion there is a real need of detached independents in this same field.

219

Adherence to any religion may be either a personal convenience or a flaming conviction. It is reckoned enough to be labelled a member of some conventional orthodox and organized religious community to be regarded as having fulfilled religious duty. Because men measure human spirituality by human conformity, history mocks them and punishes their error with evils and crimes, with sordid happenings and brutal deeds. Whatever faith a man attaches himself to, outside the faith of his forefathers, will depend partly on his intellectual level and partly on his personal inclinations. If he is sincere, he will illustrate the difference between the social inheritance and profound conviction motives, as well as demonstrate the superiority of the conscious adoption of a faith after wide search and comparative examination over the mere inheritance of a faith after geographical accident or chance of birth. For the source and form of religious belief have usually been the parents of the believer. Men accept their faith from their fathers and never question it. Yet is what his forefathers happened to believe in religion a valid standard of what is true in religion? What shall it profit a man if he enters a religious building merely because his neighbours expect him to go, or if he takes part in a religious gathering for the same reason that soldiers take part in military drill? It is impossible for those held in creedal chains or organizational straitjackets to keep their judgement free and their thinking unconditional. A respect for the human personality cannot submit entirely to the extremism which would impose a rigid straitjacket of total authoritarianism. Indeed, a man is likely to be harmed by it. This happens as soon as he allows his leaders to imprison him in the tradition or enslave him in the institution. He is then no longer able to benefit by, and is instead robbed of, all the other knowledge or inspiration available outside the little space in which he is shut. The men of this era have to be led closer to the freedom of their higher self. No organization can do this because all organizations necessarily demand fealty and impose bondage.

220

There is a wide difference between people who come by their religion through inward private conviction and those who come by it through outward social convenience.

221

The self-deception into which the masses fall is to start their thought about religion with the presumption that it must necessarily be organized, institutionalized, traditional, and professionalized if it is to be genuine religion at all.

222

People are easily impressed by size, tradition, wealth, prestige. They are overawed by a "great" religion with many fine churches, a long past history, and a well-organized structure. They will follow such a religion even though its ministers are spiritually dead whereas they will not even look twice at a man who is shining with the Overself's light and permeated through and through with the consciousness of God's presence.

223

It is one thing to accept a religion through traditional authority and another to accept it through a search for truth.

224

What faith a man chooses for himself, if he goes so far as to reject his ancestral faith, is partly a matter of temperament, partly of past experience and present opportunity, partly of moral character and intellectual development.

225

The real trouble is that many mistake tradition for religion. When they can learn the profound difference between these two things, when they can appreciate that a social relic is not a spiritual force, they will become truly religious.

226

A worship which is daily, and not weekly, is required of him who is really religious.

227

Freedom from the limitations of membership in organized religion may be good but anchorage in its harbour is in another way also good. Each man decides for himself.

228

At some point down the line of being born by family into a particular religious persuasion, the first ancestor to have the courage—unless he was forced by ruling tyranny or bribed by social ambition—to become a convert must be applauded. He may have been mistaken, his mind weak enough to let itself be misguided, but he did have the faith that he was moving from an inferior religious form to a superior one.

229

It is he who has chosen to remain in the church into which he was brought by birth or to join the one which pleases him better. It is he who must answer for the decision, bear the responsibility. The institution has its own but that is separate.

230

Too often we meet men holding at the same time beliefs which are contradictory. This is mostly pertaining to their respect for science and their reliance on intellect in professional matters being kept from colliding with their religious dogmas and prejudices.

231

In most cases people stay with their inherited creed but in others they seek and find one which reflects their own inclinations, character, or limitations.

232

Where a religion is organized and codified, validated by long tradition, and spread by a large number of people, the question of its truth is not a pressing one to its followers.

233

To keep one's religious affiliation through heredity or habit but to live without daily reverence or active faith—this is not true religion; it is pseudo-religion. Yet this is precisely what conventional hypocrisy so lazily accepts.

234

The herd of men and women are so hypnotized by the prestige of an institution that they never stop to question the truth of the institution. This is why Jesus was persecuted and Socrates was poisoned.

235

The largest followings of religious groups belong to the least rational and least inspired ones. And the followers are there usually because their parents were there, not because they have thought their way into these groups.

236

A wide experience of men shows up the strange fact that they may be well-talented, brilliantly executive, or acute reasoners, yet their religious beliefs will often be kept in closed compartments, unaffected by their mental powers, undisturbed by their excellent judgement, and hence quite primitive and quite irrational.

237

Some men, all too many men, are as stupid in their religious belief and practice as they are clever in their business ideas and activity. If they were to manage their businesses in the same credulous unreasoning and superstitious way in which they follow their religion, they would go bankrupt.

Grading teaching to capacity

238

Why did primitive races bring a highly spiritual wisdom to rest on the same pillow as barbaric superstition? The question is easily answered by asserting "the need of grading teaching to capacity."

239

Instruction in religion and all other subjects must be adapted to the level of the learner, or time and energy will be wasted, while the desired result will not be obtained.

240

Let us not deny the need of so many millions for a personal relationship with their God merely because we have found truth and satisfaction in an impersonal one. Are they to have nothing to look up to because they are unable to stretch their minds into that rarefied atmosphere? Is it not better that they do the more essential thing and acknowledge the existence of a Higher Power rather than fail to worship It at all?

241

The first work of religion is to bring the highest mystical ideas within the reach of the lowest mental capacity. It does this by symbolizing the ideas or by turning them into myths.

242

Unless there is an equal level between the understanding of a student and the communication of a teacher, there can be no complete success in the teaching. Hence a competent teacher first puts himself *en rapport* with the mind of the student. It is because the sages did this that they found it necessary to set up personal gods, priestly guides, and organized sacred institutions for the benefit of the masses. But this must not be taken to mean that the sages themselves believed in such gods, revered such guides, honoured such churches, or regarded them as eternally useful or always necessary and their dogmas valid for all future ages.

243

The simple masses can understand better that there is a God who answers prayers or responds to ceremonial invocations than that God is impersonal and transcendent.

244

The physical and mental images of religion exist because men need, and must necessarily make, symbols of That which they cannot conceive directly.

245

Is it not better to give to those who are unable to comprehend that there is a divine reality—which is anyway beyond human grasp—a symbol which stands for it and which can be grasped by ordinary human faculty or human sense? At the least it will remind them of it, at the most it will help to lead them to acknowledge its factuality.

246

The mass of people who believe in a transcendent power seek for more than a symbol or form to express it. They seek also for a channel, an embodiment, something or someone seeable and touchable through which it can find an outlet.

247

Those who are unable to formulate any concept of the formless Power in which they are rooted, and therefore unable to worship it, must worship a man instead. Hence the saviours and gurus, their religions and scriptures, the churches and temples.

248

In religious myth and legend, in sacred ritual and ceremony, there are symbols and allegories which are useful for meeting the mass-mentality but which offer much more to the educated one.

249

The masses are susceptible to, and impressed by, the colourful pageantry of religious processions, religious symbols, and kindred outward suggestions which awaken pious feeling.

250

The man of developed reason will feel its need less, or even not at all, but the unevolved multitude is moved emotionally and impressed mentally by ceremony. It preserves tradition, satisfies gregariousness.

251

The fact is that orthodox religion is usually a compromise between the truth and the lie, a concession to human weakness to which the truth must be offered wrapped up in the lie.

252

It would be cruel to tell the uninstructed many that the God they worship exists only in their imagination and superstition. But it would be equally cruel to let them always remain as children and keep the truth from them.

253

He should be sparing with his ideas for spiritually elevating the masses. The first aim must be not to sail over people's heads into the clouds. Otherwise he becomes a mere dreamer, while nothing tangible is achieved. It is better to give the masses one ounce of idealism in a pound of realism, and thus ensure its being swallowed successfully, than to give them a full pound's worth and have it totally rejected. No doubt they are spiritually sick, but they must be treated with homeopathic doses where teaching is concerned. This approach illustrates one of the practical differences between mysticism and philosophy. Indeed, it is often possible to tell from the character of its practical proposals for dealing with a deplorable social problem or reforming an unsatisfactory public situation, how far any theory of life is true to the facts of life.

254

Just as young children are more influenced by the world of the five senses than by the conclusions of reason, so many whose adulthood is still largely physical rather than mental are more influenced by what they see, hear, and feel, rather than by reason or intuition. Such persons are far from being ready for philosophy and could never give assent to its teachings. They lack discrimination and are led by appearances. They are impressed by "signs," that is, physical miracles, cures, and demonstrations, as proof of God-given power. Few of them would be willing to forsake their ego-directed lives and take to the way of living which Jesus—in contradistinction from his Church—really preached. But all of them may make excellent followers of an inwardly devitalized mass religion.

255

If, in the past, the truth has been dressed up in ecclesiastical myths, that could not be helped. It was in the nature of things and in the nature of man. It was also in the conditions of communication in bygone ages when most men could neither read nor write. Symbols and fables were useful in the intellectual childhood of the race.

256

Religions which have invented myths to suit the mentality of the multitude, who put up symbols to which they can attach meanings, are behaving quite logically. But man cannot live by invention and symbolism alone. As he grows up, evolves, gets more educated, his need is for the Reality behind them.

257

Many of the Gods worshipped in ancient cultures—Western or Eastern—are simply states of being. They are not to be regarded as living personages but as symbols of that higher state of being. For the masses, their picture and form may represent a useful object of worship, since it is difficult to form abstract conceptions of such states. For us who study philosophy, they represent conditions superior to our present one and to whose attainment we should aspire.

258

The sage could not transmit his knowledge to the masses except by presenting a remote symbol of it, a picturesque reflection. But this caused it to lose its vivid immediacy and its personal actuality. Yet so only could religion be born.

259

The sages had to face the fact that the masses under their or their pupils' care were inferior in mentality to themselves, and that their knowledge of the significance of the universe could only be communicated effectively through the use of symbols, suggestions, and images rather than through plain statements of fact. Hence the whole content of folklore and religion was invested in those days with its sacred character not because of what it said but because of what it did not say.

260

Those who cling to tribal legends and magical rites as essentials of religion, who put them on the same level as theological affirmations and moral injunctions, have never understood religion.

261

We can hope to understand folklore, myth, early religion, and savage beliefs only when we understand that these are the first, faint foreshadowings of philosophic truth created for the benefit of primitive minds by better informed ones. The savage was taught to think in terms of what he could easily visualize; consequently, he was taught to see the invisible in the visible, to feel the presence of spirits (that is, shadowy human or animal forms) as lurking in trees in order to explain their growth and life, as escaping from dead bodies in order to explain that the dead man continued to survive, or gigantically sized and placed in the sky in order to explain the processes and movements of Nature. How else could the intelligent leader teach these ungrown minds the truths that the mind of a man did not die with his body, or that mind was forever producing thoughts of the universe? Thus, these primitive "superstitions" are semi-symbolical and they rest on a philosophical foundation.

262

Religion *as we usually know it* touches only the periphery of the spiritual life. It is truth brought to bed with mental incapacity. It is a presentation to the gross senses of man of what is by its very nature entirely supersensual. Its exposition is not only elementary and narrow but necessarily incomplete.

263

It is a sign of the primitive mentality to believe in the personal actuality of a purely mythical and symbolic figure. Yet such faith is not to be despised and rejected as valueless, since it is a fact that the imagination can take hold of such a personal and pictorial representation much more easily than it can of an impersonal and abstract concept.

264

The easiest way for religion to account for the various forces of nature and laws of the cosmos to simple minds was to personify them. When it came to the Supreme force and Supreme mind, it had to personify that too. Thus, its limited and human conception of God is easier for the masses to grasp than the higher and truer one.

265

The savage mind bases its religion on fear, the cultured mind on faith. This proves the position taken by philosophy, that there is an evolutionary movement in religious concepts as there is in social customs.

266

It cannot be said that these truths have been kept from the masses. Rather, the masses' own limitations have kept them from these truths.

267

Emerson's scorn of the "mummery" of Catholic pageants and processions which he saw in Italy is intellectually understandable but spiritually unwarranted. Such festival shows have this effect, that in the mentally unevolved masses they keep alive the remembrance of historic figures and values in their religion, while in the mentally evolved they provide satisfaction for aesthetic needs or symbolic ones. Whatever promotes a mood of reverence is to be welcomed.

268

The mentality which has not been developed to perceive anything beyond the touchable and seeable, which cannot itself comprehend the abstract and metaphysical, this—the mentality of the masses—has to receive a simpler form of spiritual food. For it there must be the more palatable and easier digested food of dogmatic religious revelation. If from the standpoint of the sage such a religious form is a concession to popular prejudice and kindergarten minds, it is not at all a hollow valueless concession. He will always regard it as most essential to the welfare of the world, provided it is kept within proper limits.

269

Primitive peoples feel and act in response to the *feelings* aroused in them. Civilized peoples behave in the same way but with this addition, that feeling now combines with immature reason and to that extent is controlled by it. This explains why it was easy for the leaders of early races to get them to submit to religion. For religion is an appeal to feeling excited through the imagination.

270

To put the masses in a lower category of development may find supporting reasons—at least in past centuries—but to try to keep them there permanently is unjust. To feed them on myth, symbol, allegory, keeping back the higher truths and not telling them the facts about their existence, is also unjust.

271

Some readers have taken exception to my statement in the eleventh chapter of *The Wisdom of the Overself* that the aborigine should be left alone to worship God in his own way. They point out the great uplift of religious conceptions which has followed the work of Christian missionaries amongst aborigines. My own observations as a traveller would endorse this claim as true in some cases but false in others. There has been welcome advance in some countries but definite deterioration in others. This is apart from social, medical, and educational work of the missionaries, for which I would bestow the highest praise. However, the point I tried to make is evidently not quite understood. I hold only that, just as philosophy should not disturb the advanced religionist's faith but yet should make a higher teaching available to him as and when his faith weakens of its own accord, so the advanced religionist should not disturb the primitive religionist's faith but should make his own higher creed available as and when it might be helpful to do so. This would still leave a clear field for Christian missionary activity in distant lands but it would regulate and limit such activity within wiser borders. When I wrote about the advisability of letting the aborigine alone, this applies only if he is satisfied with his religion. It is not wrong to interfere when he begins to find fault with it. I did not mean to cause doubts about the value of propagating higher and more spiritual types of religion amongst primitive peoples. On the contrary, such propaganda should certainly continue, although it ought to be less offensively, less ignorantly, and less dishonestly practised than it has been in the past. It should be there, on the spot, available for those primitives who are nearing the level where they can begin to profit by it. Between the primitive tribesman, blindly obeying his patriarchal leaders and unthinkingly following his traditional customs, and the modern city-dweller, the difference is unmistakable. It is a difference on the one hand of more liberated individuality and on the other of more developed intelligence. Hence, the kind of teaching which historically suited the one is unsuited to the other. The missionary has his place in the world of religions, and especially so when he is the bearer of a more developed religion, but that place is not, as he thinks, an unrestricted one.

272

We need not accept a primitive form of religious revelation if our own intellect has developed too far beyond such a level. But we ought not despise those who do accept it, who find in it an answer to their need of belief in the higher power. However imperfect and unevolved, it is at base an affirmation that God is.

273

The man whose idea of himself is strictly limited to his little ego, and who is excessively attached to it, will naturally tend to form an idea of God as being a kind of gigantic person.

274

It is not true religion but rather impious irreligion to present the formless, limitless, sense- and thought-transcending infinitude of the Deity as a capricious tyrant and angry giant. To make It into an exaggerated human entity is to minify and slander It.

275

But most people, certainly the common folk, want a human God, one who shows emotion and responds to theirs.

276

It satisfies the demand on the part of the populace for a powerful supernatural being only if God is made masculine in gender, just as it satisfies their demand for a magnified father only if God is made humanly personal. They must have an anthropomorphic deity.

277

The Myth, given out to the populace, to the human mind at a simple naïve and unevolved level, is not intended for nor acceptable to the human mind at a high-cultured level. For this, nothing less than the Fact will do. For the others the Myth is, as a high Tibetan lama said recently (and privately), "like a sweet given to children because they like it so much."

278

Religion of the popular, mass kind makes its demand upon belief, not upon intellect. The priest or clergyman is not concerned with the question whether his offering is true: it is simply a dogma to be blindly accepted, an arrangement which suited the simple illiterate masses of earlier times and still suits those of our times in backward lands.

279

The truth could not be expressed in all its fullness to those whose cultural level was so different from today's. If they were given less, it is because they could not comprehend more.

280

It was perfectly correct for primitive peoples to feel and obey this deep longing to glorify their hereditary rulers and to worship their high priests.

281

We find that not a little in popular religion is nothing more than a thinned-down materialism.

282

The masses are not sensitive to the mystical, nor comprehensive of the philosophical. They must be reached through the physical senses. Hence religion is their path.

283

School the immature to enjoy and appreciate truth, prepare them for it, give them a chance to learn its elementary phases: this is a better way to stop their estrangement from religion.

ORGANIZATION, CONTENT OF RELIGION

Clergy

If we are to keep religion inspired; we must keep its ministers and priests inspired; that is, we must keep their *hearts* open to the sacred presence, their minds *alive* to the sacred Truth.

2

Who are the real bishops, priests, clergymen, and preachers of God's church? They are those who show, by the way they live and think, that they have found the spiritual self and follow the spiritual laws. And this is true whether they wear a clerical garb or a layman's suit.

3

Let the churchless man follow his own way but let him not deny the priest's path—it too is a service to those who are helped by ceremony and chants.

4

The objection that no intermediary ought to come between man and God needs to be kept in its place and confined to the limits of reasonableness. That a section of the people should be specially ordained and specially trained in religion and theology as a clergy is not in itself a bad thing, even though it could be abused and turned into a bad thing. That another section should be willing to live a disciplined, ascetic, and secluded life devoted to meditation and study is also not necessarily bad and anti-social, although again it also could become so if the purpose of all this is wrongly understood.

5

To transmit thoughts which have come out of some celestial plane, or feelings which hold a man by their delicate charm, to make one's way into ever-deepening states of tranquillity or of revelation and later return to

point at life's higher possibilities—these also are forms of religious attendance and, in some instances, even of priestly services.

6

Jesus, the first and best Christian, set an example for all later professed
Christians to follow. He did not preach in return for payment. He did not
turn religion into a profession. He even told those whom he sent forth as
apostles to carry no purse. If therefore we wish to understand one reason
why the Church does not represent him, here it is. The apostle Paul made
tents so that he could pay his own way while spreading the Christian
message. Modern spiritual teachers could not do better than follow this
excellent example. Their instruction should be given free. Hence they
should either earn their own living or have their own financial resources.
Thus, the new clergy will not labour for hire but for love. They will draw
no salary for their teaching and preaching, but will draw it from their
worldly work. Having learned how to earn their own living first, they will
be beholden to no one, dependent on no organization, but will have the
freedom to speak as the Spirit of Truth bids them speak. The old idea was
to preach and serve at the cost of the clergy's hearers. The new idea will
impel the minister to preach and serve at his own cost. When religion is
pure, however, there will be no professional clergy. Its ministers will then
have to earn their livelihood from a different source. Thus they may remain undefiled in motive and inspiration.

7

The mere title or position of priest, minister, clergyman does not sanc-
tify a man if he lacks the inner sanctity.

8

I have a distaste for "professional" spirituality. It took some years to
develop. It not only includes the teachers, guides, and ministers but also
the special kind of jargon they use in their communication.

9

By professional spirituality I mean that which is labelled as a priesthood
by an established organization, an authoritative hierarchy, and accepted by
the people as such. And I mean also that which is self-labelled by members
of the laity who take on a title like "Swami," who stand before the public
to preach and teach, who wear a special dress or uniform or robe.

10

All priests should be instructed in the exercises of meditation.

11

Only when meditation is officially restored among the highest positions
in spiritual life will religions be able to rise to their most important level.
Only when laymen can find available, whenever they wish to accept it,

both instruction in the art and retreats where it can be practised with the least obstruction, will the religious organizations be able to render their best service, their best fulfilment. For this it is which makes men connected in the most intimate way possible—within human limitations, of course—with the Overself.

12

It is not only those professional persons like priests, clergy, and monks who minister to the religious needs of men and women, but also the writers and artists, the rulers and leaders, the educators and the authorities, who must teach them the necessity and importance of aspiration towards spiritual goals.

13

Fate has put the priest in the position he holds; the necessity of earning a livelihood doing work on which others depend is an honourable one; and the Church as an influential organization has its definite place in society, a space in which the minister can play a worthy part. If he holds the ideal of service and seeks to infuse a little more light and life into those entrusted to his spiritual care, and if he does this with wisdom and discretion, he may do much good. He should grade his teaching to suit the minds of hearers, reserving for the intelligent few those doctrines which the others could not grasp or would resent emotionally. He must teach fables to intellectual children but the more mature deserve better stuff.

14

Even the clergyman who is trying to reach simple country folk would do well occasionally to drop a hint for the benefit of the few who are ready to receive initiation into mystical practices.

15

Clergymen can render better service to their flocks when they deepen their own inner life.

16

The minister who is able to instruct his flock serves them, but the minister who is able to inspire them serves them better.

17

When religion becomes a professional job, when men make their living by it, its reality vanishes, its hypocrisy appears.

18

It is not enough for a priest to have learning and virtue; he needs also to have inspiration. It is not enough that he performs correctly the outward gestures and ceremonial movements required of him or chants the proper sentences prescribed for him.

19

The ecclesiastic too commonly suffers from spiritual pride, too often makes empty pretense to superiority.

20

There are priests who lose their own faith and become spiritually impotent, so that in the end they preach to empty churches. They cannot help themselves, much less help others, cannot give consolation, much less give truth.

21

Why should we not consider some of the great writers like Plato and Thoreau as spiritual prophets, as holy in their way, and as illuminative to their fellows, as Christ himself?

22

Exaggerated statements by enthusiastic devotees or confused imaginations passed on by naïve ones come from the laymen. For deliberate removals and even insertions responsibility lies with the professional class.

23

Narrow-minded ecclesiastics look with horror at any and every departure from rigid orthodoxy and insist on a mechanical legalistic following of the form of every detail.

24

It is more important in their view to preserve the institution of which *they* are a part than to serve the people.

25

If there is to be an institution or organization and if it must have a head, experience leads the impartial observers to prefer unhesitatingly the elective principle to that of hereditary succession.

26

The benediction of a bishop possesses grace and power only if the bishop himself is an inspired man, not because he is a member of the institutional hierarchy.

27

If the words of a priest or a clergyman contain the message of true spirituality and carry comfort to suffering men, the latter might walk many miles to hear him; but if they do not contain them, they might probably walk miles to avoid him! How many clergymen have said all that they had to say in their very first sermon, since which they have added nothing new? Yet although they have had nothing further to preach, they continue to preach it boringly for the remainder of their lifetime! The people of this hapless epoch seek the bread of an inwardly-ravishing spiritual experience; they are offered instead the stones of inwardly-dulling intellectual gabble.

28

There are doctrines which belong to the spiritual infancy of the race, others to its spiritual adolescence. A prophet, a minister, or a priest who offers them to spiritual adults makes himself ridiculous.

29

The finished product of the theological seminary who takes his first pulpit with much education but little inspiration, may know his dogmas but is unlikely to know "the peace which passeth understanding."

30

Religion has suffered from the impostures of wily priests and the hollowness of boring services. But it has survived because of the nobility of inspired priests and the truth of fundamental beliefs.

31

If the clergy are to free themselves from this corruption of doctrines, this degeneration of mood, this hollowness of rite, the first step is to free themselves of ignorance of the true meanings of religious doctrine, the religious mood, and religious rites. Then only religion itself becomes intelligent and its following become sincere. It then worships the One Spirit, not any one person.

Church and State

32

If the clergy are to be supported by anyone else rather than by their own work, it should be by the worshippers themselves, and not by the State.

33

No church can keep its primitive spirituality unless it keeps its political independence. And this in turn it cannot have if it accepts a preferred position above other churches as a state establishment. It was not the leader of Russian atheism but the leader of the Russian Orthodox Church itself, the late Patriarch Segius, Metropolitan of Moscow, who admitted that the disestablishment of the State Church in his country by the Bolsheviks was really "a return to apostolic times when the Church and its servants did not deem their office a profession intended to earn their living." Such were his own words.(P)

34

There is no way, opening, or gate to God through the State, but only through the individual human being. The establishment and entrenchment of a State Church is based on an illusion, but the Communist disestablishment of religion *in general* is based on a much bigger illusion.

35

Faith in any religious creed and the following of any religious system should not be imposed by the State nor financed by it nor identified with it, but should be left entirely to the individual conscience and support. Even authorities, as history proves, are capable of making mistakes.

Religious symbols

36

Protestants, Calvinists, and Muhammedans who reject excessive symbolism, such as we find in Hinduism and Catholicism, make a good point in refusing to attach too much importance to the symbol, to the appeal to the senses of the body. But the fact remains that for the mass of people who until lately were untutored, simple, and overworked, symbolism did come within their mental reach and thus enabled them to get something from religion which in higher forms they might be unable to approach.

37

True religion is often fostered in a man by the use of a symbol. If a visible representation of the invisible God helps a man's worship, he is entitled to use it. If he has need of a symbol of the Infinite Spirit—be it man, angel, or Incarnation—to help him feel that It is something more than an abstract conception, that It may become existent and real, then its use is of assistance. If the symbol evokes a higher mood for the worshipper, it is an effective and worthy and honourable device which is unaffected by its failure to do this for others. It is one use of the symbol to lead him from the familiar outer plane of awareness to the unfamiliar inner one, to throw a bridge over which his mind can cross into perceptions beyond its everyday zone. He has passed from the tyrannous rule of exterior attractions to the gentle sway of interior ones. Until the time comes when the external symbol is no longer needed, he would be as foolish to cast it aside prematurely as another would be to refuse it altogether. But if he begins to believe that this image is thereby permeated with divine power in its own right, he begins to go astray. The worship of any false deity is the degradation of reason. Hindu pilgrims make their threefold ceremonial perambulation around smug idols and expect marvel and miracle in return. Reason denounces these futile propitiations of an unheeding deity.

38

Unless he possesses enough intuitional and metaphysical capacity, there is no way in which the believer may make contact with the Real except indirectly through the use of a Symbol. This can mediate between the limited degree his capacity has reached and the ineffable degree that can alone make the contact. The mediation is indirect, however, because it makes use of the senses, the imagination, the capacity to believe, or even of the ego itself. Consequently the result is incomplete. There is no way of completing it without passing first into mystical religion and, later, into philosophical religion.

39

The symbols of a religion may mean much where there is faith in them or else recognition of their true inner meaning. But they may also mean little where there is neither. Yet in the end, one should not stop with adoring them or with despising them, but move on to the reality they represent. For the believer, this is something on the spiritual plane; for the sceptic, it is a figment of the superstitious imagination. Only the actual, firsthand, personal investigation of it will determine what it is, if properly done. And this is what philosophy proposes—and does.

40

The same religious symbol which, at an early stage, helps a man to advance spiritually may, at a later stage and after its inner meaning has been well grasped, become a hindrance to further advance.

41

Beauty and Goodness, as we witness them on earth, are symbols of the divine. The failure to recognize this is responsible for much misery and suffering. The commandment "Thou shalt have no other God before me" meant that the highest of all desires should not be sought among earthly things. It did not mean especially the physical gold, bronze, or other metal images that the unfaithful worshipped—these were only symbolic of those earthly things.

42

To take every descriptive statement in most scriptures only literally betrays want of intelligence, but to take it only allegorically betrays a want of balance. The gods and goddesses of scriptures and mythologies are but popular explanatory principles of the one and only Divine principle. They are more easily comprehended by the masses than abstract metaphysical teachings.

43

In religion, metaphysical *principles* become symbolized by mythological *persons*. Thus Adi Buddha, the primeval Force, becomes the first historic Buddha, while Christos, the Higher Self, becomes the man Jesus. Thus the universal gets shrunken into the local.(P)

44

The dangers and downfall of every religion begin when its symbols are taken as substitutes for its realities, and when attendance at its public services replaces efforts at individual development.(P)

45

Man worships through the particular form which tradition and environment suggest to him. In his ignorance he gives the form more importance than it deserves until it comes at last to stand between him and God, a barrier to be broken down if he would find God.

46

In Christian symbolism the vertical line of the cross stands for spiritual aspiration, and its horizontal line stands for earthly desire.

47

If he is to use his religious symbol or spiritual guide philosophically, he ought to direct his mind to the truth behind the one and the reality behind the other. He should not leave it solely with the outer form.

48

The symbolic meaning of so many religious, ritual sacrifices involving the killing of animals on an altar was that the beholders should slay the beast within themselves.

49

They are right in honouring the sacred symbols of their religion, but wrong in letting those symbols extinguish knowledge of the reality for which they stand.

50

As understood by the masses, the gods—whether of India or Greece—never existed: but their figures were used to create significant myths and helpful symbols.

51

The Symbol which has become overused and devitalized, which is almost dead through being taken too much for granted, may prove inadequate and even misleading.

52

Several antique religions make the Virgin Mother a chief feature. Why stretch the credible so far to accept literally what is, after all, only a symbolism? The pure in heart—that is, the ego-free—shall see God—that is, shall give birth to the awareness of a new life within them.

53

The language used, the fables told as if they were history, may not be acceptable to an honest well-educated mind. But it could still, if it wished, accommodate them and remain within the fold of its traditional religion by taking them allegorically, not literally.

Places of worship

54

The simple feeling of religious reverence which we have on entering a church building, even though we may not believe in the doctrines of the sect to which it pertains, if stretched to a farther extent becomes the deep feeling of mystical communion which we have on entering the advanced degree of meditation.

55

Every temple, ancient or Oriental, if built on a philosophically traditional plan, acts also as a diagram of the human mind, with the shrine representing the Overself.

56

The deep heavy clang of a temple bell reverberates in the inner being of its hearers. The musical chimes of a church bell seek to attract worshippers, and each sound works in its own way as a sacred reminder.

57

It is right that the principal cathedrals, temples, and mosques of religion should be built on a majestic plan to impress those who go there to worship and to express the faith of those who put the buildings up. Such structures are not only symbolic of the importance of religious faith, but also conducive to the humility with which worship should be conducted.(P)

58

A building specifically planned and built for religious purposes only, holding an assembly of people who meet there to direct their minds and feelings towards the divine power, kept orderly and quiet so that its atmosphere becomes saturated with worship, prayers, chants, and meditations—such a building is inevitably more attractive to anyone who seeks to use it for the same purposes.

59

It is right and proper that a building put to a sacred use should be reserved for it and kept apart from profane activities.(P)

60

It is understandable that they would like to keep the serene aura of such a place uncontaminated by negative thoughts and mean, entirely self-enwrapped emotions.

61

In some rose-stained-glass-windowed church one may sense the strong atmosphere of true devotion so acutely that one instinctively falls on bended knee in humble prayer and in remembrance that self is nought, God is all.(P)

62

God is Mind and they that would worship it in truth must worship it mentally. The ostentatious ceremonies set up by paid professionals enable men and women to obtain pleasing emotional effects but they do not enable them to worship God. A building becomes a sacred temple when it ceases to hear phonographic mumblings and when it ceases to witness theatrical mimicries, and when it provides a fitting place where its visitors can engage in undisturbed silent and inward-turned communion with their own deeper Mind.(P)

63

A church's architectural form, a temple's sunward orientation and rhythmic music, a mosque's geometric decoration, and a synagogue's galleried arrangement are helps to each religion's expression of itself.

64

The visual effect of those temples, with their towers and carvings, upon the people is a successful reminder of sacred duties, mental and physical.

65

Temples or churches where men babble of God (whom they have not known) might be better used if men themselves kept silent therein. Then, after a while and little by little, God might speak to them.

66

They too often forget that the temple is not greater than the god.

67

The great height and grand interior of a cathedral or an important church are intended to create a mental impression, on the worshipper, of the importance of religion.

68

Although the mental impressions and emotional reactions which follow entry into a Greek temple, a Christian church, or a Muhammedan mosque are distinctly different, the architectural intention is the same—uplift to a higher plane.

69

The church building should arouse or confirm or strengthen religious aspiration when a man first beholds it and then enters it.

70

Temple: The rows of kneeling people, the chanting, the choir, the painted pictures and figures, the robed priests, the dim coloured lights—all contribute to set this place apart and produce an unearthly atmosphere.

71

What is the use of these temples of traditional religion when the gods have deserted them, when the only things in them are a bit of stone or metal, an idol, when truth and compassion, honesty and sincerity, spirituality and service are absent?

72

The symbolism that is built into the walls of church or temple, that is enacted in its ceremonies and rites, may be translated by a philosophical mind into philosophical meanings.

73

Thought, interest, attraction, wonder, and enquiry concerning God are not necessarily stirred up only in the buildings specifically planned for religious purposes; it may happen elsewhere.

74

One of the Indian seers actually prayed to God asking to be forgiven for having gone to the temple so often, visits which by their very nature seemed to reject the truth that God is everywhere.

Ceremonies and rituals

75

These grave ceremonies and beautiful rituals, which mean nothing at all to those practical men who feel no response to religion, mean comfort, inspiration, hope, mystery, and wonder to those who do.

76

If sacramental worship helps to put you into a reverent mind, take advantage of it. If ritual and ceremony seem hollow and meaningless and powerless, turn aside. But do not condemn them. Others *may* benefit.

77

The controversy between those who believe ritual to be indispensable and those who believe it to be irrelevant nearly always ignores four truths which, understood, dismiss the controversy itself—as ordinarily carried on—as futile. The first is that any means that adapts the truth to the limitation of intelligence which is present in the masses is useful *to those masses*. The artistic symbolism of ritual is such a means. The second is that the idolatry which the puritan objects to in ritual, reappears in his own use of mental images and limiting attributes, or anthropomorphic terms in thought, speech, and literature about God. The third truth is that the puritan's means is obviously adapted to a higher grade of intellect than the ritualist's and that one day the physical worship will have to give way through evolution to metaphysical worship. The fourth truth is that since each means helps different groups of men, its advocates should not attempt to impose it on a group to whom it is unsuited and consequently unhelpful. The diverse levels of human minds must be recognized. If it is wrong for the ritualist to interfere with the non-ritualist who has outgrown this level, the latter needs to be tolerant of the former who has something more to exploit in the lower level.(P)

78

Both Jesus and Buddha sought to remove bloody sacrifices from the institutional religion which surrounded them.

79

Any rite or ceremony which reminds men of their spiritual duties, which instigates them to worship the higher power, which helps them to concentrate on it, which creates the feeling of its presence, and which excites them to love it, has justified its existence.

80

For the mass of mankind and for beginners on the Way, any outer ritual or physical method which turns the mind away from earthly things, which lifts it up from total immersion in the lower interests of the personal ego to recognition of and aspiration toward its divine source, has its place and value in human life. But its spiritual merit depends on the extent to which it provokes a mental or emotional—that is, an inner—result. A mechanical co-operation with the ritual, empty of such a heartfelt result, is useless and, instead of being virtuous, may become harmful by creating a complacency which deceives the worshipper and a hypocrisy which deceives society.

81

Correct ideas of the place of asceticism and the proper form it should take are too seldom held. This is just as true of religious ritual.

82

Liturgical ceremonies which touch the deeper feelings are not less useful than inspired texts which touch the deeper thoughts.

83

The ceremonial observance of festival dates, the ritualistic participation in church or temple services, and the following of liturgical usages have their chief value in being first steps for the masses towards faith in a higher power and fervour in devotional attitudes. If a truly illumined priest is present during any of them and, more especially, if he performs a leading role, this value is transcended.

84

It is not hard to surrender to the hypnotic and repetitious choral chants, to the dim flickering lights, to the authoritatively voiced liturgies. Whether the result be only a spectacular theatrical show emotionally received or a vital communion spiritually uplifting depends largely on the celebrant of the rite.

85

If cold intellectuality looks on these ancient sacraments as mere outward shows, participated in as hypocritical routine, fervent piety looks on them as foundations which have supported the established religion and maintained its importance through the centuries.

86

Respectful ceremonials and huge buildings are not in themselves hollow, empty, and hypocritical materialistic forms, although they may become so with time. They are intended to impress the observer's mind, kindle appropriate feelings, and overwhelm him into submission by the power of suggestion.

87

Animal sacrifices do not belong in any way to the worship of God but to the worship of demons. They come near to, and are even used in, some forms of black magic. Whenever temples were turned into slaughterhouses in the past, and in certain lands still today, religion takes its lowest form, becomes pseudo-religion. Still lower were the rites of human sacrifice. Both kinds are concessions to, or expressions of, the killing instinct so marked in unevolved humans.

88

Have no use for a spirituality that only puts itself on show.

89

If church bells remind people of the existence of churches, and if churches remind them of the existence of religion, both serve a useful purpose. But this is not to say that all must go to an external church. Those who can find the spirit and practice of religion from within themselves do not need to; they may, if they wish, but it is not a necessity for them.

90

No sacred performance, ceremony, or rite gives anyone enlightenment, salvation, absolution, or inner strength without the real presence of the higher power. But this can manifest itself anywhere, and when one is completely solitary.

91

Insofar as a religious rite succeeds in arousing the proper attitude of reverence, enchaining the thoughts to a loftier centre than usual, and bringing the worshipper into contact with a genuinely inspired priest, it deserves an honoured place.

92

No formal rite of circumcision, as in Judaism and Islam, no mechanical baptism, as in sects of Christianity, can have the slightest actual virtue in spiritually affecting a child. All that it can do is to affect him post-suggestively by providing a remembrance in adult years of his dedication to a Faith to be secretly held, an Ideal to be earnestly followed.

93

The real use of any physical ceremony in religion can be only to help the worshipper who is not able to arrive at the same mood by metaphysical understanding.

94

Within one and the same church there should be place for such diverse expressions as those who can find stimulus only in rituals as well as those who can find it only in non-ritualistic worship. There should be place for mystics and thinkers as well as for the simple sense-bound masses.

95

Why not be large enough to tolerate both the ritualistic and the rationalistic in the same system, for each has its place and does its service?

96

The liturgy and vestments are but a door to the Real Presence.

97

We do not hear the voice of God in the priest's voice. We can hear it only within the mind's stillness. We do not commune with God through pageantry and ceremony. We commune through self-relaxation and self-surrender.

98

The magical value of any sacrament lies not in itself but in the faith it arouses, the reverence it suggests, and the reminder it gives. If a man can believe, revere, and remember God by any other means, such as reading, for instance, and if the sacrament has no effect upon him, he is not obliged to participate in it. But if a sacramental form helps him to either the remembrance or the aspiration of divine reality, why should he not take advantage of it? It is true that ritual which helps man to concentrate on a value higher than the material ones is certainly useful to him. But it is not indispensable to him. At the last, no sacramental symbol, no external rite can give what a man's Overself alone can give. Although the chief function of external rites is to direct the mind towards internal ideas, a mechanical ceremony of itself has no moral value. One may ask how far do the collective incantations and public prayers of organized religion lead to any tangible results? The mistake is not in creating or continuing these ceremonial systems themselves, these processions and observances, but in forcing them upon people who have no inner affinity with them, who feel no need for them and no help from them. Liturgical symbolism and ecclesiastical rite may exalt and satisfy the emotions but they do not go beyond this. They do not carry out their claim to constitute for the participant a direct sacramental means of grace. Those who administer such sacraments are invested with no higher authority than a merely human one. We must not believe that any paid professional has a better right to assume the status of intermediary between God and man than does an unpaid amateur. In fact, it often is better to believe the opposite. The confusion of clerical power with authentic spirituality is a common mistake. There is no real relation between the two. This is because it is not the ethics of a holy man which clerics seek to spread, but the power of a worldly institution. It is not faith in an immaterial reality whose propagation is their prime aim, but faith in a material hierarchy. When it has become outworn, the inner mental attitude which gave it birth and the accompanying feeling which gave it justification are no longer active. Consequently, its followers do not know why they are following it and act mechanically or, quite often, hypocritically. A ceremonial observance which carries no inner meaning and gives no mental uplift to those who partake in it becomes even worse than useless. It becomes a deception. There is a further danger when ceremonial symbolism becomes more important than moral principle. It is then that a religion falls into risk of betraying itself. Philosophy appreciates the services of organized religion and objects only when it loses itself in mere externals, when it sets up its own ecclesiastical organization and liturgical forms as all-important to man's salvation. The greatest dangers to its purity are the corrupt forms that men give to it and the selfish institutions that men set up in it. The seeds of destruction are implanted by karma and germinated by time whenever a religious form fails to serve humanity.

99

If anyone wants the processions and banners, the lights and incense, the priestly robes and litanies of ritualism as essential to his feelings for religion, let him have them. But if he insists on imposing these things on others who do not share the same feeling, he acts wrongly.

100

The creed and doctrine of a religion, its rites and sacraments, its communions and prayers, hold or lose their value according to the inspiration with which they were created, the character and conduct which they demand, the proportion of truth they contain.

101

If it is the business of religion to guide faith and not to supply knowledge, to promote moral feeling and not to stimulate rational intelligence, it would be well if those who are officially in charge of religious institutions were occasionally to remind themselves and their flocks not to become so immersed in its forms and customs as to forget the ultimate aim of the institution. Ceremonies which become more and more mechanical as they become more and more familiar, also arouse less and less inner response, stimulate less and less true reverence, and are apt to turn religious services into empty shows. To take a human ecclesiasticism for a divine religion or a showy ritualism for divine worship is a sign of intellectual childhood. It is perfectly proper in its own time. But systems and customs must grow up, like the child itself. Formalized religion is too often dead religion. "In the opinion that my body is completely extinct they pay worship in many ways to the relics, but me they see not. . . . Repeatedly am I born in the world of the living," observes Buddha in *Saddharma Pundarika*. There is no nutriment here for matured human minds or true human lives. This is why we neither support any external organization nor encourage the following of any personal teacher. This is why we practise, and counsel others to practise, a balanced individualism.

102

When people work themselves into too much emotionalism in religious dancing or singing, there is departure from, or inability to reach, that inner calm wherein alone the Spirit can visit us. These orgies of religious zeal do not yield true insight.

103

The gorgeous ceremonials and censered picturesque rituals of a religion appeal to those of aesthetic feeling, impress those of simple unsceptical minds.

104

It is partly to prevent the doctrines and teachings from fading out of men's minds and memories that they have been put into ceremony and song, symbol and bible, ritual and record.

105

What is it but a few sounds heard in the ears of men? Without the private experience of a glimpse—even only a single one in a whole lifetime suffices—what kind of conception can they form of it that will be accurate and trustworthy? What meaning can it carry to them at all?

106

For, after all, the really important factor is what happens *inside*, what is felt and thought, and less what is being done and said or sung under the imposed formula of the outside ritual.

107

Incense may be used for religious purposes in ceremonies and worship, but less devout persons use it to help smoke out mosquitoes, while more aesthetic ones find its fragrance and colour attractive.

108

All forms of external sacramental worship become worthwhile if they are used as jumping-off steps into real devotion.

109

All gurus and disciples, ceremonials and initiations belong to duality, relativity.

110

The services of aspiration expressed in song are an excellent feature of some churches and chapels.

111

Throughout the Orient, at least, if not in other parts of the world, rituals, sacrifices, and ceremonies have been a large source of income for the priestly order.

112

It is inevitable that where people tend to exaggerate the external, sacramental form so disproportionately, they will tend to overlook the power within the form.

113

A rite, a ceremony, or an image is of worth to anyone only insofar as it brings him, however slightly, closer to a sense of holiness, a feeling of reverence, and a recognition of mystery.

Relics

114

The exhibition of relics, the erection of shrines, or the creation of memorials, statues, paintings, and sects to record the name of a saint or prophet or holy man is useful to impress his attainments upon the minds of others living long after he has gone, and perhaps to inspire them to do something for themselves in the same direction.(P)

115

They believe that in touching these objects left by holy men or in visiting these places where such men resided, they touch holiness itself. A few even believe that they commune with it.

116

"Spare me, and take your absurdities elsewhere!" exclaimed Goethe a few days before he died in rejection of the belief in holy relics—in this case an Apostolic thumb-bone.

Scriptures

117

If you study the history of religion, you will find that prophets of the highest order, like Buddha, Krishna, and Jesus, did not write their messages in books. Every writer of a religious revelation or mystical inspiration belongs to spheres below that on which the great prophets stood. Their work at best is incomplete and at times imperfect. Therefore we should not look for perfection in it. Nevertheless, it is necessary to help lead people in their journey towards the Ever-Perfect and the message reaches those who are not yet ready for the final quest. To understand this situation, we must understand first of all that the truth is beyond all intellectual formulation. A book is the product of the intellect. The truth in its purity can be communicated only in silence and only to the awakened intuition. Hence the great prophets felt that the pen would be a limiting instrument to use. But why then did they use the instrument of speech which also is a mental expression? The answer is partly that in almost all cases their speech was directed to individuals, whereas books are not, and partly because of their being able to give some measure of help towards the understanding of truth through the impact of auras. The spoken words became merely supplementary to the interior and intuitive help.

118

Among the other chief purposes, it was the work of a priestly class as in Hinduism or of a learned class as in Islam to study and learn their scripture, thus preserving and protecting it. For in those days there was no printing. The scripture itself was treated with the greatest respect as containing the record and memorial of the prophet's revelation.

119

It is better to use the term "inspired book" than the term "divine revelation." The one is more scientific, more in tune with modern psychological knowledge; the other raises religious doubts and theological arguments when the assertion is made that it never originated in a human brain.

120

All scriptures are valuable as inspirers of faith and uplifters of minds but none is essential as the absolute arbiter of creed.

121

They do not understand that in setting up the text of some scripture as the last authority, they are worshipping a graven image as much as Moses' faithless followers did of old.

122

So much misinterpretation of sacred scriptures, and especially of the

Bible both in its Jewish and Christian parts, has been rife in the past that it has been used to support contrary opinions. This shows how much fancy and speculation go into these opinions.

123

The great variety of interpretations of religious texts may reveal only the different capacities of the interpreters' imaginative power in many cases but it may also attest their different levels of awareness.

124

Sacred writings are not necessarily those alone which conventional opinion labels as such. Any writing which uplifts the mind, ennobles the character, and imparts a feeling of reverence for the higher power is a sacred one.

125

From the philosophical standpoint, the entire chapter of Genesis in the Old Testament is both an allegorical legend and a divine revelation at remote remove.

126

The undeveloped mentality may be allowed to take the Book of Genesis as historical fact, in the same way and for the same reasons that children may be allowed to take any fairy tale as fact. But the developed mentality ought to know better, ought to take Genesis as an allegory and its scenes, personages, and events as symbolical.

127

There are several interpretative schools of semi-mysticism which devote their energies and spend their time finding new meaning in old texts. They lose themselves on some scripture and torture it into agreement with their own particular teachings. They might be better employed in finding reason first, rather than finding incorrect imaginary meanings in sacred books.

128

There are mystically minded students who spend much, too much, of their time juggling with esoteric interpretations of scriptural texts or tortuously hatching out from these texts confirmations of their own beliefs. My experience is that most passages of sacred scriptures and most happenings in profane fortune are open to as many mystical interpretations as there are mystically minded persons to make them. Such quotations of divine writ and such ascriptions to divine intervention prove nothing.

129

It is easy to fall into the errors of so many sectarian enthusiasts who see so much more in simple texts than the writers ever dreamed of.

130

Such grave and great distortions, interpolations, and eradications have some scriptures undergone in the course of their history and manipulation, it is no wonder that sects compete in common ignorance with one another.

131

A writing can be as much a piece of religious work as one so labelled, even though it is not dealing with a religious subject. It depends on the writer himself, his attitude and character, his knowledge and grade of consciousness.

132

In these ancient scriptures the religious babblings of primitive men are found strangely confounded with the philosophic reflections of wise ones.

133

Those who find allegorical significances in religio-mystical bibles, or who attach symbolical meanings to historical sacred records, need to be especially balanced and discriminating in such activities.

134

Scriptural texts have accommodated so many different interpretations in the past, and still do, that prudence should precede acceptance, patience should attend suspense.

135

It is a grave error to found man's moral life on the say-so of any tribal collection of outdated stories and maxims. A scripture is acceptable not because it is a scripture, but because and to the extent of the truth it contains. Also, not everyone who knows how to read can extract the true meaning from holy scriptures. No scripture, no gospel ever fell from the skies. Somewhere, some man took up a writing instrument and composed the one with which his name is associated. And because he was a man, however divinely inspired, the production was a human act and therefore a fallible one. A book is not a sacred image. It is not something to be revered merely because its typeset pages are printed in black ink on white paper. If we set it up as an authority, we fall into the fallacy of authoritarianism. Medieval debates about angels dancing on needle points or Mosaic cosmogonies are equally unreal today.

136

Those who think that because a statement appears in sacred scripture such appearance terminates all further controversy upon a question are deluding themselves. They base their unqualified assent upon the undeniable fact that the ancient sages knew what they were talking about, but they ignore the other fact that some of their followers did not. They do not know that the scriptural texts have been peppered with later interpolations or debased with superstitious additions and are consequently not always reliable. But even if they were, still, the human mind must keep itself unfettered if it would achieve truth.(P)

137

The biblical sages have told to all human races, not only to the Hebrew race, truths which, being eternal, are as needed in the twentieth century A.D. as they were in the twentieth century B.C. There is no statement in the Book of Proverbs, for instance, which requires revising and bringing up to date, or which can be dismissed as discarded religious superstition.

138

The Authorized Version of the New Testament is so clean-cut, so forthrightly spoken and yet picturesque, that it comes near to being a work of poetic art. It never forgets its purpose—to tell us the story of a man of God and to teach us what to do with our life.

139

Jesus spoke in Aramaic but the written texts of his teaching came to us in Hebrew, Greek, and Latin. Buddha spoke in Pali but at least half his followers got the written teaching in Sanskrit. The possibility of mistranslation through symbolic, metaphorical, or allegorical expressions being taken literally; or through esoteric-mystic experiences being only half-understood; or through terms with two different meanings being used; or through simple ignorance, is an ever-present peril.

140

The simply constructed, unforgettably inspired sentences of Jesus may be picked out in the four Gospels from those which have been interpolated by later men. Why this interpolation, it may be asked? Because they *wrote down* the words, as we have them today, after original bearers were themselves dead. Because with the passage of years and the passing down from mouth to mouth, remembrance may be faulty. Because human mentality may misinterpret the facts. Because human desire may exaggerate them. Because the fatal influence of an ambitious emperor forced organization and institutionalism on believers to serve his own ends and secured the necessary interpolations for this purpose on the theory that the end—monopoly and stability of power through the union of religion and State—justified the means.

141

Those who wish to understand their Christianity better should make this experiment. Let them procure Doctor Moffatt's translation of the Bible into modern English. It lacks the beauty of the King James Version, and can never take its place, but it amply compensates for that lack by the clearer expression and the fresher insights it gives. The two versions are needed together, side by side.

142

Esoteric meanings of the Bible: "Jehovah" means "Who is and who will be." "Israel" means "to see God."

Conceptions of God

143

The God a man believes in will reflect something of his own moral character, mental capacity, upbringing, tendencies, and education. There is no such person as an unbiased, unprejudiced believer. For God being unknown, the man has to substitute his own idea for direct knowledge. It makes no difference that this idea has been supplied to him by other men, through tradition, authority, reading, or hearing. They projected their own concept onto God and he has enough affinity with them to share their limitations.

144

God has made man in His own image, says the Bible. Man has made God in his own image, says the critical science of comparative religion. Understanding this, we can understand why the African savage imagines God in the form of a magnified tribal chief of terrifying aspect. It is not easy, however, to proceed on a higher plane and understand that it is for much the same reason that highly evolved civilized men have made God a great Artist or a great Logician or a great Architect or a great Mathematician. Yet it really is so. Such concepts represent the Supreme seen under the limitations of the beholder's personality. Therefore they are only partial and inadequate. The Infinite Power not only includes all these aspects but necessarily transcends them. So far as the human intellect can form a complete and correct idea of God it can form it only by bringing the whole personality to the effort and not merely a fragment of it.

145

Whatever men may say or write about the divine will always fall short of the actuality. This is so for three reasons. First, the Real transcends thoughts and their clothes, words. Without personal experience of it, and achieved insight into it, the intellect yields opinion only. Second, each man sees and says from his own standpoint, gives his own reaction to the divine. This is always an individual one. Third, there are many aspects of the divine. Muhammed listed no less than one hundred, without exhausting them. So far their totality has eluded description. Let no one insist on *his* own picture of the divine as being the whole one. Let no one set up *his* favoured symbol of it and exclude all the others from the right of worship.

146

We do not mean that the concept of God is an untenable one: we do not assert that it should be totally dropped. We mean only that in the light of our latest knowledge, as gleaned from such sciences as physics, astronomy, anthropology, archaeology, comparative religion, and psychology, the hour has arrived to restate this concept in a modern way. The concept itself remains, but the semantic content which is put into it must be rectified and purified. The fictions about God which were fashionable in older times have been largely exploded, but the *fact* of God's existence remains what it always must be—the greatest and grandest in the universe.

147

However false a man's idea of God may be, the basic instinct which is behind the idea's acceptance still remains a true one.

148

The God whom they worship may be a fiction of their own brains, but It is not a baseless fiction. The essence of the concept is true enough; only its form is false.

149

Whether he knows it or not (and if he is a sage he will surely know but if he is a religionist he may not), the Christian mystic, the Hindu pundit, the Buddhist monk, the Taoist priest, and the Muhammedan theologian talk of one and the same Principle under different names.

150

Each group gives a different name to the Parent of the universe, calls it Brahma or Jehovah, Allah or Tao, but all groups really direct their worship to one and the same God.

151

The self-existent Principle of Life which is its own source was given the same name by prophets of three different religions: "I AM" is the appellation of God in Judaism, Zoroastrianism, and Hinduism.

152

No dogma is more utterly materialistic than that which would compress the infinite unbounded Spirit into a physical human form, a personal human self, and worship that as a God. Nor could any other dogma so utterly falsify truth than that which would make a single religion, a single church, or a single man be sole repository of God's revelation to the human race. They are not religious truths, they are merely concessions to human weakness and human egos. They are exhibitions of the infirmity of human understanding.

153

The man who goes into a church because he believes that all the other churches are wrong, is going to a kindergarten school. When experience has schooled him through many births, he will learn the first lesson—that God is no respecter of churches but comes to the threshold of all, and nowadays too often to none.

154

The elementary religionist protests that he cannot form a conception of an impersonal God and that It could not exist. The philosophic religionist answers that he cannot form a conception of a personal God and that no other than an impersonal one could exist.

155

When I feel the divine presence in my heart, I acknowledge God as Personal; but when, going deeper in silent contemplation, I vanish in the infinite immeasurable Void, I must afterwards call Him Impersonal.

156

The old theology invested God with the quality of man. It belittled the Infinite power and imputed petty motives to the motiveless. Such a theology really worshipped its own thought of God, not God in reality, its own cruel and pitiful concept of the Inconceivable. Can we wonder that it provoked atheism and led to agnosticism when the human race began to outgrow its intellectual childhood? However fitted to that early stage of our growth, such an idea is unfitted to this mid-twentieth century of our history. We must and can face the truth that God is not a glorified man showing wilful characteristics but a Principle of Being, of Life, and of Consciousness which ever was and therefore ever shall be. There is only one Principle like that, unique, alone, the origin of all things. The imagination cannot picture it, but the intuition can receive some hint of its solitary grandeur. Such a hint it may receive through its worship of its own source, the Overself which links man with this ineffable power, the Divine Spirit within him which is his innermost Self. The personal concept of Deity was intended to satisfy the race's childhood, not to enlighten the race's adulthood. The time has come to do away with such a false concept and to accept the purity of this philosophic truth.(P)

157

Let us not be misled by the wide-flung nature of the theological belief in a personal god. For this single primal error introduces a whole host of other errors in its train. (a) The error of the observed Nature apart from the observer. This error is involved in the notion of a separate Creator. (b) The error of teaching a beginning and ending to the world. If matter ever existed in any form, its underlying essence would never completely disappear, whatever the changes it underwent and however numerous they were. (c) The error of the belief that something—the world—was created out of nothing. (d) The error of the belief that time, space, and motion could have been created, for the same reason. Their very existence implies that infinite duration, infinite space, and perpetual motion must also exist—which would negate their own supposed creation. (e) The error that God is all-benevolent and merciful yet creates an immense multitude of living creatures only for the sake of seeing them endure sorrows and tribulations of every kind, finally crushing them with the bitterest blow of all—death. (f) The delusion that we are entering into communion with this God (when we are only communing with our own imaginings about Him).

158

Words or names like "OM," "Allah," and "Mana" were never invented by ordinary men; they were revealed to seers. They are the true natural expressions for the corresponding ideas of God.

159

The Bible's first commandment is "Thou shalt have no other Gods before me." What is the meaning of a "god" here? It means something which is the object of worship. That thing can be money, fame, or sex: it is not at all necessarily an idol, a force, or a being.

160

What any religion, creed, or cult proclaims about God is almost always true as to God's existence, but is not always true as to God's nature.

161

The primitive man fears God. He seeks to propitiate this distant and awful power by offering sacrifices. The positive value of this view is the recognition that a power higher than himself does exist and does affect the course of his life. The civilized man reverently believes in, and gladly worships, God, who is felt to be much closer and like a benevolent parent. The element of fear is still not eradicated but it is very largely reduced.

162

If the arguments of atheism are studied, they will all be found directed against the idea that God is a Person, the mental image which has been set up and which presents God as an enlarged and glorified semi-human being.

163

Religion worships a Personal God through symbols but nondualism sees and seeks union with what is behind them, the Impersonal Reality.

164

The discovery that God *is* may be beyond our own experience, but it need not be beyond our faith.

165

The divine presence is outside time, and those who seek it through ceremonies, practices, or methods measured inside time can find looking-glass images but not the original presence.

166

Many people have so meditated upon their concept of God, that they have become one with the concept and not one with God, as they vainly delude themselves. The concept is not reality.(P)

167

The idea of a personal God as a loving father naturally appeals to, and greatly helps, the intellectually young. Children everywhere feel acutely the need of, and depend upon, such a parent. But when they grow up and become adult, they learn to practise a large measure of self-reliance. In the same way, with the more advanced concept of Deity, the love remains but the being is depersonalized.

168

It will not avail us to practise self-deception. Let us think for a moment of how many millions of men and women implored God to bring this bitter war to an end during its first year but found God deaf, how many millions repeated this request during its second year with the same sad result. Those who would force this narrow and petty picture of God upon others, deny and blaspheme the true God in the very act. Whoever reflects upon this unsatisfactory conception of a deity subject to racial bias, arbitrary favouritism, and other limitations of human personality, must repudiate it. And if it is not repudiated by millions it is only because they never pause to reflect long enough nor deeply enough on such a matter.

169

They project their own mental picture of their prophet or saviour, and it is this only that they see and worship. This projection becomes a barrier between them and the reality, which is by its very presence rendered inaccessible to them.

170

Tibetan texts admit frankly what other religious documents fail to admit, that the crowds of gods whose forms fill temple altars and wayside shrines are virtually "the play of one's own mind," that all the pageantry of worship, chants, music, and prayers is directed to symbolic figures.

171

We all worship God as best we can. But the ignorant perceive and honour only the veils of liturgy, dogma, and ceremony which enwrap Him, whereas the wise thrust the veils aside and worship Him as He is.

172

It is necessary to remind the orthodox from time to time of what one of the greatest and sincerest of orthodox Episcopalian clergymen reminded his audience in a Philadelphia church. He himself dwelt in the holy Presence and knew what he was talking about when he startled them by exclaiming: "God is not an Episcopalian."

173

The concept of God as Father or Father-Mother is a true one but still only an elementary one. The man who rises to the understanding of God as that in which his own self is rooted holds a truer concept.

174

Most people worship at an idol's shrine even when they honestly believe they are worshipping God. For they accept the imaginary personification of the Infinite Power which popular religion sets before them, and bow before it.

175

The atheist asserts that God does not exist, the religionist claims that He does, while the agnostic declares that both are talking nonsense because it is utterly impossible for the human mind, with all its limitations and conditioning, to get at the truth of this matter, since it can know only its own states.

176

Those who feel they must apply a personal pronoun to Deity should do so. But they in turn should accord equal liberty to others who are unable to share this feeling, and not regard them as apostates or heretics.

177

Those who can only believe in a God who has taken up his abode in some institution, some established organization, are and always have been in the majority.

178

The unconscious belief that there is a divine power back of the universe prevails even in the materialist, the sceptic, and the atheist. Only he conceives of it in his own deficient way, limits it to some force issuing from it, and gives it a different name.

179

There are such wide differences among the ideas about God which men, groping to get out of their ignorance, hold, that they might find it more useful to start by examining their equipment for the task.

180

Whatever evidence in disproof of God's existence is provided by thought can refer only to a personal God of popular religions rather than to an impersonal God of an intellectual elite.

3

RELIGION AS PREPARATORY

The religious life, if earnestly followed and conscientiously sustained, carries the devotee only part of the way towards worship of, and communion with, God. It is only a preparatory school. For both morally and intellectually it is a kind of compromise, yielding to a certain degree of the lower nature's rule and accepting beliefs that violate reason. This satisfies him only because he has not made perfect purity and perfect truth his standards.

2

To deny the immense value of the ordinary religion in its own place and to those who have yet to gain its rewards would be to break off the lower rungs of the ladder whereby men must climb to what is the ultimate goal of all religion.

3

The general line of inner development for the human race is in the first stage right action, which includes duty, service, responsibility. In the second stage religious devotion appears. This engenders worship of the higher power, moral improvement, holy communion. The third stage is mystical and involves practice of meditation to get a more intimate communion. The fourth stage is the awakening of need to understand truth and know reality. Its completed product is the sage, who includes in himself the civilized man, the religionist, the mystic, and the philosopher.(P)

4

Organizations are for most people the only way of receiving religious help or acquiring religious belief. This, however, does not mean that they will always remain so, for a time comes when they are seen for what they are—elementary stages usually, intermediary stages sometimes.

5

When a man comes to the attitude that it is not sufficient for him to receive religion at second hand as a creed or a conviction, when he must receive it directly as an actual experience in his own life, when he can pray with Flemish Thomas à Kempis, "Let it not be Moses or the Prophets that speak to me, but speak thyself," he is ready to move up from the first and lowest grade to the second and middle one. Such a one will then put himself in a position—which he did not occupy before—of being able to move forward to the central point of all religion, which is the personal revelation of the Overself, God's Deputy, in the heart of the individual man.

6

The sceptic, the anthropologist, and the philosopher of Bertrand Russell's type say that religion arose because primitive man was terrified by the destructive powers of Nature and endeavoured to propitiate them or their personifications by worship and prayer. They say further that civilized man, having achieved some measure of control over natural forces, feels far less in need of religious practices. This is an erroneous view. Religions were instituted by sages who saw their need as a preparatory means of educating men's minds for the higher truths of science and philosophy.(P)

7

Codified religion is not the final truth. It is but the vestibule of Mysticism, which is the vestibule of Philosophy, which is the vestibule of Truth. He who tarries in any vestibule is a sluggard, unfit for entrance into the innermost chamber where Truth's treasure lies.

8

Religion as popularly organized, with priesthoods and hierarchs, vestments and incense, ceremonials and rites, liturgies and scriptures, churches and temples, is an excellent first step for most people but not for all people.

9

The religious path is only a way leading at its end to the still higher mystical path. It does not bring its followers directly into the presence of God, as they believe, but rather to the beginning of a further way which alone can do so.

10

Yet the worship that is given by the multitude to an imagined God is not without value. It is an initiation, a preparation, and a training for the worship that will one day be given to the real God. It is an archway through which they pass on their way to philosophic worship.

11

The ancient division of men into three grades of spiritual development was expressed variously in different countries. In India, the *Bhagavad Gita* placed lowest the man whose mentality was inert and dull, next the man whose understanding was coloured by emotion or distorted by passion, and highest the man of clear and balanced intelligence.

12

The ceremonies and beliefs of institutional religions are useful, even necessary, on the level of consciousness for which those religions have been created; but they do not assist the mind to rise to the higher levels of metaphysical and, especially, philosophical religion. For these are concerned with a far higher quality.

13

The Ultimate meaning and social significance of religion will be hidden from us so long as we do not understand that it represents the appeal to the first of the three stages of growth in human mentality. The latter begins with the primitive, arrives at the civilized, and finishes with the philosophic stage. We have only to study the fruits of anthropological research to become aware of this truth. Ultimate truth being beyond the intellectual range of savage society, its wiser leaders unfolded a faith suited to their followers' capacity and needs, a faith which worked perfectly well and was indeed the best faith for such people. It ill becomes us to sneer at their superstitions, therefore, merely because we are totally unable to place ourselves into sympathetic relationship with their primitive environment. Their beliefs became superstitions only when those who led them did not realize that capacity for change and growth must be allowed for when the tribes had outgrown their first faith. Therefore, such esotericism does not mean that the masses are condemned to wear forever the badge of intellectual backwardness.

14

A man on the second level will not be able to accept the ideas or practices of a man who lives higher up on the third one. It would be unreasonable to expect such acceptance.

15

It is as erroneous to take the popular form of a religion as being all there is to it, as to take the symbolic statements of that form in a literal sense. Deeper than this form is a mystical layer and deeper still a philosophic lore.

16

The mission of religion is to take mankind through the first stage of the road to spiritual self-fulfilment. It can succeed in this mission only as it leads its adherents to regard religion more and more as a personal matter, less and less as a corporate one.

Doubt

17

It is not enough for one's religious faith to be fervent; it ought also be intelligent.

18

Simple minds can be taught to accept the symbols of religion as realities and the metaphors of its dogmas as truths, but cultivated minds submit with difficulty.

19

All religion rests ultimately in some kind of revelation—that is, on the appeal to faith. The first impulsive reply of modern man must be to doubt.

20

The reality in religion is true, but what too often passes for religion may be quite untrue. Doubt of what is false in it may be faith in, and consequent upon worship of, the real Deity.

21

The capacity to defy religious superstition is needed if a man is to discover religious truth.

22

The abatement of faith in a particular sacerdotal organization is not alarming in itself, but the abatement of faith in the Supreme Power which works for righteousness is indeed alarming. How many people have forsaken institutionalized religion not because they have lost faith in the existence of the Supreme Power but because they have lost faith in the representative character of the institution itself, not because they do not feel the need of religion but because they feel the need of a purer and better religion? If they have not found any other creed to replace the one they have outgrown, they may still turn for inward solace directly to the Supreme Power itself.

23

One may have truly religious feelings yet still be critical of a religious environment which practises hypocrisy or supports superstition.

24

Although organized religion is rendering a great and necessary service to the mass of people, there are still a few individuals who need a somewhat deeper understanding of the truth which such religion is teaching. If they pursue their enquiries they will not only be able to gain this understanding but also be rewarded by inner peace.

25

At a certain distance along the way, the institution or organization which may have helped him in the past now bars his way. Instead of serving his highest purpose it arouses questions, doubts, criticisms.

26

If he is sufficiently developed as a human being, he finds himself wondering at this existence of his and of his world. And if he becomes serious enough to look around for the answers which others have given to his questions, he can easily become bewildered by the contradictory results.

27

The traditional ancient historical religion into which a man is born, and which he accepts unquestioningly, is comforting and secure in his young days. But with adult maturity and the intellect coming more into play, his faith may become disturbed.

28

Questions about the assumptions of religion, uncertainties about its fulfilment of promises, doubts, and distresses may cause him many a pang during this difficult period.

29

The religious devotee does not care to trouble himself with such questions but all the same he cannot keep them out for all time. The human mind is so constructed that under the pressure of experience or the nurturings of evolution it desires, nay even demands, to know. Both desire and demand may be feeble at first and limited in extent. But they will emerge as inevitably as bud and leaf emerge, and find troubling utterance.

30

Those whose hearts could receive a nobler faith, whose heads could absorb a truer one, need not remain captives to an inferior one.

31

A philosophically based religion would give all its worshippers a chance to move up higher whenever they wished, felt ready, or began to express doubts.

32

There are two ways open: either advance into another religion or sect, or sink a shaft into the religion already held and go down deeper and deeper until its ultimate Source is found.

33

The type of religion which seeks to frighten men by the ever-burning fires of hell is for the naïve. Tradition supports it but education destroys it. By education we do not here mean the memorizing of opinions but the unfolding of the capacity to think rightly.

34

As man's intelligence develops he needs to be fed with religious nutriment beyond the simpler forms and faiths of popular religion. If this is not offered he becomes indifferent or atheist.

35

When religious faith is shattered by some distressing event of the personal life, this very loss may lead to gain. For it may be a prelude to a deepening and enriching of that faith.

36

People seek to escape from the soul's solitariness by keeping close to mass organizations, including even the religious ones of traditional churches. Here they find shelter and gregarious comfort. But a day comes when crisis crashes through the one and disturbs the other. Once again they are left alone with the soul.

37

He must look upon the elaborate ceremonials and simple dogmas as a cradle where his growth began, his limbs first extended themselves. But he cannot stay in the cradle forever if he is to become a youth and an adult.

38

Religious devotion, worship, aspiration, start a man on the way by occupying his feelings. But a time may come when he may wish also to know and understand more about the mysterious object of his devotion. It is then that he must prepare to get into deep waters, must hold his breath and take the plunge into philosophic thought.

39

There is no need for anyone to leave his own religion, but there is a need for him to go deeper into it.

40

The human being cannot be kept forever in the child state, neither physically nor mentally, neither in the home nor in the church. This must be recognized if society is to have fewer problems, less friction, more understanding, and more harmony.

41

The concrete image for worship was originally given for all those who needed something physically visible and touchable to hold their attention and keep it fixed on the idea of God. It was a means of fostering concentration. The masses were helped thereby. For others it was a useful reminder. But more developed minds who are able to grasp a metaphysical or abstract idea, as well as those who feel quite cool to external rites and constantly repeated ceremonies, need not let the less developed ones tyrannize over them and make them hypocritically worship, or take part in, what bores them utterly. They may claim their freedom and replace the idol by the sacred Idea, substitute for the rite an inner reverence for the Higher Power.

42

When a movement's inner life hardens into an organization, when its teaching petrifies into a formulated dogmatic creed, when its advocates and elders and guides become parasites on all the others, it may be time to quit.

43

We may give up hollow religious rites, if they have become meaningless and repugnant to us, and yet we need not give up religion itself. The two are distinct.

44

It is better to go one's own spiritual way and walk at one's own private pace than to tread the path of an organized church in steps set for us by professional priests.

45

To insist on primitive forms of religion being offered to, and honoured by, those who have reached the threshold of mental maturity, is like insisting on grown-up men playing with toys or grown women with dolls.

46

When the questions concern the spiritual meaning of life, the spiritual techniques of communion, or the spiritual nature of man, and when they are strongly and earnestly felt, it is the pressure of the answer itself working upon the mind from within that is forcing the questions into the focus of attention. It may take years before the man can unite the two, however.

47

Those who go to church for reasons of social conformity or self-interest, not for reasons of inner need, are on a lower level of evolution than those who refuse to go to church at all because their intellect cannot bring itself to believe in what is taught there.

48

Whether to conform to orthodox religion or make an open break with it must depend partly on the prompting he intuitively feels and partly on his family, social, and business circumstances. If a rupture might do external harm and create great friction, and if he does not feel a strong urge to make a break, then why do so? In that case it would not be hypocrisy to conform but simple prudence. The world being what it is, it is not possible to live in it and yet achieve complete independence. On the other hand, if the intuitive leading takes him away from obedience to these practices then he should obey conscience.

49

The legal, official, and conventional nature of established churches mesmerizes the great mass of people into the belief that here only is the truth, and that outside them lies false religion. The man who is beginning to hear the call of his higher self may often need to resist the power of this mass-suggestion.

50

Few men can accept their traditional religion in its entirety; they accept it only in part.

51

So far as established religion limits the evil-doing of its followers, it renders a useful social service. But this does not help those who, so far from needing such bounds set upon their deeds, are positively active in doing good. Still less does it help the few who have felt the urge to seek the Spirit's absolute truth above all the things of this world.

52

We may accept much that is given out by a man, a religion, or a teaching without sanctioning everything else that comes from the same source. All of it is not necessarily wisdom and virtue.

53

That which appears as enlightening Truth to one man appears as dangerous heresy to another man. These are not mere differences of opinion but of evolutionary growth.

54

Those who venture beyond the boundaries of established orthodoxy are justified in their exodus if they feel insufficiently or improperly nourished within those boundaries.

55

The free man will not take kindly to rigidly binding dogmas, may even come to feel spiritually suffocated by them.

56

The masses have their ready-made religion; the seeker must form his own.

57

Doubt has shaken the belief in a merciful and benevolent Deity but has not much shaken belief in the Deity's existence.

58

The rise to a higher level from a hollow, merely formal and outward religious life to a simple childlike trust in, and inward devotion to, God is excellent. But those who are unable to put aside their intellects so easily may ask for something more.

59

The Christian who has outgrown conceptions of an elementary nature and needs more substantial spiritual food is faced with his own special situation and religious difficulties. He must begin to get for himself some glimpse of the True Self by way of personal experience.

60

It is no sin on the part of any man but rather an intellectual duty critically to investigate for himself the formalized systems of unyielding dogma which, in the name of tradition, claim his belief.

61

It was a Justice of the United States Supreme Court, Mr. O.W. Holmes, who wrote in a private letter with reference to the orthodox religious doctrines which had been inculcated in him in his mid-nineteenth-century childhood: "But how can one pretend to believe what seems to him childish and devoid alike of historical and rational foundations?" The intellectual eminence which had brought this man to such a high position brought him also to such a questioning.

62

The religious individualist who is unwilling to put his mind under the yoke of any organization, who is unaffiliated with any group, has at least as much chance to find truth as the members of such organizations and groups and, as history shows, most probably a better one.

Inner worship is superior

63

We must distinguish between the ritualistic forms of outward religion and the mental and transmental states, the emotional and intuitional experiences of inward religion.

64

People who turn away from religion, even if they believe vaguely that there is a God, because the distance between both is immeasurable, may be startled to learn that God is also very near, is indeed within themselves.

65

True Spirituality is an inward state; mere religiosity an outward one.

66

Enshrined in the secrecy of everyman's Holy of Holies, hidden in the depths of his heart, there is a point where he may find his indestructible link with God.

67

The kind of religious worship which is expressed through outer things, through physical rituals, objects, sounds and processions and movements, is intended chiefly for those people who cannot practise the inner worship of silent moveless meditation. The first is easier but the other is superior.

68

The only value of theology is a negative but still useful one: to tell the student to ascend higher and give himself up to the practice of advanced thought-free mystical meditation.

69

The public demonstration of one's religion in church or temple does not appeal to all temperaments. Some can find holiest feelings only in private. Those in the first group should not attempt to impose their will on the others. Those in the second group should not despise the followers of conventional communion. More understanding between the two may be hard to arrive at, but more tolerance would be a sign that the personal religious feeling is authentic.(P)

70

Men who imagine that if they take part in the ritual of a cult they have done their religious duty are dangerously self-illusioned. By attaching such a narrow meaning to such a noble word, they degrade religion. We have progressed in religion to the extent that whereas ancient man sacrificed the animal *outside* him upon the altar of God-worship, modern man understands that he has to sacrifice the animal *inside* him. The external forms of religion are not its final forms. Jesus ordered one convert to worship "in spirit and in truth," that is, *internally.* The two phases of worship—external and internal—are not on the same level; one is a higher development of the other.(P)

71

A fourteenth-century German churchman, John Tauler, said: "Let the common people run about and hear all they can, that they may not fall into despair or unbelief; but know that all who would be God's, inwardly and outwardly, turn to themselves and retire *within.*"

72

There is a vast difference between the man for whom religion means an organization, a numbered group, attendance at a formal ceremony, a set of creedal beliefs, and an official authority on matters of right or wrong—and the man for whom it means a vivid inner experience, enlightening and pacifying, joyous and gracious.

73

A man must find holiness in his own mind before he can find it in any place, be it church, ashram, monastery, or temple. He must love it so much that he constantly thinks about it, or thinks about it so much that he begins to love it, before he can find its real quality anywhere.

74

Set forms of prayer, fixed formulas, and ready-worded phrases are for the multitudes who have little capacity for creating their own. It makes the going easier for them when they are told or taught what to say. But those who have more capacity should not feel themselves bound so rigidly: they should feel themselves free to express their devotional feelings in their own way and own words.

75

In the deep stillness we learn no creed, are taught no dogma. Only outside it, only among quarrelling men, are we saddled with the one and strapped down with the other.

76

So long as they look for the sources of religious truth, power, hope, and goodness outside themselves, so long will they have to suffer from the imperfections and limitations of such sources.

77

The man who wants something broader than the pettiness of most religious creeds, nobler than most religious ethics, truer than most religious teaching, will have to step out of every religious cage and look where Jesus told him to look—within himself.

78

Those who formerly could not bring themselves to believe that God exists are dumbfounded when they discover that He not only exists but even exists within themselves.

79

Men go on pilgrimage to this or that holy place, city, man, or monastery. But in the end, after all these outer journeys, they will have to make the inner journey to the divine deputy dwelling in their own hearts.

80

Too often religion amounts to coddling the ego of the believers and worshippers, both in its existence in this world and in the next one. This merely creates illusions that will later have to be struggled against for release.

81

The man who accepts doctrines, obeys commandments, follows blindly, shifts responsibility to the organization of which he is a member. But his attempt fails. The karma is not only collective but personal. The man as an individual cannot escape.

82

No religion today can claim to be the sole and true inheritor of its Prophet's message. There is no unity in any of them; there is plenty of dissension and sectarianism when it comes to definitions, creeds, and observances. This really means that the individual follower, in relying on tradition to support him here, is trying to push off—unconsciously perhaps—his personal responsibility for his acceptance of it. But it remains there still!

83

When he no longer looks only to the established tradition offered him by others but also and more deeply into his own inner consciousness, he is then following the way pointed to by Jesus and Buddha and Lao Tzu. For this is how and where the soul reveals itself.

84

If many like to share their religious emotions with others in full public view, they are entitled to do so. But if this activity is done with the desire to be seen, to be admired in approval, to this extent the emotion is adulterated and rendered worthless, because it is ego-worshipping instead of God-worshipping.

85

Those who believe they honour a religion by attending its services and ceremonies are not seldom deceiving themselves. It is they themselves who are honoured by the contact.

86

Men and women go to church, mosque, synagogue, or temple, ostensibly to worship the higher power; but what is the good, if when they are there their thoughts are preoccupied with their personal affairs and are thus not really in the church or holy building, but in their egos? They might as well have stayed at home if they don't intend to make an effort to let go and to look up.

87

It is nonsense to assert that people who come together for worship touch a stronger holiness than those who pray alone. What happens is that two forces are at work: first, the power of society, of public opinion, and the crowd to incite and shame them into attending open services where they see and are seen; second, a central place or building reserved for such visible worship and heard prayer *suggests* that divine influence is active there.

88

The way in which some people flock to join organized groups is often an indication on their part of some unconscious or unexpressed doubt, for it is an indication of their need to strengthen their faith by getting the support of numbers. But this is only a spurious support because the faith is inside them, whereas the group is outside!

89

We can truly worship God without ever entering a religious building, opening a religious book, or professing a religious membership.

90

Prayer which is private and individual is superior in quality and sincerer in tone than prayer which is public and collective.

91

Religion will gain in honesty and lose in hypocrisy, society will gain in peaceableness and lose in quarrelsomeness, when religion itself becomes a private affair—so private that even two friends of different faiths will ordinarily neither display their interest in nor talk about them. Their reverence will then express itself just as well and even more sincerely in private religion than in public worship.

92

If prayers are merely said by rote, mechanically or perfunctorily, little or nothing need be expected from them.

93

The dogma, ritual, creed, and sacramental worship of religion exist only to lead up to this inner phase: they are not ends in themselves.

94

The beautifully carved figure which was to have acted as a symbol to men of their higher possibilities and as a reminder of their duty to realize them, becomes over-worshipped, its correct use forgotten and true place misconceived. In this manner materialism penetrates religion, as it does in several other ways.

95

Whether a man accords his allegiance to Salt Lake City or to Rome, to the Mormon revelation or the Catholic credo, is really of more importance to the institutions involved than to the man himself. For in the end his salvation depends on what he is rather than on what the institution is.

96

When Jesus said, "Knock and it shall be opened to you," he meant knock at the door within yourself. No amount of knocking at the doors of organizations outside yourself will bring this result.

97

The altar at which he humbly prays is deep within his mind; the god to which he gives reverent homage is there.

98

Too many people have been mistaught by religion to evade their obligations and to deny their responsibilities by trying to put them into God's hands merely because it is unpleasant or uncomfortable to the ego to deal with them themselves.

99

The more importance is placed upon the inner life by a religion, the less is development given to ritualism.

100

If you depend too much on the external, you will become weaker to the same extent internally.

101

It has been observed that most religious hymns are about ourselves, few only are about God.

102

They worship their own ego and call it God!

103

It is only by relegating religion from being a public to being a private affair that those two typical religious nuisances—intolerance of other beliefs and interference with other people's lives—can be got rid of.

104

We must take a higher position than ordinary religion offers and come face to face with the mystery that is Mentalism. The nonbeing of the universe, the nonduality even of the soul may be too mathematical a conclusion for our finite minds; but that this matterless world and all that happens in it is like a dream is something to be received and remembered at all times. We are important only to ourselves, not to God. All our whining and praying, chanting and praising, gathering together and imagining that this or that duty is required of us is mere theatre-play: Mind makes it all. In this discovery we roll up the stage and return to the paradox of what we really are—Consciousness!

Mysticism and religion

105

Mysticism is religion come to flower. The yearning for security against fears, which religious belief and ceremony satisfy in an elementary way, is still further and much more fully satisfied by mystical experience in an advanced way.

106

When religion is of the socially visible, publicly attended kind, it serves the people in a limited way. When it is of an extremely private, quiet silent meditative kind, it penetrates their mystical essence.

107

Faith in the soul is the first step and is provided by religion. Knowledge of the soul is the second step, and is provided by mysticism.

108

The religionist has a vague intuitive feeling that there is something higher than the daily round, someone behind the universe, and some kind of existence after death. The mystic has developed this intuition into definite insight into his own relation to this mystery: he knows he has a soul.

109

Religion was devised to assist the masses. Mysticism was designed to assist the individual. When religion has led a man to the threshold of deeper truths behind its own, its task is done. Its real value is attained in mysticism. Henceforth, the practice of mystical exercises can alone assure his further spiritual progress. For mysticism does not rest upon the shifting sands of faith or the uncertain gravel of argument, but upon the solid rock of experience. The first great move forward in his spiritual life occurs when he moves from religion to mysticism, when he no longer has to go into some stone building or to some paid mediator to feel reverential towards God, but into himself. Mysticism is for the man who is not in a hurry, who is willing to work persistently and to wait patiently for consciousness of his divine soul. The others who have not the time for this and who therefore resort to religion must live by faith, not by consciousness. The man who wishes to rise from sincere faith and traditional belief in the soul to practical demonstration and personal experience of it must rise from religion to mysticism. Mysticism seeks to establish direct contact with the divine soul, without the mediation of any man and without the use of any external instrument. Hence it must seek inward and nowhere else. Hence, too, the ordinary forms and methods of religion are not necessary to it and must be dropped. When the mystic finds the divine presence enlightening and strengthening him from within, he cannot be blamed for placing little value upon sacramental ceremonies which claim to achieve this from without. Nor is he censurable if he comes to regard church attendance as unnecessary and sacramental salvation as illusory. If a man can find within himself the divine presence, divine inspiration, and divine guidance, what need has he of church organization? It can be useful only to one who lacks them.(P)

110

If the transition from religion to mysticism is to be conveniently made, it must be gradually made. But this can be done only if the teachers of religion themselves approve and promote the transition. But if they do not, if they want to keep religion imprisoned in ecclesiastic jail-irons, if they persist in a patriarchal attitude which indiscriminately regards every member of their flock as an intellectual infant who never grows up, the transition will happen all the same. Only it will then happen abruptly and after religion itself has been discarded either for cynical atheism or for bewildered apathy.(P)

111

Religion brings the truth *to* him only in part and, too often, in symbol—only from outside himself and by secondhand revelation. Mysticism brings *him* to the truth from inside himself and by personal experience.

112

Without this mystical dimension, religion lies at its most elementary level.

113

Under the half-dead conservatism of religious tradition and dogmas there lie concealed a group of profound truths and ulterior meanings. They are needed today much more than those relics are needed. Yet the irony is that the men who teach those traditions have all the prestige of great institutions to support them whereas the mystic who perceives those undisclosed truths stands alone and has little or no prestige. So the masses continue to echo the empty babble of their religious leaders, or else repudiate religion altogether and become either indifferent or hostile to it.

114

Valuable and respected as the Catholic mystics were as guides to mystical knowledge and practice, most of them still remain biased and unscientific guides. Allowance must be made for this difference of attitude with which they approach the subject, from that with which a modern mind—freed from prejudice, superstition, and organizational ties—approaches it. Even so outstanding and leading a mystic as Saint John of the Cross, who is considered to have reached the goal of complete union, limited his reading to four or five books, of which one was *Contra Haereses*, and confined his writing by his proclaimed intention "not to depart from the sound sense and doctrine of our Holy Mother the Catholic Church."

115

Mysticism is not to be confused with any religion. Mysticism can drop all the religions from its hold and yet be unaffected. No religion can help the true mystic, but he can help any religion with which he cares to establish contact. His presence alone inside any fold will give it more than a momentary grandeur and cause men to look on an old Church with new respect. This is why mysticism can stand on its own feet, and why it does not need the doubtful legends and theatrical liturgies of institutional religion.

116

When a man has outgrown the tutelage of religion and tired of the barren negative period of agnosticism which succeeds it, he is ripe for the tutelage of mysticism.

117

A sincere Church would do everything to encourage, and nothing to hinder, its members taking to the mystical quest. For this would be the best sign that it honestly sought to consummate its own work for the individual benefit rather than its own.

118

The assertion that, in certain cases, heresy can be true religion and orthodoxy false, may seem incredible to those who have not the necessary evidence to prove it. Yet Buddha and Jesus and Muhammed were, in their time, heretics. How many others have died unknown, canonized as saints or revered as sages in the minds and remembrances of only a small number of persons? And how many of them, had it been their mission to declare themselves openly, would have been rejected, calumniated, or persecuted?

119

Mysticism is larger than religion and ought not to be confounded with it; yet paradoxically it takes in religion and does not deny it. It fulfils and consummates religion and does not retard it.

120

We must not confuse the truly mystical life with either a religious one or an ethical one. The latter two are merely elementary and preparatory to the former.

121

More than three hundred years ago, a wonderful little woman took the Galilean at his word. She put all her emotional strength into aspiration and meditation and succeeded in achieving an exalted state by practising a simple method. When her own heavenly peace was sufficiently stabilized, she began to think of others, of how she could help them attain it too. She was not so selfish as to be satisfied with her own satisfaction alone. So she journeyed from city to city and from village to village in religious yet religionless France, lighting the candles of human faith with a divine taper. Such was the spiritual darkness of the time that her success was immediate, and such was her own Christlike power that it was amazing. Crowds flocked gladly to her side, listened eagerly to her words, and endeavoured faithfully to follow her instructions. Her doctrine came to be called "Quietism" because she showed people how to quieten their personal thoughts and emotions and thus become aware of the impersonal heaven behind them, the kingdom within. She was no heretic. She drew frequently from Jesus' own recorded words to explain or illustrate her teaching. Yet she did not speak from dead pulpits in churches but from living ones in the fields. The clergy became seriously alarmed. Such activities could not be countenanced, they said. They petitioned the authorities against her, as the Jewish priests had once petitioned the Roman authorities against Jesus. She was thrown into prison and the jailer turned his key on her dismal abode, where she was shut in for a long period of years. Such was the story of poor Madame Guyon.

She was also denounced by the Church, as were her followers, for

having fallen into the sin of spiritual pride. This was because of the assertion that outward practices and ritualistic acts were no longer needed by
those who could find inspiration within. This teaching is quite correct but
politically wrong. Out of respect for, or fear of, the Church's great power
in those times, as well as out of consideration for the mass of people who
were still unable to rise above their dependence on such outward ceremonies, Madame Guyon could have worked longer if she had worked
quietly and privately, not openly and publicly. She could have instructed
her followers, first, not to talk about the teaching to any person who was
not ready for it, and second, not to communicate it even to those who
were ready without the safeguard of complete secrecy.

Do you wish to penetrate to the essence of this episode? Here it is. A
bishop of that time naïvely let the cat out of his theological bag! He said:
"This woman may teach primitive Christianity—but if people find God
everywhere what is to become of us?"

"*What is to become of us?*" Six short words but what a tremendous
commentary they contain! When religion was about to become a living
actuality in the lives of common people whose hearts were moved by the
enlightening words of Mme. Guyon through personal realization of its
loftiest truth, when it was ready to inspire them from hour to hour with
inward peace and outward nobility, the official exponents of Christianity
interfered and prevented it because of their selfish fears! They did not see
and perceive the ultimate danger to themselves, and the immediate shame
on their teaching, of such a situation. Well may the thinker have repeated
the poet's lines about the mills of the Gods grinding slow but exceedingly
small, for when the French Revolution broke out and spread its ugly
malignant fury over the land, when the so-called Goddess of Reason was
set up on her throne in the very midst of Notre Dame Cathedral, and
when all France was rocking in the great upheaval which retributive destiny and rebellious demagogues had conspired to bring upon her, fifty
thousand French priests fled from persecution, imprisonment, and even
death. To appear on the streets of Paris in those days wearing the cleric's
garb was to court the punishment of death itself.

122

The mystical phase is to be acquired without dropping the religious
phase, although he may wish to modify it.

123

If religion is to save what is best in itself, it must not only set its house in
order but must admit the mystical practices into its system of instruction.
It must become less exteriorized and more interiorized, more mystical.

Stone-built sanctuaries are many in every town and village of the land. But those that truly light the mind are few. Yet there is one with doors wide open to all, great enough to include every city in the country yet narrow enough to exclude the dull materialist, the ruthlessly cruel, and the poisonously selfish. This is the sanctuary of the inner Self. From this mystical standpoint the institutional side of every religion is its least important side. To understand a religion in this way we must first become heretics; we must cast off conventional views which blind the mind's eyes. We need no longer worry ourselves over the hotly debated question of whether or not Christ was born of a virgin mother, for instance, but we do need to give our time and thought to finding that which Christ represents within ourselves. Christ can live again within our hearts, as he himself taught, which means we must look for him inside ourselves much more than inside a Church building.

124

The disuse of outward sacraments and the distaste for church organization which mark the life-history of several mystics, come from the vigour and independence with which they must shield the growing plant of inner life, and from the reorientation of trust with which they turn from all man-made things to God alone.

125

When spiritual yearnings become more insistent but perhaps more indefinable, it may be that the mystical depths of religion are calling him away from its shallow surfaces.

126

The mystic unfolds his higher individuality. The more he does so, the more he tends to draw away from the organization which acts as custodian of his outer religion.

127

Fanatical religion killed Hypatia, conventional religion lynched Pythagoras, respectable religion poisoned Socrates, authority-worshipping religion crucified Jesus.

128

It is historical fact that a number of those who successfully deepen their spiritual life by contemplation practice may develop anti-ritualistic attitudes. This is why mystics have been tolerated, even venerated, and alternately treated as heretics and persecuted.

129

Ecclesiastic hierarchies do not welcome, even discourage, the claim to personal inspiration in their own times. A fresh revelation of deific power is regarded as a fresh danger. For the new voice may be listened to in place of the old parrot-like repetitions!

130

Because time brings to instituted religions growth, and that brings power, success, wealth, and prestige—with all their corruptions and infidelities—all religions' principles need to be periodically re-established. This is why contemporary mystics and prophets are always needed and why they should be given a hearing.

131

So long as so many of the authorized guardians of religion fail to appreciate the fact that mysticism is the very core of their doctrine, so long will they lack the glowing inspiration, the broadening view, and the beneficial strength which religion at its best can and ought to give.

132

What the religious man feels by instinct or faith, the mystical man knows by experience or revelation.

133

It remains a historical fact that the man who has discovered truth finds more opposition within the formal established church of his religion than outside it, more who will accept it among laymen than among professional ministers and theologians. This is regrettable, because the latter ought to be the first to welcome his discovery. But organizational ego, plus personal timidity or cowardice, get in the way.

134

So long as people are overwhelmed by the official prestige of established churches and overawed by their historic tradition, so long will it be futile to expect wide recognition of, and proper honour for, the authentic revelations of a true contemporary mystic.

135

The individual mystic's lack of status is regrettable but expectable. For it is the penalty he must pay for refusing to be overawed by the dogmas current in his time and the traditions inherited from his people's past. What chance has this teaching when its adherents form only a small unrecognized entirely scattered cult whereas the adherents of orthodoxy are numbered by the million, and even those of unorthodoxy are numbered by the thousand or hundred? Must all importance, all truth, all significance in religion be limited to organized groups alone? Are there no inspired persons and no ordinary individuals who do not choose to belong to any such groups at all? Why should orthodoxy and unorthodoxy, merely because they are organized into churches and labelled as denominations, alone represent the voice of religion?

136

The inspired individual who has climbed Sinai on his own feet and received the Tablets of God's Law with his own hands has merely a small fraction of the power, influence, and prestige of the be-robed representative of organized religion, who knows God only at second hand and through others, who has no inspiration with which to bless men and no real power to save them.

137

What is the difference between Quietism and Mysticism? Quietism is Roman Catholic and seems to have been solely devotional-mantra, repetition japa singing, ascetical in order to find personal salvation, whereas Mysticism is a generic term for all religions and seems to be positive living in God plus illumination.

138

So long as official religions held the highest places, so long the Enlightened, the knowers and the seers, were left to walk alone or to think in secret or to stifle their words.

139

There are austere anti-mystic theologians just as there are hidebound anti-mystic ecclesiastics.

140

The devotional life of religion finds its culmination in the meditative life of mysticism. Devotion can be practised *en masse* but meditation is best done in solitude. Religion can be organized but mysticism is best left to the individual.

141

If we mix the mystical with the religious standpoint, the result will be confusion and misunderstanding. They must be kept apart and in their proper places.

142

Those who have touched the mystical level in what they have deeply believed and deeply experienced are much less likely to be dogmatic, narrow religionists.

143

The gulf between ritualistic religion and mystical religion is the gulf between a metaphor and a fact.

144

It would be sheer folly for even an organized form of mysticism to compete with organized religion. The votaries of mysticism are and will remain a minor group. But insofar as their challenge acts as a successful irritant, they may help orthodox religion to improve itself.

145

The Roman Catholic Bishop of Cochin told me a few years ago that he disapproved of mysticism because it could very easily lead, and had historically led, to intellectual and spiritual anarchy and was therefore dangerous. Another Roman Catholic, G.K. Chesterton, the brilliant English author and journalist, told me nearly thirty years ago that he disapproved of mysticism because it could very easily lead to moral anarchy and evil behaviour, and had indeed done so. Yet both men were quite willing to accept mysticism provided it was fenced around by the limitations and regulations, the dogmatic definitions and supervisory direction imposed by their Church.

146

It is the constant contention of ecclesiastical authorities that mystics who find sufficient guidance and teaching in waiting upon the inner light, who disregard all outward supports, expose themselves to deception and error and the Church to anarchy and disintegration. Their contention is correct enough. Nevertheless the argument is not adequate enough to prohibit the practice of mysticism altogether. For, on the first count, the mystic can be taught how to protect himself against these perils. On the second one, not many people are willing or ready to become mystics and there are more than enough left to keep the Church busy while those who are ready can still be helped by the Church.

147

This insistence on the rigorous following of external forms, together with this neglecting of the internal spirit which should be the main object of those forms, is more harmful in the mystical world than in the religious one.

148

That which religion worships as from a distance, mysticism communes with as an intimate.

149

Many believe, some suspect, but few know that there is a divine soul in man.

4

PROBLEMS OF ORGANIZED RELIGION

On criticism and scepticism

The criticism of religious truths arises not only out of its confusion of pure religion with ecclesiastical religion, but, in the case of other persons, out of a low character rather than a lofty ideal. It is then destructive and unscrupulous, taking meanings and deliberately distorting them to suit its own purposes. It is then sincere only in its selfishness and adequate only in its materialism, not only seeking all the defects of the attitude it proposes to replace but also inventing many imaginary ones. It lives by criticism and feeds on conflict. It cunningly entraps those who are so troubled by present world conditions as to have lost hope, enthusiasm, courage, and faith on the one hand, and on the other those who are so troubled by these conditions as to have become unbalanced, violent, irrational, and cruel. To both, the phraseology of conventional religion, politics, society, and economics has become hollow. To both, the feebleness and foolishness of our entire social structure have become apparent. But both are wrong.

2

Unfair and untrue criticism by sceptics may well be ignored, but too often in the past religions have failed to benefit themselves by looking into justifiable criticism from believers. This failure has strengthened superstition and weakened real religion.

3

Instead of being vexed over the rise of scepticism and indifference or grieved over the fall of religious influence, they should seek the causes and adjust faith to reason and truth.

4

If a teaching can make a man more hopeful when accepted, more peaceful when studied, and more intuitive when applied, then it deserves respect, not scorn.

5

When we speak here of the dangers of atheism and the darkness of materialism, we do not refer to those brave, intelligent men who have protested against superstitious religions and pious exploitation. That which they opposed was not genuine religion at all, but the satanic pretense of it. It is an historic and unfortunate fact that such pretense is too often successful.

6

Every man who receives the Life-Force from his inner being yet denies its existence, who is sustained by the Overself's power yet decries those who bear witness to it, sins against the Holy Ghost. This is the real meaning of that mysterious sentence in the New Testament which refers to such a sin.

7

Each person has some kind of faith; this includes the person whose faith reposes in scepticism.(P)

8

In making unfaith their faith, the scoffing have taken the first step forward out of superstition on a long road whose course will be spiral and whose end will be religious once again. But because the impulse behind this step is so largely selfish and passionate, so negative in emotional feelings and erroneous in intellectual convictions, it is a dangerous one. In getting rid of the evil of superstition, they have invited other evils, equally bad and even worse, to replace it.

9

Whether religion itself be totally eclipsed or newly revived, the fundamental truth from which it rises is always hidden deep in the subconscious mind of man. Life itself, the very drive behind the whole universe, will force the atheist one day to seek it and will give him no rest until he finds it.

10

It would be true to say that the materialism of our time is an agnostic rather than an atheistic one. People are indifferent to the question of whether there is or is not a higher power, rather than being deliberate deniers of its existence.

11

The atheists who see only the weaknesses of religion and not its services denounce it as false and injurious. They seize on the undoubted harm done by religious exploitation and religious superstition as a pretext for themselves doing infinitely greater harm by proclaiming all religious feeling to be mere illusion. They point also to the mental aberrations of individual mystics to denounce all mysticism as an even greater illusion. But to stamp out every manifestation of religious life and mystical enlightenment would reduce man to the level of the brute, albeit a cunning intellectual brute.

12

How pitiful the suggestion of Marx that religion is an invention of human imagination to enable one class—the sacerdotal—to prey on the people, and another class—the upper—to exploit the people, or the assertion of Polybius that it is an invention of society for its own protection to maintain order among men and prevent them from running amok into anarchy by following their own individual wills entirely. That it has been used for such purposes historically is correct, but the religious instinct is a very real thing and rises from a very real source.

13

The theory, based on economics, according to which religion was invented to help despoil the working class is unscientific: it is also unworthy of those who boast that they are led by reason. The very adherence to such a theory proves that they are led much more by strong emotion.

14

He alone can be an atheist who has never experienced a glimpse, or who has been caught and become embedded in a hard dry intellectualism, or in whom ethics and conscience have withered.

15

The egoistic fool, with his intellect puffed up by a little learning, sets out to criticize everything, including the belief in God. Let us be humbler, awed by the thought of the World-Mind's unchanging identity and unbroken infinity.

16

Too often a man thinks that his problem is solely personal, whereas it is most probably common to all mankind. Most men and women have or will have to face it at some time; for the basic problems of the human situation are really few, and part of the work of a religious prophet is to give guidance in a general way as to how rightly to deal with these problems. Those atheistic Communists who reject pure religion along with their rejection of sectarian religion, reject also a hand stretched out to help them. In their madness they ignore every prophet's warning against violence and hatred, against unscrupulousness and greed, and set out consciously to create sorrow for themselves.

17

The spread of atheistic movements is something to be sadly deplored. But if they are the inevitable reaction against sham religion we are forced to accept them as historical necessity. This necessity is, however, quite temporary and if atheism is put forward or permitted to remain as ultimate truth, then it becomes as morally disastrous to humanity as the falsity against which it is unconsciously opposed by the dialectic movement of racial destiny.

18

Those psychoanalysts who would stamp all religious instinct as a sexual derivation and those materialists who would stamp all religious belief as a social exploitation exhibit neither a profound psychology in the one case nor an accurate realism in the other. What they assert is only sometimes and somewhere true, not always and everywhere true.

19

The atheistic leaders of our time have tried to banish the concept of God. They have succeeded in doing so for large numbers of people, especially young people. But what is true in the concept will reappear in men's minds again, for it is eternal. It cannot be banished although it can be covered over for a time.

20

A time comes when he outgrows the elementary doctrines and popular observances, when prayer and ceremonial, scripture and asceticism have no further usefulness for him. But this does not entitle him to denounce them to the world, to destroy their place in life, or to dissuade others from using them.

21

It is wrong of those who feel they receive no blessing, no spiritual gain of peace, from a church sacrament to scorn as superstitious others who feel with joy that they do receive it.

22

"You snivelling priest," exclaimed Voltaire, "you are imposing delusions upon society for your own aggrandizement."

23

If a man believes he is nothing else than a human electrical machine, why should he pay any attention to moral character?

24

It is enough to make two statements about the Russians—first, the government in all its departments officially opposes religion; second, the highly influential Communist Party makes atheism an article of belief before membership is granted—to understand why and predict that either self-reaction or self-destruction awaits them. There may be no future also for the Russian Orthodox Church—narrow, intolerant, and materialistic as it *was*—but religion in a larger, purer, and truer sense must one day return because of the innate need for it.

25

Sceptics find one religion as untrustworthy as another because all religions are founded on belief in the existence of an Unknown and—to them—unknowable Entity.

26

The atheist who believes that morality is supported by religion to help keep the populace obedient may be partly right and partly wrong. But he falls into error if he believes that religion was invented solely for this purpose.

27

The illusionist religions, which reject all values and virtues in the world in which we humans have to live, give us little to hope for or live for. It is not surprising that most of the masses under their influence have lived a half-animal existence.

28

In Germany and Austria there were in 1933 over a million members of Freethought organizations; in Czechoslovakia in 1938 there were a million persons who declared themselves to belong to no religious body.

29

The outdated scepticism of earlier science and the moral ineffectualness of the later Church have helped those Communists who brand religion as an instrument of intellectual domination and indirectly of economic exploitation.

30

God is invoked on every side but there is no sign that he has ever been involved in our affairs, say the sceptics. If he reigns, he does not rule!

31

All too many have shaken themselves free from religious superstition without having replaced it by religious truth.

Cycles of inspiration, decay

32

The history of most religious organizations is a history of pure motives mixed with impure ones, of spiritual aspiration mixed with human exploitation, of reverence mixed with selfishness, intuition with superstition, and prayerful petition with arrogant exclusiveness.

33

History shows that nearly every religion moves through the same timeworn cycle of phases—from purity and reality and fellowship through organization and literalness and external expansion to hypocrisy and exploitation and tyranny. All religious influence historically passes through these stages of rise and fall. It begins by expressing an elementary portion of divine truth and by promoting a simple standard of human morality. It ends by opposing the truth and defending immorality. In its purity and vitality, it suffuses the hearts of its votaries with goodwill towards other men and hence draws them closer together. But in its degradation and devitalization it poisons the hearts of its slaves with intolerance towards other men and thus sets them farther apart. The declension of a religious movement begins at the point where the external organization of it begins to replace the internal feeling of it. The intuition is then gradually forgotten and the importance of funds, buildings, officials, prestige, and power rises egoistically and ambitiously in its stead. In the end the inner reality is all but lost, only its mocking shadow remains. It might be said that in its early unformed state, the movement spiritually exhilarates men but in its later institutional state it materially exploits them. It is therefore necessary to make a clear-cut distinction between a religion in its original pure form and in its later corrupt form. Time corrupts every religion. The history of Christianity confirms this cyclic nature of religion. It arose outwardly amidst bitter suffering and violent death; it began to fall inwardly amidst gilded prosperity and exaggerated pomp.

34

By "religion" is meant here not any particular one but the entire cluster of authentic sacred revelations throughout the world. No particular world-religion is referred to in our criticism. What is to be said is true of them all, although more true of some and less of others.

35

The vitality of a religion is most apparent in its primitive unorganized form, as the purity of a religion is most apparent in its apostolic phase.

36

As the inward sense of being dedicated followers of a Way, a Truth and a Life fades away with the efflux of time, so religious vision narrows, moral aspiration slackens, declarations of rigid dogma are insisted on, the abidance by a group of outward customs and rules is enforced, individuality is crushed as heresy, the zeal for self-improvement is replaced by the zeal for meddling with the affairs of others, petty differences are exaggerated, and pure creative spirituality is killed. Every established religion seems historically to pass down through such a degenerative process to a dry sterile condition. It seems not possible to keep the movement on the high level at which the prophet started it.

37

Neither the minds that gather around a prophet nor those who diffuse his influence and teaching in later centuries are likely to be equal to his own. To that extent, therefore, their understanding of him and his teaching is likely to be inferior to his own. This distance from him has the one advantage, however, that it brings them more on a level with the multitude whom they themselves wish to influence or convert.

38

Dull followers in the generations soon to come falsify his ideas, and selfish ones degrade them. Such is the disagreeable truth about every prophet's fate. Receiving the pure teaching is a sacrament but upholding its degenerated forms is a sacrilege.

39

If you realize the extraordinary length of time of the real history of man, and not merely the history which is taught in schools, you will realize also that many religions have come and completely disappeared. Why should we think that these religions which we now know must continue to exist permanently? They are only tools which are used by God so long as they are effective but thrown aside when they are worn out.

40

Time is like a river which is forever flowing onwards, which can never turn back, and which sweeps religions and races before it. This is why those who look for a triumphant and lasting revival of any particular religion deceive themselves. Revivals have occurred and will occur, but history shows how transient they are and philosophy shows why this must be so.

41

People are being deceived by the renewed vitality of some old religions, by their conversions, activities, and literature, into believing that they are witnessing a veritable and durable renaissance with a long bright future before it. This is particularly true of Christians, Hindus, and Muslims. But what are they really witnessing? It is nothing more than the dying flicker of sunset, the sudden blaze before darkness falls.

42

History teaches the same story about all the religions. They begin as faiths, freely held in the heart; they culminate as creeds, imposed like shackles upon the mind. The myth of an almost ecclesiastical infallibility is maintained by the church leaders in their own interests.

43

There comes a time in the life of each traditional religion when it becomes the enemy of true religion. History tells us this; psychology predicts its inevitability.

44

Although atheism appears when religion makes much more fuss over the appearance of virtue than over its reality, mysticism also appears when sufficient time has elapsed to demonstrate the intuitive barrenness of such decadent religion as well as the moral danger to its followers.

45

After the death of the guru, we see the hard outlines of a new sect in the making, the forming of an ecclesiastic hierarchy with new episcopate and new priesthood, the increasing disposition to detect heresy or schism and shut out those who exhibit the capacity, if not the courage, to think for themselves, the rise of personal ambitions and the seeking of private advantage. The honest, let alone passionate, pursuit of truth gradually vanishes.

46

When men transfer their faith to another religion, cult, or system of thought, it not only shows that the force behind the new one is greater than that behind the old one, but may also show that the World-Idea, which includes karma, is itself the force promoting the successful rival.

47

In those first few centuries when Christianity was a pure and vital religion, the name Christian meant one who believed in the existence of this higher power and surrendered his heart to its loving presence. The name Muslim (our western "Muhammedan") had much the same meaning in the early days of Islam's history. It signified one who had submitted his lower self to the Divine, resigned his personal will to the higher will of God. Such submission was not regarded as being only moral; it was also psychological. That is, it was to rule consciousness as well as conduct. Hence it was a difficult achievement following a long endeavour rather than a mere verbal assent made in a single moment.

48

When convention becomes stagnant and kills the living element in custom or religion, it suffocates the growing element in man's soul.

49

Creeds will come and go, being at their best the results of the working of human minds striving to comprehend divine glimpses. They are necessarily imperfect.

50

Most religions were constructed gradually, shaped by time and history. This is most true of Judaism and Christianity, least true of Hinduism and Buddhism.

51

The corruptions of religious doctrine and the conventions of religious society keep out the true spirit of the prophet behind the religion itself.

52

Little sects may become large churches. The movement towards truth may become an institution which hinders truth. The persecuted Christians of the fourth century became the persecuting Inquisition of the fourteenth. Given enough time white may turn black.

53

There are two chief justifications for the existence of a religion: (a) its influence upon the character and actions of people for the better; (b) its dim intimation of world meaning. But when a religion fails to prevent wickedness or to convince men that their existence has a higher purpose, it deserves to decline—and does.

54

The impulse which originated each existing religion has largely worked itself out, leaving stark error and pseudo-religion as its current offering. Even the error has come in the end to assume the form of an authentic tradition!

55

The visible difference between religion in its primitive purity and in its aged decadence is the best argument for the periodical need of a new religion.

56

Not only Buddhism but also Islam and Judaism originally banned the artistic representation of man's form in religious symbolism. Why? Because it commonly led to worship of idols, of the form of the human formulator of that particular religion.

57

If during a prophet's lifetime legends spring up which are only half-true or even wholly untrue, what is likely to happen after his death? This is one reason why religions are said to be based on faith.

58

The debasement of a religion usually runs parallel to the increment of its organization.

Accretions, distortion, corruption

59

A study of religious origins will reveal that much which today passes as established religion is merely accretion: it was added in the course of time. Tradition—now regarded as sacrosanct—was once innovation. It is often the opinion of later men overlaid on the Master's words.

60

The farther we get from the Prophet's time, the more difficult it becomes to discover exactly what he taught. Sects multiply in his name, each with a different doctrine. Imaginations and interpolations, distortions and caricatures become part of the received teaching. As if this were not enough, personal ambitions and institutional exploitations add to the confusion.

61

The defect in human nature which makes it stress the person rather than the power using him, the letter rather than the spirit, is responsible in part for the deterioration of religion. Let men beware of a personality worship which is carried blindly to idolatrous extremes. Let them beware, also, of unquestionably receiving ideas about religion which have been propagated by its ministers and missionaries. It is not group effort but individual effort that counts on the quest. The prophets and teachers helped people in groups and churches only because of the need of economizing their own time and energy, not because this was more efficacious. Those who quote Jesus: "Where two or three are gathered in my name, there shall I be in the midst of them" in rebuttal, are self-deceived. Words like these were never spoken by Jesus. They were interpolated by cunning priests. The populace, a term in which from the standpoint of intelligence we must include different members from all social strata from lowest to highest, is led to accept contradictions and obscurities out of a regard for religious authority which paralyses all independent thinking.

62

It is a tragedy of all history that the names of Men like Jesus, who came only to do good, are invariably exploited by those who fail to catch their spirit and do more harm than good. Formal entry into any religious organization relates a man only to that organization, not at all to the Prophet whose name it claims. No religious institution in history has remained utterly true to the Prophet whose name it takes, whose word it preaches, whose ethic it inculcates. A religious prophet is mocked, not honoured, when men mouth his name and avoid his example. No church is a mystical body of any prophet. All churches are, after all, only human societies, and suffer from the weaknesses and selfishnesses, the errors and mistakes, inseparable from such societies. It is a historical fact that where religious influence upon society has bred the evils of fanaticism, narrow-mindedness, intolerance, superstition, and backwardness, their presence may be traced back to the professional members and monkish institutions of that religion. Priestcraft, as I have seen it in certain Oriental and Occidental lands, is often ignorant and generally arrogant. Throughout the world you may divide clergymen and priests into two categories—those who are merely the holders of jobs and those who are truly ministers of religion.(P)

63

If you want the truth as it was really taught, remember that you will get from the historic official teaching of the later followers a tampered, interpolated, excised, weighted, and moulded doctrine.

64

When the truth of recompense is perverted, it becomes fatalism. Then the aspirations to evolve personally and improve environmentally are arrested, while responsibility for inaction or action is placed outside oneself.

65

More and more as I came to understand religion, to separate its truths from its fables, I discovered how the Master's teaching had been corrupted or distorted, truncated, or stressed in the wrong places. This happened more in some faiths than in others, and differently in one from the other. It happened in Judaism and Buddhism, in Islam and Christianity.

66

The theologians must take their share of responsibility for the enormous extent and power of materialism today, for their absurd squabbles about unreal or remote issues and their silly dogmatics about matters of which they can *know* nothing have repelled large numbers who seek to use their God-given faculty of reason and their capacity to observe facts.

67

There is a long distance from the rhetorical urges intended to create religious frenzy to the calm statement intended to evoke religious intuition.

68

Worse than the degeneration of doctrine has been the degeneration of ethics. A man best proves what he is by his conduct, an institution or society by its deeds. For verbal preaching may be mocked by contradictory practice. The expounders and hierarchs of religion are rightly expected to set good standards for the supposedly weaker masses, but sacerdotal cupidity and ecclesiastical intolerance, the ignoble lust for power and the ignorant hatred of other faiths, have far too often disappointed expectation.

69

The institutions, the credos, the scriptural documents even, of a religion are man-made. Even if and where they are made under divine inspiration, it may not have been present all the time.

70

What is left of a religion after thousands of years of man-handling by biased or prejudiced parties should be received with critical, independent judgement.

71

The temples and churches, the synagogues and mosques of old established religions have become empty of true spirituality, their thresholds profaned by lack of genuine interest, true faith, or real obedience to religion's dictates. The basic commandments of the founders of religion, simple though they be, are seldom given the importance they deserve. In short, the sacred name of religion is violated daily, year after year, century after century.

72

The only way to retain Faith is to regenerate it. Churchianity must become Christianity. Its failure became plain during the War, when a situation existed where the Japanese nominal followers of the peace-bringing Buddha spread murder and pillage across Asia and where the German nominal followers of the love-bringing Jesus spread hatred and aggression across Europe, in some cases with the sanction and under the blessing of their local priests and national High Priests and in all cases without a firm protest and resolute opposition by the whole weight of their organizational influence against such betrayal of what both Buddha and Jesus stood for. Here history but repeats itself. It was not the atheists who crucified Jesus but the priests. It was not the atheists who drove Buddhism right out of India but the priests.

73

People are easily deceived by the stature to which religions have grown into thinking that they have achieved assured stability. An institution which has reached great size has not necessarily reached great success. It is necessary to look beneath the illusion of numbers and the skin of popularity. Spiritual degeneration and decrepitude are still what they are even if they are spread among millions of people. When we try to understand the causes of such disintegration, we are inevitably led to the conclusion that religion wrongly understood and wrongly expounded breeds distrust, exploits ignorance, and disrupts society. How do ordinary people arrive at their understanding of a religion, then? They arrive at it through the guidance of official exponents. Therefore the latter bear a larger responsibility for the downfall of their own faith than they usually realize. They have often invoked judgement of God on others; have they ever observed how history has invoked the judgement of God on them? So far as the mission of an institution consists in assuming the austere role of a prophet and making the glowing message of such a man freely available to simple toiling folk, so far as its presence in society acts as a check on human character, which would otherwise degenerate and permit evils more serious than existing ones to spring up, it possesses something which the people profoundly need; it has a most valuable service to render for which it must live, and it can face its critics as indifferently as Jesus faced his persecutors. But so far as the institution has come to mean something glaringly different or has come to constitute a professional means of livelihood for certain individuals, merely by seating them on the chair of sanctity, or has associated itself with pointless dogmas which outrage human intelligence, it has certainly become something so unchristian and useless that the continued fall of its influence need surprise none.

74

An organization is required to transmit the services of religion whether it be an elaborate Church with three continents under its wing or an obscure sect with a single preacher located in a small room. The personnel of this organization constitute its living value, for theirs is the duty of giving right guidance to its followers. If prelates and priests understand the higher purport of religion they will slowly uplift their flock and deem it their duty to serve rather than to enslave them. For instance, they will gradually replace the notion of an angry or cruel God to be propitiated through devotional communion. If however they fail to understand this purport, they will misunderstand it. And as they are notoriously and tenaciously conservative, they will apply this quality—so admirable when it bespeaks loyalty to true and virtuous things—in wrong directions such as the dissemination of outworn, unimportant dogmas or the support of barbarous customs, untenable doctrines, false history, and worthless rites—nearly all of which do not belong to the faith in its primitive purity but are mutilations or accretions originating from the mediocre minds of ignorant interpolators or the selfish hearts of greedy interpreters. This will lead slowly to the next step, which is to use the organization primarily for their selfish benefit. When this happens the people naturally lose their faith in them as well as in the rites and dogmas, the ethical value of their religion wanes, and enemies arise both inside and outside its frontiers to bring it crumbling to the ground in the long course of time.

75

Religion as shaped by history is not the same as religion as propagated by the prophet.

76

If religions lose their original inspiration, if their texts get corrupted and their priests get worldly, it is relevant to enquire whether such deteriorations can be avoided. The imperfections of human nature warn us that *total* avoidance is impossible.

77

How many a prophet has been crucified afresh by his alleged followers who persecuted and oppressed in his name! How often has his teaching been caricatured by giving it a false application to serve personal interests or support emotional hatreds!

78

Religion is supposed to raise a man's moral quality, diminish his hatred, and curb his selfishness, but too often in history it has failed to do so. But it is not only religion that is at fault: it is also the stubbornness of man himself.

79

When a religion, suffering from decay and inertia, asks us to give reverence to tradition more than we give it to God, it fails in its own mission.

80

When the ceremonies and forms of religion have become a tangled network, when the primal simplicity of its sanctities has been lost underneath the fussy elaborations of its dogmas, it becomes sterile and unhelpful: from the highest point of view, such religion becomes irreligion.

81

If the immature are taught nothing better than the incredible and half-credible assertions, the foolish tales they have hitherto been told, why wonder that religious faith and church attendance turn into religious hypocrisy?

82

It is right and proper to continue a good tradition, to keep a spiritual inheritance from the past which has intrinsic worth; but it is not right to demand enslavement to such tradition and inheritance so that nothing new may enter or be said.

Sectarianism

83

The atmosphere of pure religion is as different from the atmosphere of sectarian organization as a natural flower is different from an artificial one.

84

Religion which wills to lead mankind into spiritual consciousness has failed to do so. Why? Because it has led him into organizations, groups, divisions, monasteries, ashrams, sectarianism, and centres. These have become the important things, not the spiritual consciousness.

85

We may honour, even revere, a place in this world, an epoch in spiritual history, a man who has been graced by enlightenment; but to depend on any particular one only is both unwise and sectarian.

86

He only has the fullest right to talk of God who *knows* God, not his idea, fancy, belief, or imagination about God. He only should write of the soul, its power, peace, and wisdom, who lives in it every moment of every day. But since such men are all too rare and hard to find, mankind has had to accept substitutes for them. These substitutes are frail and fallible mortals, clutching at shadows. This is why religionists disagree, quarrel, fight, and persecute both inside and outside their own groups.(P)

87

Since truth can be looked at from different standpoints, since it has different aspects, it is desirable that there should exist a variety of doctrines and views. Where the attempt is made to congeal it into a fixed creed, for all time, a sect is created and sectarian prejudices are introduced.

88

A sect is not open to truth: it closes the door upon what it has, will not scrutinize whether it be truth or not, will not admit new formulations. And by sects I mean groups with many millions of adherents or a few hundreds. The larger they are, the more accustomed to power they are, and the less open they are when traditional formulations no longer meet contemporary needs.

89

No membership of any church, temple, or ashram will save you if it becomes a cause of narrowing down ideas, relationships, mind—of sectarianism.

90

It is the wrong idea they have of the sect which constitutes their enslavement, not necessarily the sect itself. With a free mind they can use its organization safely.

91

Why has every historic religion divided itself into sects, why has no religious and no mystical organization yet escaped being severed by sectarianism or cut by schism? The answer can be found partly in the different needs of different types of human individuals, and partly in the imperfections and weaknesses of human character. It is because men have not risen into the full truth, because their understanding has not been freed from egoism nor their feelings from bias, that they fall into mean and petty sectarianism. In this pitiful condition, they imagine God to care only for members of their own sect and no other! The work of adverse forces seeking to pervert, materialize, or nullify the original inspired teaching must also be taken into account.

92

Those who look for an earthly heaven and spiritual millennium round the corner of the widespread adoption of some cult are sure to be disappointed. Their credulity shows they understand neither why nor how cults are formed, nor what human nature still is. That people will shed overnight their conventional forms of religious subservience on the one hand, and their selfishness and violence, their ignorance and uncontrol on the other hand, is a naïve belief which only naïve unphilosophic cults could foster.

93

It was a seventeenth-century clergyman, Christian Hoburg, who dared to publish a pamphlet, albeit pseudonymously, which contained such statements as "All Churches are sectarian" and "Christ is unknown to all the Churches."

94

All the revolts against orthodoxy, against organization, against dogma, acquire an enthusiastic following which ultimately ends up with another orthodoxy, another organization, another set of dogmas.

95

My plaint against them is that they are parrots, endlessly repeating and babbling the answers which original minds gave thousands of years ago. They are quite noncreative, and too often quite sectarian under their pretense of non-sectarianism.

96

Not only do organized religions split off into sects, but there are further splits of sects within sects.

97

There are benefits and disadvantages in old, established, traditional religions. But if the disadvantages stay too long or become too strong, they obstruct the basic purpose of religion. If their doctrines hamper religious aspiration or tyrannize over men, they are rendering a disservice. If symbols are taken too literally they may bind men to idol-worship and they may become substitutes for reality. Even an effort to propagate non-sectarian views, to cull what is good or essential from various quarters—as theosophy was to a large extent an attempt—even such a movement is likely, in the end, to become itself sectarian.

98

Schisms are found inside most religions: they are not less free from the ego's activity than politics and commerce.

99

Most blind followers of a sect do not attempt to understand the metaphysical and practical problems involved but simply take sides against the one who is being personally vilified.

100

The earnest pleas of Saint Paul could not stop dissensions among the faithful during his own lifetime: "I beg of you, brethren, be perfectly united in the same mind and in the same judgement." It has not stopped them dividing into bickering sects and contending cliques during the many centuries since his lifetime. Only when we understand the limitations of religion shall we understand why his plea was a utopian dream.

101

A religion might possibly gain universal support one day, but unless its devotees had touched and kept the philosophic level, sects would eventually appear within it to break the uniformity and disturb the harmony.

Intolerance, narrowness, persecution

102

None save Mind Itself can know what Mind is. No person can form an idea of Mind which is at all adequate. No one can create a mental picture which is correct. No one can formulate a concept which corresponds to the actuality of Mind. All results suffer from human limitations. If accepted by any religious creed they become idols worshipped in vain. If this be so it becomes clear that religious intolerance and religious persecution are evil human failings masquerading as virtues exercised on behalf of faith in the true God!

103

The notion that some sect, some people, or some race has been chosen to fulfil a special mission upon earth is a notion which is to be found in every nation that a philosopher can visit and in every epoch of history that he can study. It is a foolish notion and a recurring fallacy. It is such teaching which has kept false ideas and foolish emotions stubbornly alive. But it will persist and go on persisting because it appeals to peoples' vanity, not because it is based on any facts. Josephus lengthily argued that Plato derived his wisdom from Hebrew lore. Nowadays the Hindu Swamis tell us that Plato borrowed it from Indian lore. 'Tis all opinion, mere opinion—the truth is that the light of wisdom can shine everywhere, on any race and at any time. No single nation or land possesses primal inspiration.

104

The devotee believes that his God is the only true God, and other people's Gods are inferior or false. His ego is thus still in the way, despite high experiences.

105

So long as each institutional religion asserts that it alone has the truth, or has more truth, or more closeness to God, or that it is the most important vehicle used by God, so long will it continue to divide men, foster prejudice and ill will, even create hate, along with whatever good it is, or is capable of, doing.

106

Every man is entitled to his own personal opinion. It is his private possession. But when he wants to communicate it to others as a universal dogma or, worse, to impose it upon them as a universal faith received from God, we are entitled to remind him that he ought to keep his affairs to himself.

107

In the end the powers of karma fall crushingly upon those who, for selfish motives, have suppressed truth and supported falsehood.

108

Jesus would have been the first to realize that the love which he enjoined on his followers was essentially the same as the compassion which Buddha enjoined on his own. Yet, uninformed, or informed but biased, religionists seek to decry the Oriental teachings by proving the alleged superiority of the Occidental—as if Jesus was not Himself an Oriental! The real secret of this attempt to classify Jesus among the Occidental races is that they happen to be Occidental: in short, it is the dominance of their egos which leads to the confusion in their concepts.

109

If prejudice favouring an inherited creed denies the full truth, bias against it blocks the path to such truth.

110

All such denigration of other spiritual paths or of other spiritual tribes is as unnecessary as it is inexcusable.

111

The history of religious bigotry is associated with the history of religious persecution. If the first is denied entry, the second cannot appear.

112

The higher power bears no labels but men invent them and, later, their descendants begin to worship the labels instead of the power. Hence religious conflicts and wars: hence, too, religious ideas and atheistic movements.

113

Wherever there is persecution *within* a religion of those who differ from the ruling authority of the period, it usually covers the fact that the persecutors are greater heretics than their victims. For the Founder did not come to preach hatred and cruelty—there is enough of that in the world for God not to need to send someone to increase it—but virtue and goodwill. So the persecutors, even if successfully established and long established, are not preaching *his* message, but their own, which contradicts it.

114

The overleaping of these sectarian labels can only help the dissolving of the sectarian frictions, quarrels, persecutions, and intolerances which in the end turn into tortures, inquisitions, hatreds, and wars.

115

If we study the history of established state religions, too often we find that the priests or clergy of the religion have been able to stir up the fanaticism of ignorant crowds to persecute or to eliminate those who dare to believe otherwise and are foolish enough to state their beliefs publicly. It must be pointed out that this tendency is most pronounced among those who follow the three Semitic religions: Judaism, Christianity, and Islam, in the order of their historic appearance. It is all to the credit of Buddhism and Hinduism that tolerance is almost a tenet of their religions.

116

When the acceptance of religious faith stirs up animosity, creates hatred, and fosters persecution, it is then no better but even worse than its rejection.

117

Criticism is the inevitable karma of superstitious credulity as hatred is the inevitable karma of unjust persecution. We heard much of the persecutions of the Russian Orthodox Church by the Bolsheviks after their revolution but little of the persecutions by the same Church before the revolution. Those who understand how karmic retribution works unerringly will find the following little paragraph, taken from a leading St. Petersburg newspaper, *Novoye Vremya*, during the year 1892, very significant. Dealing with accounts given by Prince Mestcherski of certain suffering endured by the Christian sect called "Old Believers" at the hands of the Orthodox State Church, in Siberia, the paper writes: "The treatment of the Buddhists is still harsher. Says the Prince, 'They are literally forced by the police, at the instance of the local clergy, to embrace Christianity. All kinds of means are resorted to; they are captured in the woods, hunted like beasts and beaten, force even being employed with pregnant women.'"

118

What strikes us most poignantly is the absence of sympathy, of love in the widest Christian sense, for all those outside each little sect. For the incompatible difference between the lofty kindness enjoined by Jesus and the petty meanness practised by the sectarians in his name is heart-saddening.

119

Religion has hardly been successful in bringing men to the most elementary and merely negative duty of refraining from killing one another. At Ayuthia, the former capital of Siam but now overgrown by jungle, I saw a lone large statue of Gautama the Buddha sadly looking out at the ruins of the city destroyed by a Burmese army two centuries ago. And both antagonists claimed to be Buddhists! At Shanghai, I saw another Buddha statue amid the debris of a wrecked temple in the suburban district of Chapei, the scene of battle in 1937, yet both the Chinese and Japanese antagonists here were partly Buddhist, and the Buddha made non-killing a prominent tenet of the ethical code which he laid down for all his followers, for monks and laymen alike.

120

Too many men have used the word God to cover their cruelties, or their follies, or their own selfishnesses!

121

The absurdity of insisting on name-labels, the narrowness of joining religious groups, attains its summit when immortal life is proclaimed as our destiny only if we belong to a particular group!

122

The journey from the narrowness of dogma to the arrogance of infallibility may take time for a religious institution to finish, but when it is finished a further journey may begin. And that is to intolerance, totalitarianism, and finally persecution.

123

The religious temperament has its puzzling contradictions. The Holy Inquisitors would have been hurt if told that they had repudiated Christ, would insistently have asserted their devotion to him. Yet for religious reasons they broke men's bodies on the torture wheel, tied them to the stake for burning. The gentle inhabitants of Tahiti shed tears copiously when Captain Cook flogged a thief on his ship, yet for religious reasons they practised human sacrifice while their priests killed their own children. A Jewish king in the early pre-Islamic Arabia persecuted those among his subjects who were Christians. Later Christian kings in Europe persecuted their Jewish subjects, while Muhammedan kings in the Middle East persecuted Jews and Christians alike!—all in the name of religion.

124

If the *Bhagavad Gita*'s statement means anything at all, it means that we ought to be tolerant to other people's worship, to the form in which they symbolize God. Pliny understood this very well when he wrote: "You are going to Athens. Respect their gods."

125

When conversion is followed by enthusiasm, this is natural, often inevitable. But when it is followed by fanaticism, the convert is put in danger and others even more so.

126

It must be remembered as a mark against exaggerated valuation of, and trust in, religious institutions and religious authority, that the Holy Inquisition not only burned or tortured infidels but even the Franciscan Brothers, good Christian Catholics who happened to become victims of the prejudice of one particular medieval Pope.

127

It is very difficult to find any organized form of religion which does not exaggerate its own value, or denigrate other forms.

128

A truly universal outlook would be free from the subtle possessiveness which wants to draw others into one's own particular fixed cult or creed and keep them there forever chained. This kind of religious attachment is not less binding, not less shutting-in to horizons, than those other, and more obvious, forms of personal, material, or emotional attachment.

129

Fanaticism is often allied with superstition using the authority of religious texts, customs, or traditions. So it passes unscrutinized and self-deluded, too often preoccupied with externals and trivialities.

130

They hold their opinions too ferociously to hold them on a basis of reason.

131

The sacred foolishness of those teachers of the path of religious devotion who reject all the other paths is still better than worldly foolishness, but it cannot form part of the philosophic ideal.

132

Where doctrine is elevated above life, it inevitably leads by a series of fatal downward steps to guarding itself by persecuting those who hold opposing views. This happened in medieval Catholic history. It happened in early Reformation history, and it happened even in American Presbyterian history.

133

The Romans, who brutally slaughtered the assembled Druids in Britain, were symbolic of the retribution which eventually punishes priestly fanaticism and of the challenge which inevitably comes to priestly superstition.

134

They are fools who do not know that though they burn ten thousand heretics this day, God will implant the same idea, if it be a true one, in ten thousand minds tomorrow.

135

So long as ecclesiastical leaders falsely teach their flocks that their own particular religion is the only one acceptable in God's eyes and that all other religions are bereft of His grace and light, so long will religion continue to give birth to strife instead of peace, prejudice instead of tolerance, hatred instead of love.

136

The Israelites did not have a monopoly of the "God's Chosen Race" belief. Milton, in his "Areopagitica," proclaimed that "God reveals Himself first to His Englishmen." Hegel, however, asserted that it was the divine decree for the Germans to lead the world. And, until Hitler's hordes smashed through their land, not a few of the mystically inclined Poles passionately believed that theirs was to be "the Messianic race." In the Far East, the Japanese cherished similar beliefs until American bombs initiated a process of revisionary thinking.

Naïve sentimentalists or distorted thinkers manufacture romantic impressions about their race religion history or country. Some dream golden-age, Eden-idyllic fantasies about the past or future that have no basis in fact. Perverted wishful thinking asks for illusion—and gets it!

False theory breaks down before personal experience of the present fact as it actually is. This is often quite painful but how else is the real truth to be established when the sayer of it is disregarded or disbelieved?

Superstition

137

We need religion, yes assuredly, but we need it freed from superstition.(P)

138

When the faculty of reverence is diverted from its proper object—the divine Power—and perverted to a base one, it becomes superstition.

139

Theological arguments which use empty words without mental substance, sacred names of non-existent entities, can be classified as superstitious.

140

Do not lose your wits over religious fables which were intended to help ungrown minds—that is, most minds—or to soothe and comfort half-grown ones needing new interpretations and better explanations. There never was a "Golden Age" where all people lived happily together, nor is there now an "Iron Age" where they all live miserably together.

141

Every superstition is a truth corrupted. Therefore when we say that religion ought to purify itself, it need in many cases only turn its superstitions inside-out to set itself right!

142

Superstition is a costly luxury which the mood of this age cannot afford to set up; it is harmful to genuine religion and useless to genuine devotees. False thoughts are so plentiful that they lie ready to the hand of man; hence he finds it easier to pick them up without effort, rather than to exert his own mind to independent thinking. In the absence of the inspiration of true religion men will accept the degradation of untrue materialism, though it is noteworthy that the younger clergy have abandoned the teaching about the creation of the universe and the origin of man which they had inherited.

143

There is no excuse for such unthinking complacency. If the powerful suggestions of tradition and environment persuade us to believe certain things heedlessly, to go on believing them throughout a lifetime is to shame and deny our thinking power. Much of what passes for religion is mere superstition. Religion raises us whereas superstition degrades us. We must seek the true face of religion under the false mask of mere spiritual legalism and hollow theological casuistry. We must cast away the accretions and have no use for what is sectarian and self-seeking and superstitious in religion.

144

Scepticism is the inevitable swing from superstition. The moral code that comes with the superstition goes with it, too. This is the worst danger of false religion.

145

There is a very real difference between right faith and superstitious faith.

146

Where religion lets itself support the superstition which, if allowed, grows like a parasite upon it, it begins to practise deception upon itself and imposture upon society. It lets go of Truth at its own peril and to its followers' harm.

147

Because millions of people share a superstition does not make it a truth.

148

The perversions of truth have been numerous. But the materializations of truth have been even more numerous. In Japan the guru of a certain Zen sect gave thirty blows with a wooden stick to an unfortunate disciple. This beating was considered to be a precious opportunity for the disciple to gain Satori (Enlightenment)! In India many a pious person or holy man who arrives on pilgrimage in Benares is told by the priests there that by bathing in the River Ganges and putting his head under the surface of the water, he will then gain spiritual enlightenment!

149

When a religious dogma prevents people from searching for the true cause of their distressed condition—whether it be personal trouble or physical disease—and hence from searching for its true remedy, it is nothing more than a superstitious belief masquerading as a religious one.

150

Puerile superstitions have intertwined themselves with every religion, or even taken their place along with golden wisdom.

Dogma

151

We have only to study history, true history, which requires a wider reference than is customary, to discover how religious dogmas develop, how private imagination and personal opinion go into their creation. They are human, not divine.

152

There are religious dogmas which are quite unreal, others which are quite inane; yet, this said, the general residue of religious teaching is solidly and substantially true. Some of it may be wrapped in mystery, which those who want to go farther can unravel with the help of mysticism or philosophy. All of it contains a perceptible message of uplift, of hope, of comfort and of guidance.

153

In the old days metaphysics fell asleep through too much reclining in the arms of my lady Church; if it woke up with the Renaissance that is because this theological flirtation was stopped.

154

False doctrines promulgated in logical form under the title of theology, false beliefs bequeathed from generation to generation and holding crude superstition: these we can well do without, but when getting rid of them, exercise discrimination, take care not to get rid of the true doctrines which theology contains and the worthy beliefs which tradition passes down.

155

It is more prudent to assert that you have some of the truth than to assert that you have the fullness of it.

156

Every organized religion must have dogmas. It could not be what it is without them. Even its first basic assumption—that there is a God—is a dogma. There is nothing wrong in its adherence to dogmas. What is wrong is adherence to false dogmas, to those whose truth is denied by the realities of existence and life.

157

Where any of the doctrines of a religion are unable to survive the tests of reason, examination, factuality, and evidence, they hide away in a part of the mind where the tests cannot get at them. This is called "resting on faith." It is a way of defending them from certain defeat. Instead of permeating the whole outlook, they are compartmentalized.

158

It is a more truly religious man who does not put his religion in fetters, manacled to hard dogma, cruel canon law, and intolerant practice.

159

These creeds and systems are interesting as records of human faith and thought, imagination and invention, but they are useless as paths to salvation. They may give comfortable hopes to their devotees but they do not repudiate the ego which fosters illusions and creates sufferings.

160

All these mystical symbolisms and metaphysical allegories become in the end obstructions which get in the way of a clear understanding of the truth.

161

It is possible that the minister of an orthodox church may be a truly enlightened individual. How, then, it will be asked, can such a person coordinate the abstract Truth of Philosophy with the popular belief of the divinity of Jesus Christ? One answer might be that he privately interprets "divinity" in a special way but publicly follows the orthodox interpretation, because of what he believes to be the necessity of making use of the best available means for leading mankind nearer to Spiritual Reality. Outwardly he might elect to appear as a representative of, say, the Church of England.

162

If the metaphysical foundations are unsound, we need not expect the moral superstructure to be safe from criticism.

163

Where faith has a false basis and a wrong direction, it may one day weaken or even collapse.

164

Those who have the heroism to turn away from outworn creedal dogmas are the real followers of their Redeemer or prophet, the real believers in God.

165

When petty quibbles about surface details and trivial idiosyncrasies of behaviour are placed on a level with the highest ethical standards in importance, we must assert our critical judgement. When external formalities are made to matter just as much as internal virtues of character, we must use our sense of discrimination.

166

When religious faith is inculcated as an attitude towards the unknown and unseen, it is rightly inculcated. But when it is advanced as the right attitude towards the irrational and impossible, it is wrongly advanced.

167

To teach the masses one thing publicly but to believe something very different privately is an attitude which has a great and grave danger—it tends to obliterate the distinction between a truth and a lie.

168

Religious teaching will be all the better when it is freed from life-prisoning and mind-fettering dogmas.

169

A belief for which there is supporting evidence ought not be put in the same category as an unfounded belief.

170

Some religious doctrines are stiflingly narrow and create a desire for the fresh air of reason and science, humanitarianism and compassion.

171

The doctrine of relativity may be applied anywhere and shows that there are no unquestionable creeds, no indisputable dogmas.

172

We can absorb the religious spirit, its emotional reverence for and intellectual fidelity to the Higher Power, without absorbing its commitments to crystallized dogma.

Institutionalism, exploitation

173

I do not know of any organization or institution which attempts to work for mankind in a religious or mystical way which has not its weaknesses, its limitations, and its evils, for remember, every organization and every institution is in the end composed of human beings and in them there is always this dual age-old conflict of good and evil.

174

In the beginning an organization is "pure," that is, seeks earnestly and sincerely to perform its proper function. In the end, its original ambition realized, its success established, it deviates into other purposes. It becomes power-hungry, tyrannical, selfish, more interested in its own perpetuation than in serving the early ideal, more eager for membership and money than in the common welfare. And this is as true of religious as of political organizations, trade unions, and commercial associations.

175

Without some organization there may result intellectual anarchy, moral indiscipline, and emotional chaos. It is also true that the man who accepts a traditional form, joins an organized group, or enters an established church benefits by the help of the tradition or institution. Hence, we are not against teachers and groups which fulfil or even only sincerely strive to fulfil these legitimate expectations. But neither in past history nor present experience are absolutely sincere institutions ever found on earth, although they may be found on paper. It would seem that to set up an organization is to introduce fresh sectarian limitations; that to institutionalize a revelation is to render null and void its spiritual inspiration; and that to totally submit faith, reason, and will to one man is eventually to invite exploitation and accept superstition.

176

The degradation, falsification, commercialization, and exploitation which men, making use of institutional religion, have made of a prophet's mission, speaks clearly of what these men themselves are made. The fact is that they are not fit to be trusted with the power which institutionalism gives them. Religion is safer and healthier and will make more genuine progress if left free and unorganized, to be the spontaneous expression of inspired individuals. It is a personal and private matter and always degenerates into hyprocrisy when turned into a public matter. The fact is, you cannot successfully organize spirituality. It is an independent personal thing, a private discovery and not a mass emotion.(P)

177

When religion identifies itself with an ecclesiastical organization and forgets itself as an individual experience, it becomes its own enemy. History proves again and again that institutionalism enters only to corrupt the purity of a religion.(P)

178

No religion will keep its original purity or inspiration if it fails to keep out its organization's own ambitions and thirst for power or wealth.

179

In religion inspiration dwindles as organization grows. Men come to worship the visible organization itself instead of the Invisible Spirit—that is to say, to worship themselves.

180

Institutional forms render their service by helping a body of teaching to survive, by giving permanence to a tradition, by enshrining and preserving valued memories.

181

Any ecclesiastical organization or any prophetic person who claims *exclusive* knowledge of higher things, *exclusive* communication with heavenly spheres, goes beyond whatever real mandate of authority it possesses. None has the right to make such a claim. Instead of honouring the organization, the latter is dishonoured by it, by its arrogance and falsity.

182

Beware of religious institutions. They are dogmatic, self-loving, unable to transcend their limitations.

183

How would old established ecclesiastical circles, of whatever creed, receive their prophet today? A little knowledge of history, of human organized society, with a little practice of imagination would soon supply an answer.

184

The true Church is an invisible one. It exists only in the hearts of men.

185

The true Church is an interior and invisible Idea, not an exterior and tangible institution.

186

Every attempt to organize religion harms it. It must be spontaneous if it is to keep its purity, personal if it is to keep its reality.

187

No system, no doctrine, and no organization can hold truth without squeezing out much of its life.

188

A religion must be transmitted from generation to generation, so its ministers and scriptures come into being. The purity of its doctrines must be maintained: so sects heresies divergencies reforms and dissents are resisted.

189

It is somewhat sad to observe, in the study of history, that the very purpose of creating an organization to preserve, to guard, and to keep pure a new religion too often becomes with time the very cause of the opposite condition. Additions are made to texts, truths are cut out from them, while the organization regards its own preservation and power as more important than anything else.

190

If there is any lesson which history can teach us, it is that absolute power always corrupts. Such unchecked domination proves in the end, and in the religious world, as bad for the dominator as for those dominated. It breeds weaknesses in him and retards the spiritual growth of his victims. This is not less but even more true when it is exercised by a group, for the risk with the creation of all institutions and organizations is that everything is thereafter done more for the sake of the institution or the organization than of the principle it was embodied to spread. That this risk is very real and almost unavoidable is proved by all history, whether in the Orient or the Occident, whether in ancient times or in modern. It is not long before a time comes when an organization defeats its own ends, when it does as much harm as good, or even more, when its proclaimed purposes become deceptive; external attacks and internal disputes increase with the increase of the organization. No religious organization is so all-wise and so all-selfless that, being entrusted with totalitarian power, it will not yield in time to the temptation of abusing that power. It will practise intolerance and paralyse free thought. The history of every religious monopoly proves this. Thus the individual's need to follow whatever faith he pleases, to think and act for himself, to find the sect that suits him best, is endangered by the monopoly's demand for blind obedience and blinder service. The organization which begins by seeking to spread truth ends by obstructing it. The inheritors of a message of peace and goodwill themselves bequeath hate and bitterness.

191

We do not need to be much learned in the chronicles of both Asiatic and European history to note the unfortunate fact that as religious institutionalism spreads and strengthens itself, religious inspiration shrinks and weakens itself. The original impulse to authentic communication with

God becomes gradually changed into an impulse to selfish exploitation of man. The climax comes when the ecclesiastical organization which was intended to give effect to the sacred injunctions of a seer or prophet not only fails to do so, but actually tries to prevent its members from trying to do so themselves. His purpose is perverted. His teaching is degraded. Thus religion, which should be a potent help to mankind's evolution, tends to become and does become a potent hindrance to mankind's evolution. For such a degradation the karmic responsibility lies heavily on its paid professionals.

192

History has shown that a monopolistic religious institutionalism invariably falls into spiritual degeneracy and inevitably ends in intellectual tyranny. The setting up of autocratic government, episcopal authority, and professional clergy is sooner or later followed by a train of corruptions and abuses. Jesus denounced the religious institutions and religious hierarchy of his time, and drew his followers out of them. Yet hardly had he passed from this earth when they began, in their atavistic reversion to traditional ideas, to recreate new institutions and new hierarchy. If it be asked why the spiritual teacher who knows the harmfulness of these ideas is not heeded by those who believe in him, the answer is first, that belief may be present yet understanding may be absent and, secondly, that the innate selfishness of men finds too easy an opportunity for exploitation through such ideas to miss falling into the temptation of propagating them. Were the truth of any religion really clear to people, all the bitter controversies and bloody persecutions of history would not have happened, and all the innumerable commentaries of theology would never have been written to prove what was so plainly evident.

193

While religion is intimately associated with ecclesiastical organization, it will be intimately associated with money and power needs also. In such a situation it can no longer remain true to its purer self but must inevitably deteriorate.

194

The harmony among religions is a fact, but unfortunately it is not a fact easily seen nor frequently supported by religious organizations in whose interest it is to oppose it.

195

If you wish to know one sign of the difference between a true religion and a half-true or untrue one, remember that the latter seeks power over men whereas the former never does.

196

Institutions are necessary to society; it is only when they become tyrannical or dictatorial that they serve evil purposes.

197

Where religions have failed it is through their institutionalism; where they have succeeded it is through whatever individualism still remained in them. Romantic illusions may keep these institutions alive, but the darkening gloom of our times shows that human welfare cannot be preserved by illusions.

198

"Thou shalt have no other God before Me!" warns the Biblical Commandment. Yet the ignorant still give to the Limited—an organization or a man—the worship which they ought to reserve for the Unlimited—God—alone.

199

For those who have little time and less inclination for the work of study, reflection, meditation, and aesthetic appreciation—namely, for the toiling masses—an attempt is made to accommodate their needs and limitations by providing them with popular religion. But human nature being what it is, sooner or later the institutions and organizations associated with religion become either semi-commercialized or turned into instruments of power. A modern Japanese thinker even went so far as to criticize them by accusing them of "stealing Heaven's Way."

200

An institution or organization is only a background for the men who work in it. It helps or hinders them, elevates or degrades them, but they are the more important factor.

201

We must separate, in our minds, institutional religion from personal religion, the outward structures they have built up historically from the inward atmosphere they have created individually. Persecutions and pogroms come more often from the first, yet without these institutions how would the texts, the teachings, and the reminders be passed down?

202

To give religion a merely institutional significance is to take the incidental for the essential. The churches and sects of religion are its least part; the influence on character and intuition is its greatest.

203

The doctrine of an apostolic transmission of divine authoritative power through human ministry and episcopates is one instance of such false but widely accepted belief. Man will never be saved by any official church.

204

When an organized religion places power over humanity before service to humanity, it loses its way; and when it becomes an instrument of persecution, it prepares its own eventual doom.

205

The sects seeking to get adherents, to commit new members to their dogmas or opinions, are not for him. For nineteen hundred years priests, captive clergymen, and pale theologians have been deliberately endeavouring to persuade people that the kingdom of heaven is to be reached within a professional organization called the Church, *and nowhere else*, as though they could be saved in a mass. Had the ecclesiastics honestly said that their organization existed to help people find the kingdom within themselves and therefore had a perfect right to receive support, nobody could cavil at them. But they have deliberately transplanted the emphasis in their own interests, and followed their master only from the safe distance of a sermon.

206

The organization which gathers round such a prophet, especially after he has left his body and cannot control them, may become an obstacle and, to some extent, even a traitor to his real value and true message.

207

When a religion organizes itself to conquer the world, the world instead conquers the religion. History tells us this time and again.

5

COMMENTS ON SPECIFIC RELIGIONS

Ancient religions

In the Mithraic cult of the Middle East, the sun was united with the Earth, fertilizing it. We call Mithraism a religion of sun worship, but the hidden God behind it was the real object of worship. Yet the final end of all the solar activity—fertilization—was not forgotten. Spirit and Matter became one, daily life of the human being became his spiritual life. Then only did the results of this fertilization—the living crops—appear. Zen *sahaja*, natural *samadhi*—this is what they mean.

2

The sacred places where Druidic priests worshipped were chosen according to knowledge—geographic, astronomic, religious, ritualistic, symbolic, and magnetic.

3

It is something in history to ponder over that in the Alban hills, a few kilometres from Rome, there was once a Temple of Orpheus where, 3000 years ago, the Orphic mysteries were celebrated, where Orphic religion prevailed with its tenets of rebirth, fleshless diet, the quest, and inner reality. It is arguable whether the two other religions which followed it in that area have brought a better message.

4

The dualism of the Persian religions—Zoroastrianism and its kindred Mithraism—is ethical but the dualism of Indian religions is metaphysical. These are two quite different definitions. But in the case of the Christian Manichaeans, whose doctrine Saint Augustine followed for a time and later renounced as a heresy, there is a strange mixture of the ethical along with the metaphysical.

Bahaism

5

Granting the fact that an incarnation has been given a special mission by God which will affect millions of souls and that he must therefore be charged with special divine power, I am unable to see in what way he can be superior to other prophets who have come into close communion with God. It would seem that he would still come within the category of Muhammed's well-known statement, "I am only a man like you." Yet the status which the Bahai faith seems to assign to Baha'u'llah is nothing less than the divinity in the flesh. How can it be possible for even Baha'u'llah to have communed with the uncomprehensible, inconceivable Godhead directly if, as he says, that Godhead is beyond all human conception? Surely no man, however saintly he may be, can escape this limitation?

6

The criticism of the differences in my books from some of the teachings of Baha'u'llah and Bahaism are partly due to misunderstanding and partly to actual divergence. The latter arises, I believe, from the fact that in these days the Bahai faith stresses organization and institutionalism, whereas in the early days it was like primitive Christianity and primitive Islam, free from these later accretions. Although history shows that every religion has followed this course, I still consider the essence of religion to be mystical and not institutional.

7

To the extent that the Bahai faith has dropped the mystical side for the organizational, to that extent it has suffered inwardly however much it has expanded outwardly. In this it follows the history of most religions, which grow and spread their influence in the world at the cost of the purity and spirituality which should lie at their core.

Buddhism

8

Buddha, this godless yet godlike man, rejected most of the Gods in the Hindu pantheon, threw aside the sacrifices, rituals, prayers, and priestcraft current in his time. Buddha is worthy of every admiration because he showed men of rational temperament, men who find it difficult to believe in a God according to the common notion and who are not devotional by nature, how to attain the same spiritual heights as those do who believe and who are religious. He made room in heaven for the rationalist, the free-thinker, and the doubter of all things. Again, those whose familiarity with the Buddha is limited to his statues, with their characteristic attitude of contemplation, often form the wrong notion that he spent his life in inactivity and meditation. On the contrary, he lived strenuously, like Saint Paul, teaching and travelling incessantly, limiting his meditation to not more than an hour or two every day. If Buddha formulated the tragedy of existence, he did not permit his resultant pessimism to paralyse him into mere apathy.

9

That Buddha, like Jesus, wanted to reach the populace, there can be no doubt, except in the minds of the prejudiced. First, he went to extraordinary, most unusual lengths to repeat his teachings from different aspects, so as to make his meaning clearer. Second, he recommended his monks to use the ordinary dialects of simple people whenever they preached Doctrines which were both complex and subtle in themselves and needed simplification anyway.

10

If Buddha did not, like most of the other Indian teachers, affirm the existence of God, he did not deny it. But the reason for this position can be found in his environment, in the Indian scene—too much superstition masquerading as religion, too little respect for reason and fact.

11

The Buddhist can readily get rid of the charge of atheism by referring to the doctrine of Buddha concerning "Amitabha"—"the infinite light of revelation . . . the unbounded light, the source of wisdom and of virtue, of Buddhahood." It corresponds to the Christians' "Logos," the Word, "the true Light that lighteth every man that cometh into the world."

12

It is amusing irony that the very rites and ceremonies which the Brahmin priests tell the masses will advance their spiritual progress were denounced by Buddha because they hinder spiritual progress!

13

It is not the prophet, not the seer, but the men who come later who found churches, establish organizations, and turn religion into a vested interest. Thus when Buddha was dying his attendant disciple, Ananda, was alarmed, according to the ancient records, and said: "The Master will not pass into Nirvana before he has arranged something about the Order?" The Buddha replied: "It would be one who would say, 'I will lead the Order' or 'The Order looks up to me' who would arrange something about it. But I did not think so. Why then should I make any arrangements about the Order?"

14

Although Zen was founded as a Buddhist sect, the Zen attitude toward humanity is far from the Buddha's, with his tender compassion. When I discussed the menace of another global war with a distinguished Japanese Zen leader, he coldly remarked that if it removed most of mankind it would be a good riddance of a nasty race! He felt no distress at the suffering involved. He seemed to look down at it as if the war were a little quarrel among little insects like destructive termites.

15

It is true that the Buddhist way is one of self-discipline and the Christian way one of discipleship, but this is so in appearance only and not in the highest schools of both ways, which are naturally esoteric; the latter approach each other much more closely. The Mahayana school, for instance, has many parallels with the Christian and has as much right to be regarded as authoritatively Buddhist as has the Southern School of Buddhism.

Christianity

16

If you want to learn what Christianity originally was, you must put together the pieces of a jigsaw puzzle, collecting them from the Protestant, the Roman Catholic, the Greek Orthodox, the Manichaean, and the Coptic Churches. Then you must add further pieces from the Alexandrian, the Russian, and the Syrian traditions.

17

The close relation between new faiths and old ones can still be readily traced in Asia, where the vestiges of the latter continue to flourish by the side of the former among aboriginal tribes. It can be traced, too, in African Egypt and Ethiopia, in lands even more accessible to the Western student of theological archaeology, by anyone who cares to venture into the Coptic churches and to examine the Coptic tradition. He will find it in many of the externals and theoretic dogmas of the simple primitive cult of Coptic Christianity, a cult whose propitiations of burning incense, unimpressive mass, cymballed music, and priestly blessings are replete with characteristics that were familiar enough to the Pharoahs. Christianity, which arose in a region midway between the Orient and the Occident, significantly moved westward first and then spread across Egypt, where it silenced the superannuated sanctuaries more quickly than in any other land. In fact,

although the worship of Jesus was so quickly triumphant in this colony of
Rome, it did not officially supplant the worship of Isis or Jupiter until the
reign of Constantine two and a half centuries later.

18

The fact that Jesus was born in the Near East and not the Far East gave
the religion that bears his name a geographical advantage and a historical
familiarity which help to explain why Buddhism and Hinduism spread in
all other directions except Westward. And the fact that the European-
American mind is much more outward bent and much more attached to
the personality than the tropical-Asiatic mind explains why Christianity
had much more affinity with and appeal to the first mind.

19

Christ spoke to the Roman world, and to some of those parts of the
Near East which were then included in the Roman Empire. Buddha spoke
to Asia. Saint Paul and Timothy felt themselves "forbidden of the Holy
Ghost to preach the Word in Asia." In short, Christianity is for the West
since its civilization grew out of the Roman one.

20

The spectacle of so many sects, hostile to one another, teaching dogmas
that Jesus never taught, raised probing questions in the minds of many
Orientals who spoke to me about the matter.

21

The Oriental ideas about the spiritual goal and methods of spiritual
practice as they appear in most Buddhist and many Hindu sects are not
likely to appeal to Occidental seekers. For they seek the dissolution of
human personality, either through merging into an inconceivable Unity or
through disappearance into an indescribable Nirvana. As a rolling wave
dissolves in the sea, as a wisp of smoke vanishes in the air, so does the
separated human life enter its ultimate state. Few Westerners are prepared
to renounce their own identity, to sacrifice their inborn attachment to
personality for the sake of such a vague goal—one moreover which seems
too much like utter annihilation to be worth even lifting a finger for! To
most Westerners it is unpleasant and terrifying to look forward to such an
end. For who gains by this goal? The man himself certainly does not. The
absolute Unity remains what it was before; so it does not gain either. If we
enquire why the goal is acceptable to the East but objectionable to the
West, the answer will be partly found in the latter's religious history.

By seeking to perpetuate for all eternity the same human personality in
the spirit world, too many orthodox church interpreters of Christ's teaching have misinterpreted it. For Christ taught in several clear sentences the
giving up of self, the denial of personality. These theologians reduced this

preachment to the practice of charity and unselfishness but kept the ego as something precious, whereas Jesus asked not only for these moral virtues, but for the immeasurably more important metaphysical-mystical virtue of rooting out the ego itself. The moral improvement of character is thus substituted for the metaphysical destruction of ego.

22

A more sympathetic study of the other Oriental religions, especially the Indian ones, would help Christians to understand better, and interpret more correctly, their own religion.

23

Those who support the sending of missionaries to foreign countries do so in the belief that they are honouring Jesus' words, "to publish the gospel to all parts of the world." But the world in his time and speech is not the world of our own. This is shown clearly by Saint Luke's allusion to it: "In those days there went out a decree from Caesar Augustus that all the world should be taxed." Here "world" stands for the empire of the Romans. It does not include the Chinese, for instance.

24

Those who are not yet ready for any other than a Christian path would not be helped by Hindu and Buddhist literature.

25

The gospel story is not a transcript from the Indian story of Krishna, as some of the critics suggest. A few of the similarities are certainly there but the explanation is a mystical one.

26

The British soldier and sailor all unwittingly prepared the way for the British dissemination of Bibles throughout the world. The British Empire has been one of the carriers of the Christian scriptures.

27

Those who know little about the origin, history, and development of religious opinions would receive a shock, or rather a series of shocks, if they were to inquire into the development of the principal Western faith and if they were able to lay hands on the necessary material. But let them be warned that they will not find such material in official sources. There was once a very voluminous literature which contained the true Christian teaching, but it was completely exterminated by the official church as soon as the latter's triumph over these so-called heresies was established. How ironical it is that reincarnation, the very doctrine which is today regarded as a heresy—that is, a perversion of true doctrine—was originally regarded as an authentic one!

28

A Christianity once existed which has long been condemned and forgotten but which is as much nearer the true teaching of Jesus as it is nearer him in time. We refer to the school of the Gnostics. Their defeat and disappearance does not lessen their truth. The Gnostic Christians of the third century accepted the pre-existence and earthly rebirths of man. With this doctrine there came naturally the law of recompense, which warns men to heed more carefully what they think and do, for the results will return equally and justly in time.

29

Gnosticism was banned as heresy by the Church Councils, its books destroyed, its teachers persecuted. The truth in it was banned indiscriminately along with the untruth. The differing sects in it were treated all alike. That during Rome's luxurious and decadent periods some sects said we should give to the spirit what is of the spirit and to the flesh what is of the flesh, and practised immorality, is true. But it is also true that other sects presented the struggle by good forces against the evil ones in most dramatic and forceful terms. Its recognition of the meaning, place, and importance of "Light" seen in meditation was a prominent and valuable feature of Gnosticism.

30

Those Christians who were closest to Jesus' time did *not* set up two categories—those in the world and those living withdrawn from it outwardly, with the second as superior. It was monks who later made this division.

31

In the third-century pagan world, hate and envy prevailed. The propertied classes were hated by the poor, the working classes hated the middle class, while the army was hated by all classes. Christianity preached love to neighbours, philanthropy towards strangers, as the Emperor Julian, though hostile, reluctantly admitted. It would bring these mutually antagonistic classes together, as the Emperor Constantine saw. Pagan religions and philosophies revealed this, too, but failed to practise it, had become cold. This is one of the reasons, apart from the alleged visionary experience of a cross in the sky, which persuaded Constantine to adopt Christianity as the official religion of the Roman Empire.

32

The early Christians who spoke of being "in Christ" were men whose intense faith, devotion, and sacrifice had lifted them into the Overself consciousness.

33

The most intellectual early Christians were those who abode in Alexandria, for it was the greatest Mediterranean centre of philosophical learning before Christianity appeared in it.

34

Chrysostom was born about 347 A.D., Tertullian about 150 A.D. The latter was the first of the Church's Latin Fathers, well educated, a brilliant scholar, with numerous friends among the learned, and a wide knowledge of the tenets teachings and customs of his time.

35

The Christian thought of Clement and Dionysius is close to the higher philosophic thought of the Indian Rishee-sages. And this is not surprising when we remember that they got their ideas in Alexandria, which was then having regular commerce with India.

36

Was not the most important council of all the Council of Nicaea, which finally settled Christian doctrines for a thousand years, but which foolishly dropped the tenet of metempsychosis as heresy after it had survived the first five centuries of *anno domino*; was not this great gathering composed of men who mostly could neither write nor read, who were stern extreme ascetics, fanatical in character and behaviour, narrow, intolerant?(P)

37

When the Romans ruled there were few means of communication, and even these were slow and difficult. Nor were there newspapers and printed books. The message of Jesus spread along Roman highways but even so took a few hundred years to find its hearers.

38

In symbolism of the Trinity, God signifies the World-Mind, Christ the Overself, and the Holy Ghost the Kundalini.

39

"I indeed baptize you with water unto repentance; but he that cometh after me is mightier than I, whose shoes I am not worthy to bear: he shall baptize you with the Holy Ghost, and with fire."—Matthew 3:11.

Water has been universally used in sacred literature as a symbol of the emotional nature of man. The fluidic character of both is the reason for the use of this symbol. What John called "baptism by water" means therefore such a cleansing of the dominance of his animal passions, desires, and appetites. Consider further that it is the tendency of water always to flow downwards in obedience to the law of gravity, and then note the striking contrast of the tendency of fire, whose sparks always soar upwards. "Baptism by fire" therefore refers to a process on an entirely higher level, not to a merely negative purification but to a positive illumination. Light is one of the effects of fire. The work of John the Baptist was concerned with clearing the way for Jesus, the light-bringer, a preparation that was not only outward and annunciatory but also inward and purificatory. John collected "followers" for Jesus; they were the masses who sought physical help and emotional comfort in their troubles and sicknesses. But Jesus, when he came in person, not only gathered all these followers but also collected "disciples"; they were those who had no necessity to seek such help and comfort, but were attracted by the Spirit itself as it shone through Jesus. They were the few who received the baptism of fire and by the Holy Ghost. Many people became followers but few became disciples.

There is, further, a difference between the baptism by the Holy Ghost and the baptism by fire. The baptism by the Holy Ghost arouses and awakens the potentialities of the dynamic Life-force, raising its voltage far above the ordinary. This process is usually accompanied by thrills, ecstasies, or mystical raptures. It represents the first awakening on the spiritual level as it filters through the partially cleansed emotional nature. Baptism by fire represents the next and highest stage after this event, when, the thrill of the new birth has subsided and when, in a calmer and steadier condition, the intelligence itself becomes illumined in addition to the feelings, thus balancing them.

40

In Love (for the highest) in Wisdom (of intuition and Intelligence) and Power (the creative energy of the Overself) we find the inner meaning of the Holy Trinity.

41

Christianity's most solemn ritual—the celebration of the Holy Eucharist—which symbolized membership by a common meal, was partly taken from the pagan Mysteries. This is the part that was brought in during a later century.

42

The public confession of sin, "sharing," as one cult calls it, is unnecessary and leads in the end to exhibitionism. The Roman Church, in the wisdom of many centuries, rightly has made the confessional a private affair, heard only by the priest, and even then the penitent only half-sees him through the gauze curtain in the booth.

43

It is a misunderstanding of the benefit of confession or sharing, which has value only if done with or before a superior person. With others it is futile or harmful.

44

Ought he not enter the confessional booth to denounce not only his sins but also his stupidities? Is it not a duty of human beings to display intelligence?

45

That the cross was a mystical symbol used in the ancient Mysteries was known to Plato. In the *Republic* he wrote: "The just man, having suffered all manner of evils, will be crucified."

46

Jesus did not construct any religious system or creed, Church or doctrine. Others did that when he was no longer there to say Yes or No. Christianity was therefore *their* creation, not his.

47

A reincarnated Jesus appearing in our century would not be able to recognize his original message in the orthodox sects of our time.

48

These three doctrines—now turned by the Church for its own motives into three dogmatic superstitions—were, and are, sacred truths before being corrupted. They are the Crucifixion, the Atonement, and the Trinity. Trinitarianism in its present form was never taught by Jesus. It came into Christian doctrine centuries after he lived.

49

Nowhere does Jesus in the publicly available sayings included in the New Testament order the formation of a clergy or preach the need of a church or lay down a ritual. Instead he gave clear precise instruction on how to pray: "Enter into thy closet, and when thou hast shut thy door, pray to thy Father which is in secret." But Paul thought differently and founded what is now misnamed Christianity.

50

The Inspired Prophets did not themselves personally organize religion. What they did was to give inspiration to those individuals who could respond to it. It was their followers, men acting on external methods, men with limited capacity, who organized and eventually exploited institutions. Indeed these followers had no alternative but to use such methods, not possessing themselves the inner depth of the prophets. The truth is that nobody has ever really organized religion, for it is a private and personal affair between each individual and his God. It is men who have organized themselves for purposes derived from their religious feelings—which is not the same as organizing religion itself. All such organizations are man-made throughout, as is also the authority they claim. There is no record in the New Testament speeches of Jesus that he himself appointed apostles. Consequently we must believe that they appointed themselves after he was no longer present among them. The basic claim of certain Churches to be a continuation of this apostolate has no ground to support it in Jesus' own statements. It is because of this claim that the Catholic Church does not theoretically recognize the right to freedom of worship on the part of other religious organizations, although in actual practice it gradually found it expedient to grant that right on practical grounds. "My kingdom is not of this world," declared Jesus. We may easily identify to which world these institutions belong, which were later organized in his name, by noting the official status which they secure in "this world." This explains the historic opposition occurring at times between the true spirit of Jesus and the worldly behaviour of his Church. It is regrettable that most people confuse an institution with the man upon whose name it may be built. There is no indication that Jesus ever wanted an organized church, but there is every indication that it was his followers who wanted it and who made it. Unfortunately, the masses do not understand this but are easily deceived into thinking that they are in touch with Jesus through his Church when in reality they are not so at all. To find Jesus they must go deep into their own hearts. There is no other way.

51

Search all the words of Jesus and you will not find the word "religion" uttered once in reference to what he was teaching. It was a way of positive living, although men have turned it into a mere social convention.

52

The truth about Jesus and about his teaching is hard to find today. For it is buried under a man-built mountain of deliberate falsification and superstitious accretion.

53

Jesus is honoured in every Christian Church by name, by chanted hymn, and by carven figure. Why does it not also honour his tremendous teaching that the kingdom of heaven is within man himself, not within the church?

54

The great Galilean was put by God among very little men. What he told them was beyond their comprehension, so they emotionalized it, sentimentalized it, organized it, and produced an all-too-human and undivine thing.

55

The severe impact of Jesus' phrases, stripped of embellishment and free from rhetoric as they are, shows up the lengthy lucubrations of official religionists for what *they* are.

56

Nowhere in the parables, nowhere in the spoken words of Jesus is there any teaching showing that he wanted an ecclesiastical hierarchy established or that he instituted a system of sacraments.

57

The so-called Holy Inquisition was quite unholy and more akin to those who persecuted the early Christians than to Christianity itself.

58

When men become enslaved by their religious symbols to the extent that they are willing to murder other men for them, or even to imprison them, when this slavery blinds their better sight and renders them fanatically intolerant of all other views, Nature deems it time to liberate both— the first from their sin, the others from their suffering. When ecclesiastics become intolerant and forget the first virtue of all religion—which is goodwill towards other men—and when they begin to persecute good men who are unable to agree with them, they not only put others in danger but also themselves. Jesus is one authority for this statement, for he warned all mankind that they would reap the circumstances sown by their conduct. Another authority is the ever-open bloodstained book of history. A good deal of true Christianity burnt itself out in the medieval fires which its more ardent advocates lit for each other and for those unfortunate infidels who knew nothing more of Christ than his name.

59

When the earth was regarded as flat, it seemed plausible to believe that God was a super-Person somewhere out in the heights of space, separate from His universe and beyond its limits. The philosophers of Alexandria never accepted this view and were later persecuted by those who did— ignorant religious fanatics.

60

The figure of Jesus has been molded into fictions by credulous, imaginative, or professionally interested priests—fictions that were acceptable to the marvel-loving taste of posterity. But no marvel could be greater than what he taught—the entry into the kingdom of heaven, which is nothing else than a conscious return to the true nature of man. Thousands of theologians have scrutinized his personality and estimated the worth of his teachings, but most of them have deluded themselves because only those who have come within the orbit of a living sage can possibly understand him or his words, in their truest significance. Jesus made an impact on the spiritual life of the West, but that impact has never been properly evaluated because it cannot be perceived in the light of Church organization but somewhere else—in the hearts of men. Although he did not properly belong to our own planet, he gave us the emphatic assurance that we too might win his realization and attainment; we too might uncover our true selves and enter the Light. Professors come and write their academic footnotes to his work, but he must be viewed for what he was—not the organizer of a Church but the planter of living, unseen seeds that fertilized in their own special way in the nature of Western man. He owed and demanded allegiance to no particular sect or school, and he paid fealty to no earthly master. He stood out only under the auroral light of divinity which shone down upon his life. He descended like an angel to dwell in the tabernacle of flesh at a time when religious life was but a guttering candle.

61

Jesus emanated love, Jesus brought truth, and Jesus incarnated forgiveness.

62

Whether Jesus was merely human or really divine is a question which may worry others but which does not trouble me. He had something to communicate and did so. He had affirmation to make, a gospel to give which supported so many people for so many centuries. That men have demeaned his message, exploited his person, and twisted his words is regrettable but, men being what they are, expectable. It is good that he came, for clearly they needed him.

63

Whether we put Christ's telling Truths into hard syllogisms and heavy intellectual dogmas which enter the mind or simple but noble phrases which are felt in the heart, we must accept them.

64

Most Christian churches and sects have claimed a spiritual monopoly. The main foundation for this claim is the sixteenth verse of the third chapter of John where the Evangelist says that Jesus is "the only begotten son of God." But nowhere in the New Testament does Jesus himself make the same assertion. On the contrary, he went out of his way to tell men, "The works that I do shall ye do also," thus refusing to put himself in a unique separate and unattainable species, which would make it impossible for other men to imitate his example or hope to attain his understanding.

65

The belief that Jesus was specially created, as no one before or since has been, is unacceptable. The belief that Jesus was one among the other great souls invested with special power is both acceptable and reasonable.

66

"Why callest thou me good?" asked Jesus. "There is none good but one; that is God." If these words mean anything, they mean that he is still a human being, however close and harmonious is his relationship with God, and that he is not to be deified.

67

When Jesus declared that he was the Way, he spoke as the infinite Christ-self in every man, not as the finite person Jesus. He meant that whoever sought God, the Father, had to come through this higher self, could not find him by any other channel. This only was the Way.

68

The Sermon on the Mount is truly representative of Jesus' teaching. It holds first place in the literature of the world; it contains the essence of practical Christianity expressed as finely as is humanly possible.

69

Jesus' Sermon on the Mount is not merely a pretty speech. It is a discipline. Therefore, it is only for his disciples. The masses who seek benefits or follow convention, not being ready for the effort, cannot be called disciples.

70

When Jesus told his adult hearers that they had to become children before they could enter the kingdom, he made what must have sounded an astonishing assertion to them. What did he mean? How are we to interpret and apply his words? There are two ideas worth noting here. First, a child enjoys living. Second, a child thinks, feels, and acts spontaneously. Both these factors are combined in its direct awareness of life, untrammelled by hesitations or obstructions imposed from without and unfiltered by colourings or opinions imposed from within.

71

I had heard from different sources—Hindu, Buddhist, Nestorian and Indian Christian—of this legend which is current in the Western Himalaya region and in Chinese Turkestan, that Jesus came as a young man to India and spent several years there before returning to Palestine.

72

We hear much of Jesus' being the friend of sinners and outcasts. But the fact was that he was also the friend of good people and society's supporters. It is true to say that his mission was chiefly to the populace, the common people, but that did not mean that he was hostile to those classes whose grammar and diction were superior and whose possessions and status were higher.

73

It is hardly credible, to those who understand, that Jesus ascended quite literally and physically "to heaven." This assertion can be credible only to those who ignore Jesus' own statement that "the Kingdom of heaven is *within* you," those who look to the *sky* for its abode. For the same reasons, Jesus' second coming is also not to be taken literally, visibly, and physically, but inwardly as an experience in the heart.

74

Christ's supposed despairing exclamation on the cross, and also his last uttered words, "My God, why hast thou forsaken me?" have been wrongly translated, according to the Nestorian Christians, one of the oldest sects, whose Bible in the Aramaic language in which Jesus spoke gives the phrase as: "My God; For this was I kept," meaning, "This is my destiny."

75

It is one more of life's singular paradoxes that such a man as Jesus, who incarnated essential goodness, who would not wish to inflict the slightest hurt on any creature, who came here among men to be appreciated, even revered, so that they might draw the return back-flow of spiritual life-current to revive a materialistic world, met so much insensitivity. So many saw nothing superior in him but denigrated him, attacked him, vilified him, and sought his death.

76

It is utterly impossible to find in the first drawings, carvings, or pictures of Christ any reference to his suffering on the Cross.

77

The orthodox view of the Bible is untenable, according to philosophic tradition. It is really a collection of books written in different centuries by men on different levels of inspiration. It mixes half-history with myth, and legend with allegory and poetry. The tribal memories of the Hebrews are put on the same level—which is a mistake—as the inspired revelations of their seers and the Mystery teachings they learned in Egypt and Chaldea. The orthodox view of Jesus is equally dispelled by philosophic insight. The man Jehoshua, who was the real figure behind the legendary one, lived a hundred years before the supposed date. Although much of the teaching associated with his name in the New Testament is actually his own, not much of the life there given is actually historical. The narrative in its pages is partly an allegory depicting a disciple's mystical journey ending in the crucifixion of his ego and partly an excerpt from Jehoshua's biography. There was no violent death, no physical crucifixion in this biography.

78

We need not torture our reason to accept these parts of the New Testament which seem incredible. If we give some of them an allegorical meaning, as being taken from the mythology of a mystery cult, and reject the others as the results of deliberate tampering with the text, as obvious interpolations, we shall be able to justify all the more our faith in the credible parts. For with them is interwoven the genuine historical narrative of the real life of the man Jesus. The result is a mixed composition, where the Annunciation and Crucifixion are not to be taken literally, but Jesus' preaching and his disciples' apostolate are. The biographic Jesus must be separated from the symbolic Christ, for the one is an earthly figure and the other a mystical concept.

79

Consider how vain, how puffed-up these mortals be when they declare that nothing less than the One Infinite Power—the Absolute Itself— deliberately incarnated as man to help them. Surely if it had such intent it would act more in accord with its own laws of progressive development and send here another mortal but a more advanced one. Such a man could be found on a more advanced planet. And this is what happened. Jesus came here from a higher planet. There was no need for God to intervene directly.

80

Benedict de Spinoza's mathematical mind led him to put into apt mathematical symbol this same criticism: "The doctrine that God took upon Himself human nature I have expressly said I do not understand. In fact, to speak the truth, it seems to me no less absurd than would a statement that a circle had taken upon itself the nature of a square."

81

There are a number of alleged portraits of Jesus, some passed down traditionally and others made in our own time by psychic means. They are not in agreement with each other. But this contradiction is resolved when we understand that each is the fruit of the artist's own idea. They are imaginative conceptions.

82

Jesus was not an ordained minister, yet his preachments have outlived many centuries. He was only a layman, yet he brought more reverential feeling for the higher power to more people than thousands of clergymen combined.

83

Jesus said: "Except you eat the body of the Son of Man and drink his blood, you have no life in you." In the Aramaic idiomatic and colloquial language the phrase means: "endure suffering and work hard." Also, "Eloï, Eloï, lämä säbächthäni," could not possibly mean, in the case of a man so advanced as Jesus was, "My God, My God, why hast thou forsaken me?" In the Aramaic common speech it becomes clear, for there it means, "My God, my God, for this (destiny) I was preserved."

84

There has been much miscomprehension of Jesus' proclamation that the kingdom of God was immanent. It did not refer to a future event but to a present fact; it was not prophetic but Vedantic. The kingdom is "at hand" always; immediacy is its correct attribute.

85

Not once in all his recorded sayings did Jesus ever refer to, or use the word, Hell.

86

Jesus is the Greek transcription of the Hebrew name Jehoshua. Christus is Latin, Khristos in the Greek, which is a title meaning "anointed," as Buddha, meaning "enlightened," is a title, and Gautama the name.

87

During the course of my studies I have been shown three portraits of Jesus which seemed to be immeasurably more authentic than the oversentimentalized, utterly unrealistic ones which the Western world self-deceptively takes so seriously. Yet all three were sufficiently different from each other for each to present a different aspect of his personality. The first was a drawing quickly made by Jacques Romans, a clairvoyant friend who died when he was nearly 100 years old. I do not know what became of this portrait. The second was an oil painting by another clairvoyant, Boyin Ra, which his widow showed me in their Swiss home. The third is a fresco in the Assembly Hall where Canons meet in Chapter of Monastery of St. Mark, Florence, by the Dominican monk and visionary Fra Angelico. In the drawing, the aspect shown was that of a man in absorbed communion with his Father. In the canvas it was a man confronting the world fully possessed by the strength of the Spirit. In the fresco it is the Christ of the Crucifixion, extraordinarily sad—for the human race. Thus the first typified Prayer in depth, the second, divine Power, and the third, mysterious melancholy, Pity. Yet they were of a *real* man, not a fanciful one.

88

In ancient Rome as in modern Europe, in Attica as in America there were, and are, humanists who reject religion as such but concede its usefulness in restraining the baser expressions of human character. If they cannot denigrate Jesus, they deride his spiritual message. They may accept him as a good man, as an ethical teacher, but not his revelation that God *is* and that man may commune with Him.

89

Jesus went to the length of denouncing as hypocrites those who were outwardly faithful in performing religious practices, but who were secretly sinning in thought.

90

Christ's mission was addressed to the common man with limited intellectual attainments. I have said so in my book *A Search in Secret Egypt*. That is why he did not publicly teach the metaphysical truths.

91

James, the brother of Jesus and an Apostle, was a vegetarian. But the theologians and historians ignore this fact which was testified to by the Judeo-Christian Hegesippus, who lived in the century following and had contact with the Palestinian circles of the Apostolic time. Moreover Hegesippus asserts that James had been brought up in this way since childhood. Does this imply that the family circle was vegetarian?(P)

92

The first need for Christian theology is to separate the teaching of Jesus from that of the unfortunately canonized Paul, who never even met him and who began to organize a Church, spread a doctrine, and formulate an asceticism of his own. This gained power and prevailed far too long, being the chief contribution to keeping people from the true Christianity.

93

If Paul had not busied himself with turning Jesus' inspiring message "The Kingdom of Heaven is within you!"—meaning it is within you *NOW*—into an ascetic message of long-drawn war against the carnal body; if he had listened better and learned more from that flash which lighted his road to Damascus, instead of returning to the bias and prejudice of his innate nature, he might have given history a higher, less Judaic, version of Christianity.

94

Some of the statements of Saint Paul are on a religious level and are very questionable; others, on a mystical level, are representative of his own but not of general experience; while still others, on the philosophical level, as in his remark to the Greeks about the Unknown God, are quite confused. But he was used to spread Christianity despite this, because of his fervent missionary temperament; and so his preachments were mainly effective and serviceable to the cause, even though they led in the end to a vast organization which was never mentioned, desired, or suggested even once by Jesus.

95

It must be said, and said quite plainly, that the Western and Near Eastern worlds would have had a better history, and Christianity would have had a stronger foundation, because truer, if Saint Paul had never been converted but had remained a Jew. For the vision on the road to Damascus, although a genuine one, was totally misinterpreted. It was a command (to stop persecuting Christians) of a solely personal nature; but he went much farther and not only began the construction of a new world-religion but shifted its emphasis from where Jesus had put it (the kingdom of heaven within men) to Jesus himself, from faith in the Christ-consciousness to faith in a crucified corpse.(P)

96

The apostle Bartholomew preached in India—this is stated by the Early Church Father Jerome, and by Eusebius in his *Ecclesiastical History*. Others add that he also taught in Persia and Egypt.

97

Quote from Saint Paul: "In Him we live and move and have our being." In Mind we have God, man, and the universe. All are of Mind, pure Being, pure Consciousness, so in Mind we humans live, move, and have our being. Is not this a mentalistic statement equivalent to the religious statement of Saint Paul? The fact that the saint arrives at it through his own personal experience and that the mentalist arrives at it either through his own deep reflection or personal revelatory experience does not alter the identity of the basic idea.

98

Pantaenus, who went as a missionary to India in the very early Christian times, was not an ordinary missionary: he was a Gnostic, a Christian mystic.

99

When pure religion descends upon the earth and makes its way among men, two things will happen. It will dissolve the false belief of the populace that they already possess it, and it will receive the opposition of religious institutions with pretensions to represent it. It was Saint Paul who started Christianity on the road which turned it into Churchianity. But he derived his Christian knowledge at second hand. He knew less about the work which Jesus sought to do on this earth than about the work which he himself sought to do. He is the true founder of the Christian Church, its first great propagator, but he is not the truest interpreter of Jesus' message. It is the Church's personal self-interest, however unconsciously present, which has made the apostle Paul the most praised Christian teacher and the most frequently mentioned one in all the sermons and writing of the clergy. Never having met Jesus, he should not be blamed for never having fully understood Jesus' teaching. The grave consequences of this misunderstanding appeared later in the form of obstacles which interposed themselves between Jesus and his true work, and which succeeded in diverting and distorting it. They were organization, dogma, hierarchy, and literalness. Where Jesus tried to create Christian individuals, Saint Paul tried to create Christian groups. This opened the door to hypocrisy, externalism, materialism, ritualism, priestcraft, persecution, and deterioration. The realizable kingdom of heaven within man had to give way to an unrealizable kingdom of God on earth. The way back to true religion must therefore lie through making a fresh start with new ideas and a fresh approach through individual self-development.

100

Without Paul, Christianity could never have had any future in Europe and would have remained and died in obscurity. Paul brought it to Greece and Rome and put it into formulations that reached the non-Asiatic mind.

101

That Saint Peter was the proper successor of Christ, with all that this assertion entails for church and bishop, is at least debatable.

102

Saint Paul had passed through the initiatory revelation given by the Greek Mystery schools, and the results show in his writings.

103

The Catholic Church is nearer to philosophy than most Protestant sects. Its mystical meditations, ascetical disciplines, metaphysical activity, and secret doctrine are some points of contact, despite its ritualism and anti-mentalistic theology.

104

Reverend C.O. Rhodes: "Protestantism makes no provision for the contemplatives and loses much as a result."

105

The contrast between the Catholic and Protestant missionary in Asia is striking. The latter has divided his allegiance, part to wife and family, part to mission. The former is free and fully devoted. The Protestant carries the double burden—family welfare and mission welfare.

106

What is your attitude towards the Pope? This is a question I am sometimes asked. My answer is: I have much respect for him as an individual. I believe he is a man who lives in prayerful fellowship with spiritual forces. I might even be willing to accept the claim that, historically and legally, he is the successor of Saint Peter, but I have not studied this point. Unfortunately, I am unable to respect His Holiness as an institution, for I am unable to accept the claim that he is the Vicar of Christ on earth. Christ's true church is not built with hands and his representative is to be found by each man in his own heart alone. [We are uncertain to which pope this para refers.—Ed.]

107

I am equally unable to accept the Roman Catholic doctrine that true saints have existed only within the Roman church and that all others are impostors, lunatics, or self-deceived.

108

Although I personally do not belong to this or any religious organization, I sympathize with Quaker ideals, respect the Quaker ethos, and admire the Quaker individual. But although the Quaker form of worship is quite lofty from the religious standpoint, it is not lofty enough from the mystical one. Its silent meditation is good, but its congregational meditation cannot attain the profound depth possible in private and solitary meditation. Moreover, its expression in uttered speech of what "the holy spirit moves us to say," although helpful from a religious standpoint, is a hindrance from the mystical one. For it disturbs the individual concentration.

A community which has always been told by its rules that the corporate form of worship is the primary and necessary one cannot leap suddenly into the blinding glare of full truth. It has to travel first from the quarter-truth to the half-truth, and so on. The Quaker method of group meditation is such an advance. It represents a loftier view of the meaning of worship because it shifts the emphasis from outward sacrament to inward holiness, from swallowed creed to quiet "waiting on the Lord." But from the true mystical standpoint, this group form is only a concession to traditional human habit and gregarious human weakness. Nevertheless, if anyone feels that membership of a religious body is essential to him, then I would recommend him to join the Society of Friends, or Quakers, as they are more popularly called. Not that I am satisfied with all their doctrines and methods, but that I consider there is more honesty and more safety amongst them, less exploitation and less insincerity than amongst any other religious denomination I know. That there is no paid class of professional clergy in the Society of Friends is undoubtedly one of the factors which contribute to this purity.

109

When Pope John announced his project for a convocation, it was a history-making piece of news. His prophetic vision showed him the need for his Church to rethink, renew, reactivate, and reinspire inside itself, not only its own body but also outside in its relations with the other Churches. The Vatican Councils which followed the Ecumenical movement are signs of the times.

110

The Eastern Orthodox Church allows the lower ranks of priest to marry, but not the higher ones. This is because the fathers considered celibacy a prerequisite to enlightenment. "Acquire chastity," enjoined Saint Ephraim, the Syrian, "that the Holy Spirit may come to dwell in thee." (The latter's writings are much read in the Mount Athos monasteries, which helps to explain why women are forbidden to visit them.)

111

What the Methodist finds at his church through group singing is not quite the same as what the Quaker finds at his Meeting-house through group silence. The one method is purely emotional, the other is passively intuitional. Both Methodist and Quaker are uplifted but there is a difference in the quality of the result.

112

Luther carried out the work for which he incarnated—the purifying of a once great religion from the selfishness and sinfulness and commercialism which had made it a hindrance that spoiled its helpfulness.

113

If men like Cardinal Newman, T.S. Eliot, G.K. Chesterton, and Graham Greene turned away from Protestantism to Catholicism despite their brilliant minds, it was not in quest of the truth but *to escape from truth*. They were poets at heart and in the Holy Church found satisfaction for their feelings. The beauty of its ritual, the mystery of its dogma, and the music of its chants appealed where intellect resigned itself to incapacity.

114

Whereas the Greek Orthodox Church gives its liturgy the primary importance, the Protestant Churches give it to the Bible.

115

The younger Luther learned much from German mystics, but the mature Luther rejected them. What he eagerly absorbed at one time he completely discarded at another time. What was truth earlier, he called "vain fantasy" later.

116

The Calvinist's stubborn ascription of salvation wholly to grace is as extreme and one-sided as the yogi's ascription of it to self-labour. It is not less extreme than the Calvinist view of fate, with its iron hardness.

117

Jesus said that the kingdom of heaven is within us: he did not say that the Church is within us.

118

Christianity in its beginnings was a mystical religion. Its only hope of recovery from the ailments which afflict it now is to return to the road it has deserted.

119

They need not look beyond Christ and Christianity for these verities but they must learn to understand Christ and interpret his message on a deeper level than the professional hierarchies have been able to do.

120

The only way in which the individual can find Jesus today is to seek for him within his own heart by the means of constant prayer and study, together with the faithful carrying out of his teachings in all daily life.

121

The initiated early Christians understood well enough that the Christ was no other than their own higher self, the Overself. This was true then; it is true now. The Christ-Babe must come to birth in a man's own heart before he can become a real Christian. The true Christian, as distinct from the merely nominal one, feels this force which enters his heart, but it is something very different from, and much superior to, mere emotion.

122

The woman of deep Christian piety who has striven to follow this path knows well that in the Christ-Self within her heart she has her greatest treasure. Its Presence is the God she is to worship. She will have learned in the past the mysterious value of tears—tears of spiritual yearning, as well as tears of worldly grief.

123

The Church that Jesus actually founded was not an ecclesiastical organization, complete with its credos, liturgies, rituals, robed prelates, and imposing buildings of its own, but a deeper awareness of being and a better outlook on life. It was therefore an unseen Church, laical rather than clerical.

124

The message of Jesus, which was so largely a call to repentant deeds and changed thoughts, is needed today by us all much more than it was needed by the Jews of his time.

125

The noble life of Jesus inspires sensitive men as few lives have done. The benign sayings of Jesus afford them matter for heartfelt ethical reflection during the peace of eventide. The terrible sufferings of Jesus have taught his weaker kindred how to bear their own personal misfortunes with strength, courage, and dignity. The true followers of Jesus have spent great sums and given much food, clothing, shelter, and education through varied praiseworthy charitable enterprises.

126

There are several matters which are not dealt with by the personal teaching of Jesus. Is it not proper therefore to regard them within the general spirit of his teaching? And where there is only a single uncertain mention of such a matter, is it not safer again to interpret it within the light of that same internal spirit rather than within the letter of mere external logic? If we do this, we will find it impossible to give to the word "church" the meaning which the materialistic mind historically gives to it. The true Christian church was an invisible one.

127

When religionists realize that Jesus' simple and eloquent sayings are more important to them than Jesus' unhistorical and less significant doings, and when they begin to look into the inward mystical experience which found expression in those sayings, they and their cause will gain much, while the dissensions and schisms, the rivalry and dispute among their churches will grow less.

128

Is it not heresy to the orthodox to proclaim that potentially every man can know, and unite with, the Christ-consciousness, and thus in effect *is* the Christ-self?

129

If the teachings of Jesus, for example, were correctly interpreted, if the teachings of the churches which use his name were freed from the ignorant accretions and veiled materialisms which he never taught, the Western people would then be so effectively helped by their religion that it would undergo an intellectual rebirth.

Hinduism

130

If the Roman Catholic faith teaches that Salvation is the highest and most desirable aim in human life, the Hindu faith teaches that freedom from rebirth is such an aim.

131

Religion teaches mythology as historical fact. The Hindu holy book *Vishnu Purana* tells of a king who massacred the male children in his country in a vain search for the divine Krishna, whose fortunes, it was predicted, would menace his own. The Jewish scriptural tale of the infant Moses and the Egyptian scriptural tale of the infant Osiris escaping from exactly the same danger are significant. We have here versions, different in time and altered by time, of one and the same event, whose original is lost in the prehistory of Central Asia. Or, alternatively, we have an equally ancient myth whose inner meaning needs to be fathomed.

132

The Hindu religion does not have congregational worship. Its temples are for the individual devotee. Its priests serve him alone, not a group of devotees.

133

Coconut is a sacred fruit, used in many or most Hindu religious ceremonies. It represents the human head, hence bloodless sacrifice. It is believed to be the only fruit without seed.

134

The study of comparative religion shows that Hinduism's "Divine Mother" is simply the Creative Energy of the universe. The name and form are merely symbolic, but have been taught to the simple masses of a pre-scientific age, being better within their grasp.

Islam

135

Sheikh Al-Alawi: "The acts of worship were prescribed for the sake of establishing remembrance of God." Here a Sufi teacher puts in a short pithy sentence the chief service of most religions.

136

Non-Islamic people react with horror and contempt when they learn from history that those who rejected the Islamic religion when proffered to them by invading armies were then given an ultimatum: "Die by the sword or become a slave for life!" But the background to these incidents needs to be seen. The Arabia of Muhammed's time was inhabited by semi-savage tribes: Islam was originally an attempt to lift them forcibly to a higher, more civilized life, and a higher view of religion. That Muhammed's followers later tried to impose Islam on more developed peoples, especially Christian and Hindu people, was wrong.

137

During the minutes of prayer, Muhammedans the world over turn concentrically in the direction of Mecca. The physical unity which they thus achieve is a fit emblem of the spiritual unity which all men will one day achieve—for all must eventually turn toward the Overself.

138

Christian Europeans who came into contact with the Saracens and learned some Sufi truths and practices started the Rosicrucian movement. The rose was a Sufi metaphor for the mystic exercise (meditation in some form). The Cross was added by these Europeans.

Jainism

139

Jain meditation is for self-contemplation or for purifying ideas and emotions or for loving and reverencing an ideal still beyond us, an ideal embodied in some historical sage but which is realized for the time being through mental union within oneself.

Judaism

140

Christ came as an obscure prophet, teacher, avatar (call him what you wish) and did not attain sufficient fame to be written about in any of the contemporary Roman imperial histories. Yet this obscure man's teachings became known throughout the world. And yet he was repulsed by the Jews, who in turn were repulsed by the people with whom they lived. Why did the Jews turn away from him? Was it not because of their failure to recognize the stronger light which he had brought them? And was his failure not due to their excessive nostalgia in looking back to the times when they were a free nation? Was it not due to their excessive fidelity to their ancient religion, to their lack of flexibility?

141

The synagogue at Nazareth which expelled Jesus and the synagogue at Amsterdam which expelled Spinoza—are these not symbols of the failure of official religion to raise itself above its own selfishness and take up its true mission? Are they not reminders of its inner bankruptcy?

142

The Jews, whose original prophet-seers must have comprehended the meaning of pure Spirit, who were forbidden to make any graven images for themselves, have made several in the form of the spirit-suffocating letter of their Torah, their Talmud, their Old Testament, their traditions and customs. All this, intended to uplift and purify, not only failed to do so but prevented them from recognizing Jesus for what he was.

143

An unpublished paper on the history and solution of the Jewish problem by P.B. gives the spiritual meaning of the mission to humanity of the Jewish people, their opportunities and failures in the past, why they were persecuted, and the great opportunity which will come to them to close their whole tragic history and enter a new, happy phase—if they will follow the advice given to them. Had they accepted Jesus two thousand years ago as a prophet from their own line, they would have saved themselves much misery. Now it is a mockery that Jesus is not followed even by so-called Christian nations. It is too late (and no longer timely) for the Jews to accept Jesus. Where, then, are they to look? The problem is stated and a solution attempted in this paper. This is the only one that would be successful as well as the only solution that is divinely commanded. [To date, this paper has not been located.—Ed.]

144

Both Buddha and Solomon were not stupefied by their royal luxury: each noted the sad side of life. "The heart of the wise is in the house of mourning; but the heart of fools is in the house of mirth," bemoaned the Israelite.

145

It is interesting to note that the philosophic ideas of the French eighteenth-century Enlightenment writers got their basic thought from Spinoza's critiques of the Hebrew Bible, despite their personal dislike of the Jews themselves. Voltaire was decidedly anti-Semitic.

146

YHWH, in Exodus 3, was the name given, to Moses, by that Presence which spoke to him out of the bush, and its derivation followed—the Hebrew root for *being*! That it became the narrowed concept of a tribal anthropomorphic god—Jahweh—is the inevitable historical consequence; that is what the tribe could take and be satisfied with.

147

Once I wandered into the prewar Ghetto of Venice—a small and uninviting quarter where the Jews were formerly made to live by law, and where a few still resided because they were too poor to live in a better place. I thought of this dark race, its long and painful history, and the words of Charles Lamb rose in my memory: "The Jew is a piece of stubborn antiquity compared to which Stonehenge was in its nonage." I saw the Wandering Jew shambling through the centuries. I pondered on his meaning. And these were my thoughts:

They could not altogether escape their strange destiny, which took them out of their native land and forced them to wander though half the world. It was their own stubborn conservatism which brought them among strange peoples, still clutching tightly to their own worn-out creed and not as missionaries of Jesus' loftier development of it. Thus instead of bringing light as they might have done, had they responded to the sacred call, they brought merely physical goods, for their cosmopolitanism found its full scope in creating and financing the import and export trade of many countries.

In a curiously distorted and obviously inferior manner, the Jews have played a historic role which is an indirect reflection of the higher role they could have played as the first wholly Christian nation. They carried earthly goods to the different nations when they might have carried unearthly ideas.

The legendary story of the Wandering Jew has a profound esoteric significance. Even the Jewish claim of being a chosen race also possesses a similar significance, albeit it is one which the Jews themselves have failed to grasp. If they are no longer a chosen race, it is for them to reflect why this is so.

The more cultured among the early Christians understood that the Overself—whom they called Christ—was the real object of their worship, the ultimate goal of their mystical endeavour, and that the man Jesus was but its Voice—like those other voices with which the Word periodically breaks its silence for the guidance of bewildered mankind.

6

PHILOSOPHY AND RELIGION

Differences, similarities among religions

The genial tolerance which affirms that all religions express something of the truth is justified. But whereas some express only a little, others express much of it.

2

The esoteric traditions have come down from remote antiquity into a large part of the Oriental and Occidental hemispheres. In most cases they were well guarded. A thorough study of them shows that they hold many dissimilarities. If some of these are due to the changes which are inevitable from one century to another, or in transposition from one climate to another, others are clearly due to irreconcilable standpoints and contradictory revelations.

3

The differences exist, and in great number, but they are mostly on the surface. The agreements exist and concern the more important matters; they are mostly at a deep level.

4

If some forms of religion are sensuous, if others are austere, all forms are expressions of some aspect only and hence incomplete.

5

In most of the creeds, cults, and systems there is some truth, a little in one, more in another, but also some error or some limitation of outlook. This is why they are all in disagreement with one another.

6

This cacophony of different and conflicting religious teachings may turn one man away from religion altogether but another to deeper and more detailed study of them.

7

We may try to make religions more tolerant by pointing to their points of agreement: this is laudable. But what is gained by ignoring or belittling the points of difference?

8

Different religions are or should be different attempts to lift mankind out of materialism.

9

Because they are different approaches, this need not mean they are antagonistic ones.

Comparative study, practice

10

No little coterie or large sect may rightly claim the sole knowledge of God, or the sole communion with Him. The very claim cancels itself out quite automatically, the mere statement of it is contradicted and refuted by the large volume of evidence gathered together in the studies of Comparative Religion, Mysticism, and Philosophy.

11

The well-informed observer, scholar, traveller knows that each cult, religion, sect, movement is but one of many. It contributes what it can to truth but it has no right to claim that it alone has all the glory of truth, or that no other has any truth. There have been insights in widely scattered groups in widely different centuries.

12

To search widely as well as variously in the records left by those who seem to have some insight is a wise procedure. How much better than remaining imprisoned in the limitations of a single geographical culture, a single period of thought! How much more likely to lead to broader, truer understanding of life!

13

His religious feeling should be broadened by comparative study of other faiths. It should be wide enough to take them in amicably even though he demurs at some of their tenets or deplores some of their history.

14

The subject of comparative religion, born in the previous century and developed in our own, attracts attention from the curious but serious study from the earnest. It is a fit and worthy field for questers, who should widen it to include comparative mysticism and metaphysics. But they should study only the best in each system and, annually, the best of the best. The worst is there, but let others, non-questers, wallow in it.

15

He will become truly religious if he ceases to remain sectarian and begins to take the whole world-wide study of religious manifestations for his province.(P)

16

Whoever limits himself in his search, faith, and acquaintance to a single book—the Bible—limits the truth he finds. Such is the position of those sects with narrow outlooks like the Lutheran Church, the Calvinists, the Jehovah Witnesses, and several other churches. They silently proclaim their own lack of culture when the bibles, texts, hagiographs, and recorded wisdom of all lands, all historic centuries, and all languages are today available or translated or excerpted.(P)

17

If anything will ever show it, the comparative study of the world's religious mysticism will show that truth, grace, spirit do not come through the historic Jesus or the historic Krishna alone, nor through the historic Christianity or the historic Hinduism alone. They can be confined to a single religious dispensation only by those who refuse to make this study or, studying, refuse to discard bias and divest themselves of prejudice while doing so. Today all who study widely and honestly know as clearly as can be that God's message has been here all the time, however impaired or imperfect its forms may be and however different his messengers may be.

18

Few take the trouble to discover what is authentic in religion and what is not. It would be a long tiring process requiring several years of extensive study involving history, theology, psychology, plus personal practice in several forms of worship, plus experience in varying moral values—and all this over wide areas of the world and through the centuries, for without knowledge of comparative religion the investigation would be an incomplete one. Ignorance is much easier. This is why scientifically minded persons become sceptics and piously minded ones become superstitious.

19

There ought to be religious education in the schools; the mistake in the past has been to narrow it down to a single creed or sect. It ought to be widened, to include the history and teachings of the world's chief religions, as well as those of persons without organized established churches.

20

Education in even elementary and certainly in secondary schools should give the pupils at least a little notion of comparative religion. This could at least be confined to biographies of founders of the world faiths together with those of celebrated saints and mystics from different lands and cultures. At college and university levels, carefully chosen tenets from their teachings could be added, and some discussion of the theologies or philosophies involved. In all this instruction the religions dealt with are to be described fairly and explained without prejudice, not criticized or judged.

21

If some pious persons raise the head in prayer, others lower it. If many Christians let their knees go down to the floor, some Muhammedan dervishes bring theirs up to the chest. If Catholics and Protestants sit on benches or chairs during church service, Greek Orthodox congregations stand during their service. Hindus and Buddhists squat cross-legged in meditation, but Indian Jains stand. All these outward forms have been shaped by tradition and so historically: fanatical insistence on them misses the point—what is going on in their minds and hearts. Not only the facts revealed by the studies of comparative religion and comparative mysticism show up the silliness of fanaticism, but even more the correct understanding of those facts.

22

If any one religion is to be taught to children and youth at State expense, then all representative religions should be taught likewise. Let it be a part of such education to know not only the life and teachings of Jesus, but also the lives and teachings of Buddha and Baha'u'lla, Krishna and Muhammed. Only so will religion in its purity rather than in its corruption be instilled. Only so will the young be liberated from the quarrels and prejudices created and kept alive by the selfish monopolies and vested interests which exploit religion for their own benefit.

23

The economy of Nature is spacious enough to have room for all these different ways and means to the common end. They are not competing rivals. A true perception accepts them and is thereby made tolerant toward them.

24

History has presented us with too many spiritual guides, prophets, sages, and saints in too many lands and through too many centuries for any single cult to claim a monopoly of revelation wisdom truth. No human formulation can give us all the fullness, so we profit by them wherever they appear. But partisans, with narrow views, ignore history and neglect the study of comparative religion.

25

The philosopher successfully reinterprets in the secrecy of his own mind the dogmas, rituals, and beliefs of every religion that history, scriptures, circumstance, or study brings into his life. Thus, too, he is able to save the truth of religion when others impatiently reject that along with the falsity of religion. It is true that the comparative study of religions, in a spirit of sympathetic detachment from all and prejudice against none, is rare. But it is a useful part of philosophic study. The rational investigator can take no scripture as finally authoritative but must take all scriptures on their merits. He understands that a religious message is partly shaped by the character and tradition of the country in which it has been delivered. Taking into consideration the various beliefs of human development, he finds it desirable that there be room for variety in religions and for freedom in thought. The Inner Voice has spoken differently to different people. The variety of religions proves not that they cancel each other out but that they arose in response to a variety of needs. Nobody will be kept out of the kingdom of heaven because he does not belong to the orthodox religion which prevails in the place where, by the accident of his birth, he happens to live. Nobody will get into the kingdom of heaven because he does belong to the orthodox religion. The right of entry will depend on quite other and quite nobler qualifications.

26

The study of comparative religion ought to be part of all educational systems to foster knowledge, replace narrow fanaticism by a reasonable tolerance, and combat superstition or persecution.

27

Such a comparative study can bring the evidence needed to dissolve ignorant intolerance and to combat religious hatred. It will show up the foolishness of denouncing heresies when most founders were, like Buddha and Jesus, themselves great heretics from the standpoint of the prevalent religions. It will show the case for a reasonable freedom of thought so that different types of people may find the path, the goal, and the form which suits them. So long as they are good morally, beneficent and helpful, there is room for most creeds.

28

So far as they are genuine expressions of the impulse to worship the Higher Power, all religions have a rightful place. But where human ambition and greed, ignorance and superstition, fanaticism and unbalance have entered into them, they render disservice or do actual harm. The study of comparative religious history is valuable.

29

There is hardly a people which did not have a large or small fragment of the higher teaching in its possession. Egyptians, Chinese, and Greeks in early times, Persians, Spaniards, and Germans in later times, were among this number. Anaximander, teaching in Europe more than two thousand years ago, ascribed the origin of the universe to a First Principle which was "the boundless, the infinite, and the unlimited."

30

When a man begins to exercise independent thought and independent judgement, when he becomes sufficiently informed through the study of comparative religion to note how devastating are the disagreements and inconsistencies with each other, he will have only one possible conclusion open to him. The various beliefs about God and the different statements about religion are as likely to be wrong as right, but the personal experiences of God are all *essentially* the same. But this conclusion reached, he passes through it out of the religious level and rises up to the mystical one.

31

Those who are really intent on finding truth will search for it as widely as their circumstances allow and think about it as often as their time allows.

32

Truth can speak for itself. It has done so since the earliest recorded times—thus incidentally defeating the theory of religious evolutionism—and has done so even in our own time.

33

The study of comparative religion is one thing, the study of comparative history of religion is another; but both demand from the student enough willingness to try to be unprejudiced.

34

The study of comparative religion must be an independent, not a partisan one.

35

The study of comparative religion along with the history of religions, and the inclusion under these heads of little-known, unorganized sects or inspired individuals, is the first step to open the eyes of blinded humanity. When most people are insufficiently educated about their own religion, it is not a surprise that they are ill-informed about that of others. Nor can this study stop there. It ought to be broadened to include the mysticism and metaphysics behind and beyond religions.

36

Comparative religion will become more scientific as it is freed from the prejudices brought to it from the images previously stamped upon other religions by half-ignorant missionaries trying to make them look childish or foolish. The spiritual insensitivity of agnostic or atheistic investigators reflects back from their encounters with other people's spiritual experiences.

37

The liberating power of the study of comparative religion comes into effect mostly outside the academic centres, outside the colleges where it is taught with a bias towards the particular religion prevailing in the country, along with a prejudice against the other religions outside it.

38

Welcome knowledge from the four points of the compass but be carefully selective in what is absorbed. Avoid sectarianism but do it wisely.

39

It is not even enough to make a comparative study of religions and mysticisms, of metaphysics and systems and practices through the centuries and around the world. Discrimination in what is found becomes necessary, evaluation and critical judgement become essential. It is then that unexamined dogmas and rigid sectarianism with the stifling attitudes they generate are more likely to be dropped. In the end a higher kind of knowledge, the intuitional, coming from a higher level of the mind, must penetrate it all. This is the beginning of the most meaningful events.

40

This larger outlook which the study of comparative religion gives to a man may set him free from being confined to dogmas of a single creed or the practices of a single religion. If he feels happier with this liberation why should he not abide by it? Why should he build walls around his faith and customs? Why must he go only into a church and not into a mosque, only into a synagogue and not into a temple? Why should he not feel free to go into all of those if he wishes—in other words, to be able to worship anywhere in any place at any time?

41

He is safe in selecting those tenets, those mystical revelations, those moral disciplines and personal regimens which form a common basis to all religious cults and systems; they are at least the best beginning.

42

Religion as profound conviction and religion as a social inheritance are vitally different. Philosophy examines religion as profound conviction because it is not the monopoly of any particular race or land but is the possession of all. There is no single religion with which philosophy identifies itself. It cannot accept what is not proved true; it may not regard a belief as false but it cannot use it as true. It does not deal in *a priori* reasoning; it assumes nothing and is thoroughly agnostic at the start. Faith and philosophy are like the lion and the lamb—they cannot easily bed together! Consequently, philosophy's approach to religious questions is comparative in method and eclectic in spirit.

43

Anthropology is another of the subjects which can yield some of its substance to the student of philosophy. So far as it traces the evolution of the God-idea and of morals from primitive to civilized, it may usefully be studied.

44

All these intellectual and imaginative activities in religion like historical research, theological speculation, and Sanskrit, Greek, or Hebrew interpretation are proper in their own place; but their value ought to be recognized as being quite limited, if contrasted with the value of direct insight.

Philosophy completes religion

45

The Quest takes him through three levels of experience. First, he travels through religious beliefs and observances. Then he discovers mystical ideas and practices. Next, he sees that the personal consolations of religion and the intuitive satisfactions of mysticism are not enough. So he adds to them the impersonal quest of truth for its own sake and thus enters the domain of philosophy.

46

Philosophy does not cancel or deny the sublime teachings of religion but endorses and supports what is incontrovertible in them. The rest it corrects or rejects.

47

In every act of religious worship—however blind it be—there is a dim realization of God's existence. It is the business of mysticism to get rid of much of this dimness and of philosophy to get rid of it altogether.

48

The statements of religion ask for our belief: they may or may not be true. The statements of mysticism ask us to seek experience of their factuality. But the statements of philosophy confirm belief by reason, check reason by intuition, lead experience to insight.

49

If we look at man's inner life from the point of view of the whole cycle of reincarnation, popular religion will be seen to be a preparation for philosophy. The idea of a personal God is admitted and belief in it is encouraged, because it is the first step towards the idea of and belief in an impersonal God. Belief that the good or ill fortunes of life are sent to us by some outside being at his whim is useful as leading the way eventually to the understanding that they come to us under the operation of eternal universal law. This is one of the reasons why philosophy does not criticize or oppose popular religion on its own ground and why it leaves it completely alone and never interferes with it.

50

A man may be holy without being wise, but he cannot be wise without being holy. That is why philosophy is necessary, why religion and mysticism are not enough, although excellent as far as they go.(P)

51

Between those who feel too weak to go farther than the simple reverence of church religion and those who feel strong enough to enter the philosophical quest in full consciousness, there is every possible degree.

52

Only those who are able to drink the strong wine of philosophy can forsake religion without losing by, or suffering for, their desertion.

53

These fine teachings may quickly be distorted by popularization or greatly cheapened when brought within reach of the common understanding. If their integrity is to go in order to make concessions to the sensate mentality, if their truth is to be adulterated in order to accommodate the mass mentality, then whatever is gained will be less than what is lost. The higher truth can and should be translated into the vulgate for a mass audience—and the attempt is being made—but no unworthy compromises should be made. After all, if men want to learn the partly true, partly false, they can do so from a hundred sources. But if they want the wholly true, how few are the sources to which they can turn! Let us keep at least these few inviolate.

54

To insist on carrying religious dogmas into philosophic truth, for example, is to insist on carrying the child-mind into adult life. Each has valuable work to do in its own place but may become useless or even harmful when set up in judgement of what is beyond its frontier. Religion is important, mysticism is important, metaphysics is important; but if we fail to distinguish between the relative degrees of such importance, if we do not estimate them separately against the larger background of philosophy, we are liable to fall into the common error of confusing their categories and values, and thus deceive ourselves.

55

The religious codes are judgements or opinions, and are absolutely necessary at the popular stage; but on the philosophic level, where truth contains the highest possible goodness as an accompaniment, inspiration from the Higher Self produces a nobler conduct.

56

From the standpoint of social need, we must be the advocate and friend of religion when it performs its proper duty of keeping men within ethical bounds. But, from the same standpoint, we should be the opponent of religion when it becomes a farcical, hypnotical, hollow show, or when it slays and tortures men for holding other beliefs. But mounting to a higher level and adopting the standpoint of what is the ultimate truth, we can be the impartial observer of religion, for then we shall see it is but an elementary stage of man's journey on the upward mountain road leading to this high goal. Whoever seeks the last word about life must not tarry at the starting point.

57

Religious institutions have always been unfriendly to philosophers. This is because they have feared philosophy.

58

When a man of superior intellectual attainments, moral stature, or intuitional feeling ends a period of doubt or search, of darkness or agnosticism, by attaching himself to a sectarian religion, and especially to a sectarian religion which attempts to impress the senses by sacerdotal pomp and ritual, as well as the mind by claims and dogmas, it is a confession of the man's mental failure, an indication of his intellectual retrogression, and an advertisement of his moral cowardice. Such a man should have gone onwards into either the mysticism of truth or the metaphysics of truth. There must have been some weakness either in his character or in his intellect which caused him to fall back so far.

59

Philosophy does not effect a conversion from one religious point of view to another, but a confirmation of what intuitive feelings and ideas are trying to tell the man.

60

Mentally disturbed or emotionally hysterical persons can neither find Truth nor produce beauty, except during temporary lucid periods. Religious cults founded by them can only attract their own kind. Art created by them can only find acceptance because of supposed daring originality. Both are unhealthy and increase the existing confusion. Truth is eminently sane. Reality is breathtakingly beautiful. Popular externalized religion must rise into internalized mysticism, but the first must avoid the danger of superstition and the second avoid aberration. This is why both attain fulfilment in the safety of philosophy.

61

They come to religion seeking consolation; he comes to philosophy seeking truth; the two aims are quite different. But in the end the philosopher experiences consolation and the religionists take a step towards truth.

62

All the outer forms of religion, all the outer rites affect their sincere devotees emotionally, but within the higher part of the ego only. But all the *samadhis* of yoga, and certainly the insights of philosophy, escape this limitation by cutting completely through emotion into its deep calm core—the real being.

63

Because religion is an easier approach, because it requires only a devotional attitude whereas philosophy requires both a devotional and an intellectual one, the one feeds the multitude, the other an elect.

64

Here is religion without ritual, inspired ministration that wears no vestment, and church attendance without leaving home.

65

Popular religion is able to do so but philosophy cannot speak directly to all persons. It can open its lips only in the presence of those who have been made ready by life to receive it.

66

Both religion and mysticism are self-enclosing activities. The defense against fears which religion offers and the transcendental experiences which mysticism offers provide personal satisfactions. But philosophy can only offer truth. It is not directly concerned with substituting one emotion for another, even if the new one is on a higher level, nor does it care whether the man has pleasing or displeasing experiences through following it.

67

Philosophy shows how a teaching which is purely religious can be re-expressed in a non-religious way.

68

If they look less to ecclesiastical institutions for spiritual satisfactions, it is not because they feel less spiritual need. It is because their needs have deepened, because they want to come to the principal points of the matter rather than the tedious, obsolete, arguable, and questionable ones.

69

The mass of men need something visible and touchable and perhaps audible if they are to believe it really exists—hence idols for primitive people, rituals and ceremonials for more developed people. But for the advanced ones, an idea needs no such symbol, as they can grasp it by mind alone.

70

A theosophy, a mixture of what is excellent in all the religions, is a breeder of tolerance and fellowship among them, a stage on the way, but still not the ultimate level. For that the seeker needs to penetrate in depth, beneath religion to mysticism, beneath mysticism to philosophy.

71

For one person who will respond to the call of philosophy, there are perhaps a thousand who can hear only the call of religion.

72

That most people are only in the first degree of religion is not their fault; they cannot help it and are not to be blamed. They are simply what their past has made them. If others have risen to the higher degrees of mysticism or philosophy it is because they have a longer fuller past behind them. Young plants are not to be reproached because they are not old trees.

73

The teaching which is suited to those who are well on the way to the final stage of spiritual development is not much help to those who are only at the first stage.

74

To rise up from the religious level calls for some metaphysical faculty, a sensitivity to subtle ideas. The mind's more abstract level must be used. Those unaccustomed to it should not let themselves be discouraged. Each attempt made at intervals helps to open the way.

75

The philosopher does not have to sing hymns, mutter mantrams, attend churches, or take part in rituals and ceremonies organized by priests and clergymen. All that is useful, necessary, and essential to the masses—for it is the limit of their spiritual exploration. He, however, has ventured much farther and he cannot stop within these narrow borders.

76

Once the individual has risen above the levels of religion it would be sheer folly to fall back into them.

77

There is no liturgy and no ritual, no hierarchy and no institution in philosophic worship, nor are they needed.

78

The philosopher joins with the atheist in resisting superstition. But they part again when this resistance is directed against atheism itself—the greatest superstition of all.

79

No doubt individual students have their own beliefs but for these they must accept responsibility themselves. Since philosophy seeks to know the Real, it is not concerned with beliefs.

80

Philosophy neither elevates any man into God nor drags God down to any man's level.

81

Religion is satisfied with the spiritual fact diluted by myth and legend, philosophy wants the fact only.

82

Ungrown and immature minds would be bored by the illuminations of philosophy. For a philosopher to argue with them combatively would be a waste of time—theirs and his. There are so many creeds, systems, and sects which are really preparatory to philosophy and which are more useful to them at their stage. When they are ready for something more fundamental, they will find their way to it.

83

Mankind is led by easy preparatory stages towards the highest philosophy. Only when they are well grounded in true religion or mysticism and sound metaphysics is the full and final revelation made to them.

84

There are some persons who could not be stopped by worldly attractions from seeking something entirely unworldly, who longed for an understanding that was true and a consciousness that was real, stable, transcendental, and peace-bestowing. They tried orthodoxy and unorthodoxy, faith and unfaith, cults and leaders, organizations and solitariness. In the end they found their peace, or rather the first step to it, when they found philosophy.

85

Thus the vaguely felt, dimly apprehended, and always symbolic truth of religion is developed into clear full direct knowledge by philosophy.

86

It is not interested in forming just another sect, in building up one more denomination.

87

That worship which the followers of popular religion give blindly, instinctively, and often mechanically is given intelligently, scientifically, and consciously by the adherents of philosophy.

88

Those who are attached to the religious creed into which they have been born have no need to discard it merely because they wish to avail themselves of the knowledge and benefits provided by philosophy, for by applying its light to the creed, to the forms and the symbols, they will find much more meaning and depth in them. Properly interpreted they will not be found contradictory. But what has been added by ignorance, miscomprehension, wilfulness, or superstition will be shown up for what it is. The Founder's great message will remain untouched, his access to the eternal verities will be vindicated. In the case of those who had previously turned away from their traditional religion into a blank agnosticism, or even a stronger atheism, their doubts will be removed. So philosophy alone serves both groups! If it refuses to support false beliefs, it equally refuses to support false negations of religious belief. It sees quite clearly through religion and atheism and can nourish the follower of both.

89

There is nothing in religion that philosophy really displaces. It simply supplements and completes, corrects and inspires mature understanding, and leads the individual to *experience* the blessed inner peace which religion, per se, can only *allude* to.

90

Religion signifies an intellectual descent when compared with Philosophy *only* when it is *separated* from Philosophy, which earnestly sets itself the task of evoking the presence of a new Faith in the hearts of men. Prayer, worship, communion, reverence, and faith in God are indispensable parts to the philosophic life. Philosophy is, for those who are willing to live it as well as to study it, a religion. They acquire the religious spirit from it even if they never possessed it before. They increase their religious fervour if they did possess it before. They finish up with a sense of their helplessness, their smallness, and their dependence. They finish up with prayer. Thus religious worship, so often denounced as the first superstition of primitive man, becomes the final wisdom of matured man.

91

Why walk into the prison of another sect? Why not walk out from all sects into freedom?

92

Because philosophy includes and extends religion, it necessarily supports it. But it does not support the erroneous dogmas and misguided practices which are cloaked under religion's mantle, nor the human exploitations which are found in its history.(P)

93

The attitude of philosophy towards proselytizing Euro-American converts to yoga and propagandizing Ramakrishna Mission swamis is naturally sympathetic, yet wisely discriminating. It refuses to associate itself solely with any particular religion, whether Eastern or Western. Hence, it is uninterested in conversions from one religion to another, unconcerned with the defense or attack, the spread or decay of any organized religion. Those who especially link it with Hinduism alone or Buddhism alone are wrong. But although philosophy has no ecclesiastical system of its own, a philosopher is free to support one if he chooses to do so. This may happen for social reasons, or family reasons, or special personal reasons.

94

Because most religions theoretically turn people towards a power holier than themselves, however high or low their concept of that power may be, there is no ground for intolerance, fanaticism, or persecution. But because these things do exist, we must ascribe their origin to the human faults of upholders of religion and to the sectarian ambition or selfish aims of its organizations. Such an atmosphere is suffocating to would-be philosophers, with their pursuit of calm, their attitude of goodwill, and their doctrine of evolutionary levels. They are perfectly willing to let others follow their own way of worship, so long as it is not morally destructive or utterly evil.

95

If religion is for the consolation of man, philosophy is for the improvement of man.

96

How far is the distance between the pale apathetic faith of a nominal religionist and this wholly intensive devotion of a philosophic life!

97

If philosophy confirms basic religious feeling, it does not do so to serve any particular sect, institution, or creed. On the contrary, it frees one from the narrowness too often associated with them.

98

Buddha said, "Proclaim the Truth"; he did not say, "Convert others to the Truth." It is for the philosopher to make it available, to open up a way for others, but not to count the gains or weigh the harvest.

99

Judged from the philosophic level, the old religious forms which are disintegrating and the new forms which are striving to replace them are both gravely imperfect.

100

Philosophy does all that religion does for a man, but it does more. It not only restores or reinforces faith in a higher Power, gives each life a higher meaning, brings consolation and support during trouble, and ennobles one's treatment of other people, but also explains the deeper mysteries of the nature of God, the universe, and man.

101

The disciplinary revelations of the Overself displace the ethical regulations of established orthodoxy and render them unnecessary.

102

Religions and cults seek to get people into their particular folds. Philosophy seeks to get them out of all folds.

103

There is hope for these teachings so long as they do not become embedded in an organized church, so long as the movement of public appreciation remains individualistic, so long as no orthodoxy gets established with its accompanying pronouncements of anathema upon heresy.

104

The religious feelings of a philosopher are not less existent than those of the outwardly pious; they are deep and delicate: yet they are untouched by sentimentality.

105

Compulsory belief in particular religious dogmas has done harm as well as good, has led to much bloodshed and hatred. Philosophy instills an air of tolerance which operates against such religiosity.

106

The principles of philosophy are its clergy. They serve its little flock, minister to its higher needs, and support it in times of stress.

107

In the presence of sectarianism, with its rivalry and recrimination, philosophy remains aloof and silent. Unlike the sects, it is concerned with universal truths that will always be valid.

108

There are no labels in the kingdom of heaven, no organizations and no ashrams either. He who affixes a label to his name, be it that of Christian or Hindu, Advaitin or mystic, affixes a limitation also, and thus bars the gateway leading to the attainment of Truth. The study of philosophy mercilessly demolishes every possible division which the history of man has established.

109

It does not seek the convinced sectarians but tries to get the ear of the intelligent laymen who are dissatisfied with orthodox doctrine.

110

The current of religious conversion, exciting though it be at the time, is likely to exhaust itself as emotion subsides. The inward growth which comes with philosophy is slower moving and deeper rooted but more lasting. The change it makes cannot be undone, the peace it leaves cannot be taken away.

111

It is not religion itself that he has outgrown but *organized* religion, not truth that he has denied but arrogant claims to monopolize truth. He does not want a heaven which is really a prison.

112

Those who have passed through the disciplines of body, intellect, and emotion are no longer on the same level as those who have not. They need a teaching appropriate in every way to their higher development.

113

All that is finest and all that is really essential in religion is not negated but carried to its fulfilment in philosophy.

Philosophy and "the faithful"

114

It is unphilosophic and imprudent to disturb anyone's religious faith. It is only when the course of events or their own mental development creates doubts and disquiet—and even then they must come seeking more satisfactory answers to their questions—that higher teaching can be given. But even then the manner in which the latter is presented is important—that is, try not to bring it into collision with those parts of their faith which they still hold, be constructive and not destructive. In that way the new teaching can be presented as a higher octave of the old one or used for reform of the old one.

115

Intolerant religious organizations which would allow no other voice, however harmless, to speak than one which echoes their own must in the end fall victim to their own intolerance; for as men through their education and contact with more developed persons come to perceive the Truth, their hostility and enmity to those religions are inevitably aroused. They will then either fall into agnosticism or into sheer atheism, or they will find their way to other and truer expressions of what religion should be if it is to fulfil its highest mission. Therefore, it is not the work of a philosopher to reverse, correct, or otherwise disturb other people's religious beliefs. If the latter are faulty and if the organization propagating them is intolerant, he may be sure that given enough time others will arise to do this negative and destructive work; and this saves him the trouble of these unpleasant tasks. His own work is a positive one.(P)

116

He will not disturb the faith of those who are satisfied with their own religion or of those who feel sure they have the truth. His ministrations are only to those who humbly call themselves seekers, who do not arrogantly feel they have arrived at the goal of truth, who are bewildered or who approach him earnestly.

117

Because of the absence of intolerance from his character, the philosopher neither desires nor attempts to impose his ideas upon others. He gives them the intellectual freedom he wants for himself.

118

He will accept the fact that a variety of attitudes and a diversity of views must exist among mankind, since the life-waves behind mankind are themselves so varied in age. The result of this will be a large willingness on his own part to let others believe what they wish so long as they do not try to force these beliefs compulsorily where not wanted.

119

They attend the church synagogue mosque most piously but the experience of the Deity as it really happens (not the ego-inflating joyous semimystic experience of popular religion and conventional mysticism) would frighten them away if described in advance. For it involves the disappearance of the ego into the Void.

120

The destruction of religion would constitute a serious loss of moral strength and mental hope to mankind. Its dogma of the existence of a higher power, its insistence that a virtuous life is rewarded and a vicious one punished, its periodical call to drop worldly thoughts and activities are values of which the multitudes cannot afford to be prematurely deprived without grave peril to their higher evolution. The philosophical student should be sympathetic to the genuine worth of religion as he should be hostile to the traditional abuses. He must not permit himself to be swept away on the emotional tide of extreme fanaticism, either by the materialistic atheists who would utterly destroy religion and persecute its priesthood in the name of science or by the blind pious dogmatists who would destroy scientific free thought in the name of God.

121

Popular religion, suited to rural peasants and city crowds, asks for simple faith, not reflective thought; questionless obedience and not critical inquiry. It is easier to follow. And besides, conformity in this matter means fewer troubles and freedom from harassment for those who have to live among others. A philosopher who pays outward deference to the religion of those around him because he wants a tranquil life is not necessarily a hypocrite. He knows what is true and what is superstitious in that religion. The truth he accepts, the other he ignores. He wants to worship God just as much as, more likely more, than the other people.

122

Religion must be regarded as a necessity for the masses, for whom it represents the best possible source of help; it is not right to disturb their faith. Nevertheless, for those who have begun to diverge from the herd and who have developed an interest in mysticism, such facts as the foregoing should be pointed out and need to be discussed.

123

Many in the prewar period had so altered their outlooks as to be somewhat sceptical of the validity of religion. But scepticism is a negative attitude which hides a real hunger, the hunger for some new truth to replace the old belief which has been found lacking. It is for us to show such minds that a rational mysticism, pruned of superstition, has much to offer them. It is also for us to show the few among them who can ascend so far that the hidden philosophy will satisfactorily fill their hunger and provide an alternative to replace what they have renounced.

124

This clinging adhesion to the institutions and organizations of religions and cults whether established or unorthodox, this lack of exploratory spirit to search out little known but superior teaching, must be recognized by the educator in philosophy. He must accept ruefully that what he has to communicate will be welcomed only by a small minority.

125

But if we do not tell others that the truth exists, how will anyone ever know about it? The answer is that telling is not a job for the incautious beginner but for the seasoned proficient.

126

In meeting with religious advocates, the student should listen courteously but not waste time arguing with them: he should keep his mental reservations to himself.

127

He will carefully avoid disturbing the faith of others but, except in special circumstances or for special motives—persecution, position, children, or mission—he will not go out of his way to encourage them. It is not his business to encourage superstition.

128

The sage seeks to descend and meet a man at his own level, and then try to lift him just a little higher. Thus he will try to give the remorselessly cruel fanatical religionist a noble view of his own faith.

129

It is not that philosophy holds a different conception about man from the religious one, but that it holds a deeper one.

130

The enlightened philosopher has no conflict with religion so long as it retains its ethical force. When a religion is crumbling, when men reject its moral restraining power, when they refuse to accept its historical incidents and irrational dogmas as being vital to living, when in consequence they are becoming brutalized and uncontrolled, as our own epoch has painfully seen, then this religion is losing its raison d'être and the people among whom it held sway are in need of help. The mass of the common people now in the West mentally dwell outside any church, and are consequently outside its disciplinary moral influence. They cannot be left to perish unguided when religion becomes just a means of duping simple minds in the interests of ruling or wealthy classes, and is no longer an ethical force. This puts the whole of society in danger, and such a religion will inevitably fall, bringing down society with itself in the crash as it did in France and later in Russia. When the old faith fails then the new is needed. Thinking men refuse to bind their reason to the incredible articles of a dogmatic creed. They refuse to swear belief in queer concepts which they find impossible to reconcile with the rest of human life and certainly with modern knowledge. The philosopher finds that religion looms against a much larger background; it is the mere shadow cast by philosophy, but for the masses the shadow suffices.(P)

131

The pious man may keep his religious denomination when he adds philosophy, so long as he does not try to keep its conformism and dogmatism and smug monopolism. The one attitude is incompatible with the other. But the original living spirit behind its beginnings, the essential reverence of the higher power, the beautiful communion, the fervent devotion—these are perfectly philosophical.

132

Philosophy can never collide with religion. Indeed it includes a cult, a worship of the higher Power. But it may and does collide with superstition masquerading as religion, and with exploitation pretending to be religion.

133

Just as the confusion of planes of ethical reference between the monastic and householder's duties has introduced error into the whole subject of yoga, so the confusion of planes of intellectual understanding between the religious and the philosophic concepts has introduced error into the whole subject of truth. Philosophy has no quarrel with religion so long as it does not go beyond its legitimate frontiers.

134

If some men find help in the regular formal observance of established religions, philosophy does not object. But if they assert that these observances should be honoured and followed by all other men, as being indispensable to their spiritual welfare, then philosophy is forced to object. We must allow tolerance in spiritual and social matters to all except those whose doctrines would subvert tolerance itself or whose action would destroy it. If we regard it as wrong to impose our religious views on others, we also regard it as wrong to allow others to impose them on us.

135

They are not asked to give up their faith in God but to broaden their idea of God.

136

The gap between the religious approach and the philosophic approach cannot be closed except by time and development. Fools ignore it only to suffer disillusionment for their trouble.

137

Philosophy is forced to support existing religious bodies not because it conceives them to be the best, but because it can find no better ones. It is grieved by their faults and imperfections, their past history and present selfishness, but it believes that a world without them would be a worse one.

138

To the ignorant sceptic, the venerable institution of religion rests on the twin pillars of superstition and prejudice, but to the philosopher these are but the incrustations of time on the real pillars, which are understanding and reverence.

139

Philosophy is always sympathetic towards religion because the parent is always sympathetic towards its offspring.

140

Just as the worship of an anthropomorphic Deity is a proper prescription for the masses, so the worship of a personal saviour is a proper prescription for them too. Philosophy warmly endorses both kinds of worship. Let it not be thought that it would obliterate them. On the contrary, it rationally explains their necessity and defends their utility. They are valuable aids to millions of people. Moreover, they yield genuine and not illusory results. However, when ignorant or intolerant persons would set up these elementary goals as the highest possible ones for all men, or as the sole paths leading to divinity, then philosophy feels it necessary to refute the ignorance of the one and to denounce the intolerance of the other.

141

If personality is denied to Universal Being, this is only because of the littleness it imposes on that Being, because it lessens and minifies. But if children, adolescents, and many or most adults need the support of such a belief to maintain religious aspiration and provide personal comfort, why not let them have it? The others, who have been educated so highly as to regard it as an illusion, are entitled to their view too. Philosophy is able to point out what is correct and what is not in both views.

142

When one talks or writes in public about popular religion, one must be cautious and careful, for it is very easy to tread on the feet of those who take popular religion quite literally and most seriously. Just as the educated Greeks and Romans could not, because they dared not, tell the masses that the various cults they worshipped were really the laws of nature, so the philosopher must be very careful if he hints that popular religion is merely the first step on the way to God—a step too often mixed with confusions and superstitions.

143

Those who have reached its higher levels and stand at the portals of philosophy can get a point of view which will harmonize all old and new religions which now compete or even conflict with each other.

Intolerance toward philosophy

144

The sage of former centuries was prudent in the presence of established religious authority. He took care to avoid being persecuted for heresy, although he did not always succeed in protecting himself against its suspicions. Even on a lesser plane, a mystic like Miguel de Molinos could not be saved by the Pope, his friend, from the dungeons of the "Holy" Office, the Inquisition. Remember that the Jesuits were hostile to the work of Molinos and also Madame Guyon because of its success. They were also jealous of his intimacy with the Pope, who lodged him in the Vatican. Plots were laid, the Inquisition was brought into their opposition, he was denounced as a heretic and, further, falsely libelled. The Jesuits succeeded in winning the French king to their cause: he used all his influence with the Papacy to have Molinos arrested. The poor victim never regained his freedom but died in the dungeons of the Inquisition some twelve years later. His books were termed "dangerous" and destroyed.

145

The so-called normal condition of the human mentality is really an abnormal one. Sanity has not yet been stamped upon the human race. That is still a perfectionist ideal which is being approached slowly, haltingly, and with many side-wanderings. The narrow, unbalanced, and confused mentalities of most people naturally react indifferently, impatiently, or intolerantly to the broad straight truths of philosophy. Nothing can be done by anyone to assist them so long as they not only do not understand this teaching but do not even care to understand it. Only when they will have sufficiently awakened to regard it as being not too absurd or too idealistic to be considered will they have attained civilized maturity.

146

The narrow-minded and little-hearted among orthodox institutions will resent his independence and protest that to allow him freedom and equality is to allow anarchy and chaos to reign.

147

This word "religion" is very often and very glibly used. Yet the meaning given it by the seers is too frequently not the same meaning given it by the hearers. Consequently history has witnessed the curious spectacle of Spinoza, whose entire life was a contemplation of God and a practice of virtue, denounced as an atheist by the Jewish ecclesiasts, and as a scoundrel by the Christian ones, of his times.

Philosophic independence, universalism

148

The philosopher who would be completely loyal to Truth will also be non-denominational in religion. Among those who boast of their formal membership in a solidly organized or socially respected church he will be a churchless outsider. The very membership they are so proud of would be an oppressive limitation to him. Intellectually he is fully justified in refusing to affix to himself any label bearing the name of any sect. His detached impartial judgement allows him to see the errors and weaknesses of all sects no less than their truths and services. He can gladly share what is true in all beliefs but not what is false in them or limiting in their followers and organizers. Yet this true position will not be what it seems from the outside. It will paradoxically be both in and out of all religions—in by reason of his deeper understanding of them than their own believers possess, and out by reason of his knowledge that the inspired Word has been spoken in many lands, among different races, to the most varied individuals. He is in by reason of his sympathy with all groping for light and all giving Light, which a religion represents, but out by reason of his inability to narrow down his receptivity to that Light through adopting a dogmatic creed or through identifying himself completely with any particular faith. He cannot for the sake of partial truth endure the imitating error. He is out too because he sees each denomination locked in on itself, restricted in outlook and inadequate in tolerance. He feels the need of a larger liberty than any of them can give him, so as to express somewhat the infinite freedom of the Spirit itself. Nor will he, for the personal or social benefit of associating with a closed congenial group, yield to the temptation of losing interest in all other groups. His intellectual attitude is the only truly catholic one, and the neutrality of his feelings is the only really universal one. He stands at the frontier between every pair of religions, a foreigner but yet a friend, serene and immobile. In all this what else is he doing except expressing not only a stricter adherence to truth but also to love? For no man, whether believer or atheist, is shut out from his circle. All men are included in it.

149

No universal rule can be laid down for the illumined man to follow in the matter of relationship to the religion into which he was born. He may adhere to it, observe all its rites, and fulfil all its requirements quite faithfully or he may anarchically reject all allegiance to it. If he follows the first alternative it will most probably be because of the need to set an example to those who still need the support of such outward and visible institutionalism and such fixed forms and dogmas. If he follows the second alternative, it is most certainly because first, his inner voice tells him to do so, second, because the hour is at hand to recall religion itself to the great verities which have largely vanished from it, and third, simply because his own temperament and disposition prefer it. This is why in history we find the strangely paradoxical actuality of some mystics following orthodoxy with pious conformity but others standing aside with heretical stubbornness.

150

In the end man will find that no church can give him what he can give himself or do for him what he must do for himself. And that is, to go back to the source of his being and seek communion there within his own mind and his own heart where God is hidden.

151

Real religion is as universal as the wind. Cut and dried religions are mere local limitations; they were originally put up as temporary trelliswork for the young souls of man to climb and grow upward, but they have become imprisoning hatches and sometimes instruments of torture. Let us look only for that which is *salient* in a religion, and we shall find ourselves set free from its lassoing limitations. We shall not arrive at its meaning by muddled talk in its favour any more than by muddled talk in its despite, for the powers of calm judgement and reasoned reflection are then stupefied. The philosophical student's attitude is simply this, that he can *begin* no discussion with acceptance of the existence of any dogma; such acceptance is only proper as the *culmination* of a discussion. He must question and cross-question every inherited belief, every acquired doctrine until he can elicit what we really know out of the mass of pseudo-knowledge, until he becomes conscious of the ignorance which is so often veiled by the mask of supposed knowledge. Through such agitated unsettlement and such sharp doubt alone can we win our way to rocklike certitude ultimately.(P)

152

The outer forms and observances, the liturgies and rituals of religion may be dispensed with by the person who has successfully opened up an inner way of communication with the higher self, so far as his own personal needs are concerned. But, for the sake of others to whom these are still necessary, he may, by way of example, continue with them, as he deems best.

153

You can no more decipher the name of his denomination than you can put the sky into a container. For he does not belong to one inwardly although he may, occasionally, for social reasons, belong to one outwardly.

154

He does not have to enter a church or temple to stand in God's presence: he is continually there.

155

Religion is for the masses of men, mysticism for the few, but philosophy is for the individual.

156

The orthodox offering of myth will never satisfy the man who has had a glimpse of the star of truth.

157

Who is willing to sacrifice his worldly interests for the sake of coming closer to the intangible Overself? Who is willing to deviate from the conventional path of mere sensuality and narrow selfishness for the sake of a mysterious intuition which bids him obey and trust it implicitly? The answer to these questions is that only a scattered minority is willing to do so, and one small enough to show up humanity's actual state as being inwardly far from knowing why it is here on earth.

158

The shelter which religion offers the masses has its correspondence in the strength which philosophy offers the few.

159

Although the philosopher is not really tied to any dogmas or tethered to any cult but is friendly to all those which are not directly evil, this does not mean he is ready to agree deferentially with all the doctrines offered to the world. He may have to point out where acceptance must stop, but he qualifies this by showing up its relativity, its dependence on a particular level.

160

If others feel the need of a creedal, dogmatic teaching to support them, of a leader to take them along, of a group to give them gregarious comfort, it is right for them to accept these things. But the philosopher feels that he must remain uncommitted, must not put up fences and barriers behind which he is to shut himself in with a leader and a group. He remembers the experience of the spiritual glimpse, when he felt that God's love was for all, and not for any special sect or society, that God's truth was greater than any creed or dogma, and that he was set free from all man-made mental, social, and spiritual cages.

161

Too intelligent to accept the nonsense which is traditionally served in the name of religion, too intuitive not to feel the worshipful reverence for a higher Power demanded by religion, he is forced to follow an independent path.

162

In answer to the question which sometimes arises, whether the aspirant could continue to remain, without hypocrisy, in communion with an orthodoxy such as the Church of England, while holding the philosophic view of Jesus, the reply is that he could certainly do so. There is absolutely no need to break away from the Church nor to give up the services of institutional religion. Philosophy makes no pronouncements against these items but leaves it entirely to each individual to make his own decision in such matters. The decision must depend upon his circumstances, temperament, and so forth. Philosophy merely says that such services are not enough in themselves to ensure illumination in the case of the believer, while in the case of the sceptic they are useless. They may have their value to quite a number of people, and if one feels the need of them or of religious fellowship, it would be quite permissible for him to continue them. This need not at all be construed as hypocrisy or cowardice. However, no one should act hastily in so vital a matter. He has not only to consider the effect of such an act upon himself, but also upon the community around him. It might even be that, although the service no longer satisfied him personally, he might have to continue it for the sake of setting an example to other, less mature persons who still fully believe in it—since they think they are receiving help from it—and who are influenced by his decisions.

163

Philosophy sees that the problem of man's attitude to God is an individual problem, that organizations can at best only contribute towards its solution and at worst retard and delay its solution. No organization can ever solve it for him. Only he himself can do so.

164

The sceptic, who has no use for religious institutions and no belief in religious experience, is far removed from the philosopher, who criticizes these things but does not reject them.

165

The experience which carries him into the pure air of the Overself carries him also high above the limitations of creeds and dogmas, sects, rituals, and groups which so arbitrarily divide men.

166

Emerson overestimated the value of individualism because he tended to overlook the fact that all the fine things he said about it were true only of those rare individuals who had attained the zenith of noble character and inspirational wisdom.

167

He has freed himself from the biased creedal trap, from the fanatic sectarian exclusiveness, from the tight limits caused by non-existent or insufficient comparative knowledge. He has yet to free himself from himself, to become detached from the egoistic way of viewing ideas, to become detached and impartial and equilibrated.

168

It is not conversion from one religion into another that a philosopher seeks to effect, such as from Christianity to Hinduism, but conversion to the inner understanding of all religions.

169

The philosopher is inwardly a non-traditionalist. Why should he, who seeks or dwells in the fullest mental freedom, condition his mind by the opinions of others or conform his life according to the beliefs of others? Why should he, who knows that the Spirit bears no labels, attach himself to any particular system of thought, values, or rites? Do not therefore expect him to belong to any creed, religion, sect that you can name or to adore its symbols and submit to its clichés.

170

The Spirit which he has touched will not let him be confined to a single religious system but enables him to perceive what is true (and what is not) in all systems.

171

He is independent and neutral towards organized religions yet at the same time friendly and understanding of them. He is unable to commit himself to all their credos or join their institutions, yet he willingly studies those credos and recognizes the need of those institutions. He needs no formal authority to endorse his attainment for he needs no following, no publicity, no patronage.

172

Such a man will be highly advanced whatever religion or sect he follows outwardly, and not as the effect of that particular group to which he belongs. The credit is his own, not the group's.

173

He who acquires a thorough and correct understanding of philosophy acquires a property that will remain in his possession throughout life. He will never change it although he may broaden it.

174

If he chooses to remain within a particular denomination, it will not be at the price of regarding it as God's chosen one.

175

The sage is in himself a non-sectarian, yet his people's need or his personal destiny, or both, may make him active on behalf of religious sects. He is mentally nonpolitical, yet the same pressure may make him work for some political cause.

176

The philosopher has no general need to identify himself with any particular religion, with its bias and limitation, but he may have a special need to do so because of personal circumstances or of service to humanity.

177

He may attend his ancestral church, temple, mosque, or synagogue if he wishes but it will not be at all necessary for spiritual comfort to do so. His obedience to the obligation is merely a gesture, an outward symbol of acknowledgment that there *is* a Higher Power worthy of homage and worship. And he makes this acknowledgment to confirm the faith of the ignorant who are not able to do more than take their religion on external authority.

178

Traditional forms and organizations have little appeal to one who draws his inspirations from today's life, and not yesterday's: still less to one who holds to the superiority of the individual intuition above all organizations and prefers it to their tyranny and dogmatism.

179

With the fuller establishment of enlightenment he comes to understand

that if he is to transcend duality he must give up the idols he has worshipped—gods and gurus.

180

He needs no religious authority to interfere with or interrupt this glorious glimpse, no theologian to bring it down to the intellectual level and
thus lose it for him.

181

Do not ask the name of his religion or the whereabouts of his church,
for he does not know anything more than that it is a faith and worship
which saturate his mind, penetrate his heart, and satisfy both, and that it
goes with him regularly everywhere he himself goes.

182

The philosopher may recite no creed and observe no sacrament, or he
may do both. He is free.

183

But if such an event as the formation of a new cult be in the destiny of
things, then he is content to let it come in its own way by the activity of
others, never by his own, and only after his death, for he will do all he can
to prevent it during his lifetime.

184

All these minor stars of religious theology and intellectual theory pale
before the bright constellation of final Truth.

185

Philosophy is profoundly religious, but it is not a religion. Men belonging to different folds may study and practise it.

186

If you regard it as a religion, then it is one which embraces all other
religions.

187

Whenever the masses begin to question, they ask, "What are we to
believe?" whereas whenever the intelligent few begin to question they ask,
"What can we know?"

188

If he is to be at all understood, he must use the names and dogmas of the
established religion, the ascendant faith, in his own declarations.

189

To accept an institution's usefulness to society generally without accepting the institution personally is his attitude.

190

A man who develops his own private approach to the spirit has as much
right to hold independent views of it as others have to hold conventional

ones. Societies rightly depend upon organized religions but they should learn to respect individuals who are unable to do so but who are not less appreciative of religious values in their loftiest sense.

191

Those who look for overnight miraculous uplifting and exalting changes in the minds of the masses are looking for rare happenings; this is for individuals only; all the others will be changed either by a long process of experience or by a shorter process of education, or, more usually, by a combination of both.

192

If ideas, truths, knowledge of enormous importance to the human race, as well as a way of life founded upon them, are not to vanish from the world altogether, a few men and women here and there must carefully preserve them and lovingly nurture them.

193

It is not a long step but rather an easy one from the universalizing of communications and transport which is such a feature of our times, to the universalizing of spiritual culture. The search for God, the quest of the Soul can now be carried on with the help of all the knowledge gleaned by all human beings everywhere. It can now be discussed in terms of basic human experiences and not mere sectarian ones.

194

This universal message is destined to flow all over the world. Its bearers will be none other than the writings of ancient and modern seers. It will bring people the opportunity to grow, to go forward. Those who will be mentally flexible enough to understand and emotionally courageous enough to accept the truth will break away from the effete tradition which holds them. The others will stubbornly prefer to remain as they are. It is not easy to desert one belief for another.

7

BEYOND RELIGION
AS WE KNOW IT

A better understanding of the religious instinct is replacing the old one. The elimination of fear and superstition as the accompaniments of this instinct are good signs of the spread of truer knowledge about it.

2

Humanity has to find a religious form to suit the coming era. It has to find something between the extreme of mere anarchy and the extreme of steel-trap institutionalism. In the first case, it becomes the victim of any and every phantasy which human imagination may throw up, which human ambition may put forth, or which human ignorance may blunder into. In the second case, it becomes the victim of a letter that kills the spirit or of a collective enslavement by outworn dogmas and selfish organizations and by mechanical worship. Humanity has to find a form which respects the individual's right to choose freely what will most help him and which to that extent leaves religion a personal matter. Yet it cannot afford to disdain the proffered hand of traditional experience, authoritative knowledge, and group association. The needed revelation must be relevant to external conditions and adequate to internal outlook. Those who are no longer attracted by church religion, who believe its claims are exaggerated and its dogmas untenable, can go forward towards higher religious truth only by going forward into a more mystical and more scientific cult. Instead of wasting time trying to resurrect the dead forms of an old faith, many people were moved up by the war closer to this point of view.

3

Religion must organize itself on a more intellectual basis to meet modern needs. It must present a fuller system, which will intelligibly explain the inner meaning of man, God, and the Universe. It must not contradict the verified knowledge of modern science. It ought no longer to attempt to outrage reason, but should go out of the way to convince it. It must be so timely and reasonable that it will give satisfying intelligent answers to the most disconcerting questions.

On the second point, it is a lesson of history that if religion is to be more rational it will have to be less ritualistic. The tendency of all external rites is to become empty and hollow. Nobody is worse off and everybody is better off when religious practices or rites which have become merely mechanical and utterly hypocritical are abandoned, whether in disbelief or in disgust. As a religion becomes less inspired, it becomes ritualistic. What it is no longer able to give men through inward power, it pretends to give them through outward forms. When the means of worship becomes an actual hindrance to communion with the Worshipped, when the worshipper is deceived by pretense of the act into belief that he has performed the act itself, it is time to call a halt. Nevertheless, ritual is useful if it helps the mind to think of diviner things and it therefore has a proper place in religion. If a religious ceremony acts as a springboard whence a man can enter more easily into a reverential mood, it has justified its value for him. This is usually the case with the peasant mentality among the lower classes and with the aesthetic temperament among the higher ones, although it is much less true of artisan town workers and city intellectuals who indeed may find it a hindrance to worship rather than a help. Religion will always be, by its nature, something of an allegory; but it need not always stick to the same set of symbols. Why should not this era find a new religious symbolism? In the end, religion will find its truer expression in the public acts and private thoughts of a man than in its own public rites. Those who would propagate it will best do so by their living example. It will then become less formal and more vital, less institutional and more free, less devoted to public parades in church, temple, or synagogue and more devoted to personal righteousness in home, factory, and field.

The practical question arises: What is to be done with orthodox religious institutions as they exist today? Much needs to be done with them. If mankind's religious leaders could broaden their vision, could recognize these truths, there would then be some hope for their institutions. If they cannot put themselves at the head of this movement, then they will have to become stragglers in its rear. The choice cannot be evaded. But first it may be said that unless the State dis-establishes religion, it will continue to get not religion in its purity but religion in its degeneration. To worship an institution merely because it is an established one, is to worship an idol. The new religious teaching must be a vocation, not a profession. Hence, teachers may receive voluntary contributions towards their expenses, but they must not be paid a prescribed salary.

If rites and ceremonies will be less needed, then the services of priests to perform them will also be less needed. The coming faith will not only be a rational and riteless one, but may also be a priestless one. It will tolerate no paid professionals to exploit it in their own interests, but will substitute direct, silent, inward communion instead. It will not mock at itself with ostentatious, theatrical ceremonies nor at truth with hollow clamour, but will substitute the remembrances of moral law in everyday conduct instead. The services of a professional priestly class were needed when the intellect of the race was still undeveloped and the masses still uneducated. But today, when men are becoming mentally individualized and when illiteracy is becoming rapidly eliminated, people can read and reflect over sacred scriptures for themselves and with their own understanding. Not only will there be no religious ceremonials, no paid clergy, but there will be no public prayers. For these, sooner or later, tend to degenerate into hollow, meaningless formalities. Here, indeed, "Familiarity breeds contempt."

Its very newness would be an attractive feature to many because it would not have had time to develop the maladies of stiffened arteries and congealed blood, but would possess an aura of hope and helpfulness, of enthusiasm and energy. The religion of the new era must be alive. It must be so radiant with inspiration that it will have something to give man, instead of weakly begging for its own support and sustenance from him. It must be effective because so long as young people are given an uninspired religion and a mistaken education, so long will they be badly equipped for the hard business of living. We say "uninspired" because not a few even of institutionalized religion's own ministers have raised their hands in helplessness as they watched the melancholy spectacle of a deserting flock and the inevitable results of an antiquated creed dwindling daily in its authority over the lives and hearts of men. In the early part of 1939, for example, it was noted that only 5 percent of the people of London thought it worthwhile to attend any place of worship. And we say "mistaken" because, to take a particularly glaring example, the German people were one of the best-educated in the whole world and yet the Nazi doctrines were able to impose successfully on the German mind.

On the third point, the postwar situation of society will depend, eventually, less upon its political arrangements and more upon its ethical decisions. If it fails to maintain enough of the idealism born during the war, then like a rudderless, propellerless ship it will be helplessly tossed about upon a stormy sea. The old values have miserably collapsed where they deserved to do so. And, unfortunately, in their fall they have dragged down some sound, ethical ones, which have not deserved to suffer in the same way but which selfish exploitation and stupid traditionalism have unfortunately associated with them. Consequently, many men have become morally perplexed and mentally hurt. Only so far as the religious faith into which he was born coincides with the reasoned faith which he has unconsciously worked out for himself, does anyone live practically by its ethics.

On the fourth requirement of the new faith, let it be noted that we need a technique which will be workable under twentieth-century conditions and understandable by the twentieth-century mind. Otherwise, we shall end up by becoming living anachronisms, human relics of an obsolete past, and consequently ineffectual dreamers. The mold into which the religious faith and mystical ideology of the postwar world will flow will not be shaped by the desires of the spiritual guides who cling closely to the half-moribund institutions and obsolete dogmas of the prewar world. If the representatives of dying and failing traditions have seen the writing on the wall, they will have seen that the future will not conform to their selfish hopes, much less obey their selfish dictates. New and different forces are inserting themselves into men's hearts. New and different ideas are rising vitally in their minds. And new guides and new institutions will perforce come into existence to assist this process where the old ones might merely suffocate it.

The universal religion, when it comes—as it will at an appropriately advanced stage of human evolution—will not be a melange of outgrown faiths which have already fulfilled their mission, but a perfectly new and timely one. That stage, however, is far off.

The fifth requirement is that a religious teaching, today, must contain these two elements: the spiritual and the social. It must develop the individual and yet regenerate society. It must kindle solitary, personal experience and promote general, public welfare. The postwar period, with all the moral confusion, economic disorders, and political complications legated to it, will open a period of great opportunity for starting a new faith which has the wisdom to combine mystical meditation with social renovation. This is evidenced by what happened in Japan, to take a single example, after the last war. In 1921, the Japanese government outlawed, in fear of its swift-rising influence, a new hybrid cult called *Omoto-Kyo*, which combined socialism, millenarianism and mysticism and which gathered a million followers in a few years and published its own daily newspaper and magazines.

There is a profound reason why the new faith must possess such an *integral* character. In ancient civilizations, the spiritual formulation preceded the social one. But in twentieth-century civilization, the social must precede the spiritual. For men and circumstances have so changed that today we can give a new significance to human life only by first giving it new economic and political creations.

It has elsewhere been explained that the evolution of the human ego is about to undergo its most momentous historic change. Hitherto, it has wandered farther and farther in its own thought from its divine source on an outgoing orbit, but henceforth it must return nearer and nearer on an ingoing one. Hitherto, it has followed an increasingly separative movement leading to selfishness, but henceforth it will have to follow an increasingly unitive one leading to balanced altruism. Therefore, the keynote of the coming age will not be individualistic competition but co-operation, not the brutal struggle of creatures with each other for mere existence but the nobler union of all for each, each for all. If the old idea was that man must struggle against man, class against class, nation against nation, race against race, the new idea will be that they must co-operate together for their common welfare. Thus, the immense significance of such a spiritual change is that it will first have a pathway cleared for it by social-economic changes. The creation of new structural forms in the social sphere will thus be part of a higher movement whose later unfoldment will operate in the religious, mystical, and philosophic spheres.

The evolution of each ego, of each entity conscious of a personal "I," passes through three stages through immense periods of time. In the first and earliest stage, it unfolds its distinct physical selfhood, acquires more and more consciousness of the personal "I," and hence divides and isolates itself from other egos. It seeks to differentiate itself from them. It feels the need to assert itself and its interests. This leads inevitably to antagonism towards them. Its movement is towards externality, a movement which must inevitably end in its taking the surface or appearance of things for reality, that is, in materialism. Here it is acquisitive. In its second and intermediate stage, it unfolds its mental selfhood and hence adds cunning to its separative and grasping tendencies, with intellect expanding to its extremest point. Here it is inquisitive. But midway in this stage, its descent comes to an end with a turning point where it halts, turns around, and begins to travel backward to its original source. In the third and last stage, the return towards its divine source continues. Its movement is now toward internality and—through meditation, investigation, and reflection—it ultimately achieves knowledge of its true being: its source, the Overself. And as all egos arise out of the Overself, the end of such a movement is one and the same for all—a common centre. Conflicts between them cease; mutual understanding, co-operation, and compassion spread. Hence, this stage is unitive.

The central point of the entire evolution is about where we now stand. Human attitudes and relations have reached their extreme degree of self-ishness, separateness, struggle, and division, have experienced the result-ing exhaustion of an unheard-of world crisis, but are beginning to reorien-tate themselves towards an acknowledgment of the fundamental unity of the whole race. Thus, war reaches its most violent and terrible phase in the second stage and then abruptly begins to vanish from human life al-together. The separatist outlook must cease. Most of our troubles have arisen because we have continued it beyond the point where it was either useful or needful.

The unequal state of evolution of all these egos, when thrown together into a conglomerate group on a single planet, is also responsible for the conflicts which have marked mankind's own history. They stand on dif-ferent steps of the ladder all the way from savagery to maturity. The backward ego naturally attacks or preys on the advanced one. Thus, the purely self-regarding ego, which was once an essential pattern of the evo-lutionary scheme—a necessary goal in the movement of life—becomes with time a discordant ingredient of that scheme, an obstructive impedi-ment to that movement. If humanity is to travel upward and fulfil its higher destiny, it can do so only by enlarging its area of interest and extending its field of consciousness. It must, in short, seek to realize the Overself on the one hand, to feel its oneness on the other.

We should preserve intact what is useful to us in the old systems, but at the same time we should create what is essential to our altered times. This is what present-day philosophy is trying to do. There are sincere religious prophets and teachers, ardent mystical swamis and monks eager to guide mankind in old dusty ways and well-trodden paths. But the special impor-tance of the philosopher's work is that he is trying to hew out a new way, to cut a new path. For he perceives what these others fail to perceive—the vital necessity of re-adjustment to the unique evolutionary change which is now taking place. The philosophic seer knows how important to the race are the future purposes and distant goals hidden in the present confused tangle of events. He knows that the evolutionary twist, which is now appearing inside the human soul, is momentous in its ultimate signifi-cance. If the war did not change human nature generally, it did change a certain number of individual human beings. Everyone knows this. But not everyone knows that the war marked a moment of profound importance in human history—the change-over from a solely egoistic extroverted and materialistic basis to a deeper one.

At an earlier stage, the evolutionary path proceeded through an increased turning outward to the senses, a growing egotism, and a developing intellect. But now it is destined that human character and endeavour must strike out new paths for themselves—must reverse these trends. This evolutionary development represents what is virtually a new beginning in the history of the present race of mankind. Cosmic forces are communicating themselves to the human mind. The most tremendous changeover of its evolution is at hand. And the same forces which are working at it from within by prompting, are also compelling it to submit itself from without by events. The great inner evolutionary changeover will be responsible for increasing tension and conflict within the individual human being, his lower self beckoning one way and his higher self beckoning another way.

All the world-shaking events of our times are compelling men and women to rise out of their habitual thoughtlessness about life. Whoever thinks that these people will be permitted to relapse into torpor again with the conclusion of the war is mistaken. For the situation today is unique. New forces have entered the planet's atmosphere which will increasingly bring powerful inner and outer pressure to bear on its inhabitants, because the ego is destined to evolve in a different direction. Hitherto it has, in most human beings, travelled farther and farther away from its hidden centre, the Overself, as it expanded its own circumference. Henceforth it will, while holding whatever is of worth in its previous gains, return closer and closer to that centre. And it will do this partly because planetary evolution has reached a point where it will enforce it and partly because it is itself so constituted that it cannot escape time by a return to the source of its own life. With the subsidence of present turmoils, the human ego will resist the realization of its spiritual possibilities less fiercely, if more subtly, than in the past. This will be a distinct and definite advance. It will show in many different phases and aspects. There is a real basis for the hope that we have seen the worst in man's conduct and that he will begin to reflect some better qualities and nobler attitudes. In this faith, we may work for a more spiritual future, sure that our efforts will not be in vain or futile. It may sustain us amid present crises when personal misfortunes bid us despair. It may enlighten us during contemporary darknesses when world events bid us fall into helpless inertia.

It would be easy to misunderstand this tenet. The assertion of such a tremendous modification in the spiritual make-up of mankind as the disappearance of human egoism from human history is certainly not made here. Such an assertion is wildly fantastic and would be and could be made with any hope of acceptance only if made to wild enthusiasts. The clinging to the "I," or the aggressive assertion of it, is something which will yield only to the intermittent batterings of constant frustrations, repeated disappointments, and frequent misfortunes—that is to say, to the experience of hundreds, if not thousands, of earthly incarnations. What is really asserted here is that:

(a) The universal crisis is a sign that we have reached a point in the process of the ego's development where the more violent and hence more extreme aspects of its inevitable struggles with other egos must be curbed in its own interest or self-destruction will ensue.

(b) The very intensity and extensity of this struggle during the war have brought about a widespread recognition of this fact.

(c) We are only at the very beginning of it now, although in a half-dozen centuries this result will have been achieved to such an extent all over the world as to be quite unmistakable. The forces which are now beginning to release themselves in mankind's character will by then increase in intensity quite rapidly. And although this has been happening on all the continents, their quickest, strongest, and fullest manifestation will occur on the North American continent. Such a development will be closely connected with the birth of a new ethnological race, which is maturing out of the American melting pot.

(d) This spiritual overturn in the ego's evolutionary life refers not to all the egos here but to the largest wave of human egos travelling our planetary path, not to all entities but only to the human ones, and not to the entire history of this earth but only to its present evolutionary cycle.

(e) At any given time, this planet will not be inhabited by more than a small number of spiritually advanced persons. Nature maintains the balance between them and the unevolved masses by constant re-adjustment. This evolutionary overturn will not, however, directly involve the entire race, but only a part of it. Those who can accept such a higher world-view are and will be heavily outnumbered by those who cannot. Small groups and scattered individuals in every part of the world will continue to respond immediately, directly, and consciously to this urge; but the response of the masses will come mainly, vaguely, and indirectly through their leaders and rulers.

(f) It does not matter, at first, that this great change in human outlook is taking place without a parallel consciousness of the inner evolutionary development, which is its real motivator. Such a deeper understanding is sure to come later. The ideology may be imperfect, but the impulsion is being felt just the same.

The new spiritual impulse which inspires all these forward movements embodying this social principle is God-sent. The old interests may struggle fiercely against it, but they cannot win against it. Forces are today entering this planet's atmosphere and pouring themselves into the humanity it bears which, owing to our having reached this unique turning point in evolution, are themselves of a unique and special character. Shadows signify the presence of light, anti-Christ the presence of Christ, and the evil forces of materialistic Nazism signify the presence of sacred powers of spiritual regeneration. If we deplore the great darkness which has fallen over this planet, we should know that it speaks of a coming dawn, as the unparalleled destructive violence of this war speaks of an unparalleled constructive peace. In other words, tremendous unreckoned spiritual energies are now in our midst and only await the ripened opportunity to manifest themselves.

Such is the coming faith, a faith suited to the requirements of men of intelligence and goodwill, capable of bringing together those whom the old religions keep divided and even hostile. No sincere well-wisher of mankind can object to the introduction of a new, genuinely inspired faith. At the very worst, it cannot harm mankind, while at the very best it may save mankind. Only the selfish guardians of uninspired, unserviceable vested interests can object to such results. But it cannot come of itself—it must come through some Man. In short, the times require a new Prophet.

There are being put forward, as religions divinely preordained for and practically suited to our times, the Ramakrishna Mission form of Hinduism and the Iranian-born faith of Bahaism. Of the the first, it need only be said that Sri Ramakrishna himself warned his disciples against forming an organized cult and that none of the old religions, however polished up they may be, really suits us today. Of the second, it is needful only to examine a few of its leading tenets to show their insufficiency. The present-day version of Bahaism, which is markedly different from its original version, rejects mysticism. But we have already seen that the needed faith must have some mystical touch about it. This rejection is all the more curious and ironical because the founder of the Bahai faith was himself a mystic and a psychic. Next, divine claims are made on his behalf. The time when reason could receive such claims is vanishing. No one man can incarnate the ineffable, unbounded Absolute Spirit. Thirdly, the Bahai faith holds that there is a progressive revelation in time and that, because it is the latest one, it is consequently the best one. Against this claim, the informed observer may well smile and match the claim of Hinduism, which holds that the oldest and primal revelation is the best one and that time only brings deterioration. Incidentally, philosophy shares neither of these views and considers them both to be self-deceptions. Nor is the Bahai claim to be the latest religion tenable today. A hundred years have passed since the first Bahai prophet appeared. Several new religions and dozens of sects have been born during that time. That only a few achieved fame has nothing to do with the argument.

The totality of Bahai mystical, self-deification claims are equally irrational in their literal form. And the Bahai religious-unification predictions have psychological roots which are unsound. Its expectations of an imminent attainment of religious unity is as groundless as its claims to possess the only divine manifestation for our age.

When they descend from piety to practice, the Bahais embrace impracticable schemes. If a certain mystically advanced ashram could not live as a harmonious, peaceable united family, how will it be possible for a merely religious Bahai world to do so? It is useless to ask humanity to outrun its present capacity, to live in a visionary's dreams or a fool's paradise. If nowhere on earth, not even amongst the most religious, most mystical, and most spiritual assemblies, fraternities, societies, or hermitages, men can live as a loving, self-sacrificing family, how can they do so when still constrained by lower outlooks? The ideal of a single human family is not immediately realizable, for it cannot be formed out of the present defective human material. To demand its instant enforcement is to label oneself an impracticable dreamer.

Considering these predictions on the level of philosophy leads to quite a different result. In both cases, we find that they arise out of emotional complexes and unphilosophic outlooks.

Hence, mystics should not hesitate to invent new and better methods suited to our times and to combine them with the best of the old ones. We know more than well that in suggesting an innovation of this kind, we lay ourselves open to become a favourable target for the critical shots of the orthodox yogis. But the twentieth century is not called upon to subscribe slavishly to the methods, disciplines, and systems of the tenth. Intelligent persons know that we cannot limit ourselves entirely to the life of the past. They have to be synthetic and to mold such elements only as they can profitably use into a fusion with present ones. So the old Indian yogas, however admirably worked out they be, are to be regarded with critical yet appreciative eyes and not simply with mute acceptance. Men of today must build up their own methods out of the needs of their own natures.

4

If so many religious tenets are falling apart or even being let go altogether, let it be remembered that not a few deserve to go. They lacked truth and held only ungrounded but long-established opinions. But the pity of it is that the other parts of religion—solid, true, worthy—have also become suspect to the confused younger minds of today.

5

Inspiration did not stop in any particular year, nor with any particular man. If it was possible then, it is possible today, and to some other man.

6

This postwar period is the most morally dangerous in all mankind's history. The breakdown of religious sanctions is inevitably more widespread than ever before. For evolution has brought millions of people to the point where irrational dogmas and unscientific beliefs have become hopelessly outmoded. Such an intellectual displacement need not be deplored because sooner or later it had to happen. But unfortunately the loss of these sanctions is accompanied by the breakdown of that which depends on them. And the most important single item among the latter is the ethical standard. People have no cause to practise virtue and fear evil when they come to believe that the one will go unrewarded and the other unpunished. The whole world has witnessed, in the barbarous wrongdoing of Hitler and his young fanatic followers, how lost to all decent living, how utterly without a conscience, how unguided by any valid sense of right or wrong, men may become when they give up religious faith but are unable to replace it by right mystical practice or correct metaphysical reasoning. They exist thereafter in a moral "no-man's-land." It is this interregnum in moral evolution between the standards set by religions and those set by mysticism or metaphysics, an interregnum where morality lapses altogether, that must necessarily constitute a period of the gravest ethical crisis and danger to mankind. The depths to which the Nazis sank amply illustrate this truth.

7

Its originator left some power behind which was partly responsible for its wide and deep spread. This is the vivifying principle behind the spread of every historic religion, a principle whose results make us exclaim with Origen, "It is a work greater than any work of man." We should regard the great originators, the great religious saviours of the human race like Jesus and Buddha, as divinely used instruments. The individual centre of power which each left behind on our planet extended for long beyond his bodily death, continued to respond helpfully to those who trusted it, but then gradually waned and will eventually terminate after a historic period has ended. No organized religion ever endures in its original form for more than a limited period. All the great religions of the earliest antiquity have perished. The originators were admittedly not ordinary men. They belonged to higher planes of thought and being. They came from spheres of consciousness superior to that of average humanity. This was highly exceptional, but it does not turn them into gods. Nor does it justify us today in living in the past and leaning on what is vanishing. For despite all lapses and regressions, humanity is now coming of intellectual age. This is one reason why it must now furnish its own teachers, must recognize and appreciate its own wise men. For in the coming age, no further descents of these superior beings like the two just named may be expected. There will be no other Messiahs than those we can evolve from amongst ourselves.(P)

8

If we gaze into the soul of modern man as it has been during the present century, we shall discern therein a state of long-drawn crisis. For two opposed and conflicting world-views have been taught him during his youth: the one religious and the other scientific and both accusing each other of being untrue. The emotional consequences of this have manifested themselves in instability, immorality, cynicism, hypocrisy, and despair. The mental consequences have manifested themselves in frustration, uncertainty, and bewilderment. So long as these two forces cannot come to terms with each other within him, so long will they exhaust and not nourish him. Such a widespread and deep crisis, such a fateful and difficult situation cannot be left unresolved for long. It is driving men to sink in bewilderment and despair, where they fail to comprehend and master it, or to rise in clarity and strength where they do. It is inevitable that man should try to unify his thoughts into a coherent system and his experiences into a coherent pattern. All traditional concepts of religion will have to be reshaped to conform to this new knowledge. If, for example, his religion tells him that the world was created five thousand years ago whereas his science tells him that it was created very much more than five million years ago, a nervous tension is set up within him which harms his mental sight and hurts his physical health. Only when he can find a satisfactory synthesis which consolidates the claims of reason and feeling without sacrificing either can he find healing of his trouble. And such a synthesis exists only in philosophy.(P)

9

New religions will come, for the demands of the intellect and the needs of the young will have to be satisfied. Some will shape themselves as movements within the existing churches, but most will shape themselves outside the churches. But even the new ones will be taken over in time by men who will form a vested interest, for the tendencies of human nature at its present stage of evolution are too egoistic. History repeats this result again and again.

10

The emphasis upon mystical insight, the respect for spiritual illumination, the desire to be a personal witness for the presence of God—these are present-day signs of religious deepening.

11

It was enough for an ancient prophet to state the truth. Today he must do more that that: he must state the reasons why it is true.

12

The prudent way of quietly and little by little dropping beliefs found to be wrong has been practised by some Churches, notably Protestant ones, but never, or rarely, by others, notably Catholic and Oriental ones.

13

The need for precise knowledge to replace vague faith is as important today in religion as in any other sphere.

14

The message for this age must satisfy its primary needs, hence must contain three elements. First, the *doctrine* that there is a divine soul in man. Second the *gospel* that it is possible through prayer and meditation and study to commune with this soul. Third, the *fact* of the Law of Recompense and hence the necessity of good thoughts and righteous deeds.

15

The time has come when religion should depend upon the certainties of universal human experience rather than the uncertainties of questioned historical events.

16

More than anything, men need today to find some kind of contact with the Higher Power which is behind them, and behind the universe.

17

It may be that religion will have to be presented in non-religious language if we are to get away from dogma that has never been questioned, from terms that have become hollow and empty, from an approach which has a boring effect. It may be that the new and more appealing presentation will use art, music, the discoveries of science, and the offering of meditation to reach the consciousness of today.

18

A religion may be reformed from within by re-inspiring and regenerating it, or from without by critically re-examining its ideas and correcting its customs.

19

Too often have people been called upon by ecclesiastical organizations to repent their ways when it is the organizations themselves which should be called upon to do so. They should abandon false teachings, renounce worldly pomp, purify selfish motives, and return to genuine religion.

20

If institutional religion is to continue an active existence, and not a decaying one, it must accept the message of the times and adapt itself to the changed new conditions.

21

Will a new world-wide religion of the future come to birth in this century? The astrologers and clairvoyants—for what their personal interpretations of the signs are worth—believe so. The old religionists think their own creed will arise rejuvenated and purified. The mystics find it in their visions and meditations. The philosopher considers it will come because it must come. But only through one man's birth and mission can its birth come. Who, What, and Where is he?

22

The commonplace forms and moralities of conventional religion are not enough for this era, when tomorrow's existence is uncertain for the whole human species, and today's mind is fed with unprecedented knowledge.

23

Even the simple assurance that there is a higher power in the universe and a loftier meaning in human existence, which religion gives—come in what shape it may—helped in the past to support life and endure death. Instruction in science at first weakened or destroyed this faith but now, through opening of the mind by relativity, nuclear physics, and biological discoveries, is beginning to confirm it, as Bacon predicted.

24

Holiness must become a reality—something vividly felt and inwardly realized—if it is to become a sincere part of religion. The consequences will then be historically shown by constructive ennobling and deepening actions, changes, or events.

25

The thoughtful man today is beginning to perceive the futility of such a shallow penetration of his own being and such a childish idea of the divine being.

26

There are young people today who have strong religious feelings, but who do not find in the traditional forms of religion sufficient satisfaction, because they do not find that they can carry it fully into their activities in the world and because they have intellectual difficulties in reconciling it with the knowledge of science.

27

The possible evils and probable dangers of venturing to reform an ancient religion are certainly there and must be recognized; but there ought not to be a total concentration on these negative sides of reform alone. The positive ones should not be ignored, the beneficial consequences in the present and to the future should not be neglected. What actually happens, the good and the bad, can be seen historically in the case of all existing and dead religions. The proper approach would not deny reforms, but measure carefully how far they can and ought to be carried out. This not only applies to the mass religions but also to the metaphysical systems and devotional theologies.

28

The Age of Faith has been succeeded by sceptic psychology, but the cycle of development is not at an end yet. For we shall return anew to our starting point, but this time it will be an intellectual Faith. We have learned to question the universe and life; we have pushed thinking to its uttermost limits; we can go no farther and must perforce sink to our knees once more in humble prayer. Then we shall acquire an unshakeable faith that will survive every question, every doubt, and that will carry us through the struggles of existence with serenity and strength.

29

The fuller entry and further permeation of religion and mysticism by science will take a few hundred years more, but will inexorably lead to the displacement of old established churches appealing to blind faith by new religions appealing to reasoned intuition.

30

War shakes the belief of mankind in a benevolent Deity. They begin to revolt against the doctrine that its hideous suffering is compatible with God's omnipotence and all-mercifulness.

31

Churches are anachronisms while the heart of man turns sick at the cold comfort of meaningless monotonous words; while the body looks up at the sky of hope and sees it turn to grey lead and tarnished brass; while the mind is tortured by despairing queries during the night that surrounds it; while faith craves for saner religion, actual and living, and is handed instead the pious aspirins of a future after-death heaven.

32

War reveals agnostic rationalism to be but a reed that breaks in one's hand. This is why the aftermath of war brings scepticism, although the presence of war brings faith to the frightened. Such is the startling contrast which the trial of scepticism and its disappointing consequences must inevitably bring about.

33

The broad masses of the people must live by accepted faith and not by reasoned enquiry; they have neither leisure, mentality, nor inclination for the latter. Consequently they have to live by religion which is ultimately and immediately based on faith. Religion is and must remain the motivating force behind their moral outlook on life. From this standpoint we have always to ask ourselves whether a religionless world would not place mankind in great jeopardy. If the defects and degeneration of old religions have caused millions to desert them, still there are vastly more millions who cling to the old dogmas simply because they have nothing else to grasp. It would therefore be an unwise, even wicked, act to abolish all religion and it would be an act which must end in failure. Those who would exterminate religious thought and practice must pause to consider the ethical breakdown which might follow. Can they offer to replace that which is taken away? They are faced with the choice of quarrelling with this view or compromising with it. But this does not mean that twentieth-century intelligence is to be insulted by offering it obsolete dogmas and ridiculous assertions; that because the multitude must have a religion therefore any worn-out creed and senseless rite will suit them. They will not. The religion that is needed by our age is a rational one.

34

When comparing the relative appeals of Christian and Buddhistic thought, remember that the weight of tradition, the power of vested interests, and the difficulty of embracing ancient forms of approach would prevent any widespread flow of the Buddhistic system in the West. The present need seems to be more for a new form that would synthesize the two systems and also add something to satisfy the special requirements of modern humanity. But the truth of the need of three progressive presentations to suit the three types—religious mystical and philosophical—has not been antiquated but only modified by present conditions.

35

Jesus today would not ask you to rely only on belief, for we can now comprehend things which were beyond the comprehension of his day. People of his time did not have the comprehension that this electric age has given us. It is through scientific comprehension of nature that the doors will open to the Light and give us greater consciousness of the One Being within us.

36

The time is approaching when orthodox religions must yield to the demand of the modern mind for doctrines that are intellectually satisfying and inspiration which is actually livable. The age of dogmatic assertion has come to an end for intelligent people and the age of scientific demonstration has come upon them. Faith can no longer convince the modern mind, but reason may and must. Modern conditions are so different that the appeal of mere dogma and myth is dwindling rapidly, though mythical explanations of the universe were necessary in pre-scientific times because the human mentality could not then grasp a better one. There are signs that this hour is almost upon us, for religious doctrines have already begun to dress themselves in the clothes of modernist philosophy and to walk in the shoes of progressed science. Nothing but good can come from the collaboration of science, philosophy, and religion, provided these terms are not limited to narrow meanings.

37

What the Western nations need to comprehend is that a large proportion of those who have been drawn into socially destructive atheistic movements fail to find satisfaction in orthodox and established religions, and that this has happened because their capacity for faith has been reduced by the development that evolution, although limited, one-sided, and unbalanced, has been working on them. Abusing and denouncing these rebels will not meet this situation. The correct way is to restate spiritual truths and laws in a scientific manner and to show that they can be saved from avoidable suffering and disaster only by learning these truths and obeying these laws.

38

The established religions are too intent on helping themselves, too forgetful of their original mission to be able to serve man sufficiently in this staggering crisis, let alone save him from its worst effects. A new force must be introduced—fresh spontaneous and sincere, unhampered by trivial pomposities, uninhibited by traditional egoisms.

39

Let us readily admit the earlier usefulness of those aged forms, but let us not desist from the search after vital, timely, and inspiring forms suited to our present needs.

40

Not by kindling the cold grey ashes of outdated religions shall we succeed in saving them. Only by facing the fact that new religions and new prophets are needed shall we save what is more important—humanity's soul.

41

What is lacking from the modern heart is a feeling of reverence in the presence of inspired men and of awe at the thought of the Power behind the universe.

42

If the old texts are to be brought to a new life today, and made to serve us too, they must be expounded by inspired men and explained by perceptive ones.

43

The widespread stimulus given to intellectual development since the opening of this scientific epoch two and a half centuries ago, and, even earlier, since the Renaissance, will reflect itself in the coming religion of the new epoch for which the world will be prepared. It will be a religion of intellect vivified by intuitive feeling, of the head balanced by the heart, sane and not superstitious. The coming of a new faith will inevitably be contested by the old ones, by those forces which are evil or materialistic, and by the selfish vested interests which profit by human ignorance.

44

Not the least of the obstacles to a spiritual revival is that the mere appearance of religion has posed as its authentic reality. When it will be openly admitted that the truths of religion have faded from the modern man's psyche, leaving only their mere shadows behind, it will be possible to do what can and should be done to revivify them. The first step will be to cast out primitive superstitions, to correct functional abuses, to democratize authority, and to get rid of hollow formalism. Yet although religion clings so desperately to what is outworn and outmoded, the desire to revive decaying creeds, techniques, and attitudes is futile; the attempt to do so is predestined to eventual failure. There is also no future for obligatory beliefs, cultural absolutisms, or imposed ideas. We have lived to witness the last desperate effort in this direction, that of Nazism, and its failure. The religious world is too hampered by its past to produce easily the new faith which mankind must construct today, if it is to survive. It is too much caught in its own medieval creation to provide dynamic leadership. If spirituality, therefore, begins to make itself felt a little among us today, it is not because of organized religion but in spite of it.

45

If many men and women have lost interest in the futilities of institutional religion they have not lost any interest whatever in the wonderful words of those grand men whose mission these institutions have purported to represent. They honour their benign sayings more than most pious people but they detest the puerile creeds and intolerant actions which were perpetrated under the shelter of such hallowed names. They revere and love those teachers who give a higher ethic to man. Although they can take no interest in the dogmatic utterances of mitred clerics and professional priests, they ever raise their minds in homage before Jesus, Krishna, Buddha, and Muhammed. If they appreciate the missions of these messianic men and receive a deeper significance in their sacred glowing utterances, they remain indifferent to the foolishness of followers who take the name of these Masters in vain, and who have strayed far from the ethical precepts. If the rebels have left behind the public observances of established religion, it is because they regard them as having degenerated into meaningless mumbo-jumbo. "Repent and return" is an old maxim but a sound one. A church which has departed from the straight and narrow road of its master can always return if it wishes. A pontiff who holds a million minds in benighted thraldom can always set them free again. A temple-priest who has battened on the trust of numerous pilgrims can always cease to be an official charlatan and help them to a higher view of God. A clergyman who entered a pulpit as his profession and not as his inspired vocation can always resign. But these decisions demand immense sincerity to make and immense courage to implement. Why should not a religion go from strength to strength, instead of from weakness to weakness? Why should it not deserve increasing success? Will not its tangible and intangible profits be greater, grander, and more enduring if it fulfils its task of emotionally comforting and morally uplifting mankind? Has not history proved such profits to be fitful and fugitive when its followers are ignobly exploited and their minds forcibly enslaved?

46

Because there will be no paid sacerdotal class, there will be no public prayers in the ideal religion. Man's mental and emotional traffic with the higher power will be a private and personal one. Therefore there will be no empty show of religiosity for the benefit of his neighbours, no chance for hypocrisy to parade itself as devotion, no mechanical phonographic repetition of phrases which time or familiarity has divested of emotional significance and mental content. For although a congregation may gather in a public building, the prayers it will silently utter, the devotions it will silently perform, will not follow a set collective form but will be quite individual. Furthermore no separate order of clergy will be set apart from or be permitted to dominate over the laity, but a democratic basis of mutual consultation will support. Thus it was a sixteenth-century German, Sebastian Franck, who wrote in one of his books that a minister of the Gospel should resign his living when he finds that his sermons bear no spiritual fruit in changed lives. Franck himself soon demonstrated his sincerity by following his own advice. The old religious faith found itself at war with reason; the ideal faith will look to reason as an ally in its own camp. That is why the religious society which is to express such a faith will inevitably refuse to submit itself to any priesthood. But this is not to say that it is to submit itself to a completely democratic system. How could it, when the tenets which it holds speak plainly of the spiritual inequality of man, of the distinctions which show themselves in moral outlook and intellectual equipment? It will find an alternative way between these two extremes, the way of honorary, unpaid, inspired expositors. It will be the birth of a new priesthood, a priesthood that could give men the inner peace they hunger for, that could inspire them with the wisdom and courage to tackle personal problems rightly, and that could show them that there is something back of life worth living for; it would not need to mortgage its services to the State. It would get all its needs voluntarily satisfied by those whom it helped. But if it could not really help men, then its failure would eventually become its own scourge. People do not want empty puerile words alone; they want new hope and new faith that their problems will be solved and life's essential worth can be found.

47

If one dares to look forward, a new religion will arise with the decay of the old; a new prophet will bring the fresh wind of divine inspiration to a dulled humanity. But both religion and its prophet must be *new*, fresh, vital.

48

The need and demand today is for explicit statement, not for enigmatic ones. They are a survival from medieval periods when religious persecution was rife and intolerant. Or they are the unhealthy symptoms of mental disorder.

49

The existing orthodox religions both in the Orient and in the Occident have lost a great part of their inner vitality and exist largely as a collection of conventional mechanical forms. It is the duty of religions to guide mankind correctly and uplift them morally. When they can no longer fulfil this function sufficiently, they slowly die off or are destroyed by their own karma. In 600 years all the existing orthodox religions will have disappeared from this planet and new ones will have arisen to replace them. This means that new prophets will be appearing among mankind in different parts of the world, of whom there will be one who will be the greatest of all. From him there will start a new religion which will spread in all the continents side by side with the other religions of more limited influence. In this world religion, the prophet will appeal to the combined intellect, feelings, intuition, and will of human beings.

This new world religion will include some simple elementary meditation as well as prayer. It will state some of the laws which govern the universe as well as human life.

In the situation which now faces us and will continue to face us for several years, what is the best way in which we can help humanity and also help ourselves? It is to remember that we can help mankind only to the extent to which we develop ourselves. In that way only can we become a channel through which spiritual forces can flow to others and in that way only can we find the true protection against the dangers that menace the world. Therefore each student should work on himself, and especially on his character, harder than ever before.

Human life is like a river which must keep overflowing onwards and not become a stagnant pool. Our era needs and must find a new inspiration, a new hope, and a new life. There was a time when it could have done these things quite peaceably but because it did not understand its own situation it is being made to do them in pain and suffering. Those who will not wake up to the hard facts of the situation will be awakened later by the terrific crash of atomic bombs, and worse.

50

The Indian *sadhu* who marks his forehead with a bond of ashes, or smears his scalp with them, or covers his whole body under them, is symbolically reminding himself that everything is destroyed in the end. This is supposed to help him abandon desires and free himself from attachments. If the same mental attitude can be developed without using ashes, why give them more importance than they deserve? It is not clear enough that what really matters are the thoughts, and that by proper education they can be trained to understand, appreciate, and hold spiritual values without resort to ash-smearing—a messy affair anyway since they have first to be prepared and then mixed with butter and lime-juice. A further supposition for the existence of this religious custom is that God himself, being depicted with three lines of ash on his forehead, is brought to mind by the custom when followed, as recommended, by ordinary laymen, and thus they are better strengthened to bear their troubles. Why then is this custom fast vanishing from India along with several others which were inaugurated in the childhood of the race? There are several reasons for this disappearance. One of them is that the higher level of intellectual education is creating a habit of questioning what is old and anachronistic. If nuclear physics is leading more and more to the superior image of God as

Universal Mind and Power rather than as glorified Man, if knowledge of meditation as a help to calm the mind when suffering is present is rippling over into the masses, the latter will exchange more and more these indirect primitive helps for direct and more advanced ones. Even Emerson, a former clergyman, predicted well over a hundred years ago that the religion of the future would be, and have to be, more intellectual to keep pace with the growth of mankind.

51

The coming faiths will be wider than the old ones, for they cannot be deeper. They will explain more to more. They will not reject intellect, nor its modern product, science, but will put both in their own place, just where they belong. Their conception of God will be infinitely more godlike than so many familiar, limited, and anthropomorphic conceptions that have been babbled in the past.

52

When the spirit of impartial research for its own sake no longer prevails, when the aspiring mind is half-strangled by narrow traditions and absurd superstitions, it is time for a fresh religious impulse to be given.

53

It was an error in the past, whose consequences the whole world is suffering today, to believe that in order to conceal the truth from the unready, untruth should be taught to them. For with the growing capacities of men, growing rebellion against being misled was certain to come.

54

What is the religious ideology which is to reign over the coming age? It must be: first, rational in form; second, effective in inspiring faith; third, powerful in uplifting character and influencing conduct; fourth, quick in meeting the requirements of modern times; and fifth, attentive to social needs.

55

If orthodox religion would as vigorously denounce its own hypocrites as it does its heretics the believing world would be better served.

56

There are movements of thought and shifts of standpoint in religious circles today which could not have been entertained last century. Even the mere fact that there has been discussed—quite apart from whether or not there have been negotiations—reunion between the Orthodox and the Anglican Churches and Protestant Churches, is highly eloquent of the change of atmosphere. In England, for example, The Fellowship of Saint Alban and Saint Sergius has done useful work in bringing together the intellectuals of Orthodoxy and Anglicanism, so that there is better understanding of one another's beliefs, more correction of errors and knowledge of agreements, where they stop and why.

57

The history of even our own unfinished century has shown unprecedented changes in every department of human life, circumstance, and thought. How then can religion escape? There are grave weighty problems which it did not have to meet in the earlier periods.

58

A merely pious attitude whose basis is blind faith and whose technique is simple prayer makes a good beginning yet is only a beginning. For the conditions through which we have to pass, the experiences which life ordains, bring about in the course of reincarnations a questioning which only philosophy can satisfy in the end. The Jew whose piety is mocked by the slaughter of six million of his co-religionists, the Hindus and Muhammedans whose meditations or prayers are interrupted by riots which remove another million from earth's scene, must sooner or later come to realize that faith is not enough, and that knowledge must be acquired to supplement it, not to supplant it. A refined understanding of cosmic purposes and cosmic laws is also needed. They find that sentimentality does not save them in their hour of need.

59

The old established and traditional religions will crumble with time and events, as they are doing more quickly in Asia, but as they pass they will carry with them what is intrinsically good for, and helpful to, the masses. Their negative attributes and disservices are regrettable, but it is not fair to note the one side without the other. The cultivation of religious reverence is a basic need on any level of human existence and comprehension.

60

There is a feeling among many more than is realized, because it is often somewhat obscure, that the contemporary conditions of life in time, which may well be the last lap for most living people, have made the finding of a satisfactory spiritual relationship to God urgent and essential, if life is to be raised from confusion and redeemed from terror. There is a vital and urgent need in human minds today of relating personal experience to the universal experience in which it has been born. Put into religious terms, it is a need of finding God.

61

In these days of criticism and revision it would be prudent for any established religion to shed its accumulated superstitions so long as the process does not affect fundamental truths.

62

What is beautiful or useful or serviceable in tradition should be kept.

63

The disaster in which European humanity found itself did not indicate the failure of Christianity, as its enemies declare, but the failure of Church-ianity. A nation without some genuine spiritual inspiration is a society without a spine. It will collapse when the big test comes.

64

Religion in its purity deserves reverence; in its decay, scepticism. When a noble tradition tails off into a mere travesty of itself, the end is near, and none ought then to complain when somebody attempts to hasten it. When honest men feel they no longer receive any spiritual help from a church, they stay away. And what help can come from those who are full of the letter but empty of the spirit?

65

Orthodox religious leaders rightly condemn the unsatisfactory nature of an education which leaves out the making of moral character, but the remedy which they offer is only a little better than the disease. For they would deform the growing rationality of the young and clip their intellectual wings by reverting to a narrow type of education based on outworn religious dogmas and unacceptable scriptural statements. The coming age will demand reason alongside its righteousness, a sharper intelligence rather than a drugged one, and a religious truth rather than religious distortion and debasement.

66

We need a bold and unconventional departure from ordinary methods of approach sanctified by time and usage.

67

Unless a religion renews itself constantly, like every living organism, and develops itself periodically in relation to the varying needs of new epochs, its doctrines will become dead, petrified formulae, its priests or ministers will become mere mechanical gramophones, and its followers will become hapless stumblers in the night.

68

Outwardly the religious situation may seem excellent, the religious institutions well-supported, but inwardly the real effectiveness may be little.

69

Those who believe that the spiritual awakening of mankind must express itself necessarily through the old faiths, the old organizations, believe that the way forwards leads backwards. The old forms may share some of the fruits of this awakening but it will be only until the new forms get strong enough to replace them more and more.

70

The religions of Europe are torpid; its cults are in a state of apathy. Those leaders who have conquered the small groups of occult and mystical students possess no influence with the people at large because they possess no spiritual power; they pour but a continuous cascade of *words*. The crowd who follows them confuses this windy rhetoric with spiritual reality.

71

Let us not be afraid of the truth: *new* bibles will appear in the history of man, his religion, and his culture. The end of revelation and inspiration is not in sight.

72

If popular institutional religion is to save itself and at the same time serve the people, then it must recognize that the time is at hand when it ought no longer stand between them and the higher truths.

73

At this late hour in cultural and educational history, men will not accept the view that they are not to look into these things, not to search for answers where knowledge seems impossible. It may well be so, but the right to search must be safeguarded.

Part 2:

THE REVERENTIAL LIFE

He who sits with humbled, bowed head and folded, clasped, or knees-rested hands, with mind and heart in awed reverence, in sincere, worshipful, and rapt absorption which is aware of nothing else than the divine presence—he is praying, is meditating, is worshipping, is in heaven already.

1

DEVOTION

All living forms everywhere embody this principle of being—the One Infinite Life-Power. It is not itself personal yet it is open to man's personal access and will respond to his invocation—provided he succeeds in establishing contact with it and provided his approach is right—but its response must come in its own way and time.

2

The devotional element belongs as much to this quest as to any other. *Adoration* of the divine soul and *humility* in the divine presence are two necessary qualities which the quester ought to develop. The first is expressed through meditation and the second through prayer.

3

Look how the smaller birds greet the sun, with so much merry chirruping and so much outpouring of song! It is their way of expressing worship for the only Light they can know, an outer one. But man can also know the inner Sun, the Light of the Overself. How much more reason has he to chirp and sing than the little birds! Yet how few men feel gratitude for such privilege.(P)

4

Why ought I to cultivate religious faith, feeling worship? Because it lifts up the feeling nature generally. Because it develops humility. Because it invites Grace. Because it is the duty of a human being in relation to its Source.

5

Krishna, in the *Bhagavad Gita*, is the individual's own higher self. He must keep his inner shrine within the heart reserved for the Ideal. He should worship there the Spirit that is birthless and deathless, indestructible and divine. Life in this world is like foam on the sea: it passes all too soon; but the moments given in adoration and obeisance to the Soul count for eternal gain. The most tremendous historic happenings on this earth are, after all, only pictures that pass through consciousness like a dream. Once the seeker awakens to the Real, he sees them for what they are. Then he will live in Its serenity, and it will no longer matter if the pictures themselves are stormy and agitated. It is the greatest good fortune to attain such serenity—to be lifted above passion and hatred, prejudice and fear, greed and discontent, and yet to be able to attend effectively and capably to one's worldly duties. It *is* possible to reach this state. The seeker may have had glimpses of it already. Someday, sometime, if he is patient, he will enter it to stay—and the unimaginably rewarding and perfect purpose of his life, of all his lifetimes, will be fulfilled.

6

He will come to perceive that his real strength lies in remembering the higher self, in remembering the quest of it, and, above all, in remembering the two with intense love, devotion, and faith.

7

If the aspirant will cultivate a feeling of reverence toward the higher power, whether it be directed toward God, the Overself, or his spiritual guide, he will profit much.

8

There is a sacred quality about one side of philosophy which ought not be underrated by those who are unattracted by anything religious.

9

When devotion, worship, and reverence are fortified by knowledge, they can one day reach a stage where notably less is desired or demanded and peace then naturally arises. Nor is a measure of peace the only gain. Virtue later follows after it, quietly and effortlessly growing.(P)

10

Metaphysical study will not weaken reverence but will rather put it on firmer ground. Metaphysical understanding will not weaken devotion but will rather more firmly establish it. What it will weaken, however, is the attachment to transient *forms* of reverence; what it will destroy is the error of giving devotion exclusively to the individual and refusing to include the Universal.(P)

11

Since true philosophy is also a way of life, and since no such way can become effectual unless the feelings are involved, it includes and cultivates the most refined and most devotional feelings possible to man.(P)

12

Nature displays her beauteous landscapes in vain if he who has wandered into her presence lacks the aesthetic reverent sensitivity to glance appreciatively at the grand vistas. Similarly, philosophy calls for a tuned-in, quieted, and reverent mentality if a man who wanders to its feet is to profit by it.

13

Our greatest strength comes from reliance on the Higher Self and faith in the Higher Laws.

14

The ancient pagan who greeted the sunrise by stretching out his arms to it and the simple Oriental who still does so obeyed true instincts of worship which civilized religions have not improved.

15

I will never tire of telling men that the Overself is as loving as any parent and that it does care for our real welfare. But we must return that love, must give our unconditional devotion, if we are to have a correct relationship with it.

16

A proneness to veneration is necessary in an aspirant: it helps him in different ways. But the sceptical and denigrating attitude which is so common in certain intellectual and social circles tends to make any manifestation of this quality quite impossible.

17

The need is for much more *bhakti*, especially during meditation, for intenser and warmer yearning to *feel* the sacred presence. It is really a need to descend from merely knowing in the head to knowing and feeling in the heart.

18

Intense devotional religious feeling is as much a part of the philosopher's character as quietly mystical intuitive feeling.

19

I have been astonished to meet Buddhists in the Orient and Theosophists in the Occident who deny the usefulness and scorn the need of devotion. How can there be any higher life without this very holy feeling, without the reverence, worship, communion, self-humbling, aspiration, and self-surrender that it embodies?

20

This deep, inner, and indescribable feeling which makes him yearn for closeness to the higher power is neither a misguided feeling nor a vain one.

21

It is a queer notion which regards a philosopher as a man without feeling, only because he has brought it under control. Not that it is altogether to his credit that he has been able to do so, for grace must share some credit too. There is plenty of feeling in his communion with the Higher Self.

22

This is the magic talisman which will strengthen and save you, even though you go down into Hades itself—this faith and love for the inner self.

23

It is a necessary moment in a man's life when he turns attention away from self to humbled recognition of the divine being which activates the planet on which he dwells. From such wondering thoughts he may be led to worshipful ones and thence to a still deeper self-forgetfulness. The climax, if it comes, will be the feeling of divine Presence.

24

Truth is not only to be known with all one's mind but also to be loved with all one's heart.

25

Reverence, awe, adoration—these are evoked by, and themselves evoke the feeling of, the Overself's presence.

26

In the French nineteenth-century Academy painter Jean-Léon Gérôme's picture *The Two Majesties*, a lion squats on a flat high rock in the desert fringe watching the setting sun. Its concentration of attention seems perfect, its interest in the golden orb is complete. The ordinary human, having no access to the precise state of animal consciousness, could even ask himself whether the lion is rapt in worship; it may have seen from a distance the desert Bedouins so engaged in their prescribed daily devotions. Certainly chimpanzees have been observed greeting the rising sun and thumping their chests in salute.

27

Reverence and homage are apparently not limited to animate beings, particularly not to human beings. We read in early Greek texts of inanimate ones, namely doors, which opened of themselves magically and uncannily on the approach of a divinity.

28

The message of philosophy in this matter may be summed up as this: Look beyond your tiny circle of awareness and forget the little "I" for a while in order to remember that greater and grander Being whence you have emanated.

29

His search for intellectual precision and scientific factuality need not and must not be allowed to dry up his heartfelt devotion and sensitive feeling.

30

Through associating reverence with knowledge both ways of spiritual self-recovery are enriched, while the man himself is equilibrated.

31

It is a mistake to believe that anyone could be a good practising philosopher if he is without warm feelings for the philosophic truth he professes to regard as important or to interpret with fidelity.

32

We need the turgid devotion of religion, the clearer devotion of mysticism, and the understanding devotion of philosophy. With each stage of ascent, there is more purity and less publicity, more real holiness and less lurking egoism.

33

To that self-existent untouched Reality, the heart in simple reverence must forever bow in homage, and the mind must make it the object of keenest meditation.

34

Devotion must be dovetailed in with knowledge, reverence must be locked together with understanding, if this inner work is not to be one-sided, unbalanced, and even, in some cases, unreliable.

35

The key word here is reverence. It ought to enter every remembrance and every meditation.

36

He has raised an altar to the unknown God in his heart. Henceforth he worships there in secret and in silence. His hours of solitude are reserved for it, his moments of privacy dedicated to it.

37

He has become conscious of the sacredness of existence.

38

If they do not come to this quest with enough reverence, they are led later to the reverence by the quest.

39

Memorable are those minutes when we sit in silent adoration of the Overself, knowing it to be none other than our own best self. It is as though we have returned to our true home and rest by its hallowed hearth with a contentment nowhere else to be known. No longer do we possess anything; we are ourselves ineffably possessed. The individual hopes and fears, sorrows and desires that have so plagued our days are adjourned for the while. How can we, how dare we hold them when our own personal being is tightly held within an all-satisfying embrace?

40

His devotion to the quest is something that he may not usually talk about to others, something that he finds himself forced to hide like a secret love. He dare not speak one word about it for fear that it will be received with utter incomprehension or open ridicule. This may be true of his family or his friends, his associates or his chance contacts. A shyness develops which may make him unable to seek help even from those who are more advanced on the same quest.

41

Without such faith or without some intuitive feeling, how can anyone rise to the true meaning of the Christian Gospels or the Hindu *Gita*?

42

We revere God best in silence, with lips struck dumb and thoughts hid deep.

43

This tender gentle and even beautiful feeling which moves him, holds him, and humbles him is worship, reverence, and holiness. He senses the higher power is closer than it normally is.

44

The word *bhakti* includes not only worship but also reverence.

45

Here we walk on holy ground, reverently adoring the Supreme.

46

Reverence is a beautiful quality when directed toward the higher power. The more it is developed the humbler a man must become in the Presence.

47

Humbly the ego bends in silent homage, held by the benign peace; and then this second self appears: it is the Overself. Gently the smiling Presence spreads around.

48

If men really wish to revere God, they may best do so by revering God's deputy in their hearts, the Overself.

49

Reverence, if it is to be true, authentic, and feelingful, will also be humble, self-abasing, and an act of the heart.

50

He is there all alone in a sanctuary no being can share with him, except Divine Being. This is the meaning of life for those who feel this loneliness as a form of suffering.

51

He is the best of worshippers who comes to Me in secret, who prays in silence, and who tells no one.

The greatest love

52

From the base to the apex of the philosophic pyramid, every stone should be chiselled with meticulous thought and ardent love.

53

Aspiration which is not just a vague and occasional wish but a steady settled and intense longing for the Overself is a primary requirement. Such aspiration means the hunger for awareness of the Overself, the thirst for experience of the Overself, the call for union to the Overself. It is a veritable power which lifts one upward, which helps one give up the ego more quickly, and which attracts Grace. It will have these desirable effects in proportion to how intensely it is felt and how unmixed it is with other personal desires.

54

Remember that no enterprise or move should be left to depend on the ego's own limited resources. The humble invocation of help from the Higher Self expands those resources and has a protective value. At the beginning of every day, of every enterprise, of every journey, and of every important piece of work, remember the Overself and, remembering, be obedient to its laws. Seek its inspiration, its power. To make it your silent partner is to double your effectiveness.(P)

55

If you want to know how to set about finding the Higher Self, Jesus has very clearly given the answer. Seek, knock, and ask; pray to it and for it— not just once but scores of times, if necessary, and always with your whole heart, lovingly, yearningly, reverently.

56

He must give himself up to the daily practice of devotional exercises in prayer and meditation. He must give up to this practice time that might otherwise be spent in pleasure or wasted in idleness.

57

What intellect cannot do because of its feebleness the aspirational feeling can do by its force.

58

The fourth state *is* attainable but his yearning for it must be wholehearted and his efforts must be sustained ones.

59

To yearn only at times for this spiritual awakeness is not enough. He must yearn for it continually.

60

To remember the Overself devotedly, to think about it frequently and lovingly, is part of this practice.

61

The quest is not a thing to be played with; that is only for those who merely talk about it. To engage in it is of necessity to devote one's entire life to it.

62

Aspiration seeks its proper level. Rising waters are difficult to dam.

63

If at times he feels a kind of holiness welling up within him let him nourish it without delay. It can expand and give the fruit more sweetness.

64

Dwelling upon the beauty and tranquillity, the wisdom and the power of the Overself, he lets thoughts move towards it of their own accord.

65

If he is to achieve his purpose, it should be clearly pictured in his mind and strongly supported by his will. It should be desired with all his being, believed in with all his heart.

66

This feeling of reverence, awe, and inner attraction should be nurtured and developed so that it may grow into a great love, an aesthetic communion which is fully satisfying.

67

That which I address as "O Mind of the World!" and whom Kabbalists address as "Master of the Worlds!"—That which is without name or face or form, That alone I worship. That upon which all things depend but itself depends on nothing, That I revere. That which is unseen by all beings but which itself sees all, That I worship.

68

Each act becomes a holy remembrance: we speak on behalf of the Divine Being, we work for It, we do everything as if we were Its agent. A letter is written, or a book composed, in this reverential spirit. Hence, Shankara writes in *Saundaryalahari*: "Let all that I do thus become Thy worship."

69

Henceforth he lives on and for the quest, killing in his heart all other desires.

70

The presence of the Great Spirit can be recognized, approached, felt, and loved.

71

Life, history, experience—each gives us the same clear message. The temple of Solomon, once a pyramid in its vast area, is felled to the ground, and its thousands of worshippers gone with it. What, then, how, and where shall we worship? Let us seek the timeless Power which transcends the centuries, let us utter no word but fall into silence, for here the voice of the little ego's thoughts is an insult. Let us go where Jesus advised—deep inside the heart. For we carry the truth within ourselves—yet how few know it—and bear the closest of ties with that Power in consciousness itself.

72

Loving attention to the Overself should not be limited to moments spent in meditation or prayer, but should form the background for all one's other thoughts.

73

Hindu scriptures enjoin worship before taking any important step in life.

74

That Being from which all beings come forth and to which they finally return—that I worship!

75

To create faith is one thing; to sustain it another.

76

Why does not the Overself show its existence and display its power once and for all? Why does it let this long torment of man, left to dwell in ignorance and darkness, go on? All that the ego is to gain from undergoing its varied evolution is wrapped up in the answer. This we have considered in *The Wisdom of the Overself* and *The Spiritual Crisis of Man*. But there is something more to be added to that answer. The Overself waits with deepest patience for him—man—to prefer it completely to everything and everyone else. It waits for the time when longings for the soul will leave the true aspirant no rest, when love for the divine will outlast and outweigh all other loves. When he feels that he needs it more than he needs anything else in this world, the Overself will unfailingly reveal its presence to him. Therefore a yearning devotion is one of the most important qualifications he can possess.

77

By thought, the ego was made; by thought, the ego's power can be unmade. But the thought must be directed toward a higher entity, for the ego's willingness to attack itself is only a pretense. Direct it constantly to the Overself, be mentally devoted to the Overself, and emotionally love the Overself. Can it then refuse to help you?

78

The way to be admitted to the Overself's presence can be summed up in a single phrase: *love it*. Not by breathing in very hard nor by blowing out very slow, not by standing on the head nor by contorting like a frog can admission be gained. Not even by long study of things divine nor by acute analysis of them. But let the love come first, let it inspire the breathing, blowing, standing, or contorting, let it draw to the study and drive to the thinking, and then these methods will become really fruitful.(P)

79

Love the Overself with your whole heart if you would have it reveal the fullness of its receptive love for you.

80

When the divine has become the sole object of his love and the constant subject of his meditation, the descent of a gracious illumination cannot be far off.

81

Love is both sunshine for the seed and fruit from the tree. It is a part of the way to self-realization and also a result of reaching the goal itself.(P)

82

The love which he is to bring as sacrificial offering to the Overself must take precedence of all other loves. It must penetrate the heart's core to a depth where the best of them fails to reach.(P)

83

He needs to hold the sacred conviction that so long as he continues to cherish the Ideal his higher self will not abandon him.

84

Amid all his mental adventures and emotional misadventures, he should never lose sight of the goal, should never permit disappointment or frailty to cause desertion of the quest.

85

The reverence of confusion, when we kneel down to seek guidance out of it, is good; but the reverence of love, when we are attracted by the soul for its own sake, is better.

86

He who is possessed by this love of truth and who is so sincere that he is willing to subordinate all other desires to it will be repaid by truth herself.

87

Only when the Overself becomes the focus of all his thinking is it likely to become the inspirer of all his doing.

88

He will come, if he perseveres with sufficient patience, to look upon his practice not as a dry exercise to which he reluctantly goes at the call of duty but as a joyous return to which he is attracted by his heart's own desire.

89

If the quest calls him to sacrifice human love, will he have the strength to do so? Will he be able to crucify his ego?

90

How close he comes to the truth may depend on how deeply he cares for it.

91

Love will have to enter his quest at some point—love for the Overself. For it is through this uniting force that his transformation will at the end be effected.

92

Unless he loves the Overself with deep feeling and real devotion, he is unlikely to put forth the efforts needed to find it and the disciplines needed to push aside the obstacles in the way to it.

93

Love of the Overself is the swiftest horse that can bear us to the heavenly destination. For the more we love It, the less we love the ego and its ways.

94

The devotional attitude will not decrease with the growth of the mystical one. It too will grow, side by side with the other. But it will cast out of itself more and more egoistic selfish interest or grasping until it becomes the pure love of the Overself for the latter's sake alone.

95

Why do we come to God's presence only with our messy problems and our dark troubles? Why only as beggars, or when unhappy, miserable, unhealthy? Can we not come to Him joyously, for His own sake, for love of Him alone?

96

"Absolute truth is *the symbol of Eternity* and no *finite* mind can ever grasp the eternal; hence, no truth in its fullness can ever dawn upon it. To reach the state during which man sees and senses it, we have to paralyse the senses of the external man of clay. This is a difficult task, we may be told, and most people will, at this rate, prefer to remain satisfied with relative truths, no doubt. But to approach even terrestrial truths requires, first of all, *love of truth for its own sake,* for otherwise no recognition of it will follow. And who loves truth in this age for its own sake?"—H.P. Blavatsky

97

His longings after the Beloved's presence alternate with his despairs of ever attaining it. Indeed the higher self seems to play hide-and-seek with him.

98

Cling by love to the real.

99

This yearning for spiritual light will at some periods be accompanied by anguish but at others by pleasure.

100

The fierce loving constant devotion, even worship, which most mothers give to their only or favoured child would be enough to carry an aspirant through all the vicissitudes of the Long Path.

101

The love which really matters is love of the Highest. All other kinds are merely cheap substitutions.

102

When the idea that a Higher Power which always was, is, and shall be, becomes impregnated with faith so strongly as to have explosive force, he comes closer to Truth.

103

A man or woman to whom fate has denied the outer human love may find that it has also offered him or her the very real feeling of divine love. In that case, he or she cannot receive the gift *in its fullness* unless he or she accepts the denial with resignation.

104

Whereas he came first to the quest out of dire need for solace in suffering failure, tragedy, or despair, he comes now out of heartfelt love for the True, the Good, the Real.

105

If men offer worship at all, it is offered to a Power infinitely wiser and grander than any condition which they dare hope to attain.

106

Some feel this aspiration for a higher life so strongly that it becomes an ache.

107

Worship and thankfulness should be reserved for the Source alone. The right way to express these is to inculcate them into one's Being.

108

He is to find his highest satisfaction, his strongest attachment, in the divine Beloved.

109

You are no longer wanting God. You are now loving God. The former is only for beginners.

110

He reserves his worship for the infinite and ineffable Unseen Being alone. He will honour, and humble himself before, the human teachers who affirm its existence, but he cannot give them the same worship.

111

The more we are devoted to the diviner attractions, the less devoted or susceptible do we become to the earthly ones. Thus the mere exercise of the faculty of veneration for something beyond ourselves gradually lifts us nearer to the desireless state.

112

Only when he comes to love it deeply and understand it instinctively can he be said to have arrived at real discipleship.

Warnings and suggestions

113

The path of devoting oneself ardently to a religious love of God ought to be trod by all. But it need not be the only path; indeed that would be undesirable.

114

A worldly refusal to honour the sacred is as unbalanced as a monastic refusal to honour the secular. In a balance of both duties, in a common-sense union of their ordained roles in a man's life lies the way for present-day man. Each age has its own emphasis; ours should be equilibrium.(P)

115

The danger of the religio-mystic devotional path is the danger into which blind faith tends to fall. A facile credulity easily takes up with a harmful—because ego-satisfying—superstition.

116

It is unphilosophical to set up a cult, a system of worship with one person—the guru—as its object. He may be respected and admired, revered and loved, but he is still human and should not be worshipped.

117

Devotion to any historic or mythological deity must end, if grace is won and if advancement be experienced, in devotion to the Overself—to pure being. Precisely the same must happen with devotion to any human guru.

118

Too often this holy and beautiful feeling deteriorates under the ego's pressure and falters into mere sentimentality.

119

The notion that any human being has anything to give which God needs—be it love, adoration, or worship—is inadmissible, notwithstanding the dogmas of some popular theology and statements of some advanced mystics like Eckhart. It would make God less than what He must be.

120

The duty of worship, whether in a public temple or a private home, exists not because God needs our praise—for he is not in want of anything—but because we need to recollect him.

121

Is he thinking of the truth or is he thinking of himself? Is he interested enough in the higher self to forget this lower one? In short, is he worshipping God or the *"me"*?

122

He prostrates himself before his own ego several times daily: this is often the only worship modern man performs.

123

When we want the inner light at least as much for its own sake as for its effects, we shall begin to get it. But to seek the effects while calling on the kingdom is to deceive ourselves.

124

When this devotional path is overstressed and not balanced with any counterpoise, when the guru is made into the object of a hysterical love-game, then the imagination leads the mind into pseudo-illuminations that are worthless for Truth. The guru himself is involuntarily made into an accommodating substitute for the friendship or love, the companionship or drama or motherhood, which the world failed to offer. The august relationship of disciple and Master is turned into a love affair, with all the egoistic accompaniments of jealousy, intrigue, exaltation, or depression that go with one. Is it not understandable why atheistic sceptics sneered at the mystical raptures of cloistered nuns who saw erotic images in their visions of embracing the Lord? Admittedly the mystical eroticism of medieval nunneries may be explained, either in part or in particular cases, by this repression of sex. But it fails to explain the other part and the other cases.

125

What is prayer but a turning to the higher unseen power in the only way that simple, spiritually untutored people know? Why deprive them of it? What is wrong about its use in organized religion is that they are not taught the further facts. First, prayer is only a beginning, its continuing development being meditation. Second, it ought not be limited to material demands but always accompanied by moral and religious aspiration. Third, it is best performed, as Jesus taught, in private and secret.

126

Although the attainment is not possible without a devotional singleness of mind, this does not mean that other interests should be banned.

127

We must distinguish between a true sincere aspiration and one which is only wishful thinking.

128

Jalaluddin Rumi, the Sufi: "When men imagine they are adoring Allah it is Allah who is adoring himself."

129

There is danger to every man who denies this inner part of his being any share in daily life, any love, reverence, and worship. This danger may appear, fully realized, in his body or mind.

130

When religious devotion never rises above the physical details of the form of its object, it becomes materialistic. When it is centered in the human details alone, it becomes hysterical.

131

It is true that many of the gods worshipped by man are clothed in *forms* that are merely the products of his own imagination. But the basic *idea* behind those forms is not.

132

The feeling of religious reverence, the attitude of humble worship, must well up of themselves in the heart. It is not enough merely to go through the external and physical motions which accompany their inner presence.

133

Any image which a man forms of God, whether it be painted, mental, or human, has a place if its familiarity helps him to worship. But it still remains an image and must one day be transcended.

134

The symbols and ceremonies need to be clearly and simply interpreted to the layman so that he may not only follow intelligently what happens at a service and why it is so, but also more strongly share emotionally in it.

135

A rite may create a mood of reverence. It is active outside him yet helps the receptive mind within.

136

If the people are shown that going to church is not and ought not to be only a social habit, they can better draw from such attendance some uplift and moral strength.

137

The intellectual mystic often rejects all those liturgical, ritual, and hierarchical aspects which are so prominent in most institutional religions. For they lead human aspiration outward whereas true mysticism leads it inwards.

138

When you are fortunate enough to discover that there is both an ashram and a guru within you, just as there is also a church and a Presence within you, you may well ask, why go hither and thither for them?

139

The three little manuals of devotion, *The Bhagavad Gita*, *The Voice of the Silence*, and *Light on the Path*, used by so many, form a perfect and excellent trio and surely belong to the philosophical teaching.

140

Recommended reading list of books

Sri Aurobindo: *Lights on Yoga*

H.P. Blavatsky: *The Voice of the Silence*

Buddha: *Dhammapada*

John Bunyan: *The Pilgrim's Progress*

Sir Edwin Arnold: (1) *The Song Celestial;* (2) *The Light of Asia*

Annie Besant: (1) *In the Outer Court;* (2) *The Path of Discipleship*

William Q. Judge: translation of the *Bhagavad Gita*

Ralph Waldo Emerson: "The Over-Soul" (essay)

Evelyn Underhill: (1) *Mysticism;* (2) *Practical Mysticism;* (3) *The Essentials of Mysticism;* (4) *The Life of the Spirit and the Life of Today*

Swami Vivekananda: Works

Sri Ramakrishna: *Sayings* [Editors' note: Three selections are available. (1) F. Max Müller, *Ramakrishna; His Life and Sayings;* (2) N. Gupta, *Sayings of Parahansa Ramkrishna* (sic); (3) Sri Ramakrishna Math, *Sayings of Sri Ramakrishna*: the most exhaustive collection of them, their number being 1120]

Brother Lawrence: *The Practice of the Presence of God*

Sri Rabindranath Tagore: *Sadhana; the realisation of life*

Jacob Boehme: (1) *The Way to Christ;* (2) *Dialogues on the Supersensual Life*

Yogi Ramacharaka: *Advanced Course in Yogi Philosophy and Oriental Occultism*

Joseph Sieber Benner: *The Impersonal Life*
Ralph Waldo Trine: *In Tune with the Infinite*
Wisdom of the East Series
Smith: (1) *Persian Mystics;* (2) *Attar*
Sheldon Cheney: *Men Who Have Walked with God*
Kahlil Gibran: *The Prophet*
F.L. Woodward (trans.): *Some Sayings of the Buddha*
Plato: Works (especially "Apology of Socrates")
Seneca: Writings and other Roman Stoic writers
Gordon Shaw: *The Road to Reality*
Albert E. Cliffe: (1) *Lessons in Successful Living;* (2) *Let Go and Let God*
David Seabury: *Help Yourself to Happiness*
Mary Strong (editor): *Letters of the Scattered Brotherhood*

2

PRAYER

Prayer is one of the oldest of human acts and one of the first of human needs.

2

"Teach us how to pray," cried the disciples to Jesus. The modern man is just as bewildered as they were. He has to learn the answer afresh.

3

The quest begins with prayer and even ends with it too. No man, whether novice or proficient, can afford to throw away this valuable means of communion, adoration, worship, and request.

4

The call for prayer which, in most religions, is timed for once or twice a day and, in the Islamic religion, for five times a day, has at least two objectives in the mind of those sages who originally framed it. The first is to act as a reminder of what one is—a soul—and where one is going—ultimately to God. The second is to rescue us from the narrowing materializing routine of work or business.

5

Prayer is very necessary. It helps to clean or purge the feelings. Prayer later leads to intuition.

Do not pray for things to happen in the way you wish them to; this is not always the same as what is best for you. Even in your daily prayers you can do something to better your character.

Most people start their prayer asking for something. That is not right; prayer is an act of devotion and love to God. It is the manifestation of the feeling that there is something higher with which it is possible to come in contact. Prayer is not only asking, it is first and foremost an act of worship and love of God. Only after that is done may you ask for something for yourself—mainly, of course, for spiritual things and not material. You should pray in solitude, if possible. But you may pray with others if they are in harmony with you.

6

There is no man so advanced that he can afford to dispense with prayer. It occupies a most important place in the philosophic aspirant's life.

7

The sceptic who deems all prayer vain and useless, who regards the reasons for it as foolish, is too often justified. But when he ceases to search farther for the reasons behind prayer, he becomes unjustified. For if he did search, he might discover that true prayer is often answered because it is nothing less than making a connection—however loose, ill-fitting, and intermittent it be—with the life-force within the universe.(P)

8

There is no one so sinful or so degraded in character that he is denied this blessed privilege of a contrite yearning for communion with his own divine source. Even the failure to have ever prayed before, even a past life of shame and error, does not cancel but, on the contrary, merely enhances this right. This granted, it will be found that there are many different forms of such communion, different ways of such prayer.(P)

9

There are those who object to the introduction of prayer into the philo-sophic life. In a world governed by the law of cause and effect, of what avail is this whining petition for unearned boons, they ask. Is it not unreasonable to expect them? Would it not be unfair to others to grant them?

These objections are valid ones. But the subject is covered with clouds. To dispel two or three of them, it is worth noting two or three facts. The first is that whether a prayer is addressed to the Primordial Being, to the Overself, or to a spiritual leader, it is still addressed to a higher power, and it is therefore an abasement of the ego before that power. When we remember the smug self-complacency of man, and the need of disturbing it if he is to listen to a truer Voice than his own, what can be wrong with such self-humbling? He will not be exempted by his petitioning from the sway of the law of cause and effect. If he seems to get an answer to his prayer we may be sure it will be for reasons that are valid in themselves, even if he is ignorant of those reasons. But how many prayers get an-swered? Everyone knows how slight the proportion is.

The man who is earnestly seeking to advance spiritually will usually be ashamed to carry any worldly desire into his sacred prayer. He will be working hard upon himself to improve, purify, and correct himself, so he need have no hesitation to engage in prayer—for the right things. He will pray for better understanding of the higher laws, clearer sight as to what his individual spiritual obligation consists in, more and warmer love for the Overself.(P)

10

It is strange that most just persons usually acknowledge having no right to get something for nothing, yet in the matter of prayer they feel no shame in requesting liberation from their particular weaknesses or habitual sins. Are they entitled to ask—often in a mechanical, importunate, or whining manner—for a result for which other persons work all-too-hard? Is it not effrontery to ask for divine intervention which should favour them while the others toil earnestly at reshaping themselves?

How then should a man pray? Should he beg for the virtues to be given to him gratis and unearned for which other men have to strive and labour? Is it not more just to them and better in the end for himself if, instead of demanding something for nothing, he prays thus: "I turn to you, O Master, for inspiration to rise above and excel myself, but I create that inspiration by my own will. I kneel before you for guidance in the problems and decisions of life, but I receive that guidance by taking you as an example of moral perfection to be followed and copied. I call upon you for help in my weakness and difficulty, my darkness and tribulation, but I produce and shape that help by trying to absorb it telepathically from your inner being." This is a different kind of prayer from the whining petitions often passing under that name, and whereas they seldom show direct, traceable results, this always shows them.(P)

11

He should not fall into the error of believing that the transition to philosophical study has exempted him from the duty of mystical practice or that the transition to the latter has exempted him from the need of religious devotion. We do not drop what belongs to a lower stage but keep and preserve it in the higher one. Aspiration is a vital need. He should become as a child at the feet of his divine Soul, humbly begging for its grace, guidance, and enlightenment. If his ego is strong, prayer will weaken it. Let him do this every day, not mechanically but sincerely and feelingly until the tears come to his eyes. The quest is an integral one and includes prayer alongside of all the other elements.(P)

12

Prayer is the mood of the lower self when it turns towards the higher self.

13

We pray to confess sin or to humble self, to commune with the Divine or to invoke Grace, in joy as well as in despair.

14

Prayer does not mean bribery, flattery, or fright.

15

Those endowed with strong critical judgement may feel that it is useless to bow the head and bend the knees in prayer. It might be better for the personal balance if they did so, but their difficulty must be recognized.

16

Buddha labelled prayer as quite useless. Jesus, on the contrary, invited his followers to frequent prayer.

17

We are called to prayer because we can achieve no success, whether in human life or in the spiritual quest, without seeking and gaining divine help.

18

In those situations wherein it is totally helpless to save itself from danger and death, every creature sends forth an anguished cry from the heart. And this is as natural to animals as to human beings. The younger animals address it to their physical mother, the older ones to the Father-Mother of all beings, God.

19

Can anyone correctly say that he can put no feeling behind prayer for spiritual light, guidance, or help because he knows so little about it or has so little faith in it? At least he realizes the need of help from an outside source and can beseech or petition whatever powers there be to give whatever help they can. Telepathy being a fact and the mental world being no less real than this one, such concentrations cannot be without some kind of value.

20

The first value of prayer is that it is a confession of personal inadequacy and, by consequence, an aspiration to personal upliftment. It is a self-humbling of the ego and the beginning of a detachment from it. It is a first step in obedience to Jesus' paradoxical proclamation, "He that loseth his life shall find it."

21

Dionysius the Areopagite said that there were three kinds of prayer: the circular, the spiral, and the direct.

22

Those who believe prayer to be a remnant of primitive superstition, outmoded in a modern spiritual life or unheeded by a higher mystical one, are wrong. The twentieth-century man may as profitably give himself to it today as the second-century man did—perhaps more profitably because he requires more help from outside himself.

23

However, if prayer is an indispensable part of the spiritual life, lower conceptions of prayer are not indispensable to a higher grade of that life.

24

Within the conception of philosophy there is room for the humblest prayerfulness as well as the acutest intelligence.

25

The Christian grace before, the Hebrew thanksgiving before and after meals, were prescribed for the same reason that the Muhammedan's brief five-times-a-day prayer was prescribed. And this was to bring the remembrance of life's higher purpose into everyday living.

26

Many philosophic students do not realize the importance of prayer and are genuinely surprised when counsel is given to preface their meditations with a few minutes of humble worship. Some protest that they do not know to What or to Whom to pray; that God as the Absolute Principle is incapable of intercommunication, whilst God as the popular dispenser of boons and woes is a mere fiction of priests and clerics. They seem to think that those who have started practising mystical exercises—and certainly those who have commenced philosophic studies—have no further need for prayer. They could not be more mistaken.

The positive gains from each stage of the Quest are never lost. Those of religion are preserved in the mystical stage, and must not be rejected; those of mysticism are retained in the third and higher degree of philosophy. Naturally, the individual advances to higher conceptions of prayer, but that is not to say he advances beyond its practice altogether. Such an atheistic attitude could never be sanctioned. Sincere prayer is a necessity and a delight to the earnest student.

To return to those who are still wondering to What or Whom they should address their prayers: it is suggested they offer them in the direction of That in whose existence they presumably do believe—their own Higher "I."

27

Too many individuals—and some of them are followers of this Quest—fail to remember the importance of simple prayer. There is not enough humbling of intellectual pride at the feet of the Higher Power and there is an obvious neglect of reverent worship in their attitudes and daily lives.

28

One must not overlook the importance of prayer, particularly at a certain stage of development. This does not mean the mechanical formula of an orthodox church, but simple, spontaneous, fervent worship—a petition for communion—directed from the heart to the Higher Self.

29

The mystic has to pass through the earlier stage of regarding the Overself as an "other" before he can arrive at the later stage of regarding it as his own essential self. Hence the need of prayer for the first stage.

30

True prayer may be any of several things: humble opening of the whole heart so that the Divine may enter if it chooses to do so, allowing endeavour to achieve silent communion with the higher power, or a selfless seeking to understand the divine will in any particular situation.

31

The suggestion that the student devote more time to prayer is made and repeated because it is believed that prayer can be of great help to his progress.

Forms of prayer

32

The devotional nature of the student should be brought out by cherishing love for the Divine, nurturing aspirations toward the Divine, and cultivating earnestness in quest of the Divine. These qualities are best expressed through the habit of daily prayer. The love will be expressed by the eager feeling with which he turns his thoughts to prayer every day; the aspiration will be revealed by the height towards which the worship will reach during the prayer and by the depth towards which his self-abasement will fall during the same time. The earnestness will be shown by the fundamental mood of endeavour after self-betterment which should underlie his whole waking life.

33

Each morning the inner work is to be prefaced by a brief prayer and physical obeisance, the first asking to be used as a channel, and the second seeking a reorientation of contact.

34

A philosopher's prayer: "That which is the ever-living presence in man: to That I turn when in trouble; on That I meditate when at rest; may That bless with its grace my entry into the other side of death."

35

It is good to pray that the coming year may find in you a more aspiring and more determined person, a calmer and better balanced seeker after truth.

36

The power of thought is greatest when it is inspired by that which is beyond thought, and so, with the approach of the Christmas–New Year season, the mystic takes others with him into this mental remembrance which is to him a form of meditation and which he believes will not be without some inner value to them.

37

Kneeling, the Western bodily attitude of prayer, expresses the mental attitude of humility. Prostration, the Eastern attitude of prayer, with the forehead bent close to the floor, carries the same mental attitude to the extreme degree—abasement.

38

Thanks for Thy presence and existence here and now.

Praise for making life on earth more bearable and more endurable when it becomes oppressive.(P)

39

The Egyptian priest knelt on the floor on his haunches, heels supporting buttocks, both arms stretched out sideways to receive invisible powers from above, the palms upturned toward heaven.

40

Prayer is at its best, and consequently most effective, when it is done in humility and love.

41

He should make use of prayer. Every day he should go down on his knees and pray for grace, offer himself in self-surrender to the higher self, and express his yearning and love for it. Such readiness to go down on his knees for a minute or two, to abase the ego's pride in prayer, is extremely valuable. This is what Jesus meant by becoming "as a little child"; this humility is inspired childlikeness, not stupid childishness.

42

It was Origen, the early Church Father, who asserted that the true posture of prayer is the standing one, where the arms are stretched out in the shape of a cross.

43

O Thou Divinity within me, (and in whom I similarly am)—may I ever remember why this earthly life must be elevated and redeemed.

44

With hands upraised, the palms and fingers steepled in the gesture of prayer, a man expresses himself, with or without voice, to the Infinite instinctively and physically.

45

"May He guide our minds," prays the Hindu every day. This is a good humbling thought.

46

At some point during your prayer surrender your personal self to God, and your personal will to His Will.

47

If you want a workable and faultless prayer, what is better than the one which Socrates habitually used, "Give me that which is best for me," or the one which some older pagan used, "May I love, seek, and attain only that which is good"?

48

In all times hands have been lifted—whether in supplication or in aspiration—before God. This is an instinctive natural gesture.

49

Hymn: "Praise God from Whom all blessings flow,
    Praise Him, all creatures here below;
    Praise Him above, Angelic Host,
    Praise Father, Son, and Holy Ghost!"

50

Buddhist form of showing homage: Place both hands together with palms touching. Raise up the arms and then bring them backward until the thumbs rest on the forehead.

51

What a privilege to carry
Everything to God in prayer!
Oh, what peace we often forfeit,
Oh, what needless pain we bear—
All because we do not carry
Everything to God in prayer!
    —nineteenth-century hymn

52

It is advisable to bring your prayer or healing treatment to an end with a silent or spoken expression of thanks to the higher power. It should be uttered with strong fervour and deep humility.

53

The Jain saint Amitagati: a) "Pray my mind, O Lord, be always at equilibrium, at home and abroad." b) "By self-analysis, self-censure, and repentance, I destroy sin."

54

Thou!
Unseen, untouched and unknown,
The only grace I beg for
Is the grace of loving Thee!
    —My prayer

55

The Seven Sacred Physical Postures and Mental Attitudes of Philosophic Worship (Essay also printed in volume 4)

The function of these postures is suggestive and helpful. They are symbolic of seven emotional attitudes. Each physical posture is to some extent an index to the feelings which actuate it. Because man dwells in a body of flesh, his bodily posture is as significant during prayer and worship as during any other activity: it becomes a sacred gesticulation.

Some mystically minded people, either because they reject all ceremonial observance or because they can see no utility in them whatever, object to using these postures. On the first ground, we answer that in philosophy such practices are not hollow rites, but valuable techniques, if performed with consciousness and with intelligent understanding. On the second ground, we answer that the exercises depolarize the physical body's earthward gravitation and render it more amenable to the entrance of spiritual currents. They clear the aura of undesirable magnetism. If anyone feels that he has no need of them, he may dispense with them.

Three remarks by Avicenna serve as an excellent introduction to the use of these postures.

"The act of prayer should further be accompanied by those attitudes and rules of conduct usually observed in the presence of kings: humility, quietness, lowering the eyes, keeping the hands and feet withdrawn, not turning about and fidgeting."

"These postures of prayer, composed of recitation, genuflection, and prostration and occurring in regular and definite numbers, are visible evidence of that real prayer which is connected with, and adherent to, the rational soul. In this manner the body is made to imitate that attitude, proper to the soul, of submission to the Higher Self, so that through this act man may be distinguished from the beasts."

"And now we would observe that the outward, disciplinary part of prayer, which is connected with personal motions according to certain numbered postures and confined elements, is an act of abasement, and of passionate yearning on the part of this lower, partial, compound, and limited body towards the lunary sphere."

—from *Avicenna on Theology*,
by A.J. Arberry

1. *Standing and remembrance.*

(a) Stand comfortably, facing towards the east or the sun. (b) Plant the feet ten inches apart, raise arms forward and upward until they are about halfway between vertical and horizontal levels, at forty-five degrees above the horizontal, and fully extended. (c) The palms of both hands should be turned away and upward. (d) The head is slightly raised and the eyes are uplifted.

Bring the mind's attention abruptly away from all other activities and concentrate only on the Higher Power, whether as God, the Overself, or the Master. The act of uplifting the arms should synchronize with decisively uplifting the thoughts. The mere fact of abruptly abandoning all activities and of practising the lifting of hands for a certain time will help to bring about the uplift of the mind.

2. *Stretching and worship.*

(a) Assume the same position of feet and arms as in the previous posture. (b) Bend in lower part of arms at elbows and bring palms of both hands flatly together, at the same time inhaling deeply. Hold the breath a few seconds. Exhale while letting arms fall.

The attitude should be one of loving, reverential, adoring worship of the Overself.

3. *Bowing and aspiration.*

(a) With feet still apart, place both hands lightly on front of the thighs. (b) Bend the trunk forward at the waistline until it is nearing a horizontal level. Take care to keep both knees rigidly straight and unbent. (c) Let the palms slide downward until they touch the knees. Relax the fingers. (d) The head should be in line with the backbone, with the eyes looking down to the floor.

By pouring the devotion and love towards the Higher Power, the feeling of a personal relation to It should be nurtured.

4. *Kneeling and confessions.*

(a) Drop down to the floor and rest the knees upon it. (b) Lift the trunk away from the heels, keeping it in a straight erect line with the thighs. (c) Flatten the palms of both hands together and bring them in front of, as well as close to, the breast. (d) Close the eyes. This, of course, is the traditional Christian prayer posture.

Remorsefully acknowledge weaknesses in character and confess sins in conduct in a repentant, self-humbling attitude. Be quite specific in naming them. Also confess the limitations, deficiencies, and imperfections one is aware of. Second, ask for strength from the Higher Power to overcome those weaknesses, for light to find Truth, and for Grace. The qualities needed to counteract them should be formulated in definite terms. This confession is an indispensable part of the philosophic devotions. When it is sincere and spontaneous, it makes a proud man humble and thus opens the first gate in the wall of Grace. It compels him to become acutely conscious of his ignorance and ashamedly aware of his weakness. The praying person humbles the ego and breaks up his vanity; therefore he must not hide his mistakes or look for excuses. Only through such frankness can the time come when he will get the strength to overcome that mistake. This confession forces the praying person down to the ground and his self-respect with him, like a humiliated beggar. In his anguish, he constantly rediscovers his insufficiency and need of help from God or God's man.

5. *Squatting and submission.*

(a) Remaining on the knees, sink down until both heels support the trunk's weight, spine and head erect, hands on thighs. (b) Lower the chin until it touches the chest. (c) The eyes should be kept half-closed.

This posture is to be done with the mind and heart together completely emptied and surrendered to the Higher Power in utter resignation of the self-will. Humbly surrender the ego and discard its pride. Pray for Grace and ask to be taken up into the Overself completely. It is a sound instinct which causes a man to bend his head when the feeling of reverence becomes strong within him.

6. *Prostrating and union.*

(a) Without rising, and keeping legs folded at the knees, bend the torso forward and incline the face as low as possible. (b) Bring the hands to rest upon the floor-rug, with palms outstretched, taut, and touching. (c) Place the forehead upon the hands. The knees should then be crouched up toward the chest. All ten toes must touch the floor. (d) Shut the eyes. The ancient Egyptian religion made *hetbu* or "bowing to the ground" an important part of its worship. The Muhammedans make bowings of the body during prayer equally important. This posture is practised widely in the Orient, but it is inconvenient to most Western people and is therefore usually withdrawn from them. If anyone, however, is much attracted to it, he may practise it.

During this posture, one should empty the mind of all thoughts and still it. Relax the emotions, open the heart, and be completely passive, trying to feel the inflow of heavenly love, peace, and blessing.

7. *Gesturing* (with thoughts concentrated on service and self-improvement).

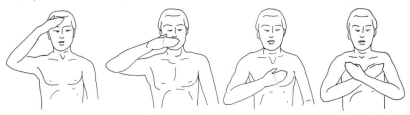

(a) So as not to lose this high mood, rise from the floor slowly and smoothly to resume ordinary activities in the world. At the same time, turn attention away from self towards others, if inclined. Intercede for them, draw blessings down upon them, and hold them up to the divine light, power, and peace. (b) Press the right hand to brow, mouth, and heart by turns, pausing at each gesture. Resolve to follow firmly the ideal qualities mentioned during the confession of posture 4. When touching the brow, resolve to do so in thoughts; when touching the mouth, resolve to do so in speech; and when touching the heart, resolve to do so in feelings.

Epilogue.

Cross and fold the arms diagonally while standing. The hands will then rest upon the chest, the fingers will point upwards toward the shoulders. In this last stage, you are to be sincerely thankful, joyously grateful, and constantly recognizant for the fact that God *is*, for your own point of contact with God, and for the good—spiritual and material—that has come your way.

56

The first part of his prayer should be spoken aloud. His lips must give his thought a physical embodiment. This is because he lives in a physical world and the prayer should start on the same level. But the second part should be silent and mental, introverted and absorbed. Yet he should not arbitrarily fix the moment of passage from the first to the second part. The change from speech to silence ought to come about of its own accord and by his own inner prompting.

57

Prayer, if it is petitionary, is best formulated just before and just after entering the stillness. In the first case, the heart is then purer and will ask more wisely. In the second case, if the silent communion has been established, and the afterglow of peace is there, the heart will then understand that the whole problem is then best left with the higher power and anxiety dismissed, that demands made from ignorance merely limit or thwart the power.

58

Prayer ought to be a reaching out to the spiritual presence of the higher power. It ought to satisfy itself with obtaining a certain intuitive feeling, above and beyond all its ordinary everyday personal feelings. Then, if it seeks something specific, it ought to ask for more light of understanding, more power of self-mastery, more goodness of heart—not for more dollars in the bank, more furniture in the home, more horsepower in the car.

59

He should not hesitate to pray humbly, kneeling in the secrecy of his private room, to the Overself. First his prayer should acknowledge the sins of his more distant past having led to sufferings in the later past or his immediate present, and he should accept this as just punishment without any rebellious feeling. Then he may throw himself on the Grace as being the only deliverance left outside his own proper and requisite efforts to amend the causes. Finally let him remember the living master to whom he has given allegiance and draw strength from the memory.(P)

60

To enter this stillness is the best way to pray.(P)

61

It is not to be, as it is with so many unenlightened religionists, nothing more than a request to be given something for nothing, a petition for unearned and undeserved personal benefit. It is to be first, a confession of the ego's difficulty or even failure to find its own way correctly through the dark forest of life; second, a confession of the ego's weakness or even helplessness in coping with the moral and mental obstacles in its path; third, an asking for help in the *ego's own strivings* after self-enlightenment and self-betterment; fourth, a resolve to struggle to the end to forsake the lower desires and overcome the lower emotions which raise dust-storms between the aspirant and his higher self; and fifth, a deliberate self-humbling of the ego in the admission that its need of a higher power is imperative.(P)

62

Do not make your request until you have first made the highest grade of your devotional worship or scaled the peak of your mystical meditation. Then only should you formulate it, and hold it before the Power whose presence you then feel.

63

He should believe that he is at that moment receiving that which he is praying for. But he should do so only if he feels no contrary indication of coldness or doubt, and only after he has made contact with the power through pure worship or meditation.

64

Whenever an emergency arises wherein you require help, guidance, protection, or inspiration, turn the thought away from self-power and bring it humbly to the feet of the higher power in prayer.

65

Prayers really begin when their words end. They are most active not when the lips are active but when they are still.

66

Many people turn to prayer through weakness in desperation and pain. Others turn through strength in the desire to establish communication or attend holy communion.

67

That which is prayed for in the turbulent desire of the ego may be wrong. But that which is prayed for in the deepest stillness of the Overself's presence will be right and, therefore, received.

68

A public place is an unnatural environment in which to place oneself mentally or physically in the attitude of true prayer. It is far too intimate, emotional, and personal to be satisfactorily tried anywhere except in solitude. What passes for prayer in temples, churches, and synagogues is therefore a compromise dictated by the physical necessity of an institution. It may be quite good but too often alas! it is only the dressed-up double of true prayer.

69

Perhaps the best solution of this problem is to combine the two: to perform private prayers in a public building as the Catholics do. But those individuals who have gone some way ahead of the mass will usually prefer to follow Jesus' advice and pray in the secrecy of their own chambers.

70

Too often prayer is mere soliloquy, a man talking to his own ego about his own ego, and heard only by his own ego. It would be far better for him to learn how to keep his thoughts silent, to put himself into a receptive listening attitude; what he may then hear may convince him that "the Father knoweth what ye need."

71

Oh, Lord, if I have any prayer at all it is, "Make the 'me' absolutely quiescent and lead me into thy utter stillness where nothing else matters but the stillness itself."

72

Prayer is of course only one part of the Quest. Prayer should be the expression of his reverence and love for the Higher Power, God, or the Soul, or whatever he likes to call it. It can be silent or not. In his prayers he should follow this worship with a confession of those defects and weaknesses which hinder his full communion with God, and, only at the end of the prayer should he ask for help in overcoming them and for light to guide him.

73

What shall he pray for? Let him aspire more intensely than ever to the Overself and ask to become united in consciousness with it, surrendered in will to it, and purified in ego.

74

If the presence of divinity is felt, no name need be uttered in invocation and no prayer need be made in petition.

75

It is wiser not to talk excessively in prayer, better to remain silent a while and thus give God a chance to speak to us.

76

Prayer and meditation are private acts for they do not concern a man's relations with other men, but with God. Therefore they should be practised privately.

77

Pray by listening inwardly for intuitive feeling, light, strength, not by memorized form or pauperized begging.(P)

78

When we are actually in the vivid presence of this holier self, we may utter our petitionary prayers, but not before.

79

The step from public worship to private communion is a step forward.

80

The Russian Staretz Silouan wrote, in the notes which he left behind when he died in monastic Mount Athos, that prayer should be so highly concentrated that each word comes forth slowly.

81

He may always rightly close his prayer by soliciting guidance and sometimes by asking for forgiveness. Such a request can find justification, however, only if it is not a request for interfering with karma, only if it comes after recognition of wrong done, perception of personal weakness, confession leading to contrition, and a real effort to atone penitently and improve morally. The eternal laws of karma will not cease operating merely for the asking and cannot violate their own integrity. They are impersonal and cannot be cajoled into granting special privileges or arbitrary favours to anyone. There is no cheap and easy escape from them. If a sinner wants to avoid hurtful consequences of his own sins, he must use those very laws to help him do so, and not attempt to insult them. He must set going a series of new causes which shall produce new and pleasanter consequences that may act as an antidote to the older ones.

Misunderstandings and misuses

82

If the world's business were to be at the mercy of every uttered petition that rises from the lips of man, then it would tumble into chaos, and life would become a bewildering maze. No!—before we talk glibly about prayer being answered, we should first distinguish between pseudo-prayers and genuine prayer.

83

The belief that the Supreme Principle of the universe can be drawn away from Its work by every call from every person, or induced to obey every request of every kind, or persuaded to cancel the operation of cosmic laws to suit one creature who dislikes its effect upon himself, is not only naïve but also insulting. For it would lessen God and dwindle him down to the status of a mere man. Ascribing more power to his own prayer really implies that there is so much less power in God.

84

Men and women who find themselves in situations of great need, or confronted by problems which render them desperate, or oppressed by sickness, loss of employment, in debt, or involved in circumstances of grave peril, are not to be blamed if they turn for help to the Source of all love. Their prayers are as legitimate as the outcries for help from every child to its mother or father. Their call for relief is pardonable and not improper. But what is unreasonable is the refusal to enquire how far they have themselves contributed to their situation and how much they must themselves do to amend it. The immature child cannot be expected to make such enquiry and its parent may have to do alone everything that is required to help it, but the grown adult has also grown into responsibilities and duties. What I am trying to say is that he must share with the higher power the work of saving himself, a work which begins with examining the past causes of his calamity, goes on to taking present steps off the beaten path on required action, and ends only in resolving on a future character or capacity which will throw out the seeds of such causes. Call this rational prayer, if you like. The act of praying is here neither wildly denounced as being quite useless, a kind of childish talking to oneself, nor foolishly praised as being the right way out of all troubles.

85

If men knew, as the seers know, how wide a gulf lies between established, organized religions and true religion itself, they would understand why the prayers of such religions, whether for national or individual objects, so often fail to reach God and get no response. On May 26, 1940, there was a mass appeal to God from every house of worship throughout England and the British Empire. The British Government declared it a National Day of Prayer for this purpose. But within a few days Belgium surrendered, and within a month France collapsed. Britain was left to fight alone. Was this the answer to her prayer? Religious prayer, when neglected at other times and resorted to only when material benefit is sought, is the greatest example of wishful thinking the world has ever known. If the response of the Almighty Deity is to be in direct ratio to the volume of the prayers He receives, if He is to be amenable only when these incantations reach a certain figure, then the Tibetan prayer-wheel deserves to be manufactured in the West by mass-production methods!

86

To regard—as W. Tudor Pole regards—the successful withdrawal from Dunkirk or the successful air battle of Britain as being the result of the Church's intercession or of the National Day of Prayer is merely to fall into superstition. Why not say that the capitulation of Belgium and the collapse of France were also due to the same cause because they also occurred about the same time? Why did not all the clergy's prayers save the thousands of British churches which were destroyed by German bombs? No—karma is more powerful than the Church, evolution more fateful than intercession; Britain was saved because both the British karma and the world's evolutionary needs demanded its saving.

87

The idea that because of national days of prayer the war took a different course than it might otherwise have taken is one that must be questioned. Since the most ancient times, nations have had such days whenever they found themselves in trouble and usually they consisted of nationwide requests that the trouble be taken from them. Merely making such a request cannot of itself alter the course of Destiny, nor influence God. True prayer should be something more, something deeper than that. There must be true repentance and not merely an attempt to escape a situation toward which one has contributed by one's own wrong thinking and wrong actions. How few are the nations who have genuinely repented; once out of trouble they have quickly resumed the same old course. One may have the greatest faith in the value and power of prayer, but in order for it to be effectual, it must be genuine and it must be practised correctly.

88

The emotional worship and wishful thinking of popular religion have not saved the millions who practise it from following leaders who led them into war and destruction, or from customs which caused sickness and spread disease. Prayer will not prove a substitute for intelligence nor prevent man experiencing the effects of his own failure to restrain his lower nature.

89

So many believe that if only they keep on begging, God will magically put into them the good qualities which they lack. Is such a great result to be achieved as simply as that? The hundreds of thousands of disappointed persons who find themselves the same as they were before, despite months and years of pouring out their emotional petitions to a crudely and childishly imagined God, show that this naïve belief is either a misuse and misunderstanding of true prayer or a mere superstition.

90

When we consider the tremendous number of public prayers which have been spoken, chanted, read, or muttered in public gatherings for so many centuries, the human race seems to have derived disproportionate profit from the practice. May it not be because the utterance has become too formal, a matter of mental repetition without the supporting inward loving devotion needed to make it real?

91

Considering that all is known to God, and that therefore all our needs must be known to him too, what is the use of offering this information to God in our prayers?

92

How useful are prayers which are set, formal, and prepared? All too often they lack individual appeal and fail to stir any feeling. Nevertheless, it would be wrong to say that they are quite useless.

93

Who has kept count of the number of ministers who prayed for sick patients, only to witness the latter get worse and die! How many relatives have gone to the bedside of their ailing one, there to pray earnestly for recovery, but the ebbing underflow of life trickled away despite their request? Nobody knows the ratio of answered prayers to unanswered ones, but everybody knows that it is a small one.

94

To utter routine prayers whose words have never received sufficient thought, or even any thought at all, is a waste of time.

95

It is a great and grave fallacy to believe that it is necessary to pray in order to be taken care of by God. The truth is that there is no moment when God is not taking care of us or, indeed, of everyone else. God is in every atom of the Universe and consequently in full operation of the Universe. This activity does not stop because we stop praying.

96

When these three signs of the most elementary stage are brought together and united—the public rite, the spoken utterance, and the set wording—there is danger of the whole prayer itself becoming a mere gabble unless the individual safeguards it by the utmost humility and sincerity.

97

Many more people than is usually admitted fall into the posture or utter the petitions of prayer without much hope that it will be effectual.

98

For so many thousands of years in the historic epoch, and for unknown thousands of years in the prehistoric epoch, men have propitiated God, and prayed for boons or relief; yet the world today is more miserable and more engulfed in suffering than ever before.

99

Father John of Kronstadt was called to the Imperial Palace to pray for the Empress, who had had only girls born to her, whereas the Tsar urgently wanted a son and heir. The holy man's prayers failed to produce the desired result. Yet at other times and with other persons, they had been granted.

100

Dogmatic or mechanical prayer is really valueless. The only effective prayer comes straight from the heart. It should be fervent, reverent, and spontaneous, expressing both idealistic aspirations and spiritual needs.

101

Offering prayers to the kind of God whom most people talk about is almost as useful, as helpful, and as rational as offering chocolates to the law of gravitation.

102

How foolish are those men who try to make their prayers heard on earth, as if God were also a man!

103

With the departure of superstitions from religion, waste of time in meaningless religious activities will also depart. What is the use of praying to the Source for those things which man himself, by using his natural capacities, can supply? He should turn to prayer only when his own efforts are in vain, an indication that it is time to turn the problem over to the Source, the Overself. How many of his illnesses, for example, come from wrong ways of living, eating, drinking, or thinking? The body has its own laws of hygiene, and the learning of them is as much part of his development during his lives on earth as the learning of spiritual laws.

104

True prayer is first fellowship, then communion, and ultimately merger. That is, it is a drawing closer and closer to the Overself. Asking for things is not even to attain the first step. Such things are merely the secondary results of prayer. They will surely come, for the Overself knows your needs, your *true* needs, and will surely take care of them.

105

The man who prays for material goods is performing a questionable act, but the man who prays for spiritual goods is performing a wiser one. The man who asks to have his troubles taken away is also acting questionably, but the man who asks for the strength and guidance to deal wisely with his troubles is more likely to get them.

106

The hour of prayer is a time not to beg but to ascend, not to be filled with thoughts of yourself but with thoughts of God. It is not to be concerned with this world but to lift the mind above it.

107

The more we use prayer for communion and worship, the less we use it for begging and petition, the more will our prayers be answered. God has given us both intelligence and will: we have the business of using as well as developing them. Prayer is not to be used as an alibi to save us from these duties.

108

Too many people do not know how to pray, or try to use meditation to satisfy their selfishness. The first group comes to prayer with the attitude "My will be done." The second group comes to meditation with worldly desires as the object of their worship. Both are doing wrong.

109

The belief many people have that they can call out in prayer to the higher power for their needs without fulfilling their obligations to that power is illogical. They ought not to be so naïve. They ought to enquire first how far, through ignorance, they are disobeying the higher laws and how far, through negligence, they are departing from the hygienic laws. The first concerns their fortunes, the second their health.

110

True prayer is not a devotional act which is done only when we happen to be frightened. It is not a temporary reaction to fear but a constant expression of faith.

111

If people pray only when they have something to ask for, if they think of God only in crises, they have only themselves to blame for their infantile spiritual growth.

112

Before you venture into the prayer of petition ask yourself first, is it really as wise to get what you seek as it seems to be; second, are you deserving of it; and third, what will you do to justify its bestowal.

113

Just as the animal cries out when in fear and the child when in need, so the adult man when in grave stress silently calls out to God for help—unless a one-sided education has stupefied his deeper instincts or a brutalized life has crushed them.

114

What usually passes for prayer seldom gets near the divine presence, remains ego-encircled and useless.

115

If an attempt is made to inform God what is required from Him by and for us, that would be wrong.

116

To pray, asking that an exception be made in their favour, is a common enough act with many people.

117

In return for the favour which they confer on the Higher Power by believing in it, they demand the satisfaction of their personal desires.

118

The true purpose of prayer is not to keep asking for some benefit each time we engage in it, but rather to express the yearning of the underself for the Overself, the attraction felt by the ego living in darkness for its parent source dwelling in light.

119

Whimpering is not praying. It is another form of the self's long littleness.

120

We will begin to get some fruit from prayer and hear less of its many failures when we begin to regard it less as a petition than as a transaction. We have to pay over our arrogant self-reliance and receive in exchange what the infinite wisdom deems best for us.

121

He may, if he wishes, add a prayer for material help but this should be done only under critical or urgent circumstances. The highest, and therefore most philosophic, use of prayer is not to beseech satisfaction of worldly desires but to beseech light into the darkness spread by those desires and to implore the soul for its strength to enter into him for the fight against animal passions.

122

The internal ego does them more harm than anything or anyone else, yet how few appeal to the Divine for protection against themselves, how many for protection against merely external evils?

123

Prayer has value to the extent that it inevitably makes man think of the higher power, but he detracts from that value to the extent that he joins that to the thought of his world by needs, desires, or problems.

124

It is better not to beg nor to demand in prayer, not even for spiritual things or help. It is more fitting to render homage to the higher power, to think of it worshipfully and reverently and humbly and, above all, lovingly.

125

When men pray it is mostly the ego praying, and for itself. If this attitude is maintained until the end of the session, God gets very little chance to say anything to the devotee.

126

Many prayers are dictated not by reverence, but by fear. This is as true of those emanating from the clergy as of those from the lay people.

127

The farther the aspirant is advanced in this Quest, the less he is likely to ask for worldly things in his prayer. In any case, all such petitioning should be strictly limited. Whoever enters a sanctuary to ask for worldly things should beware how far he goes in this direction, and how often he goes there.

128

When prayer is not selfish commerce but holy communion, when it is not worldly minded but spiritually minded, when it seeks the inner Ideal rather than the outer Actual, it has the chance of becoming effectually realized.

129

"If thou canst do what He enjoins on thee, He will do what thou dost ask assuredly," said Awhadi, a medieval Persian mystic. This is the key to prayer. Failure results from ignorance of this key.

130

It is a human and pardonable urge of the devout believer to bring forward specific requests, however trivial, as the main thought in prayer, and to do so repeatedly. This is the little ego petitioning God as a big Ego. It shows faith; it is a part of religion at that level, which is a low one. Personal prayers ought to be the exception, not the rule, and limited to graver matters. Later they may be limited to spiritual matters, and, in the end, left out altogether.

131

It is a great temptation to pray for named persons or for particular things.

132

This begging for personal favours through religious prayer may be a waste of time, especially where it demands divine intervention to escape the consequences of its own acts. But it may also be a prompting to acknowledge the existence of a higher power, a humbling of the ego.

133

Immeasurably better than begging God for things is to beg him for himself.

Human petition, divine response

134

Self-purification is the best prayer, self-correction is the most effectual one.(P)

135

It is good and necessary to practise confession in one's prayer at all times but especially so in distressful times. If one is praying for deliverance, it is not enough merely to ask for it—indeed, that would be egocentric, childish, and useless. One should also ask in what way one is responsible for, or has contributed toward, the making of the trouble from which escape is sought. Nothing should be hidden that can help to bare this guilt. The natural inclination to blame others or protect one's self-esteem should be resisted. Nor should one confess only moral sins; it may be that the cause lies in intellectual incapacity, poor discrimination, or lack of balance.

136

It is common to pray for help to overcome our shortcomings, and this is right; it is even more common to pray to escape the painful results of our shortcomings, but this is not right. Their results are needed for our development and if God took them away from us we would be robbed of a chance to make this development.

137

Man does not always know what is good for him, let alone what is best for him. Moreover, his mistakes may involve others and bring them suffering too.

138

When faced with problems which seem beyond adequate solution by reason or experience or counsel, take it as an indication that you are to put them to divine intervention. Ask during the time of prayer or meditation for the illuminating idea.

139

Too many believe in their own weakness, and in prayer implore or request a higher being to bestow upon them a personal power, virtue, or capacity felt to be lacking in themselves. Yet they, too, have latent inner resources, untapped and awaiting exploitation.

140

The stresses and strains have been increasing in intensity. In our time, life is like climbing a steep rocky path. It does not permit us to rest. It calls us to overcome internal struggle and external opposition. One of the Indian Emperor Akbar's spiritual guides was the Jain master Myoe Syonin. When a friend asked him to offer a prayer on his behalf, Syonin answered: "I pray every morning and every evening for the sake of all beings, and I am sure that you are also included among them."

141

He who can kneel down in utter humility and spontaneously pray to his higher self out of a genuine desire to elevate his character, will not pray in vain.

142

If the confession of sins and faults is an indispensable part of philosophic prayer, striving to forsake those sins and faults must be made an active part of the daily life after prayer.

143

Beware what you pray for. Do not ask for the truth unless you know what it means and all that it implies and nevertheless are still willing to accept it. For if it is granted to you, it will not only purge the evil out of you but later purify the egoism from your mind. Will you be able to endure this loss, which is unlikely to be a painless one?

144

It is better to pray to be led into truth, for then, as Jesus knew and remarked, "All these [other] things shall be added unto you."

145

If anyone claims to have enough faith to pray, let him have a little more faith and act out his prayer in conduct. This is the way to get an answer!

146

Everyone seeks in prayer forgiveness of the consequences of sin, but few seek freedom from the sin itself. That entails hard personal effort, but success in it could bring forgiveness also.

147

The aspirant who finds himself separated, either by force of circumstances or by deliberate desertion, from someone he cares for, may follow the conventional way of praying that the other person should come back to him, or he may follow the philosophic way of praying that he shall come to truth and peace and strength.

148

The kind of prayer which tries to coax God into bestowing something which he wants but cannot get by his own effort presupposes that the thing is for his benefit.

149

A particular problem should be carried into prayer again and again until the solution is found.

150

Why always importune God to answer your prayers? Try sometimes to answer them yourself.

151

It is one sign of progress when we stop informing the higher power of our need, which It must already know. It is another sign of progress when we stop expecting from It some boon which we ought to set about getting for ourselves.

152

If a man will not contribute towards his own welfare by at least attempting to improve himself, what is the use of his constant prayers to God for it?

153

To ask God to do for us what we should be capable or willing to do for ourselves is to show laziness and express dishonesty. We have no right to do this and such prayers consequently are futile.

154

Meditation in a solitary place remote from the world may help others who are still in the world, but only under certain conditions. It must, for example, be deliberately directed towards named individuals. If it floats away into the general atmosphere without any thought of others, it is only a self-absorption, barren to others if profitable to oneself. It can be turned toward the spiritual assistance of anyone the practiser loves or wishes to befriend. But it should not be so turned prematurely. Before he can render real service, he must first acquire the power to do so. Before he can fruitfully pray for persons, he must first be able to draw strength from that which is above all persons. The capacity to serve must first be got before the attempt to serve is made. Therefore he should resist the temptation to plunge straightaway into prayer or meditation on behalf of others. Instead he should wait until his worship or communion attains its highest level of being. Then—and then only—should he begin to draw from it the power and help and light to be directed altruistically towards others. Once he has developed the capacity to enter easily into the deeply absorbed state, he may then use it to help others also. Let him take the names and images of these people with him after he has passed into the state and let him hold them there for a while in the divine atmosphere.(P)

155

It is a commonly used religious formula to say "God will take care of him," or "May God bless him," or "May God forgive him." To utter such words, even mechanically and automatically, is better than to utter words burning with resentment and antagonism against someone who has injured us, or tingling with nervousness and fear for someone who is meeting with trouble. But most often they have no positive value, especially where they have become almost meaningless and empty through excessive familiarity and frequent repetition.

That would not be the case if immediately after speaking these words the person sat down and considered deeply, earnestly, and adequately their full semantic meaning and connections. There would then be a creative building up of the correct mental attitude towards the other man, which would keep away negative thoughts about him, generate a happier feeling about the situation concerning him, or assist to bring about a better relationship with him.

Such a procedure is excellent. But it is mainly an intellectual operation. For those who are travellers upon the Quest of the Overself there is a still higher one available which would use spiritual forces and which is much more effective in making the blessing come literally true.

This they can do by temporarily dismissing from the mind the problem connected with the other person and then calmly taking as a subject of meditation the metaphysical nature of the Overself, how impersonal it is, and how glorious are its attributes. Then they should bring ardent aspiration into the meditation and try to lift themselves into that pure, beautiful atmosphere. When they feel that, to some extent anyway, they have succeeded in doing so, they should stay there for a while and let themselves be thoroughly bathed in its large impersonal peace. Finally, it is at this point only, and not earlier, that, before descending and returning to ordinary life, they may take up afresh the thought of the other person and of the situation connected with him. They should commend him to the care and ministration of this beneficent Spirit. Here is the real way to make the words of these all-too-familiar blessings come true.

156

The best kind of prayer which we can make for another person is uttered without words—that is, by leading him to the stillness; the lesser kind is to beg for him by voiced sound.

157

He is neither to pity nor to despise those whose weaknesses are very pronounced, but he is to wish to help them. If actual aid seems beyond his capacity, he can at least turn them over during the peak period of his meditation hour to the care of the higher power. In this way he makes some kind of a mental link for them with this power.

158

If he will mentally release the relative or friend from his personal fears and anxieties concerning her, she will benefit. She will be helped by his telepathic and auric radiation mentally supporting her by this positive thinking. Mental possessiveness must be abandoned and the girl turned over to God's care in his mind.

159

If you seek to invoke the divine grace to meet a genuine and desperate physical need or human result, seek first to find the sacred presence within yourself and only after you have found it, or at least only after you have attained the deepest point of contemplation possible to you, should you name the thing or result sought. For then you will not only be guided whether it be right to continue the request or not, but you will also put yourself in the most favourable position for securing grace.(P)

160

The highest help we can give another person is not physical but spiritual. And in giving it we benefit ourselves too. For the lofty mood, the loving thought, the peaceful feeling, the full confidence in higher power that we seek to transmit in prayer or meditation to him, must be first created within ourselves. From that creation, we benefit as well as he. Yes, we may introduce the remembrance of other persons, toward the close of our meditation, and pray silently on their behalf. The wonder is that this remembrance, this prayer, this meditation for another may have some effect, although we may be in Canada and the other in Africa. Like a radio broadcast, it reaches out to him.

161

He has no right to bring other persons into his meditation or prayer unless they are aware and willing that he should do so or unless his own motives are absolutely pure and his own knowledge of what he is doing is absolutely true. Much less does he have the right to draw them to the performance of his desires at the expense of their own integrity as individuals.

162

In the exercise of intercessory prayer, first seek to make contact with the higher power by aspiring to it and dwelling upon its nature and attributes. Then, when you feel the presence of this power—and it is ineffectual to do so before—think of it as protective. Next, think of the person whose protection you seek and place him in the presence and hold him there.

163

All those who remember instances of successful prayer bringing large sums of money, as George Miller's and Saint Francis' prayers for the institutions they founded, ought also remember that these were ego-free prayers for the welfare of others: they were not for personal benefit.

164

A person who has not yet found the peace and power of the Overself is in no position to give blessings to other persons.

165

If the attempt at intercession—be it healing, helping, or blessing—is successful, he will feel exultant as the sensation of power flows through him.

166

If petitionary prayer, whether for self or others, is possible at a certain stage of meditation, it is impossible at a deeper stage.

167

He cannot be aware of any individual human while he is deeply enfolded by that state, but shortly before entering it, or shortly after emerging from it, he may be. This makes intercessory prayer and meditation a real possibility.

168

When he is able to bring himself to practise this bestowal of silent blessing upon all others, and to practise it both lovingly and universally, he will find it a quick cure for the trouble of nervous self-consciousness. Instead of feeling uneasy in the presence of certain persons or of a crowd, he will feel poised. Why is this so? Because he is drawing Grace down to himself. This secret was seen by Oscar Wilde when he said: "One cannot search for love. It comes to us unbidden, when we give love to others."

169

The counsel that you are not promiscuously to interfere with other persons in order to improve them, or unwisely to involve yourself in their lives in order to help them spiritually, does not mean that you are to do nothing at all for them. You may, if you wish, take them beneficently into your prayer or meditation to bestow blessing.

170

Those who write a blessing at the end of a letter but who lack the spiritual power to make it real, waste their time. Those who read the feeble words may feel pleasantly hopeful but are the victims of their own imaginations.

171

He feels infinity with others and that is enough reason to include them in the circle embraced by his meditation. He needs no other reason.

172

He who is a follower of this Path may help another by holding a mental picture of him in his own thought at the end of meditation, and by invoking the protective blessing of the Overself upon his name in prayer.

173

The quick recovery of a loved one prayed for in the silence is a remarkable illustration of the power of the spirit. Before such a circumstance he must indeed humble himself. While he was going through great agony, all the time his Higher Self was present in him. It gave him the chance to react in a higher way than the conventionally egoistic one. By rising to the occasion, he too could benefit as well as the one whom he loved.

174

There was the case of a man who lost his leg in the war. What could a student do for his friend? The thing he could do would be to hold him, when finishing a prayer or a meditation, in the thought of the Infinite Power—to hold the belief that he is completely taken care of by that Power and that all is well with him because it enfolds him. He should not attempt to work out any details such as wishing that his friend's second leg should be saved. He should leave all the results to the Power, and not introduce his personal ideas about the matter.

175

He should hold the person, the friend, or relative about whom he is troubled in this helpful and healing presence that he has found in the stillness. In this way he may employ the mystical art of intercession for another's benefit.

176

Do not give any "suggestion." All that is necessary is to pray to be used in whatever way best for the other person's spiritual benefit.

177

Intercessory meditation may be practised for the benefit of others, the illumination of others, and the healing of others. But these intercessions should never precede communion with the source; they should always follow it. All petitions are best presented at the end of a prayer, never at its beginning.

178

Both prayer and receptivity are needed. First we pray fervently and feelingly to the Overself to draw us closer to it, then we lapse into emotional quietness and patiently wait to let the inner self unfold to us. There is no need to discard prayer because we take up meditation. The one makes a fit prelude to the other. The real need is to purify prayer and uplift its objectives.(P)

179

Whereas prayer is a one-way conversation with the higher power, you being the talker, meditation is a reversal of this situation, for you become the listener. The praying devotee expresses what is in his own mind but the silent meditator is impressed by ideas from a diviner mind. In prayer man brings himself to the attention of God but in meditation God brings himself to the attention of man.

180

It is true that I have written almost nothing about prayer in my published books. This is because I thought that such an enormous amount of literature on the subject already existed. The philosophical approach to prayer, and conception of it, is somewhat different from the traditional one. It should act as a preface to meditation and as a help to prepare one to enter meditation.

181

In prayer we are trying to speak to God. In meditation we are trying to let God speak to us. There lies one difference.

182

A further difference between prayer and meditation is that in prayer, when successful, there is felt an intimacy with the Holy but not an identity with it, as is the case in the latter.

183

When prayer reaches its highest manifestation, it closely resembles meditation.

184

Every philosophic aspirant should devote a little time to prefacing meditations or studies with a worshipful, devoted, and reverent supplication of the higher self for enlightenment.

185

The praying devotee regards the object of his worship as being outside himself, whereas the meditating one regards it as being inside himself.

186

The correct order is to follow prayer with the declaration and to follow them in turn with meditation.

187

More than four hundred years ago a Dominican monk, Louis of Granada, affirmed: "Contemplation—is the most perfect prayer."

188

Prayer not only must be used as a suitable preface to meditation, but may also be effectively used as a help to meditation. Where an aspirant is unable to calm his restless thoughts, in addition to the constant daily regular effort to do so—for perseverance is part of the secret of success—he may pray to the higher self to take possession of his mind. Such prayer must be deeply heartfelt, constantly repeated, and animated by a longing to get away from the peaceless ego.

189

If there is response to prayer, who or what is it that responds? The orthodox religionist believes that it is a personal and interested God with whom he establishes contact in prayer. The philosophical religionist knows that it is his own higher self, his divine soul, that he reaches. All that the first expects in the way of consolation strength and help from his personal God, the second also expects from his own soul. Thus the results in practice are somewhat the same; it is the interpretation of their origin that differs.

190

Prayer begins to make itself heard and get itself answered when the praying one begins to penetrate his own within-ness, to experience his own spiritual selfhood. For the only God he can reach, and the only one who will help him, is the God in him, the Overself.

191

From the moment that a man looks for God in himself, his prayers begin to have a chance of being heard. When, before that moment, he looked for God as far off, outside of and unconnected with himself, the prayers were unable to make themselves heard and consequently unable to get answered.

192

It seems to be a law of the inner life that we have to ask for the inner help that is needed long long before it begins to manifest.(P)

193

Whether this effective power be deep within the inner self or out beyond in the universe is more of theoretical concern than practical; what matters is that it really does exist and we really can at times enter into active relation with it by an inner act. And that act is expressed through prayer in some cases or meditation in others. If all the conditions created by us are right, the response of the medium of power will be reciprocal and effectual, thus augmenting our own power in connection with our need.

194

His prayers and longing, his aspirations and yearnings are not in vain. They are all heard, let him be assured of that. But their fulfilment must necessarily come in the Overself's time, not his own. A seed cannot shoot up all at once into a tree. The processes of growth in nature satisfy the criterions of soundness, although they dismay the criterions of sentimentality.

195

The answer to prayer may come in a wholly unexpected way that we neither desire nor like. It may come as an apparent misfortune, for that may be the real "good" for us just then.

196

If the response to prayer could set aside universal laws for the sake of those who pray, then the universe would become a chaos.

197

Even where prayer is correct in form and spirit, it may be followed up by an incorrect attitude. Many are the cases I have observed where this has happened, where half the answer has already come in internal guidance or external contact with some man or book or circumstance but, because the mind had been made up beforehand to a preconceived solution, it was not recognized for what it was, and was either ignored or rejected.

198

He may carry such problems into his prayers. The answers do not necessarily come at the time of the prayer itself, but may only come some time later, maybe days or even weeks later.

199

Such is the untouched depth of the human being that when a man prays to God he really prays to himself, his Overself.

200

The praying ego will have its prayer answered if it gets taken up momentarily by the Overself, and swallowed by it. But although the answer will be the right one, it may not be the desired one.

201

The Power to whom prayer should be addressed—for Its Grace, Its Self-Revelation and Guidance—is one's own higher self, the Overself.

202

In praying, the aspirant should direct his prayer to the only God he can *know*, that is, the God-Principle within himself—his own Divine Soul.

203

The man who finds God within himself feels no need to pray to a God who is to be sought and addressed outside himself.

204

Where the response to prayer is so direct definite and unmistakable, it is mostly because the devotee has touched this infinite power through and in his Overself. This does not mean that the Deity has intervened to set laws, decrees, or circumstances aside for this one man's personal benefit. It means rather that he has himself drawn on his own latent godlike capacity. This can happen only when the attitude of prayer becomes so intense and so concentrated that it is really a form of meditation.

205

If the sincere desire of his heart is echoed by a prayer that expresses humility and requests guidance, it will be heard. Although he may receive no answer for quite a time, sooner or later it will come.

3

HUMILITY

The need

We complain that there is no response to our prayer for uplift or light. But that is because there is no propriety in our approach. The intellectually gifted comes with his arrogance and the artistically gifted with his vanity, while each man comes with his pride. The correct approach was described by Jesus: "Become as a little child"; for then we become humble, feel dependent, and begin to lay the ego aside. With that the door to the Overself opens and its grace begins to shine through.

2

The need of self-humbling before the Overself (which is not the same as self-humbling before other men) is greatest of all with the aspirant of an intellectual type. The veil of egotism must be lifted, and with his own hand pride must be humbled to the dust. So long as he believes he is wise and meritorious for entertaining spiritual aspiration, so long will the higher self withhold the final means for realizing that aspiration. As soon as he believes he is foolish and sinful the higher self will begin by its Grace to help him overcome these faults. Then, when his humility extends until it becomes a realization of utter helplessness, the moment has come to couple it with intense prayer and ardent yearning for Divine Grace. And this humility towards the higher self must become as abiding an attitude as firmness towards the lower one. It must persist partly because he must continually realize that he needs and will forever need its Grace, and partly because he must continuously acknowledge his ignorance, folly, and sinfulness. Thus the ego becomes convinced of its own unwisdom, and when it bends penitently before the feet of the Overself it begins to manifest the wisdom which hitherto it lacked. Instead of wasting its time criticizing others, it capitalizes its time in criticizing itself. In old-fashioned theological language, he must consider himself an unworthy sinner and then only does he become able to receive Grace. He should measure his spiritual stature not by the lower standards of the conventional multitude, but by the loftier standards of the Ideal. The one may make him feel smug, but the other will make him feel small.

3

Concentration is often a passport to spiritual attainment, but it needs the visa of Humility to make it an impeccable document.

4

We must be humble enough to recognize how imperfect we are, but instructed enough to recognize that the ego-covered part of us is shiningly divine. Thus both humility and dignity must be brought together in our make-up and reconciled and balanced.

5

Undue humility can be a fault, although not so repugnant a fault as undue arrogance. The first trait underestimates itself and thus refrains from what it clearly ought to attempt. The second overestimates itself and tries to do what it lacks the fitness for. Moreover, the first is too apt to depend on others until it becomes incapable of leading an independent life, while the second is too slow to seek expert advice which might save it from falling into failure or error.

6

What the ego's pride cannot do, the Overself's humility may. It is always worth trying this better way, even if it be a self-mortifying way.

7

Rare is the person who can witness his ego crushed to the ground and yet never forget his divine parentage, so that his mental equilibrium is not broken—who can be lifted up to the glorious heights of the Overself and yet remain humbly human.

8

Let us have enough courage to face life yet let us not forget the need of enough humility to face our creator.

9

"Thou standest not by thine own strength—from the invisible art thou sustained each moment."—*Bustan* of Saadi

10

If the need to communicate either in prayer or in meditation with that higher power is not felt by a man, his intellect may be too powerful or his pride too strong.

11

The last lesson to learn is an ancient one: be willing to be humble. For it was refined in pitiless fire and shaped by a holy communion.

12

There is no entry here for the proud, the conceited, the self-pedestalled. They must first be humbled, shorn, and shamed. They must drop to the ground on their knees, must become weeping beggars and wounded mendicants.

13

If he presents a firm assured face to the world, to protect his place in it, he presents a far humbler one to the Overself.

14

The proud heart of man must be humbled before the Overself will reveal itself to him.

15

There are certain times and certain experiences which a man must approach humbly and uncritically if he is to benefit by them.

16

Somewhere along this Quest humility and modesty become necessary acquisitions.

17

What is all our knowledge but trivial scratches in the sand?

18

When we come to know more fully and more really what we are, we have to bow, humbled, in heartfelt adoration of the Mind of the World.

19

Humility is needed, yes, but it should not be misplaced. It is not in self-effacement before other men nor in abasing oneself before them that we advance spiritually, as so many ignorantly think, but in self-effacement and self-abasement before the Divine.

20

The humility needed must be immensely deeper than what ordinarily passes for it. He must begin with the axiom that the ego is *ceaselessly* deceiving him, misleading him, ruling him. He must be prepared to find its sway just as powerful amid his spiritual interests as his worldly ones. He must realize that he has been going from illusion to illusion even when he seemed to progress.(P)

21

The Long Path seeks humility in order to abase and thin down the ego. But although pride is full of ego, even humility implies you are still thinking about it.

22

Let him not mistake mere timidity for true humility.

23

Do not confuse true humility with the false modesty which deprecates its own status.

24

Yet this repentance, this remorseful conviction of our personal un-worthiness, ought not to paralyse our hopes for the future by stamping us with an inferiority complex.

25

It is so difficult to make a success of success. When the head is turned by it or swelled with it, danger appears and failure may follow.

26

He should not imagine that he is being humble when he is merely being servile.

27

There is a difference between the morbid and exaggerated self-abase-ment often found in ascetic circles and this true humbleness.

28

He will bow to nothing that is visible.

29

There are a number of people who call themselves "advanced" but the truth is that they have merely advanced into a cul-de-sac, whence they will one day have to return.

30

Let us be humble where it is right to be so but let us not forget that when humility becomes personal cowardice and disloyalty to truth, then its virtue is transformed into vice.

31

If he is over-sensitive to other persons to the point of always yielding to their wishes, always saying only what will please them, and that without emotional conflict or mental indecision, then his self-damaging condition is a false and futile egolessness.

32

No man need take himself so seriously that he thinks the world's happi-ness or understanding depends on him. The world found these things before he was born and can find them again.

33

If the spiritual preferment which grace seems to indicate inflates his vanity, then one day it will desert him.

34

It is an ironic truth that on every level of development, from the most primitive to the most cultivated, from the most materialistic to the most spiritual, every man says, "I know!" He says this either quite openly in discussion or quite unconsciously in attitude. Real humility is a rare quality. This amazing arrogance is generally self-justified by supporting experiences or vindicating feelings of the individual himself.

35

It is good to enrich intelligence but not at the cost of increasing spiritual pride. It is well to enjoy the glad uplifts of mystical presence but the afterglow ought to make him humbler still.

36

With the personal arrogance that credits all its powers to itself, he will surely lose them. With the personal humility that refers them to their true source, he will not.

37

"Convict our pride of its offense in all things, even penitence."—W.H. Auden

38

Too often the quester, after a certain number of years, wants to be admired for his magnificent spirituality. But too often, in another mood, he enters the confessional to be humiliated for his great egoism.

39

Spiritual pride has rightly been listed by the Christian saints as a source of deception, and as the last of the traps into which the would-be saint can fall. A man may be quite holy and well self-controlled, but if he notices these two attainments with self-complacency, or rather self-congratulation, he at once strengthens the ego—although he transfers his excellence from worldly to spiritual matters.

40

The simple recognition of one's own stature need not become a matter for pride or conceit.

41

It is a false humility and moral cowardice that lead a man to pretend he does not know how tall he is.

42

There are mystics who have developed a considerable depth of meditation. They come back from their session of practice feeling the peace they have touched, but at the same time they come back smugly satisfied with the experience and especially with the attainment it seems to point towards. This is not enough. Even if they go apparently to the apex of the stillness, the ego has travelled with them. They may be aware of where they have been, but they were aware that they were aware. Thus there was duality in what *they* thought was unity. Do not praise the ego for having found God. It was Grace which brought about the discovery. It was not the ego. It is true that the beginner needs humility but it is even more true that the advanced man needs even more humility.

The practice

43

Humility, sensitivity, and emotional refinement are essential qualities which must be developed. Even more necessary is the daily practice of humble worship, devotion, and prayer.

44

The cultivation of reverential, prayerful, humble worship is needed to attract Grace. The putting aside of pride, self-conceit, and complacency is indispensable in order to assume the correct attitude during such worship. At such a time the saying of Jesus "Except ye be as a little child . . ." is directly applicable. The shy reticence of the Overself cannot be overcome without utter humility on the practitioner's part. Of course, this is the attitude to be adopted during devotions, not during worldly activity.

45

Man naturally shrinks from acknowledging frankly his defects and mistakes, his weaknesses and vanities. Yet such acknowledgment is the beginning of his salvation.

46

What are the attributes of a little child? A child has a flexible mind. It has not become mentally set or prejudiced by a collection of conceptions about life. It is fresh. Its head is not stuffed with a lot of so-called education. It is ready to learn—in fact, it is learning all the time. And the child has also a simplicity of spirit. It does not become complicated, tied up with all sorts of conjectures imposed by societies or families or newspapers. It has not become prejudiced by caste or environment. Moreover the child has not yet developed the strong sense of personality which adults have. Above all, the child is humble, it is teachable, it is willing to learn. This is what we need too. Humility is the first step on this path. We should realize how little we really know when confronted by the great mysteries of life. And even what we believe we do know, we cannot be too sure of in an age when the doctrine of relativity has undermined our bases. We must understand that what seems true today may seem false tomorrow. Many of the most widespread truths of last century have now been thrown overboard. Don't hold any doctrine too tightly.

47

Some seekers seize the goddess Truth by the throat and would fain strangle her in their efforts to embrace; I would suggest to them that to yield the hand to her like a child and to be led may compass their designs more quickly and surely.

48

To be humble is to be willing to admit the galling fact that one's own shortcomings of character or intelligence (and not other people's) were mostly responsible for most of one's troubles.

49

The higher he climbs, the humbler he becomes. Only he will not make an exhibition of his humility to the world, for it is not needed there and might even harm him and others. He will be humble deep down in his heart where it is needed, in that sacred place where he faces the Over-self.(P)

50

The practice of humility, especially in the form of obedience in monastic systems, is intended to subjugate the personal will and lessen self-love.

51

He has to kneel before his higher self and confess how weak, how ignorant, and how foolish a being he is. And then he has to pray for grace, to ask like a beggar for a little strength light and peace. Such daily recurring prayer is only a beginning of what he has to do but it is a necessary part of that beginning.

52

These great truths require great humility in a man to receive them. The bigoted and the prejudiced lack it.

53

He must be humble enough to admit errors in thought and conduct, never hesitating to retrace his steps when on the wrong road.

54

Let him not cover his weaknesses nor pretend to be what he is not.

55

Only so far as he is willing to confess his failings and shortcomings is there hope to remedy them. Herein lies the true esoteric importance and value of the exoteric practice of "confession of sins." (But this is no justification of the particular forms and historical abuses which such a practice has assumed in certain religions.)

56

The chief value of such confession lies in the ego giving up its habitual self-justification, the everlasting alibi-finding, its complacent and smug acceptance of itself. Such confession gives a jolt to the ego's vanity and self-righteousness by exposing its own weakness.

57

Such confession of sinfulness, wrong thinking, bad character, and mistaken deeds is valuable not only because it brings these defects to the surface and exposes them to the full light of conscious attention, but also because its effects upon the penitent himself are so humbling.

58

The days when he could speak glibly and assuredly on the most recondite phases of spirituality gradually go. A new humility comes to him.

59

It is safer to plead guilty than to give ourself the benefit of the doubt about our weaknesses. Let us confess them and tread on the ego's pride, even if they are not clear or strong.

60

Humility: See all men and women according to the Holy Ghost that is within them; always remember that the outer picture is still being worked on.

61

By maintaining the humility of the learner and the questing spirit of a seeker, he improves his own usefulness as a channel to help other people.

62

At first this humbling sense of his own sorry insufficiency will overwhelm him. He sees himself at his worst. Remorse for the past, anguish over the present, hopelessness for the future will momentarily blacken his outlook. This is a necessary step in the purificatory movement of his quest.

63

We must first acknowledge our guilt, we must have the courage to confess our errors and cast out our self-righteousness, before we can hope to start the new life aright.

64

With the onset of this overpowering sense of sin and in the hypercritical examination of conscience which it induces, he will react gloomily against, and condemn severely, his whole past.

65

His attitude need not be utterly pessimistic. He may say to himself, "If I have made a mistake, very well; I am undergoing a process of spiritual trial and error. Some errors are inevitable, but I shall catch up with them, study them, understand their results, and wring their meaning and their lessons out of them. In that way they will become steps which I shall mount towards Truth. If I suffer calamities of my own making, I will stand aside, calm, impersonal, and detached, and take the sting out of them by this ego-free attitude. In the long-range point of view it is not what I want but what I need that matters; and if I need the correction of adversity or calamity it is better that I have it."

66

The nearer his understanding comes to this higher Self, the humbler he becomes and the less likely is he to boast about this uncommon condition.

67

He needs to cultivate some degree of inward humility. There may be a tendency in his disposition to be somewhat strongly self-centered, proud, and overconfident. The best way and the quickest way in which he could begin to cultivate such humility would be through becoming a child again in the act of prayer.

68

There is much that we must let stand as inexplicable, must accept as a mystery, and thus avoid falling into the trap of smooth intellectual theories. We ought not demand what the human mind, because it is finite, has no right to demand.

69

For the man who has a strong ego, the religious approach with its cultivation of humility, its confession of sinfulness, and its redirection of emotion away from personality is the best to be recommended, if accompanied by some of the Philosophical Discipline's restrictions of the ego. However, such a person usually refuses to drink the medicines he most needs and therefore continues to remain involved in troubles of his own creation.

70

He must accept the chagrin of humbled pride, the bitter taste of self-accusing truth.

71

At such a time he feels that his entire past was a horrible series of self-deceptions.

72

To confess sins of conduct and shortcomings of character as a part of regular devotional practice possesses a psychological value quite apart from any other that may be claimed for it. It develops humility, exposes self-deceit, and increases self-knowledge. It decreases vanity every time it forces the penitent to face his faults. It opens a pathway first for the mercy and ultimately for the Grace of the higher Self.

73

He has emotionally to crawl on hands and knees before the higher power in the deepest humility. This kills pride, that terrible obstacle between man and the Soul's presence.

74

The ego must acknowledge its own transiency, confess its own instability, and thus become truly humble.

75

Humbly to accept our limitations, after long experience and repeated test, is also a form of wisdom. The innate tendencies that make us what we are from birth may prove too strong for our will to oppose successfully. Yet even if the leopard cannot change his spots, time may mellow their hard black to soft grey.

76

The Abbé Saint-Cyran's advice to a nun may be pertinent here: "It is against humility to want to do extraordinary things. We are not saints to do as the saints have done. One must hold oneself humbly in mediocrity and live in a certain disguise, so that people will see only ordinary things in you."

77

They are still frail and fallible mortals even though they are seeking and sometimes even glimpsing a state beyond all weakness and error.

78

He must come to see that his own strength is too limited, his capacity to help himself too small for a total self-reliance to be able to bring him through this quest successfully. Association with someone more advanced or, failing that, constant petition for the Soul's grace, will then be seen as indispensable.

79

Only when his ego's pride has been shattered, only when he has become depressed by future prospects and humiliated by present failure, is a man more likely to listen to the truth about himself.

80

Most of us are on the lowest slopes of the mountain; some of us have climbed to the middle slopes; very, very few have reached the peak.

81

It is not abject cringing humility but utter dependence which is called for by the Higher Power.

82

When affliction seems too hard to be borne any longer, when man has come to the end of his endurance, what other recourse has he than to fall on his knees or to cry out in humility?

83

The poignant feeling of hopeless aridity and helpless dependence on Grace brings one's ego very low.

84

When, with the arrogance beaten out of him by events which are stronger than himself, a man turns in humility to the higher power, he obeys a natural instinct.

85

When he sees how feeble are his resources and how formidable are his problems, he may see also the need of receiving help from outside or beyond himself.

86

To call himself a philosopher might be presumptuous when he is really a would-be philosopher, a student of the theory and the practice, a candidate trying for the philosophic goal.

87

To the wandering Indian *sadhu* or the cloistered Christian recluse of medieval times, Machiavelli's scorn for the person who has no social position in life is meaningless. For the holy man help must come from the higher power, not from other men.

88

Too often man has to have his ego crushed, has to be pushed into sorrow and even despair, before he is willing to turn his head upward or to bend his knees in prayer to the unseen power.

89

The more he is humbled by his failures, the more is he likely to find a way out of them.

90

A sharply critical, dryly intellectual aspirant who has had many troubles in his worldly life and physical health has had the opportunity of working out a lot of hard destiny. But it will not be without compensation if out of his suffering he develops a more religious attitude towards life, a fuller acceptance of the insufficiency of earthly things and human intellect, a greater throwing of himself into self-humbling prayer and upon the Grace. He is the type and temperament which must emphasize the religious, devotional approach to Truth and confess his helplessness. In this way he will begin to rely less on his own ego, which is his real enemy and hindrance to his true welfare.

91

When life seems to lose its meaning, when action seems in vain and ambition futile, when depression besets one like a dark cloud, the ego begins to feel its helplessness, its dependence on forces outside itself.

4

SURRENDER

In the end we have no choice. The head must bend, consentingly, to the higher power. Acceptance must be made. Some kind of communion must be established.

2

When we can fully accept the truth that God is the governor and manager of the universe, that the World-Mind is behind and controlling the World-Idea, then we begin to accept the parallel truths that all things and creatures are being taken due care of and that all events are happening under the divine will. This leads in time to the understanding that the ego is not the actual doer, although it has the illusion of doing, working, and acting. The practical application of this metaphysical understanding is to put down our burdens of personal living on the floor and let Providence carry them for us: this is a surrender of the ego to the divine.

3

If you identify with the little ego *alone*, you may believe and feel that you have to solve your problems *alone*. In that case, the burden will be heavier than it need be. But if you recognize that this planet has its own governor, the World-Mind, you need not feel forlorn, since you are included in the world.

4

Every problem that worldly men solve in a strictly worldly way leads to new ones. On this plane it has always been so. There is only one way to gain a final solution—transfer the problem to the celestial plane.

5

The ego does not give itself up without undergoing extreme pain and extreme suffering. It is placed upon a cross whence it can never be resurrected again, if it is truly to be merged in the Overself. Inner crucifixion is therefore a terrible and tremendous actuality in the life of every attained mystic. His destiny may not call for outer martyrdom but it cannot prevent his inner martyrdom. Hence the Christ-self speaking through Jesus told his disciples, "If any man will come after me let him deny himself and take up his cross daily and follow me."

6

Are we to wander with all our burdens from a hapless birth to a hopeless death? Or shall we surrender them?

7

It is when a man breaks down and finally admits that he cannot go on, that both he and his life must change—it is at such a moment that he is close to the guidance and help of the Overself, if only he can recognize them and is willing to accept them.

8

When life in the world becomes so formidable or so frightening that in desperation or bewilderment, panic or mental unbalance, the idea of suicide seems the only way out, then the time has come for a man to cast his burden on the Higher Power.

9

There is a panacea for all troubles. It is to turn them over to the Overself. This is a daring act; it will demand all your faith and all your understanding, but its results are proven. They are not available, however, for the lazy drifters and idle dreamers, for the insincere would-be cheaters of the Overself, and for the superstitious seekers of something-for-nothing.

10

Blessed are those who can find or keep this faith that, in spite of all unpleasant contradictory appearances, the course of human life will in the end be upward and the goal of human life will be spiritual self-fulfilment.

11

To try solving his problems by himself, without resort to a higher power, is to bring to bear upon them all his ignorance and unwisdom, all his faults and deficiencies, all his incapacities and maladjustments. How, using such imperfect tools, can he bring about a perfect result? How, for instance, can a muddled confused mind bring about any other than a muddled confused result of the efforts to solve his problems? How can his own unaided efforts be other than antagonistic to a correct solution?

12

He will come to the point where he will give up the burden of always trying to *do* something for his spiritual development, the burden of believing that it rests entirely upon his own shoulders.

13

The higher guidance may not be recognized or felt until after all efforts end in frustration, until the intellect retreats and obeys, until planning ends and surrender begins.

14

If you cannot see the proper way to deal with your problem, if making a right decision or coping with a difficult situation seems too much for you, if all the usual guides to action prove insufficient or unhelpful, then it is time to hand the trouble over to the Superior Power.

15

When a sensitive man loses faith in his own goodness, and even his own capacities, to the point of despairing hopelessness, he is really ready to pray properly and practise utter dependence upon the Higher Power's grace. When he realizes that the evil in himself and in other men is so deep and so strong that there is nothing below the surface of things he can do, he is forced to turn to this Power. When he abandons further trust in his own nature and clings to no more personal hopes, he really lets go of the ego. This gives him the possibility of being open to grace.

16

When a person is converted from one religion to another which is more ancient, more grandiose, or when a sceptic turns religious before dying, it is because he has reached a point when he feels helpless and his defenses have broken down. He must depend on other men, on other powers than his own, for now he has none. He is like a man lost in the desert, eager to accept anyone, any living thing, as a rescuer. What has happened? The profounder answer is that his ego has been completely crushed and he is ready to surrender.

17

The surrender of every problem as it arises to the higher self, the renouncing of personal will in the matter, and the readiness to accept intuitive guidance as and when it comes provide a superior technique and yield better results than the old ways of intellectual handling and personal planning alone.

18

So long as he is more afraid of giving up the ego than he is desirous of gaining the consciousness beyond it, so long will he dwell in its gloom.

19

He who has not learned to lower his head before the higher power, to surrender his personal aims to the World-Idea, to submit his desires to the need for self-governance, will suffer in the end.

20

Having worked to the utmost upon himself, but finding that a stable spiritual consciousness still eludes him, he has no recourse except to submit his further development to a higher power than his own will and then wait and let it work upon him.

21

Submit to the World-Idea—or suffer. Resign yourself to the higher course of things: go along with it—and be at peace!

22

When the ship on which the Muhammedan mystic Ibrahim ibn Adham was travelling was endangered by a storm, his companions begged him to pray for help. He retorted: "This is not the time to pray, it is the moment to surrender."

23

What the Hindus call detachment and what the Muhammedans call submission to God's will are really one and the same.

24

If we concentrate attention only on the miseries and distresses which afflict us, then we have to depend on our own intellect to find a way out of them. If, however, we turn concentration in the opposite direction, that of the Overself, and deposit our troubles there, we gain a fresh source of possible help in dealing with them.

25

When it seems humanly impossible to do more in a difficult situation, surrender yourself to the inner silence and thereafter wait for a sign of obvious guidance or for a renewal of inner strength.

26

In the end, after many a rebellion, he learns to trust God and accept his lot, like a tired old man.

27

To surrender is to know one's own incompetence and to put one's life in wiser hands.

28

No one finds that the pattern of his experience of life conforms to what he wished for in the past or wishes for now, so everyone in the end must learn acceptance.

29

The passage from black despair to healing peace begins with learning to "let go." This can refer to the past's crippling pictures, the present's harsh conditions, or the future's grim anticipations. To what then can the sufferer turn? To the Overself and its divine power.

30

The resignation which is advisable when circumstances are unalterable need not be a grim and hopeless one.

31

He has tried to manage his life by himself through all these years, but the results have been too deplorable too frequently. Is it not time to let the Overself take over?

32

When he has exhausted every means of finding a right and reasonable solution to his problem, it is time to hand it over to the higher self. Let him not indulge in self-pity under the delusion that he is indulging in self-abasement. There is a total difference between the two emotional attitudes, for the first will only weaken his capacity for the spiritual quest whereas the second will only strengthen it.

Avoid self-deception

33

There are great dangers in falling into a supine attitude of *supposed* submission of our will, an attitude into which so many mystics and religionists often fall. There is a profound difference between the pseudo-surrendered life and the genuine surrendered life. It is easy enough to misinterpret the saying "Thy will be done." Jesus, by his own example, gave this phrase a firm and positive meaning. Hence this is better understood as meaning "Thy will be done *by me*." A wide experience has revealed how many are those who have degenerated into a degrading fatalism under the illusion that they were thereby co-operating with the will of God; how many are those who have, through their own stupidity, negligence, weakness, and wrong-doing, made no effort to remedy the consequences of their own acts and thus have had to bear the suffering involved to the full; how many are those who have failed to seize the opportunity presented by these sufferings to recognize that they arose out of their own defects or faults and to examine themselves in time to become aware of them and thus avoid making the same mistake twice. The importance of heeding this counsel is immense. For example, many an aspirant has felt that fate has compelled him to work at useless tasks amid uncongenial surroundings, but when his philosophic understanding matures, he begins to see what was before invisible—the inner karmic significance of these tasks, the ultimate educative or punitive meaning of those environments. Once this is done he may rightly, and should for his own self-respect, set to work to free himself from them. Every time he patiently crushes a wrong or foolish thought, he adds to his inner strength. Every time he bravely faces up to a misfortune with calm impersonal appraisal of its lesson, he adds to his inner wisdom. The man who has thus wisely and self-critically surrendered himself may then go forward with a sense of outward security and inward assurance, hopeful and unafraid, because he is now aware of the benign protection of his Overself. If he has taken the trouble to understand intelligently the educative or punitive lessons they hold for him, he may then—and only then—conquer the evils of life, if at the same time of their onset, he turns inward at once and persistently realizes that the divinity within offers him refuge and harmony. This twofold process is always needful and the failures of Christian Science are partially the consequence of its failure to comprehend this.(P)

34

Most people who state that they have submitted their financial affairs to a higher power find things going from bad to worse. This point must be clarified. There is not actual surrender, but only self-deception, if it is made before reason, will, and self-reliance have been exhausted. There is no such easy escape out of difficulties, financial or otherwise, as mere verbal assertion of surrender. Education comes by negotiating difficulties, not by running away from them in the name of surrender. True surrender can only be made when one is mature enough. Life is a struggle for all; only the wise struggle ego-lessly, but they struggle all the same. They have to because the adverse element in Nature is forever at war, tearing down where they build, stimulating strife where they give peace, and enslaving minds where they lead to freedom.

35

There are those who believe that the mystical surrender to God's will means that they are to sit with folded hands, inert and lethargic. They believe also that to co-operate with Nature, to alter or to interfere with it, is blasphemous. It is not for them to try to make other men better, although they do try to make themselves better. Because they see that they can do little in every direction, they decide to do nothing. The humility behind this view must be appreciated, but the lack of rationality may not.

36

Giving up the ego does not require us to give in always to other people. That would be weakness.

37

This surrender of the future does not imply idleness and lethargy. It does imply the giving up of useless worry, the abandonment of needless anxiety.

38

If anyone refrains from using his own initiative and depends on the Overself for answers to his questions, for solutions to his practical problems before he is psychologically ready for such dependence, then he invites trouble.

39

The intuitive sensitivity of the artist and the discriminating intellect of a scientist are needed to keep that delicate balance which knows when to assume responsibility for one's own decision, action, and life and when to shift this responsibility to a higher power. The novice's statement that he commits his life into God's hands is not enough, for obviously if he continues to repeat the same foolish judgements and the same guilty conduct as before this commitment, his life still remains in the personal ego's hands. If his commitment is to be effective, it must be accompanied by the duty of self-improvement. Surrender to a higher power does not relieve him of this duty; on the contrary, it compels him more than ever before to its carrying out. The shifting of personal responsibility is achieved only when the awakening of consciousness to the higher self is itself achieved. The mere desire and consequent say-so of the aspirant does not and cannot become factual until then. He may seek to relieve himself of the pressure of obligation and the irritation of obstacles by this device, but the relief will be merely fictional and not factual.(P)

40

Such a prudent aspirant will surrender himself to no exterior organization but only to the interior Overself. He will permit no human group to annex his will and direct his thought, for they are to serve the Divine alone.

41

Surrender to the Higher Self is one thing; apathetic resignation to life is another. The one act gives birth to, or is the consequence of, mystical intuition. The other merely shuts out or prevents the arisal of such intuitions.

42

All talk of doing God's will becomes meaningful only if we are ourselves aware of God's existence. All talk of trust in God is meaningless if we are ourselves unaware of God's presence.

43

This practice must not be abused. It is premature and wrong to try to hand over a problem to the higher power before it has been thoroughly analysed and impersonally related to the causative factors within oneself.

44

We render much lip service to the theme of doing God's will; hundreds of writers, speakers, and clergymen utter its praise; but how few take a practical opportunity of giving it real expression by giving up the ego.

45

It is correct that we may trust absolutely to the higher power. But mystics should first be sure that they have found it and are not merely trusting some subconscious aspect of their ego. Otherwise they will be abusing the principle of inner guidance, falsifying the doctrine of inner light, even though they feel they are acting correctly in their own judgement.

46

It is a bias of certain religious persons to attribute to the will of God what is plainly the work of ego, or weather, or circumstances.

47

We must look within ourselves for the deliverance of ourselves. Nowhere else can we find it and no one else can effect it.

48

If the problem is really handed over to the Higher Power he is released from it. This lifts the feeling of being burdened with it. But if the feeling still remains, then he has deceived himself, has not truly committed it except outwardly in mumbled words.

49

If he is to surrender the conscious will, it should be only to the divine will.

50

The surrender to the Overself must not be misinterpreted as surrender to lethargy, to lack of initiative, or to absence of effort. It means that before initiative rises and before effort is made, a man will first look to the Overself for inspiration. When such inner guidance and rational thinking speak with united voice, then he can go forward with a plan, a faith, or a deed, sure and unafraid and confident.

51

To cast our ultimate reliance on the universal mind which, supporting all things as it does, can well support us, is a rule that works unfailingly. Only it must not be practised prematurely, for then the man will have the mere show of the thing instead of the real thing itself. He must first prepare for such a relation by developing himself sufficiently.

52

Such resignation does not mean that he shall let himself be always put upon, that he shall uphold truth, principle, justice, and goodness for others but deny them to himself.

53

This turning of a problem or a situation over to God may be real humility but it may also be a cowardly evasion of an unpleasant decision or difficult act.

54

Why do these religio-mystics worry about anything happening against

God's will? Do they not believe that, regardless of what they or others may do, everything will happen in conformity with that will anyway?

55

This blind abject apathy of many fatalistic Orientals is based, not on real spirituality, but on fallacious thinking. "Because the whole universe is an expression of God's will, and because every event happens within the universe, therefore every calamity must be accepted as expressing God's will." So runs the logic. The best way to expose the fallacy lurking in it is to place it by the side of a countersyllogism: "Because the whole universe is an expression of God's will, and because every individual resistance of calamity happens within the universe, therefore such resistance is the expression of God's will!"

56

There is a right and a wrong way of surrendering the outer life. To surrender it to one's own sorry foolishnesses or hallucinations, and call them God, leads to disaster. Yet this is precisely what many beginners in mysticism do.

57

Self-surrender does not mean surrender to someone else's ego, but rather to the Overself. Merely giving up one's own will to perform the will of somebody else is personal weakness and not spiritual strength; it is to serve the fault and negative qualities of other persons rather than to serve their spiritual life.

58

He is to turn it over to the higher power. He may do this for wrong motives to evade harsh facts and escape unpleasant consequences. In this case there will be no contact and no success.

59

Self-surrender should not signify merely letting others do what they wish with him or to him, but rather letting the higher nature work within and through him.

60

It is easy to ignore the fact that the cause of one's failure is one's own shortcoming, to cover incompetence in the management of earthly life by loud reiteration of trust in Providence—in short, to deceive oneself.

61

When dependence upon grace becomes total, when all effort is believed to be useless, when personal striving is renounced entirely, then the very belief which should have been fortifying becomes paralysing.

62

"It never consists in a sluggish kind of doing nothing so that God might do all," dryly wrote John Smith, seventeenth-century English philosophical mystic, about this struggle for truth and goodness within men's souls.

63

It is not a slavish and sentimental putting up with all that happens which is required.

64

Let no one confuse the calm delightful irresponsibility of such a planless life with the vague indolent irresponsibility of selfish or unbalanced men. There is a wide chasm between them.

65

"Trust your life to God" is an excellent maxim. But it does not mean, as some seem to believe, "Think foolishly or behave wickedly and trust to God to enable you to escape the painful karmic consequences of your wrong thought or action." If that were true the educative value of experience would be lost and we would go on repeating the same sins, the same errors. If that were true we would not grow up morally or mentally.

Accept responsibility

66

The ordinary mystic who has surrendered his will to the Overself is like a man floating downstream in a boat with his eyes turned up to the sky and his hands folded in his lap. The philosophic mystic who has surrendered his will to the Divine is like a man floating downstream with his eyes gazing ahead, on the look-out, and his hands keeping firm hold of the rudder to steer the boat. The first man's boat may crash into another one or even into the riverbank at any moment. The second man's boat will safely and successfully navigate its way through these dangers. Yet both men are being supported and propelled by the same waters, both mystic and philosopher have given their self and life to the Divine. Nevertheless, the consequences are not and cannot be the same. For the first despises and refuses to use his God-given intelligence.

67

To be truly resigned to the will of God—a demand made on the Muhammedan, the Hindu, and the Christian alike—does not necessarily mean blindly accepting all that happens as perfect, unquestionable, or best. According to the occasion, it may mean one or another of these things. But it may also mean looking with open eyes and intelligent mind at the course of events in order to understand them impersonally and then, this achieved, comprehending that given the factors and persons involved, only this could have happened.

68

It is for him to do whatever practical wisdom calls for in each situation but, having done that, to relinquish the results to the higher power for better or for worse.

69

It is true that every happening in the outer life can be accepted as being good for the inner life, that the most calamitous situation can be taken as God's will for us. But it is also true that unless we ask—and correctly answer—in what sense it is good and why it is God's will, we may fail to seek out and strive to correct the fault in us which makes it good and providential. For each situation presents not only the need and opportunity of recognizing a higher power at work in our life, but also a problem in self-examination and self-improvement.

70

The indispensable prerequisite to mystical illumination is self-surrender. No man can receive it without paying this price. Any man in any degree of development may pay it—he has to turn around, change his attitude, and accept the Christ, the higher self, as his sovereign. But once this happens and the Grace of illumination descends, it can affect the self only as it finds the self. An unbalanced ego will not suddenly become balanced. An unintellectual one will not suddenly become learned. His imperfections remain though the light shines through them.(P)

71

There is surely room for both surrender and self-reliance in a healthy life.

72

Where is the evidence that this trial, this suffering, was really the divine intention towards him, and not the consequences of his own stupidity or his own weakness?

73

If a man can give up his fears and anxieties to the higher self, because he is convinced that it is better able to manage his problems than the egoistic self, because he believes in trusting to its wisdom rather than to his own foolishness, yet does not evade the lessons implicit in those problems, his surrender becomes an act of strength, not of weakness.

74

It is right to say resignedly that it is God's will when we find ourselves in misfortune. But to content ourselves with such a half-truth is dangerous. It blinds our present perceptivity and bars our future advancement. Without perceptivity, we cannot accurately read the situation. Without advancement, we repeat mistakes and duplicate sufferings. A wiser statement would add the second half-truth, whose absence imperils us: that we ourselves often are largely the cause of our misfortune, that God's will is only the universal law of consequences bringing us the results of our own thinking or doing, our own tendencies or nature. Yes, let us submit to the divine will, let us surrender in acquiescence to what it sends us. But what will it profit us if we do so blindly, dumbly, and without comprehension? Is it not better to remember that it sends us what we have earned or what we need, either for self-perfection or self-purification? And, remembering, should we not seek out the lesson behind what is sent us and thus be able to co-operate intelligently with it? Then the Overself's will truly becomes our own. Are we not as aspirants to be distinguished from the multitude in several ways and not least in this, that we must try to learn from our experiences instead of letting them be useless and futile?

75

Swami Ramdas states in his autobiography: "It is beyond Thy humble slave to know the reason. Every move Thou givest to the situation of Thy servant is considered by him to be for the best." There are two statements here which are questionable and arguable. *Every* move? For how many of them arise as a direct result of his own character or capacities or tendencies or of those he associates with? How many situations are of his own direct personal making? If any particular situation in which he finds himself is caused by karma out of a previous birth, it is an inevitable one, not necessarily the best one from a practical viewpoint. It just *had* to happen. Of course, he could turn it to good by adopting the philosophical attitude toward it, but then that is true of *every* possible situation without exception. Where all of them may be regarded as the best, none is. The word then loses its meaning.

What are the correct facts behind Ramdas' claim? Because he surrendered his life to God, and sincerely renounced the world in doing so, God certainly guided or helped him in return at certain times, and brought about situations on other occasions. To this extent Ramdas' faith was fully justified. But because Ramdas' human self was still the channel through which he had to express himself, the individual temperament, characteristics, and intellect contributed also to giving a shape to the other situations or developments. His unfamiliarity with Western civilization led quite directly to certain results of his world tour. Had he been more familiar with it, these results would have been markedly different. Yet Ramdas told me personally that God had arranged every step of his way on this tour! This is not, of course, a personal criticism of Ramdas, who is one of my beloved friends, but a brotherly discussion of a topic on which he has often written or spoken and always in this manner. His conclusions seem to me, in the light of both the philosophic instruction I have received and the observations of mystical circles I have made, to be confused. It is *not* beyond us to know the reason for some situations; indeed, it is part of our development to learn the reason. And it is *not* God who intervenes in every petty incident or trivial circumstance of His devotee's life.

Those who refuse to exercise the reasoning faculty with which the divine World-Idea has endowed them will certainly believe that it is "God's will" for mishaps, disappointments, frustrations, or ill health to happen to them which, by proper thought or care, could have been avoided or diverted. They have been confused about the fact that outside of limited free will, God's will is inescapably and compulsively acting upon them, but within that limited freedom their own will may reign as it chooses.

76

"Trust in God but keep your powder dry" was as useful a maxim in a recent century as "Trust in God but keep your arrows sharp" might well have been in an earlier one.

77

We ought not to expect man to give what he is not yet ready to give. Only in the measure that he recognizes a higher purpose to be fulfilled will he renounce the ego which hinders that fulfilment.

78

Insofar as the whole of his future must be surrendered to his Higher Self, the planning of it through his ego-mind cannot be allowed. He resigns himself to God's will in this matter because he realizes that it will bring him only what is best for him or only what is needed by him or only what has been earned by him. He believes that God's will is a just will. Yet within the frame of reference of the intuition which may come to him as a result of this self-surrender, he may allow the intellect to plan his course and to chalk out his path. The intellect may function in the arrangement of his personal life, but it must function in full obedience to the intuition, not to the ego. Hence if he makes any plans for the future, he does so only at the Higher Self's bidding.

79

Where he depends on things events or persons too excessively, they may take an unfavourable turn and he will be thrown back on himself again and again. This kind of experience, taken to heart rightly, may quicken his spiritual progress; but taken wrongly, it may only arouse personal bitterness. If he intelligently accepts the suffering that the Overself, under the law of recompense, brings him, the evil will be transmuted into good. If he blindly clings to a completely egoistic attitude, he fails to show his discipleship.

80

Before we can do God's will we have to find out what it is.

81

Where, despite his best efforts, he finds that he cannot control the course of events, he should accept it as being the higher will, the ordained destiny. Where he can control it, he should seek to learn from and obey the inner voice in what he does.

82

That is true willpower which acts from the deepest part of our being, which sets the ego aside instead of expressing it. Not only can it thrust heredity aside and master surroundings, but then only is "Thy will" done by us.

83

Both ordinary mysticism and philosophic mysticism teach surrender to God's will, in any situation. But whereas the first is content to do so blindly, the second adds clear sight to its surrender. The first is satisfied with ignorance because it is so happy, so peaceful as a direct result of surrendering the ego's will. The second likewise enjoys the happiness and peace but uses its intelligence to understand the situation.

84

Having handed his life over to the higher power, he has handed his future over, too. But although much that will happen to him will not be of his own planning, he need not paralyse his will and negate his reason. They have their place and may be used, especially to work out the details of what he is led to do by intuition, or by inner guidance.

The process

85

His destination is also his origin. But if you say that he was born in the eternal Spirit, the question arises how can time, which is placed outside eternity, bring him to eternity. The answer is that it does not bring him there, it only educates him to look for, and prepares him to pass through, the opening through which he can escape. Need it be said that this lies at the point where ego surrenders wholly to Overself?

86

So few seem to know that surrender of the ego—what Jesus called denying self and also losing life—must be absolute. It does not stop with the more obvious and grosser weaknesses, the so-called sins. It must include surrendering the clinging to religious organizations and beliefs, religious dogmas, and groups. The attachments which hold us to the self are not only concerned with material possessions and material things. They are also concerned with social conventions and prejudices, with inherited habits and traditions. We remain deluded by the self until we are denuded of the self.

87

He is to sacrifice all the lower emotions on the altar of this quest. He is to place upon it anger, greed, lust, and aggressive egoism as and when each situation arises when one or another of them shows its ugly self. All are to be burnt up steadily, if little by little, at such opportunities. This is the first meaning of surrender to the higher self.(P)

88

No candidate could enter the King's Chamber and be initiated therein into the Greater Mysteries without stooping in emblematic submission beneath the low doorway at its entrance. For no man may attain adeptship without surrender of his personal egoism and his animal nature.

89

From the day that he abandons the egoistic attitude, he seeks no credit, assumes no merit. Hence Lao Tzu says: "Those most advanced in Tao are the least conspicuous of men."

90

Attempt to use no personal power. Rather get into meditation and quiet the person more and more until you can get away from yourself altogether. Turn the matter over to the Overself in the perfect faith that it has all the power needed to handle the situation in the best way. Having done that, do nothing further yourself, refrain from the slightest interference. Simply be the quiet spectator of the Overself's activity, which you will know to be occurring by its visible results, for its processes are mysterious and beyond all human sight.

91

Do not let the ego try to manage your worldly life. Do not let it even manage your search for truth! It is faulty and fallible. Better to cast the burden on the higher self and walk by faith, not knowing where you are going, not seeing what the future is.

92

Release your problems. Work in the Silence—until the Silence rules. The Infinite Intelligence will then take over your problems—to the extent that you release them to it.

93

When the ego is truly given up, the old calculating life will go with it. He will keep nothing back but will trust everything to the Overself. A higher power will arrange his days and plan his years.

94

But before he can even attempt to surrender the underself, he must first begin to feel, however feebly and however intermittently, that there *is* an Overself and that it is living there deep within his own heart. Such a feeling, however, must arise spontaneously and cannot be manufactured by any effort of his own. It does not depend on his personal choice whether he experience it or not. It is therefore an unpredictable factor; he cannot know when it is likely to come to him. This indeed is what makes this quest so mysterious. For such a feeling is nothing else than a manifestation of grace. Hence an old Sanskrit text, the *Tripura*, says: "Of all requisites Divine Grace is the most important. He who has entirely surrendered to his larger self is sure to attain readily. This is the best method." Without the divine grace (Faiz Ullah), the Sufis say, man cannot attain spiritual union with Him, but they add that this grace is not withheld from those who fervently yearn for it.

95

The more he becomes conscious of that thing in himself which links him with the World-Mind, the more he becomes conscious of a higher power back of the world's life, a supreme intelligence back of the world's destiny. It is consequently back of his personal destiny, too, and bringing him what he really needs to fulfil the true purpose of his earthly existence. With this realization he becomes content to surrender it to God's will, to abandon all anxiety for the future, all brooding over the past, all agitation over the present.

96

No man can penetrate into the being of the Overself and remain an ego-centered individual. On the threshold he must lay down the ego in full surrender.

97

The moth which throws itself into the candle's flame has practised self-annihilation. The man who lets himself be used by the Overself does the same, but only to the extent that he lets go.

98

You will have turned over the matter or problem if certain signs appear: first, no more anxiety or fretting about it; second, no more stress or tension over it; third, no more deliberating and thinking concerning it.

99

The extraordinary thing is that when, putting aside the ego-desires, we selflessly seek to know the divine will for us in any given circumstances, the answer brings with it the strength necessary to obey it.

100

If he wants the full Grace he must make the full surrender. He should ask for nothing else than to be taken up wholly into, and by, the Overself. To ask for occult powers of any kind, even the kind which are called spiritual healing powers, is to ask for something less than this.

101

Whatever happens in the world around him, he will so train his thoughts and feelings as to keep his knowledge of the World-Idea, and his vision of its harmony, ever with him.

102

The student should not habitually think that the problems with which he believes himself beset are really as grave as they appear. If he can let go, relax, and surrender his entire life with all its circumstances, and even all its aspirations, to the Higher Power, he should then patiently await the outcome of this surrender, in whatever form it manifests itself.

103

If he really surrenders his life to the Higher Power and turns over his sense of responsibility to It, he will be unable to act selfishly in his relationship with others, but will consider their welfare along with his own.

104

If he turns his problem over to the Overself in unreserved trust, he must admit no thoughts thereafter of doubt or fear. If they still knock at his door he must respond by remembering his surrender.

105

He will learn to live by faith where he cannot live by sight, to accept happenings against which the ego rebels and to endure situations which reason denounces.

106

Jesus said, "Take no thought of the morrow." What did Jesus mean? If we know to whom Jesus was speaking and the path along which he was trying to lead his hearers, we shall know also what he meant. It was certainly not that they should do nothing at all for the morrow; it was not that they should give no attention to it. It was that they should not fret and worry over the morrow; they should accept the duty imposed upon them to take care of the morrow, but reject all anxiety as to its outcome. They should not think that their little egos must manage everything, but they should have some faith also that the higher power can operate in their lives.

107

The real meaning of the injunction, so often delivered by spiritual prophets, to give up self is not a humanitarian one and does not concern social relations with other men. It is rather a psychological one, a counsel to transfer attention from the surface self to the deeper one, to give up the personal ego so as to step into the impersonal Overself.

108

"I tell you that the very holiest man in outward conduct and inward life I ever saw had never heard more than five sermons in all his days," was the testimony of old Dr. John Tauler. "When he saw how the matter stood he thought that was enough, and set to work to die to that to which he ought to die, and live to that to which he ought to live."

109

The real meaning of these constant injunctions to practise selflessness is not moral but metaphysical and mystical. It is to give up the lower order of living and thinking so as to be able to climb to a higher one.

110

Humbly recognizing our dependence on it, we must open our minds and offer our hearts to God.

111

He renounces the possession of his own thoughts and the performance of his own deeds. Henceforth they belong to the higher self.

112

It is the poor ego which worries and struggles to come closer to perfection. But how can the imperfect ever transform itself into the perfect? Let it cease its worry and simply surrender itself to the ever-perfect Overself.

113

The shoulders of the aspirant must be strong enough to bear the bitter blows of destiny without getting bowed down. He has placed his life utterly in the hands of the gods, and he must be ready to suffer with a sublime fortitude.

114

Whether in the artist's adoration of beauty or the mystic's aspiration toward the Glimpse, there must be willingness to turn from the present state to a fresh one. This is behind that denial of the ego, to which Jesus referred.

115

If the ego is led into surrender to the Overself, must it also be led to the guillotine? Can it not continue to live upon this earth, purified and humbled as it now must be, sharing a new inner life with the Overself?

116

All that he seems to be must dissolve to let the new self arise.

117

We achieve a total surrender of the ego only when we cease to identify ourselves with it. In this aspiration is the key to a practical method of achievement.

118

We may know God only by losing self, we may not lose self without experiencing pain. This is the inner meaning of the crucifixion.

119

If a problem or a life is to be handed over to the Higher Power for management or guidance, this can only be done if the faith is there to force a real turning-around from ego to counter-ego, from intellect or passion to inner quiet.

120

He is to receive passively what Grace bestows positively. Hence the need of a surrendered attitude.

121

Practise referral of doubts, questions, needs, requests to the Higher Power. Do not depend on the ego alone.

122

To surrender life to TRUTH is to desert the baser standards of conduct which have hitherto held us. It means that henceforth we will no longer consult our own comfort and convenience, but will accept the leading of the inner Master, no matter into how hard a path he may direct us.

123

"There is a principle which is the basis of things, which all speech aims to say, and all action to evolve, a simple, quiet, undescribed, undescribable presence, dwelling very peacefully in us, our rightful lord; we are not to do, but to let do; not to work, but to be worked upon; and to this homage there is a consent of all thoughtful and just men in all ages and conditions."—Emerson

124

To turn to the Higher Power and to wait patiently for its direction or support is a good practice but it must be remembered that one can only turn to a Higher Power by turning away from the ego.

125

He begins with turning his problems over to the higher unseen Power: he ends by turning himself over to it. This is what is also called "surrendering to God" and "taking refuge in Him alone."

126

The finite mind of man can not take possession of the Infinite Power any more than the little circle can contain the large one. At the point where the two come into contact there must be surrender, self-surrender, a willingness to let go of its own self-centre, its own instinct of self-preservation.

127

To die to one's self is to let go of all attachments, including the attachment to one's own personal ego. In some ways it is like the act of passing away from the fleshly body.

128

It happens by itself, this mysterious point where his own activity stops, when he surrenders to the feeling of the grace which suddenly comes within the glimpse of his horizon, when its presence is unmistakable surrender, offered of its own accord at the bidding of thinking, but gently and peacefully.

129

What it is necessary for him to do is really to surrender his fears and anxieties, whether concerning himself or those near and dear to him, or those who, he thinks, want to hurt him. He should surrender all these to God and be himself rid of them. For this is what giving up the ego truly means. He would then have no need to entertain such negative thoughts. They would be replaced by a strong faith that all would be well with him. To the extent that he can give up the little ego with its desires and fears, to that extent he invites and attracts divine help in his life.

130

It may be helpful for him to try a new angle on his spiritual problems. This is to stop striving and to wait with surrendered will for the higher power. This power is there within him and without him and knows his need. Let him stop being tense, stop working and striving. Let him even stop studying for realization of this presence, but let him just ask prayerfully for it to take hold of him.

131

The surrendering of his life to the Overself does not depend wholly upon his own efforts. He cannot bring it about as and when he wills. He can bring about the prerequisite conditions for this manifestation. He can fervently yearn for it, but the last word depends upon the Overself, upon

Grace. The Grace comes in time if it is wanted strongly enough, and then he steps out of the shadows into the sunshine and a benign assurance is born in the heart. Of course this can never be the result of metaphysical striving alone but only of a coordinated, integral effort of thought, feeling, and action. But whoever can arrive at it will surely be able to endure life's problems as well as, and perhaps much better than, he who has to endure and struggle without it.

132

We struggle to find God, we long after what seems unattainable, and we must hold nothing back, must yield all, surrender all, until the ego melts with every fetter that belongs to it.

133

This humble self-surrender is not the same as the supine resignation of the coward. On the contrary, it is an attitude of the brave.

134

To believe in the powers of the Overself is to believe rightly, but to suppose that those powers can be attained without complete self-suppression is to believe superstitiously. Few are ever able to exercise them because few are ever willing to pay the requisite price.

135

If we turn ourselves over to the higher power, surrendering our personal spiritual future to it, we must also turn over the personal physical future, with all its problems, at the same time.

136

"Whatever you do, offer it to Me," said Krishna. This implies constant remembrance of the Higher Power, which in turn saves those who obey this injunction from getting lost in their worldly life.

137

He who surrenders his future to the Higher Power surrenders along with it the anxieties and cares which might otherwise have infested the thought of his future. This is a pleasant result, but it can only be got by surrendering at the same time the pleasurable anticipations and neatly made plans which might also have accompanied this thought. "Everything has to be paid for" is a saying which holds as true in the realm of the inner life as it does in the marketplace. The surrender of his life to the Higher Power involves the surrender of his ego. This is an almost impossible achievement if thought of in terms of a complete and instant act, but not if thought of in terms of a partial and gradual one. There are parts of the ego, such as the passions for instance, which he may attempt to deny even before he has succeeded in denying the ego itself. Anyway, he has to make clear to himself the fact that glib talk of surrender to God is cancelled if he does not at the same time attempt to surrender the obstructions to it.(P)

138

When a man consciously asks for union with the Overself, he unconsciously accepts the condition that goes along with it, and that is to give himself wholly up to the Overself. He should not complain therefore when, looking forward to living happily ever after with a desired object, that object is suddenly removed from him and his desire frustrated. He has been taken at his word. Because another love stood between him and the Overself, the obstruction had to be removed if the union were to be perfected; he had to sacrifice the one in order to possess the other. The degree of his attachment to the lesser love was shown by the measure of his suffering at its being taken away; but if he accepts this suffering as an educator and does not resent it, it will lead the way to true joy.

139

The Inner Being will rise and reveal Himself just as soon as the ego becomes sufficiently humbled, subdued, surrendered. The assurance of this is certain because we live forever within the Love of God.

140

Within his heart, he may call or keep nothing as his own, not even his spirituality. If he really does not want to cling to the ego, he must cling to nothing else. He is to have no sense of inner greatness, no distinct feeling of having attained some high degree of holiness.(P)

141

Once he grasps that the higher part of his being not only knows immeasurably more than he what is good for him, but also possesses infinitely more power than he does to bring it about, he is ready to enter upon the surrendered life. He will no longer complacently assume that his imperfect mentality is wise enough to guide him or his faltering ego strong enough to support him. He will no longer predetermine his decisions or his doings. He realizes that other forces are now beginning to enter his life and mind, and his part is not to obstruct them but to let them do *their* work. The more his own passivity meets their activity, the better will this work be done.

Its effect

142

From the time when the Overself holds this ego in its enfolding embrace, he sees how its divine power brings great changes in his life, renders great service to others, and effects great workings in their outlook without his own effort in such directions. Therefore he cannot help concluding that it is competent to do all that is required to be done, that the ego may remain utterly quiescent, the body utterly still, and the whole man unemployed, and yet every need can be safely left to the Overself for attention. Thus, without an attempt to render service, nevertheless service is mysteriously rendered. It suffices if he leaves all activity to It, does nothing himself, and plays the role of an unaffected spectator of life.

143

He who has the courage to put first things first, to seek the inner reality which is changeless and enduring, finds with it an ever-satisfying happiness from which nothing can dislodge him. This got, it will not prevent him seeking and finding the lesser earthly happinesses. Only he will put them in a subordinate and secondary place because they are necessarily imperfect, liable to change and even to go altogether. And then if he fails to find them or if he loses them after having found them, he will still remain inwardly unaffected because he will still remain in his peace-fraught Overself. This is as true of the love of man for fame as it is true of the love of man for woman. The more he looks in things and to persons for his happiness, the less he is likely to find it. The more he looks in Mind for it, the more he is likely to find it. But as man needs things and persons to make his existence tolerable, the mystery is that when he has found his happiness in Mind they both have a way of coming to him of their own accord to complete it.

144

He who puts himself at the Overself's disposal will find that the Overself will in turn put him where he may best fulfil his own divine possibilities.

145

The unfulfilled future is not to be made an object of anxious thought or joyous planning. The fact that he has taken the tremendous step of offering his life in surrender to the Overself precludes it. He must now and henceforth let that future take care of itself, and await the higher will as it comes to him bit by bit. This is not to be confounded with the idle drifting, the apathetic inertia of shiftless, weak people who lack the qualities, the strength, and the ambition to cope with life successfully. The two attitudes are in opposition.

The true aspirant who has made a positive turning-over of his personal and worldly life to the care of the impersonal and higher power in whose existence he fully believes, has done so out of intelligent purpose, self-denying strength of will, and correct appraisal of what constitutes happiness. What this intuitive guidance of taking or rejecting from the circumstances themselves means in lifting loads of anxiety from his mind only the actual experience can tell. It will mean also journeying through life by single degrees, not trying to carry the future in addition to the present. It will be like crossing a river on a series of stepping-stones, being content to reach one at a time in safety and to think of the others only when they are progressively reached, and not before. It will mean freedom from false anticipations and useless planning, from vainly trying to force a path different from that ordained by God. It will mean freedom from the torment of not knowing what to do, for every needed decision, every needed choice, will become plain and obvious to the mind just as the time for it nears. For the intuition will have its chance at last to supplant the ego in such matters. He will no longer be at the mercy of the latter's bad qualities and foolish conceit.(P)

146

He is fortunate who hears the summons from within and obeys it. For despite its demands, it brings him ever closer to peace of mind.

147

Johanna Brandt came with little money and no friends to a strange land with a work of service to humanity's physical and spiritual health. She said that within a short time, "When it became necessary to have a secretary, a woman with great executive ability stepped forward and offered her services. Her rooms were placed at my disposal for the reception of visitors." This is an illustration of the truth that whoever is animated by the quest ideal will find that whatever and whoever becomes necessary to this true and best life will come into it at the right time.

148

When Jesus declared: "Whosoever shall say unto this mountain be thou removed, it will be," he did not mean the word *mountain* to be taken literally—surely that is perfectly obvious—but symbolically or poetically. Here it signifies problems. Whoever adopts the right attitude to them, the attitude explained in the heart-lifting words of this wondrous message, will find them removed from troubling his mind.

149

Five hundred years before Jesus said, "Seek ye first the kingdom of heaven and all these things shall be added unto you," Lao Tzu, a Chinese sage, said: "If you have really attained wholeness, everything will flock to you."

150

Emotional worry, whether it be worry about worldly and personal affairs or even about the spiritual quest, will vanish if one surrenders one's life to the Overself entirely. That is the only way to enjoy real freedom from worry; that is inner peace.

151

The total acceptance of this higher will changes life for us. It affects our relations with other people and brings some measure of serenity into ourselves.

152

Once this direction from within, this reception of the Overself's voice, is accepted, whatever comes to us from without falls into intelligible pattern. It is for our good even when its face is forbidding: it is helpful even when it is painful. For we no longer judge it egoistically and therefore wrongly. We seek its true meaning, its hidden message, and its place in the divine orderliness.

153

Anxieties subside and worries fall away when this surrender to the Overself grows and develops in his heart. And such a care-free attitude is not unjustified. For the measure of this surrender is also the measure of active interference in his affairs by the Divine Power.

154

When he has made this surrender, done what he could as a human being about it and turned the results over completely to the higher self, analysed its lessons repeatedly and taken them deeply to heart, the problem is no longer his own. He is set free from it, mentally released from its karma, whatever the situation may be physically. He knows now that whatever happens will happen for the best.

155

His confidence in the reality and beneficence of the higher power will increase as his experience of its inner working and outer manifestation grows.

156

There is a strikingly parallel thought in the *Bhagavad Gita* which confirms the New Testament's injunction, "Seek ye first the kingdom of heaven and all these things shall be added unto you." In the Indian scripture, Krishna, the Indian Christ, enjoins his disciple Arjuna: "Whoever worships Me and Me alone with no other thought than the worship of Me, the care of his welfare I shall take upon myself."

157

We become free from aims and ambitions: we are able to forgo all plans and projects.

158

He will feel all personal pride and claims ebb out of his being as the higher self takes possession of him. An utter humility will be the result. But this is not the same as a sense of inferiority; it will be too serene, too noble, and too satisfying for that.

159

Such a surrender to the higher self brings with it release from negative tendencies, liberation from personal weaknesses.

160

If he attains and maintains a harmony with the Overself (for which he must pay the price of submission to it) then the Overself will help him for it is being allowed to do so.

161

Courage in the face of a risky situation, an uncertain future, a harassing present, comes easily and spontaneously to the man who surrenders his self-will and submits to God's will.

162

The Overself—when you are fortunate enough to find it—will provide for and protect you, comfort and support you.

163

He who places his mind in Me enjoys Joy!

164

Once we accept the soul's existence, faith in its power and worship of its presence follow by deduction.

165

By escaping this common dependence on the ego, he enters into a dependence on the Overself. This, in one way, is utterly blind, because it may or may not show him even one centimetre of the path ahead; for he is led, like a little child, by the mysterious No-thing that is the higher power. But in another way, it confers greater freedom, openness, and flexibility.

166

So long as he has entrusted his life to the Overself wholeheartedly, on the practical as well as on the theoretical level, why should he entertain anxious thoughts about it? Rather should he let the Overself do whatever thinking about his welfare is needed, since he has handed over responsibility.

167

He who is faithful to his inner call at all times, whether in ideals, ego-sacrifice, meditation practice, or the like, loses nothing of worldly advantage in the end—except what ought to be let go. Providence is rightly named.

168

Saint John of the Cross: "If you fail not to pray, God will take care of your affairs, for they belong to no other master than God, nor can they do so . . . . God takes care of the affairs of those who love Him truly without their being anxious concerning them."

169

The Higher Power has given us the intelligence with which to solve these matters of practical daily life. When the human will has been truly surrendered, this Power may be counted on to guide—and guide aright.

170

The serenity of the Overself never varies and consequently the man who accomplishes the complete surrender to it is unvaryingly serene and unshakeably tranquil.

171

To the degree that he can surrender his mind to the higher self, to that degree does he surrender the worries and fears that go along with it.

172

Men love their egos more than anything else, or those extensions of their egos which are their families. But if and when the lesser self submits to the higher self, which is Egohood, this love is harmonized with love for the Overself.

173

If he has really turned his life over to the higher power, then he need not crease his brow trying to work out his own plans. He can wait either for the inner urge to direct him or for new circumstances to guide his actions.

174

The same power which has brought him so far will surely carry him through the next phase of his life. He must trust it and abandon anxieties, as a passenger in a railroad train should abandon his bag by putting it down on the floor and letting the train carry it for him. The bag represents personal attempts to plan, arrange, and mold the future in a spirit of desire and attachment. This is like insisting on bearing the bag's weight himself. The train represents the Higher Self to which the aspirant should surrender that future. He should live in inner Peace, free from anticipations, desires, cares, and worries.

175

He need no longer seek things essential to his life or needful to his service; they themselves will come seeking him.

176

He has nothing more to do, at this stage, than to give up the ego and give in to the Overself. This done, all that matters will be done, for from that time his farther way will be shown to him, and his subsequent acts guided, by the Overself.

177

The notion of making up an itinerary well in advance appeals to the time-bound calculating intellect but not to the spirit-led intuition.

178

He wastes no time on recovering the past or looking into the future.

179

Only when a man has reached this harmony with Nature's intent for himself can he unfailingly trust events as truly being what God wills for him.

180

Now that Grace is at work within him in response to his self-surrender, he may cease his struggles at self-improvement in the sense that he need no longer feel fully responsible for it. This does not mean at all that he is to become so careless as to throw away all the fruits of previous efforts. If this were to happen it would be evidence of a weakening setback rather than of a true surrender.

181

His life is no longer planned out meticulously in advance; he begins to live by the day, and cannot say what he will do within a month or a year, until the time actually nears or finally arrives.

182

A time comes when there is no longer any feeling of control and resistance, and discipline and opposition, simply because there is no longer any striving for an ideal to be attained. Having handed himself over to the higher power, he has handed both struggle and ideal over too.

183

At this stage he will tend more and more to stop counting on fixed, pre-thought plans for future movement, actions, or arrangements, to let the guidance of the moment take over, through the silent voice of intuition.

184

He finds that having attained this liberation of his will from the ego's domination, his freedom has travelled so far that it loses itself and ceases to be free. For it vanishes into the rule of his higher self, which takes possession of him with a completeness and a fullness that utterly hoop him around. Henceforth, its truth is his truth, its goodness is his goodness, and its guidance his obedience.

185

He who has turned all problems over to the Overself is no longer faced with the problem of solving each new problem that arises. He is free.

186

Jesus had no where to lay his head. He wandered from place to place, teaching without price as he wandered. Wherever he went he was at home in the complete confidence that Providence was taking care of him.

187

With this serene acceptance of Life, this glad co-operation with it and willing obedience to its laws, he begins to find that henceforth Life is for him. Events begin to happen, circumstances so arrange themselves, and contacts so develop themselves that what he really needs for his further development or expression appears of its own accord.

188

When a man has reached this stage, where his will and life are surrendered and his mind and heart are aware of divine presences, he learns that it is practical wisdom not to decide his future in advance but rather to let it grow out of itself like corn out of seed.

189

His struggle for survival has ended. Henceforth his life has been entrusted to a higher power.

190

He knows, having aligned himself harmoniously with the higher power that supports the universe, that it surely can and will support the little fragment of the universe that is himself. A sublime confidence that he will be taken care of in the proper way pervades him in consequence.

191

Few know the quiet security of having this inner anchorage, the secret power generated by this surrender of flesh to spirit.

192

Those who sincerely and intelligently live according to the philosophical ideal as best they can, surrendering the ego to the Overself continually, receive visible proof and wonderful demonstration of a higher presence and power in their lives. They can afford to trust God, for it is no blind trust.

193

He will be shown some way of dealing with his problem whether it leads to overcoming or to submission, to amendment or to sidestepping.

194

Either he will be inwardly directed to a certain move with successful results, or without any effort of his own something will happen of itself to bring them about. Whether he himself makes the right move at the right moment or whether someone else does it for him, a higher cause will be at work for the man who truly relies on the higher forces of the Spirit.

195

In that wonderful state the feeling of tension, the troubling by fear, and the suffering from insecurity vanish away. Why? Because the particular problems involved have been taken over by the Overself. Also, because no negative thinking is possible in that peaceful atmosphere. From this we may deduce an excellent practical rule for daily living: surrender *all* problems to the Overself by turning them out of your mind and handing them over, but not in the wrong way by refusing to face them. (*The Secret Path* and *The Quest of the Overself* show the right way.) Jesus taught the same method in simpler language: Psalm 55 holds out the promise "Cast thy burden upon the Deity, and he shall sustain thee." And in the *Bhagavad Gita*, among the final words addressed to the troubled Prince Arjuna, there is almost identical counsel.

196

The universal power will sustain him simply because he has surrendered himself to it. Failure in the true sense, which, however, is not always the apparent one, will then be impossible.

5

GRACE

Grace is a cosmic fact. If it were not, then the spiritual outlook for the human race, dependent entirely on its own efforts for the possibility of spiritual progress, would be poor and disheartening.

2

Grace is the indrawing power, or inward pull, of Overself, which, being itself ever-present, guarantees the ever-presence of Grace.

3

There is either great ignorance or grave confusion as regards grace, some serious errors and many smaller ambiguities. There is need to understand exactly what it is, the principal forms it takes, how to recognize its presence, and how its workings show themselves.

4

Grace is the benign effluence of the Overself, the kindly radiation from it, ever-present in us. The theological use of this term to mean particular help given by God to man to enable him to endure temptation and act rightly is a serious and arbitrary narrowing down of its original meaning. It may mean this sometimes, but it also means the loving mercy God shows to man, which appears variously as enlightenment of the mind or relief of the heart, as change of outward physical conditions or a dynamic revolution-working energy acting on the aspirant or on his life.

5

Out of the grand mystery of the Overself, the first communication we receive telling us of and making us feel its existence is Grace.

6

The rejection of the idea of Grace is based on a misconception of what it is, and especially on the belief that it is an arbitrary capricious gift derived from favouritism. It is, of course, nothing of the kind, but rather the coming into play of a higher law. Grace is simply the transforming power of the Overself which is ever-present but which is ordinarily and lawfully unable to act in a man until he clears away the obstacles to this activity. If its appearance is considered unpredictable, that is because the karmic evil tendencies which hinder this appearance vary considerably from one person to another in strength, volume, and length of life. When the karma which generated them becomes weak enough, they can no longer impede its action.(P)

7

By grace I mean the manifestation of God's friendliness.(P)

8

The Overself extends its grace to all men, but not all men are able to get it. This may be due to different reasons, some physical and others, the most numerous, emotional or mental.

9

There have been many objections to the introduction of the idea of Grace in these writings. It is too closely associated with theology for these objectors' liking, too much connected with a God who favours some but neglects others. Grace was never taught by Buddha, they point out. And to those who have plodded wearily year after year along what seems an unrewarding spiritual quest, the idea either mocks their plight or is simply a remnant of theological imagination—unfactual and untrue. These critics are right in part, wrong in part. If Saint Paul used this term and concept "Grace" several times but may be thought too religious to be considered authoritative by modern seekers of a scientific bent, let them remember that Ramana Maharshi of India also used it several times and yet his bent was quite mystical and philosophic.

10

What I mean by Grace may easily be misunderstood, or only half-understood. Its full meaning is only partly suggested by the Tamil word *arul*—divine blessing—and the Greek word *charis*—free and beautiful gift.

11

Grace is either a gift from above or a state within, a help of some kind or an experience reverently felt.

12

It is a whisper which comes out of the utter silence, a light which glimmers where all was sable night. It is the mysterious herald of the Overself.

13

There are little graces, such as those which produce the glimpse; but there is only one great Grace: this produces a lasting transformation, a deep radical healing and permanent enlightenment.

14

Indian critics who reject my statements about Grace are requested to consider the meaning of *prasada*—so often associated with the greatest holy men. If it does not mean Grace of God or guru, what does it mean? I refer them also to their own scriptural *Svetasvatara Upanishad* which especially states that *prasada* is needed for salvation.

15

To deny the reality of grace is to call into question the presence, in nearly all religions, of an intercessory element—Allah's mercy, God's pardon, Rama's help, or Buddha's compassion. This element has been greatly exaggerated perhaps, or grossly materialized, but it is still there under the superstition.

16

The wicked cannot always be judged by appearances. Some illumination may suddenly be granted because of past good deeds or intensity of suffering. The Higher Self is infinitely accommodating to human weakness and, also, infinitely patient; compassion is its first attribute.

17

Grace is here for all. It cannot be here for one special person and not for another. Only we do not know how to open our tensioned hands and receive it, how to open our ego-tight hearts and let it gently enter.

18

There is a power which inspires the heart, enlightens the mind, and sanctifies the character of man. It is the power of Grace.

19

The grace of an infinite being is itself infinite.

20

The doctrine of grace may easily lead to a supine fatalism if unclearly understood, but it will lead to intense self-humbling prayer if clearly understood.

21

The sceptical view that Grace is a superstition prompted by our human self-regarding and self-favouring nature, that it could have no place on the high altitude of truly divine attributes, is understandable but erroneous.

22

"My Grace is sufficient for thee." What does this sentence mean? For an answer we must enquire first, who pronounced it and second, in what context it was spoken.

23

Those who reject the concept of grace will have to explain why the *Bhagavad Gita* declares, "This Spiritual Self reveals itself to whom it chooses," and why the New Testament asserts, "Neither doth anyone know the Father but . . . he to whom it shall please the Son to reveal him."

24

Those Indian critics who have rejected my inclusion of Grace and stamped it as an alien Christian idea do not belong, and could not have belonged, to the great Southern region of their country, with its far purer Brahmin knowledge (because less subject to admixture by repeated Northern invasion). The mystical literature of that region is quite familiar with *arul*, a Tamil word which has no other and no better equivalent than "Grace."

25

The Grace is always present since the Infinite Power, from which it originally comes, is always present.

26

Grace does not depend on God's intervention in any favouritistic or arbitrary manner. It is not an effect of God's whim or caprice. It falls like sunlight on all, the good and evil alike. Each individual can receive it, according to the quantity of obstacles he removes from its path.

27

Grace comes from outside a man's own self although it seems to manifest entirely within himself.

28

So hidden is the manifestation of Grace and so mysterious is its operation, that we need not wonder why men often deny its very existence.

29

R.W. Emerson put it pithily: "Into grace all our goodness is resolved." These were his words, as far as I can remember them.

30

That is the real Grace which depends neither upon any other person nor upon himself.

31

In the religious symbolism of the Islamic faith, the crescent figure stands for the reception of Grace, as well as for the man who is perpetually receiving grace—that is, the mystic who has perfected himself.

32

I know that many dispute the existence of Grace, especially those who are Buddhistically minded, strictly rational, and they have much ground for their stand. My own knowledge may be illusory, but my experience is not; from both knowledge and experience I must assert that through one channel or another Grace may come: dutiful, compassionate, and magnanimous.

33

If he offers himself to the divine, the divine will take him at his word, provided his word is sincerely meant. The response to this offer when it comes is what we call Grace.

34

There has been some questioning about the idea of Grace. It is accepted by the Christians and Hindus and denied by the Buddhists and Jains. However, even those who accept it have confused and contradictory ideas concerning it. In a broad general sense it could be defined as a benevolent change brought about without the person's own willpower, but rather by some power not commonly or normally his own. But because we have with us residues of former reincarnations in the form of karma, it is impossible for most persons to distinguish whether any happening is the result of karma or of Grace. But sometimes they can, for instance, if they wake up in the morning or even in the middle of the night remembering some difficulty, some situation or problem, but along with it feeling a Higher Presence and then with this feeling beginning to see light upon the difficulty or the problem and especially beginning to lose whatever distress, inquietude, fear, or uncertainty may have been caused by it. If they feel that the negative reactions vanish and a certain peace of mind replaces them, and especially if the way to act rightly in the situation becomes clear, then they are experiencing a Grace.

35

People have curious ideas about what grace really is. So few, for instance, seem to see that in opening themselves up to the beauties of nature or of music and art they would be inviting the attention of grace too. Grace is not just an arbitrary religious factor.

36

It is grace which inspires our best moves, and which enables us to make them.

37

If Grace does not exist, why does the *Bhagavad Gita* contain the statement: "To him whom the Overself chooses, to him does It reveal Itself"? And why did the early Christian Father Clement, whose writings are considered authoritative, state: "It is said the Son will reveal Himself to whom He wishes"? (The Homilies, Vol. xvii, p. 278, Ante-Nicene lib.)

38

Grace may be defined as the Overself's response to the personal self's aspiration, sincerity, and faith, lifting up the man to a level beyond his ordinary one. This working in us (as contrasted with the working *by* us) begins in deep passive stillness and ends in mental, emotional, and even physical activity.

It is true that grace is given, but we ourselves help to make its blessing possible by the opening of self to receive it, the silencing of self to feel it, and the purifying of self to be fit for it.

An unknown mysterious thing inside the self is drawing him to it. He is groping his way, but it constantly eludes him. There must be something very beautiful there, which the subconscious recognizes, for the feeling of being attracted will not leave him and only grows stronger if by remaining passive, meditative, he will let it.

Its transmission

39

If the existence of grace is granted, the question of its means of transmission arises. Since it is a radiation issuing from the Overself, it can be directly bestowed. But if there are internal blockages, as in most cases there are, and insufficient force on the man's part to break through them, then it cannot be directly received. Some thing or person outside him will have then to be used as a means of indirect transmission.(P)

40

When a person is crushed by events and falls to his knees in prayer, his ego is temporarily crushed at the same time. After the prayer has been formulated, whether aloud or mentally, there are a few moments of complete exhaustion, of complete rest, which follow it. There is then temporary stillness and it is in this stillness that the Grace which is always emanating from the inner Being is able to do its healing and helping work. At the same time there may also be a corresponding external activity of a beneficial character.

Ascending to a higher level and studying the case of the aspirant on the Quest who by the practice of meditation deliberately brings about such moments of stillness, we see that he too opens a door to Grace. At this point it is necessary to clear away some confusion which often makes its appearance in spiritual literature and most especially in Indian literature. There we find an insistent and reiterated declaration of the absolute necessity of finding a guru so that by his Grace the aspirant may be helped towards enlightenment. When I say Indian literature I mean of course Indian Hindu literature, because in the Buddhist literature this insistence is generally absent and the aspirant is told to do the necessary work and he will get the natural result. The aspirant who has silently called for help may find that his call is answered by the appearance of a book or a person or a circumstance from whom he receives the help needed at the time. In the case of the appearance of a person, this may or may not be his destined guru, but it will be someone sufficient for the moment. The point is that what is called the guru helps prepare the right conditions which allow the inner Presence to make itself felt or which let it do its gracious work. The real help comes from this Grace—from the aspirant's own spiritual being, from himself. Saswitha, the Dutch healer, once said that he used his patients' own healing energy in order to treat them. Where did this healing energy come from? It came from their own subtler bodies, that is, from themselves; but Saswitha created the necessary conditions which enabled it to be released—when he was successful.

41

Grace is not necessarily bestowed deliberately or conferred personally. It may be received from someone who does not even know that he is its source. It may manifest through nothing more than the physical meeting between these two, or through a letter from one to the other, or even through the mere thinking about one of them by the other person. But, however obtained, Grace has its ultimate source in the mysterious Overself. This is why no man, however saintly, exalted, or advanced, can really give it to anyone: he can only be used by the higher power for this purpose, whether aware or unaware in the surface part of his mind of what is happening.

42

Ask for your share of the divine nectar and it shall not be withheld from you. Indeed, those who have turned from the peaceful hearth that is their due, to move through the gloomy houses of men to dispense it, have done so because of the dark flood of secret tears that break daily through the banks of human life.

43

Grace flows in wavelengths from the mind of an illuminated man to sensitive human receivers as if he were a transmitting station. It is by their feeling of affinity with him and faith in him that they are able to tune in to this grace.

44

No one but a man's own Being gives him grace. From the moment when he lays his head prostrate before It, and returns again and again to that posture, mentally always and physically if urged, grace is invoked.(P)

45

He may receive grace directly from its source in the infinite love, power, and wisdom of the Overself, or indirectly through personal contact with some inspired man, or still more indirectly through such a man's intellectual or artistic productions.

46

The philosophic concept of Grace is different from, and not to be confounded with, the popular religio-theologic one. The latter carries arbitrariness, caprice, and favouritism within it. The former has nothing of the kind. Despite its mysteriousness, it often follows the fulfilment of certain conditions by the seeker; but even when it does not appear to do so, it is a legacy from causes set going in earlier lives on this earth. The notion that it is dispensed in an arbitrary manner by the Higher Power is to anthropomorphize that Power, to regard it as a glorified man. This is nonsense to anyone who can reflect correctly and think deeply on the Power's real nature. The notion of caprice is to make the manifestation of Grace an affair of mere whimsy, an emotion of the moment, a passing mood. This simply could not be, for grace descends from a plane which transcends such things. Lastly, the notion of favouritism is usually applied in connection with a guru, a holy man, or a godlike man. If such a man is really, fully, and profoundly illumined, he has goodwill to all other people, wishes that all shall come to the Light, not just those he favours or who favour him. His grace is always there, but men must be able to recognize him and accept it. He is *always* ready to share his experience of the divine ever-presence with everyone, but not everyone is ready to receive it. In short, grace is what comes to you from an inspired book, or a blessed letter, or a few moments of relaxation.

47

To expect help to come to us through God when it should and could come to us only through man, is one fallacy. To expect it to come through some "master" when it should and could come only from oneself, is another.

48

It is possible for someone to make Grace a living presence either through divine utterance or through extraordinary quietness.

49

Grace is not imparted by any sacrament of any church, although sometimes the state of mind engendered by intense faith in such a sacrament may open the believer to such impartation. The Quakers have several instances in their history of having received grace, yet they have no sacraments.

50

Whether he be a recipient of the Overself's healing grace, or its teaching grace, or its protective grace, the source remains one and the same.

51

Whatever and whoever an adept brings into the Overself's light will eventually be conquered by that light.

52

Grace may be willed and yet not manifest; may not even be thought of, and yet manifest. Someone hears the sound of a sage's voice, and lo! he begins to feel an inner glow without the sage seeking to do anything or knowing what is occurring.

53

No man has the right or capacity to dispense grace, but some men may sometimes be used by the higher power in effecting its own dispensations.

54

I do not use the term *grace* in the narrow sense given it by one of the world religions, that it flows to recipients only through the outward sacraments and ritualized communions of that Church, but in the wide sense that philosophy gives it.

55

It was not Christ's death that brought his grace into the human world, but his life.

56

It is not the teacher's business to impose his own will on the other, but to help the introduction and working of Grace in the other.

57

No words can re-create these moments of grace so well as music. Think of the blessed gift which mankind has received through such works as Handel's *Messiah* and Bach's *Christmas Oratorio*.

58

There has been too much abuse of the idea of special channels of grace and too many claimants have made unwarranted declarations.

59

Each time he deliberately holds loving thought towards anyone—whether disciple or not—he extends grace to that person.

60

Although the glimpse is the chief form taken by Grace, it would be a mistake to believe that it is the only form. There are other and different ones.

61

The man who fervently believes that Christ has the power to forgive his sins is not wrong. But his interpretation of his forgiver is wrong. The Christ who can do this for him must be a living power, not a dead historical personage. And that power is his own Christ-self, that is, Overself.

62

We do not mean by grace that lasting union with the Overself can be given from without by the favour of another man.

63

A master must use words to impart his teaching but he need not use them to impart his Grace.

64

The translator into German of *The Wisdom of the Overself* went to Egypt for a three-week rest to avoid nervous collapse after the death of a most beloved person, who she believed was her twin soul. While she was staying at a hotel in Luxor, various shoeshine men came there and sat outside, offering their services to guests. One day an elderly Arab appeared among them, with a striking face and an even more striking radiation of tranquillity. She was so drawn to him that she let him polish her shoes in preference to the one who usually did them. When he finished she paid him four piasters (which was double the normal payment), because she felt so comforted by his presence. He immediately returned half the money to her, saying, "The Lord will look after the needs of tomorrow. Two piasters are enough for today." He never came again to the hotel, but she constantly thought of him and his peace, to have something to save her from utter despair. After she had returned to Europe still grieving and depressed, he appeared to her in a dream surrounded by light and blessed her. When she awoke, his mental image still seemed there, but it said, "This is the last time I shall come to you. From now on you must take care of yourself." He never reappeared, but she slowly recovered thereafter.

65

That grace can come only through the benison of a minister appointed by some church, and no other channel, is mere superstition. It can come through any man who is inspired, or any book written by such a man, even if he dwells outside all churches. If a parson or a priest has himself entered into the source of Light, he can become a channel for it, but not otherwise.

66

This belief in a master's grace appears in Moorish countries of North Africa, where it is said in spiritual circles that the more time spent in the company of one who is blessed with spiritual power, the more do we absorb some of his power in the reflected form of "baraka."

67

Another channel for grace's manifestation is through circumstances. These may provide the right surroundings, the right persons, and the right happenings for it.

68

It is not for him to know in advance in what form the revelation will come, whether it will be an intuition, a strong pressure, a dream, or a particular happening, words read in a book, a phrase dropped from someone's lips, a mood engendered by music, art, Nature.

69

No Maharishee, no Aurobindo, no Saint Francis can save you. It is the Holy Spirit which saves man by its Grace. The ministrations of these men may kindle faith and quiet the mind, may help you to prepare the right conditions and offer a focus for your concentration, but they offer no guarantee of salvation. It is highly important not to forget this, not to deify man and neglect the true God who must come to you directly and act upon you directly.(P)

Karma and forgiveness

70

Some have difficulty in understanding the exact place in the scheme of things of Grace. If they believe in the law of recompense, there seems to be no room left for the law of Grace. It is true that man must amend his conduct and correct his faults; that no escape from these necessary duties can be found. But they can be done alone or they can be done with the thought, remembrance, and help of the Overself. This second course introduces the possibility of Grace. It can enter only if the first has been followed and only if the aspiration has succeeded in lifting the consciousness to the Overself. A moment's contact will suffice for this purpose. What happens then is that the inner change is then completed and the remaining, unfulfilled karmic consequence is then annulled. There is no giving of "something for nothing" here, no breakdown of the law of recompense. The ego must use its will to repent and amend itself, in any case.

71

The forgiveness of sin is no myth, but it can become a fact only after the sinner has done penance and sought purification.

72

He who has himself sinned and suffered for his sin, who has attained inner understanding of it and made repentant atonement for it, who has then felt in his heart the benign grace of being forgiven—such a person can easily extend pardon to those who wrong him and compassion to those who wrong themselves by wronging others.

73

There are three types of Grace: firstly, that which has the appearance of Grace but which actually descends out of past good karma and is entirely self-earned; secondly, that which a Master gives to disciples or aspirants when the proper external and internal circumstances exist—this is in the nature of a temporary glimpse only but is useful because it gives a glimpse of the goal, a sense of the right direction, and inspiring encouragement to continue on the Quest; thirdly, when a man attains the fullest degree of realization, he is enabled in some cases to modify overhanging negative karma or in others to negate it because he has mastered the particular lessons that needed to be learned. This is particularly evident when the Hand of God removes obstructions in the path of his work. The philosophic conception of Grace shows it to be just and reasonable. It is indeed quite different from the orthodox religious belief about it, a belief which regards it as an arbitrary intervention by the Higher Power for the benefit of its human favourites.(P)

74

By this grace the past's errors may be forgotten so that the present's healing may be accepted. In the joy of this grace, the misery of old mistakes may be banished forever. Do not return to the past—live only in the eternal Now—in its peace, love, wisdom, and strength.

75

We have the authority of Lao Tzu that there is such a thing as pardon. He says: "For what did the ancients so much prize this Tao? Was it not because by it those who had sinned might escape?"

76

Would forgiveness be an impossible nullification of the law of karma? Is there no way out of one karmic consequence leading to and creating a further one in an endless and hopeless series? I believe an answer to the first question has been given by Jesus, and to the second by Aeschylus. Matt. 12:31: "Therefore I tell you, every sin and blasphemy will be forgiven men," was Jesus' clear statement. As for the difficult problem propounded by the second question, consider the solution suggested by Aeschylus: "Only in the thought of Zeus, whatever Zeus may be." Karma must operate automatically, but the Power behind karma knows all things, controls all things, controls even karma itself, *knows and understands when forgiveness is desirable.* No human mind can fathom that Power; hence Aeschylus adds the qualifying phrase, "whatever Zeus may be." Forgiveness does not destroy the law of karma; it complements the work of that law. "All of us mortals need forgiveness. We live not as we would but as we can," wrote Menander nearly four hundred years before Jesus' time.

77

The notion of grace as given out in popular religion was helpful perhaps to the masses but needs a large revision for the philosophic seekers. It is not granted at the whim of a Personal God nor solely after deserving labours for it. It is rather more like a steady permanent emanation from a man's own Overself, always available, but of which he must partake by himself. If at times it seems to intervene specially on his behalf, that is an appearance due to the immense wisdom in timing the release of a particular good karma.

78

Just as this generation has lived to see the experience of gravity upset by the weightlessness experiences of spacemen, so in all the generations there have been those who have found the experience of karma upset by grace and its forgiveness.

79

When the ego's total submission is rewarded by the Overself's holy Grace, he is granted pardon for the blackest past and his sins are truly forgiven him.

80

Grace will shatter the power of an evil past.

81

To make the result dependent on Grace alone would be to deny the existence and power of the universal law of recompense. The need of effort can only be ignored by those who fail to see that it plays an indispensable part in all evolution, from the lowly physical to the lofty spiritual.

82

Who can tell the miraculous power of the Overself? Its Grace may lift the most degraded of men into the most exalted.

83

A man who has sinned, erred, or been mistaken much and wakened up at last to what he has been doing, will instinctively seek first for affectionate understanding and sympathetic forgiveness. The more he has strayed, the more he needs them.

84

It is not possible to have the punishment of past errors remitted until we ourselves let them go by taking their lessons fully and fairly to heart.

85

Buddha found himself in a land where degenerate priestcraft had cunningly persuaded the masses to believe that every sin could be expiated, and its present or future effects in destiny circumvented, by some paid-for ritual, sacrifice, or magic. He tried to raise the moral level of his people by denying the pardon of sin and affirming the rigorous governance of karmic law, the strict unalterability of unseen justice. Jesus, on the contrary, found himself in a land where religion proclaimed harshly, "An eye for an eye, a tooth for a tooth." He too tried to raise the moral level of his people. But a wisdom not less than Buddha's made him meet the situation by stressing forgiveness of sins and the mercy of God. "The law of recompense brings every man his due and no external religious form can change its working" is, in effect, the gist of much Buddhist teaching. "True," Jesus might have said, "but there is also the law of love, God's love, for those who have the faith to invoke it and the will to obey it." Let us grant that both the prophets were right if we consider the different groups they were address-ing, and that both gave the kind of help that was most needed by each group. Let no one deny to divinity a virtue which is possessed by human-ity. The higher self's response to the ego's penitence is certain. And such response may stretch all the way to complete forgiveness of sins.

86

The failure to appreciate the role of grace because of faith in the law of karma is as deplorable as the tendency to exaggerate it because of faith in a personal deity.

87

Such is the wonder of grace that the worst sinner who falls to the lowest depths may thereafter rise to the loftiest heights. Jesus, Buddha, and Krishna have plainly said so.

88

Those who believe that the universe is governed by law and that human life, as a part of it, must also be governed by law, find it hard to believe in the forgiveness of sins, and the doctrine of Grace of which it is a part. But let them consider this: that if the man fails to appropriate the lesson and to amend his conduct, if he lapses back into the old sins again, then their forgiveness automatically lapses too. The law of recompense is not negated by his forgiveness but its own working is modified by the parallel working of a higher law.

89

The Overself acts through inexorable law, yes, but love is part of the law. Grace violates no principle but rather fulfils the highest principle.

90

Grace can be a ripening of karma, or a response to a direct appeal to a higher power, or can come through a saint's appeals. Faith in the Power is rewarded by grace. If the appeal fails, adverse karma must be too strong. Materialists do not make such appeals, so they receive no Grace unless the accumulation of good deeds brings good karma.

91

Lift up your eyes from the ground to the sun of a justified hope. We have it on the authority of Jesus that there is mercy or forgiveness for the worst sinners if they set about obtaining it in the right way. And as you do not come anywhere near that category, surely there is some hope and some help for you too.

92

The notion that we must qualify for Grace before we can receive it may not, apparently, hold true in some cases. But even there the laws of reincarnation and recompense will supply the missing connections.

93

There is hope for all because there is Grace for all. No man is so sinful that he cannot find forgiveness, cleansing, and renewal.

The power of the Other

94

Where is the hope for mankind if there is no Grace, only karma? If it took so many ages to collect the karmic burden we now carry, then it will take a similar period to disengage from it—the forbidding task will continue throughout every reincarnation until the man dies again and again—unless the individual collector, the ego, is no longer here to claim it. But to cancel its own existence is impossible by its own efforts, yet possible by its non-effort, its surrender, its letting in the Higher Power, by no longer claiming its personal identity. The coming in, when actualized, *is* Grace for it is not his doing.

95

The aspirant who depends solely on his own unaided efforts at self-improvement will nevertheless one day feel the need of an outside power to bestow what he cannot get by himself. The task he has undertaken cannot be perfectly done or completely done by himself alone. He will eventually have to go down on his knees and beg for Grace. The ego cannot save itself. Why? Because secretly it does not want to do so, for that would mean its own extinction. So unless he forces it to seek for Grace, all his endeavours will bring him only a partial result, never a fully satisfactory one. Those who say that the idea of Grace violates the concept of universal law do not look into it deeply enough. For then they would see that, on the contrary, it fulfils the law of the individual mind's effort, which they believe in, by complementing it with the law of the Universal Mind's activity inside the individual, which they ought also to believe in. God cannot be separated from man. The latter does not live in a vacuum.

96

The destiny of the ego is to be lifted up into the Overself, and there end itself or, more correctly, transcend itself. But because it will not willingly bring its own life to a cessation, some power from outside must intervene to effect the lifting up. That power is Grace and this is the reason why the appearance of Grace is imperative. Despite all its aspirations and prayers, its protestations and self-accusations, the ego does not want the final ascension.

97

The case for Grace is that only the Overself can tell us what the Overself is, can teach us about itself. The ego-intellect cannot do so; the senses certainly cannot; and ordinary experience seems far from it.

98

No man can render himself so independent of bodily appetites and human desires that they cannot sway his judgements or decisions, unless he is inwardly supported and strengthened by grace.

99

The "me" is in us, and attempts to destroy it and to remove its existence from consciousness yield here and there only to reappear later. Only grace can effectively overcome its tyranny. Surrender to the Overself by constantly turning toward it ends the struggle and brings peace. The ego then lies, obeisant, the victim and no longer the victor.

100

It does not lie within man's power to gain more than a glimpse of this diviner life. If he is to be established firmly and lastingly in it, then a descent of grace is absolutely necessary. Artificial methods will never bring this about. Rites and sacrifices and magical performances, puzzling over Zen koans or poring over the newest books, will never bring it.

101

The closer he comes to the Overself, the more actively is the Grace able to operate on him. The reason for this lies in the very nature of Grace, since it is nothing other than a benign force emanating from the Overself. It is always there but is prevented by the dominance of the animal nature and the ego from entering his awareness. When this dominance is sufficiently broken down, the Grace comes into play more and more frequently, both through Glimpses and otherwise.(P)

102

The Holy Spirit's light alone can open his understanding and that of those around him.

103

Grace acts as a catalytic agent. Where a man is unable to liberate himself from the animal and the ego, it assists him to do so. Where rule of the mechanical responses of his senses, his glands, and his unconscious complexes holds him captive to an established pattern, it sets him free.

104

Nothing that you do can bring about this wonderful transformation, for it is not the result of effort. It does not depend on the power of your will or the strength of your desire. It is something which can only be done to you, not by you. It is the result of your absorption by another and higher Force. It depends on Grace. It is more elusive yet more satisfying than anything else in life.

105

Most things may be acquired by violent effort, but not Grace.

106

It is the power of the Other which pulls him upward out of his attachments to body and earth, cajoling him to do what he cannot do of himself—let go. This power, when so felt, we call grace.

107

Let him leave some room in his calculations for grace. The conquest of self, and certainly the negation of self, must in the end be a gift of the Lord.

108

When the ego knows that it is beaten, when it gives up its strivings, efforts, and goals, when it lies prostrate and calls out to the higher Power in despair or surrender, there is then a chance that the Grace will appear. However, lest there be any misunderstanding on this point, it must be said that this is only one way for Grace to appear, and there are other ways not so unhappy and much more joyous.

109

Where man fails, Grace succeeds. Where his ego laughs at all his efforts to dislodge it, he has to surrender it in humility before the guru or God, whose grace alone can do what his own act cannot do.

110

It is not within the power of man to finish either the purificatory work or its illumination-sequel: his Overself, by its action within his psyche, must bring that about. This activating power is grace.

111

Grace is not a fruit which can be artificially forced. It must be left to ripen of itself.

112

What he is unable to attain by all his efforts will, if he is blessed by Grace, be given him unexpectedly and suddenly when all desire for it has lulled.

113

Grace is a necessity before the ego can go up in the blaze of divine energy.

114

What Grace does is to draw the man's attention away from himself, from his ego, to the Overself.

115

Since grace does not depend immediately and directly on the man himself, on what he thinks and does, he cannot *make* a glimpse happen by any act of will. At best he can draw nearer the source of this experience.

116

Many have failed to disidentify themselves from their thoughts, despite all attempts. This shows its difficulty, not its impossibility. In such cases, grace alone will liberate them from their thought-chains.

117

When the ego is sufficiently crushed by its frustrations or failures—and sooner or later this may happen to most of us—it will turn, either openly or secretly, to the admission that it needs outside help. And what other help can it then find than Grace, whether mediated directly from the Overself or indirectly through a master?

118

The ego, the personal limited self, cannot lift itself into the Higher Self, and if the student at times has felt dismally powerless to make progress by self-effort, he will have learned the priceless lesson of the need of Grace.

119

He cannot take any virtue to himself because he did not make the change by himself. It was a gift—the gift of Grace.

120

The supreme effect of Grace, its most valuable benefit, is when its touch causes the man to forfeit his ego-dominance, when it takes away the personal obstruction to the Overself.

121

Only when the ego, thwarted and disappointed, hurt and suffering, finds that it cannot sufficiently change its own character, is it ready to beg, out of its helplessness, for Grace. So long as it believed that by its own power it could do so, it failed. And the way to ask for Grace is to sit perfectly still, to do nothing at all, since all previous doing failed.

122

Since the very "I" which seeks the truth and practises the meditation is itself so illusory, it cannot attain what it seeks or even practise with success, unless it also receives help from a higher source. Only two such sources are possible. The first and best is the Overself's direct grace. This must be asked for, begged for, and wept for. The next best is the grace of a master who has himself entered into truth-consciousness.

123

He may come at length to the disconcerting conclusion that his spiritual hopes would never be fulfilled. But in doing this he is not allowing for the unknown X-factor, the higher and mysterious Overself.

124

The revelation which brings one's own consciousness into coincidence with the Overself comes only by Grace.

125

When a man's strivings mature, the insight dawns of itself. Yet he cannot tell which day this is to be, cannot precipitate the wondrous event by his own will. For this depends on grace.

126

We need the power it gives, the understanding it bestows, and the solace it brings.

127

If he insists on clinging to the ego, he makes it impossible to know truth, approach God, or experience the timelessness of reality. Only an outer intervention can then help him, only the Grace coming direct or through some human channel.

128

"By him is He realized to whom He is full of grace," says the *Katha Upanishad*.

The significance of self-effort

129

Just as we have to look at the world in the twofold way of its immediate and ultimate understanding, so we have to find enlightenment in a twofold way through our own self-creative efforts and through the reception of Grace.

130

Grace is the hidden power at work along with his spirit's aspiration and his efforts at discipline. This does not mean that it will continue to work if he drops both aspiration and effort. It may, but more often it will not.

131

It seems a tiring and endless task, this, of tracking down the ego and struggling with it in its own lair. No sooner have we given ourselves the satisfaction of believing that we have reached its last lair and fought the last struggle than it reappears once again, and we have to begin once more. Can we never hope to finish this task? Is the satisfaction of victory always to be a premature one? When such a mood of powerlessness overwhelms us utterly, we begin at last to cast all further hope for victory upon Grace alone. We know that we cannot save ourselves and we look to the higher power. We realize that self-effort is absolutely necessary to our salvation, but we discover later that it is not enough for our salvation. We have to be humbled to the ground in humility and helplessness before Grace will appear and itself finish the work which we have started.

132

It is important to note that in the *Bhagavad Gita* the introduction of the subject of Grace and its actual descent upon the disciple Arjuna come only at the very end of the book—after Arjuna, by patient discipleship, has really earned it. Without Grace there is no entry. We may strive and weep, but unless the Grace falls on us we cannot enter into the kingdom of Heaven. How and when it should come depends partly upon our karma, partly upon our yearning, and partly upon the channel which God uses.

133

The passing over into higher consciousness cannot be attained by the will of any man, yet it cannot be attained without the will of man. Both grace and effort are needed.

134

If all his efforts are concentrated on self-improvement, then the circle of his thinking will be a small and limited one. The petty will become over-important in his own eyes and the insignificant will become full of meaning. It is needful to balance the one attitude with another—surrender to and faith in the power of Grace.

135

Constant self-effort can thin down the egoism but not eliminate it. That final act is impossible because the ego will not willingly slay itself. What self-effort does is to prepare the way for the further force which can slay it and thus makes the operation timely and its success possible. What it further does is to improve intelligence and intuition and to ameliorate the character, which also prepares the individual and attracts those forces. They are nothing else than the pardoning, healing, and, especially, the transforming powers of Grace.

136

To make any spiritual venture explicitly efficacious and to bring it to complete success, certain conditions must first be fulfilled. Most of them can be provided by the venturer himself but a few of them must come from outside himself. These are grace and favourable destiny.

137

However much he exerts his intellect he cannot reach the final revelation, the clearest enlightenment, for this is a gift of grace.

138

While he patiently waits with surrendered will for the oncoming of divine Grace, he directs conscious effort to improve himself and thus, incidentally, deserves it.

139

It is not by special intervention that the divine grace appears in his life. For it was there all the time, and behind all his struggles, as a constant unbroken radiation from the Overself. But those struggles were like the hoisting of sails on a ship. Once up, they are able to catch the wind and propulsion begins automatically.

140

Only the double viewpoint does justice to the double truth that both personal effort and bestowed grace are needed, or that both ego and Overself are present.

141

When your efforts have brought you to a certain point, then only do they get pushed aside or slowly drawn away by another power—your higher Self. What really happens is that the energy or power which you are using spontaneously ignites. It is that which enables you to do, to get done, to achieve. The all-important point is that the active power is not your own will, but is really a direct visitation of what we must call Grace. It is strongly felt, this experience of the higher power or higher Self.

142

A man can look to his own knowledge and his own actions to carry him a long distance on this path, but in the end he must look to grace for final results.

143

He cannot bring this enlightenment into being—much less into permanent being—by his own willpower. It can only come to him. But although striving for it may probably end in failure, the masses' indifference to it is worse. For whereas he will at least be open to recognize and accept it when it does happen to come, their doors of perception will be shut to it, or, bewildered and frightened, they will run away from it.

144

Man has no power of his own to command Grace but he does have the power to turn away from smug satisfaction with his own ego and throw himself at the feet of the Overself—the source of Grace.

145

He who told us to note the lilies of the field also told us the parable of the talents. Whatever the divine Grace brings us, it brings it *through* our personal effort.

146

When he becomes acutely aware both of the sacred duty of self-improvement and of the pitiful weakness which he brings to it, the need of getting the redeeming and transforming power of Grace follows logically. He is then psychologically ready to receive it. He cannot draw Grace to himself but can only invoke and await it.

147

In the end, and after we have tried sufficiently long and hard, we find that the knot of self cannot be untied. It is then that we have to call on grace and let it work on us, doing nothing more than to give our consent and to accept its methods.

148

It is a simple error to attribute to grace what properly belongs to his own nature, but it is spiritual arrogance to attribute to his own power what properly belongs to Grace.

149

If he fails but persists despite the failures, one day he will find himself suddenly possessed of the power to win, the power to achieve what had hitherto seemed impossible for his limited ability. This gift—for it is nothing else—is Grace.

150

If grace had to depend solely on human merit, if it had to be fully worked for and earned, it would no longer be grace. It really depends on the mysterious will of the higher power. But this is not to say that it comes by the caprice of the higher power. If a man puts himself into a sufficiently receptive attitude, and if he applies the admonition "Be still and know that I am God," he is doing something to attract grace.

151

When he has worked and worked upon himself as well as he is able, but comes in the end to acknowledge that success in getting rid of his weaknesses is beyond his power, he is ready to realize the need of Grace. And if it comes—for which such realization is essential—he will discover that final success is easy and, sometimes, even instantaneous with Grace.

152

If he thinks that the result depends wholly upon his personal endeavours after holiness, he is wrong. But if he does little or nothing to control himself because he waits for the Grace of God or the help of a master to come into his life, he is also wrong.

153

The idea of conquering his own lower nature solely by his own efforts does not allow any room for Grace. It would be better to find a more balanced approach. He needs to learn in his efforts that they cannot of themselves bring all he seeks. The first step to attract Grace is to humble himself in prayer and to confess his weakness.

154

When he has passed successfully through the last trial, overcome the last temptation, and made the last sacrifice of his ego, the reward will be near at hand. The Overself's Grace will become plain, tangible, and wholly embracing.

155

Belief in the reality of Grace and hope of its coming are excellent. But they are not to be turned into alibis for spiritual sloth and moral sin.

156

The strength needed for sustained mystical contemplation must come at first from his own ego's persistence but will come in the end from the Overself's Grace.

157

Although personal effort and the will toward self-mastery do much to advance him on this quest, it is grace, and grace alone, which can advance him to the goal in the last stages or assist him out of an impasse in the earlier ones.

158

First, he must attempt to lift himself upwards, taking the needed time and making the needed effort. Then he will feel that some other force is lifting him gratuitously—this is the reaction, Grace.

159

To come into the consciousness of the Overself is an event which can happen only by grace. Yet there is a relation between it and the effort which preceded it, even though it is not an exact, definite, and universally valid relation.

160

We must exert our own will and strength to prepare the way for, and make us receptive to, the divine grace. Thus the one complements the other; both are necessary parts of the World-Idea.

161

Jesus has said that it is Grace which starts and keeps a man on the way to God, even though his heart and will have to make their effort also. Ramana Maharshi confirmed this statement.

162

How can the ego's self-effort bring about the grand illumination? It can only clear the way for it, cleanse the vehicle of it, and remove the weaknesses that shut it out. But the light of wisdom is a property of the innermost being—the Soul—and therefore this alone can bring it to a man. How can the ego give or attain something which belongs to the Overself? It cannot. Only the divine can give the divine. That is to say, only by grace can illumination be attained, no matter how ardently he labours for it.

163

No man is excluded from that first touch of Grace which puts him upon the Quest. All may receive it and, in the end, all do. But we see everywhere around us the abundant evidence that he will not be ready for it until he has had enough experience of the world, enough frustration and disappointment to make him pause and to make him humbler.

164

The aspirant who cries out in despair that he is unable either to make progress or to get a mystical experience and that Grace seems absent or indifferent does not understand that he has within himself, as every man has, a place which is the abode of Grace. When I say every man, I mean every human being—which includes the vast multitudes of non-aspirants too. Just as the exhausted athlete may with some patience find what he calls his second wind, so the man whose thought, feeling, will, and aspiration are exhausted may find his interior deeper resource; but this requires patience and passivity. The need to hope, to wait, and to be passive is the most important of all.

165

Some Questers become depressed and discouraged when they learn that grace is the final essential ingredient for success on the Quest. This seems to put the issue out of their hands and to make it a matter of luck. They are taking too negative an attitude. It is true that grace is not subject to their command, but the atmosphere which attracts it, the conditions in which it can most easily enter, are subject to him.

166

God's Grace is the spark which must fall into human effort to make it finally effective.

167

We may wander about and wait for Grace to come or we may follow a disciplined way of working for it.

168

If the Overself's Grace does not come to the help of a man, all his exertions will be fruitless. But, on the other hand, if he does not exert himself, it is unlikely that the Grace will come at all.

169

His part is to open a way, remove obstructions, gain concentration, so that the Overself's grace can reach him. The union of both activities produces the result.

170

He is not asked to free himself from all feeling, nor to throw out all desire, but to attain a measure of calm. This can come through a twofold source. First, he must learn and cultivate self-control. Second, his aspiration and purification must succeed in attracting grace.

Preparing for grace

171

The fact of Grace being an unpredictable descent from above does not mean that we are entirely helpless in the matter, that there is nothing we can do about it. We can at least prepare ourselves both to attract Grace and to respond aright when it does come. We can cleanse our hearts, train our minds, discipline our bodies, and foster altruistic service even now. And then every cry we send out to invoke grace will be supported and emphasized by these preparations.

172

When his strongest passion is to make real the presence of the Soul and when he demonstrates this by the strivings and sacrifices of his whole life, he is not far from the visitation of Grace.

173

Let him feel even in the very heat of this world's activity that his Guardian Angel is ever with him, that it is not farther away than his own inmost heart. Let him nurture this unshakeable faith, for it is true. Let him make it the basis of all his conduct, try to ennoble and purify his character incessantly, and turn every failing into a stepping-stone for a further rise. The quest winds through ups and downs, so he must make despair a short-lived thing and hope an unkillable one. Success will not depend on his own personal endeavours alone, although they are indispensable; it is also a matter of Grace and this he can get by unremitting prayer, addressed to whatever higher power he believes in most, and by the compassion of his guide.

174

If he wants the grace he must do something to earn it, such as attend to the wastage of time on trivial or even harmful (because negative) gossip and activities; purify his character; study the revelations of sages; reflect on the course of his life; practise mind-stilling and emotional discipline.

175

When the Quest becomes the most important activity in a man's life, even more important than his worldly welfare, then is Grace likely to become a reality rather than a theory in his life too.(P)

176

The commonest way, the most usual way, of attracting grace was indicated by the Carthusian monk Guiges, more than eight hundred years ago: "It would be a rare exception to gain [the degree of] contemplation without prayer. . . . Prayer gains the grace of God."

177

Swami Ramdas gives the advice that the way to get Grace is to pray for it. The philosophical point of view is that one must *both* pray and pay for it.

178

It is said that grace is given only to a few chosen persons and that no matter how hard a man works on himself, unless he is fortunate enough to receive it, the illumination he wants will evade him. This teaching sounds depressing because it seems to put us at the mercy of caprice, favouritism, or arbitrariness. But the mystery of grace is not so mysterious as that. We are *all* children of God: there are no special favourites. Grace can come to all who seek it, but they must first make themselves ready to receive it. If they thirst, hunger, and seek with their whole heart and body, and if in addition they make the gestures of penance, self-denial, and purification both to prove their sincerity and to help achieve this readiness, it is inconceivable that the grace will not come to them in the end.

179

It is deeply sacred, yet could only have been brought forth through the ardent seekings and intense sufferings of a very human being.

180

A man must first recognize his weaknesses, admit his deficiencies, and deplore his shortcomings if Grace is to come to him. By that act and attitude of self-abasement he takes the first step to opening the door of his inner being to its presence. This is a necessary procedure but it is still only a first step. The second is to call out for help—whether to God or man—and to keep on calling. The third step is to get to work upon himself unremittingly and amend or elevate his character.

181

By forgiving those who have harmed us, we put ourselves in the position of earning forgiveness for the harm we ourselves have done.

182

The need for this purification arises from the need to remove obstruc-

tions to the inflow of the blessed feeling of Grace, the light of new understanding, and the current of higher will.

183

Those who are asking the Overself to give them its greatest blessing, its
grace, should ask themselves what *they* have been willing to give the
Overself—how much time, love, self-sacrifice, and self-discipline.

184

These repeated prayers and constant aspirations, these daily meditations
and frequent studies, will in time generate a mental atmosphere of receptivity to the light which is being shed upon him by the Grace. The light
may come from outside through a man or a book, or it may come from
inside through an intuition or an experience.

185

It is true that Grace is something which must be given to a man from a
source higher and other than himself. But it is also true that certain efforts
made by him may attract this gift sooner than it would otherwise have
come. Those efforts are: constant prayer, periodical fasting.

186

The man who has the courage to be his own bitterest critic, who has the
balance to be so without falling into paralysing depression as a result, who
uses his self-analysis so constructively that every shortcoming is the object
of constant remedial attention—he is the man who is preparing a way for
the advent of Grace.

187

Grace is always being offered, in a general way, but we do not see the
offer; we are blind and so pass it by. How can we reverse this condition
and acquire sight? By preparing proper conditions. First, mark off a period
of each day—a short period to begin with—for retreat from the ordinary
out-going way of living. Give up this period to in-going, to meditation.
Come out of the world for a few minutes.

188

The pursuit of virtue and the practice of self-control, the acceptance of
responsibility for one's inner life—these things are as necessary as grace,
and help to attract it.

189

Whoever invokes the Overself's Grace ought to be informed that he is
also invoking a long period of self-improving toil and self-purifying affliction necessary to fit him to receive that Grace.

190

He may fall into dismay at times but should never let it become despair.
This helps grace to come.

191

The fact is that the higher power dispenses grace to all, but not all are able, willing, or ready to receive it, not all can recognize it and so many pass it by. This is why men must first work upon themselves as a preparation.

192

What can anyone do to get Grace? He can do three things: first, want it ardently; second, prepare within himself the conditions which invite and do not obstruct it; third, meet a Master.

193

The conditions which help to make Grace possible include first, a simpler life than that of modern thing-ridden civilization; second, communion with, and veneration of, Nature.

194

The ultimate secret of Grace has never been solved by those who do not know that previous reincarnations contribute to it. Some men receive it only after years of burning aspiration and toil but others, like Francis of Assisi, receive it while unprepared and unaspiring. The ordinary candidate cannot afford to take any chance in this matter, cannot risk wasting a lifetime waiting for the unlikely visitation of Grace. He had better offer his all, dedicate his life, and surrender his loves to one all-consuming passion for the Overself, if he wants the power of Grace to flow into him. If he is unable to give himself so totally, let him do the next best thing, which is to find someone who has himself been granted the divine Grace and who has become inwardly transformed by it. Let him become such a man's disciple, and he will then have a better chance of Grace descending on him than he would have had if he walked alone.

195

The gift of grace is ever available—but on terms—yet few care to benefit by it. This is for different reasons with each person. However, it may be summarized by saying that the effort to lift self out of self is too hard and so is not only not made, but also not desired.

196

The aspiration which mounts upward from his heart is answered by the grace which descends downward into it.

197

If he makes himself worthy of grace, he need not worry about whether he will ever receive it. His earnest strivings will sooner or later merit it. And this is the best way to render its bestowal a likely happening.

198

Grace needs a prepared mind to receive it, a self-controlled life to accept it, an aspiring heart to attract it.

199

If he tries to fulfil these conditions of sincere self-preparation, and if he tries to practise service, compassion, and kindliness, Grace will come and its meaning will be found. For Grace holds a significance that is very close to love, to unselfish love. What he has given to others will be returned to him by the law of recompense.

200

Those who seek grace should do something to deserve it. Let them practise forgiveness of others who have injured them; let them extend mercy to anyone in their power or needing help from them; let them stop slaughtering innocent animals. This will really be as if they were granting grace themselves. What they give to others, they may expect to receive themselves.

201

It has been said that the Short Path is absolutely necessary because the ego on the Long Path cannot by all its own efforts attain enlightenment. The higher individuality must come into play, and that entry onto the scene is called grace. This does not mean an arbitrary intervention, favouring one person and repulsing another. It comes by itself when the proper conditions have been prepared for it, by the opening or surrender of the self, by the turning of the whole being to its source. This openness, surrender, or passivity to the Other is not to be attained by quietening the thoughts alone. The mind is open then but it has to be opened to the highest, directed to the highest, aspiring to the highest. Otherwise, there is the mere passivity of the medium, or of the thought-reader, without the divine presence.

202

If grace is tardy in coming, look to the ego's willingness to follow the path chalked out for it, whether by outer guide or inner voice. Has he been unwilling to obey the higher will when it conflicted with his own?

203

The Grace comes into his mind when thoughts are still and quiet, and into his life when ego is stilled and relinquished.

204

If he cannot compel or command grace, he can at least ask, work, and prepare for it. For if he is not prepared properly by understanding he may not be willing to submit when it *does* come, if the form it takes is not to his liking.

205

Grace, from a source above and beyond himself, is the last answer to all his questions, the last solvent of all his problems, when his own intellect fails with the one and his own management cannot cope with the other. And the first prayerful call for the gift must go forth by way of silencing the confusion within himself and stilling the tumult within his mind. The ego must recognize its own natural untrustworthiness and must pause, stop its persistent activity, in passive meditation.

206

Two things are required of a man before Grace will manifest itself in him. One is the capacity to receive it. The other is the co-operation with it. For the first, he must humble the ego; for the second, he must purify it.(P)

207

When a man feels the authentic urge to walk a certain way, but cannot see how it will be possible either because of outer circumstances or of inner emotions, let him trust and obey it. For if he does so, the Grace of the Overself will manipulate these circumstances or alter his feelings accordingly. But it will do this so as to lead to his further growth and real need, not for satisfaction of his personal desires or his supposed wants. Let him accept its leading, not the ego's blindness.(P)

208

The real bar to the entry of grace is simply the preoccupation of his thoughts with himself. For then the Overself must leave him to his cares.(P)

209

If there is any law connected with grace, it is that as we give love to the Overself so do we get grace from it. But that love must be so intense, so great, that we willingly sacrifice time and thought to it in a measure which shows how much it means to us. In short, we must give more in order to receive more. And love is the best thing we can give.(P)

210

The student may throw himself with full assurance on the mercy of the Higher Power, ask for forgiveness of past error, and pray for the descent of Grace. He will be knocking very loudly at the door of the Overself, and gradually he will find that his own weakness was but the shadow of coming strength, his own helplessness but the precursor of coming Grace.

211

In all spiritual situations where some help, light, or protection is sought, allow for the X-factor—grace. Try to invoke it by entering the silence, keeping the entire self bodily and inwardly still.

212

Confession is a good practice when it is a sincere honest recognition that certain actions of the past were wrong actions, whether they were merely imprudent or wholly evil; that they ought never to have been committed; and that if faced by similar situations again he will try his utmost not to commit them. Remorse, penitence, and a desire to make amends are the emotional feelings which ought to accompany the intellectual recognition if it is to have effective value in the future. According to custom, there are three ways in which confession can be made. There is the way of certain religions, which enjoin the presence of an ordained priest. This is useful mainly to adherents of these religions who can bring themselves to have faith in both the dogmas and the priests. But whether done in a religious atmosphere or not, confession to another person possesses worth only if that other is really of a spiritual status superior to the sinner's own and not merely claiming or pretending it. If this safeguard is present, then confession releases the tension of secretly held sins. Secondly, there is the way of some sects and cults, which enjoin the presence of a group. This too is useful only to fellow believers, and useful in a very limited way. It offers emotional relief. But it degenerates all too easily into egoistic exhibitionism. It is certainly much less desirable than the first way. Private confession done in solitude and directed toward one's own higher Self is the third way. If the sinner experiences a feeling of being inwardly cleansed, and subsequently shows no tendency to repeat the sin, he may know that his confession has been effective and that the Overself's Grace has come to him in response to the act. It is a mistake to believe, however, that a single act of confession is all that is needed. It may be, but most often such response comes only as the climax of a series of such acts. It is also a mistake to believe that any confession has any value if the sinner's ego is not abjectly humiliated and made to feel not only its foolishness and unworthiness but also its dependence on the higher power for help in attaining wisdom and self-mastery.

213

He needs the humility to admit that it is only as the Overself permits itself to be known that it is known at all. That is to say, it is only by grace that this blessed event ever happens.

214

When Christ called his hearers to repentance, he did not mean that they should leave their present state of "sin" and return to a previous state supposedly virtuous. He meant that they should leave the old altogether and go forward into something entirely new.

215

Few men find their way to the real prayer for Grace before they find their hearts broken, their minds contrite.

216

In his reception of grace, whether during the temporary mystic state or during an entire life period, he needs to be perfectly passive, unresistant, if he is to absorb all the benefit. Nevertheless, a certain kind of activity must be apparent in the early stage when he must take part in the operation by putting down the ego and its desires, attitudes, or clingings.

217

When a man begins to see the error of his ways, to repent greatly and lament deeply about them, it is a sign that Grace is beginning to work within him. But how far the Grace will go and whether it will carry him into a religious conversion or still farther, into a mystical experience, no one can predict.

218

Endorsement of the moral value of confession should not be mistaken as an endorsement of the institutional value of absolution. There are churches which require confession from their believers and which give absolution in return. The kind of confession philosophy advocates is secret, private, individual, and made in the depth of one's own heart, quite silently. The kind of absolution philosophy recognizes is grace given by the individual's own higher Self, just as silently and as secretly as the confession itself should be made. No church and no man has the power to absolve him from his sins, but only his higher self.

219

When the ego is willing to let its own tyranny be cancelled—and it never does so unless it has been crushed to the ground by the fates or by philosophy—when it comes to the end of its tether and gives up, the grace of the Overself is the response.

220

We should not egotistically interfere with the working of grace when it comes but should let ourselves be borne unresistingly and, as it were, helplessly upon its gentle current.

221

Some Oriental mystics of the Near Eastern Islamic faith often used a phrase in their talks with me that captured my attention but evaded their definition. It is easy to see why this was so. The phrase was "the opening of the heart." What this means can only be known by a personal experience. The intellect may talk and write about it but the end product will be hollow words unless the feelings talk or write about it themselves. For the experience of opening a door to the entry of grace and love must be felt personally.

222

Having done all he could do by his own strivings, being aware that he has travelled so far by the power of self-dependence, he now realizes that he can do no more except throw himself humbly on the Grace. He must wait patiently for its coming to complete, by its power transcending his own, what has thus been started.

223

Sorrow for a wrong course of life, the resolve to abandon it, and the readiness to make definite amendments are prerequisites to secure Grace.

224

As the desires depart, they leave the heart vacant for tenancy by the Overself.

225

We must make way for the Overself if we desire its presence. But we can do so only by pushing aside the objects, the conditions, and the beings who block the path into our consciousness, through our attachment to them. Removing them will not fulfil this purpose but severing the attachments will fulfil it.

226

It is not the lack of grace that really accounts for our situation, but the lack of our co-operation with the ever-existing grace.

227

In the end Nature will respond to his aspiration. Patience must be cultivated.

228

When he can come to this point and say, "Without this inner life and light, I am nothing," when he reverses the world's values and seeks the Value-less, he is ready for the initiation by Grace.

229

The internal work of Grace is only possible if the aspirant assents to the direction it is taking and supports the transformation it is effecting. If it is severing him from an attachment which he is unwilling to abandon and if he withholds his consent, the Grace itself may be forced to withdraw. The same may happen if he clings to a desire from which it seeks to free him.

230

If no one in this world can achieve perfection but only approach it, the personal realization of this fact at the proper time and after many efforts will lead to a deep humility and surrender. This may open the door of one's being to Grace, and thence to the beatific experience of the Overself, the Ever-Perfect.

231

Let Grace in by responding positively to the Teaching and by letting go of the ego.

232

Grace is not a one-way operation. It is not, as a few erroneously believe, getting something free. There is nothing free anywhere. For when the Grace starts to operate it will also start to dispel those negative qualities which obstruct it. They will resist, but if you adopt the correct attitude of self-surrender and are willing to let them go, they will not be able to resist long. But if you hold on to them because they seem a part of yourself, or because they seem "natural," then either the Grace will withdraw or it will lead you into circumstances and situations that remove the obstructions forcibly, and consequently painfully.

233

There is a point where self-effort must cease and self-abasement must begin. Not to recognize it is to show conceit and hinder Grace.

234

The highest object of worship, devotion, reverence—what the Hindus name *Bhakti*—is that which is given to the World-Mind—what Hindus call *Ishvara*. But remember always that you are present within It and It is ever present within you. So the source of grace is in you too. Silence the ego, be still, and glimpse the fact that grace is the response to devotion that goes deep enough to approach the stillness, is sincere enough to put ego aside. Help is no farther off than your own heart. Hope on!

The mysterious Presence

235

The divine grace brings a man not what he asks but what he needs. The two are sometimes the same but sometimes not. It is only with the wise that they always coincide; with others they may stand in sharp conflict.

236

Even if a man does not respond to it, the divine presence in the world is itself a grace. Even if he is quite unaware of its being in his heart, his centre, its guidance and the intuitive thoughts which may arise are manifestations of grace.

237

There is a difference of opinion about the alleged inaccessibility of the Overself. Among those who call themselves mystics in the West and yogis in the East, some claim that every man may justifiably hold the hope of penetrating to the transcendental realm of Overself, provided he will give the necessary time and effort. But others claim that the certainty which attends scientific processes is not found here, that a man may spend a lifetime in searching after God and fail in the end. This uncertainty of result is absent from standardized laboratory processes and present only in experimental ones. There is a mystery here, both in the object and the operation of the search. It cannot be solved by the intellect, for it is the mystery of Grace.

238

In the early stages of spiritual progress, Grace may show itself in the bestowal of ecstatic emotions. This encourages him to pursue the Quest and to know that he is so far pursuing it rightly. But the purpose gained, the blissful states will eventually pass away, as they must. He will then falsely imagine that he has lost Grace, that he has left undone something he should have done or done something he should not have done. The true fact is that it is Grace itself which has brought this loss about, as constituting his next stage of progress, even though it affords no pleasure to his conscious mind, but only pain. His belief that he has lost the direct contact with the higher power which he formerly enjoyed is wrong: his actual contact was only an indirect one, for his emotions were then oc-cupied with themselves and with their pleasure in the experience. He is being separated from them so that he may be emptied of every desire and utterly humbled in his ego, and thus made ready for the time when joy, once regained, will never leave him again. For he is now on the threshold of the soul's dark night. In that state there is also a work being done for him by Grace, but it is deep in the subconscious mind far beyond his sight and beyond his control.(P)

239

Indeed, the hour may come when, purified from the ego's partiality, he will kiss the cross that brought him such agony and when, healed of his blindness, he will see that it was a gift from loving hands, not a curse from evil lips. He will see too that in his former insistence on clinging to a lower standpoint, there was no other way of arousing him to the need and value of a higher one than the way of unloosed suffering. But at last the wound has healed perfectly leaving him, as a scar of remembrance, greatly in-creased wisdom.

240

There is an incalculable factor in this game of self with Overself, an unpredictable element in this quest—the Grace!

241

As he pores reminiscently over the book of his past history, he will come to see how Grace entered into it by denying him some thing that he then ardently desired but whose acquisition would later have been a calamity or an affliction.

242

If outer events bring him to a position where he can bear them no longer and force him to cry out to the higher power in helplessness for relief, or if inner feelings bring humiliation and recognition of his dependence on that power, this crushing of the ego may open the door to grace.

243

The Overself's grace meets us just at the point where our need is greatest, but not necessarily the one we acknowledge as such. We must learn to let it do what it wants to do, not necessarily what we want it to do.

244

When the Overself's Grace is the real activating agent that is stirring up his petition, the coming event has cast its shadow before. When this is the case, the meaning of Emerson's cryptic sentence, "What we pray to ourselves for is always granted," becomes luminously revealed.

245

If he could penetrate into the so-called unconscious levels of his mind, he might find, to his utter amazement, that his enemies, critics, or domestic thorns-in-the-flesh are the very answer to his prayer for Grace. They fully become so, however, only when he recognizes them as such, when he perceives what duty or what self-discipline they give him the chance to practise.

246

The grace is bestowed in spite of his negative qualities, in spite of his ego's assertiveness: no one knows why or when it first reaches him.

247

Rufus Jones, eminent Quaker, made such a study and had to conclude, "There is a mystery about spiritual awakenings which will always remain unexplained." Nevertheless those who have studied the working of Grace with the added equipment of the philosophic and esoteric knowledge which he lacked find it more explicable, although still somewhat unpredictable.

248

The connection between the manifestation of grace and the kind of person to whom it comes is sometimes inexplicable. It comes not at all, or it comes sporadically, or it comes so completely that he is changed forever.

249

We dare not leave Grace out of our reckonings. Yet, because it is such an incalculable factor, we cannot put it in!

250

The passage from an earthly attitude to a spiritual one is accompanied either by intense suffering or by intense joy but always by intense feeling.

251

The longer grace is withheld, the more is it appreciated when finally vouchsafed.

252

It is not often easy to discern the why and wherefore of its operations and manifestations. Grace does not conform to human expectations, human reasonings, or human modes. It would not be divine if it always did that.

253

The course of each individual quest, its ecstasies and sufferings, is not easily predictable. The factors of karma and Grace are always present and their operation in different life situations may always be different and cannot be foreseen.

254

Grace may be granted at any unexpected time. We supply the channel but do not determine the means.

255

Although all this working of Grace takes place outside the level of ordinary consciousness—whether above or beneath it is a matter of the point of view—nevertheless it influences that consciousness far more than most people suspect.

256

The advent of Grace is so unpredictable that we dare not even say that Grace will come into action only after a man consciously and deliberately seeks God and practises self-purification. We may only say that it is more likely to come to him then.

257

In our own time the case of Aldous Huxley shows how a scientific agnostic is moved unwillingly toward the intellectual acceptance of truth. The case of Simone Weil shows how a Marxist materialist is moved just as unwillingly to an even farther distance—the direct experience of what she had to call God and the utter submission of the ego which permanently followed that experience. Both cases illustrate the mysterious and unpredictable character of Grace.

258

It is a mystery of Grace that it will come looking for one who is not pursuing truth, not looking for holiness, not even stumbling towards any interest in spirituality. And it will capture that person so completely that the character will totally change, as in Francis of Assisi's case, or the world view will totally change, as in Simone Weil's case.

259

The Overself can work in him—without his knowledge or help—to unfold, balance, or integrate him.

260

Grace happens. But to whom, when, and where, cannot be said with certainty, at best only with probability.

261

It is possible to chart out a course for man whereby he may move step by step towards the discovery of his own divine Overself, and with it the beauty and dignity in life. But it is not possible to say at what point in his movement the working of Grace will manifest itself.

262

Many who ask for Grace would be shocked to hear that the troubles which may have followed their request were actually the very form in which the higher power granted the Grace to them.

263

The influx comes at its own sweet will: he cannot grasp at it. It has to happen of itself. This enforces a full measure of humbleness and a wide stretch of patience on his part.

264

In a dozen different places Jacob Boehme declares that his wonderful illumination was a gift of Grace and that he had done nothing to deserve it. Although in a few other places he balanced this declaration with the idea that he was being used as a serving vessel from which others could draw the teaching given him, the fact remains that he did not aspire to be the recipient of a revelation and was astounded when it came.

265

The Grace works from his centre outward, transforming him from within, and therefore its earliest operation is unknown to his everyday mind.

266

The workings of Grace cannot always be judged by their temporary emotional effects. It depends on the particular circumstances, special needs, and evolutionary stage of a man as to whether these effects will be joyous or melancholy. But in the end, and when he enters into the actual consciousness of the sacred Overself, he will feel intense happiness.

267

Sometimes we are pushed to perform deeds which turn out to be our finest ones, or our most fortunate ones, although at the time we did not know this. Who is the pusher? In those cases it is either karma or grace.

268

Sometimes the Overself does its recondite work in the arid desolation of "the soul's dark night" but sometimes in the rapturous awakening to the new life of spring.

269

The psychological laws governing the inner development of spiritual seekers often seem to operate in most mysterious ways. The very power whose presence he may think has been denied him—Grace—is taking care of him even when he is not conscious of this fact. The more the anguish, at such a time, the more the Higher Self is squeezing the ego. The more he seems to be alone and forsaken, the closer the Higher Self may be drawing him to Itself.

270

Grace breathes where it will. It does not necessarily follow the lines set by man's expectation, prayer, or desire.

271

The Overself's grace will be secretly active within and without him long before it shows itself openly to him.

272

The grace may be barely felt, may come on slowly for many months, so that when he does become aware of its activity, the final stage is all he sees and knows.

273

Those who will not pause to philosophize about life are sometimes forced to do so by illness or distress. Although this brings suffering to the ego, to the aspirant it brings grace, latent in him.

274

The effect may not show itself immediately; in most cases it cannot, for most people are insensitive. But in such cases it will show itself eventually.

275

Grace has no favourites. Its working is characterized by its own mysterious laws. Do not expect it in return for faith alone, nor for just effort alone. Try both.

276

Because grace is an element in this enterprise, the question where will he stand in ten years' time is not answerable.

277

He may be disappointed because he is not more consciously aware of being helped. The forms which spiritual help takes may not always be easily recognizable because they may not conform to his wishes and expectations. Moreover, the kind of help given in this manner may require a period of time to elapse between its entry on the subconscious level and its manifestation on the conscious level. This period varies in actual experience with different individuals, from a few days to a number of years. Its exact duration is unpredictable because it is individual in each case. God alone knows what it is, but its final eruption is sure.

278

He may know that the work of Grace has begun when he feels an active drawing from within which wakes him from sleep and which recurs in the day, urging him to practise his devotions, his recollections, his prayers, or his meditations. It leads him from his surface consciousness to his inner being, a movement which slowly goes back in ever-deepening exploration and discovery of himself.(P)

279

A certain momentum will be imparted to his aspirations. During all this time the spiritual forces have been slowly maturing in mental regions below consciousness. Their eruption will be sudden and violent.

280

The weeping, begging, and worshipping through which the seeker passes is a result of Grace which occurred when, deciding to give up the ego, he felt a great peace. It is an emotional upheaval of an agonizing kind but it soon passes. He will then feel much calmer, more aspiring, and less worldly in character. This permanent change is a reorientation of the love forces; the Sufis call it "the overturning of the cup of the heart." In view of its being both auspicious and beneficial, he should not worry about it, but be patient and have hope.

281

The force which becomes active in his meditation—and which is associated with Grace—will also become active in waking him up from sleep in the morning, or even earlier. It will lead him immediately into the thought and practice of loving devotion to the higher self. He may even dream of doing his practice during the night. This will fill him with great joy. The force itself is a transforming one.

282

All he can do is to accept the inner gift when it is offered, which is not so easy or simple a feat as it sounds. Too many people brush it off because its beginnings are so delicate, so faint, as not to point at all plainly to their glorious consequences.

283

A shadow cast by the light of oncoming Grace sometimes appears as a fit of weeping. Without outer cause, the tears stream without stop or else sadness wells up without mitigation. But most often the cause does exist.

284

If a man misses the chance when grace is offered him internally by impersonal leadings or externally by a personal master, he will have to wait several years before the possibility of its recurrence can arise, if it does arise at all. In the same form, unobstructed by the disadvantages accumulated during the years, it can never arise again. Therefore it behooves him to be heedful that spiritual opportunity does not pass him by unrecognized or unseized. In this affair, the heart is often a better guide than the head, for the intellect doubts and wavers where intuition inclines and impels.

285

If this happens, if he surrenders himself unreservedly to the first faint growth of Grace within his innermost heart, then its blessing will eventually fructify gloriously.

286

The sudden, unexpected, and violent agitation of the diaphragm for a few moments may be a favourable phenomenon. It signifies a visitation of Grace from the Overself, a visitation which is the precursor of coming intellectual change and spiritual redirection.

287

It is one sign of coming Grace when he begins to despise himself for his weaknesses, when he begins to criticize his lower nature to the point of hating it.

288

When the Grace at last overcomes the inner resistance of the ego, the latter breaks down and the eyes often break into tears.

289

The simple working of inward Grace is the essential mystical experience; the extraordinary clairvoyant accompaniments are not.

290

Saint Thomas Aquinas: "Whoever receives Grace knows by experiencing a certain sweetness, which is not experienced by one who does not receive it."

291

It is most important to recognize what is happening—a visitation of Grace—and to respond to it at once. This means that everything else must be dropped without delay.

292

True sacredness is not something which anyone can pick up in his hands, examine, and identify at once. It is impalpable, as subtle and as delicate as perfume.

293

When Grace takes the form of spiritual enlightenment, it may catch him unawares, enter his consciousness unexpectedly, and release him abruptly from the protracted tensions of the quest.

294

The awakening to spiritual need, although often productive of longing and sadness, is also often a sign of the preliminary working of Grace.

295

Sometimes the Grace is felt psychically as a spiritual current actually pouring in through the head, although its posture may be inwardly shaped to the upturned tilt at one time or the bowed depression at another time.

296

When his aspiration rises to an overpowering intensity, it is a sign that Grace is not so far off.

297

Let us look for those wonderful moments when grace has been bestowed and peace has been felt. Let us stop all this busy business awhile, and stand still. Let us listen for awhile for then we may hear the Word which God is forever speaking to man.

298

In its presence it is easier to cast off some of the cares of life and, for the more practised, even feel some inner calm. Such moods are spiritual in the finer meanings of the word.

299

The wonderful effect of profound sleep is not only the recovery of the physical body's energy but much more the man's return to himself, his spiritual self, the pure universal consciousness. Note that all this happens without any effort on his part, without any use of the personal will. It is all done *to* him. Grace acts in the same way.

300

When the grace descends, whether from some action or attitude of one's self, or apparently without cause from outside one's self, if it is authentic, it will seem for the brief while that it lasts as if one has touched eternity, as if life and consciousness are without beginning and without end. It is a state of absolute contentment, complete fulfilment.

301

I dislike the word "bliss"—so often used in translating *ananda*. Surely "beatitude" is the word measuring more clearly the experienced feeling.

302

He may be one of the fortunate ones who can call down upon themselves the workings of Grace. When he feels the urge to weep for no apparent reason he should not resist, as it is a sign of the working of Grace upon him. The more he yields to this urge the more quickly will he progress. This is an important manifestation although its inner significance will not be understood by the materialistic world.

303

The seeker need not be worried about frequent weeping spells, but must be patient and have hope. Such actions assist him in bringing about permanent changes for the better in his character.

304

He is aware that a new force, more powerful than his own normally is, has risen up and taken command of his whole being.

305

When he reaches this stage, he will cease to waver, either in allegiance to the doctrine or in practice of the discipline. He will be steadfast.

306

The need to be alert against negative suggestions, to guard himself mentally against divergent or degrading ideas, exists for a time but not for all time. When Grace begins its operation, the danger from these sources vanishes, for the possibility of his being attracted by or open to them itself vanishes. The Grace enfolds him like a mantle.

307

As the light of Grace begins to fall upon him, he becomes aware of the tendencies and propensities, the motives and desires which obstruct or oppose the awakening into awareness of the Overself.

308

If it is individual effort which has to make the long journey from ignorance to illumination, it is divine Grace which has secretly and silently to lead the way for it.

309

Grace settles the intellect on a higher level and stabilizes the emotions with a worthier ideal.

310

If his mastery of self is established on well-earned and well-worked-for inward grace more than on outward will, then it is well sealed and cannot break down, cannot be wrecked by the lusts and hates, the greeds and passions which agitate ordinary humanity.

311

Grace works magically on the man who opens himself humbly and sensitively to receive it. His personal feelings undergo a transformation into their higher impersonal octaves. His very weaknesses provoke occasions for gaining effortlessly their opposite virtues. His selfish desires are turned by Grace's alchemy into spiritual aspirations.

312

The man's effort must be met by the Overself's Grace. What he does attracts what the Overself gives. This he can understand. But what he seldom knows, and finds hard to understand, is that in certain cases the aspiration which impels such effort is itself impelled by Grace.

313

Wherever you read in history of a religious martyr who was filled with supernatural serenity in the midst of terrible torture, be sure that he was supported by the Overself. The consciousness of his divine soul had, by its grace, become stronger than the consciousness of his earthly body. If you wish, you may call it a kind of mesmerism, but it is a divine and not a human mesmerism.

314

There will be moments when a tendency to sin will suddenly be checked by an invading power which will work against the lower will.

315

When the power of Grace descends into his heart, no evil passion or lower emotion can resist it. They, and their accompanying desires, fade and then fall away of themselves.

316

From that time he will feel increasingly yet intermittently that a force other than his own is working within him, enlightening his mind and ennobling his character. The Overself's Grace has descended on him.

317

His innate tendencies may still be there for a time—they constitute his karma—but the grace keeps them in check.

318

With the coming of Grace, his development takes on a life of its own and is no longer to be measured in direct ratio to his effort.

319

After the descent of grace, he feels lifted by a power stronger than his own above the stormy passions and unpleasant greeds, the petty egotisms and ugly hatreds which agitate the mass of mankind.

320

He experiences a veritable rebirth, an inspiring renewal of all his being, a feeling of liberation from darkness, weakness, and moral blindness.

321

He may watch the working of Grace in its varied manifestations both within himself and in his personal relationships.

322

Grace is a powerful stimulus. It descends from a higher source, urges us to perfect our nature, equips us to complete it. Thus we are lifted up to its own higher level.

323

That enlightenment is a transfiguring event which not only revolutionizes general outlook but also changes moral character, there is testimony enough for anyone in the archives of mystical biography. The old self is laid aside as too imperfect, the old weaknesses are drowned in the overwhelming tide of Grace which pours through the man and his life.

324

The truth is that the Overself's power has worked upon him in advance of his own endeavours. The urge to seek a close and conscious relationship with it, the decision to enter upon the quest—these very thoughts stemmed from its hidden and active influence.

325

The emptied and stilled mind opens the way for the grasp of divine grace. The latter may then gather us up into its fold, leaving behind the ego's conceit and the body's passion. But when it is time for us to return to the world's nervous restlessness, to its tumult and jarring noise, we find how far humanity has fallen.

326

The ineffable peace and exquisite harmony which take hold of his heart are the first results of grace.

327

In the end all this aspiration supported by practical effort attracts Grace. He finds that he is not alone, that in becoming its recipient not only is a glimpse vouchsafed him but also some part of him has now an unassailable faith no matter what vacillations, questionings, or lapses the strains of life, the moods of ill health, or the changes of fortune may do to his thoughts for a time.

328

A new understanding has been gained. It is a possession that may be kept, with care, as long as he lives. Of how many other possessions may this be said?

Index for Part 1

Entries are listed by chapter number followed by "para" number. For example, 1.192 means chapter 1, para 192, and 5.33, 35 means chapter 5, paras 33 and 35. Chapter listings are separated by a semicolon. Please note also that, for the reader's convenience, the first number in the right-hand running heads throughout the text indicates chapter number.

Index for Part 2

Entries are listed by chapter number followed by "para" number. For example, 5.218 means chapter 5, para 218, and 2.9, 37 means chapter 2, paras 9 and 37. Chapter listings are separated by a semicolon. Please note also that, for the reader's convenience, the first number in the right-hand running heads throughout the text indicates chapter number.

The 28 Categories from the Notebooks

This outline of categories in *The Notebooks* is the most recent one Paul Brunton developed for sorting, ordering, and filing his written work. The listings he put after each title were not meant to be all-inclusive. They merely suggest something of the range of topics included in each category.

1 **THE QUEST**
   Its choice —Independent path —Organized groups — Self-development —Student/teacher

2 **PRACTICES FOR THE QUEST**
   Ant's long path —Work on oneself

3 **RELAX AND RETREAT**
   Intermittent pauses —Tension and pressures —Relax body, breath, and mind —Retreat centres —Solitude — Nature appreciation —Sunset contemplation

4 **ELEMENTARY MEDITATION**
   Place and conditions —Wandering thoughts —Practise concentrated attention —Meditative thinking — Visualized images —Mantrams —Symbols —Affirmations and suggestions

5 **THE BODY**
   Hygiene and cleansings —Food —Exercises and postures —Breathings —Sex: importance, influence, effects

6 **EMOTIONS AND ETHICS**
   Uplift character —Re-educate feelings —Discipline emotions — Purify passions —Refinement and courtesy —Avoid fanaticism

7 **THE INTELLECT**
   Nature —Services —Development —Semantic training — Science —Metaphysics —Abstract thinking

8 **THE EGO**
   What am I? —The I-thought —The psyche

Will in the World

ALSO BY STEPHEN GREENBLATT

Hamlet in Purgatory

Practicing New Historicism (with Catherine Gallagher)

Marvelous Possessions: The Wonder of the New World

Learning to Curse: Essays in Early Modern Culture

Shakespearean Negotiations:
The Circulation of Social Energy in Renaissance England

Renaissance Self-Fashioning: From More to Shakespeare

Sir Walter Ralegh: The Renaissance Man and His Roles

Three Modern Satirists: Waugh, Orwell, and Huxley

EDITED BY STEPHEN GREENBLATT

The Norton Anthology of English Literature (general editor)

The Norton Shakespeare (general editor)

New World Encounters

Redrawing the Boundaries:
The Transformation of English and American Literary Studies

Representing the English Renaissance

Allegory and Representation

Will in the World

HOW SHAKESPEARE
BECAME SHAKESPEARE

Stephen Greenblatt

W. W. NORTON & COMPANY
New York · London

Book design by Judith Stagnitto
Production manager: Amanda Morrison

ISBN 0-965-93118-8

W. W. Norton & Company, Inc., 500 Fifth Avenue, New York, N.Y. 10110

W. W. Norton & Company Ltd., Castle House, 75/76 Wells Street, London W1T 3QT

TO JOSH AND AARON, ONCE AGAIN,
AND NOW TO HARRY

Contents

Preface

A YOUNG MAN from a small provincial town—a man without independent wealth, without powerful family connections, and without a university education—moves to London in the late 1580s and, in a remarkably short time, becomes the greatest playwright not of his age alone but of all time. His works appeal to the learned and the unlettered, to urban sophisticates and provincial first-time theatergoers. He makes his audiences laugh and cry; he turns politics into poetry; he recklessly mingles vulgar clowning and philosophical subtlety. He grasps with equal penetration the intimate lives of kings and of beggars; he seems at one moment to have studied law, at another theology, at another ancient history, while at the same time he effortlessly mimes the accents of country bumpkins and takes delight in old wives' tales. How is an achievement of this magnitude to be explained? How did Shakespeare become Shakespeare?

Theater, in Shakespeare's time as in our own, is a highly social art form, not a game of bloodless abstractions. There was a type of drama in the age of Elizabeth and James that did not show its face in public; known as closet dramas, these were plays never meant to be performed or even printed. They were for silent reading in the privacy of small, prefer- ably windowless rooms. But Shakespeare's plays were always decisively out of the closet: they were, and are, in the world and of the world. Not only did Shakespeare write and act for a cutthroat commercial entertain- ment industry; he also wrote scripts that were intensely alert to the social and political realities of their times. He could scarcely have done other- wise: to stay afloat, the theater company in which he was a shareholder had to draw some 1,500 to 2,000 paying customers a day into the round wooden walls of the playhouse, and competition from rival companies was fierce. The key was not so much topicality—with government cen- sorship and with repertory companies often successfully recycling the same scripts for years, it would have been risky to be too topical—as it was intensity of interest. Shakespeare had to engage with the deepest desires and fears of his audience, and his unusual success in his own time suggests that he succeeded brilliantly in doing so. Virtually all his rival playwrights found themselves on the straight road to starvation; Shake- speare, by contrast, made enough money to buy one of the best houses in the hometown to which he retired in his early fifties, a self-made man.

This is a book, then, about an amazing success story that has resisted explanation: it aims to discover the actual person who wrote the most important body of imaginative literature of the last thousand years. Or rather, since the actual person is a matter of well-documented public record, it aims to tread the shadowy paths that lead from the life he lived into the literature he created.

Apart from the poems and plays themselves, the surviving traces of Shakespeare's life are abundant but thin. Dogged archival labor over many generations has turned up contemporary allusions to him, along with a reasonable number of the playwright's property transactions, a marriage license bond, christening records, cast lists in which he is named as a performer, tax bills, petty legal affidavits, payments for serv- ices, and an interesting last will and testament, but no immediately obvi- ous clues to unravel the great mystery of such immense creative power.

The known facts have been rehearsed again and again for several centuries. Already in the nineteenth century there were fine, richly detailed, and well-documented biographies, and each year brings a fresh crop of them, sometimes enhanced with a hard-won crumb or two of new archival findings. After examining even the best of them and patiently sifting through most of the available traces, readers rarely feel closer to understanding how the playwright's achievements came about. If anything, Shakespeare often seems a drabber, duller person, and the inward springs of his art seem more obscure than ever. Those springs would be difficult enough to glimpse if biographers could draw upon letters and diaries, contemporary memoirs and interviews, books with revealing marginalia, notes and first drafts. Nothing of the kind survives, nothing that provides a clear link between the timeless work with its universal appeal and a particular life that left its many scratches in the humdrum bureaucratic records of the age. The work is so astonishing, so luminous, that it seems to have come from a god and not a mortal, let alone a mortal of provincial origins and modest education.

It is fitting, of course, to invoke the magic of an immensely strong imagination, a human endowment that does not depend upon an "interesting" life. Scholars have long and fruitfully studied the transforming work of that imagination on the books that, from evidence within the plays themselves, Shakespeare must certainly have read. As a writer he rarely started with a blank slate; he characteristically took materials that had already been in circulation and infused them with his supreme creative energies. On occasion, the reworking is so precise and detailed that he must have had the book from which he was deftly borrowing directly on his writing table as his quill pen raced across the paper. But no one who responds intensely to Shakespeare's art can believe that the plays and poems came exclusively from his reading. At least as much as the books he read, the central problems he grappled with as a young man—What should I do with my life? In what can I have faith? Whom do I love?— served throughout his career to shape his art.

One of the prime characteristics of Shakespeare's art is the touch of the real. As with any other writer whose voice has long ago fallen silent and whose body has moldered away, all that is left are words on a page, but even before a gifted actor makes Shakespeare's words come alive, those words contain the vivid presence of actual, lived experience. The poet who noticed that the hunted, trembling hare was "dew-bedabbled" or who likened his stained reputation to the "dyer's hand," the playwright who has a husband tell his wife that there is a purse "in the desk / That's covered o'er with Turkish tapestry" or who has a prince remember that his poor companion owns only two pairs of silk stockings, one of them peach-colored—this artist was unusually open to the world and discovered the means to allow this world into his works. To understand how he did this so effectively, it is important to look carefully at his verbal artistry—his command of rhetoric, his uncanny ventriloquism, his virtual obsession with language. To understand who Shakespeare was, it is important to follow the verbal traces he left behind back into the life he lived and into the world to which he was so open. And to understand how Shakespeare used his imagination to transform his life into his art, it is important to use our own imagination.

Acknowledgments

I T   I S   A   T O K E N of the special delight Shakespeare bestows on everything that even the many debts I have incurred in writing this book give me deep pleasure to acknowledge. My remarkably gifted colleagues and students at Harvard University have been an unfailing source of intellectual stimulation and challenge, and the university's fabled resources—above all, its celebrated libraries and their accomplished staff—have enabled me to pursue even the most arcane questions. The Mellon Foundation gave me the precious gift of time, and the Wissenschaftskolleg zu Berlin provided the perfect setting to complete the writing of this book. I am grateful for the opportunities I had to try out my ideas at the Shakespeare Association of America, the Bath Shakespeare Festival, New York University, the Lionel Trilling Seminar at Columbia University, the Leo Lowenthal Memorial Conference, Boston College, Wellesley College, Hendrix College, the Einstein Forum, and, on multiple occasions, Marlboro College and the Marlboro Music Festival.

The idea of *Will in the World* originated years ago during conversations I had with Marc Norman, who was then in the early stages of writing a film script about Shakespeare's life. The script was the germ of a celebrated movie, *Shakespeare in Love*, but my own project lay dormant until my wife, Ramie Targoff, gave me the sustained encouragement, intellectual and emotional, to pursue it. Crucial advice and assistance came from Jill Kneerim, and my friends Homi Bhabha, Jeffrey Knapp, Joseph Koerner, Charles Mee, and Robert Pinsky each gave me more of their time, learning, and wisdom than I can ever hope to repay. I have benefited too from the help and probing questions of many other friends, including Marcella Anderson, Leonard Barkan, Frank Bidart, Robert Brustein, Thomas Laqueur, Adam Phillips, Regula Rapp, Moshe Safdie, James Shapiro, Debora Shuger, and the late Bernard Williams. Beatrice Kitzinger, Kate Pilson, Holger Schott, Gustavo Secchi, and Phillip Schwyzer have been tireless and resourceful assistants. With exemplary patience and insight, my editor, Alane Mason, continued to work on the manuscript of my book through the course of her pregnancy, and, by something of a miracle, she somehow managed to finish on her due date.

My deepest and most richly pleasurable debts are closest to home: to my wife and my three sons, Josh, Aaron, and Harry. Only the youngest, by virtue of being a toddler, has been spared endless conversations about Shakespeare and has not directly contributed his ideas. But Harry, who came into the world 104 years after the birth of his namesake, my father, has taught me how breathtakingly close we are to lives that at first sight seem so far away.

A Note to the Reader

AROUND 1598, still relatively early in Shakespeare's career, a man named Adam Dyrmonth, about whom next to nothing is known, set out to list the contents of a collection of speeches and letters that he had transcribed. Evidently, his mind began to wander, because he began to scribble idly. Among the jottings that cover the page are the words "Rychard the second" and "Rychard the third," along with half-remembered quotations from *Love's Labour's Lost* and *The Rape of Lucrece*. Above all, the scribbler repeatedly wrote the words "William Shakespeare." He wanted to know, it seems, what it felt like to write that particular name as one's own. Dyrmonth might have been the first to be driven by this curiosity, but he certainly was not the last.

As Dyrmonth's scribblings suggest, Shakespeare was famous in his own lifetime. Only a few years after Shakespeare's death, Ben Jonson celebrated him as "the wonder of our Stage" and the "Star of poets." But at the time such literary celebrity did not ordinarily lead to the writing of biographies, and no contemporary seems to have thought it worthwhile to collect whatever could be found out about Shakespeare while his memory was still green. As it happens, more is known about him than about most professional writers of the time, but this knowledge is largely the consequence of the fact that England in the late sixteenth and early seventeenth century was already a record-keeping society and that many of the records survived, to be subsequently combed over by eager scholars. Even with this relative abundance of information, there are huge gaps in knowledge that make any biographical study of Shakespeare an exercise in speculation.

What matters most are the works, most of which (the poems excepted) were carefully assembled by two of Shakespeare's longtime associates and friends, John Heminges and Henry Condell, who brought out the First Folio in 1623, seven years after the playwright's death. Eighteen of the thirty-six plays in this great volume, including such masterpieces as *Julius Caesar, Macbeth, Antony and Cleopatra*, and *The Tempest*, had not appeared in print before; without the First Folio they might have vanished forever. The world owes Heminges and Condell an immense debt. But beyond noting that Shakespeare wrote with great facility—"what he thought," they claimed, "he uttered with that easiness that we have scarce received from him a blot in his papers"—the editors had little or no interest in furthering biography. They chose to arrange the contents by genre—Comedies, Histories, and Tragedies—and they did not bother to note when and in what order Shakespeare wrote each of his plays. After many decades of ingenious research, scholars have reached a reasonably stable consensus, but even this time line, so crucial for any biography, is inevitably somewhat speculative.

So too are many of the details of the life. The Stratford vicar John Bretchgirdle noted in the parish register the baptism of "Gulielmus filius Johannes Shakspere" on April 26, 1564. Though anything can be called into question, that much seems beyond a reasonable doubt, but the scholars who subsequently fixed Shakespeare's date of birth as April 23—on the assumption that there was ordinarily a three-day interval at the time between birth and baptism—were engaged in speculation.

One further and potentially more consequential example will give readers a sense of the scope of the problem. From 1571 to 1575 the schoolmaster in the Stratford grammar school was Simon Hunt, who had received his B.A. from Oxford in 1568. He would thus have been

William Shakespeare's teacher from the age of seven to eleven. Around July 1575, Simon Hunt matriculated at the University of Douai—the Catholic university in France—and became a Jesuit in 1578. This would seem to indicate that Shakespeare's early teacher was a Catholic, a detail that is consistent with a whole pattern of experiences in his youth. But there is no hard-and-fast proof that Shakespeare attended the Stratford grammar school—the records for that period do not survive. Moreover, another Simon Hunt died in Stratford in or before 1598, and it is at least possible that this second Simon Hunt, rather than the one who became a Jesuit, was the schoolmaster. Shakespeare almost certainly attended the school—where else would he have acquired his education?—and the coincidence of the dates and the larger pattern of experiences make it highly likely that the schoolmaster from 1571 to 1575 was the Catholic Hunt. But in these details, as in so much else from Shakespeare's life, there is no absolute certainty.

Will in the World

CHAPTER 1

Primal Scenes

LET US IMAGINE that Shakespeare found himself from boyhood fascinated by language, obsessed with the magic of words. There is overwhelming evidence for this obsession from his earliest writings, so it is a very safe assumption that it began early, perhaps from the first moment his mother whispered a nursery rhyme in his ear:

> Pillycock, pillycock, sate on a hill,
> If he's not gone—he sits there still.

(This particular nursery rhyme was rattling around in his brain years later, when he was writing *King Lear*. "Pillicock sat on Pillicock-hill," chants the madman Poor Tom [3.4.73].) He heard things in the sounds of words that others did not hear; he made connections that others did not make; and he was flooded with a pleasure all his own.

This was a love and a pleasure that Elizabethan England could arouse, richly satisfy, and reward, for the culture prized ornate eloquence, cultivated a taste for lavish prose from preachers and politicians, and expected even people of modest accomplishments and sober sensibilities to write poems. In one of his early plays, *Love's Labour's Lost*, Shakespeare created a ridiculous schoolteacher, Holofernes, whose manner is a parody of a classroom style that most audience members must have found immediately recognizable. Holofernes cannot refer to an apple without adding that it hangs "like a jewel in the ear of *caelo*, the sky, the welkin, the heaven" and that it drops "on the face of *terra*, the soil, the land, the earth" (4.2.4–6). He is the comical embodiment of a curriculum that used, as one of its key textbooks, Erasmus's *On Copiousness*, a book that taught students 150 different ways of saying (in Latin, of course) "Thank you for your letter." If Shakespeare deftly mocked this manic word game, he also exuberantly played it in his own voice and his own language, as when he writes in sonnet 129 that lust "Is perjured, murd'rous, bloody, full of blame, / Savage, extreme, rude, cruel, not to trust" (lines 3–4). Concealed somewhere behind this passionate outburst are the many hours a young boy spent in school, compiling long lists of Latin synonyms.

"All men," wrote Queen Elizabeth's tutor, Roger Ascham, "covet to have their children speak Latin." The queen spoke Latin—one of the few women in the realm to have had access to that accomplishment, so crucial for international relations—and so did her diplomats, counselors, theologians, clergymen, physicians, and lawyers. But command of the ancient tongue was not limited to those who actually made practical, professional use of it. "*All* men covet to have their children speak Latin": in the sixteenth century, bricklayers, wool merchants, glovers, prosperous yeomen—people who had no formal education and could not read or write English, let alone Latin—wanted their sons to be masters of the ablative absolute. Latin was culture, civility, upward mobility. It was the language of parental ambition, the universal currency of social desire.

So it was that Will's father and mother wanted their son to have a proper classical education. John Shakespeare himself seems to have had at most only partial literacy: as the holder of important civic offices in Stratford-upon-Avon, he probably knew how to read, but throughout his life he only signed his name with a mark. Judging from the mark she made on legal documents, Mary Shakespeare, the mother of England's greatest writer, also could not write her name, though she too might have acquired some minimal literacy. But, they evidently decided, this would not suffice for their eldest son. The child no doubt began with a "hornbook"—a wooden tablet with the letters and the Paternoster printed on a piece of parchment covered with a thin sheet of transparent horn—and with the standard primary school text, *The ABC with the Cathechism.* (In *The Two Gentlemen of Verona,* a lover sighs "like a schoolboy that had lost his ABC"[2.1.19–20].) Thus far he was only acquiring what his father and possibly even his mother may have possessed. But probably starting at age seven, he was sent to the Stratford free grammar school, whose central educational principle was total immersion in Latin.

The school was called the King's New School, but it was not new and it had not been founded by the king who was honored in its name, Elizabeth's short-lived stepbrother Edward VI. Like so many other Elizabethan institutions, this one wore a mask designed to hide origins tainted with Roman Catholicism. Built by the town's Guild of the Holy Cross in the early fifteenth century, it was endowed as a free school by one of its Catholic chaplains in 1482. The schoolhouse—which survives more or less intact—was a single large room above the guildhall, reached by a flight of external stairs that were at one time roofed with tile. There may have been partitions, particularly if an assistant teacher was teaching very young children their ABCs, but most of the students—some forty-two boys, ranging in age from seven to fourteen or fifteen—sat on hard benches facing the schoolmaster, sitting in his large chair at the head of the room.

By statute, the Stratford schoolmaster was not allowed to take money for his instruction from any of the students. He was to teach any male child who qualified—that is, anyone who had learned the rudiments of reading and writing—"be their parents never so poor and the boys never so unapt." For this he received free housing and an annual salary of twenty pounds, a substantial sum at the high end of what Elizabethan schoolmasters could hope to make. The town of Stratford was serious about the education of its children: after the free grammar school there were special scholarships to enable promising students of limited means to attend university. This was not, to be sure, universal free education. Here as everywhere else, girls were excluded from both grammar school and university. The sons of the very poor—a large proportion of the population—also did not go to school, for they were expected to begin work at a young age, and, besides, though there was no fee, there were some expenses: students were expected to bring quills for pens, a knife for sharpening the quills, candles in winter, and—an expensive commodity—paper. But for the sons of families of some means, however modest, a rigorous education, centered on the classics, was accessible. Though the Stratford school records from the time do not survive, Will almost certainly attended this school, fulfilling his parents' desire that he learn Latin.

In the summer the school day began at 6 A.M.; in the winter, as a concession to the darkness and the cold, at 7. At 11 came recess for lunch—Will presumably ran home, only three hundred yards or so away—and then instruction began again, continuing until 5:30 or 6. Six days a week; twelve months a year. The curriculum made few concessions to the range of human interests: no English history or literature; no biology, chemistry, or physics; no economics or sociology; only a smattering of arithmetic. There was instruction in the articles of the Christian faith, but that must have seemed all but indistinguishable from the instruction in Latin. And the instruction was not gentle: rote memorization, relentless drills, endless repetition, daily analysis of texts, elaborate exercises in imitation and rhetorical variation, all backed up by the threat of violence.

Everyone understood that Latin learning was inseparable from whipping. One educational theorist of the time speculated that the buttocks were created in order to facilitate the learning of Latin. A good teacher was by definition a strict teacher; pedagogical reputations were made by the vigor of the beatings administered. The practice was time-honored and entrenched: as part of his final examination at Cambridge, a graduate in grammar in the late Middle Ages was required to demonstrate his pedagogical fitness by flogging a dull or recalcitrant boy. Learning Latin in this period was, as a modern scholar has put it, a male puberty rite. Even for an exceptionally apt student, that puberty rite could not have been pleasant. Still, though it doubtless inflicted its measure of both boredom and pain, the King's New School clearly aroused and fed Will's inexhaustible craving for language.

There was another aspect of the very long school day that must have given Will pleasure. Virtually all schoolmasters agreed that one of the best ways to instill good Latin in their students was to have them read and perform ancient plays, especially the comedies of Terence and Plautus. Even the clergyman John Northbrooke, a killjoy who in 1577 published a sour attack on "dicing, dancing, vain plays or interludes with other idle pastimes," conceded that school performances of Latin plays, if suitably expurgated, were acceptable. Northbrooke stressed nervously that the plays had to be performed in the original language, not in English, that the students should not wear beautiful costumes, and, above all, that there should be no "vain and wanton toys of love." For the great danger of these plays, as the Cambridge scholar John Rainolds noted, was that the plot may call for the boy who is playing the hero to kiss the boy who is playing the heroine, and that kiss may be the undoing of both children. For the kiss of a beautiful boy is like the kiss of "certain spiders": "if they do but touch men only with their mouth, they put them to wonderful pain and make them mad."

In fact it is almost impossible to expurgate Terence and Plautus: take out the disobedient children and sly servants, the parasites, tricksters, whores, and foolish fathers, the feverish pursuit of sex and money, and you have virtually nothing left. Built into the curriculum, then, was a kind of recurrent theatrical transgression, a comic liberation from the oppressive heaviness of the educational system. To partake fully of the liberation, all you needed, as a student, was a histrionic gift and enough Latin to get the point. By the time he was ten or eleven, and perhaps earlier, Will almost certainly had both.

No surviving records indicate how often the Stratford teachers during Will's school years had the boys perform plays or which plays they assigned. Perhaps there was a time, a year or so before Will left school, when the teacher—Oxford-educated Thomas Jenkins—decided to have the boys perform Plautus's frenetic farce about identical twins, *The Two Menaechmuses.* And perhaps on this occasion, Jenkins, recognizing that one of his students was precociously gifted as both a writer and an actor, assigned Will Shakespeare a leading role. There is hard evidence from later in his life that Shakespeare loved this particular play's combination of logic and dizzying confusion, the characters constantly just missing the direct encounter and the explanation that would resolve the mounting chaos. When he was a young playwright in London casting about for the plot of a comedy, he simply took over *The Two Menaechmuses*, added a second set of twins to double the chaos, and wrote *The Comedy of Errors*. The comedy was a great success: when it was performed at one of London's law schools the students rioted trying to get seats. But for the talented schoolboy in the King's New School, this future triumph would have seemed almost as implausible as the zany events depicted in the play.

In Plautus's opening scene, Menaechmus of Epidamnum squabbles with his wife and then goes off to visit his mistress, the courtesan Erotium (women's parts as well as men's would have been played by the boys in Will's class). Before Menaechmus knocks at her door, it swings open and Erotium herself appears, ravishing his senses: "Eapse eccam exit!" ("Look, she's coming out herself!"). And then in this moment of rapture—the sun is bedimmed, he exclaims, by the radiance of her lovely body—Erotium greets him: "Anime mi, Menaechme, salve!" ("My darling Menaechmus, welcome!").

This is the moment that anxious moralists like Northbrooke and Rainolds most feared and hated: the kiss of the spider boy. "Beautiful boys by kissing," writes Rainolds, "do sting and pour secretly in a kind of poison, the poison of incontinency." It is easy to laugh at this hysteria, but perhaps it is not completely absurd—on some such occasion as this, it is possible that the adolescent Shakespeare felt an intense excitement in which theatrical performance and sexual arousal were braided together.

Long before performances in school, Will may already have discovered that he had a passion for playacting. In 1569, when he was five, his father, as the bailiff—that is, the mayor—of Stratford-upon-Avon, ordered that payments be made to two companies of professional actors, the Queen's Men and the Earl of Worcester's Men, which had come to town on tour. These traveling playing companies would not have been an especially impressive sight: some six to a dozen "strowlers" carrying their costumes and props in a wagon, compelled by circumstances, as one contemporary observer wryly put it, "to travel upon the hard hoof from village to village for cheese and butter-milk." In fact the usual rewards would have been slightly more substantial—a pound or two in cold cash, if they were fortunate—but not so great as to make the players turn up their noses at whatever free cheese and buttermilk they could cadge. Yet to most small boys it would all have been unspeakably thrilling.

The arrival in provincial towns generally followed a set pattern. With a flourish of trumpets and the rattle of drums, the players swaggered down the street in their colorful liveries, scarlet cloaks, and crimson velvet caps. They proceeded to the house of the mayor and presented the letters of recommendation, with wax seals, that showed that they were not vagabonds and that a powerful patron protected them. In Stratford in 1569 they would have come to Henley Street, to the boy's own house, and they would have spoken to his father with deference, for it was he who would decide whether they would be sent packing or allowed to post their bills announcing the performances.

The first performance was known as the Mayor's Play, and it was usually free to all comers. Stratford's bailiff would certainly have been expected to attend this, for it was his privilege to determine the level of the reward to be paid out of the city coffers; he would, presumably, have been received with great respect and given one of the best seats in the guildhall, where a special stage had been erected. The excitement of this occasion was not limited to small boys: municipal records in Stratford and elsewhere routinely recorded broken windows and damage to chairs and benches caused by mobs of unruly spectators jostling for a good view.

These were festive events, breaks in the routines of everyday life. The sense of release, always bordering on transgression, was why some stern town officials occasionally turned the players away, particularly in times of dearth, sickness, or disorder, and why the players were not permitted to perform on Sundays or during Lent. But even the most puritanical mayors and aldermen had to think twice about annoying the aristocrats whose liveries the players proudly wore. After all, at the end of each performance in these country towns, the players would kneel down solemnly and ask everyone present to pray with them for their good lord and master—or, in the case of the Queen's Men, for the great Elizabeth herself. Hence, even when they were forbidden from performing, the troupes were often sent off with a gratuity, bribed in effect to go away.

John Shakespeare, the records indicate, did not send the players on their way. He permitted them to play. But would he have taken his five-year-old son to see the show? Certainly other fathers did. In his old age, a man named Willis, born the same year as Will, recalled a play (now lost), called *The Cradle of Security*, that he saw in Gloucester—thirty-eight miles from Stratford—when he was a child. On arriving in town the players, Willis wrote, followed the usual routine: they presented themselves to the mayor, informed him what nobleman's servants they were, and requested a license for performing in public. The mayor granted the license and appointed the company to give their first performance before the aldermen and other officials of the town. "At such a play," Willis remembered, "my father took me with him and made me stand between his legs, as he sat upon one of the benches, where we saw and heard very well." The experience was a remarkably intense one for Willis: "This sight took such impression in me," he wrote, "that when I came towards man's estate, it was as fresh in my memory as if I had seen it newly acted."

This is probably as close as it is possible to get to Will's own primal scene of theatricality. When the bailiff walked into the hall, everyone would have greeted him and exchanged words with him; when he took his seat, the crowd would have grown quiet in the expectation that something exciting and pleasurable was about to happen. His son, intelligent, quick, and sensitive, would have stood between his father's legs. For the first time in his life William Shakespeare watched a play.

What was the play that the Queen's Men brought to Stratford in 1569? Records do not show, and perhaps it does not matter. The sheer magic of playing—the fashioning of an imaginary space, the artful impersonations, the elaborate costumes, the flood of heightened language—may have been enough to capture the young boy forever. There was, in any case, more than one occasion for the spell to be cast. Troupes came repeatedly to Stratford—the Earl of Leicester's Men in 1573, for example, when Will was nine years old, the Earl of Warwick's Men and the Earl of Worcester's Men in 1575, when he was eleven—and each time the thrilling effect, initially enhanced by the child's sense of his

father's importance and power, may have been renewed and strengthened, the clever devices stored away as treasured memories.

For his part, Shakespeare's contemporary Willis remembered all his
life what he had seen at Gloucester: a king lured away from his sober,
pious counselors by three seductive ladies. "In the end they got him to lie
down in a cradle upon the stage," he recalled, "where these three ladies,
joining in a sweet song, rocked him asleep, that he snorted again; and in
the meantime closely conveyed under the cloths wherewithal he was covered, a vizard, like a swine's snout, upon his face, with three wire chains
fastened thereunto, the other end whereof being holden severally by
those three ladies; who fall to singing again, and then discovered his face,
that the spectators might see how they had transformed him." The spectators must have found it very exciting. Some of the older ones probably
remembered the swinish face of Henry VIII, and all in the audience
knew that it was only under special circumstances that they could publicly share the thought that the monarch was a swine.

Young Will is likely to have seen something similar. The plays in
repertory in the 1560s and '70s were for the most part "morality plays," or
"moral interludes," secular sermons designed to show the terrible consequences of disobedience, idleness, or dissipation. Typically, a character—
an embodied abstraction with a name like Mankind or Youth—turns
away from a proper guide such as Honest Recreation or Virtuous Life
and begins to spend his time with Ignorance, All-for-Money, or Riot.

> Huffa, huffa! Who calleth after me?
> I am Riot, full of jollity.
> My heart is light as the wind,
> And all on riot is my mind.
> (*The Interlude of Youth*)

It is rapidly downhill from here—Riot introduces Youth to his friend
Pride; Pride introduces him to his glamorous sister Lechery; Lechery
lures him to the tavern—and it looks like it will all end badly. Sometimes
it does end badly—in the play Willis saw, the king who is transformed

into a swine is later carried away to punishment by wicked spirits—but more typically, something happens to awaken the hero's slumbering conscience just in time. In *The Interlude of Youth*, Charity, reminding the sinner of Jesus's great gift to him, frees him from the influence of Riot and restores him to the company of Humility. In *The Castle of Perseverance*, Penance touches Mankind's heart with his lance and saves him from his wicked companions, the Seven Deadly Sins. In *Wit and Science*, the hero Wit, asleep in the lap of Idleness, is transformed into a fool, complete with cap and bells, but he is saved when he catches sight of himself in a mirror and realizes that he looks "like a very ass!" Only after he is sharply whipped by Shame and taught by a group of strict schoolmasters—Instruction, Study, and Diligence—is Wit restored to his proper appearance and able to celebrate his marriage to Lady Science.

Relentlessly didactic and often clumsily written, morality plays came to seem old-fashioned and crude—any summary of them will make them sound boring—but they were in vogue for a long period of time, extending into Shakespeare's adolescence. Their blend of high-mindedness and exuberant theatrical energy pleased an impressively broad range of spectators, from the unlettered to the most sophisticated. If these plays had little or no interest in psychological particularity or social texture, they often had the canniness of folk wisdom along with a strong current of subversive humor. That humor could take the form of a swine-snouted king, but it more often centered on the stock character known generally as the Vice. This jesting, prattling mischief-maker—bearing in different interludes names such as Riot, Iniquity, Liberty, Idleness, Misrule, Double Device, and even, in one notable instance, Hickscorner—embodied simultaneously the spirit of wickedness and the spirit of fun. The audience knew that he would in the end be defeated and driven, with blows or fireworks, from the stage. But for a time he pranced about, scorning the hicks, insulting the solemn agents of order and piety, playing tricks on the unsuspecting, plotting mischief, and luring the innocent into taverns and whorehouses. The audience loved it.

When Shakespeare sat down to write for the London stage, he drew upon those rather creaky entertainments that must have delighted him as a child. He learned from them to give many of his characters emblematic names: the whores Doll Tearsheet and Jane Nightwork and the sergeants Snare and Fang in *2 Henry IV*, the drunken Sir Toby Belch and the puritanical Malvolio ("ill will") in *Twelfth Night*. On rare occasions he went further and brought personified abstractions directly onto his stage— Rumour, in a robe painted full of tongues, in *2 Henry IV*, and Time, carrying an hourglass, in *The Winter's Tale*. But for the most part his debt to the morality plays was more indirect and subtle. He absorbed their impact early, and they helped fashion the foundations, largely hidden well beneath the surface, of his writing. That writing builds upon two crucial expectations the morality plays instilled in their audiences: first, the expectation that drama worth seeing would get at something central to human destiny and, second, that it should reach not only a coterie of the educated elite but also the great mass of ordinary people.

Shakespeare also absorbed specific elements of his stagecraft from the moralities. They helped him understand how to focus theatrical attention on his characters' psychological, moral, and spiritual life, as well as on their outward behavior. They helped him fashion physical emblems of this inner life, such as the withered arm and hunchback that mark the crookedness of Richard III. They helped him grasp how to construct plays around the struggle for the soul of a protagonist: Prince Hal poised between his sober, anxious, calculating father and the irresponsible, seductive, reckless Falstaff; the deputy Angelo, in *Measure for Measure*, given the reins of power and put to the test by his master the duke; Othello torn between his faith in the celestial Desdemona and the obscene suggestions of the demonic Iago. And above all, they provided him with a source for a theatrically compelling and subversive figure of wickedness.

The Vice, the great subversive figure of the moralities, was never far from Shakespeare's creative mind. With mingled affection and wariness, Hal refers to Falstaff as "that reverend Vice, that grey Iniquity" (*1 Henry IV*, 2.5.413); the mordantly funny, malevolent Richard III likens himself to "the formal Vice, Iniquity" (3.1.82); and Hamlet describes his wily, usurping uncle as "a vice of kings" (3.4.88). The word "vice" does not have to be directly invoked for the influence to be apparent: "Honest Iago," for example, with his air of camaraderie, his sly jokes, and his frank avowal of villainy, is heavily indebted to this figure. It is no accident that his diabolical plot against Othello and Desdemona takes the form of a practical joke, an unbearably cruel version of the tricks played by the Vice.

It may seem strange at first that the lovable Falstaff should find himself in the company of cold-hearted murderers like Claudius and Iago. But Shakespeare learned something else essential to his art from the morality plays; he learned that the boundary between comedy and tragedy is surprisingly porous. In figures such as Aaron the Moor (the black villain in *Titus Andronicus*), Richard III, and the bastard Edmund in *King Lear*, Shakespeare conjures up a particular kind of thrill he must have first had as a child watching the Vice in plays like *The Cradle of Security* and *The Interlude of Youth*: the thrill of fear braided together with transgressive pleasure. The Vice, wickedness personified, is appropriately punished at the end of the play, but for much of the performance he manages to captivate the audience, and the imagination takes a perverse holiday.

The authors of the morality plays thought they could enhance the broad impact they sought to achieve by stripping their characters of all incidental distinguishing traits to get to their essences. They thought their audiences would thereby not be distracted by the irrelevant details of individual identities. Shakespeare grasped that the spectacle of human destiny was, in fact, vastly more compelling when it was attached not to generalized abstractions but to particular named people, people realized with an unprecedented intensity of individuation: not Youth but Prince Hal, not Everyman but Othello.

To achieve this intensity, Shakespeare had as much to free himself from the old morality plays as to adapt them. He felt free to discard many aspects of them altogether and use others in ways their authors could never have imagined. At times he greatly intensified the fear: Iago is immeasurably more disturbing—and more effective—than Envy or Riot. At other times he greatly intensified the laughter: the Vice's trickery and delight in confusion turns up in Puck in *A Midsummer Night's Dream*, but the wickedness has been entirely leached away, leaving only the mischievousness. So too if the ass's head placed on Bottom strikingly recalls the swine's snout placed on the face of the king, the heavy weight of moral instruction has been entirely lifted. Bottom, to be sure, is asinine, but it takes no magical transformation to reveal that fact. Indeed, what is revealed is not so much his folly—he does not have one moment of embarrassment or shame, and his friends do not laugh at him—as his intrepidity. "This is to make an ass of me," the ass-headed Bottom stoutly declares, when his friends have all run away in terror at his appearance, "to fright me, if they could; but I will not stir from this place, do what they can" (3.1.106–8). He is surprised at the Fairy Queen's passionate declaration of love, but he takes it in his stride: "Methinks, mistress, you should have little reason for that. And yet, to say the truth, reason and love keep little company together nowadays" (3.1.126–28). And he is entirely at ease in his new body: "Methinks I have a great desire to a bottle of hay. Good hay, sweet hay, hath no fellow" (4.1.30–31). When the ass's head is finally taken from him, he does not experience a moral awakening; rather, as Puck puts it, he merely peeps at the world once again with his own fool's eyes.

Here, and throughout his career, Shakespeare altogether scrapped the piety that marked the plays he saw in his youth. The underlying structure of those plays was religious. Hence they often climaxed in a moment of vision that signaled the protagonist's redemption, a vision that pointed beyond the everyday and what was familiar to a truth that exceeded mortal understanding. In the words of St. Paul's Epistle to the Corinthians, words deeply familiar to Shakespeare and his contemporaries from endless repetitions in church, "The eye hath not seen, and the ear hath not heard, neither have entered into the heart of man" those things that God has prepared (1 Corinthians 2:9, from the Bishops' Bible [1568], the version Shakespeare knew and used most often). "I have had a most rare vision," Bottom begins, when he is returned to his human shape. And then, in a series of fits and starts, he tries to recount it:

I have had a dream past the wit of man to say what dream it was. Man is but an ass if he go about t'expound this dream. Methought I was—there is no man can tell what. Methought I was, and methought I had—but man is but a patched fool if he will offer to

say what methought I had. The eye of man hath not heard, the
ear of man hath not seen, man's hand is not able to taste, his
tongue to conceive, nor his heart to report what my dream was.
(4.1.199–207).

This is the joke of a decisively secular dramatist, a writer who deftly
turned the dream of the sacred into popular entertainment: "I will get
Peter Quince to write a ballad of this dream. It shall be called 'Bottom's
Dream,' because it hath no bottom, and I will sing it in the latter end of
a play" (4.1.207–10). The joke reaches out a long way—to the solemni-
ties of the pulpit, to the plays that the professional playing companies
took to the provinces when Shakespeare was a boy, to the amateur actors
who performed cruder versions of these plays, and perhaps to the young,
awkward Shakespeare himself, filled with visions his tongue could not
conceive and eager to play all the parts.

There must have been many such moments in Will's life at home.
The very young boy could have amused his family and friends by imitating what he had seen on the raised platform of the Stratford town-hall
stage or on the back of the traveling players' cart. And as he grew older
and more independent, his exposure to playacting was not restricted to
Stratford: the touring companies crisscrossed the Midlands, performing
in neighboring towns and manor houses. A stage-struck youth could
have seen most of the great actors of the time performing within a day's
ride of his home.

Theatrical life in the region by no means depended solely upon the
visits of professional troupes. Towns in the vicinity of Stratford, as in the
rest of the country, had seasonal festivals, when the members of guilds and
fraternities donned costumes and performed in traditional plays. For an
afternoon, ordinary folk—carpenters and tinkers and flute makers and the
like—paraded before their neighbors as kings and queens, madmen and
demons. Coventry, eighteen miles away, was particularly vital; when he was
young, Will could have been taken to see the Hock Tuesday play there. The
second Tuesday after Easter, Hock Tuesday traditionally initiated the summer half of the rural year and was celebrated, in many places, by women
tying up passersby with ropes and demanding money for charity. In

Coventry the men and women had a special way of marking the festival: they staged a rowdy commemoration of an ancient English massacre of the Danes, an event in which Englishwomen were said to have displayed particular valor. The annual reenactment enjoyed considerable local fame and may have drawn, among its spectators, the Shakespeare family.

In late May or June, in the time of long, sweetly lingering twilights, they could also have seen one of the great annual Corpus Christi pageants, plays presenting the whole destiny of mankind from the creation and the Fall to the redemption. These so-called mystery cycles, among the great achievements of medieval drama, had survived into the later sixteenth century in Coventry and in several other cities in England. Associated originally with a grand procession to honor the Eucharist, the production of a mystery cycle was a major civic enterprise, involving large numbers of people and significant expenditure. At various places in the city, usually on specially built scaffolds or carts, a part of the cycle—the story of Noah, the angel of the Annunciation, the raising of Lazarus, Jesus on the Cross, the three Marys at the tomb, and so forth—was performed by pious (or simply exuberantly histrionic) townspeople. Particular guilds usually assumed the costs and the responsibility for the individual pieces of the cycle, at times with particular appropriateness: the shipwrights undertook Noah, the goldsmiths the Magi, the bakers the Last Supper, and the pinners (men who made pins and needles) the Crucifixion.

Protestant reformers were understandably hostile, for they wished to dismantle the traditional Catholic culture and rituals out of which these pageants arose, and they campaigned hard to put the performances to an end. But the plays were not strictly Catholic, and the civic pride and pleasure in them was intense, so they lingered, in the teeth of opposition, into the 1570s and '80s. In 1579, when Will was fifteen, he and his family could still have seen them performed at Coventry. Something of their power—their way of constructing a shared community of spectators, their confidence that all things in the heavens and the earth can be represented onstage, their delicious blending of homeliness and exaltation—left its mark upon him.

These events were particularly spectacular instances of seasonal festivities that shaped Will's sense of the year and conditioned his later understanding of the theater. Many of the traditional holidays had withered under attacks, both from those who thought the calendar offered working people too many occasions to play and from those who thought that particular customs were tinged with Catholicism or paganism. But the moralists and the religious reformers had not yet managed to discipline the festive year into relentless sobriety. "I came once to a place, riding on a journey homeward from London," wrote the great Protestant bishop Hugh Latimer in 1549,

> and I sent word over night into the town that I would preach there in the morning because it was holy day. . . . The church stood in my way, and I took my horse, and my company, and went thither. I thought I should have found a great company in the church, and when I came there, the church door was fast locked. I tarried there half an hour and more, at last the key was found, and one of the parish comes to me and says: "Sir, this is a busy day with us, we cannot hear you, it is Robin Hood's Day. The parish are gone abroad to gather for Robin Hood. . . ." I was fain there to give place to Robin Hood.

A traditional May game probably kept the parish busy that day—on May Day people had long celebrated the legend of Robin Hood, with raucous, often bawdy rituals.

Thirty-four years later an irascible polemicist, Philip Stubbes, reiterated the complaint:

> Against May, Whitsunday, or other time, all the young men and maids, old men and wives, run gadding overnight to the woods . . . where they spend all the night in pleasant pastimes, and in the morning they return, bringing with them birch and branches of trees. . . . But the chiefest jewel they bring from thence is their Maypole, which they bring home with great veneration, as thus: they have twenty or forty yoke of oxen, every ox having a sweet nosegay of flowers placed on the tip of his horns; and these oxen draw home this Maypole (this stinking idol, rather) which is cov-

ered all over with flowers and herbs, bound round about with strings from the top to the bottom, and sometimes painted with variable colors, with two or three hundred men, women, and children following it with great devotion. And thus being reared up with handkerchiefs and flags hovering on the top, they strew the ground round about, bind green boughs about it, set up summer halls, bowers, and arbors hard by it. And then fall they to dance about it, like as the heathen people did at the dedication of the idols, whereof this is a perfect pattern, or rather the thing itself.

Stubbes was writing in 1583, when Will was nineteen. Even if Stubbes sullenly exaggerated the pervasiveness and vitality of the ancient folk customs—customs whose attractiveness comes across despite his pious horror—he was not making it up: traditional festivities, though constantly under attack, endured throughout the late sixteenth century and beyond.

What might Will have participated in, growing up in Stratford and its surrounding countryside? Men and women and children, their faces flushed with pleasure, dancing around a Maypole, decked with ribbons and garlands. A coarse Robin Hood show, with a drunken Friar Tuck and a lascivious Maid Marion. A young woman garlanded with flowers as the Queen of the May. A young boy dressed as the bishop and paraded through the streets with mock gravity. A belching, farting Lord of Misrule who temporarily turned the world upside down. Topsy-turvy days when women pursued men and schoolboys locked the teachers out of the classroom. Torchlight processions featuring men dressed as fantastic animals, "wodewoses" (wild men), and giants. Leaping morris dancers—from their supposed Moorish origin—with bells around their knees and ankles, cavorting with dancers wearing the wickerwork contraption known as the Hobbyhorse. Bagpipers, drummers, and fools dressed in motley carrying baubles and pigs' bladders. Drinking contests, eating contests, and singing contests at sheep-shearing and harvest-home festivals. Most interesting of all, perhaps, at Christmastime there was the mummers' play, featuring a madman, his five sons—Pickle Herring, Blue Breeches, Pepper Breeches, Ginger Breeches, and Mr. Allspice—and a woman named Cicely (or, on occasion, Maid Marion). The madman first fights with the hobbyhorse and with a "wild worm," that is, a dragon. The sons then decide to kill their father; interlocking their swords around his neck, they force him to kneel down and make his will, before dispatching him. One of the sons, Pickle Herring, stamps his feet upon the ground and brings the father back to life. The play—or perhaps, with its seasonal occasion, primordial rhythms, and indifference to realism, it should be called a ritual—lurches toward its end with the father and sons wooing Cicely together and then with grotesque sword dances and morris dances.

These folk customs, all firmly rooted in the Midlands, had a significant impact upon Shakespeare's imagination, fashioning his sense of theater even more than the morality plays that the touring companies brought to the provinces. Folk culture is everywhere in his work, in the web of allusions and in the underlying structures. The lovers who meet in the Athenian woods in *A Midsummer Night's Dream* are reminiscent of May Day lovers; the deposed Duke Senior in the Forest of Arden in *As You Like It* is likened to Robin Hood; the drunken Sir Toby and, still more, Falstaff are Lords of Misrule who turn the order of things topsy-turvy; and, as queen of the feast, the garlanded Perdita in *The Winter's Tale* presides over a rustic sheep-shearing festival, complete with dancing swains and maidens and a sly, light-fingered peddler.

The author of *The Winter's Tale* was not a folk artist, and he made it clear in many ways that he was not. A sheep-shearing festival performed on the stage of the Globe as part of a sophisticated tragicomedy was not in fact a sheep-shearing festival; it was an urban fantasy of rural life, informed by knowing touches of realism but also carefully distanced from its homely roots. Shakespeare was a master of this distancing; if he had a sympathetic understanding of country customs, he also had ways of showing that they were no longer his native element. The Athenian lovers are not in fact in the woods to celebrate the May; Duke Senior bears no real resemblance to Robin Hood; the queen of the sheep-shearing festival is not a shepherd's daughter but the daughter of a king; and if an old, mad father becomes the object of murderous attack by his children, it is not in the grotesque comedy of the mummers' play but in the sublime tragedy of *King Lear*. No one can stamp upon the ground and make Lear or his daughter Cordelia spring back to life. Sir Toby and Falstaff come closer to the actual way in which Lords of Misrule functioned—they do for a limited time overturn sobriety, dignity, and decorum—but Shakespeare went out of his way to depict them after their disorderly reign is over: "What, is it a time to jest and dally now?" Prince Hal shouts in a rage, throwing the bottle of sack at Falstaff (*1 Henry IV*, 5.3.54). "I hate a drunken rogue," moans Sir Toby, beaten and hungover (*Twelfth Night*, 5.1.193–94).

But there was nothing defensive in the ways Shakespeare distanced himself, no stiff-necked insistence on his sophistication or learning, no self-conscious embrace of the urban or the courtly. He had deep roots in the country. Virtually all of his close relatives were farmers, and in his childhood he clearly spent a great deal of time in their orchards and market gardens, in the surrounding fields and woods, and in tiny rural hamlets with their traditional seasonal festivals and folk customs. When he was growing up, he seems to have taken in everything about this rustic world, and he did not subsequently seek to repudiate it or pass himself off as something other than what he was. The cultivated Elizabethan literary critic George Puttenham writes snobbishly of "boys or country fellows" who listened with delight to blind harpers and tavern minstrels singing old romances and who enjoyed the carols sung at Christmas dinners and at the old-fashioned wedding feasts known as bridales. Will was almost certainly one of those country fellows. He doesn't seem to have been anxious about such pleasures, though he subsequently moved in circles that laughed at their rusticity. He simply took them with him to London, as his possession, to be used as much or as little as he liked.

Shakespeare was anything but indifferent to being counted as a gentleman. But his concern for his station in life, his longing for social success, and his fascination with the lives of aristocrats and monarchs did not entail the erasure of the world from which he came. Perhaps he simply loved the world too much to give any of it up. Instead, he used his boyhood experiences—as he used virtually all of his experiences—as an inexhaustible source of metaphor.

In one of his earliest history plays, *2 Henry VI* (written around 1591), Shakespeare has the ambitious, conniving Duke of York explain that he has lured the headstrong Kentish peasant Jack Cade into rebellion. "In

Ireland have I seen this stubborn Cade" fight against a troop of soldiers,
York remarks,

> And fought so long till that his thighs with darts
> Were almost like a sharp-quilled porcupine;
> And in the end, being rescued, I have seen
> Him caper upright like a wild Morisco,
> Shaking the bloody darts as he his bells.
>   (3.1.360, 362–66)

Shakespeare himself had in all likelihood not served in the wars and had
never seen a soldier's thighs pierced with arrows, but as a country boy, he
had almost certainly seen his share of sharp-quilled porcupines. He had
also almost certainly seen his share of morris dancers—"wild Moriscos"—
leaping about in a kind of ecstasy. From such sights he constructed his
astonishing image of the unstoppable Cade. More important, from the
accumulation of such sights and sounds and rituals he constructed his
sense of the magic of the theater.

But it was not only these traditional folk rituals, with their illusory
but compelling air of timelessness, that exercised a powerful imaginative
influence upon him; a particular event in his neighborhood, widely noted
at the time, seems to have strongly marked his vision of the theater. In the
summer of 1575, when Will was eleven, the queen had gone to the Midlands on one of her royal progresses—journeys, accompanied by an enormous retinue, on which, bejeweled like a Byzantine icon, she displayed
herself to her people, surveyed her realm, received tributes; and all but
bankrupted her hosts. Elizabeth, who had already visited the area in 1566
and again in 1572, was the supreme mistress of these occasions, at once
thrilling and terrifying those who encountered her. In 1572 she was
greeted officially by the Recorder of Warwick, Edward Aglionby, a local
dignitary whom the Shakespeares would probably have known. Aglionby
was a learned and imposing figure, but in the presence of the queen he
trembled. "Come hither, little Recorder," the queen said, holding out her
hand for him to kiss. "It was told me that you would be afraid to look
upon me or to speak so boldly; but you were not so afraid as I was of you."

No one, least of all the "little Recorder" himself, would have believed that polite fiction from the daughter of Henry VIII.

The climax of the 1575 progress was a nineteen-day stay—from July 9 to 27—at Kenilworth, the castle of the queen's favorite Robert Dudley, the Earl of Leicester. Kenilworth is located some twelve miles northeast of Stratford, which would have been caught up, like the entire region, in the feverish preparations for the visit. John Shakespeare, a Stratford alderman at the time, was too insignificant a figure to have got very close, in all likelihood, to the elaborate entertainments that were staged for the queen by the man she called her "eyes," but it is certainly conceivable that he took his son Will to glimpse what they could of the spectacles: the grand arrival of the queen, greeted with speeches by Sibylla, Hercules, the Lady of the Lake, and (in Latin) an emblematic poet; fireworks; a dialogue between a Savage Man and Echo; a bearbaiting (a "sport" in which mastiffs attacked a bear chained to a stake); more fireworks; a display of acrobatics by an Italian; and an elaborate water pageant.

Leicester, whose hold on the queen's favor had been slipping and who clearly regarded this as an occasion on which nothing should be omitted that might conceivably bring her pleasure, also arranged for a set of rustic shows. The shows were the equivalent of the mock-authentic cultural performances done in our own time for visiting dignitaries or wealthy tourists; they included a bridale and morris dance, a quintain (a sport of tilting at targets), and the traditional Coventry Hock Tuesday play. These folk entertainments were of the kind that had been attacked by moralists and strict reformers, as Leicester understood perfectly well. He also understood that the queen took pleasure in them, was hostile to their puritanical critics, and would be sympathetic to an appeal to allow them to continue.

Will may have watched these pieces of his own local culture staged for the grand visitors. He would at the very least have heard the events described in loving detail, and he is also likely to have encountered an elaborate written description of them in a marvelous long letter by a minor official— "clerk of the council chamber door"—Robert Langham, or Laneham. The letter, inexpensively printed and widely circulated, would have been useful reading for anyone who was in the business of trying to entertain the queen—and Shakespeare was shortly to go into that business.

Langham's letter makes clear that the performance of the Hock Tuesday play was a carefully stage-managed piece of cultural politics. Certain "good-hearted men of Coventry," led by a mason named Captain Cox, had learned that their neighbor, the Earl of Leicester, was entertaining the queen. Knowing that he was eager to make his sovereign "gladsome and merry" with all pleasant recreations, the Coventry artisans petitioned that they might renew their old show. They thought that the queen would particularly enjoy the commemoration of the ancient massacre because it showed "how valiantly our English women for love of their country behaved themselves." This appeal to the queen's special interest was part of a defensive strategy that Langham conveniently summarizes: "The thing, said they, is grounded on story, and for pastime wont to be played in our city yearly, without ill example of manners, papistry, or any superstition, and else did so occupy the heads of a number that likely enough would have had worse meditations." The claims here turn out to be ones that would be repeated again and again throughout Shakespeare's lifetime, both in the justification of particular plays and in defense of the stage in general: the play in question is based on history ("grounded on story"), it is a traditional form of entertainment, it is free from ideological contamination and immorality, and it is a distraction from potentially dangerous thoughts, "worse meditations." That is, members of the audience who might otherwise be plotting mischief—brooding on injustice, for example, or longing for the old religion, or hatching rebellion—would have their minds safely occupied by the spectacle of the ancient massacre of the Danes.

What was the problem, then? Why did the Hock Tuesday play, which had "an ancient beginning and a long continuance," need to be defended at all? Because, the artisans acknowledged, it had been "of late laid down"— that is, banned. The men scratched their heads and said they could not quite understand it: "They knew no cause why." Then, as if it suddenly occurred to them, they came up with an explanation: "unless it were by the zeal of certain of their preachers, men very commendable for behavior and learning, and sweet in their sermons, but somewhat too sour in preaching away their pastime." The performance at Kenilworth, then, was not simply a way of amusing the queen; or rather, in any attempt to amuse the queen there was always a half-hidden agenda. Here the agenda was to get the queen to pressure the local clergy to halt the campaign against a beloved local festivity: "they would make their humble petition unto her highness that they might have their plays up again."

Despite the careful planning for the Hock Tuesday performance—the show took place directly below the queen's window—the occasion was botched. Too many things were going on at once—the bridale and the dancing drew away the queen's attention, and she was further distracted by "the great throng and unruliness" of the crowd that had been allowed into the courtyard (into which an eleven-year-old boy may have made his way). Elizabeth managed to see only a bit of the play. After all their rehearsals and strategizing, the men of Coventry must have been crushed. But then, unexpectedly, all was saved—the queen commanded that the performance be repeated on the following Tuesday. It was a success: "Her Majesty laughed well." The town players, rewarded with two bucks upon which to feast and with five pieces of silver, were ecstatic: "What, rejoicing upon their ample reward, and what, triumphing upon the good acceptance, they vaunted their play was never so dignified, nor ever any players afore so beatified." And in the Coventry records for the next year there is a crucial confirmation of their triumph: "Thomas Nicklyn Mayor. . . . This year the said mayor caused Hock Tuesday, whereby is mentioned an overthrow of the Danes by the inhabitants of this city, to be again set up and showed forth."

"Her Majesty laughed well." Said to have cost Leicester the staggering sum of a thousand pounds a day, the Kenilworth festivities were an enormous machine designed to produce those laughs—along with admiration, wonder, and delight—from the remarkable, unpredictable, dangerous woman who ruled the country. The spectacles were elaborate and arresting, but the attention of the Earl of Leicester—and no doubt of many others in the crowd—would have been intensely focused on a single person. If a wide-eyed young boy from Stratford did see her, arrayed in one of her famously elaborate dresses, carried in a litter on the shoulders of guards specially picked for their good looks, accompanied by her gorgeously arrayed courtiers, he would in effect have witnessed the greatest theatrical spectacle of the age. As the queen once candidly remarked of herself, "We princes are set on stages in the sight and view of all the world."

Shakespeare continued to be fascinated throughout his entire career by the charismatic power of royalty—the excitement awakened in crowds, the trembling in otherwise strong men, the sense of awesome greatness. Long after he had come to understand the dark sides of this power; long after he had taken in the pride, cruelty, and ambition that it aroused, the dangerous plots that it bred, the greed and violence that it fostered and fed upon, Shakespeare remained in touch with the intoxicating pleasure and excitement royalty aroused. At the close of his creative life, in the play originally called *All Is True* and known today as *Henry VIII*, he still drew on this excitement, imagining the birth of the radiant queen whom he may have first glimpsed at Kenilworth in 1575. For there *was* a first time that he glimpsed her—if not at Kenilworth, then somewhere else, in a procession or a grand entertainment or a court reception—and his imagination was certainly fired by what he saw. And the events at Kenilworth, whether young Will saw them for himself or listened to eyewitness accounts of them or simply read Langham's letter, seem to have left traces in his work.

In the single most extravagant entertainment Leicester staged for the queen during her long stay, a twenty-four-foot-long mechanical dolphin rose up out of the waters of the lake adjacent to the castle. On the back of the dolphin—in whose belly was concealed a consort of wind instruments—sat the figure of Arion, the legendary Greek musician, who sang, as Langham put it, "a delectable ditty" to the queen. "The ditty in metre so aptly endited to the matter," Langham recalled,

> and after by voice so deliciously delivered; the song by a skilful artist into its parts so sweetly sorted; each part in its instrument so clean and sharply touched; every instrument again in its kind so excellently tunable; and this in the evening of the day, resounding from the calm waters, where presence of her Majesty and longing to listen had utterly damped all noise and din; the whole harmony conveyed in time, tune, and temper thus incomparably melodious. With what pleasure . . . with what sharpness of conceit, with what

lively delight this might pierce into the hearers' hearts, I pray you imagine yourself as you may, for so God judge me, by all the wit and cunning I have, I cannot express, I promise you.

Years later, Shakespeare seems to have remembered this luminous spectacle in *Twelfth Night*, when the sea captain tries to reassure Viola that her brother may not have drowned in the shipwreck: "like Arion on the dolphin's back," he tells her, "I saw him hold acquaintance with the waves" (1.2.14–15).

More strikingly, in *A Midsummer Night's Dream* (written in the mid-1590s, when Shakespeare was about thirty), the playwright's imagination drew on the scene at Kenilworth in crafting a gorgeous compliment to Elizabeth. The queen probably attended one of the early performances of the comedy—perhaps the earliest, if, as many scholars think, it was written for an aristocratic wedding that she graced with her presence—and the company obviously felt that a piece of flattery was called for. But Shakespeare did not simply break the illusion and have the players turn to address the queen. Instead, he slipped in a passage of prince-pleasing mythology that takes the form of a memory. The memory—of an occasion when Cupid took aim at the "fair vestal thronèd by the west" (2.1.158)—clearly alludes to Leicester's attempt, some twenty years earlier, to charm the queen. "Thou rememb'rest," the Fairy king Oberon asks his principal assistant, Puck,

> Since once I sat upon a promontory
> And heard a mermaid on a dolphin's back
> Uttering such dulcet and harmonious breath
> That the rude sea grew civil at her song
> And certain stars shot madly from their spheres
> To hear the sea-maid's music?
>
> (2.1.148–54)

It is worth reading the last three lines aloud for oneself to see how perfectly they serve as an exquisite instance of "dulcet and harmonious breath." Eerily beautiful, they conjure up, across the gap in time, the fireworks visible from afar—as far as twenty miles away, according to one observer—along with a fantastical version of the water pageant. The speech goes on to bow graciously toward the aging Elizabeth's cult of virginity: Cupid's arrow missed its mark, and "the imperial vot'ress passèd on, / In maiden meditation, fancy-free" (2.1.163–64). Having delivered this exquisite compliment to the queen, the play resumes its momentarily suspended plot. The arrow intended for the fair vestal, Oberon explains to Puck, fell instead on a little western flower. When placed on the eyelids of a sleeping man or woman, the juice of this flower will make the person dote on the next live creature that he or she sees. It is this device, love juice, mistakenly applied to the wrong eyelids, that occasions the wild confusions of the play.

The glimpse of the dolphin's back is only an isolated moment in *A Midsummer Night's Dream,* a decorative flourish. But the lines about the mermaid's song, though irrelevant to the plot, speak to something deeply important in the play and in the playwright's imagination. The memory of Kenilworth served to evoke the power that song has to create hushed order and to excite an almost frenzied attention. This paradox—art as the source both of settled calm and of deep disturbance—was central to Shakespeare's entire career. As a dramatist and a poet, he was simultaneously the agent of civility and the agent of subversion. This double vision in him might well reach back to the astonishing spectacle, mounted close to his home when he was eleven years old: a huge, restive sea of spectators quieted by the queen's presence, with everyone straining intently to listen to the song of Arion, the primordial poet.

What Shakespeare articulated in *A Midsummer Night's Dream* was a deep cultural fantasy that Leicester's entertainments extravagantly tried to embody. The fantasy was of a world of magical beauty, shot through with hidden forces and producing a free-floating, intense erotic energy to which all creatures, save one alone—the "fair vestal thronèd by the west"—had to succumb. Reality could never have approached this dream: the fireworks were hardly stars starting from their spheres; there was no sea, only an unruly crowd by the castle lake; the fair vestal was a middle-aged woman with rotting teeth; the mechanical dolphin would have looked no better than expensive floats usually look; and the figure on the dolphin's back was neither Arion nor a mermaid but a singer named Harry Goldingham. As an unpublished contemporary account of the festivities relates, the singer was not in good voice:

> There was a Spectacle presented to Queen Elizabeth upon the water, and amongst others, Harry Goldingham was to represent Arion upon the Dolphin's back, but finding his voice to be very hoarse and unpleasant when he came to perform it, he tears off his Disguise, and swears he was none of Arion, not he, but even honest Harry Goldingham; which blunt discovery pleased the Queen better than if it had gone through in the right way.

The queen's gracious response managed to salvage the enchantment of the afternoon, even in the face of its apparent crumbling. Something similar could be said about any production of *A Midsummer Night's Dream*: the spectators do not see fairies flying through the moonlit woods near Athens; they see a troupe of all-too-human actors tramping about onstage. But the risk of disillusionment only seems to enhance the experience of wonder.

Leicester got the effect he wanted by means of an enormous capital outlay. Shakespeare offered a vastly less expensive magic: the players in *A Midsummer Night's Dream* entertain the wild hope that they might be rewarded with a pension of sixpence per day apiece. For the playwright relied not on elaborate machinery but on language, simply the most beautiful language any English audience had ever heard:

> I know a bank where the wild thyme blows,
> Where oxlips and the nodding violet grows,
> Quite overcanopied with luscious woodbine,
> With sweet musk-roses, and with eglantine.
> There sleeps Titania sometime of the night,
> Lulled in these flowers with dances and delight.
>
> (2.1.249–54)

Shakespeare, who had already written such plays as *The Taming of the Shrew* and *Richard III*, was capable of a very different kind of dramatic speech, altogether tougher and leaner, but in *A Midsummer Night's Dream* he gave full scope to what is, to borrow one of the adjectives he uses here, luscious poetry.

Among Shakespeare's plays, *A Midsummer Night's Dream* is one of the very few for which scholars have never located a dominant literary source; its vision of moonlit, fairy-haunted woods evidently sprang from more idiosyncratic and personal imaginative roots. Shakespeare was able to tap into his close-up knowledge of "the barky fingers of the elm" or "a red-hipped humble-bee on the top of a thistle" (4.1.41, 11–12). He was also, if this account of his childhood is correct, able to tap into firsthand experiences of the swirling delights of May Day and Hock Tuesday and into memories of the lavish, visionary entertainments Leicester staged in order to please his royal guest.

If Shakespeare's sense of the transforming power of theatrical illusions may be traced back to what he heard about or saw for himself in 1575 at Kenilworth, his sense of the coarse reality that lies beneath the illusions may very well go back to the same festive moment. Virtually the whole last act of *A Midsummer Night's Dream* is given over to a hilarious parody of such amateur theatrical entertainments, which are ridiculed for their plodding ineptitude, their naïveté, their failure to sustain a convincing illusion. The Hock Tuesday play, performed by the Coventry artisans for the queen and her courtiers, is transmuted into "A tedious brief scene of young Pyramus / And his love Thisbe: very tragical mirth" (5.1.56–57), performed by the Athenian artisans for the highborn couples joining in wedlock. The newlyweds, and the audience of *A Midsummer Night's Dream*, take pleasure in laughing at the grotesque absurdities of the play and the spectacular incompetence of the players, "Hard-handed men that work in Athens here, / Which never laboured in their minds till now" (5.1.72–73). One of the blundering artisans in *A Midsummer Night's Dream*, Snug the Joiner, even seems to mimic Harry Goldingham's "blunt discovery" of his actual identity. The dim-witted Snug, cast as a lion, has from the start been worried about the role, and all of the players are concerned that he will frighten the ladies. Hence, when he plays his part, he pulls a Harry Goldingham:

> You, ladies, you whose gentle hearts do fear
>   The smallest monstrous mouse that creeps on floor,
> May now perchance both quake and tremble here
>   When lion rough in wildest rage doth roar.
> Then know that I as Snug the joiner am
> A lion fell. . . .
>
> (5.1.214–19)

Sure enough, the comic ineptitude pleases the ruler. "A very gentle beast," says Duke Theseus, "and of a good conscience" (5.1.222). The performance gets what these performances always longed to get: the smile of the great. "Her Majesty laughed well."

A Midsummer Night's Dream—written some twenty years after the Kenilworth festivities—marks the adult playwright's access to some of the most memorable scenes of his childhood, and at the same time it marks the distance he had traveled from home. By 1595, Shakespeare clearly grasped that his career was built on a triumph of the professional London entertainment industry over traditional amateur performances. His great comedy was a personal celebration of escape as well as of mastery. Escape from what? From tone-deaf plays, like Thomas Preston's *A Lamentable Tragedy, Mixed Full of Pleasant Mirth, Containing the Life of Cambises, King of Persia*, whose lame title Shakespeare parodied. From coarse language and jog trotting meter and rant pretending to be passion. From amateur actors too featherbrained to remember their lines, too awkward to perform gracefully, too shy to perform energetically, or, worst of all, too puffed up with vanity to perform anything but their own grotesque egotism. The troupe of artisans who perform "Pyramus and Thisbe"—the weaver Nick Bottom, the bellows-mender Francis Flute, the tinker Tom Snout, the joiner Snug, the tailor Robin Starveling, and their director, the carpenter Peter Quince—are collectively an anthology of theatrical catastrophes.

The laughter in act 5 of *A Midsummer Night's Dream*—and it is one of the most enduringly funny scenes Shakespeare ever wrote—is built on a sense of superiority in intelligence, training, cultivation, and skill. The audience is invited to join the charmed circle of the upper-class mockers onstage. This mockery proclaimed the young playwright's definitive passage from naïveté and homespun amateurism to sophisticated taste and professional skill. But the laughter that the scene solicits is curiously tender and even loving. What saves the scene of ridicule from becoming too painful, what keeps it delicious in fact, is the self-possession of the artisans. In the face of open derision, they are unflappable. Shakespeare achieved a double effect. On the one hand, he mocked the amateurs, who fail to grasp the most basic theatrical conventions, by which they are to stay in their roles and pretend they cannot see or hear their audience. On the other hand, he conferred an odd, unexpected dignity upon Bottom and his fellows, a dignity that contrasts favorably with the sardonic rudeness of the aristocratic spectators.

Even as he called attention to the distance between himself and the rustic performers, then, Shakespeare doubled back and signaled a current of sympathy and solidarity. As when borrowing from the old morality plays and folk culture, he understood at once that he was doing something quite different and that he owed a debt. The professions he assigned the Athenian artisans were not chosen at random—Shakespeare's London theater company depended on joiners and weavers, carpenters and tailors—and the tragedy they perform, of star-crossed lovers, fatal errors, and suicides, is one in which the playwright himself was deeply interested. In the period he was writing the "Pyramus and Thisbe" parody, Shakespeare was also writing the strikingly similar *Romeo and Juliet*; they may well have been on his writing table at the same time. A more defensive artist would have scrubbed harder in an attempt to remove these marks of affinity, but Shakespeare's laughter was not a form of renunciation or concealment. "This is the silliest stuff that ever I heard," Hippolyta comments, to which Theseus replies, "The best in this kind are but shadows, and the worst are no worse if imagination amend them." "It must be your imagination, then, and not theirs," is her rejoinder (5.1.207–10)—the spectators' imagination and not the players'—but that is precisely the point: the difference between the professional actor and the amateur actor is not, finally, the crucial consideration. They both rely upon the imagination of the spectators. And, as if to clinch the argument, a moment later, at the preposterous suicide speech of Pyramus—

> Approach, ye furies fell.
>   O fates, come, come,
>   Cut thread and thrum,
> Quail, crush, conclude, and quell
>   (5.1.273–76)

—Hippolyta finds herself unaccountably moved: "Beshrew my heart, but I pity the man" (5.1.279).

When in *A Midsummer Night's Dream* the thirty-year-old Shakespeare, drawing deeply upon his own experiences, thought about his profession, he split the theater between a magical, virtually nonhuman element, which he associated with the power of the imagination to lift itself away from the constraints of reality, and an all-too-human element, which he associated with the artisans' trades that actually made the material structures—buildings, platforms, costumes, musical instruments, and the like—structures that gave the imagination a local habitation and a name. He understood, and he wanted the audience to understand, that the theater had to have both, both the visionary flight and the solid, ordinary earthiness.

That earthiness was a constituent part of his creative imagination. He never forgot the provincial, everyday world from which he came or the ordinary face behind the mask of Arion.

CHAPTER 2

The Dream of Restoration

A STRATFORD LEGEND, recorded around 1680 by the eccentric, gossipy biographer John Aubrey, held that Will Shakespeare, apprenticed to be a butcher like his father, occasionally took a turn at slaughtering the animals: "When he killed a calf, he would do it in a high style, and make a speech." The inquisitive Aubrey, trying to find out how young Shakespeare solved the problem of work and discovered his vocation, wanted to know what happened between the time that he left school, presumably at some point in the late 1570s or early 1580s, and the time, in the early 1590s, that he was first noted as a professional actor and playwright in London.

The mystery of what Shakespeare was up to in what scholars have dubbed the "Lost Years"—the years when he dropped from sight and left no traces in the documents of a notably record-keeping society—has generated mountains of speculation. Legends, some more or less plausible, began to emerge about seventy-five years after his death, that is, when those who could possibly have known him personally had all died off but people were still alive who could, in their younger years, have encountered his contemporaries and sought out information about him.

Though Aubrey's story about butchery is implausible—John Shakespeare was not a butcher and would not have been permitted by trade regulation to slaughter animals—it is a safe bet that from boyhood on Will had helped his father in the family business, the making and selling of gloves from the shop that occupied part of the family's handsome double house on Henley Street.

No doubt he wrote poems in his spare moments, but his family would hardly have toiled to subsidize his idleness. Paper was expensive. A pack of paper that, neatly folded and cut, yielded about fifty small sheets would have cost at least fourpence, or the equivalent of eight pints of ale, more than a pound of raisins, a pound of mutton and a pound of beef, two dozen eggs, or two loaves of bread. Perhaps young Will carved his verses, like Orlando in *As You Like It*, on trees. All the same, he would have been expected to work. Indeed, there is an odd trace of the kind of contribution to the glove trade his special talents as a poet offered. Alexander Aspinall came to Stratford in 1582 to be master at the King's New School, shortly after Will had finished his schooling there but when his younger brothers presumably were in attendance. In the seventeenth century, someone wrote down in a commonplace book—a notebook in which it was customary to record memorable or curious things—verses that accompanied a pair of gloves sent by Master Aspinall to the woman he was then courting:

> The gift is small, the will is all.
> Alexander Aspinall

The gloves were presumably bought at John Shakespeare's shop, for the posy was noted as a trace of the famous poet: "Shaxpaire upon a pair of gloves that master sent to his mistress." Instead of making a career writing plays, Will could have stayed at home and eked out a living as the writer of personalized jingles into which he slyly inserted his own name.

He did not, in fact, leave it all completely behind: gloves, skins, and leather show up frequently in the plays, in ways that seem to reflect an easy intimacy with the trade. Romeo longs to be a glove on Juliet's hand, so that he could touch her cheek. The peddler in *The Winter's Tale* has scented gloves in his pack "as sweet as damask roses" (4.4.216). "Is not parchment," asks Hamlet, "made of sheepskins?" "Ay, my lord," replies Horatio, "and of calf-skins too" (5.1.104–5). The officer in *The Comedy of Errors* wears a calf-skin uniform—he resembles "a bass viol in a case of leather" (4.3.22); Petruchio, in *The Taming of the Shrew*, has a bridle made of sheep's leather; the cobbler in *Julius Caesar* resoles shoes made of neat's leather; tinkers, according to *The Winter's Tale*, carry sow-skin bags. When Shakespeare wanted to convey the fantastical world of the fairies in *A Midsummer Night's Dream*, he played with miniaturized versions of this trade: the "enamelled skin" shed by snakes is "wide enough to wrap a fairy in," and the Fairy Queen's followers war with bats "for their leathern wings / To make my small elves coats" (2.1.255–56, 2.2.4–5).

For Shakespeare, leather was not only a means of providing vivid detail but also the stuff of metaphor; it evidently came readily to mind when he was putting together his world. "A sentence is but a cheverel glove to a good wit," quips the clown Feste in *Twelfth Night*, remarking on the ease with which language can been twisted, "how quickly the wrong side may be turned outward" (3.1.10–12). Young Will, assisting his father in the glover's shop, no doubt observed the qualities of good "cheverel"—fine kidskin valued for its elasticity and pliability—and they made a strong impression on him: "O, here's a wit of cheverel," Mercutio teases Romeo, "that stretches from an inch narrow to an ell broad [big stretch: an ell was forty-five inches]" (*Romeo and Juliet*, 2.3.72–73). "Your soft cheveril conscience," the reluctant Anne Boleyn is told in *Henry VIII*, would receive the king's gifts, "If you might please to stretch it" (2.3.32–33).

John Shakespeare bought and sold wool as well as leather. Here he was violating the laws that restricted this business to authorized wool merchants. But the illegal trade, called wool brogging, was potentially lucrative, and he had the range of contracts both in the town and in the countryside to make it seem worth the risk. To make his deals, John would have had to travel to sheep pens and rural markets, and he is likely to have taken his eldest son with him. Here too Will's imagination seems to have borne the imprint long after. We are constantly "handling our ewes," says the shepherd in *As You Like It*, explaining why he and his fellows do not kiss their hands in the manner of courtiers, "and their fells, you know, are greasy" (3.2.46–47). And when the rustic in *The Winter's Tale* carefully reckons how much his shearing is likely to bring, he uses terms—"wether," meaning a castrated ram; "tod," meaning twenty-eight pounds of wool—that Will would have heard as a child at his father's side: "Let me see. Every / 'leven wether tods, every tod yields pound and odd shilling. Fifteen hundred shorn, what comes the wool to?" (4.3.30–32). When in the nineteenth century the wing of the house that had served as John Shakespeare's shop needed a new floor, fragments of wool were found embedded in the soil beneath the floorboards.

Other traces of the shop on Henley Street and the surrounding countryside are preserved in the plays and poems. A legal document, dated three years before Will's birth in 1564, describes his father as an "agricola," Latin for farmer. Long after he settled in Stratford, John Shakespeare not only dealt in agricultural commodities but also contin- ued to buy and lease farmland around Stratford. Will must have been out in the country with his father and his mother all the time. (An inhabitant of Elizabethan Stratford, a town with only some two thousand inhabi- tants, was, in any case, only a short stroll away from the surrounding farms and woods.) One of the most beautiful and appealing aspects of his imagination is the ease, delicacy, and precision with which he enters into the lives of animals and describes the vagaries of the weather, the details of flowers and herbs, and the cycles of nature. He enters deftly as well into the business cycles of nature. "I am shepherd to another man," says Corin in *As You Like It*, explaining to his visitors why he cannot offer them hospitality, "And do not shear the fleeces that I graze." This is not an urban fantasy of shepherds piping melodies on oaten flutes, but an altogether more realistic world. "My master is of churlish disposition," the shepherd adds.

> Besides, his cot, his flocks, and bounds of feed
> Are now on sale, and at our sheepcote now
> By reason of his absence there is nothing
> That you will feed on.
>
> (2.4.73–75, 78–81)

Though he had intimate knowledge of the country—he had seen the inside of a shepherd's "cot" (cottage) and knew that the grazing rights, the "bounds of feed," would have been sold along with the flocks—William Shakespeare was not essentially a countryman, nor, despite his origins, was his father. Indeed, the son was powerfully struck less by his father's rural wisdom than by his moneylending, for which he was twice taken to court in 1570, and by his property transactions, the real-world model for the maps, deeds, and conveyances that figure so frequently in the plays. The core biographical records of the poet's adult life are real estate documents. Biographers have often lamented the plethora of these documents in the place of something more intimate, but Shakespeare's lifelong interest in property investments—so unlike that of his fellow playwrights—may be more intimate a revelation than has been readily understood to be.

Will's early years, in any case, must have been strongly marked by his father's impressive entrepreneurial energy and ambition. John Shakespeare, the son of a tenant farmer from the small village of Snitterfield, was rising in the world. In the late 1550s he had made his first decisive move upward by wedding Mary Arden, the daughter of the man from whom his father had rented land. The Arden name was itself a significant piece of social capital: the family was one of Warwickshire's most distinguished, tracing its lineage back to the Domesday Book, the great record of property holdings compiled for William the Conqueror in 1086. The Arden properties occupy four long columns in that record, and the great expanse of forest to the north and west of Stratford was still in Shakespeare's time known as the Forest of Arden.

Mary's father, Robert, was by no means a prominent member of this family; he was simply a prosperous farmer who kept seven cows, eight oxen for the plough, two bullocks, and four weaning calves. If the inventory made at the time of his death is any indication, the household had no table knives, forks, or crockery—domestic signs of social distinction in a period when ordinary folk ate with their fingers from wooden plates—and owned no books. In the Arden household, the most visible marks of culture were "painted cloths"—the low-cost equivalent of tapestries, typically captioned with sententious mottoes—of which the inventory lists two in the hall, five in the chamber, and four in the bedroom. (When he wrote *The Rape of Lucrece,* Shakespeare ironically recalled their homely lessons: "Who fears a sentence or an old man's saw / Shall by a painted cloth be kept in awe.") It is not clear that anyone in the household could read the mottoes on their painted cloths; perhaps they simply liked the effect of the writing on the walls.

In a world that took kinship seriously, it meant something to be related, if only distantly, to such a distinguished and wealthy man as Edward Arden of Park Hall, the great house near Birmingham. Arden was a name for anyone with social ambition to conjure with, and a name was by no means all the riches that Mary's dowry held. Though she was the youngest of eight daughters, Mary was her father's favorite. When he died in 1556—commending his soul, like a good Catholic, "to Almighty God, and to our blessed Lady Saint Mary, and to all the holy company of heaven"—he left his youngest daughter a tidy sum of money and his most valuable property, a farm called Asbies in the village of Wilmcote, along with other lands. John Shakespeare married well.

There is no record of precisely when John decided to leave the farm in Snitterfield and move to Stratford, where he must have apprenticed himself to a glover, but his neighbors were quick to recognize his virtues. In 1556, when he was still in his twenties, he was elected an ale-taster for the borough, one of the inspectors of bread and ale. The position was for people deemed "able and discreet," who would not "let for favor or for hatred but do even right and punish as their minds and consciences would serve." In the following years he held a steady succession of municipal offices: constable, in 1558–59 (responsible for keeping the peace); affeeror (responsible for fixing fines not set by statute); chamberlain, from 1561 to 1565 (responsible for the property of the corporation, including collecting revenues and paying debts and overseeing building repairs and alterations); alderman, in 1565; bailiff, in 1568–69; and chief alderman, in 1571.

This is the record of an impressively solid citizen and a locally distinguished public man, someone liked and trusted. In the patriarchal world of Tudor Stratford none of these positions was taken lightly. The constables in the year John Shakespeare served struggled to maintain order at a time of intense suspicion and the risk of communal violence between Catholics and Protestants. The aldermen looked into the lives of residents who were said to be living "immorally"; they could order the arrest of servants who had left their masters or apprentices who ventured out of doors after the curfew hour of 9 P.M.; they decided whether a wife who was said to be a "scold" should be tied to the "cucking stool" and ducked in the waters of the Avon. And the Elizabethan bailiff had powers that are hardly conveyed by our notion of a mayor: no one could receive a stranger into his house without the bailiff's permission. Several of John Shakespeare's offices involved regular contact with the magnates of the region: the lord of the manor, the Earl of Warwick, whose ancestors had held Stratford as a feudal fiefdom in the Middle Ages; wealthy gentlemen like Sir Thomas Lucy, who entertained the queen at his house in nearby Charlecote; the influential and learned bishop of Worcester, Edwin Sandys. Stratford was not directly ruled by any of these imposing figures; it was an independent town, having been incorporated as a royal borough in 1553. But the big men exercised considerable power as well as prestige, and local officials would have had to possess great skills of tact and cunning in order to uphold their rights. John Shakespeare must have been good at the task; he would not otherwise have been entrusted with his offices.

Then, around the time Will reached his thirteenth year, things began to turn sour for his buoyant, successful father. One of the fourteen aldermen of Stratford, John Shakespeare had been marked absent from council meetings only once in thirteen years. Abruptly, beginning in 1577, he ceased to attend meetings. He must have had very good friends on the council, for they repeatedly exempted him from fines, reduced his assessments, and kept his name on the roster. At one time he had given generously to the poor, but now his situation had changed. When in 1578 the corporation voted to levy every alderman fourpence per week for poor relief, "Mr John Shaxpeare" among the sitting aldermen was exempted. The exemption was an exceptional gesture of kindness—not all aldermen in financial difficulties were treated with comparable consideration. It was repeated when he was given an extremely low assessment for the expenses of equipping the town's constabulary: four men with bills, three men with pikes, and one man with a bow and arrow. There must have been something unusually appealing and useful about the man, something that kept his colleagues hoping that he would somehow or other right himself and return to public affairs. But still he did not resume attending meetings, and still he seems to have had difficulty paying his dues, even the reduced levies. Finally, in 1586, after years of nonattendance, Shakespeare's name was struck from the roll; he had by that time ceased to be a person who counted for much in Stratford. His public career had ended, and his private situation had clearly deteriorated.

John Shakespeare needed money. He needed it urgently enough by November 1578 to do what Elizabethan families dreaded and resisted doing: he sold and mortgaged property. And not just any property: in a few years' time he disposed of virtually all of his wife's inheritance. Piece by piece, in exchange for ready cash, the properties she brought to the marriage slipped through the fingers of her improvident husband. An interest in land in Snitterfield, where his father had farmed, was sold for four pounds; Asbies was let for a nominal rent, presumably in exchange for a payment up front; and in 1579 another house and fifty-six acres at Wilmcote were mortgaged for forty pounds to his wife's brother-in-law, Edmund Lambert, of Barton-on-the-Heath. This cash evidently vanished quite quickly. When the borrowed money came due the next year, John was unable to repay it, and the property was lost. Years later, he twice sued to try to get the land back, claiming that he had in fact proffered payment, but the courts found for Lambert. All Will's mother, Mary, had left of what she brought to the marriage was the Arden name.

The most striking glimpse of John Shakespeare's financial situation is provided by evidence of the inquisitive eyes of the queen's officers. The government was anxious to enforce religious uniformity. Though the queen had declared that she did not want to rip open each individual's soul and inquire into private beliefs, she wanted to pressure as many of her subjects as she could to observe at least the outward forms of official Protestant belief. Once a month at a minimum, everyone was expected to attend Sunday services of the Church of England, services in which the Protestant Book of Common Prayer would be used and in which the ministers would deliver one of the homilies, or state-sponsored sermons, written by the central religious authorities. People who broke the law requiring regular church attendance were subject to fines and other punishments. The fines were relatively small and manageable until 1581; thereafter, in the wake of a systematic crackdown on religious dissidents, they became astronomical.

In the autumn of 1591 the government ordered the commissioners of every shire in the land to draw up a list of those who did not come monthly to church. John Shakespeare's name turns up on the list prepared by the local officials, but in a category set apart by a note: "We suspect these nine persons next ensuing absent themselves for fear of processes." Some months later the commissioners filed their report and reiterated the explanation: "It is said that these last nine come not to church for fear of process for debt." If the explanation is accurate and not a cover for religious dissent, then the onetime bailiff of Stratford and justice of the peace was staying in his house on Sundays—and, presumably, many other days as well—to avoid arrest. The public man had become a very private man.

By 1591, when John Shakespeare was making himself scarce, his eldest son had almost certainly flown the coop: the next year he is first mentioned as a London playwright. But his father's humiliating position was only the latest scene in a drama that had been long unfolding and that must have shaped Will's entire adolescence. As he came of age, Will would have been keenly aware that something had gone seriously wrong. He could not have been indifferent to what he saw; his father's standing in the world was sinking exactly at the time when he, the oldest son and heir, was about to emerge as an adult.

What was the cause of the decline? Then, as now, there were business cycles—the last decades of the sixteenth century were particularly difficult in the Midlands—and in hard times people are obviously less likely to purchase luxury goods like elegant gloves. But many prominent merchants in comparable situations weathered hard times and personal disasters. Another Stratford chamberlain, Abraham Sturley, lost his house in a fire that swept through several streets of the town on September 22, 1594, and never fully recovered financially, but he managed to keep his eldest son, Henry, at Oxford and to send his second son, Richard, to

Oxford the next year. Another prominent Stratford citizen, William Parsons, lost his house in the same fire, but he too managed to send his son to Oxford and to serve as alderman and magistrate. John Shakespeare's debts, mortgages, fines, and losses and his sudden and precipitous disappearance from public life suggest something more than the consequences of a cyclical downturn in the glove trade.

A far likelier cause was a sharp government crackdown on one of the key sources of his income. In the wake of wool shortages in the mid-1570s, the authorities decided that the fault lay with the "broggers," men like John Shakespeare, who had already been twice denounced for illegal transactions. In October of 1576 the queen's principal advisers, the Privy Council, ordered wool traders in for questioning; in November they temporarily suspended all wool trading; and in the following year they required all known wool broggers to post bonds of one hundred pounds—a very large sum—as a surety against any further illegal dealings. This was all terrible news for John Shakespeare.

Matters were made worse by another financial blow. In 1580 the Crown issued a long list of names—over two hundred—and demanded that everyone listed appear on a specified day in June at the Queen's Bench in Westminster to be bound over to "keep the peace towards the queen and her subjects." John Shakespeare's name was on the list. "Binding over"—roughly equivalent to a restraining order—was a key low-level policing and crime-prevention method in the sixteenth and seventeenth centuries. Upon someone's swearing an oath that he feared for his life or well-being or the well-being of the entire community, the court could issue an order requiring the suspected malefactor to appear in order to guarantee his good behavior and to post a bond—a surety—to this end. The surviving records do not reveal who swore an oath against John Shakespeare or why. Was it because of his wool brogging, or some drunken quarrel for which he had been denounced, or a suspicion that he held the wrong religious beliefs? He somehow managed to find four guarantors for his appearance, and he agreed reciprocally to serve as guarantor for one of them. But on the June date neither John nor his guarantors appeared—again their absence has never been explained—and they forfeited their money. John was fined twenty pounds for himself and twenty pounds for John Audley, the Nottingham hatmaker for whom he had agreed to pledge. In the wake of his other difficulties, this was money he could not spare.

The impact upon his family appears to have been severe. Unlike the sons of Sturley and Parsons, Will conspicuously did not go to Oxford, nor did John Shakespeare's other sons. In the early eighteenth century the Shakespeare biographer and editor Nicholas Rowe wrote that John Shakespeare sent his eldest son to the Stratford grammar school, where he learned some Latin, "but the narrowness of his Circumstances, and the want of his assistance at Home, forc'd his Father to withdraw him from thence, and unhappily prevented his further Proficiency in that Language." Rowe believed, incorrectly, that John Shakespeare had had ten children, and the rest of the account may be equally incorrect. But the story of the son's being taken out of school in order to help at home would certainly be consistent with the documented financial straits of the late 1570s. At a certain point it may have seemed an absurd luxury to have his eldest son parsing Latin sentences.

"My father charged you in his will to give me good education," Orlando complains to his wicked brother in the pastoral comedy *As You Like It*. "You have trained me like a peasant, obscuring and hiding from me all gentleman-like qualities" (1.1.56–59). A good education marked the difference between a gentleman and a peasant. And yet Shakespeare did not, from all appearances, harbor any regrets about failing to attend Oxford or Cambridge; he did not show signs of a frustrated vocation as a scholar. For that matter, nothing in his works suggests any very sentimental feeling about school: Jaques' vision in the same comedy of "the whining schoolboy with his satchel / And shining morning face, creeping like snail / Unwillingly to school" does not convey nostalgia for a lost happiness (2.7.144–46). Nor does the scene of Latin instruction in *The Merry Wives of Windsor*, a scene that must have come quite close to Shakespeare's own direct memories of the King's New School. "My husband says my son profits nothing in the world at his book," Mistress Page complains to the Welsh pedagogue Sir Hugh Evans, whereupon Evans—in the Welsh accent that struck English ears as funny—puts little William through his paces:

EVANS: What is "*lapis*," William?
WILLIAM: A stone.
EVANS: And what is "a stone," William?
WILLIAM: A pebble.
EVANS: No, it is "*lapis*." I pray you remember in your prain.
WILLIAM: "*Lapis*."
EVANS: That is a good William.

(4.1.11–12, 26–32)

The tedium of rote learning is deftly recalled, as is the punning—preferably, obscene punning—that must have been the schoolboy Shakespeare's principal psychic relief from this tedium. This language lesson manages to turn the genitive into the genitals and to make us hear the word "whore" in the Latin for "this":

EVANS: What is your genitive case plural, William?
WILLIAM: Genitive case?
EVANS: Ay.
WILLIAM: *Genitivo: "horum, harum, horum."*
MISTRESS QUICKLY: Vengeance of Jenny's case! Fie on her! Never name her, child, if she be a whore.

(4.1.49–54)

These dirty jokes surfaced in abundance whenever Shakespeare gave a thought to Latin lessons or indeed to any language lessons at all. "Comment appelez-vous les pieds et la robe?" asks the French princess in *Henry V*, trying to learn the English words "feet" and "gown." Her tutor's reply discombobulates her: "*De foot*, madame, et *de cown*." In "foot" she and the audience (or at least the members of the audience in on the joke) hear the French word *foutre*, "fuck," and in the slightly mangled pronunciation of "gown" she hears *con*, "cunt."

CATHERINE: *De foot* et *de cown?* O Seigneur Dieu! Ils sont les mots de son mauvais, corruptible, gros, et impudique, et non pour les dames d'honneur d'user. [O Lord God! Those are evil-sounding words, easily misconstrued, vulgar, and immodest, and not for respectable ladies to use.]

(3.4.44–49)

If this stuff is not, in truth, infinitely amusing, it still can generate chuckles after four hundred years, and it would have served to lighten the burden of an exceedingly long school day. But it is certainly not the glimpse of a lost vocation. Ben Jonson wrote scholarly footnotes to his Roman plays and his classicizing masques; Shakespeare laughed and scribbled obscenities.

The end of his formal schooling must have meant more time for Will in the glove trade, getting to know the qualities of cheverel and deerskin. All the Shakespeare children probably helped in the family business. But after the late 1570s, there may not have been much of a business left to help in. Will's younger brother Gilbert, born in 1566, is described in town records as a "haberdasher," and Edmund, born in 1580, followed Will to London and became an actor. No records survive of how a third brother, Richard, born in 1574, spent his almost forty years of life. He too probably did not become a glover; if he had something to do with the father's business, and certainly if he had been a success at it, he is likely to have left a trace.

It often happens, Hamlet tells Horatio, that there is "some vicious mole of nature" in men (1.4.18.8), some inborn propensity or weakness, that ruins what would otherwise be an altogether admirable life. The particular fault on which Hamlet focuses his brooding attention is heavy drinking, a Danish national custom, he says, "More honoured in the breach than the observance" (1.4.18). Other nations call us drunkards, Hamlet complains, and with this charge sully our reputation:

> and indeed it takes
> From our achievements, though performed at height,
> The pith and marrow of our attribute.

(1.4.18.4–6)

Hamlet's extended meditation on this fault makes for a rather strange passage—extraordinarily intense, as if the thoughts were forcing themselves into speech, but at the same time oddly irrelevant, since his crafty, calculating uncle and his confederates are not elsewhere in the tragedy notably depicted as drunkards. One of the texts of *Hamlet* simply cuts the lines, as if they represented a false start, an idea Shakespeare decided not to pursue.

Is this a further clue to the cause of the father's decline? Did the man who served in 1556 as the borough ale-taster drink himself into deep personal trouble? In the mid-seventeenth century, when the public began to be curious about the life of their greatest playwright, Thomas Plume, archdeacon of Rochester, jotted down something he had been told about the Stratford glover, "a merry-cheeked old man" whom someone had seen once in his shop and questioned about his celebrated son. "Will was a good Honest Fellow," the father is said to have replied and then added, as if he had been challenged, "but [I] durst have cracked a jest with him at any time." The anecdote comes too late to be reliable as an eyewitness account, but does it contain a trace of the actual person, genial, good-natured, at once proud of his son and a touch competitive with him, and, possibly, "merry-cheeked" from something more than good humor or advancing age?

Throughout his career, Shakespeare kept thinking about drunkenness. He registered the disgust eloquently voiced by Hamlet. But he was also fascinated by the delicious foolishness, the exuberant cracking of jests, the amiable nonsense, the indifference to decorum, the flashes of insight, the magical erasure of the cares of the world. Even when he depicts the potentially disastrous consequences of alcohol, Shakespeare never adopts the tone of a temperance tract, and in *Twelfth Night* the drunk and disorderly Sir Toby Belch delivers the decisive put-down of the puritanical Malvolio: "Dost thou think because thou art virtuous there shall be no more cakes and ale?" (2.3.103–4). In a luminous scene in one of the greatest of the tragedies, *Antony and Cleopatra*, the rulers of the world become soused, join hands, and dance "the Egyptian bacchanals" (2.7.98). Even grave, calculating Caesar is caught up, against his will, in the muddle-headed revelry: "It's monstrous labour when I wash my brain, / An it grow fouler." "Gentle lords, let's part," he says, looking at the faces of those about him and feeling his own flushed face. "You see we have burnt our cheeks" (2.7.92–93, 116–17).

If Caesar's cold sobriety marks him as likely to prevail in the struggle for power, it also marks him as far less appealing than the riotous, great-spirited Antony. True nobility in *Antony and Cleopatra*—nobility not of blood alone but of character—has an affinity with excess, a perception that extends to many of Shakespeare's plays and carries the force of a conclusion drawn from life. John Shakespeare may have never seemed more like a nobleman to his observant, imaginative child than when he was in his cups, his cheeks burning.

But heavy drinking is associated in the plays with clowns, buffoons, and losers as well as kings. And an early play, *The Taming of the Shrew*, brings drunkenness literally close to home in the figure of Christopher Sly, who is noisy, impotently belligerent, and entirely unwilling to pay for the glasses he has broken. When the tavern hostess calls him a rogue and threatens to call the constable, the drunken beggar grandly stands on his family honor—"The Slys are no rogues. Look in the Chronicles—we came in with Richard Conqueror" (Induction 1, lines 3–4)—and then promptly falls asleep. A few moments later, a nobleman decides to trick the beggar into thinking he is a lord, and the baffled Sly clutches at a more homely sense of his identity: "What, would you make me mad? Am not I Christopher Sly—old Sly's son of Burton Heath, by birth a pedlar, by education a cardmaker, by transmutation a bearherd, and now by present profession a tinker? Ask Marian Hacket, the fat ale-wife of Wincot, if she know me not." (Induction 2, lines 16–20).

Shakespeare wrote this comedy shortly after he moved to London, and it bears vivid traces of the district around Stratford: Barton-on-the-Heath, where his cousins the Lamberts lived; Wincot, where dwelled a Hacket family he probably knew; perhaps Sly himself, since there was a Stephen Sly living in Stratford. It must have amused Shakespeare, in a quiet, private way, to introduce these familiar details onto the urban stage in order to give a realistic air to his depiction of rustic folly. Perhaps, like his comic character, he too felt dazed by his recent transmutation. He had gone from a provincial nobody to a professional actor and playwright in the great city of London, and he used the details to remind himself of who he was—old John Shakespeare's son of Stratford. The character of Christopher Sly is hardly a depiction of his father—a man whose accomplishments and social standing were far higher—but perhaps the drunkenness, the family pride, the mounting debts, and the unwillingness or inability to pay seemed as reminiscent of home as the familiar place-names Barton-on-the-Heath and Wincot.

Shakespeare's greatest representation of drunkenness is Sir John Falstaff, the grotesquely fat knight whose reiterated call for a white wine imported from Spain and the Canaries serves virtually as his motto: "Give me a cup of sack." In the second part of *Henry IV*, Falstaff delivers an ecstatic rhapsody to the virtues of "sherry-sack"—that is, sack from Jerez, in Andalusia—a mock-scientific analysis of its power to inflame both wit and courage:

> A good sherry-sack hath a two-fold operation in it. It ascends me into the brain, dries me there all the foolish and dull and crudy vapours which environ it, makes it apprehensive, quick, forgetive, full of nimble, fiery, and delectable shapes, which, delivered o'er to the voice, the tongue, which is the birth, becomes excellent wit. The second property of your excellent sherry is the warming of the blood, which, before cold and settled, left the liver white and pale, which is the badge of pusillanimity and cowardice. But the sherry warms it, and makes it course from the inwards to the parts' extremes; it illuminateth the face, which, as a beacon, gives warning to all the rest of this little kingdom, man, to arm; and then the vital commoners and inland petty spirits muster me all to their captain, the heart; who, great and puffed up with his retinue, doth any deed of courage. And this valour comes of sherry. (4.2.86–101)

Of course, the playwright could have heard the prototype of this encomium to drink in the alehouse or made it all up from scratch. But in the context of the trajectory that led the once prosperous bailiff to hide in his house from creditors, the end of this speech is striking: "If I had a thousand sons, the first human principle I would teach them should be to forswear thin potations, and to addict themselves to sack" (4.2.109–11). Perhaps in the wake of the family's financial decline, this was what Will took to

be his father's first principle, the legacy the crumbling glover had decided
to leave him.

But this did not mean that Will had to accept the legacy. One of the
earliest anecdotes about Shakespeare reports that though he was good
company, he was not a "company keeper"—he "wouldn't be debauched,
and if invited to, writ: he was in pain." Aubrey recorded this around 1680,
many years after the playwright's death, but it is peculiar enough as a recollection to suggest that it might be authentic. "He was in pain." Stories
of drinking contests with village boozers or drunken flights of wit at the
Mermaid Tavern or thousand-pound gifts from enamored aristocrats are
far more the stuff of legend than a propensity to decline invitations with
a polite excuse and to stay at home. A certain steadiness, in any case, rings
true: it would be hard otherwise to imagine how Shakespeare could have
done what he did—learn his parts and perform them onstage, help to
manage the complex business affairs of the playing company, buy and sell
country real estate and agricultural commodities, compose exquisitely
crafted sonnets and long poems, and for almost two decades write on
average two stupendous plays a year.

Shakespeare depicted heavy drinkers from close-up—he noted the
unsteadiness of their legs, the broken veins in their nose and cheeks, their
slurred speech—and he did so with an unusual current of understanding,
delight, even love. But his sympathy was braided together with other elements, including the overwhelming sense of waste that Hamlet articulates. He saw in Sir Toby Belch a parasite who sponges off his niece,
ruthlessly gulls his supposed friend Sir Andrew, and richly deserves the
thrashing he receives at the hands of the effeminate boy he thought he
could bully. He saw in Falstaff something roughly similar—a gentleman
sinking into mire—but darker and deeper: a debauched genius; a fath-
omlessly cynical, almost irresistible confidence man; a diseased, cowardly,
seductive, lovable monster; a father who cannot be trusted. The drunkenness that in both cases seems linked to gaiety, improvisational wit, and
noble recklessness is unnervingly disclosed at the same time to be part of
a strategy of cunning, calculation, and ruthless exploitation of others.
Invariably, a failed strategy: the grand schemes, the imagined riches, the
fantasies about the limitless future—all come to nothing, withering away

in an adult son's contempt for the symbolic father who has failed him. "God save thee, my sweet boy!" exclaims Falstaff, when he sees Hal in triumph in London. "I know thee not, old man," Hal replies, in one of the most devastating speeches Shakespeare ever wrote.

> Fall to thy prayers.
> How ill white hairs become a fool and jester!
> I have long dreamt of such a kind of man,
> So surfeit-swelled, so old, and so profane;
> But being awake, I do despise my dream.
>   (*2 Henry IV*, 5.5.41, 45–49)

These are words written deep within the history play, words spoken by the newly crowned king of England to his exceptionally amusing, exceptionally dangerous friend. Yet it is difficult to register the overwhelming power and pathos of the relationship between Hal and Falstaff without sensing some unusually intimate and personal energy.

HOW DID THE SON of the failing glover make it into the theater? In the absence of any documentary traces, the principal evidence, pored over for clues by generations of ardent admirers, is the huge body of work that Shakespeare left behind, the plays and poems that spark the interest in the life in the first place and provide tantalizing hints of possible occupations he might have followed.

The strong presence of legal situations and terms in his plays and poems—used, for the most part, accurately, and infiltrating scenes where one would least expect them—has led to the recurrent speculation that he worked in the office of a local attorney, someone who handled minor lawsuits, title searches, and the like. No doubt much of the work would have been boring, but it would have put food on the table and would have fed his appetite for new words and fanciful metaphors. It is easy to imagine the law clerk, engaged in the humdrum task of sealing documents,

letting his imagination wander—as the schoolboy had done over his
Latin lessons—and conjuring up erotic visions. A few years later, the
visions, still carrying the traces of their modest origin, take the form of
the goddess of love in hot pursuit of the beautiful young huntsman. "Pure
lips, sweet seals in my soft lips imprinted," says panting Venus, pleading
for another kiss,

> What bargains may I make still to be sealing?
> To sell myself I can be well contented,
> So thou wilt buy, and pay, and use good dealing;
>   Which purchase if thou make, for fear of slips
>   Set thy seal manual on my wax-red lips.
>   (*Venus and Adonis*, lines 511–16)

The image of the imprint in wax might, in this account of Shakespeare's
life, represent not only the imagined kiss but also the hard impact of his
months or years of legal work on the poet's imagination.

Perhaps. But the strong presence in his work of terms from the
leather trade seems a convincing personal trace only because of the objective likelihood that Will worked in his father's shop. Once we get away
from the near certainty of this experience, we run into Shakespeare's
uncanny ability to absorb vocabulary from a wide range of pursuits and
his lightning transformation of technical terms into the intimate registers
of thoughts and feelings. It is true that the absorption is not uniform—
though in the course of his life he bought and sold houses, for example,
he picked up relatively few terms from architecture and the building
trades—but the general phenomenon is broad enough and intense
enough to defy using language as a clue to any occupation he formally
pursued. He undoubtedly took in legal language and concepts, but he
also was remarkably attuned to theological and medical and military language and concepts. Was he directly involved in all of these professions
too? A young man without prospects, he could have run off to the army
fighting a nasty campaign in the Netherlands—so some, impressed by
his theatrical command of military jargon, have speculated. He could,
from his evident fascination with sea voyages, have found a place on a

ship bound for America—"To seek new worlds," as Sir Walter Ralegh put it, "for gold, for praise, for glory." But the actuarial likelihood of his making it back home from such adventures was exceedingly small. And none of these possible professions adequately accounts for the trajectory that led from Stratford to London. Indeed, each seems only to lead away from the place that most matters in his life, the theater.

The most obvious access to the theater companies for a talented young man was through apprenticeship. But Will's marriage license places him securely in Stratford in November 1582, at the age of eighteen, and the baptismal records of his children —Susanna, christened on May 26, 1583, and the twins Hamnet and Judith, christened on February 2, 1585— strongly suggest that he still lived there or at the very least continued to make regular visits. Apprentices were usually taken on as adolescents and were not allowed to marry (let alone to father children in their late teens). Still, the skills that theatrical apprentices acquired provide a clue to some of the things that the young Shakespeare must have been learning to do, however he earned his living, in the years after he left school.

The last will and testament of Augustine Phillips, one of Shakespeare's fellow actors, business partners, and friends (he left his "fellow" Shakespeare a "thirty-shilling piece in gold") provides some sense of these skills: "I give to Samuel Gilborne, my late apprentice, the sum of forty shillings, and my mouse-coloured velvet hose, and a white taffety doublet, a black taffety suit, my purple cloak, sword and dagger, and my bass-viol. I give to James Sands, my apprentice, the sum of forty shillings, and a cittern, a bandore, and a lute, to be paid and delivered unto him at the expiration of his term of years in his indenture of apprenticeship." Money was only part of the bequest. Both the former apprentice Gilborne and the current apprentice Sands also received valuable tools of the trade: costumes, weapons, and musical instruments. The fact that James Sands had to wait for his bequest until his term of service was up suggests Phillips had his company's interests uppermost in mind: he did not want the young actor, inherited money and musical instruments in hand, to offer his services to a rival troupe.

The terms of Phillips's will indicate something of the expectations playing companies had of their actors. First, actors were supposed to be gifted musicians, able to play at least the impressive range of string instruments that Phillips evidently played—the guitar-like cittern, the mandolin-like bandore (from which we get the word "banjo"), the immensely popular lute, and the bass viol. Second, they were expected to be able to fight—or at least convincingly to mime fighting—with sword and dagger. More generally, they had to be agile: there is often dancing, as well as fighting, in Elizabethan drama, and all performances of plays, whether tragic or comic, ended with complex dances. (It takes some adjustment to imagine the players in *Hamlet* or *King Lear* brushing off the stage blood at the play's end, joining hands, and performing a set of elaborate figures, but so they did.) Third, as the bequests strongly imply, they were expected to wear clothes gracefully: Phillips's "mouse-coloured velvet hose" were no doubt designed to show off his legs—in this period of long dresses, it was men's legs, rather than women's, to which eyes were drawn.

The musical ability, sword fighting, and above all the costly clothing of velvet and silks (for taffeta in this period referred to a kind of plain-woven silk) together point to what was probably the most significant aspect of the Elizabethan actor's training: players were supposed to be able to mime convincingly the behavior of gentlemen and ladies. That is, boys and men, drawn almost entirely from the 98 percent of the population that were not "gentle," had to assume the manner of the upper 2 percent. Not all the parts in the plays, of course, were of the gentry, and some actors no doubt specialized in lower-class roles, but these were repertory companies in which most of the actors were expected to play a range of social types. And it is clear from the budgets of the playing companies that they were willing to invest a great deal of money in making the impersonation of the gentry convincing. Their single largest expense, apart from the physical building itself, was the cost of costumes—the gorgeous, elaborate clothes that audiences expected to see gracing the bodies of the actors playing the parts of lords and ladies.

There is a paradox here. Actors were classified officially as vagabonds; they practiced a trade that was routinely stigmatized and despised. As "masterless men"—men without a home of their own or an honest job or an attachment to someone else's home—they could be arrested, whipped, put in the stocks, and branded. (This is why they described themselves legally as the servants of aristocrats or as guild members.) And yet the heart of their enterprise was a representation of the upper classes persuasive enough to delight a discriminating audience that included real gentlemen and ladies. Augustine Phillips was bequeathing to his apprentices the tools of a trade that much of the time required them to learn how to look and act like their betters. Phillips himself evidently wanted to carry the performance outside the walls of the playhouse: he simply bought a coat of arms to which he had no claim at all, an act for which he was subsequently attacked by an official of the College of Heralds known grandly (after the badge of office that he wore) as the Red Dragon Pursuivant.

We scarcely know for ourselves, let alone for a person who lived four hundred years ago, how someone acquires a particular vocational desire. Will's love of language, his sensitivity to spectacle, and a certain erotic thrill in make-believe may all have played a part in drawing him to the stage. But, in the light of Shakespeare's family circumstances—a mother who could trace her family to the important Ardens of Park Hall, a father who had risen in the world only to sink down again—the focus of Elizabethan theatrical impersonation is deeply suggestive. Will may have been attracted to the trade of acting in part because it so centrally involved the miming of the lives of the gentry. As a practical strategy, this was, of course, absurd: becoming an actor or even a playwright was probably the worst imaginable route toward social advancement, something like becoming a whore in order to become a great lady. But as the legends of whores who become great ladies suggest, there is at work in certain professions a powerful mimetic magic. Onstage Shakespeare could be the person that his mother and father said he was and that he felt himself to be.

Even without a formal theatrical apprenticeship, Will must have acquired much of what he needed during his Stratford adolescence. Local talent abounded; filled with linguistic exuberance and rich fantasy, Will could have studied the lute with one of his accomplished neighbors, dancing with another, swordsmanship with still another. Observing his reflection in a glass or his shadow on a wall, he could have recited grand-sounding speeches and practiced courtly gestures. And with his mother's link to the Ardens of Park Hall and his father's faded but still notable distinction, he could have arrived at the sense that he could confidently carry off the role of a gentleman and fulfill his parents' dreams.

John Shakespeare had once had great expectations, a vision of the arrow of the family's fortunes that his accomplishments would propel toward a glorious future. At the height of his wealth and prestige—in 1575 or '76, just before his downward slide began—he had applied to the College of Heralds for a coat of arms, an expensive process a person undertook not only to confer honor on himself but also to enhance the status of his children and grandchildren. To be granted a coat of arms— not to buy one on the sly, as Phillips tried to do, but to obtain one offi- cially—was to rise above playacting to the thing itself.

Elizabethan society was intensely, pervasively, visibly hierarchical: men above women, adults above children, the old above the young, the rich above the poor, the wellborn above the vulgar. Woe betide anyone who violated the rules, forgetting to cede place to someone above him or attempting to pass through a door before his betters or thoughtlessly sit- ting somewhere at church or at a dinner table where he did not belong. William Combe, the squire of a town near Stratford, sent a person named Hicox to Warwick Jail and refused bail because he "did not behave himself with such respect in his presence it seemeth he looked for." The social elite lived in a world of carefully calibrated gestures of respect. They demanded constant, endlessly reiterated signs of deference from those below them: bowing, kneeling, doffing hats, cringing. There was virtually no respect for labor; on the contrary, it was idleness that was prized and honored. Dress was the opposite of democratizing—nothing could be further from Shakespeare's world than a culture in which mag- nates and workmen often wear the same clothes. It wasn't simply a ques- tion of money. By royal proclamation, silks and satins were officially restricted to the gentry. Actors were exempted, but outside of the play- house they could not legally wear their costumes. In general, treatment by government officials and by the courts was drastically different for the upper classes than it was for those at the bottom. Even executions were distinct: hanging for the base, beheading for the elite.

To pass from the status of yeoman—the term used to describe John

Shakespeare, even after he had left the land and established himself in business—to the status of gentleman was a major step, a virtual transformation of social identity. There were many fine gradations in Elizabethan society, but the key division was between the gentry and the "common," or "baser," sort. The division was routinely mystified as a matter of blood, an immutable, inherited characteristic. But at the same time it was possible to cross the boundary, and everyone knew the ways it could be done. "As for gentlemen," writes one canny contemporary observer, Sir Thomas Smith,

> they be made good cheap in England. For whosoever studieth the laws of the realm, who studieth in the universities, who professeth the liberal sciences, and, to be short, who can live idly and without manual labor and will bear the port, charge, and countenance of a gentleman, he shall be called master, for that is the title which men give to esquires and other gentlemen. . . . And, if need be, a King of Heralds shall also give him for money arms newly made and invented, the title whereof shall pretend to have been found by the said herald in the perusing of old registers.

"Who studieth in the universities": not only was this something inconceivable for the yeoman and glover John Shakespeare, but it was also something he conspicuously failed to see that his eldest son do. But all was not lost. The key requirement, if you are climbing into the ranks of the elite, is to live like a gentleman—that is, you have to "live idly" and to maintain a certain level of conspicuous expenditure. The next requirement is to hide the ladder—that is, you have to pretend that you are already there. You do so, Smith notes, by acquiring a coat of arms from an institution, the College of Heralds, which was in the peculiar business of concealing social mobility by reinventing the past. In exchange for money, the herald pretends that he has discovered in the old registers what he—or the applicant—is in fact fabricating.

It was not quite as simple as Smith's wry account suggests. To be an "armiger," someone entitled to bear a heraldic device, one had to meet certain requirements overseen by a bureaucracy headed by the Garter King-of-Arms, the chief of the College of Heralds. In John Shakespeare's case, it was civic office that helped to confer eligibility: "If any person be advanced into an office or dignity of public administration," one expert on these matters held, "be it either Ecclesiastical, Martial, or Civil . . . the Herald must not refuse to devise to such a public person, upon his instant request and willingness to bear the same without reproach, a coat of Arms." The bailiff of Stratford was just such a "public person," and accordingly, when he submitted a sketch for his arms to the college, John Shakespeare must have been confident that his application would be granted. But though you could not legitimately simply buy a proper coat of arms—one that you and your descendants could proudly bear forever, as an acknowledged right—you most definitely had to pay for it. The heralds' fees were high. When his financial circumstances worsened, ascent to the status of gentleman must have seemed a hopeless extravagance or perhaps a mockery, like a beggar dreaming of a crown. John Shakespeare's application was shelved and forgotten.

But not, it seems, by his oldest son. Decades later, in October 1596, the process was renewed. The old sketch—"Gould. On A Bend Sables, a Speare of the first steeled argent. And for his Creast or Cognizance a falcon, his winges displayed Argent. Standing on a wrethe of his Coullors. Suppourting a Speare Gould. Steeled as aforesaid sett uppon a helmett with mantelles & tasselles"—was pulled off the shelf, where it had gathered dust; once again John Shakespeare's claim was reviewed and, this time round, approved. Who reinstituted the application, provided the necessary information, and paid the fees to the notoriously greedy, arrogant, and irascible head of the London College of Heralds, Sir William Dethick? Not the elderly glover and his wife, whose financial situation had not, in all likelihood, greatly improved, and not, with any likelihood, the provincial haberdasher Gilbert, the apparent nonentity Richard, the unsuccessful actor Edmund, or the unmarried sister Joan. The obvious answer is William, already prospering handsomely in the London theater.

Why should he have gone to the trouble? Most obviously, by helping his father complete the process, the playwright, in an act of prudential, self-interested generosity, was conferring gentle status on himself and his children. Will had by this time no doubt played gentlemen onstage, and he could carry off the part outside the playhouse as well, but he and others would always know he was impersonating someone he was not. He now had the means to acquire legitimately, through the offices his father had once held, a role he had only played. He could legally wear outside of the theater the kinds of clothes he had been wearing onstage. For a man singularly alert to the social hierarchy—and Shakespeare spent most of his professional life imagining the lives of kings, aristocracy, and gentry—the prospect of this privilege must have seemed sweet. He would sign his last will and testament "William Shakespeare, of Stratford upon Avon in the county of Warwick, gentleman." His heirs and their offspring would be ever further from the glover's shop and, for that matter, the playhouse; they would have the luxury of taking their gentility for granted and laying claim without irony to the motto that someone—again, in all probability, Will himself—had devised to accompany the shield and crest: *Non sanz droict.*

"Not without right." Is there a touch of defensiveness in that motto, a slight sense that the claim to gentlemanly status might raise eyebrows? If so, the insecurity would not belong to the impecunious glover but to his successful playwright son. For whatever John Shakespeare's problems—drink or foolish loans or whatever—he did in fact legitimately possess the social standing, through the offices he had held in Stratford, to lay claim to the status of a gentleman. Not so his son. There were few occupations for an educated man more stigmatized socially than player. That Shakespeare was acutely aware of the stigma can be surmised from the sonnets, where he writes that, like the dyer's hand, he has been stained by the medium he has worked in. It was with such a consciousness of social shame—the sense of what it means to go up and down, making oneself a motley to the view—that he may have come up with the family motto, half-defiant, half-defensive.

The clerk who wrote down the words on the draft of the grant of arms made a telling mistake—either unconsciously or with sly sarcasm—that he had to strike out: he twice wrote "Non, Sanz Droict." The comma in effect turns the motto into an official rejection: "No; without justification." The correction was made, the motto was finally written correctly, and the arms were granted. But for Will the insecurity—or at least the sense of incongruity—is unlikely to have vanished, for there were jokes and unpleasant reminders. Most manifestations of social policing—raised eyebrows, wry faces, ironic witticisms, teasing—are evanescent and hardly outlast a day or two, let alone four hundred years. But in this case, perhaps because the volume of insult was high, perhaps because Will was sufficiently a public figure, traces of it survive. In the satiric comedy *Every Man Out of his Humour*, performed at the newly erected Globe by the Lord Chamberlain's Men in 1599, Ben Jonson has a rustic buffoon named Sogliardo pay thirty pounds for a ridiculous coat of arms, to which an acquaintance mockingly proposes the humiliating motto "Not Without Mustard." As a member of the Lord Chamberlain's Men, Will would have listened to this insult again and again in rehearsal and in performance. He probably laughed uncomfortably—how else does someone get through this kind of teasing?

In 1602 his discomfort would have been renewed when a disgruntled genealogist, the York herald Ralph Brooke, filed a formal complaint against the Garter King-of-Arms, Sir William Dethick, for abusing his authority by elevating base people to a status they did not merit. Brooke drew up a list of twenty-three such cases. "Shakespear ye Player" was the fourth name on the list.

Shakespeare was a witty mocker of pretensions and must have known that he would be exposing himself to this embarrassment. He may have felt that the social cachet was worth wincing for, but a further key to his action may lie in the specific remarks penned on the drafts that Dethick drew up in granting the renewed request on behalf of John Shakespeare. These remarks must have been based on information provided by the person paying for the application, information that could then be verified, if the officials were acting responsibly, by the College of Heralds. There is, of course, no reference to the glover's shop or the illegal trade in wool and other commodities. Along with a vague reference to the distinction of the petitioner's ancestor, who allegedly did "faithful and valiant service" to King Henry VII, though no record of this service or its reward has emerged, Dethick notes that "the said John hath married the daughter and one of the heirs of Robert Arden of Wilmcote," that he had served as a justice of the peace and the bailiff of Stratford, and that he had "lands and tenements of good wealth and substance," worth five hundred pounds.

By 1596 this was all something of a dream, akin to Christoper Sly's "we came in with Richard Conqueror." John Shakespeare was hardly destitute—despite his losses, he still had possessions—but he had ceased to be what the application claimed he was: a "man of good substance." The story Will likely told the Garter King-of-Arms—a story about a man whose ancestors had served the king, a man who had married an heiress bearing a distinguished name, a man who had risen to high civic office, in short a man of good substance—erased or undid the man who mortgaged away his wife's property, who could not leave his house for fear of arrest for debt, and whose relations with his fellow townspeople had so deteriorated by 1582 that in that year he petitioned for sureties of the peace against four men "for fear of death and mutilation of his limbs." In this application, John Shakespeare had not only been restored to his lost position; he had been raised to a position he never quite held.

The dream of restoration haunted Shakespeare throughout his life. In *The Comedy of Errors,* a merchant of Syracuse, in search of his lost twins, is arrested in the rival city of Ephesus and is threatened with death if he cannot pay a heavy fine. At the end of a zany tangle of confused identities, in which one of his sons is arrested for debt by a leather-clad officer (of the type that used to accompany the bailiff John Shakespeare), the father is reunited with the twins and with their mother, the beloved wife from whom he had been separated in a shipwreck thirty-three years before. The merchant's life is spared, his fine is forgiven, the son's debt is settled, and the family is magically restored. In *The Merchant of Venice*, a wealthy merchant loses all of his wealth in a series of shipwrecks and is about to be carved up by a merciless Jewish creditor, until, through a clever interpretation of the law, he regains everything he has lost and acquires the creditor's money as well. In *Twelfth Night*, the son and daughter of a nobleman are separated from one another and shipwrecked on the coast of Illyria. The son wanders through his life as if he is in a dream. The daughter takes a new name and pretends she is a young man, Cesario. In her assumed identity, she has suffered a steep loss in social standing—Cesario is a servant—but even in her disguise she clings to her origins. "What is your parentage?"

asks the proud countess, and the servant replies, "Above my fortunes, yet my state is well. / I am a gentleman." The countess is smitten:

> I'll be sworn thou art.
> Thy tongue, thy face, thy limbs, actions, and spirit
> Do give thee five-fold blazon.
>
> (1.5.247–49, 261–63)

"Five-fold blazon": in his speech, looks, movements, though not in his clothes or occupation, Cesario bears a gentleman's coat of arms. And when the brother and sister finally encounter one another by chance, they lay claim to their displaced identities:

> SEBASTIAN: What countryman? What name? What parentage?
> VIOLA: Of Messaline. Sebastian was my father.
>
> (5.1.224–25)

Not only are they restored to their proper social identities, but they each make a marriage above their station, the young woman to the Duke of Illyria, the young man to a great heiress.

In none of these cases is restoration entirely straightforward. The Syracusan merchant gets back a family that had, because of the disastrous shipwreck, never actually lived as one. The Venetian merchant, who despises usury, not only recoups his maritime losses; he is also given "in use" half the accumulated wealth of the Jewish moneylender. The twin brother and sister are not so much restored to one another or to their lost identities as they are linked through their new spouses, Viola marrying the duke who has long been madly in love with the countess, Sebastian's immensely wealthy bride. And the social-climbing success is strangely shadowed by the figure of the countess's steward Malvolio, who dreams of making the match that Sebastian succeeds in making.

Malvolio serves as the shadow side of Shakespeare's own fascination with achieving the status of a gentleman. He is, says the waiting gentle-woman Maria, who hates him, "an affectioned ass that cons state without book and utters it by great swathes"—that is, he memorizes and recites the dignified and high-flown language of his betters. And he is a narcissist: "the best persuaded of himself, so crammed, as he thinks, with excellencies, that it is his grounds of faith that all that look on him love him" (2.4.132-35). He suffers from what Shakespeare in the sonnets characterizes as his own besetting "Sin of self-love": "Methinks no face so gracious is as mine. / No shape so true, no truth of such account" (62.1, 5–6). Out of these qualities, Malvolio's enemies will work their revenge, which will be to make him a "common recreation" (2.3.121).

What is ridiculed in Malvolio, then, is not simply ill nature or puritanical severity but rather the dream of acting the part of a gentleman. And the ridicule comes very close to describing the process by which any actor, including Shakespeare himself, must have learned his trade. "He has been yonder i' the sun," Maria tells her fellow conspirators, "practising behaviour to his own shadow this half-hour" (2.5.14–15). When he comes close enough to be overheard, what the mockers witness is someone rehearsing a fantasy: "To be Count Malvolio!" "Now he's deeply in," one of the conspirators whispers. "Look how imagination blows him" (2.5.30, 37–38). The audience is then invited to watch someone enter a part—"deeply in"—and improvise a scene, complete with costume, props, dialogue, and what actors call a backstory:

> Having been three months married to her, sitting in my state . . . Calling my officers about me, in my branched velvet gown, having come from a day-bed where I have left Olivia sleeping . . . And then to have the humour of state and—after a demure travel of regard, telling them I know my place, as I would they should do theirs—to ask for my kinsman Toby. . . . Seven of my people with an obedient start make out for him. I frown the while, and perchance wind up my watch, or play with my — [*touching his chain*] some rich jewel. (2.5.39–54)

Malvolio is about to be lured into the trap that has been laid for him, the trap that will lead to yellow cross-garters, inappropriate smiling, imprisonment as a madman, and cruel humiliation. One of the greatest comic plots in all of Shakespeare, it draws deeply on the playwright's inner life, including a strong current of ironic laughter at the whole project—his own and that of his parents—of laying claim to a higher status.

Shakespeare found the pleasures and ironies of restoration inexhaustibly fascinating, even in his tragedies and tragicomedies. At the climax of *King Lear*, the old king's wicked daughters are defeated, and, after all his losses and his atrocious sufferings, the king is restored to "absolute power" (5.3.299). But it is too late: his beloved daughter Cordelia is dead in his arms, and he dies in an agony of despair mixed with the delusive hope that she might still be alive. A similar fate befalls Timon of Athens, who finds when he has lost his wealth that he has no friends and goes off to live alone in the woods. Digging in the earth for roots to eat, he finds gold, the last thing he desires, and once again becomes, to his virtually fatal disgust, an immensely wealthy man. And in *The Winter's Tale*, King Leontes, after sixteen years, recovers the wife and daughter whom his paranoid jealousy had seemed to destroy. But the wide gap in time is not so simply erased: his wife, Leontes remarks, "was not so much wrinkled, nothing / So agèd" as the woman he has recovered (5.3.28–29), and other victims of his jealousy—his only son, Prince Mamillius, and his faithful counselor Antigonus—do not miraculously return from the grave. The emotion of restoration is powerfully present—the sense that what was seemingly irrevocably lost has been reclaimed against all hope and expectation—but the recovery is never quite what it seems: the past that is recovered turns out to be an invention or a delusion or, in the worst case, an intensification of loss.

Near the very end of his career Shakespeare returned one more time to this plot structure, giving it in almost pure form in *The Tempest*: a ruler is thrust from his dukedom, cast out to sea in a leaky boat with his infant daughter, and shipwrecked on a strange island; years later, through the exercise of his magic, he triumphs over his enemies and recovers his lost realm. These are familiar, highly traditional motifs, and yet the peculiar intensity with which Shakespeare repeatedly embraces the fantasy of the recovery of a lost prosperity or title or identity is striking.

There is no direct relation between the staging of various forms of restoration in Will's plays and the renewal of the lapsed application for the status of gentleman. Art rarely emerges so transparently from the circumstances of life and would be far less compelling if it did. Shakespeare was in the business of reaching thousands of people, none of whom had any reason to be interested in the business affairs and social status of a Stratford glover. But there were many ways in which he might have tried to reach his audience, and his fascination with a particular set of stories—his sense that these might work and, still more, that he might have it in him to work with them—does not seem entirely random. Though his imagination soared to faraway places, the fantasies that excited his imagination seem often to have had their roots in the actual circumstances of his life or rather in the expectations and longings and frustrations generated by those circumstances. Hence, in settings as remote as the mythical Athens of *A Midsummer Night's Dream* or the romantic Bohemia of *The Winter's Tale*, there are notes that take us back to the young man who grew up on Henley Street in Stratford and dreamed that he was a gentleman. Sometime in his late adolescence, the young man awoke to find that the dream had fled, along with his mother's dowry and his father's civic stature. But, as we have seen, he did not give it up, either in his life or in his art.

Again and again in his plays, an unforeseen catastrophe—one of his favorite manifestations of it is a shipwreck—suddenly turns what had seemed like happy progress, prosperity, smooth sailing into disaster, terror, and loss. The loss is obviously and immediately material, but it is also and more crushingly a loss of identity. To wind up on an unknown shore, without one's friends, habitual associates, familiar network—this catastrophe is often epitomized by the deliberate alteration or disappearance of the name and, with it, the alteration or disappearance of social status. Shakespeare's characters repeatedly have to lay claim to a gentility that is no longer immediately apparent, all of its conventional signs having been swept away by the wild waves.

In Will's imagination his father's failure might have seemed a shipwreck, but the Shakespeares had no secure grasp of gentlemanly status to begin with. The family was at best only just about to become gentle, acquiring the coat of arms for which his father had applied. It is possible, of course, that his mother had filled her eldest son with tales of the Ardens of Park Hall or even of Turchill of the Forest of Arden, the lordly ancestor whose lands merited four columns in the Domesday Book. In that case, Will could have dreamed that the family was just about to recover, through his father's civic offices, the status that had at one time belonged by birthright to the Ardens. This dream too seems to have stayed with him. In 1599, three years after the old application for the coat of arms was revived, almost certainly at his instigation and expense, Will was in all likelihood the person behind another successful application to the College of Heralds, this time for the right to add (the technical term is "impale") the Arden arms to what is now described as "the Ancient coat of Arms" of the Shakespeares. In the end only the Shakespeare arms appeared on his funeral monument, but the symbolic statement is clear: I am not someone who can be treated like a hired servant or whipped like a vagabond; I am someone who does not merely pretend onstage to be a gentleman; I am a true gentleman, entitled to bear arms both by virtue of my father's distinguished service to the queen and by virtue of my mother's distinguished family. And, half-concealed, another symbolic statement: I have with the fruits of my labor and my imagination returned my family to the moment before things began to fall apart; I have affirmed the distinction of my mother's name and restored my father's honor; I have laid claim to my lost inheritance; I have created that inheritance.

CHAPTER 3

The Great Fear

EVEN IF WILL in his late teens or early twenties had decided clearly that he wanted to become an actor, he was in fact not likely simply to have headed off to London to seek his fortune onstage, stopping along the way to pick up a few pennies for food and lodging by singing and juggling. A person uprooted from his family and community in Elizabethan England was generally a person in trouble. This was a society deeply suspicious of vagrancy. (Shakespeare would later make much in his works of the tribulations of the uprooted and unprotected.) The age of questing knights and wandering minstrels was over—if indeed it ever existed except as a fantasy. Itinerant friars and pilgrims had certainly existed, and within living memory, but the religious orders had been dissolved by the state and the pilgrimage sites had been shut down and smashed by zealous reformers. There were wanderers on the roads, but they were exceedingly vulnerable. Unaccompanied, unprotected women could be attacked and raped almost with impunity. Unaccompanied men were less desperately at risk, but they too needed all the protection they could get. Trades that required travel were heavily regulated—every peddler and tinker was required to have a license from two

justices of the shire in which he resided, and anyone not so licensed could
be officially or unofficially victimized. An able-bodied beggar or idle
vagrant could by statute be seized and brought before the local justice of
the peace for interrogation and punishment. Being able to sing and dance,
juggle or recite speeches was no excuse: among those who were to be
classed as vagrants, the Vagabond Act of 1604, continuing earlier statutes,
includes players of interludes, fencers, bearwards, minstrels, begging scholars and sailors, palmists, fortune-tellers, and others. If the vagrant could not
show that he had land of his own or a master whom he was serving, he was
tied to a post and publicly whipped. Then he was either returned to his
place of birth—to resume the work he was born to do—or put to labor or
placed in the stocks until someone took him into service.

A very small number of people lived lives of privileged idleness, but
most inhabited a society of scarcity with no patience for anyone who did
not, as Shakespeare put it, commit his body to painful labor. And the
fruits of that labor, in theory at least, were supposed to be earned by people who knew and kept their place. Social regulations were amazingly
harsh: lest the whip and the stocks seem too lenient, a mid-sixteenth-
century statute ordered that vagabonds were to be branded and put to
forced labor as slaves. Even if such draconian statutes were not strictly
enforced—and the evidence is too scanty to be certain—this clearly was
not a culture in which a provincial young man uncertain of his future and
in need of an income to feed his wife and three small children would venture off fancy-free to the big city in the hope that, as Dickens's Mr.
Micawber puts it, something would turn up.

The seventeenth-century gossip John Aubrey jotted down something that strongly suggests that Will did not immediately find a place in
a theater company or move directly from Stratford to London in search
of employment. "He had been in his younger years," Aubrey wrote, "a
schoolmaster in the country." Most of Aubrey's gossip about Shakespeare
needs to be taken with a grain of salt, but this particular item has more
authority than most, for he noted its source as the actor William Beeston.
Beeston was the son of Shakespeare's former colleague in the Lord
Chamberlain's company, Christopher Beeston. This, therefore, is a piece
of biographical information that can be traced directly back to someone

who actually knew Shakespeare. (They acted together, records show, in the 1598 production of *Every Man in His Humour*.) No one has been able to establish with certainty where "in the country" Shakespeare was a teacher, but many scholars have come to take seriously a controversial claim, first made in 1937, that he spent a period of time, perhaps two years, in Lancashire, employed by an immensely wealthy Catholic gentleman, Alexander Hoghton, and then, upon Hoghton's death, by his friend Sir Thomas Hesketh, of nearby Rufford.

The vicious, murky world of Tudor religious conflict will help to explain why an adolescent boy, fresh from school, might have ventured from the Midlands of England to the north, how he could have had a connection with a powerful Catholic family there, and why that family would have bothered to employ someone like him rather than a licensed schoolmaster with an Oxford or Cambridge education.

Stratford had nominally become Protestant, like the rest of the kingdom, when in 1533 Henry VIII—bent on getting a divorce and on seizing the enormous wealth of the monasteries—had himself declared "Supreme Head of the Church in England." Officially, England had decisively broken away from Rome. But in matters of religious belief, families in early-sixteenth-century England were characteristically fractured, and many individuals were similarly fractured inwardly. It would have been an unusual extended kin group that did not have at least some of its members holding on to the old faith, an unusual convert to Protestantism who did not feel on occasion at least some residual Catholic twinges, and an unusual lay Catholic who did not feel a current of national pride and loyalty when Henry VIII defied papal authority. This ambivalence remained true even during the reign of Henry's son, Edward VI, from 1547 to 1553, when England's ruling elite moved decisively to a serious embrace of Protestant doctrine and practice. But significant steps were taken in these years to make a return to Catholicism, even in imagination, more difficult.

Salvation, the leaders of the new English church said, came not through the Mass and the other rituals of Roman Catholicism, but through faith and faith alone. Now it was not only the venerable monasteries and the celebrated pilgrimage sites that came under attack. The altarpieces, statues, crucifixes and frescoes that filled the churches were declared to be idols, designed to lure the people into ignorance and superstition. They were defaced, whitewashed over, or smashed, and the zealous vandals went on to attack other time-honored ways of acting out the faith, including rituals, pageants, and plays.

The most exalted moment in the Catholic service had been the Elevation of the Host. The gorgeously arrayed priest, his back to the congregation and partly concealed behind a screen surmounted by a large crucifix, would lift up the consecrated wafer. At that moment, a bell was rung, and the faithful would look up from their private prayers and strain to see the piece of bread that had miraculously been transformed into the body and blood of God. Protestant polemicists had a range of hostile nicknames for the Host—"Round Robin," "Jack in the Box," "Worms' Meat," and the like—and comparably insulting terms for the Mass, including "the Pope's Theater."

The Mass was an impressive performance, they conceded, but it was all a histrionic fake, a tissue of lies and illusions. The theater might have its value—zealous Protestants like John Bale, who wrote anti-Catholic plays, clearly thought so—but it had no business infecting worship. There was no miraculous transformation of the substance of the bread, as the Catholics claimed, only a solemn act of commemoration, which should be conducted not at an altar but at a table. Faith should rest not on a gaudy spectacle but on the word of God, not on alluring images but on texts. The only certain guide was Scripture. It was a scandal, religious reformers repeatedly complained, that the Holy Bible had been deliberately kept out of the hands of lay men and women (English translations deemed heretical had been burned in great bonfires by the Catholic authorities) and thereby confined to a Latin translation mumbled by priests. In the 1520s, aided by the printing press, Protestants moved to make an English version, shaped by the principles of the Reformation, widely available and to encourage the literacy that would give ordinary people access to what they called the plain, unvarnished truth. They moved as well to translate the liturgy into English and promulgate the Book of Common Prayer, so that all believers would understand the service and pray in unison in their own mother tongue.

This was the crucial moment in the development of the English language, the moment in which the deepest things, the things upon which the fate of the soul depended, were put into ordinary, familiar, everyday words. Two men above all others, William Tyndale and Thomas Cranmer, rose to the task. Without them, without the great English translation of the New Testament and the sonorous, deeply resonant Book of Common Prayer, it is difficult to imagine William Shakespeare.

The achievement did not come lightly. Too radical for the doctrinally conservative Henry VIII, Tyndale was driven in the 1520s to the Continent, where eventually he was captured and garroted to death by the Catholic authorities. During the reign of Edward VI, Cranmer, as archbishop of Canterbury, led the Protestant reforms, but when the sickly Edward died in 1553 the throne passed to his sister, the Catholic Mary Tudor. Mary moved at once to reverse direction, and Cranmer, along with other leading Protestants who had not managed to escape to Germany or Geneva, was burned at the stake at Oxford in 1556. The memory of these executions—which formed the core of John Foxe's great Protestant *Book of Martyrs*—haunted the later sixteenth century and sharpened the violently anti–Roman Catholic sentiments of the committed reformers.

When Mary died childless in 1558, the wheel turned once again: the twenty-five-year-old Elizabeth quickly made it clear that she would return the country to the religious course upon which it had embarked under the reign of her father and, still more, that of her brother. Though cautious about unleashing extreme reforms, the queen signaled her Protestant views at a procession on January 14, 1559, the day before her coronation. At the Little Conduit in Cheapside, she took the English Bible proffered to her by an allegorical figure of Truth, kissed the book, held it aloft, and then clasped it to her breast. When some days later at Westminster Abbey monks bearing incense, holy water, and candles approached to offer her their blessings, she dismissed them roughly: "Away with those torches," she commanded; "we can see well enough by daylight." In the months that followed, altarpieces and statues that had been reerected were taken down, altars were again transformed into simple tables, and the ancient Catholic liturgy was replaced by the Book of

Common Prayer. The Catholic priests who had emerged from what they regarded as the nightmare years under Edward VI were compelled either to conform to the Protestant doctrine or to vanish once again. Either they fled into exile abroad, or, more dangerously, they took on disguises and hid themselves in the houses of Catholic gentlemen.

At first repression was relatively mild. Queen Elizabeth made it clear that she was interested more in obedience and conformity than in purity of conviction. She had, as Bacon said, neither the desire nor the intention to "make windows into men's hearts and secret thoughts." What she wanted was an outward act of adherence to her authority and to the official religious settlement. Specifically, she wanted regular attendance at the state-sanctioned church services, whereupon the authorities would abstain from asking such questions as, Do you inwardly long for the old Catholic sacraments? Do you believe in the existence of purgatory? Do you think that priests have the power to grant absolution? Do you think that if a mouse eats a consecrated communion wafer, it has eaten the body and blood of Christ? Her officials generally followed suit, if sometimes grudgingly, until the moment came in which they felt that the Protestant religious settlement was in danger.

That moment came when William Shakespeare was six years old. In May 1570 a well-to-do Catholic, John Felton, nailed to the door of the bishop of London's house a papal bull excommunicating Queen Elizabeth. The pope, Pius V, added an order to all her Catholic subjects "that they presume not to obey her, or her monitions, mandates, and laws," lest they too be excommunicated. Felton was tortured, convicted of treason, and executed. English Catholics were regarded with greatly intensified suspicion.

Why should the pope—who was subsequently beatified and made a saint—have put the faithful in such an impossible position? Because in his view and that of many others, Elizabeth was the only serious obstacle to the return of wayward England to the Catholic faith. He was confident that most ordinary English men and women retained their ancient religious loyalty, and his agents had conducted a survey in 1567 that disclosed that fifty-two of the English peers were either staunch Catholics or well disposed to the Catholic Church and only fifteen were firmly committed

Protestants. The question was whether this religious loyalty could be turned into political action, and the pope decided that it could. The papal bull initiated a nightmarish sequence of conspiracy and persecution, plot and counterplot that continued throughout Elizabeth's long reign.

STRATFORD EXPERIENCED THE SAME sudden shifts, tensions, and ambiguities that marked much of the realm all through the sixteenth century. The monasteries and nunneries in the area had been sacked in the 1530s and '40s, and certain local families—among them the Lucys of Charlecote—had enriched themselves with the spoils. Then in the 1550s, when John Shakespeare moved to Stratford, the surrounding area was dotted with pyres on which local Protestant leaders— Laurence Saunders, at Coventry; John Hooper, at Gloucester; Hugh Latimer, at Oxford; among many others—were burned to death by the resurgent Catholics under Queen Mary. At the accession of Elizabeth, Catholic leaders were now in their turn in serious trouble, though in the first years of her reign the queen, both by temperament and policy, preferred fines, dismissal, and imprisonment to judicial murder. In Stratford the Catholic priest Roger Dyos, who had baptized the Shakespeares' first child, Joan, was dismissed, replaced by the staunchly Protestant John Bretchgirdle. It was Bretchgirdle who on April 26, 1564, christened the Shakespeares' first son, "Gulielmus filius Johannes Shakspere." Religious upheaval aside, it was not a propitious moment to enter the world: by July the town was ravaged by bubonic plague, killing fully a sixth of the population before the winter. Nearly two-thirds of the babies born that year in Stratford died before they reached their first birthday. Perhaps Mary Shakespeare packed up and took her newborn to the country for several months, away from the pestiferous streets.

For parents of John and Mary Shakespeare's generation, the world into which they brought their children must have seemed strange, unsettling, and dangerous: within living memory, England had gone from a highly conservative Roman Catholicism—in the 1520s Henry VIII had fiercely attacked Luther and been rewarded by the pope with the title "Defender of the Faith"—to Catholicism under the supreme headship of the king; to a wary, tentative Protestantism; to a more radical Protestantism; to a renewed and militant Roman Catholicism; and then, with Elizabeth, to Protestantism once again. In none of these regimes was there a vision of religious tolerance. Each shift was accompanied by waves of conspiracy and persecution, rack and thumbscrew, ax and fire.

Most people found it possible to keep their heads down, do what they had to do in order to conform to the official line, and reconcile their conscience to the shifts in doctrine and practice. Accommodation in the interests of survival led some to acquire a certain skeptical detachment from the strong claims made by both sides, claims made in the name of love and yet enforced by torture and execution. But for those who believed that the fate of their eternal souls depended upon the precise form of worship—and that, after all, is what the strong claims were about—the shifts in official belief and regulated practice must have been excruciating. Local communities were ruptured, friendships were broken, families were torn asunder—parents against children, wives against husbands—and inner lives tormented with pity and fear.

It was not only the pious who found it difficult to keep their heads down (or, more precisely, their heads on); it was also the ambitious. Major figures—powerful aristocrats, important magnates, members of the queen's Privy Council—were of course expected to stand up and be counted, and so too were small-scale civic leaders like John Shakespeare. As a constable in 1558–59, he had to keep the peace between Catholics and Protestants in the tense year of transition from the reign of the Catholic Mary to that of the Protestant Elizabeth. No doubt he had difficult moments, but at least he could maintain, if he wished, an air of studied neutrality. But as chamberlain, alderman, and bailiff, he had to act to carry out the policies of the regime, and that meant something more than keeping the peace.

A few months before Will's birth and in the years that followed, Chamberlain John Shakespeare oversaw the "reparations" of Stratford's fine Guild Chapel. "Reparations" here was a euphemism. What it meant was that he paid the workmen who went in with buckets of whitewash and ruined the medieval paintings—St. Helena and the Finding of the Cross, St. George and the Dragon, the murder of St. Thomas à Becket, and, above the arch, the Day of Judgment—that covered the church walls. Their task was not quite finished: the workmen also broke up the altar, putting a simple table in its place, and pulled down the rood loft—a gallery, surmounted by a cross, that separated the nave from the choir and displayed to the faithful the image of the crucified God. Town authorities proceeded to sell off the gorgeous vestments worn by the Catholic priests who had once celebrated the mystery of the Mass. It is worth pausing over these acts: John Shakespeare did not directly do any of them, and, in all likelihood, he did not single-handedly make the decision to have them done, but he was responsible for them, answerable both administratively—in the form of signed accounts presented on January 10, 1564, March 21, 1565, and February 15, 1566—and morally.

What were the changes for which he was paying? They were the material manifestations of the reformed religion, calculated acts of symbolic violence against the traditional Catholic religious observance, ways of compelling the community to acknowledge the new order and to observe its practices. Somewhere within the actions there is a theology, subtle doctrinal and philosophical arguments by relentlessly sober intellectuals. But the deeds in Stratford, for which the chamberlain disbursed the payments, were not subtle: men with hammers, awls, and grappling hooks violently changed the appearance of the church and the form of worship that would take place within it.

Paymaster for the ideological vandals, John Shakespeare acted officially as a committed Protestant, the agent of the Reformation in Stratford. On the town council, he voted to dismiss the Catholic steward Roger Edgeworth and to hire the Protestant Bretchgirdle—an unusually well-educated man, with a library that contained humanist classics as well as theology—to replace the Catholic curate. It is difficult to gauge how earnestly John Shakespeare oversaw these actions. He could have regarded them with the enthusiasm of a zealot, and yet the picture as a whole suggests a more complicated attitude.

The same town council that hired the new vicar Bretchgirdle also hired for the King's New School a succession of impressively learned schoolmasters who had surprisingly strong Catholic connections. The schoolmasters would have had to put in an appearance of conformity to the Anglican church—for such appointments would have been officially approved by the staunchly Protestant Earl of Warwick and the bishop of Winchester—but each evidently harbored loyalty to the ancient faith. Judging from their choices, John Shakespeare and his colleagues cannot have been too eager to identify old believers or apply any ideological test to those who would teach Stratford's children. On the contrary, they allowed—winked at or perhaps even connived at—the teaching of the young not merely by those who might have had some residual regard for the cult of the saints or the Virgin but by those who evidently possessed a deep Catholic commitment. Originally from Lancashire, in the north of England, where the old faith was clung to most tenaciously, Simon Hunt, Will's teacher between the ages of seven and eleven, took the drastic step of leaving Stratford in 1575 for the Continent to attend the Catholic seminary at Douai and, eventually, to become a Jesuit. Why drastic? Because the decision meant that he would either spend the rest of his life in exile or return to England in secret, knowing that the authorities would hunt him down, if they could, and execute him as a seditious traitor. During his years as Stratford schoolmaster, Hunt evidently did not keep his convictions entirely to himself. He seems to have taken at least one of the students from the school with him to Douai— Robert Debdale, who was about seven or eight years older than Will. The Debdales from nearby Shottery were a Catholic family, and Hunt may have had his eye out for other promising children of recusants. He may have taken an interest in William Shakespeare, whose mother was related, albeit distantly, to one of the area's major Catholic families and may even have been related to the Debdales.

The defection of Hunt and Debdale did not seem to deter the Stratford authorities when they chose the next schoolmaster: Thomas Jenkins, a graduate and fellow of St. John's College, Oxford, had a letter of recommendation from the Catholic founder of that college, Sir Thomas White. Like all other Oxford and Cambridge colleges, St. John's was officially Protestant—no other affiliation would have been permitted in an educational institution—but it had the reputation of welcoming

Catholics who were willing to conform and profess loyalty to the queen. This double consciousness—a tenaciously held inward Catholic faith coupled with a steadfast public adherence to the official religious settlement—was widespread in England, where there were many so-called church papists. Jenkins, who would have known and may have studied with the brilliant Catholic scholar Edmund Campion, also a fellow at St. John's, is likely to have been adept at maintaining this delicate balance. The pious Campion himself managed to stay for several years within the bounds of conformity—during which time he deeply impressed the Protestant Earl of Leicester and Queen Elizabeth herself with his brilliance—but in 1572 he embarked for Douai on a course that led him to the priesthood, enlistment in the Jesuits, a teaching post in Prague, and a return to England as a clandestine missionary.

Thomas Jenkins taught in Stratford for four years, from 1575 to 1579, and hence must have been, together with Simon Hunt, a significant schoolteacher in Will's life. Then, at about the time Will would have left the King's New School, Jenkins resigned his post and was succeeded by another Oxford graduate, John Cottam. Like Simon Hunt a native of Lancashire, Cottam, who presumably taught Shakespeare's younger brothers and whom Will certainly came to know, also had strong Catholic connections. His younger brother, Thomas, had gone abroad, after graduating from Oxford, and taken orders as a Catholic priest.

In June 1580 the schoolmaster's brother secretly returned to England as part of the mission led by Campion and a fellow Jesuit, Robert Parsons. Thomas Cottam was intending to go to the neighborhood of Stratford—specifically, to the village of Shottery. He carried a letter of introduction from his close friend and fellow priest, Robert Debdale, who had only five years earlier attended the Stratford grammar school. Debdale had entrusted Cottam with several Catholic tokens—a medal, several Roman coins, a gilt crucifix, and strings of rosary beads—for his family and urged them in his letter to "take counsel" from the messenger "in matters of great weight."

Cottam never reached Shottery. He had made the mistake on the Continent of confiding in a fellow English Catholic named Sledd. Sledd turned out to be an informer, and he provided a precise description of

Cottam to the authorities. "Searchers," as they were called, were watching for him at the ports, and he was arrested as soon as he disembarked at Dover. He had a brief moment of remission: the man in whose custody he was placed to be brought to London turned out to be a secret Catholic, and he let his prisoner escape. But in December 1580, when this custodian in turn was threatened with imprisonment, Thomas Cottam turned himself over to the authorities.

Determined to pry from Cottam his innermost secrets, officials in the Tower employed one of their most horrible devices, the scavenger's daughter. This instrument of torture was a hoop of iron that slowly closed around the prisoner's spine, bending it almost in two. Evidently, the government did not get enough from their interrogation to warrant an immediate trial. Instead, they kept their prisoner in the Tower almost a year, until they had captured other members of the mission. Cottam was then arraigned as a traitor, together with the others, in November 1581. On May 30, 1582, he was executed in the grisly way designed to demonstrate the full rage of the state: he was dragged on a hurdle through the muddy streets to Tyburn, past jeering crowds, and then hanged, taken down while he was still alive, and castrated; his stomach was then slit open and his intestines pulled out to be burned before his dying eyes, whereupon he was beheaded and his body cut in quarters, the pieces displayed as a warning. Robert Debdale met the same fate a few years later.

The Stratford council must have been shaken by the arrest of Thomas Cottam. It was one thing to have quietly hired three Catholic schoolmasters in succession; quite another to have a Catholic priest, suspected of treason, apprehended on his way to the neighborhood, in all likelihood to visit his schoolmaster brother as well as the Debdales. In December 1581, a month after Thomas's arraignment, John Cottam resigned from his position at the King's New School in Stratford and returned to the north. The council may informally have suggested that he leave, or, alternatively, he may simply have felt more comfortable back in Catholic Lancashire, at a safe distance from the vigilant Warwickshire sheriff, Sir Thomas Lucy, who had long been active in ferreting out priests in disguise and their recusant allies.

Why would the state have been so concerned about a young Oxford-educated priest carrying a few beads? From the perspective of the Catholics, such a person was a heroic idealist, abandoning all prospect of tranquility, career, honor, comfort, and family and risking his life daily to serve the embattled community of the faithful. Ordained at a seminary on the Continent and then smuggled back into a kingdom that had become the mortal enemy of his religion, a priest like Cottam would hope to elude informers and find shelter in the house of a sympathetic Catholic. There, disguised as a domestic servant or a child's tutor, he would preach, celebrate communion at a clandestine altar, hear confession, administer last rites to the dying, and perhaps, as Robert Debdale did, conduct exorcisms. From the perspective of the Protestants, he was at best a poor, deluded fool and, more likely, a dangerous fanatic, a conspirator in the service of a foreign power. He was, that is, a traitor, directed by his sinister masters in Rome and willing to do anything to return England to the power of the pope and his allies.

Protestant fears were not ungrounded. The Roman Catholic Church had invited English Catholics to rebel, and the meaning of this invitation was made explicit in 1580, when Pope Gregory XIII proclaimed that the assassination of England's heretic queen would not be a mortal sin. The proclamation was a clear license to kill. It was precisely at this time that the priest Thomas Cottam, with his small packet of Catholic tokens, was arrested on his way to the vicinity of Stratford. Small wonder that his brother's tenure as the town's schoolmaster was abbreviated: John Shakespeare and his fellow council members—and particularly those who had close Catholic kin—must have felt queasy. The trail could quite easily have led to them.

Such fears might seem absurd, for the schoolmaster John Cottam had done nothing wrong. But it will not do to underestimate the mood of paranoia and the reality of threat all through these dangerous years. The assassination of Elizabeth, early in her reign, would almost certainly have changed everything in the religious climate of England. And if it was in hindsight unreasonable to fear, as many people did, that thousands of English Protestants would be massacred as the French Huguenots had been, it was by no means irrational to suspect conspiracies—there *were* many—or to fear that some English Catholics would welcome and support a foreign invasion. The widespread persecution of Catholics made such support virtually inevitable; from this distance, what seems extraordinary is how many pious English Catholics remained loyal to a regime that was intent on crushing them.

Already by the acts that established the Church of England, the Mass was outlawed; it was made illegal to hold any service, except those contained in the Book of Common Prayer. A fine of one shilling was imposed for failure regularly to attend the parish church. In 1571, after the papal bull of excommunication, Parliament made it treason to bring into the country any papal bull or to call the queen a heretic. It was also illegal to go abroad for ordination or to bring into England or to receive any devotional object, "tokens, crosses, pictures, beads or other such like vain things from the Bishop of Rome." In 1581, in the wake of the Jesuits' clandestine mission, Parliament made it treason to reconcile oneself or anyone else to the Catholic Church with the aim of dissolving allegiance to the monarchy. By 1585 it was treason to *be* a Catholic priest, and by law it was illegal (and after 1585 a capital offense) to harbor priests or, knowingly, to give a priest aid or comfort. The penalty for failure to attend Protestant services in the local parish was raised to an astronomical twenty pounds per week. Though the fine cannot have been imposed very often, it hung, as a threat of ruin, over everyone who stayed away from church. Even the very few who could afford to pay such a penalty began to imitate poorer Catholic families: once their children reached the age of sixteen—the age at which the fines took effect—parents would send them to distant neighborhoods, where they were less likely to be caught by the oppressive system.

If Thomas Cottam had been apprehended in Stratford, there might well have been house-to-house searches, conducted by the sheriff. His arrest in London spared the local Catholic population that full-scale terror, but the Jesuit mission of 1580 and the tangled conspiracies of the ensuing years led to intensified rumormongering, spying, and sporadic raids on suspect recusant houses. Many of those houses harbored secrets that close scrutiny could have uncovered, and the house on Henley Street might not have been exempt. For example, if Will's mother, Mary, was a pious Catholic, like her father, she may have kept religious tokens—a rosary, a medal, a crucifix—very much like those seized on the person of the priest. And if the searchers had done a thorough job—and they were on occasion notoriously thorough, ripping open virtually everything in every room—they might have found a highly compromising document to which John Shakespeare had apparently set his name: a piously Catholic "spiritual testament," belying his public adherence to the Reformed faith.

The original document is lost—its contents are known only through a transcript—but given the risks attending such a declaration of faith, the survival of any trace of it at all is remarkable. In the eighteenth century a master bricklayer, retiling the house that had once belonged to the Shakespeares, found the six-leaf manuscript, sewn together with thread, between the rafters and the tiling. The manuscript, minus the first page, eventually reached the great editor of Shakespeare Edmond Malone, who published it but then, subsequently, had doubts about its authenticity, noting certain anomalies in the handwriting and spelling. That authenticity, though it remains open to question, was considerably bolstered by the discovery in the twentieth century of the document's source, a formulary written by the great Italian statesman and scholar Cardinal Carlo Borromeo. The Jesuits Campion and Parsons stayed with Borromeo in Milan, on their way to England, and could have received the text directly from him then. Translated and printed, with spaces left blank for the insertion of the names of the faithful, copies were smuggled into England and secretly distributed. Campion himself may have given them out when he passed through the Midlands, stopping in Lapworth, twelve miles from Stratford, where his host was the staunch Catholic Sir William Catesby, a relative by marriage of the Ardens. John Shakespeare could have received his copy from any number of people involved in the clandestine network of Jesuit sympathizers whom Lucy and the other Warwickshire officials were attempting to destroy.

The "spiritual testament" conflicts wildly with the iconoclastic violence that Chamberlain John Shakespeare authorized and paid for. What this suggests is that for Will, when he was growing up, there was not only a split between his father and mother, the former the active agent of the

Reformation in Stratford, the latter in all likelihood a Catholic, but also a split within his father. One side of him was the alderman who voted to dismiss Stratford's priest and replace him with a Reformed minister, the official who signed off on the whitewashing of the old frescoes and the smashing of the altar, the smiling public man who negotiated on behalf of the city with zealous Protestants like Thomas Lucy. The other side of him was the man whose name appeared on the "spiritual testament," who prayed for the special protection of the Virgin Mary and his personal saint, St. Winifred, who expressed an intense sense of his unworthiness as a "member of the holy Catholic religion." This was presumably the official who helped to hire the Catholic schoolmasters Hunt, Jenkins, and Cottam; and perhaps it was even the recusant who stayed away from church services and had his friends on the council cover his absence with the claim that he was worried about arrest for debt.

Perhaps the secret Catholic was the real John Shakespeare, and the Protestant civic officer was only the worldly, ambitious outward man. Alternatively, perhaps John Shakespeare, securely Protestant for most of his adult life, only briefly returned (during an illness, say, or simply to placate his wife) to the Catholicism he had left behind. Did John Shakespeare's eldest son know the truth? Could he have been sure which was the "real" father—the one who was moving up in the world or the one who kept the peace at home and perhaps in his heart by succumbing to the old fears and longings? He might have sensed that his father was playing a part, without ever knowing securely where the boundary lay between fiction and reality. He might have overheard whispered arguments between his father and mother and observed furtive acts. And at some point—to continue this line of speculation—he might have reached a strange but plausible conclusion: his father was both Catholic and Protestant. John Shakespeare had simply declined to make a choice between the two competing belief systems. Many of the people Will had encountered—the schoolmasters Simon Hunt, Thomas Jenkins, and John Cottam were presumably all examples—lived double lives: they outwardly conformed to the official Protestant religious settlement, at least enough to secure their jobs, but they inwardly adhered to the old faith. But John Shakespeare, his son may have observed, was something else. He wanted to keep both his options open—after all, he had seen enough of the world to know that there might be a drastic change of direction again; he wanted to cover himself in relation both to this life and to the afterlife; he was convinced that both positions, however incompatible they might seem to be, were possible to hold at once. He had not so much a double life as a double consciousness.

And Will? By the time he was leaving school in 1579–80, when he was fifteen or sixteen years old, had he come to acquire a comparable double consciousness? Shakespeare's plays provide ample evidence for doubleness and more: at certain moments—*Hamlet* is the greatest example—he seems at once Catholic, Protestant, and deeply skeptical of both. But though the adult Shakespeare was deeply marked by the religious struggles, what the adolescent believed (if he himself even knew what he believed) is wholly inaccessible. Out of a tissue of gossip, hints, and obscure clues a shadowy picture can be glimpsed, rather as one can glimpse a figure in the stains on an old wall.

It is odd and striking that several of Stratford's schoolmasters had connections to distant Lancashire, the part of the country where adherence to Catholicism remained particularly strong. John Cottam's family property there was only ten miles from one of the principal residences of the wealthy and influential Catholic Alexander Hoghton. As the scholar Ernst Honigmann and others have suggested, Cottam could have been asked by the Hoghtons to recommend a promising young man to be a teacher to their children—not a licensed schoolmaster, someone who would have to be certified as a Protestant by the local bishop, but a private tutor for a large household. He could have proposed Will Shakespeare, who had just left school and who, since his father's financial difficulties precluded his attending university, was looking for employment. Cottam would have been careful not only to find someone who possessed sufficient educational accomplishments—as it happened, he hit upon the most staggeringly talented young man in the kingdom—but also to find a good Catholic. For the devout Hoghtons almost certainly illegally harbored priests, along with illegal ritual objects and a large collection of banned or suspect books, and they would have wanted as servants only those whom they could trust to keep their dangerous secrets.

The small clue that Shakespeare sojourned in Lancashire has nothing in any obvious way to do with religion, Catholic or Protestant. Instead, it points to the theater. In his last will and testament, dated August 3, 1581, the dying Alexander Hoghton bequeathed all his "instruments belonging to musics [*sic*], and all manner of play clothes" to his brother Thomas, or, if Thomas does not choose to keep and maintain players, to Sir Thomas Hesketh. The will added, "And I most heartily require the said Sir Thomas to be friendly unto Fulk Gyllome and William Shakeshafte now dwelling with me and either to take them unto his service or else to help them to some good master." "Shakeshafte" is not "Shakespeare," and skeptics have pointed out that many local people were surnamed Shakeshafte. But in a world of notoriously loose spelling of names—in various records Marlowe is also Marlow, Marley, Morley, Marlyn, Marlen and Marlin— it is close enough, in conjunction with the Cottam-Hoghton connection, Shakespeare's future profession, and other small hints to have convinced many scholars that it refers to Stratford's Will.

The precocious adolescent—recommended by Cottam as intelligent, reasonably well educated, discreet, and securely Catholic—would have come north in 1580 as schoolmaster. The terms of the will suggest that he soon began to perform, at first probably only recreationally and then with increasing seriousness, with the players that Alexander Hoghton kept. Whatever his skills as a teacher, those he possessed as a player would have immediately brought him to the special attention of the household and its master, and the charismatic appeal of the young player would have enabled him—like Cesario in *Twelfth Night*—quickly to overleap other, older servants and become one of the trusted favorites. After Hoghton died in August 1581, Shakespeare could have passed briefly into the service of Hesketh and then might have been commended—as Hoghton had requested—to someone else. The likeliest candidate is a powerful neighbor of Hesketh's who was even more interested in drama. That neighbor, Henry Stanley, Lord Strange, the fourth Earl of Derby, and his son Ferdinando, employed (and, in the case of Ferdinando, even wrote for) a talented, professionally ambitious group of players who were licensed by the Privy Council as Lord Strange's Men. The principal players—Will Kempe, Thomas Pope, John Heminges,

Augustine Phillips, and George Bryan—formed the core of the London company with which Shakespeare would later be associated, the Lord Chamberlain's Men. The precise chronology of Shakespeare's link with this group cannot be determined, but the link eventually formed the center of his professional career, and it is at least possible that the initial contact—a momentous acquaintance to be renewed later—was made in the north of England in 1581.

Will's life, if he actually sojourned in the north, would have been a peculiar compound of theatricality and danger. On the one hand, a life of open, exuberant display, where for the first time Will's talents—his personal charm, his musical skills, his power of improvisation, his capacity to play a role, and perhaps even his gifts as a writer—were blossoming in performances beyond the orbit of his family and friends. His performances would not have been exactly public, but neither were they simply private after-dinner entertainments. The Heskeths were immensely wealthy, while the Hoghtons and, still more, the Stanleys were feudal magnates. They were representatives of a world of riches, power, and culture that had not yet been completely assimilated into the centralizing, hierarchical scheme of the Tudor monarchy, just as they had not yet been assimilated into the state religion. With small armies of retainers and followers; with crowds of allies, relations, and tenants; with pride fed by the obsequious deference of all around them; and with generosity reinforced by their craving for reputation as "householders," they entertained large companies of guests in banqueting halls that could easily serve as theaters. The brilliance of the performances in those halls redounded to the credit of the magnanimous host. Fulk Gyllome's improvisational skills and gifts as an actor are unknown, but William Shakespeare's proved sufficient to get him a place a few years later in London's leading playing company. As for his imaginative power, if only the smallest fraction began to show itself in the halls of the wealthy Lancashire gentlemen, its intensity would more than explain the dying Hoghton's benevolence.

On the other hand, Will would have lived a life of secrets, where even the lowliest servant knew things—a locked cabinet containing the chalice, books, vestments, and other objects with which to celebrate Mass; mysterious strangers bearing ominous rumors of Mary, Queen of

Scots, or of Spanish armies; mutterings of conspiracies—that could, if revealed, bring disaster upon the family. Lancashire in this period was tense with expectation, suspicion, and anxiety. The moment that Will is likely to have sojourned there is precisely the moment that the Jesuit Campion headed in the same direction, seeking the relative security afforded by the most stubbornly Catholic of the queen's subjects. Lancashire, in the view of the queen's Privy Council, was "the very sink of popery, where more unlawful acts are committed and more unlawful persons held secret than in any other part of the realm." On August 4, 1581, the day after Alexander Hoghton commended Shakeshafte to his friend Sir Thomas Hesketh, the Privy Council ordered a search for Campion's papers "at the house of one Richard Hoghton"—Alexander's cousin—"in Lancashire." And later that year, at a time when Will may have been in his service, Hesketh was thrown into prison for failing to suppress recusancy in his household. The atmosphere at the entertainments in which Will would have performed was compounded of festivity and paranoia.

The mission, led by Campion and Robert Parsons, had aroused the piety of Catholics and deeply alarmed the government. Not only had the pope effectively sanctioned the assassination of the queen, but an expeditionary force led by a Catholic Englishman, Nicholas Sander, had recently landed in Ireland in an attempt to spark an uprising against the Protestant colonists. The attempt had failed miserably: after unconditionally surrendering on November 10, 1580, some six hundred Spanish and Italian troops and their Irish allies, including several women and priests, were all massacred by English soldiers led by Walter Ralegh. The cold-blooded ferocity of the English response was presumably meant to chill any future invasion plans, but no one could doubt the determination of the pope and his allies to topple the Elizabethan regime and reclaim the realm. Even those English Catholics who were steadfastly loyal to Elizabeth—and there were many—must have felt some stirring of hope that the slow, relentless strangulation of their faith might somehow be reversed by the missionary piety and heroic determination of the Jesuits.

Catholics throughout the country secretly read and circulated a remarkable document that came to be known as "Campion's Brag," in which the onetime Oxford don, the object of an intense national search, explained his mission. "In this busy, watchful and suspicious world," he wrote in a tone of almost jaunty resignation, it was likely enough that he would eventually be caught and pressed to reveal his designs. Therefore, to save everyone time and trouble, he offered in advance a plain confession. He had not been sent to meddle in politics; his charge was "to preach the Gospel, to minister the Sacraments, to instruct the simple, to reform sinners, to confute errors." He knew, of course, that the authorities would claim that these activities, undertaken by a Catholic priest, were precisely what it meant to meddle in politics, and he knew that their response would be violent. But he and his companions were "determined never to give you over, but either to win you heaven, or to die upon your pikes." As for the charges of an international conspiracy, a sinister "enterprise" to invade and conquer England, he boldly played with them:

> And touching our Society, be it know to you that we have made a league—all the Jesuits in the world, whose succession and multitude must overreach all the practices of England—cheerfully to carry the cross you shall lay upon us, and never to despair your recovery, while we have a man left to enjoy your Tyburn, or to be racked with your torments, or consumed with your prisons. The expense is reckoned, the enterprise is begun; it is of God, it cannot be withstood. So the faith was planted: so it must be restored.

The sublime confidence that Campion exuded here was evident also in the challenge that gave his pamphlet its nickname: though he would be loath, he wrote, to say anything that would sound like an "insolent brag," he was confident enough of the transparent truth of the Catholic faith that he would undertake to debate any Protestant alive. His words have an odd ring to them, as if he were living not in a world of conspiracies, spies, and torture chambers but in a world in which scholars mount their books and ride out to chivalric contests: "I am to sue most humbly and instantly for the combat with all and every of them, and the most principal that may be found: protesting that in this trial the better furnished they come, the better welcome they shall be."

For Campion, the cruelty of the English Protestant authorities was a sign of their fear of open debate and hence a sign of their despair. He followed up his challenge with a longer, more scholarly work in Latin—the *Ten Reasons*—which he originally intended to call *Heresy in Despair*. This work he somehow planned during months in which he managed to evade the agents sent to capture him, months of shifting disguises, frequent moves from house to house, terrifying alarms, narrow escapes. He wrote it during the only period and in the only place in which he had enough time, protection, and access to books to sit and write: in the late winter and early spring of 1581 in Lancashire. And even there, in the north, he was forced every few days to make sudden shifts in his hiding place in order to confound the government spies and informers. Dressed as a servant, he scurried from one recusant household to another, guided by a former student and his wife. "By them," writes Campion's fine nineteenth-century biographer Richard Simpson, "he was led to visit the Worthingtons, the Talbots, the Southworths, the Heskeths, Mrs. Allen the widow of the Cardinal's brother, the Houghtons, the Westbys, and the Rigmaidens—at whose house he spent the time between Easter and Whitsuntide (April 16)."

The Heskeths and the Hoghtons: it is altogether possible, then, that in the guarded spaces of one or the other of these houses Will would have seen the brilliant, hunted missionary for himself. Campion's visits were clandestine, to be sure, but they were not narrowly private affairs; they brought together dozens, even hundreds of believers, many of whom slept in nearby barns and outbuildings to hear Campion preach in the early morning and to receive communion from his hands. The priest—who would have changed out of his servant's clothes into clerical vestments—would sit up half the night hearing confessions, trying to resolve moral dilemmas, dispensing advice. Was one of those with whom he exchanged whispered words the young man from Stratford-upon-Avon?

Let us imagine the two of them sitting together then, the sixteen-year-old fledgling poet and actor and the forty-year-old Jesuit. Shakespeare would have found Campion fascinating—even his mortal enemies conceded that he had charisma—and might even have recognized in him something of a kindred spirit. Not in piety, for though Will (in this version of events) was a staunch enough Catholic at this point in his life to be trusted with dangerous secrets, there is no sign in his voluminous later work of a frustrated religious vocation. But Campion—a quarter century older than Will—was someone who came from a comparably modest family; who attracted attention to himself by his eloquence, intelligence, and quickness; who loved books yet at the same time was drawn to life in the world. His was a learned but not an original mind; rather he was brilliant at giving traditional ideas a new life through the clarity and grace of his language and the moving power of his presence. Witty, imaginative, and brilliantly adept at improvisation, he managed to combine meditative seriousness with a strong theatrical streak. If the adolescent knelt down before Campion, he would have been looking at a distorted image of himself.

The Jesuit too, perhaps, even in a brief encounter, might have noticed something striking in the youth. Campion was a gifted teacher who had, in safer times, written a discourse on education. The ideal student, Campion wrote, should be born of Catholic parents. He should have a mind "subtle, hot, and clear; his memory happy; his voice flexible, sweet, and sonorous; his walk and all his motions lively, gentlemanly, and subdued; and the whole man seeming a palace fit for wisdom to dwell in." His years at school should plunge him into the classics: he must become intimate with "the majesty of Virgil, the festal grace of Ovid, the rhythm of Horace, and the buskined speech of Seneca." And the good student is not merely the passive receptacle of high culture; he is an accomplished musician, a budding orator, and a gifted poet. In short, he is—if the harried fugitive Campion had occasion to observe him at all closely—the young Shakespeare.

Well, not quite. For Shakespeare was not on his way to the further studies—in philosophy, mathematics, astronomy, Hebrew, and, above all, theology—that Campion's scheme of education envisaged. Moreover, in one key respect he had already no doubt violated the spirit of the plan, and he would go on to violate it as completely as possible. The ideal student is to study and to write poetry, Campion said, but with one significant exception: he is never to read or to write love poetry.

For his part, whether he actually met Campion in person or only heard about him from the flood of rumors circulating all through 1580 and 1581, Will may have registered a powerful inner resistance as well as admiration. Campion was brave, charismatic, persuasive, and appealing; everyone who encountered him recognized these qualities, which even now shine out from his words. But he was also filled with a sense that he knew the one eternal truth, the thing worth living and dying for, the cause to which he was willing cheerfully to sacrifice others as well as himself. To be sure, he did not seek out martyrdom. It was not his wish to return to England; he was doing valuable work for the church, he told Cardinal William Allen, in his teaching post at Prague. But he was a committed soldier in a religious order organized for battle, and when his general commanded him to throw his body into the fight, against wildly uneven odds, he marched off serenely. He would have taken with him young Shakespeare or anyone else worth the taking. He was a fanatic or, more accurately, a saint. And saints, Shakespeare understood all his life, were dangerous people.

Or perhaps, rather, it would be better to say that Shakespeare did not entirely understand saints, and that what he did understand, he did not entirely like. In the huge panoply of characters in his plays, there are strikingly few who would remotely qualify. Joan of Arc appears in an early history play, but she is a witch and a whore. King Henry VI has a saintly disposition—"all his mind is bent to holiness / To number Ave-Maries on his beads" (*2 Henry II*, 1.3.59–60)—but he is pathetically weak, and his weakness wreaks havoc on his realm. The elegant young men in the court of Navarre swear to live a "Still and contemplative" existence, the lives of ascetic soldiers who war against "the huge army of the world's desires" (1.1.14, 10), but *Love's Labour's Lost* shows them quickly succumbing to charms of the princess of France and her ladies. The severe Angelo in *Measure for Measure* is a man who "scarce confesses / That his blood flows" (1.3.51–52), but he soon finds himself contriving to compel the beautiful Isabella, a novice in a nunnery, to sleep with him. Isabella, for her part, is impressively true to her chaste vocation, but her determination to preserve her virginity, even at the cost of her brother's life, is something less than humanly appealing.

There are many forms of heroism in Shakespeare, but ideological heroism—the fierce, self-immolating embrace of an idea or an institution—is not one of them. Nothing in his work suggests a deep admiration for the visible church. Several of his conspicuously Catholic religious figures—Friar Laurence in *Romeo and Juliet* is an example—are fundamentally sympathetic, but not because they are important figures in the church hierarchy. On the contrary, Shakespeare's plays almost always depict powerful prelates as disagreeable, and his little-known history play *King John*, though set in the early thirteenth century, attacks the pope in highly charged, anachronistically Protestant terms. How dare the pope, King John indignantly asks the papal legate, attempt to impose his will upon a "sacred king"?

> Thou canst not, Cardinal, devise a name
> So slight, unworthy, and ridiculous
> To charge me to an answer, as the Pope.
> Tell him this tale, and from the mouth of England
> Add thus much more: that no Italian priest
> Shall tithe or toll in our dominions;
> But as we, under God, are supreme head,
> So, under him, that great supremacy
> Where we do reign we will alone uphold
> Without th'assistance of a mortal hand.
>
> (3.1.74–84)

This coarsely explicit piece of Protestant pope-baiting is by no means the sum of Shakespeare's mature attitude toward the Catholicism in which he had been immersed as a young man. And it certainly cannot tell us what the young man felt if and when he stood in the presence of the fugitive Jesuit. But the only sainthood in which Shakespeare seems passionately to have believed throughout his life derives precisely from the subject matter and emotions that Campion wished his students at all costs to avoid: erotic sainthood.

ROMEO: O then, dear saint, let lips do what hands do:
  Then pray; grant thou, lest faith turn to despair.
JULIET: Saints do not move, though grant for prayers' sake.

ROMEO: Then move not while my prayer's effect I take.
[*He kisses her*]
Thus from my lips, by thine my sin is purged.
JULIET: Then have my lips the sin that they have took.
ROMEO: Sin from my lips? O trespass sweetly urged!
Give me my sin again.
[*He kisses her*]
JULIET: You kiss by th' book.
(1.5.100–107)

There are traces of Catholicism here, of a kind that Campion would immediately have recognized, but the theology and the ritual practice have been wittily turned into desire and its fulfillment.

The beautiful, playful lines from *Romeo and Juliet* were written in the mid-1590s, some fifteen years after the moment when Shakespeare may have encountered Campion. But the sly blend of displacement and appropriation, the refashioning of traditional religious materials into secular performance, and the confounding of the sacred and the profane are characteristic of virtually the whole of Shakespeare's achievement as dramatist and poet. In *A Midsummer Night's Dream*, written relatively early in his career, the beds of the newly wed couples are blessed, as they would have been in a popular Catholic practice outlawed by the Protestants, but it is not with holy water; rather, the fairies sprinkle them with "field-dew consecrate" (5.2.45). And in *The Winter's Tale*, written near its end, there is an ecstatic description of a solemn ritual conducted by priests dressed in "celestial habits," but the "grave wearers" of those habits are not celebrating the Mass; rather, what is being described is the Delphic oracle:

I shall report,
For most it caught me, the celestial habits—
Methinks I so should term them—and the reverence
Of the grave wearers. O, the sacrifice—
How ceremonious, solemn, and unearthly
It was i'th' off'ring!
(3.1.3–8)

This is not a parody of the Mass, but it is also not exactly a sly tribute, slipped under the censor's eye. Instead, the lines and much else like them in Shakespeare's work suggest how completely he had absorbed Catholicism for his own poetic purposes. Those purposes were light-years from Campion's, and the distance might already have been apparent even—or perhaps especially—in Lancashire in 1581.

There is not only the matter of Will's temperament—a lack of religious vocation, a skeptical distance from the missionary's ardent faith, an adolescent's awareness of the claims of his own flesh. Though he was only a young servant, Will could easily have noticed something beyond its religious conviction about the strange, dangerous world he had come to inhabit. The north was a traditional site of resistance to the centralizing authority of the Crown, and the families in whose houses he lived and worked skirted close to treason. All of Shakespeare's early history plays—the plays with which he made a name for himself in London in the early 1590s—were concerned with rebellion, which he consistently conceived of as a family affair. These plays were safely set in the England of the fifteenth century, and the events were taken from the chronicles, but Shakespeare had to draw upon more than his reading to give his characters the touch of reality. His imagination was populated by powerful, restive, ambitious men and women who were willing to take extreme risks in playing the dangerous games of power. His image of these people could well have been taken from the families he would have closely observed during a sojourn in the north.

What this suggests is that if he actually saw Campion in 1581 Shakespeare would even then probably have shuddered and recoiled inwardly, pulling away from the invitation, whether implicit in the saint's presence or directly and passionately urged, to shoulder the cross and join in a pious struggle for the Catholic faith. Will had, as Hoghton's will suggests, been making a mark—probably for the first time in his life—as an actor; he had begun to sense what he was capable of doing and what he had within him. And he was not going to get caught up in a glorious, treasonous, suicidal crusade. If his father was both Catholic and Protestant, William Shakespeare was on his way to being neither.

Shakespeare—assuming that he is the Shakeshafte of Hoghton's will—stayed in Lancashire at least until August 1581, before heading back to Stratford. Campion had left the area earlier; he had been ordered by Parsons to return to the vicinity of London to oversee the secret printing of his *Ten Reasons*. Working hurriedly and in great danger, the printers managed to finish the task in time for the Oxford University commencement on June 27: the students and fellows who filed into St. Mary's Church found hundreds of bound copies waiting for them on their seats. A few weeks later, on his way back to Lancashire, Campion was trapped, arrested, taken to the Tower, and thrust into a cell aptly nicknamed "Little Ease." After four days of painful confinement—the cell did not permit the prisoner either to stand or to lie flat—he was suddenly taken out, carried under guard to a boat, and rowed to the mansion of the immensely powerful Earl of Leicester, the man who had been poised years before to be his patron. Leicester was joined by the Earl of Bedford and two secretaries of state. More astonishing still, Queen Elizabeth herself was in the room. They asked him why he had come to England. For the salvation of souls, he answered, whereupon Elizabeth asked him directly if he acknowledged her as his queen or no. "Not only as my queen," Campion replied, "but also as my most lawful governess." That word "lawful" did not escape the queen's attention; could the pope, she asked, "lawfully" excommunicate her? Could he discharge her subjects of their obedience? These were what Campion described as "bloody questions, and very pharisaical, undermining of my life." He could not, he grasped at once, give the answers she was demanding, the answers that would not only enable him to go free but would also, as the queen made clear, bring him riches and honors. He was taken back to the Tower, where he was interrogated, tortured on the rack, tried for treason, and then, with Thomas Cottam and the others, executed.

Will would only have been able to follow these terrible events through rumor and perhaps through the government's highly distorted printed reports. He would certainly have heard of Campion's capture—that was national news—and he would have heard too, no doubt with special anxiety, that Campion had, under torture, revealed the names of many of his hosts. (The extent of his confession, much trumpeted by the authorities, is still in dispute, though the pattern of subsequent arrests in

Lancashire and elsewhere, along with Campion's own words on the scaffold, indicates that he revealed more than he would have wished.)

Shakespeare might also have heard or read about an extraordinary event that intervened between the Jesuit's capture and his execution. The authorities clearly had been nettled by Campion's "brag"—his challenge to debate anyone on the merits of Catholicism—and by the clandestine publication of *Ten Reasons*. One day at the end of August, Campion was taken from his cell without warning and brought into the chapel of the Tower. There, in the presence of the guards, other Catholic prisoners, and such privileged members of the public as could crowd in, he was confronted with two Protestant theologians, Alexander Nowell, the dean of St. Paul's, and William Day, the dean of Windsor. The theologians, seated at a table piled with books and notes, were celebrated debaters. At another table two other distinguished but hardly neutral figures, William Chark, the preacher of Gray's Inn, and William Whitaker, the Regius Professor of Divinity at Cambridge, were poised to act as notaries. The prisoner would get his debate, but the government would set the stage and the rules.

Campion objected that he had had no time to prepare, had no notes and no books, and that he had been subjected to "hellish torture." The lieutenant of the Tower, Sir Owen Hopton, had the effrontery to declare that the prisoner "was scarce pinched and that it might rather be termed a cramping than racking." Responding with dignity that he himself "could best report, and be most truest judge, because he felt the smart," Campion accepted—as he had no choice but to accept—the grossly unfair terms of the debate. He then proceeded, by what appears to be a near-universal consensus, to annihilate his opponents. The authorities were chagrined. In the weeks that followed, bringing in fresh debaters and sharply restricting the scope and form of Campion's answers, they staged three further debates—this time without permitting any Catholic auditors—until they were satisfied that they could declare victory. They then brought Campion to the scaffold at Tyburn, hanged him, and chopped his body in quarters before a huge crowd of observers. One of the bystanders, a Protestant named Henry Walpole, was close to the place where the hangman was throwing the pieces of Campion's body into a vat of boiling water. A drop of the water mixed with blood splashed out upon his clothes, and Walpole felt at once, he said, that he had to convert to Catholicism. He left for the Continent, became a Jesuit, and was sent back to England, where he too was arrested and executed as a traitor. Such are the works of saints and martyrs.

Not surprisingly, Shakespeare never referred openly to Campion. Perhaps in *King Lear* there is a disguised recollection of the fugitive priest and his fellow missionaries in the figure of the innocent Edgar, viciously slandered by his bastard brother and forced to assume a disguise and flee for his life. "I heard myself proclaimed," the outlawed Edgar declares;

> And by the happy hollow of a tree
> Escaped the hunt. No port is free; no place,
> That guard, and most unusual vigilance,
> Does not attend my taking. Whiles I may 'scape,
> I will preserve myself. . . .

> (2.3.1–6)

But Edgar is not a missionary, and Shakespeare may have felt, more than anything else, the desire to distance himself from what had in the winter and spring of 1581 come dangerously close, and an overwhelming relief that he had not been drawn into the nightmare of persecution, torture, and death.

By the next year, Will was back in Stratford. Perhaps he had, after all, agreed to take one small risk, something to do with the unfortunate Thomas Cottam and whatever matters of "great weight" he had intended to convey to the family of Robert Debdale in the village of Shottery, two miles from Stratford. For shortly after he returned home, Will evidently began to walk along the path that led through the fields to Shottery. Did he have a secret message for the parents of the fugitive priest? It is impossible to say. But that the eighteen-year-old boy was in the village is certain, for there he met the eldest daughter of an old acquaintance of his father, a staunchly Protestant farmer named Richard Hathaway, who had died the year before. Anne Hathaway was twenty-six years old. In the summer of 1582—as if to mark his decisive distance from Campion, from the deep piety and the treasonous murmurs, from the scavenger's daughter and the horrible scaffold—Will was making love to her. To this secret life too there were momentous consequences, of a very different kind. By November they were married, and six months later their daughter Susanna was born.

CHAPTER 4

Wooing, Wedding, and Repenting

I F WILL RETURNED to Stratford in 1582 in the wake of a tense
sojourn in Lancashire, if he agreed to go to Shottery that summer
to convey a risky message or pass along a secret religious token to
the Debdales, then his wooing of Anne Hathaway was manifestly a rebellion against the empire of fear. Anne's world was the dia-
metrical opposite of the dangerous world to which he may have been
exposed: the powerful all-male bonds formed by Simon Hunt, the
schoolmaster who had gone off to the seminary with his student Robert
Debdale; the conspiracy to protect Campion, Parsons, Cottam, and the
other Jesuit missionaries; the secret sodality of pious, suicidal young
men. But even if the circumstances were far less dire, even if Will were
merely an inexperienced Stratford adolescent whose principal social
points of reference had been his family and the boys at the King's New
School, Anne Hathaway must have represented a startling alternative.
Will's family almost certainly leaned toward Catholicism, and Anne's
almost certainly leaned in the opposite direction. In his will, Anne's father,
Richard, asked to be "honestly buried," the code phrase for the simple,
stark burials favored by Puritans. Anne's brother Bartholomew also asked

for such a burial, "hoping to arise at the Latter Day and to receive the reward of His elect." "His elect": these are people far different from Campion or, for that matter, the Catholic Ardens to whom Shakespeare's mother was related.

Anne Hathaway represented an escape in another sense: she was in the unusual position of being her own woman. Very few young, unmarried Elizabethan women had any executive control over their own lives; the girl's watchful father and mother would make the key decisions for their daughter, ideally, though not always, with her consent. But Anne—an orphan in her midtwenties, with some resources left to her by her father's will and more due to her upon her marriage—was, in the phrase of the times, "wholly at her own government." She was independent, in a way virtually ordained to excite a young man's sexual interest, and she was free to make her own decisions. Shakespeare's lifelong fascination with women who are in this position may have had its roots in the sense of freedom Anne Hathaway awakened in him. He would have felt a release from the constraints of his own family, a release too, perhaps, from the sexual confusion and ambiguity that Elizabethan moralists associated with playacting. If the imaginary schoolboy performance of Plautus had any equivalent in reality—if Will ever experienced a disturbing erotic excitement in acting a love scene with another boy—then Anne Hathaway offered a reassuringly conventional resolution to his sexual ambivalence or perplexity.

Quite apart from this imaginary resolution—whose appeal, albeit temporary, is not to be underestimated—Anne offered a compelling dream of pleasure. So at least one might conclude from the centrality of wooing in Shakespeare's whole body of work, from *The Two Gentlemen of Verona* and *The Taming of the Shrew* to *The Winter's Tale* and *The Tempest*. Lovemaking, not in the sense of sexual intercourse but in the older sense of intense courting and pleading and longing, was one of his abiding preoccupations, one of the things he understood and expressed more profoundly than almost anyone in the world. That understanding may not have had anything to do with the woman he married, of course, and, theoretically at least, it need not have had anything to do with his lived experience at all. But the whole impulse to explore Shakespeare's life arises from the powerful conviction that his plays and poems spring not only from other plays and poems but from things he knew firsthand, in his body and soul.

The adult Shakespeare is very funny about the love antics of rustic youths. In *As You Like It*, for example, he mocks the besotted bumpkin so in love with a milkmaid that he kisses "the cow's dugs that her pretty chapped hands had milked" (2.4.44–45). But somewhere lurking behind the laughter may be a distorted, wry recollection of Shakespeare's own fumbling adolescent efforts, efforts that were perhaps more amply rewarded than he had anticipated. By the summer's end, Anne Hathaway was pregnant.

Shakespeare's marriage has been the subject of almost frenzied interest, ever since a great nineteenth-century bibliophile, Sir Thomas Phillipps, found an odd document in the bishop of Worcester's registry. The document, dated November 28, 1582, was a bond for what was in the period a very large sum of money, forty pounds (twice the annual income of the Stratford schoolmaster; eight times the annual income of a London clothworker), put up in order to facilitate the wedding of "William Shagspere" and "Anne Hathwey of Stratford in the Dioces of Worcester maiden."

The couple—or someone close to the couple—wanted the marriage to take place without delay. The reason for the haste was not specified in the bond, but for once there is a properly documented explanation: the baptism six months later—on May 28, 1583, to be exact—of their daughter Susanna. The language of the bond notwithstanding, a "maiden" Anne Hathaway of Stratford in the diocese of Worcester was definitely not.

Normally, a wedding ceremony could take place only after the banns—the formal declaration of an intent to marry—had been publicly proclaimed on three successive Sundays in the local parish church. The interval that this process necessarily entailed could be compounded by the vagaries of canon law (the code of ecclesiastical rules and regulations), which did not permit the reading of banns during certain periods in the church calendar. In late November 1582 such a prohibited period was fast approaching. By submitting a sworn assurance that there were no impediments of the sort that the banns were designed to bring to light, it was possible, for a fee, to obtain a dispensation, enabling a marriage license to be issued at once. But to back up the sworn assurance, there had to be a way to indemnify the diocesan authorities and to guarantee that something—a prior contract to marry, for example, or the objection of a parent to the marriage choice of a minor, or a covenant not to marry until the end of a term of apprenticeship—would not unexpectedly turn up, solemn oaths notwithstanding, and send the whole business into court. Hence the bond, which would become void if no impediment surfaced.

It is not known if Will's parents approved of the marriage of their eighteen-year-old son to the pregnant twenty-six-year-old bride. Then as now, in England eighteen would have been regarded as young for a man to marry; the mean age upon marriage for males in Stratford in 1600 (the earliest date for which there are reliable figures) was twenty-eight. And it was unusual for a man to marry a woman so much his senior; women in this period were on average two years younger than their husbands. The exceptions were generally among the upper classes, where marriages were in effect property transactions between families and very young children could be betrothed. (In such cases, the marriages were not consummated until years after the wedding, and the newlyweds often waited a very long time before they began to live together.) In the case of Anne Hathaway, the bride had something of an inheritance, but she was hardly a great heiress—in his will her father had stipulated that she was to receive six pounds thirteen shillings fourpence on her marriage—and a financially embarrassed, communally prominent John Shakespeare might have hoped that his son's bride would bring a larger dowry. Had they bitterly objected, Shakespeare's parents could have made a legal fuss, since their son was a minor. (The age of majority was twenty-one.) They did not do so, perhaps because, as legal records show, Shakespeare's father had been acquainted with Anne's father. Still, it is likely that in the eyes of John and Mary Shakespeare, Will was not making a great match.

And Will? Through the centuries eighteen-year-old boys have not been famously eager in such situations to rush to the altar. Will might, of course, have been an exception. Certainly, he was able as a playwright to imagine such impatience. "When and where and how / We met, we wooed, and made exchange of vow / I'll tell thee as we pass," Romeo tells Friar Laurence on the morning after the Capulet ball; "but this I pray, / That thou consent to marry us today" (2.2.61–64).

Romeo and Juliet's depiction of the frantic haste of the rash lovers blends together humor, irony, poignancy, and disapproval, but Shakespeare conveys above all a deep inward understanding of what it feels like to be young, desperate to wed, and tormented by delay. In the great balcony scene, though they have only just met, Romeo and Juliet exchange "love's faithful vow" with one another. "If that thy bent of love be honourable, / Thy purpose marriage," Juliet tells Romeo at the close of the most passionate love scene Shakespeare ever wrote, "send me word tomorrow." When she knows "Where and what time thou wilt perform the rite," she declares, "All my fortunes at thy foot I'll lay, / And follow thee, my lord, throughout the world" (2.1.169, 185–86, 188–90).

Hence the urgency of Romeo's visit to the friar early the next morning, and hence the wild eagerness of Juliet for the return of her nurse, whom she has sent to get Romeo's response. "Old folks, many feign as they were dead," the young girl complains, "Unwieldy, slow, heavy, and pale as lead." When the nurse finally trundles in, Juliet can scarcely pry the all-important news from her:

> NURSE: I am a-weary. Give me leave a while.
>   Fie, how my bones ache. What a jaunce have I!
> JULIET: I would thou hadst my bones and I thy news.
>   Nay, come, I pray thee speak, good, good Nurse, speak.
> NURSE: Jesu, what haste! Can you not stay a while?
>   Do you not see that I am out of breath?
> JULIET: How art thou out of breath when thou hast breath
>   To say to me that thou art out of breath?
>   The excuse that thou dost make in this delay
>   Is longer than the tale thou dost excuse.
>
>   . . . .
>
>   What says he of our marriage—what of that?
>   (2.4.16–17, 25–46)

Exasperated impatience has never been more deftly and sympathetically chronicled.

Romeo's urgency is sketched rather cursorily; it is Juliet's that is given much fuller scope and intensity. Similarly, it is eminently likely that Anne, three months pregnant, rather than the young Will, was the prime source of the impatience that led to the bond. To be sure, this was Elizabethan and not Victorian England: an unmarried mother in the 1580s did not, as she would in the 1880s, routinely face fierce, unrelenting social stigmatization. But the shame and social disgrace in Shakespeare's time were real enough; bastardy was severely frowned upon by the community, as the child would need to be fed and clothed; and the six pounds thirteen shillings fourpence would only be given to Anne when she found a husband.

The substantial bond to hurry the marriage along was posted by a pair of Stratford farmers, Fulke Sandells and John Rychardson, friends of the bride's late father. The young bridegroom and father-to-be may have been grateful for this handsome assistance, but it is far more likely that he was a reluctant, perhaps highly reluctant, beneficiary. If the playwright's imagination subsequently conjured up an impatient Romeo, eager to wed, it also conjured up a series of foot-dragging bridegrooms shamed or compelled to wed the women with whom they have slept. "She is two months on her way," the clown Costard tells the braggart Armado, who has seduced a peasant girl. "What meanest thou?" Armado demands, trying to bluster his way out of the situation, but Costard insists: "She's quick. The child brags in her belly already. 'Tis yours" (*Love's Labour's Lost*, 5.2.658–63). Armado is no romantic hero; like Lucio in *Measure for Measure* and Bertram in *All's Well That Ends Well*, he is treated with irony, distaste, and contempt. But these may have been precisely the feelings evoked in Shakespeare when he looked back upon his own marriage.

In one of his earliest works, the *1 Henry VI*, he had a character compare a marriage by compulsion to one made voluntarily:

> For what is wedlock forcèd but a hell,
> An age of discord and continual strife,

Whereas the contrary bringeth bliss,
And is a pattern of celestial peace.
(5.7.62–65)

The character is an earl, cynically persuading the king to make what will
be a bad match, but the dream of bliss seems valid enough, along with the
sense that "wedlock forcèd" is an almost certain recipe for unhappiness.
Perhaps at the time he wrote those lines, in the early 1590s, Shakespeare
was reflecting on the source of his own marital unhappiness. Perhaps too
there is a personal reflection in Richard of Gloucester's sly observation
"Yet hasty marriage seldom proveth well" (*3 Henry VI*, 4.1.18) or in
Count Orsino's advice in *Twelfth Night*:

Let still the woman take
An elder than herself. So wears she to him;
So sways she level in her husband's heart.
(2.4.28–30)

Of course, each of these lines has a specific dramatic context, but they
were all written by someone who at eighteen years of age had hastily
married a woman older than himself and then left her behind in Stratford. How could he have written Orsino's words without in some sense
bringing his own life, his disappointment, frustration, and loneliness, to
bear upon them?

Suspicion that Will was dragged to the altar has been heightened by
another document. The bond for the grant of a marriage license to
Willam Shagspere and Anne Hathwey is dated November 28, but the
Worcester archives also record a marriage license dated one day earlier,
November 27, for the wedding of William Shaxpere and Anne Whatley
of Temple Grafton. As there were other Shakespeares in Warwickshire, a
different William could conceivably have happened to wed at just this
time. Assuming, however, that such a coincidence would be unlikely, who
on earth is Anne Whatley of Temple Grafton, a village about five miles
west of Stratford? A woman Will loved and was hastening to marry until

he was strong-armed by Sandells and Rychardson into wedlock with the pregnant Anne Hathaway?

The possibility has a novelistic appeal: "And so he was still riding to Temple Grafton in cold November," wrote Anthony Burgess in a fine flight of fancy, "winter's first harbingers biting. Hoofs rang frosty on the road. Hard by Shottery two men stopped him. They addressed him by name and bade him dismount." But most scholars have agreed with Joseph Gray, who concluded in 1905, after extensive study, that the clerk who entered the names on the license simply became confused and wrote Whatley instead of Hathaway. Most scholars imagine too that Will was in some measure willing. But the state of his feelings at the time of his wedding is not known, and his attitude toward his wife during the subsequent thirty-two years of marriage can only be surmised. Between his wedding license and his last will and testament, Shakespeare left no direct, personal trace of his relationship with his wife—or none, in any case, that survives. From this supremely eloquent man, there have been found no love letters to Anne, no signs of shared joy or grief, no words of advice, not even any financial transactions.

A sentimental nineteenth-century picture shows Shakespeare at home in Stratford, reciting one of his plays to his family—his father and mother listening from a distance, a dog at his feet, his three children gathered around him, his wife looking up at him adoringly from her needlework—but such a moment, if it ever occurred, would have been exceedingly rare. For most of his married life he lived in London, and Anne and the children apparently remained in Stratford. That in itself does not necessarily imply estrangement; husbands and wives have often been constrained for long periods to live at a considerable distance from one another. But it must have been exceptionally difficult in Shakespeare's time to bridge this distance, to keep up any intimacy. All the more difficult, of course, if, as seems likely, his wife Anne could not read or write. Of course, most of the women in his world had little or no literacy, but the commonness of the condition does not change the fact: it is entirely possible that Shakespeare's wife never read a word he wrote, that anything he sent her from London had to be read by a neighbor, that anything she wished to tell him—the local gossip, the health of his parents, the mortal illness of their only son—had to be consigned to a messenger.

Perhaps the optimists are right and their relationship, notwithstanding the long years apart, was a good one. Biographers eager for Shakespeare to have had a good marriage have stressed that when he made some money in the theater, he established his wife and family in New Place, the fine house he bought in Stratford; that he must have frequently visited them there; that he chose to retire early and return permanently to Stratford a few years before his untimely death. Some have gone further and assumed that he must have had Anne and the children stay with him for prolonged periods in London. "None has spoken more frankly or justly of the honest joys of 'board and bed,'" wrote the distinguished antiquarian Edgar Fripp, pointing to lines from *Coriolanus*:

> I loved the maid I married; never man
> Sighed truer breath. But that I see thee here,
> Thou noble thing, more dances my rapt heart
> Than when I first my wedded mistress saw
> Bestride my threshold.
>
> (4.5.113–17)

But if these lines were, as Fripp thought, a recollection of the dramatist's own feelings many years before, the recollection was far more bitter than sentimental: they are spoken by the warrior Aufidius, whose rapt heart dances at seeing the hated man he has long dreamed of killing.

It is, perhaps, as much what Shakespeare did *not* write as what he did that seems to indicate something seriously wrong with his marriage. This was an artist who made use of virtually everything that came his way. He mined, with very few exceptions, the institutions and professions and personal relationships that touched his life. He was the supreme poet of courtship: one has only to think of the aging sonneteer and the fair young man, panting Venus and reluctant Adonis, Orlando and Rosalind, Petruccio and Kate, even twisted, perverse Richard III and Lady Anne.

And he was a great poet of the family, with a special, deep interest in the murderous rivalry of brothers and in the complexity of father-daughter relations: Egeus and Hermia, Brabanzio and Desdemona, Lear and the fearsome threesome, Pericles and Marina, Prospero and Miranda. But though wedlock is the promised land toward which his comic heroes and heroines strive, and though family fission is the obsessive theme of the tragedies, Shakespeare was curiously restrained in his depictions of what it is actually like to be married.

To be sure, he provided some fascinating glimpses. A few of his married couples have descended into mutual loathing: "O Goneril!" cries the disgusted Albany, in *King Lear*. "You are not worth the dust which the rude wind / Blows in your face." "Milk-livered man!" she spits back at him. "That bear'st a cheek for blows, a head for wrongs: . . . Marry, your manhood! mew!" (4.2.30–32, 51–69). But for the most part, they are in subtler, more complex states of estrangement. Mostly, it's wives feeling neglected or shut out. "For what offence," Kate Percy asks her husband, Harry (better known as Hotspur), in *1 Henry IV*, "have I this fortnight been / A banished woman from my Harry's bed?" She has in point of fact committed no offence—Hotspur is deeply preoccupied with plotting a rebellion—but she is not wrong to feel excluded. Hotspur has chosen to keep his wife in the dark:

> But hark you, Kate.
> I must not have you henceforth question me
> Whither I go, nor reason whereabout.
> Whither I must, I must; and, to conclude,
> This evening must I leave you, gentle Kate.
> (2.4.32–33, 93–97)

The rebellion is a family affair—Hotspur has been drawn into it by his father and his uncle—but though the fate of his wife will certainly be involved in its outcome, the only knowledge she has of it is from words she has overheard him muttering in his troubled sleep. With bluff, genial misogyny Hotspur explains that he simply does not trust her:

> I know you wise, but yet no farther wise
> Than Harry Percy's wife; constant you are,
> But yet a woman; and for secrecy
> No lady closer, for I well believe
> Thou wilt not utter what thou dost not know.
> And so far will I trust thee, gentle Kate.
>
> (2.4.98–103)

The words are all good-humored and exuberant, in the way most of the things Hotspur says are, but the marriage they sketch is one at whose core is mutual isolation. (The same play, *1 Henry IV*, gives another, more graphic vision of such a marriage in Edmund Mortimer and his Welsh wife: "This is the deadly spite that angers me: / My wife can speak no English, I no Welsh" [3.1.188–89].)

Shakespeare returned to the theme in *Julius Caesar*, where Brutus's wife, Portia, complains that she has been deliberately shut out of her husband's inner life. Unlike Kate Percy, Portia is not banished from her husband's bed, but her exclusion from his mind leaves her feeling, she says, like a whore:

> Am I yourself
> But as it were in sort or limitation?
> To keep with you at meals, comfort your bed,
> And talk to you sometimes? Dwell I but in the suburbs
> Of your good pleasure? If it be no more,
> Portia is Brutus' harlot, not his wife.
>
> (2.1.281–86)

The question here and elsewhere in the plays is the degree of intimacy that husbands and wives can achieve, and the answer Shakespeare repeatedly gives is very little.

Shakespeare was not alone in his time in finding it difficult to portray or even imagine fully achieved marital intimacy. It took decades of Puritan insistence on the importance of companionship in marriage to change the social, cultural, and psychological landscape. By the time Milton published *Paradise Lost*, in 1667, the landscape was decisively different. Marriage was no longer the consolation prize for those who did not have the higher vocation of celibacy; it was not the doctrinally approved way of avoiding the sin of fornication; it was not even principally the means of generating offspring and conveying property. It was about the dream of long-term love.

But it is not clear how much of this dream could have been envisaged when Will agreed, whether eagerly or reluctantly, to marry Anne Hathaway. It is no accident that Milton wrote important tracts advocating the possibility of divorce; the longing for deep emotional satisfaction in marriage turned out to depend heavily upon the possibility of divorce. In a world without this possibility most writers seemed to agree: it was better to make jokes about endurance, pass over most marriages in discreet silence, and write love poetry to anyone but your spouse. Dante wrote the passionate *La vita nuova* not to his wife, Gemma Donati, but to Beatrice Portinari, whom he had first glimpsed when they were both children. So too Petrarch, who was probably ordained as a priest, wrote the definitive European love poems—the great sequence of sonnets—to the beautiful Laura, and not to the unnamed, unknown woman who gave birth to his two children, Giovanni and Francesca. And in England, Stella, the star at which Sir Philip Sidney gazed longingly in his sonnet sequence *Astrophil and Stella*, was Penelope Devereux, married to someone else, and not his wife, Frances Walsingham.

It was reasonable to hope for stability and comfort in marriage, but not for much more, and if you did not find anything that you wanted, if relations deteriorated into sour-eyed bitterness, there was no way to end the marriage and begin again. Divorce—even as an imagined solution, let alone a practical one—did not exist in 1580 in Stratford-upon-Avon, not for anyone of Shakespeare's class, scarcely for anyone at all. Like everyone who wedded at that time, he married for life, whether the marriage turned out to be fulfilling or disastrous, whether the person he had chosen (or who had chosen him) continued after a year or so to touch his heart or filled him with revulsion.

Yet diminished cultural expectations can at best only partially explain Shakespeare's reluctance or inability to represent marriage, as it were, from the inside. For he did in fact register the frustrated longing for spousal intimacy, though he attributed that longing almost exclusively to women. Along with Kate Percy and Portia, there is Shakespeare's most poignant depiction of a neglected wife, Adriana in *The Comedy of Errors*. Since *The Comedy of Errors* is a farce and since it is based on a Roman model that has absolutely no emotional investment in the figure of the wife—Plautus jokingly has her put up for sale at the close of his play—it is all the more striking that Shakespeare registered so acutely her anguish:

> How comes it now, my husband, O how comes it
> That thou art then estrangèd from thyself?—
> Thy 'self' I call it, being strange to me
> That, undividable, incorporate,
> Am better than thy dear self's better part.
> Ah, do not tear away thyself from me;
> For know, my love, as easy mayst thou fall
> A drop of water in the breaking gulf,
> And take unmingled thence that drop again
> Without addition or diminishing,
> As take from me thyself, and not me too.
>
> (2.2.119–29)

The scene in which these words are spoken is comical, for Adriana is unwittingly addressing not her husband but her husband's long-lost identical twin. Yet the speech is too long and the pain too intense to be altogether absorbed in laughter.

Though the comedy rushes on to madcap confusion and though at the play's end Adriana is blamed (erroneously, as it happens) for her husband's distracted state— "The venom clamours of a jealous woman / Poisons more deadly than a mad dog's tooth" (5.1.70–71)—her suffering has an odd, insistent ring of truth. The situation seized Shakespeare's imagination, as if the misery of the neglected or abandoned spouse was something he knew personally and all too well. Amid the climactic flurry of recognitions, the play does not include, as it would have been reasonable to expect, a scene of marital reconciliation. In *The Comedy of Errors*, as in most of his plays, the substance of such a reconciliation—what it would mean fully to share a life—seems to have eluded him.

Occasionally, as in *The Winter's Tale*, there is a glimpse of something more than a frustrated craving for intimacy. Hermione, nine months pregnant, manages lightly to tease her husband, Leontes, and her teasing discloses marital emotions that go beyond anxious dependence. Leontes, who has been trying unsuccessfully to persuade his best friend to extend his already lengthy visit, enlists his wife's aid. When his wife succeeds, Leontes pays her a hyperbolic compliment whose potential awkwardness Hermione immediately seizes upon:

> LEONTES: Is he won yet?
> HERMIONE: He'll stay, my lord.
> LEONTES: At my request he would not.
>   Hermione, my dearest, thou never spok'st
>   To better purpose.
> HERMIONE: Never?
>
> (1.2.88–91)

As befits a play fantastically sensitive to intonation, there is nothing on the surface of these simple lines to suggest that anything is going wrong. But perhaps Hermione has already sensed something slightly edgy in Leontes' response, and she instinctively tries to turn it into marital playfulness:

> HERMIONE: Never?
> LEONTES: Never but once.
> HERMIONE: What, have I twice said well? When was't before?
>   I prithee tell me. Cram's with praise, and make's
>   As fat as tame things.
>
> (1.2.91–94)

There is here, as so often in the ordinary conversation of husbands and wives, at once nothing and everything going on. As befits convention,

Hermione calls Leontes her lord, but she speaks to him on easy, equal footing, mingling sexual banter and gentle mockery, at once welcoming her husband's compliment and making fun of it. Grasping his initial misstep, Leontes quickly qualifies what he has said, turning "Never" into "Never but once," and then gives his pregnant wife what she says she longs for:

> Why, that was when
> Three crabbèd month had soured themselves to death
> Ere I could make thee open thy white hand
> And clap thyself my love. Then didst thou utter,
> "I am yours for ever."
>
> (1.2.103–7)

This is one of the most extended marital conversations that Shakespeare ever wrote, and despite its slight air of formality—husband and wife are speaking, after all, in the presence of their close friend and others—it is powerfully convincing in its suggestion of entangled love, tightly coiled tension, and playfulness. Leontes and Hermione can look back with amusement at their shared past. They are not afraid to tease one another; they care what each other thinks and feels; they still experience sexual desire even as they go about forming a family and entertaining guests. But it is precisely at this moment of slightly edgy intimacy that Leontes is seized by a paranoid fear of his wife's infidelity. At the end of the catastrophic events brought on by this paranoia, there is a moving reconciliation scene, but Hermione's words then are focused entirely on the recovery of her lost daughter. To Leontes, whom she embraces, Hermione says precisely nothing.

The Winter's Tale suggests that the marriage of Leontes and Hermione could not sustain—and could certainly not recover—the emotional, sexual, and psychological intimacy, at once so gratifying and so disturbing, that it once possessed. So too in *Othello*, a tragedy with strong affinities to *The Winter's Tale*, Desdemona's full, bold presence in the marriage—

That I did love the Moor to live with him,
My downright violence and storm of fortunes
May trumpet to the world

(1.3.247–49)

—seems to trigger her husband's homicidal jealousy. But perhaps it is wrong even to speak of that particular relationship as a marriage: it seems to last something like a day and a half before it falls apart.

At least these *are* couples. Many of the significant married pairs in Shakespeare have been divorced by death long before the play begins. For the most part it is the women who have vanished: no Mrs. Bolingbroke, Mrs. Shylock, Mrs. Leonato, Mrs. Brabanzio, Mrs. Lear, Mrs. Prospero. Very infrequently there is a faint trace: Shylock's wife was named Leah, and she gave her husband a turquoise ring that their daughter Jessica heartlessly trades for a monkey. Even less frequently, there is a tiny hint, such as this one from *A Midsummer Night's Dream*, of what has taken a missing woman from the world: "But she, being mortal, of that boy did die" (2.1.135). But for the most part Shakespeare doesn't bother.

Demographers have shown that the risks of childbirth in Elizabethan England were high, but not nearly high enough to explain the wholesale absence of spouses from the plays. (Shakespeare's mother outlived his father by seven years, and despite their age difference, his own wife would also outlive him by seven years.) Clearly Shakespeare did not want a *Taming of the Shrew* in which Mrs. Minola would have her own ideas on her daughters' suitors or a *King Lear* in which the old king's wife would dispute his plans for retirement.

There are few happy marriages in all of literature, just as there are rather few representations of goodness. But most eighteenth- and nineteenth-century novels have an important stake in persuading the reader that the romantic young couple, with whose wedding the work ends, will find their deepest fulfillment in each other, even if most of the marriages actually depicted in the course of the narrative are humdrum or desperate. In Jane Austen's *Pride and Prejudice*, Mr. and Mrs. Bennett have a miserable relationship, as do Charlotte Lucas and the asinine Mr. Collins, but Elizabeth Bennett and Darcy will, the reader is assured, beat the odds. Shakespeare, even in his sunniest comedies, had no stake in persuading his audience of any such thing.

"Men are April when they woo, December when they wed," says Rosalind in *As You Like It*. "Maids are May when they are maids, but the sky changes when they are wives" (4.1.124–27). Rosalind may not herself believe what she says—disguised as a young boy, she is playfully testing Orlando's love for her—but she articulates the cynical wisdom of the everyday world. In *The Merry Wives of Windsor*, there are the same hard-edged sentiments tumbling inadvertently from the mouth of the simpleton Slender: "if there be no great love in the beginning, yet heaven may decrease it upon better acquaintance, when we are married and have more occasion to know one another. I hope upon familiarity will grow more contempt" (1.1.206–10). What is envisaged is an almost inevitable sequence summed up in Beatrice's succinct formula, from *Much Ado About Nothing*: "wooing, wedding, and repenting" (2.1.60).

The tone in which these views are uttered is not so much gloomy as humorous and jauntily realistic, a realism that does not actually get in the way of anyone's wedding. At the play's end Beatrice and Benedick too will embark on marriage, as do all the other lovers in Shakespearean comedy, despite the clear-eyed calculation of the likely consequences. Part of the magic of these plays is to register this calculation without inhibiting the joy and optimism of each of the couples. Shakespeare expended little or no effort to persuade the audience that these particular pairs will be an exception to the rule; on the contrary, they themselves give voice to the rule. The spectators are invited to enter into the charmed circle of love, knowing that it is probably a transitory illusion but, for the moment at least—the moment of the play—not caring.

Shakespeare's imagination did not easily conjure up a couple with long-term prospects for happiness. In *A Midsummer Night's Dream*, the love between Lysander and Hermia vanishes in a second, while Demetrius and Helena will cherish each other as long as the love juice sprinkled in their eyes holds out. In *The Taming of the Shrew*, a pair of good actors can persuade audiences that there is a powerful sexual attraction half-hidden in the quarreling of Petruccio and Kate, but the end of the play goes out of its way to offer two almost equally disagreeable visions of marriage, one in which the couple is constantly quarreling, the other in which the wife's will has been broken. The end of *As You Like It* succeeds only because no one is forced to contemplate the future home life of Rosalind and Orlando or of the rest of the "country copulatives," as Touchstone calls them (5.4.53). Since Viola keeps on the male attire with which she has disguised herself, *Twelfth Night* relieves the audience of the burden of seeing her dressed as a demure young woman; even at the end of the play Orsino seems betrothed to his effeminate boyfriend. Nothing about their relationship in the course of the play suggests that they are well matched or that great happiness lies ahead of them. In *The Merchant of Venice*, Jessica and Lorenzo may take pleasure together in spending the money they have stolen from her father, Shylock, but their playful banter has a distinctly uneasy tone:

> LORENZO: In such a night
>   Did Jessica steal from the wealthy Jew,
>   And with an unthrift love did run from Venice
>   As far as Belmont.
> JESSICA: In such a night
>   Did young Lorenzo swear he loved her well,
>   Stealing her soul with many vows of faith,
>   And ne'er a true one.
>
>   (5.1.14–19)

The currents of uneasiness here—mingling together fears of fortune hunting, bad faith, and betrayal—extend to Portia and Bassanio and even to their comic sidekicks Nerissa and Graziano. And these are newlyweds with blissful prospects compared to Hero and the callow, cruel Claudio in *Much Ado About Nothing*. Only Beatrice and Benedick, in that play and indeed among all the couples of the principal comedies, seem to hold out the possibility of a sustained intimacy, and then only if the audience discounts their many insults, forgets that they have been tricked into wooing, and assumes, against their own mutual assertions, that they genuinely love each other.

  It is worth pausing and trying to get it all in focus: in the great succession of comedies that Shakespeare wrote in the latter half of the

1590s, romantic masterpieces with their marvelous depictions of desire and their cheerfully relentless drive toward marriage, there is scarcely a single pair of lovers who seem deeply, inwardly suited for one another. There is no end of longing, flirtation, and pursuit, but strikingly little long-term promise of mutual understanding. How could earnest, decent, slightly dim Orlando ever truly take in Rosalind? How could the fatuous, self-absorbed Orsino ever come to understand Viola? And these are couples joyously embarking on what officially promise to be good marriages. There is a striking sign that Shakespeare was himself aware of the problem he was posing in the romantic comedies: a few years after these plays, sometime between 1602 and 1606, he wrote two comedies that bring the latent tensions in virtually all these happy pairings right up to the surface.

At the close of *Measure for Measure,* Mariana insists on marrying the repellent Angelo, who has continued to lie, connive, and slander until the moment he has been exposed. In the same strange climax, Duke Vincentio proposes marriage with Isabella, who has made it abundantly clear that her real desire is to enter a strict nunnery. As if this were not uncomfortable enough, the duke punishes the scoundrel Lucio by ordering him to marry a woman he has made pregnant. "I beseech your highness, do not marry me to a whore," Lucio pleads, but the duke is implacable, insisting on what is explicitly understood as a form of punishment, the equivalent of "pressing to death, whipping, and hanging" (5.1.508, 515–16). *All's Well That Ends Well* is, if anything, still more uncomfortable: the beautiful, accomplished Helen has unaccountably fixed her heart on the loutish Count Bertram, and in the end, despite his fierce resistance to the match, she gets her nasty bargain. There cannot be even the pretence of a rosy future for the mismatched pair.

In both *Measure for Measure* and *All's Well That Ends Well,* virtually all the marriages appear to be forced upon one party or another, and the pattern of celestial peace seems infinitely remote. The sourness at the end of these famously uncomfortable plays—often labeled "problem comedies"—is not the result of carelessness; it seems to be the expression of a deep skepticism about the long-term prospects for happiness in marriage, even though the plays continue to insist upon marriage as the only legitimate and satisfactory resolution to human desire.

There are two significant exceptions to Shakespeare's unwillingness or inability to imagine a married couple in a relationship of sustained intimacy, but they are unnervingly strange: Gertrude and Claudius in *Hamlet* and the Macbeths. These marriages are powerful, in their distinct ways, but they are also upsetting, even terrifying, in their glimpses of genuine intimacy. The villainous Claudius, fraudulent in almost everything he utters, speaks with oddly convincing tenderness about his feelings for his wife: "She's so conjunctive to my life and soul," he tells Laertes, "That, as the star moves not but in his sphere, / I could not but by her" (4.7.14–16). And Gertrude, for her part, seems equally devoted. Not only does she ratify Claudius's attempt to adopt Hamlet as his own son—"Hamlet, thou hast thy father much offended," she chides him after he has staged the play-within-the-play to catch his uncle's conscience (3.4.9)—but, more telling still, she heroically defends her husband at the risk of her own life, when Laertes storms the palace. Bent on avenging the murdered Polonius, Laertes is out for blood, and Shakespeare here provided, as he often did at crucial moments, an indication within the text of how he wanted the scene staged. Gertrude apparently throws herself between her husband and the would-be avenger; indeed, she must physically restrain the enraged Laertes, since Claudius twice says, "Let him go, Gertrude." To Laertes' demand, "Where is my father?" Claudius forthrightly answers, "Dead," whereupon Gertrude immediately adds, "But not by him" (4.5.119, 123–25).

In a play heavily freighted with commentary, those four simple words have received little attention. Gertrude is directing the murderous Laertes' rage away from her husband and toward someone else: Polonius's actual murderer, Prince Hamlet. She is not directly contriving to have her beloved son killed, but her overmastering impulse is to save her husband. This does not mean that she is a co-conspirator—the play never settles the question of whether she knew that Claudius murdered old Hamlet. When Claudius confesses the crime, he does not do so to his wife but speaks to himself alone, in his closet, in a failed attempt to clear his conscience in prayer.

The deep bond between Gertrude and Claudius, as Hamlet perceives to his horror and disgust, is based upon not shared secrets but an intense mutual sexual attraction. "You cannot call it love," declares the son, sickened by the very thought of his middle-aged mother's sexuality, "for at your age / The heyday in the blood is tame." But he knows that the heyday in Gertrude's blood is not tame, and his imagination dwells on the image of his mother and uncle "In the rank sweat of an enseamèd bed, / Stewed in corruption, honeying and making love." The dirty-minded obsession with the greasy or semen-stained ("enseamèd") sheets calls up a hallucinatory vision of his father—or is it an actual haunting?—that provides a momentary distraction. Yet as soon as the ghost vanishes, the son is at it again, pleading with his mother to "Refrain tonight" (3.4.67–68, 82–83, 152).

If spousal intimacy in *Hamlet* is vaguely nauseating, in *Macbeth* it is terrifying. Here, almost uniquely in Shakespeare, husband and wife speak to each other playfully, as if they were a genuine couple. "Dearest chuck," Macbeth affectionately calls his wife, as he withholds from her an account of what he has been doing—as it happens, arranging the murder of his friend Banquo—so that she can better applaud the deed when it is done. When they host a dinner party that goes horribly awry, the loyal wife tries to cover for her husband: "Sit, worthy friends," she tells the guests, startled when Macbeth starts screaming at the apparition, which he alone sees, of the murdered Banquo sitting in his chair.

> My lord is often thus,
> And hath been from his youth. Pray you, keep seat.
> The fit is momentary. Upon a thought
> He will again be well.
>
> (3.4.52–55)

Then, under her breath, she tries to make him get a grip on himself: "Are you a man?" (3.4.57).

The sexual taunt half-hidden in these words is the crucial note that Lady Macbeth strikes again and again. It is the principal means by which she gets her wavering husband to kill the king:

> When you durst do it, then you were a man;
> And to be more than what you were, you would
> Be so much more the man.
>
> (1.7.49–51)

If these taunts work on Macbeth, it is because husband and wife know and play upon each other's innermost fears and desires. They meet on the ground of a shared, willed, murderous ferocity:

> I have given suck, and know
> How tender 'tis to love the babe that milks me.
> I would, while it was smiling in my face,
> Have plucked my nipple from his boneless gums ·
> And dashed the brains out, had I so sworn
> As you have done to this.
>
> (1.7.54–59)

Macbeth is weirdly aroused by this fantasy:

> Bring forth men-children only,
> For thy undaunted mettle should compose
> Nothing but males.
>
> (1.7.72–74)

The exchange takes the audience deep inside this particular marriage. Whatever has led Lady Macbeth to imagine the bloody scene she describes and whatever Macbeth feels in response to her fantasy—terror, sexual excitement, envy, soul sickness, companionship in evil—lie at the heart of what it means to be the principal married couple conjured up by Shakespeare's imagination.

What is startling about this scene, and about the whole relationship between Macbeth and his wife, is the extent to which they inhabit each other's minds. When Lady Macbeth first appears, she is reading a letter from her husband that describes his encounter with the witches who have prophesied that he will be king: "'This have I thought good to deliver thee, my dearest partner of greatness, that thou mightst not lose the dues of rejoicing by being ignorant of what greatness is promised thee.'" He cannot wait until he gets home to tell her; he needs her to share the fantasy with him at once. And she, for her part, not only plunges into it immediately but also begins almost in the same breath to reflect with studied insight upon her husband's nature:

> It is too full o'th' milk of human kindness
> To catch the nearest way. Thou wouldst be great,
> Art not without ambition, but without
> The illness should attend it. What thou wouldst highly,
> That wouldst thou holily; wouldst not play false,
> And yet wouldst wrongly win. Thou'dst have, great Glamis,
> That which cries 'Thus thou must do' if thou have it,
> And that which rather thou dost fear to do
> Than wishest should be undone.
>
> (1.5.9–11, 15–23)

The richness of this account, the way it opens up from the first simple observation to something almost queasily complicated, is vivid evidence of the wife's ability to follow the twists and turns of her husband's innermost character, to take her spouse in. And her intimate understanding leads her to desire to enter into him: "Hie thee hither, / That I may pour my spirits in thine ear" (1.5.23–24).

Shakespeare's plays then combine, on the one hand, an overall diffidence in depicting marriages and, on the other hand, the image of a kind of nightmare in the two marriages they do depict with some care. It is difficult *not* to read his works in the context of his decision to live for most of a long marriage away from his wife. Perhaps, for whatever reason, Shakespeare feared to be taken in fully by his spouse or by anyone else; perhaps he could not let anyone so completely in; or perhaps he simply made a disastrous mistake, when he was eighteen, and had to live with the consequences as a husband and as a writer. Most couples, he may have told himself, are mismatched, even couples marrying for love; you should never marry in haste; a young man should not marry an older woman; a marriage under compulsion—"wedlock forcèd"—is a hell. And perhaps, beyond these, he told himself, in imagining *Hamlet* and *Macbeth*, *Othello* and *The Winter's Tale*, that marital intimacy is dangerous, that the very dream is a threat.

Shakespeare may have told himself too that his marriage to Anne was doomed from the beginning. Certainly he told his audience repeatedly that it was crucially important to preserve virginity until marriage. Though she calls the vows she has exchanged in the darkness with Romeo a "contract," Juliet makes it clear that this contract is not in her eyes the equivalent of a marriage (as some Elizabethans would have held) and that she must therefore on that night leave Romeo "unsatisfied" (2.1.159, 167). Once protected by the wedding performed by the friar—not a social ritual in *Romeo and Juliet* but a sacrament hidden from the feuding families—Juliet can throw off the retiring coyness expected of girls. The young lovers are splendidly frank, confident, and unembarrassed about their desires—they are able, as Juliet puts it, to "Think true love acted simple modesty" (3.2.16)—but their frankness depends upon their shared commitment to marrying before enacting these desires. That commitment confers upon their love, rash and secret though it is, a certain sublime innocence. It is as if the formal ceremony of marriage, performed as the condition of sexual consummation, had an almost magical efficacy, a power to make desire and fulfillment, which would otherwise be tainted and shameful, perfectly modest.

In *Measure for Measure*, written some eight years after *Romeo and Juliet*, Shakespeare came closer to depicting the situation in which he may have found himself as an adolescent. Claudio and Juliet have privately made solemn vows to one another—"a true contract," Claudio calls it—and have consummated their marriage without a public ceremony. His wife is now visibly pregnant—"The stealth of our most mutual entertainment / With character too gross is writ on Juliet" (1.2.122, 131–32). When the state embarks on a ruthless campaign against "fornication," Claudio is arrested and condemned to die. What is startling is that he seems ready to concede the point. Without the public ceremony, his "true contract" appears worthless, and in lines saturated with self-revulsion, he speaks of the fate that looms over him as the result of unrestrained sexual appetite:

> Our natures do pursue,
> Like rats that raven down their proper bane,

A thirsty evil; and when we drink, we die.
(1.2.108–10)

The natural desire that can be so frankly and comfortably acknowledged within the bounds of marriage becomes a poison outside of it.

The intensity of the dire visions of premarital sex and its consequences may have had much to do with the fact that Shakespeare was the father of two growing daughters. His most explicit warnings about the dangers of premarital sex take the form, in *The Tempest*, of a father's stern words to the young man who is courting his daughter. Yet in Prospero's lines from this play, written late in his career, there is a sense that Shakespeare was looking back at his own unhappy marriage and linking that unhappiness to the way in which it all began, so many years before. "Take my daughter," Prospero says to Ferdinand, and then adds something halfway between a curse and a prediction:

> If thou dost break her virgin-knot before
> All sanctimonious ceremonies may
> With full and holy rite be ministered,
> No sweet aspersion shall the heavens let fall
> To make this contract grow; but barren hate,
> Sour-eyed disdain, and discord, shall bestrew
> The union of your bed with weeds so loathly
> That you shall hate it both.
> (4.1.14–22)

These lines—so much more intense and vivid than the play calls for—seem to draw upon a deep pool of bitterness about a miserable marriage. Instead of a shower of grace ("sweet aspersion"), the union will inevitably be plagued, Prospero warns, if sexual consummation precedes the "sanctimonious ceremonies." That was precisely the circumstance of the marriage of Will and Anne.

Even if these bleak lines were a summary reflection on his own marriage, Shakespeare was not necessarily doomed to a life without love. He certainly knew bitterness, sourness, and cynicism, but he did not retreat into them, nor did he attempt to escape from them by renouncing desire. Desire is everywhere in his work. But his imagination of love and in all likelihood his experiences of love flourished outside of the marriage bond. The greatest lovers in Shakespeare are Antony and Cleopatra, the supreme emblems of adultery. And when he wrote love poems—among the most complex and intense in the English language, before or since— he constructed a sequence of sonnets not about his wife and not about courtship of anyone who could be his wife but about his tangled relationships with a fair young man and a sexually sophisticated dark lady.

Anne Hathaway was excluded completely from the sonnets' story of same-sex love and adultery—or at least almost completely. It is possible, as several critics have suggested, that sonnet 145—"Those lips that love's own hand did make"—alludes to her in its closing couplet. The speaker of the poem recalls that his love once spoke to him the terrible words "I hate," but then gave him a reprieve from the doom that the words seemed to announce:

> "I hate" from hate away she threw,
> And saved my life, saying "not you."

If "hate away" is a pun on Hathaway, as has been proposed, then this might be a very early poem by Shakespeare, perhaps the earliest that survives, conceivably written at the time of his courtship and then casually incorporated into the sequence. Such an origin might help to explain its anomalous meter—it is the only sonnet in the sequence written in eight-syllable, rather than ten-syllable, lines—and, still more, its ineptitude.

He could not get out of it. That is the overwhelming sense of the bond that rushed the marriage through. But he contrived, after three years' time, not to live with his wife. Two days' hard ride from Stratford, at a safe distance from Henley Street and later from New Place, he made his astonishing works and his fortune. In his rented rooms in London, he contrived to have a private life—that too, perhaps, is the meaning of Aubrey's report that he was not a "company keeper," that he refused invitations to be "debauched." Not the regular denizen of taverns, not the familiar companion of his cronies, he found intimacy and lust and love with people whose names he managed to keep to himself. "Women he won to him," says Stephen Daedalus, James Joyce's alter ego in *Ulysses*, in one of the greatest meditations on Shakespeare's marriage, "tender people, a whore of Babylon, ladies of justices, bully tapsters' wives. Fox and geese. And in New Place a slack dishonoured body that once was comely, once as sweet, as fresh as cinnamon, now her leaves falling, all, bare, frighted of the narrow grave and unforgiven."

Sometime around 1610, Shakespeare, a wealthy man with many investments, retired from London and returned to Stratford, to his neglected wife in New Place. Does this mean that he had finally achieved some loving intimacy with her? *The Winter's Tale*, written at about this time, ends with the moving reconciliation of a husband and wife who had seemed lost to one another forever. Perhaps this was indeed Shakespeare's fantasy for his own life, but if so the fantasy does not seem to correspond to what actually happened. When Shakespeare, evidently gravely ill, came to draw up his will, in January 1616, he took care to leave virtually everything, including New Place and all his "barns, stables, orchards, gardens, lands, tenements" and lands in and around Stratford, to his elder daughter, Susanna. Provisions were made for his other daughter, Judith; for his only surviving sibling, Joan; and for several other friends and relatives, and a modest donation was made to the town's poor, but the great bulk of the estate went to Susanna and her husband, Dr. John Hall, who were clearly the principal objects of the dying Shakespeare's love and trust. As he left the world, he did not want to think of his wealth going to his wife; he wanted to imagine it descending to his eldest daughter and thence to her eldest son, yet unborn, and thence to the son of that son and on and on through the generations. And he did not want to brook any interference or hindrance in this design: Susanna and her husband were named as the executors. They would enact the design—so overwhelmingly in their interest—that he had devised.

To his wife of thirty-four years, Anne, he left nothing, nothing at all. Some have argued in mitigation of this conspicuous omission that a widow would in any case have been entitled to a life interest in a one-third share of her deceased husband's estate. Others have countered that thoughtful husbands in this period often spelled out this entitlement in their wills, since it was not in fact always guaranteed. But as a document charged with the remembering of friends and family in the final disposition of the goods so carefully accumulated during a lifetime, Shakespeare's will—the last trace of his network of relationships—remains startling in its absolute silence in regard to his wife. The issue is not simply that there are none of the terms of endearment—"my beloved wife," "my loving Anne," or whatever—that conventionally signaled an enduring bond between husband and wife. The will contains no such term for any of those named as heirs, so perhaps Shakespeare or the lawyer who penned the words simply chose to write a relatively cool, impersonal document. The problem is that in the will Shakespeare initially drafted, Anne Shakespeare was not mentioned at all; it is as if she had been completely erased.

Someone—his daughter Susanna, perhaps, or his lawyer—may have called this erasure, this total absence of acknowledgment, to his attention. Or perhaps as he lay in his bed, his strength ebbing away, Shakespeare himself brooded on his relationship to Anne—on the sexual excitement that once drew him to her, on the failure of the marriage to give him what he wanted, on his own infidelities and perhaps on hers, on the intimacies he had forged elsewhere, on the son they had buried, on the strange, ineradicable distaste for her that he felt deep within him. For on March 25, in a series of additions to the will—mostly focused on keeping his daughter Judith's husband from getting his hands on the money Shakespeare was leaving her—he finally acknowledged his wife's existence. On the last of the three pages, interlined between the careful specification of the line of descent, so as to ensure that the property would go if at all possible to the eldest male heir of his daughter Susanna, and the bestowal of the "broad silver-gilt bowl" on Judith and all the rest of the "goods, chattel, leases, plate, jewels, and household stuff" on Susanna, there is a new provision: "Item I gyve vnto my wife my second best bed with the furniture."

Scholars and other writers have made a strenuous effort to give these words a positive spin: other wills in this period can be found in which the best bed is left to someone other than the wife; the bequest to Anne could have been their marriage bed (the best bed possibly being reserved for important guests); "the furniture"—that is, the bed furnishings, such as coverlets and curtains—might have been valuable; and even, as Joseph Quincy Adams hoped, "the second-best bed, though less expensive, was probably the more comfortable." In short, as one biographer in 1940 cheerfully persuaded himself, "It was a husband's tender remembrance."

If this is an instance of Shakespeare's tender remembrance, one shudders to think of what one of his insults would have looked like. But the notion of tenderness is surely absurd wishful thinking: this is a person who had spent a lifetime imagining exquisitely precise shadings of love and injury. It is for legal historians to debate whether by specifying a single object, the testator was in effect attempting to wipe out the widow's customary one-third life interest—that is, to disinherit her. But what the eloquently hostile gesture seems to say emotionally is that Shakespeare had found his trust, his happiness, his capacity for intimacy, his best bed elsewhere.

"Shine here to us," John Donne addressed the rising sun, "and thou art every where; / This bed thy center is, these walls, thy sphere." Donne may have been the great Renaissance exception to the rule: he seems to have written many of his most passionate love poems to his wife. In "The Funeral," he imagines being buried with some precious bodily token of the woman he has loved:

> Who ever comes to shroud me, do not harm
>   Nor question much
> That subtle wreath of hair, which crowns my arm.

And in "The Relic" he returns to this fantasy—"A bracelet of bright hair about the bone"—and imagines that whoever might open his grave to add another corpse will let the remains alone, thinking "that there a loving couple lies." For Donne, the dream is to make it possible for his soul and that of his beloved "at the last busy day" to "Meet at this grave, and make a little stay."

Shakespeare's greatest lovers—Romeo and Juliet, in the sweet frenzy of adolescent passion, and Antony and Cleopatra, in the sophisticated, lightly ironic intensity of middle-aged adultery—share something of the same fantasy. "Ah, dear Juliet," poor, deluded Romeo muses in the Capulet tomb,

> Why art thou yet so fair? Shall I believe
> That unsubstantial death is amorous,
> And that the lean abhorrèd monster keeps
> Thee here in dark to be his paramour?
> For fear of that I still will stay with thee,
> And never from this pallet of dim night
> Depart again.
> (5.3.101–8)

When Juliet awakes and finds Romeo dead, she in turn hastens to join him forever. So too, feeling "Immortal longings" in her, Cleopatra dresses to meet and to marry Antony in the afterlife— "Husband, I come" (5.2.272, 278)—and victorious Caesar understands what should be done:

> Take up her bed,
> And bear her women from the monument.
> She shall be buried by her Antony.
> No grave upon the earth shall clip in it
> A pair so famous.
> (5.2.346–50)

So much for the dream of love. When Shakespeare lay dying, he tried to forget his wife and then remembered her with the second-best bed. And when he thought of the afterlife, the last thing he wanted was to be mingled with the woman he married. There are four lines carved in his gravestone in the chancel of Stratford Church:

> GOOD FRIEND FOR JESUS SAKE FORBEARE,
> TO DIGG THE DUST ENCLOASED HEARE:
> BLESTE BE YE MAN YT SPARES THES STONES,
> AND CURST BE HE YT MOVES MY BONES.

In 1693 a visitor to the grave was told that the epitaph was "made by himself a little before his death." If so, these are probably the last lines that Shakespeare wrote. Perhaps he simply feared that his bones would be dug up and thrown in the nearby charnel house—he seems to have regarded that fate with horror—but he may have feared still more that one day his grave would be opened to let in the body of Anne Shakespeare.

CHAPTER 5

Crossing the Bridge

IN THE SUMMER of 1583 the nineteen-year-old William Shake-speare was settling into the life of a married man with a newborn daughter, living all together with his parents and his sister, Joan, and his brothers, Gilbert, Richard, and Edmund, and however many servants they could afford in the spacious house on Henley Street. He may have been working in the glover's shop, perhaps, or making a bit of money as a teacher's or lawyer's assistant. In his spare time he must have continued to write poetry, practice the lute, hone his skills as a fencer—that is, work on his ability to impersonate the lifestyle of a gentleman. His northern sojourn, assuming he had one, was behind him. If in Lancashire he had begun a career as a professional player, he must, for the moment at least, have put it aside. And if he had had a brush with the dark world of Catholic conspiracy, sainthood, and martyrdom—the world that took Campion to the scaffold—he must still more decisively have turned away from it with a shudder. He had embraced ordinariness, or ordinariness had embraced him.

Then sometime in the mid-1580s (the precise date is not known), he tore himself away from his family, left Stratford-upon-Avon, and made his way to London. How or why he took this momentous step is unclear, though until recently biographers were generally content with a story first recorded in the late seventeenth century by the clergyman Richard Davies. Davies wrote that Shakespeare was "much given to all unluckiness in stealing venison and rabbits, particularly from Sir ———— Lucy, who had him oft whipped and sometimes imprisoned and at last made him fly his native country to his great advancement." The early-eighteenth-century biographer and editor Nicholas Rowe printed a similar account of the "Extravagance" that forced Shakespeare "both out of his country and that way of living which he had taken up." Will had, in Rowe's account, fallen into bad company: he began to consort with youths who made a practice of deer poaching; in their company, he went more than once to rob Sir Thomas Lucy's park at Charlecote, about four miles from Stratford.

> For this he was prosecuted by that gentleman, as he thought, somewhat too severely; and in order to revenge that ill usage, he made a ballad upon him. And though this, probably the first essay of his poetry, be lost, yet it is said to have been so very bitter, that it redoubled the prosecution against him to that degree, that he was obliged to leave his business and family in Warwickshire, for some time, and shelter himself in London.

By the mid-eighteenth century this story had acquired a sequel related by Dr. Johnson: having fled his home "from the terror of a criminal prosecution," Will found himself alone in London, without money or friends. He picked up enough to live on by standing at the playhouse door and holding the horses of those that had no servants. "In this office he became so conspicuous for his care and readiness," Johnson writes, "that in a short time every man as he alighted called for *Will. Shakespear*, and scarcely any other waiter was trusted with a horse while *Will. Shakespear* could be had. This was the first dawn of better fortune." There is something appealing about Shakespeare as the patron saint of parking lot attendants, but few biographers of the last two centuries have taken this story seriously. The problem in part is that archival scholars began to recognize that Shakespeare's family, even in the period of his father's decline, remained part of a network of kin and friends; that his father never lost everything; and that therefore the vision of the uprooted young man holding horses at the playhouse door, in penury and isolation, is unlikely.

As for the deer-poaching story itself, though four independent versions were in circulation by the later seventeenth century, recent biographers have treated it too with comparable skepticism. For one thing, Sir Thomas Lucy did not have a deer park at Charlecote at the time in question; for another, whipping was not a legal punishment for poaching in this period. But these arguments are not decisive. While Lucy did not keep an enclosed park at the time that Shakespeare would have been caught poaching, he did maintain a warren, an enclosed area where rabbits and other game, possibly including deer, could breed. And he was evidently not indifferent to his property rights: he hired keepers to protect the game and watch for poachers, and he introduced a bill in Parliament in 1584 against poaching. As for whipping, it may not have been a legal punishment, but the justice of the peace may have been inclined to teach the young offender a lesson, particularly if he suspected that the poacher and his parents might be recusants. No doubt it would have been improper for Sir Thomas Lucy, as justice of the peace, to sit in judgment on a case in which he himself was the alleged victim, but it would be naive to imagine that local magnates always stayed within the letter of the law or carefully avoided conflicts of interest. After all, the story refers to Shakespeare's sense of ill-usage—that is, to his being treated worse than he felt he deserved to be treated for what he was caught doing.

The question, then, is not the degree of evidence but rather the imaginative life that the incident has, the access it gives to something important in Shakespeare's life and work. The particular act with which he was charged has by now ceased to have much meaning, and the story correspondingly has begun to drop away from biographies. But in Shakespeare's time and into the eighteenth century the idea of deer poaching had a special resonance; it was good to think with, a powerful tool for reconstructing the sequence of events that led the young man to leave Stratford.

For Elizabethans deer poaching was not understood principally as having to do with hunger; it was a story not about desperation but about risk. Oxford students were famous for this escapade. It was, for a start, a daring game: it took impressive skill and cool nerves to trespass on a powerful person's land, kill a large animal, and drag it away, without getting caught by those who patrolled the area. "What, hast not thou full often struck a doe," someone asks in one of Shakespeare's early plays, "And borne her cleanly by the keeper's nose?" (*Titus Andronicus*, 2.1.93-94). It was a skillful assault upon property, a symbolic violation of the social order, a coded challenge to authority. That challenge was supposed to be kept within bounds: the game involved cunning and an awareness of limits. After all, one was not supposed to beat up the keeper—then misdemeanor turns into felony—and one was not supposed to get caught. Deer poaching was about the pleasures of hunting and killing but also about the pleasures of stealth and trickery, about knowing how far to go, about contriving to get away with something.

Throughout Shakespeare's career as a playwright he was a brilliant poacher—deftly entering into territory marked out by others, taking for himself what he wanted, and walking away with his prize under the keeper's nose. He was particularly good at seizing and making his own the property of the elite, the music, the gestures, the language. This is only a metaphor, of course; it is not evidence that young Will engaged in actual poaching. What we know, and what those who originally circulated the legend knew, is that he had a complex attitude toward authority, at once sly, genially submissive, and subtly challenging. He was capable of devastating criticism; he saw through lies, hypocrisies, and distortions; he undermined virtually all of the claims that those in power made for themselves. And yet he was easygoing, humorous, pleasantly indirect, almost apologetic. If this relation to authority was not simply implanted in him, if it was more likely something he learned, then his formative learning experience may well have been a nasty encounter with one of the principal authorities in his district.

For in all the versions of the story something went wrong: Shakespeare was caught and then treated more harshly than he felt was appropriate (and indeed than the law allowed). He responded, it is said, with a bitter ballad. Versions of the ballad have predictably surfaced—none of them interesting as poetry or believable as Shakespeare's actual verses. "If lowsie is Lucy, as some volke miscalle it, / Then Lucy is lowsie whatever befall it," etc. More interesting is the idea that Shakespeare must have responded to harsh treatment with an insulting piece of writing, presumably an attack on Lucy's character or the honor of his wife.

Modern biographers are skeptical largely because they believe that Shakespeare was not that kind of person and that Lucy was both too powerful and too respectable to be slandered. "In public feared and respected, Sir Thomas in his domestic affairs appears to have been not unamiable," observes one of Shakespeare's most amiable and brilliant biographers, Samuel Schoenbaum. "He wrote testimonial letters for an honest gentlewoman and an ailing servant." But the late-seventeenth-century gossips who circulated the story may have had a better understanding of that world. They grasped that a man like Lucy could combine geniality and public-spiritedness—entertaining the queen at Charlecote, keeping a company of players, acting boldly and decisively in times of plague—with ruthless violence. They knew that it was dangerous to write anything against a person in authority—you could be charged with "scandalium magnatum," slandering an official—and at the same time that such writing was the prime weapon of the powerless. Above all, they believed that something serious must have driven Shakespeare out of Stratford, something more than his own poetic dreams and theatrical skill, something more than dissatisfaction with his marriage, and something more than the limited economic opportunities in the immediate area.

They doubted, in other words, that Shakespeare simply wandered off to London in search of new opportunities. Whether he was helping in his father's failing business, or working as a poor scrivener (a noverint, as it was sometimes called) in a lawyer's office, or teaching the rudiments of Latin grammar to schoolboys, they believed that without some shock Shakespeare would have continued in the rut that life had prepared for him. With the family's lands mortgaged, his education finished, no profession, a wife and three children to support, he had already begun to deepen that rut for himself. Rumormongers heard something that led them to believe that trouble with authority drove him out and that the authority in question was Sir Thomas Lucy. They thought too that something Shakespeare wrote was involved in the trouble.

Early biographers not only went in search of the missing satiric poem but also carefully scanned Shakespeare's printed works for traces of his early encounter with the angry justice of the peace. Centuries ago both Rowe and Davies pointed to the opening scene in *The Merry Wives of Windsor*, in which Shakespeare depicts pompous Justice Shallow complaining that Falstaff has killed his deer and threatening a Star Chamber suit. Shallow stands on his dignity; he is, as his nephew Slender says, "a gentleman born," one who "writes himself 'Armigero' in any bill, warrant, quittance, or obligation: 'Armigero.'" "Ay, that I do, and have done any time these three hundred years" (1.1.7–11). Laughter is directed at the self-importance that is crystallized in the lovingly reiterated Latinism "Armigero," one who bears a coat of arms. The mockery ripples across a whole class of gentry inordinately proud of their birth and eager to maintain a distinction between their inherited status and that of mere upstarts. (Some argued in this period that a family must have had a coat of arms for at least three generations before it could be securely identified as authentically armigerous.) But Rowe and Davies suggest that Shallow was intended specifically as a dig at Sir Thomas Lucy, Will's persecutor for the crime of deer poaching.

This suggestion is apparently borne out by the ensuing flurry of jokes on the heraldic symbol of the Lucy family, a freshwater fish called a luce. It is not only Shallow who writes himself "Armigero," adds Slender: "All his successors gone before him hath done't, and all his ancestors that come after him may. They may give the dozen white luces in their coat" (1.1.12–14). There follows an exchange that is by now almost entirely obscure—it is cut in most modern performances—and that even in Shakespeare's time would have been difficult to follow. It depends upon a series of puns unintentionally generated by Sir Hugh Evans, the Welsh parson who pronounces "luces" as "louses" and "coat" as "cod"—Elizabethan slang for "scrotum." As in the schoolroom scene from the same play, obscenities are scribbled in the margins of respect. The dialogue manages, with a perfect miming of innocence, to deface the Lucy coat of arms.

But if this is the case—if Shakespeare was taking symbolic revenge on the proud man who had humiliated him and persecuted him over some infraction or other—then it was a muted, delayed, and half-hidden revenge. *The Merry Wives of Windsor* was written in 1597–98, at least a decade after events that might have driven Shakespeare out of Stratford. Closer to those events, as if to placate his persecutor, the playwright had gone out of his way in one of his earliest plays, *1 Henry VI,* to present an admirable portrait of a Lucy ancestor, Sir William Lucy.

The "Armigero" satire was hardly violent or bitter—it was the quietly mocking laughter of someone whose wounds were no longer raw. And it was a laughter that did not insist on identifying its object outside the charmed circle of the play. Very few of the members of the audience could have picked up on the specific allusion to a Warwickshire notable: it was there—if it was there at all—principally for the playwright himself and a small group of his friends. And in laughing at a person who is proud of his coat of arms, the playwright was also quietly turning the laughter back upon himself. For *The Merry Wives of Windsor* was written immediately in the wake of Shakespeare's own successful attempt to write himself "Armigero" by renewing his father's application for gentlemanly status. Perhaps it was only the achievement of the coat of arms that enabled him to make fun of Lucy and at the same time to distance himself from his own social desire.

Shakespeare was a master of double consciousness. He was a man who spent his money on a coat of arms but who mocked the pretentiousness of such a claim; a man who invested in real estate but who ridiculed in *Hamlet* precisely such an entrepreneur as he himself was; a man who spent his life and his deepest energies on the theater but who laughed at the theater and regretted making himself a show. Though Shakespeare seems to have recycled every word he ever encountered, every person he ever met, every experience he ever had—it is difficult otherwise to explain the enormous richness of his work—he contrived at the same time to hide himself from view, to ward off vulnerability, to forswear intimacy. And in the case of his encounter with Thomas Lucy, he may, by the late 1590s, have buried inside light public laughter the traces of an intense fear that had once gripped him.

Even after he had moved to London and established himself as an actor and playwright, Shakespeare might not have been able to conceal entirely that as a young man he had fallen afoul of a Warwickshire magnate. But he had ample reason to recast and to sanitize whatever it was that had sent him packing. Hidden within the legend of Thomas Lucy's deer park may have been a more serious trouble, which the poaching episode, whether or not it actually occurred, at once represented and concealed. Long before he floated the hints in *The Merry Wives of Windsor*, Shakespeare may in his private conversation have told the story of a slightly comical misadventure to account for his departure from Stratford. The story might have served as a convenient cover, all the more convenient if it had at least some basis in fact: it acknowledged that Lucy played a role, but a role that could be parodied in no more disturbing a figure than Justice Shallow. It acknowledged too that Shakespeare was in trouble, but trouble of the kind, more winked at than prosecuted, for which Oxford students were famous. The far more serious threat that Lucy would have posed—his role not as defender of his game but as relentless persecutor of recusancy—was effaced, and Stratford took on the tranquil glow of a sleepy country town.

But in the 1580s ordinary life in Stratford, as elsewhere, had not been tranquil. The capture, trial, and execution of Campion and the other Jesuit missionaries had by no means settled the religious struggles in England. It was not only a matter of international plots and the ambitions of the great. Even if he was altogether untouched by fantasies of martyrdom, even if he had plunged into the everyday concerns of a family man in a provincial town, Shakespeare could not have lived his life as if there were no questions about belief. No one with any capacity for thought at this moment could have done so.

Many men and women in England—more radical Protestants as well as Catholics—were dissatisfied with the religious settlement and felt that they could not worship as they wished. Shakespeare unquestionably knew such people; members of his own family may have been among them. For the more pious, the experience must have been anguishing: they believed that their eternal salvation, and the salvation of their kin and fellow countrymen, depended upon their form of worship and upon the faith that this worship expressed. This is why, for example, a young Warwickshire gentleman, John Somerville of Edstone, began in the summer of 1583 to spend a great deal of time in intense conversation with a gardener on the estate of his father-in-law. The conversation was not about the flowers; the man dressed as a gardener was Hugh Hall, a Catholic priest, whom his father-in-law secretly harbored.

Will Shakespeare was at this point a virtual nobody, the knockabout son of a failing glover; John Somerville, educated at Oxford, was wealthy, wellborn, and well connected. But there could have been a distant family link between these two young men from Warwickshire: Somerville had married the daughter of Edward Arden of Park Hall, the head of the family probably distantly related to Mary Arden, Shakespeare's mother. And these possible cousins may both have had implanted in them from childhood the same longing to restore England to the old faith.

But if Will was moving away from this longing, John Somerville was being drawn more and more dangerously into its power. The priest Hugh Hall—according to the prosecutor's account, at the trial of Hall and Somerville—had talked to him about the plight of the Catholic Church in England; the hopes that lay in the beautiful, shamefully mistreated Mary, Queen of Scots; and the moral corruption of Henry VIII's bastard daughter, the excommunicated Queen Elizabeth. He rehearsed some of the scabrous gossip about the queen's favorite, Robert Dudley; reminded the young man that the pope had explicitly freed Englishmen from any obligation to obey her; and approvingly recounted a Spanish Catholic's recent attempt to assassinate the Protestant Prince of Orange.

At the same time, probably by coincidence, Somerville's sister gave him a translation of a book by the Spanish friar Luis de Granada, *Of Prayer and Meditation*. Printed in Paris in 1582, the book opened with a letter by the translator, Richard Harris, lamenting the rise of Schism, Heresy, Infidelity, and Atheism in England. These evils were dark signs that the world was nearing its end, Harris argued, and that Satan was frantically struggling to make a last demonic triumph. It behooved young noblemen and gentlemen in particular, he wrote, to "remember what great inclination ye have unto virtue more than others of obscure parentage, and base estate."

Somerville was deeply moved. The book seems to have pushed the young man toward a desperate determination: he would single-handedly rid the country of the viper on its throne. On October 24, 1583, attended by a single servant whom he soon dismissed, he slipped away from his wife and two small daughters and set out for London. He did not make it very far. At an inn about four miles distant, where he stopped for the night, he was overheard shouting to himself that he was going to shoot the queen with his pistol. He was immediately arrested, and a few days later found himself under interrogation in the Tower of London.

The authorities clearly understood that the young man was deranged, but, taking his wild threats seriously or simply using them as an excuse to settle old scores, they immediately moved to arrest his wife, his sister, his father-in-law and mother-in-law, the priest Hugh Hall, and others. Convicted of treason, Somerville and his father-in-law were condemned to be executed. The young man managed to hang himself in his cell the night before the sentence was to be carried out, but that did not prevent the authorities from cutting off his head to display as a warning. Edward Arden, who was probably not guilty of more than overt Catholic piety and the choice of a mad son-in-law, met the full, grisly fate of a traitor. Their severed heads, impaled on pikes, were set up on London Bridge.

In Stratford-upon-Avon Will would at the very least have heard endless talk of these events, and if the distant family link meant something to him—and the fact that he eventually attempted to "impale" the Shakespeare coat of arms with that of the Ardens implies that it did— then he would clearly have been interested in them. He may simply have felt relief that he had distanced himself from whatever Catholic intrigues he may have encountered, but there are several odd clues that suggest a more complex attitude.

Shakespeare had evidently read and absorbed the Catholic book that had fatally influenced Somerville. Behind Hamlet's melancholy brooding in the graveyard—"Dost thou think Alexander looked o' this fashion i'th' earth? . . . And smelt so? Pah!" (5.1.182–85)—probably lies Luis de Granada's meditation on the horror of the grave: "What thing is more esteemed than the body of a prince whiles he is alive? And what thing is more contemptible, and more vile, than the very same body when it is dead? Then do they make a hole in the earth of seven or eight foot long, (and no longer though it be for Alexander the Great, whom the whole world could not hold) and with that small room only must his body be content." This and many other echoes may only show that the two young Warwickshire men, so different in their character and fate, shared some of the same cultural points of reference.

A more intriguing link between Somerville and Shakespeare is not a shared book but a shared persecutor. The principal local agent in the sweep of the neighborhood after Somerville's arrest—the justice of the peace who busied himself with the arrests, the searches of suspected Catholic houses, the examination of servants, and the like—was Sir Thomas Lucy.

Lucy, born in 1532, had long wielded considerable influence in the area. Married at the age of fourteen to a wealthy heiress, he had built a great house at Charlecote, where Queen Elizabeth herself had visited in 1572 and presented his daughter (as noted in the careful list of gifts that the Crown compiled) with an enameled butterfly between two daisies. Lucy's account books show that he employed about forty servants, including a troupe of actors, referred to in the Coventry records as "Sir Thomas Lucy's Players."

Lucy had strong Protestant credentials. As a boy he had been tutored for a period by John Foxe, who subsequently wrote a Reformation classic. *Acts and Monuments*, better known as Foxe's *Book of Martyrs*, is a history of those who sacrificed their lives in the service of the true, Reformed religion. The book, which all English churches were required to purchase, includes near contemporaries who had been burned at the stake during the reign of Mary Tudor and also their precursors, famous proto-Reformers like Sir John Oldcastle, Lord Cobham, who had been executed in 1417.

In the months when Foxe lived as a tutor at Charlecote, his hugely influential history was not yet written and perhaps not even conceived, but the deep conviction behind it—the belief that England was God's chosen agent in the apocalyptic struggle against the Antichrist and his demonic agent, the Roman Catholic Church—was already strong within him and seems to have influenced his young charge. Thomas Lucy became an energetic agent of the most militant Protestant faction in the state. Knighted by the Earl of Leicester, he served in Parliament, where he distinguished himself for his work on a bill against priests disguising themselves as servingmen and, more generally, for his vehement support of the cause of the Reformation.

At the time of Somerville's arrest, Lucy was a principal figure in the commission empowered, in the wake of the Jesuit mission, to ferret out Catholic conspirators. He was a dangerous man, not treacherous or malicious perhaps, but tough, fiercely determined, and ruthless in the pursuit of what he regarded as God's own cause. He was specifically interested in the kin of Edward Arden—the government seemed to regard this as a family conspiracy—and he could have heard rumors that John Shakespeare's wife Mary was related to Edward Arden's wife Mary. John Shakespeare, from the time that he was bailiff of Stratford, would have known Lucy and understood what he was capable of. If the Shakespeares harbored Catholic sympathies, they would have had cause for alarm.

The local Catholic community was frightened and hastened to hide any incriminating papers or religious objects. "Unless you can make Somerville, Arden, Hall the Priest, Somerville's wife and his sister to speak directly to those things which you desire to have discovered," wrote the secretary of the Privy Council to his superiors in London, "it will not be possible for us here to find out more than is found already, for that the Papists in this county greatly do work upon the advantage of clearing their houses of all shows of suspicion." The remark provides a glimpse of something rarely reported in detail, though it must have been a frequent enough occurrence: Catholic families scurrying to burn or bury incriminating evidence—a rosary, a family crucifix, a picture of a favorite saint—while the government agents hammer at the doors, impatient to begin their search. On Henley Street in Stratford, the Shakespeare family may have been busy hiding their "shows of suspicion."

Their fear would not have ended with the deaths of Somerville and Arden. In 1585 Sir Thomas Lucy returned to Warwickshire from a year in Parliament with a new achievement to boast of: he had helped to promote a bill "against Jesuits, seminary priests, and other such-like disobedient persons." The bill met with unanimous approval, but on its third reading a solitary member of Parliament, William Parry, arose and denounced it as "a measure savoring of treasons, full of blood, danger, and despair to English subjects, and pregnant with fines and forfeitures which would go to enrich not the queen, but private individuals." He was immediately arrested and examined. When it came out that Parry was ambiguously implicated in a tangle of Catholic conspiracies against the queen, Lucy was at the forefront in petitioning for his execution as a traitor. Parry was hanged and disemboweled on March 2, 1585. All the ministers in the land were instructed to deliver sermons condemning attempts to assassinate God's chosen ruler, Queen Elizabeth, and celebrating her escape from the wicked traitor.

The triumphant Lucy must have been more militant and more vigilant than ever. And, after all, in the mid-1580s, with constant talk of conspiracies to kill the queen and put her imprisoned cousin, the Catholic Mary, Queen of Scots, on the throne, it made sense to be vigilant. Members of the Privy Council and hundreds of Protestants throughout the country took an oath to kill any Catholic pretender to the throne, in the event that Elizabeth was assassinated. There were dark rumors that Spain's Philip II was assembling a fleet large enough to carry an army across the English Channel in an invasion that would be abetted by treasonous English Catholics. It was in this time of extreme tension that Shakespeare may have run afoul of Lucy and decided that he had to get out.

Judging from the birth of his twins in February 1585, it seems likely that Shakespeare remained in Stratford at least until the summer of 1586, but at some point shortly after he turned his back on his wife and children and made his way to London. A piece of personal good fortune may have come his way, making the escape possible. Perhaps he had encountered Lord Strange's Men during his sojourn in the north and had renewed contact with them, perhaps he learned of another troupe of touring players that happened to be in need of an extra actor. The Earl of Leicester's Men were at nearby Coventry and Leicester in 1584–85 and in Stratford-upon-Avon in 1586–87, as were the Earl of Essex's Men. The Lord Admiral's Men were at Coventry and Leicester in 1585–86 and again in Leicester in 1586–87, and the Earl of Sussex's Men followed a similar itinerary.

The most intriguing possibility that scholars have explored in recent years concerns the Queen's Men, at the time the leading touring company in the country. The Queen's Men were in Stratford in 1587, and they were shorthanded. For in the nearby town of Thame, on June 13 between 9 and 10 P.M., one of their leading actors, William Knell, had been killed in a drunken fight with a fellow actor, John Towne. The inexperienced Shakespeare was not likely to have stood in for the celebrated Knell, but in the sudden shifting of the parts, the Queen's Men may have had a place for a novice. And if this were the company in which Shakespeare got his start, he would have had particular reason to be cautious about disclosing any residual Catholic loyalties or any trouble, aside from deer poaching, with Thomas Lucy. For the Queen's Men, scholars have argued, had been established in 1583 to spread Protestant propaganda and royalist enthusiasm through the troubled kingdom.

If any of these companies offered to take him on as a hired man, however modest the salary, Shakespeare would have had the happy occasion to leave Stratford. Of course, to his wife and three very small children, the departure might not have seemed such a piece of good fortune: even if he promised to send them money and to return home as soon or as often as possible, his leaving would inevitably have seemed an abandonment. The meaning of that abandonment—its justification, if there was any—could not at this moment have been at all clear. From an ethical point of view, if he cared to reflect about what he was doing, he might have been hoping for what a modern philosopher, thinking about Paul Gauguin's abandonment of his family in order to pursue his art, has termed "moral luck." That is, if Shakespeare felt he had something important within him that he could only realize by turning away from his domestic obligations, he could only hope to justify his actions if he actually succeeded. He stood in need of moral as well as financial luck.

Assuming that Shakespeare attached himself as a hired man to a playing company, it is not likely that this company headed immediately for London. If in June 1587 he was taken on by the Queen's Men, for example, the company would have continued to tour the towns and hospitable noblemen's houses of the Midlands. By August of that summer, the company, or part of it—for the Queen's Men often divided into touring branches—had gone to the southeast, perhaps providing the young man his first glimpse of the chalk cliffs at Dover (which later figure so powerfully in *King Lear*). The company then worked its way through towns like Hythe and Canterbury toward the capital. Such a route would have given Shakespeare the chance in a comfortingly familiar provincial setting to hone his skills: to learn some of the dance steps, figure out how to change his costume quickly, convincingly swell out a crowd scene or a battle, and begin to grasp the repertoire. He had to be a quick study—no one who did not possess an exceptional memory and a remarkable gift for improvisation could have survived in the competitive world of the Elizabethan theater. His work suggests that he had an almost unique gift for plunging into unfamiliar worlds, mastering their complexities, and making himself almost immediately at home. Still, the most seasoned actor, let alone a neophyte, must have felt a rush of nervous energy on approaching London.

LONDON WAS A CITY of newcomers, flooded every year with fresh arrivals from the country, mostly men and women in their late teens and early twenties, drawn by the promise of work, the spectacle of wealth and power, the dream of some extraordinary destiny. For many their destiny was an early death: rat-infested, overcrowded, polluted, prone to fire and on occasion to riot, London was a startlingly unsafe and unhealthy place. To the ordinary degree of hazard—appallingly high by our own standards—was conjoined the ravages of epidemic diseases. The worst of these, bubonic plague, swept through the city again and again, spreading panic, wiping out whole families, decimating neighborhoods. Even in years spared by the plague, the number of deaths recorded in London's parish records always exceeded the live births. And yet the city kept growing, a seemingly irresistible lure.

The bulk of the burgeoning populace lived and worked within the small area bounded to the south by the Thames and on the other sides by a high crenellated stone wall originally built by the Romans some fourteen hundred years earlier. The wall was pierced by a series of gates some of whose names—Ludgate, Aldgate, Cripplegate, Moorgate—still resonate for Londoners today, long after the structures themselves have vanished. Even in Shakespeare's time, when the wall was more or less intact, it was becoming less visible: the old, wide moat, still deep enough earlier in the century to drown unwary horses and men, was being filled up, and the new land was leased out for carpenters' yards, garden plots, and tenements "whereby," as one contemporary observer noted, "the city wall is hidden."

The eastern edge of the walled city was marked by the massive, grim Tower of London, begun by William the Conqueror; the west, by old St. Paul's Cathedral, which boasted the longest nave in Europe. Further to the west, along the north bank of the Thames, was a succession of mansions, formerly the London residences of the princes of the church and now, in the wake of the Reformation, the seats of powerful aristocrats and royal favorites. The glittering upstart Sir Walter Ralegh, for example, entertained his guests where the bishops of Durham had once held court, and the Earl of Southampton lived in the grand house of the bishops of Bath and Wells. Each of these residences had its own riverside mooring from which the wealthy owners with their liveried attendants could be rowed further upriver to the royal palace at Whitehall for an audience with the queen or to a session of Parliament close by. If they were less fortunate, they could also be rowed downriver to the Tower of London, where they would enter, heartsick and trembling, by Traitor's Gate.

With its crush of small factories, dockyards, and warehouses; its huge food markets, breweries, print shops, hospitals, orphanages, law schools, and guildhalls; its cloth makers, glassmakers, basket makers, brick makers, shipwrights, carpenters, tinsmiths, armorers, haberdashers, furriers, dyers, goldsmiths, fishmongers, booksellers, chandlers, drapers, grocers, and their crowds of unruly apprentices; not to mention its government officials, courtiers, lawyers, merchants, ministers, teachers, soldiers, sailors, porters, carters, watermen, innkeepers, cooks, servants, peddlers, minstrels, acrobats, cardsharps, pimps, whores, and beggars, London overflowed all boundaries. It was a city in ceaseless motion, transforming itself at an unprecedented rate. In his old age, the great London-born antiquary, John Stow, wrote at the end of the sixteenth century a remarkable survey of his city, carefully noting the thousands of changes he had witnessed in his own lifetime. A single example: when he was a boy, Stow recalled, there was an abbey of nuns of the order of St. Clare, known as the Minories, where he went to fetch "many a halfpenny of milk . . . always hot from the kine" from the abbey farm. The abbey was demolished—a casualty of the Reformation—and in its place, Stow wrote, there were now "fair and large storehouses for armour and habiliments of war." As for the farm, its new owner first used it for the grazing of horses and then subdivided it into garden plots that produced enough revenue so that the farmer's son and heir now lived "like a gentleman."

The oligarchy of aldermen, with the sheriffs and mayor, struggled to keep some control of the city through an elaborate system of regulations, but enforcement was complicated by the sheer pressure of numbers and by the existence of numerous precincts, known as liberties, that were exempt from their jurisdiction. Decades earlier, these precincts—the Black Friars, the Austin Friars, the priory of Holy Trinity, Aldgate, or the Minories where Stow went for his halfpenny of milk—had been large monasteries, with outbuildings, spacious gardens, and farms, and as such had enjoyed ecclesiastical exemptions from city codes. After the Reformation, the monks and nuns were all gone, and the buildings and land had passed into private hands. But the exemptions remained, enabling the owners to flout any attempt by the city fathers to stop activities—such as performing plays—that they regarded as nuisances or scandals.

Moreover, ringing the city were sprawling suburbs that were virtually without regulation of any kind. Within living memory, these precincts were still quite open and uncrowded. Stow recalled that near Bishopsgate, when he was a young man, there were "pleasant fields, very commodious for citizens therein to walk, shoot, and otherwise to recreate and refresh their dull spirits in the sweet and wholesome air." Now, he complained, this area, like others, had been turned into "a continual building throughout" of filthy cottages, small tenements, kitchen gardens, workshops, refuse heaps, and the like, "from Houndsditch in the west as far as Whitechapel and further towards the east." Not only had the once-beautiful approaches to the city been sullied, but the traffic had become horrendous: "The coachman rides behind the horse tails, lasheth them, and looketh not behind him; the drayman sitteth and sleepeth on his dray, and letteth his horse lead him home." And what made it worse, Stow wrote, was that young people seemed to have forgotten how to walk: "The world runs on wheels with many whose parents were glad to go on foot."

There were other bustling cities in England, and, if he had traveled, the young Shakespeare could conceivably have seen one or two or them, but none was like London. With a population nearing two hundred thousand, it was some fifteen times larger than the next most populous cities in England and Wales; in all of Europe only Naples and Paris exceeded it in size. Its commercial vitality was intense: London, as one contemporary put it, was "the Fair that lasts all year." This meant that it was fast escaping the seasonal rhythms by which the rest of the country lived; and it was escaping too the deep sense of the local that governed identity elsewhere. It was one of the only places in England where you were not surrounded by people who knew you, your family, and many of the most intimate details of your life, one of the only places in which your clothes and food and furniture were not produced by people you knew personally. It was in consequence the preeminent site not only of relative anonymity but also of fantasy: a place where you could dream of escaping your origins and turning into someone else.

That Shakespeare had this dream is virtually certain: it lies at the heart of what it means to be an actor, it is essential to the craft of the playwright, and it fuels the willingness of audiences to part with their pennies in order to see a play. He may also have had more private motives, a desire to escape whatever had led him into difficulties with Thomas Lucy, a desire to escape his wife and his three children, a desire to escape the glove and illegal wool trade of his improvident father. In his plays, he repeatedly staged scenes of characters separated from their familial bonds, stripped of their identities, stumbling into unfamiliar territory: Rosalind and Celia in the Forest of Arden; Viola on the seacoast of Illyria; Lear, Gloucester, and Edgar on the heath; Pericles in Tarsus; the infant Perdita in Sicily; Innogen (or Imogen) in the mountains of Wales; and all the humans on the spirit-haunted island in *The Tempest*.

Few of these scenes, however, depend upon the idea of the city. London may have been the principal staging ground for fantasies of metamorphosis, and it was certainly the site where Shakespeare remade himself, but it did not in an immediately obvious way shape his own theatrical imagination. In *The Alchemist* and *Bartholomew Fair*, his colleague Ben Jonson showed himself passionately interested in the city in which he grew up, the stepson of a master bricklayer living in Hartshorn Lane, near Charing Cross. Other contemporary London-born playwrights, such as Thomas Dekker and Thomas Middleton, similarly interested themselves in the lives of ordinary citizens: shoemakers, whores, shopkeepers, and watermen. But what principally excited Shakespeare's imagination about London were its more sinister or disturbing aspects.

In his very early history play *2 Henry VI*, Shakespeare depicted a band of lower-class Kentish rebels, led by the clothworker Jack Cade, descending on London to overthrow the social order. Cade promises a kind of primitive economic reform: "There shall be in England seven halfpenny loaves sold for a penny, the three-hooped pot shall have ten hoops, and I will make it felony to drink small beer" (4.2.58–60). The rebels—"a ragged multitude / Of hinds and peasants, rude and merciless" (4.4.31–32)—want to burn the records of the realm, abolish literacy, break into prisons and free the prisoners, make the fountains run with wine, execute the gentry. "The first thing we do," famously says one of Cade's followers, "let's kill all the lawyers" (4.2.68).

In a sequence of wild scenes, poised between grotesque comedy and nightmare, the young Shakespeare imagined—and invited his audience to imagine—what it would be like to have London controlled by a half-mad, belligerently illiterate rabble from the country. Something about the fantasy seems to have released a current of personal energy in the neophyte playwright, himself only recently arrived in the capital. While the upper-class characters in this early history play are for the most part stiff and unconvincing—the king in particular is almost completely a cipher—the lower-class rebels are startlingly vital. It is as if Shakespeare had grasped something crucial for the writing of plays: he could split apart elements of himself and his background, mold each of them into vivid form, and then at once laugh, shudder, and destroy them.

He emphasized the destruction, as if to insist that these illiterate, rebellious yokels, these loudmouthed butchers and weavers, had absolutely nothing to do with the playwright himself. "Die, damnèd wretch, the curse of her that bore thee!" exclaims the prosperous country squire who eventually kills Cade (5.1.74), and then, as if killing were not enough, thrusts his sword into the dead man's body. What is being destroyed with such gleeful vehemence is not only an enemy of property but an enemy of the kind of person that Shakespeare understood himself to be. It is possible to detect a disguised self-portrait in Cade's first victim. "Dost thou use to write thy name?" Cade asks an unfortunate clerk seized by the mob. "Or hast thou a mark to thyself like an honest plain-dealing man?"

> CLERK: Sir, I thank God I have been so well brought up that I can write my name.
> ALL CADE'S FOLLOWERS: He hath confessed—away with him! He's a villain and a traitor.
> CADE: Away with him, I say, hang him with his pen and inkhorn about his neck.
>
> (4.2.89–97)

These are lines written by a playwright whose parents signed with a mark and who was probably the first in his family to learn to write his name.

At the same time it is possible to detect Shakespeare on the other side as well, in the rebels swarming toward London with their fantasies of wealth and their intimate knowledge of humble trades.

> SECOND REBEL: I see them! I see them! There's Best's son, the tanner of Wingham—
> FIRST REBEL: He shall have the skins of our enemies to make dog's leather of.
>
> (4.2.18–21)

Tanning was Shakespeare's father's trade—and, in all likelihood, his own too: "dog's leather" was what they called inferior leather used in glove making. He was oddly close, then, to these grotesques, startlingly close even to their leader, Jack Cade, with his claim to be "of an honourable house" (4.2.43), his inveterate pretending, his dream of high station.

Shakespeare was dramatizing something from the chronicles—he characteristically mined these books, particularly Edward Hall's *The Union of the Two Noble and Illustre Families of Lancaster and York* and Raphael Holinshed's *The Chronicles of England, Scotland, and Ireland*, for the materials of his history plays. And he pushed Cade, the fifteenth-century rebel, still further back into the past by adding details drawn from the Peasants' Revolt of 1381. But just as Ephesus in *The Comedy of Errors* is far more a portrait of Shakespeare's contemporary London than of ancient Asia Minor, so too the medieval England in *2 Henry VI* is suffused less with the otherness of the past than with the familiar coordinates of Shakespeare's own present.

And it is the London crowd—the unprecedented concentration of bodies jostling through the narrow streets, crossing and recrossing the great bridge, pressing into taverns and churches and theaters—that is the key to the whole spectacle. The sight of all those people—along with their noise, the smell of their breath, their rowdiness and potential for violence—seems to have been Shakespeare's first and most enduring impression of the great city. In *Julius Caesar*, he returned to the spectacle of the bloodthirsty mob, roaming the streets in search of the conspirators who have killed their hero Caesar:

THIRD PLEBEIAN: Your name, sir, truly.
CINNA: Truly, my name is Cinna.
FIRST PLEBEIAN: Tear him to pieces! He's a conspirator.
CINNA: I am Cinna the poet, I am Cinna the poet.
FOURTH PLEBEIAN: Tear him for his bad verses, tear him for his
    bad verses.
CINNA: I am not Cinna the conspirator.
FOURTH PLEBEIAN: It is no matter, his name's Cinna. Pluck but his
    name out of his heart, and turn him going.
THIRD PLEBEIAN: Tear him, tear him!

                                                    (3.3.25–34)

This urban mob, rioting for bread and threatening to overturn the social order, figures as well in *Coriolanus*. And it is this same mob—"Mechanic slaves / With greasy aprons, rules, and hammers"—that Cleopatra imagines watching her being led captive through the streets of the great city. The very thought of smelling their "thick breaths," as they cheer the triumph of Rome, is enough to confirm her in her determination to commit suicide (*Antony and Cleopatra*, 5.205–7).

Even when his scene is Rome, Ephesus, Vienna, or Venice, Shakespeare's fixed point of urban reference was London. Ancient Romans may have worn togas and gone hatless, but when the rioting plebeians in *Coriolanus* get what they want, they throw their caps in the air, just as Elizabethan Londoners did. Only in his very early history play, however, did Shakespeare place this London crowd firmly in the city in which he lived and worked, without disguise. "Here sitting upon London Stone," says the megalomaniac Cade, referring to a famous landmark on Cannon Street, "I charge and command that, of the city's cost, the Pissing Conduit run nothing but claret wine this first year of our reign" (4.6.1–4). "So, sirs, now go some and pull down the Savoy," he tells his followers; "others to th' Inns of Court—down with them all" (4.7.1–2). As in a poor man's utopian dream, the law courts will be destroyed and the fountains will run with wine. Small wonder that the middle-class citizens flee in panic and the urban lower classes—"The rascal people" (4.4.50)—rise up in support of the rebels.

When the insurgents get their hands on one of their most hated enemies, Lord Saye, Cade lays out the charges against him:

> Thou hast most traitorously corrupted the youth of the realm in erecting a grammar school; and, whereas before, our forefathers had no other books but the score and the tally, thou hast caused printing to be used and, contrary to the King his crown and dignity, thou hast built a paper-mill. It will be proved to thy face that thou hast men about thee that usually talk of a noun and a verb and such abominable words as no Christian ear can endure to hear. (4.7.27–34)

The paper mill and the printing press are anachronisms—neither existed in England at the time of Cade's rebellion—but that does not matter: Shakespeare was interested in the sources of his own consciousness, the grammar school that took him away from the world of the score and tally (the stick on which people reckoned their small debts) and into the world of the printed book.

Shakespeare was fascinated by the crazed ranting of those who hate modernity, despise learning, and celebrate the virtue of ignorance. And it is characteristic of him even here—when he was imagining those who would have attacked his own identity—that he heard not only the grotesque stupidity but also the grievance:

> Thou hast appointed justices of peace to call poor men before them about matters they were not able to answer. Moreover, thou hast put them in prison, and, because they could not read, thou hast hanged them when indeed only for that cause they have been most worthy to live. (4.7.34–39)

It is mad to think that felons should be spared because they are illiterate, but Cade is lodging a protest against an actual feature of English law at the time that seems equally mad: if an accused felon could demonstrate that he was literate—usually by reading a verse from the Psalms—he could claim "benefit of clergy"; that is, he could, for legal purposes, be classified by virtue of literacy as a clergyman and therefore officially be subject to the jurisdiction of the ecclesiastical courts, which did not have the death penalty. The result in most cases was that the literate thief or murderer went scot-free, though only once: the perpetrator who successfully claimed benefit of clergy was branded with a T for thief or an M for Murderer, and a second offense was fatal. Hence Cade's otherwise incomprehensible charge makes perfect sense: "thou hast put them in prison, and, because they could not read, thou hast hanged them." And hence some of the otherwise incomprehensible rage against nouns and verbs and grammar schools: Cade commands that Lord Saye, along with his son-in-law, Sir James Cromer, be beheaded. "Let them kiss one another," he orders, when their heads are returned to him on poles, "for they loved well when they were alive." Pleased with the spectacle, he proposes parading through London: "with these borne before us instead of maces will we ride through the streets, and at every corner have them kiss." The grisly sight is meant to excite further bloodshed. "Up Fish Street!" he shouts. "Down Saint Magnus' Corner! Kill and knock down! Throw them into Thames!" (4.7.138–39, 142–44, 145–46).

Saint Magnus' Corner was at the northern end of London Bridge, the place where Shakespeare himself may have first set foot in the city. He would, in all likelihood, have been traveling with the troupe of actors he had joined. Perhaps, as they approached the capital, they joked about the rebellious butchers and weavers who long ago had marched on London. The playing company, in any case, would have wanted to attract attention to themselves, to let the populace know that they were back in the city and that they were performing at a particular place and time. In their gaudiest clothes, beating drums and waving flags, they would have timed their arrival and sought the busiest route; if they were approaching from the south, they would have marched up Southwark High Street and across London Bridge.

This, then, might well have been Shakespeare's initial glimpse of London: an architectural marvel, some eight hundred feet in length, that a French visitor, Etienne Perlin, called "the most beautiful bridge in the world." The congested roadway, supported on twenty piers of stone sixty feet high and thirty broad, was lined with tall houses and shops extending out over the water on struts. Many of the shops sold luxury goods—fine silks, hosiery, velvet caps—and some of the buildings themselves commanded attention: you could buy groceries in a two-story thirteenth-century stone building that had formerly been a chantry dedicated to St. Thomas à Becket where Masses were once sung for the souls of the dead. From the breaks between the buildings there were splendid views up and down the great river, especially to the west; overhead there were scavenging birds, wheeling in the air; and in the river hundreds of swans, plucked once a year for the queen's bedding and upholstery.

But one sight in particular would certainly have arrested Shakespeare's attention; it was a major tourist attraction, always pointed out to new arrivals. Stuck on poles on the Great Stone Gate, two arches from the Southwark side, were severed heads, some completely reduced to skulls, others parboiled and tanned, still identifiable. These were not the remains of common thieves, rapists, and murderers. Ordinary criminals were strung up by the hundreds on gibbets located around the margins of the city. The heads on the bridge, visitors were duly informed, were those of gentlemen and nobles who suffered the fate of traitors. A foreign visitor to London in 1592 counted thirty-four of them; another in 1598 said he counted more than thirty. When he first walked across the bridge, or very soon after, Shakespeare must have realized that among the heads were those of John Somerville and the man who bore his own mother's name and may have been his distant kinsman, Edward Arden.

A father and his son-in-law, their severed heads grinning on poles across from one another. "Let them kiss one another, for they loved well when they were alive." The severed heads he saw on the bridge must have made an impact upon his imagination, and not only as demonstrated in the Cade scenes of *2 Henry VI*. If he had spent some dangerous months in Lancashire, Shakespeare would already have imbibed powerful lessons about danger and the need for discretion, concealment, and fiction. These lessons would have been reinforced in Stratford, as tensions rose and rumors of conspiracy, assassination, and invasion spread. But the sight on the bridge was the most compelling instruction yet: keep control of yourself; do not fall into the hands of your enemies; be smart, tough, and realistic; master strategies of concealment and evasion; keep your head on your shoulders.

Hard lessons for a poet and an actor aspiring to be heard and seen by the world. But some such lessons may have caused Shakespeare to reach a decision that has since made it difficult to understand who he was. Where are his personal letters? Why have scholars, ferreting for centuries, failed to find the books he must have owned—or rather, why did he choose not to write his name in those books, the way that Jonson or Donne or many of his contemporaries did? Why, in the huge, glorious body of his writing, is there no direct access to his thoughts about politics or religion or art? Why is everything he wrote—even in the sonnets—couched in a way that enables him to hide his face and his innermost thoughts? Scholars have long thought that the answer must lie in indifference and accident: no contemporary thought that this playwright's personal views were sufficiently important to record, no one bothered to save his casual letters, and the boxes of papers that may have been left to his daughter Susanna were eventually sold off and used to wrap fish or stiffen the spines of new books or were simply burned. Possibly. But the heads on the pikes may have spoken to him on the day he entered London—and he may well have heeded their warning.

CHAPTER 6

Life in the Suburbs

H E HAD GROWN UP in a world where the fields began just at the end of the street, or at most within a few minutes' walk. Now all around him, extending for miles beyond London's crumbling city walls, were tenements, warehouses, small vegetable gardens, workshops, gun foundries, brick kilns, and windmills, along with stinking ditches and refuse heaps. Shakespeare made his acquaintance for the first time with the suburbs. He discovered what it was to pine for open country.

Londoners too liked to walk out into the fields to take some fresh air—the familiar joy of the countryside was intensified by a widespread belief that the plague was airborne, carried by foul smells. City dwellers passed through the crowded, reeking streets sniffing nosegays or stuffing their nostrils with cloves. In their rooms they burned scented candles and fuming pots to keep the city's pestilential stench at bay. The sweet country air was regarded as literally lifesaving—hence the rush out of the city, during times of plague, by those who could afford to leave and hence too the ordinary craving for a stroll in the fields.

Setting out from the center of the city, an energetic walker could still fairly quickly reach hedged pastures where cows peacefully grazed or ground where laundresses pegged their washing and dyers stretched cloth tautly on what were known as tenter frames or tenterhooks (from whence our phrase "to be on tenterhooks"). And though in Shakespeare's time the open spaces to which Londoners had once had easy access had already begun to disappear, other attractions drew people through the gates or across the river to the suburbs. Many taverns and inns, some of them quite venerable—the famous Tabard Inn, where Chaucer's pilgrims started their journey to Canterbury, was located in Southwark, on the south bank of the Thames—offered food and drink and private rooms in a world that had almost no privacy. In Finsbury Field, to the north of the city, archers could stroll about shooting at painted stakes and trying to avoid passersby. (In 1557 a pregnant woman out for a walk with her husband was struck in the neck by a stray arrow and killed.) Other places of amusement included firing ranges (for practicing pistol shooting), cock-fighting pits, wrestling rings, bowling alleys, places for music and dancing, platforms upon which criminals were mutilated or hanged, and an impressive array of "houses of resort," that is, whorehouses. Moralists denounced the latter with particular fierceness, of course, and demanded that they be closed, but the moves against them by city authorities always fell short. In *Measure for Measure*, a play set in a Vienna that looks and sounds like London, the ruler, embarking on a campaign of moral reform, gives an order to pull down the "houses of resort in the suburbs" (1.2.82–83). The order is not carried out.

The congested city, then, was effectively surrounded by an all-purpose entertainment zone, the place where Shakespeare spent much of his professional life. His imagination took it all in, even things that at this distance seem quite negligible. He was forcefully struck, for example, by the game of bowls, particularly by the way the ball with the off-center weight swerved, so that you hit your target only by seeming to aim elsewhere. The image came to him repeatedly as a way of figuring the surprising twists of his cunningly devised plots. So too with archery, wrestling, tilting at posts called quintains, and the whole range of Elizabethan sports and contests: when he did not actually depict them (like in the wrestling scene in *As You Like It*), he used them again and again as images.

Shakespeare's imagination was excited as well by the less innocuous amusements of the suburbs. Henry VIII bequeathed to his royal children a love of seeing bulls and bears "baited," that is, penned up in a ring or chained to a stake and set upon by fierce dogs. The bulls—on occasion "wearied to death" for sport—seem to have been more or less anonymous, but the bears acquired names and personalities: Sackerson, Ned Whiting, George Stone, and Harry Hunks (the latter blinded to increase the fun). The game was something of an English specialty—in their travel journals foreign tourists frequently noted that they took in the sight, and Queen Elizabeth treated visiting ambassadors to it. The cost of keeping the animals was defrayed by making it an entertainment available to the public: large crowds paid admission to the great circular wooden arenas to see the spectacle. In a popular variation, an ape was tied to the back of a pony, which was then attacked by the dogs: "To see the animal kicking amongst the dogs, with the screams of the ape," wrote one observer, "beholding the curs hanging from the ears and neck of the pony, is very laughable."

"Be there bears i'th' town?" asks the asinine Slender, in *The Merry Wives of Windsor*; "I love the sport well" (1.1.241, 243). Shakespeare clearly visited the bear garden in person—he had professional reasons to be interested in what crowds were excited by—but evidently he was less wholeheartedly enamored. The sport, he saw wryly, served to make the Slenders of the world feel more like real men. "I have seen Sackerson loose twenty times, and have taken him by the chain," Slender boasts. "But I warrant you, the women have so cried and shrieked at it that it passed. But women, indeed, cannot abide 'em. They are very ill-favoured, rough things" (1.1.247–51).

Elizabethans perceived bears as supremely ugly, embodiments of everything coarse and violent, and Shakespeare repeatedly echoed this view, but he also grasped something else: "They have tied me to a stake. I cannot fly," says Macbeth, his enemies closing in around him, "But bear-like I must fight the course" (5.7.1–2). This was hardly a sentimental account of either bearbaiting or murder—Macbeth is a traitor who deserves what he gets in the end—but it suspended the coarse laughter of the arena and got at something almost unendurable about the spectacle.

Why did Elizabethan and Jacobean people, including, notably, the Tudor and Stuart monarchs who were its special patrons, enjoy something so brutal and nasty? (Though there was an attempt to revive the "royal sport" at the end of the seventeenth century, it never really recovered from the blow it suffered when seven bears were shot to death in 1655 by Puritan soldiers.) The answer is as difficult to determine as it is to explain why we love our own cruel spectacles. But one key is found in a remark by Shakespeare's contemporary Thomas Dekker: "At length a blind bear was tied to the stake, and instead of baiting him with dogs, a company of creatures that had the shapes of men and faces of Christians (being either colliers, carters, or watermen) took the office of beadles upon them, and whipped Monsieur Hunks till the blood ran down his old shoulders." What the crowds saw in this instance, at least, was a grotesque—and therefore amusing—version of the disciplinary whippings that were routinely inflicted throughout society: parents frequently whipped children, teachers whipped students, masters whipped servants, beadles whipped whores, sheriffs whipped vagrants and "sturdy beggars." The spectacle in the arena had an odd double effect that Shakespeare would immeasurably intensify. It confirmed the order of things—this is what we do—and at the same time it called that order into question—what we do is grotesque.

London was a nonstop theater of punishments. Shakespeare had certainly witnessed corporal discipline before he came to London—Stratford had whipping posts, pillories, and stocks—but the frequency and ferocity of sentences meted out on public scaffolds at Tower Hill, Tyburn, and Smithfield; at Bridewell and the Marshalsea prisons; and at many other sites both within and outside the city walls would have been new. Almost daily he could have watched the state brand, cut, and kill those it deemed offenders. London's many established punishment grounds did not exhaust the locations of these spectacles: in some cases of murder the offender's right hand was cut off at or near the place where the crime was committed and the bleeding malefactor was then paraded through the streets to the execution site. Such spectacles were virtually inescapable for anyone who lived in the great city.

What was it like to walk through these streets? To see such sights every few days? To live in a city where popular entertainments mirrored these constant torments in the whipping of blind bears or, for that matter, in the performance of tragedies? Whether or not Shakespeare went out of his way to witness the gory rituals of law and order (there were other playwrights who were more interested in competing with the public torturer and hangman), they figure repeatedly in his plays. Lavinia's ghastly fate in *Titus Andronicus*—her hands lopped off, her tongue cut out—would have been easy for Elizabethan actors to represent in graphic, realistic detail, for they had seen such things performed in the flesh on scaffolds in the suburbs, near the playhouse. And when Shakespeare's characters displayed the bloody heads of Richard III or Macbeth, members of the audience could easily have compared the simulation with the real thing.

Shakespeare was not simply giving the vulgar crowd what they craved; he himself was manifestly fascinated by the penal spectacles all around him. His fascination was not the same as endorsement; indeed it included a strong current of revulsion. The most terrible scene of torture in his works—the blinding of the Earl of Gloucester in *King Lear*—is, the playwright makes clear, unequivocally the act of moral monsters. But the horror with which this particular wicked act is depicted is not the same as a blanket repudiation of his society's savage judicial punishments. When at the end of *Othello* the wicked Iago refuses to explain why he has woven his vicious plot—"Demand me nothing. What you know, you know. / From this time forth I never will speak word"—the agents of the Venetian state are confident that they will get some answer from him: "Torments will ope your lips" (5.2.309–10, 312). And even if they do not succeed—Iago remains silent for the remainder of the play, and nothing encourages us to believe that torments will lead him to alter his resolution—the Venetians are determined to exact some vengeance on the villain for what he has done. Indeed they will, as the official of the state explains, use all of their ingenuity in order to intensify and prolong his agony:

> If there be any cunning cruelty
> That can torment him much and hold him long,
> It shall be his.
>
> (5.2.342–44)

Though torturing Iago cannot revive Desdemona or restore Othello's ruined life, *Othello* encourages the audience to accept the legitimacy of this proposed course of action: it is a gesture, however inadequate, toward repairing the damaged moral order. State torture is part of the world as Shakespeare and his audience experienced and thus imagined it, and not only from the special perspective of tragedy. In the glow at the end of one of Shakespeare's happiest comedies, *Much Ado About Nothing*, when all the dark suspicions have been vanquished and the bitter misunderstandings have been resolved, there is still time to think ahead to the rack and the thumbscrew. The schemes of Don John the Bastard—a kind of inept Iago—have been exposed, and the villain has fled. Claudio and Hero have been reconciled and are about to join that most delicious couple, Beatrice and Benedick, in marrying. The merry Benedick calls for music—"let's have a dance ere we are married"—when word is brought that Don John has been captured. "Think not on him till tomorrow," Benedick says, speaking the play's closing words, "I'll devise thee brave punishments for him. Strike up, pipers" (5.4.112–13, 121–22).

This then is the answer, or at least part of the answer, to the question of what it was like to live in such a city as London, amidst the endless, grim spectacles of penal justice. The spectacles were part of the structure of life and were accepted as such; the trick was to know when to look and when to look away, when to punish and when to dance. In close proximity to the sites of pain and death were sites of pleasure—the punishment scaffolds of the Bankside were close to the brothels—and these too seized Shakespeare's imagination. Whorehouses ("stews") figure frequently in his plays—Doll Tearsheet, Mistress Overdone, and their fellow workers in the sex industry are quickly but indelibly sketched, along with assorted panders, doorkeepers, tapsters, and servants. He depicted brothels as places of disease, vice, and disorder, but also as places that satisfy ineradicable human needs, bringing together men and women, gentlemen and common people, old and young, the educated and the illiterate, in a camaraderie rarely found elsewhere in the highly stratified society. Above all, he depicted them as small businesses that struggle against high odds—stiff competition, rowdy or indifferent clients, hostile civic authorities—to make a modest profit.

These qualities closely linked whorehouses in Shakespeare's imagination, and probably in that of most of his contemporaries, with another suburban institution, one that had only recently come into its own and that was the center of his professional life. The theater, which did not exist as a freestanding structure anywhere in England when Shakespeare was born, at once conjoined and played with almost everything that the "entertainment zone" had to offer: dancing, music, games of skill, blood sports, punishment, sex. Indeed, the boundaries between theatrical imitation and reality, between one form of amusement and another, were often blurred. Whores worked the playhouse crowd and, at least in the fantasies of the theater's enemies, conducted their trade in small rooms on-site.

A foreign visitor to London in 1584 described the elaborate spectacle he had witnessed in Southwark one August afternoon:

> There is a round building three stories high, in which are kept about a hundred large English dogs, with separate wooden kennels for each of them. These dogs were made to fight singly with three bears, the second bear being larger than the first and the third larger than the second. After this a horse was brought in and chased by the dogs, and at last a bull, who defended himself bravely. The next was that a number of men and women came forward from a separate compartment, dancing, conversing and fighting with each other: also a man who threw some white bread among the crowd, that scrambled for it. Right over the middle of the place a rose was fixed, this rose being set on fire by a rocket: suddenly lots of apples and pears fell out of it down upon the people standing below. Whilst the people were scrambling for the apples, some rockets were made to fall down upon them out of the rose, which caused a great fright but amused the spectators. After this, rockets and other fireworks came flying out of all corners, and that was the end of the play.

"That was the end of the play": few today would classify this gory, gaudy spectacle as theater, but in Elizabethan London the baiting of animals and the performing of plays were curiously intertwined. They both aroused the ire of the city authorities, fretting about traffic congestion, idleness, disorder, and public health—hence the location of performances in places like Southwark, outside the jurisdiction of the aldermen and mayor. They were attacked in similar terms by moralists and preachers, threatening divine vengeance upon all who took pleasure in filthy, godless shows. They attracted crowds of common people and at the same time were patronized and protected by aristocrats. They even took place in strikingly similar buildings. Indeed, one of these buildings—the Hope playhouse—served for both bearbaiting and playacting: in Ben Jonson's *Bartholomew Fair*, performed there in 1614, one of the characters refers to the stench that still lingered from the previous day's sport. The Hope was owned by the pawnbroker, moneylender, and theatrical impressario Philip Henslowe, who also owned whorehouses. London entertainments—and the money they generated—all, in some sense, flowed into one another.

At the same time, the theater, which had (with the exception of the Hope) genuinely differentiated itself from all other types of arenas, was a remarkably important innovation. Playacting in purpose-built playhouses (as opposed to candlelit private halls, innyards, and the backs of wagons) had only recently come to London, significantly later than blood sports. A map of Southwark from 1542 already shows a bullring on High Street, but it was not until 1567 that a prosperous London grocer, John Brayne, put up the city's first freestanding public playhouse, the Red Lion, in Stepney. The enterprise was a bold one—nothing of the kind had been built in England since the decline and fall of the Roman Empire. Very little is known about the Red Lion—it may have been pulled down or transformed to other uses very quickly—but to the intrepid Brayne it must have seemed a promising speculation, for nine years later he was at it again, in a far more important venture. This time he took a business partner, his brother-in-law James Burbage, a joiner by trade who had turned actor under the patronage of the Earl of Leicester. Burbage's carpentry skills were probably at least as important as his playacting, for he played a major role in constructing the complex polygonal timber building that the entrepreneurs called simply the Theater.

The name befits the notion of the Renaissance, in the literal sense of a rebirth of classical antiquity: in 1576 the relatively unfamiliar word "theater" self-consciously conjured up ancient amphitheaters. Not surprisingly, then, the Theater was almost immediately attacked from the pulpit for being made "after the manner of the old heathenish Theatre at Rome." Burbage and Brayne were wise to build it on land they had leased in the liberty of Holywell in the suburb of Shoreditch, outside the Bishopsgate entrance to the city. Here, on the site of what had been a priory of Benedictine nuns, the enterprise was subject to the queen's Privy Council rather than the city. The preachers could fulminate and the city fathers could threaten, but the show would go on.

When Shakespeare came to London, he had seen and acted in plays, but he had never before seen a freestanding playhouse. Probably it had already been described to him in detail, perhaps carefully sketched by a family member who had been to London or by a friend, but there was a moment when he set foot in one for the first time. He saw a rectangular elevated platform, jutting out into the middle of a large yard surrounded by tiered galleries. The yard, for the "groundlings" to stand and watch the play, was open to the elements, but the stage was covered by a painted canopy—known as "the heavens"—supported by two columns. The stage, five feet above the ground, had no protective railings—an actor in the midst of a sword fight had to keep a sharp sense of where he was. Set into the stage was a trapdoor that led to a storage space known as "hell," which could be used to powerful theatrical effect. At the back of the stage was a wooden wall with two doors, for entrances and exits, and between them, in some theaters, a central curtained space that could be opened for formal entrances or for more intimate scenes. Above these doors on the back wall ran a gallery partitioned into rooms for the highest-paying spectators. The central part of this gallery could be used for staging scenes: if not at once then very soon after, Shakespeare began to imagine the ways he might use that space, say, as a balcony or the high parapet of a castle wall.

With no lighting and nothing more than minimal scenery, there would have been little scope for creating the types of illusions routinely used by modern theaters, but audiences have proved again and again that they do not need to be plunged into darkness in order to imagine the night or to see papier-mâché trees in order to conjure up a forest. What Elizabethan audiences did take seriously was the illusionistic effect of clothes; behind the back wall of the stage was a "tiring house," where the actors could don their elaborate costumes, costumes that were carefully protected from the rain by the overhanging canopy. The whole design was wonderfully functional and flexible. The handsome guildhalls and the private halls of the nobility and gentry in which the touring companies performed had their advantages, but the actors had constantly to rethink the show, altering the blocking to fit each different space and working around features that were never intended to accommodate performances. Any young actor or aspiring playwright up from the provinces must have felt on entering a London playhouse that he had died and gone to theatrical heaven.

That heaven had the agreeable quality of looking at least in certain respects reassuringly familiar. An open space, surrounded by galleries, was reminiscent of the innyards in London and throughout the country where plays were occasionally performed in the open air. (More often they were performed in large rooms.) The innkeepers—or housekeepers, as they were called in this period—rented space, along with costumes and props, to itinerant players who would, at the end of the performance, pass the hat among the crowd. By the time he reached London young Will may have collected the pennies himself more than once, though the companies in the 1580s had also begun to experiment with charging for admission at the inn door. The new Theater and the other public theaters that were built in its wake were run on different principles, but the proprietors similarly called themselves housekeepers, as if they simply owned an inn (presumably, this is why we still speak of dimming the "houselights" or of playing to a "full house").

Burbage and Brayne's investment, in fact, included an inn, the Cross Keys on Gracechurch Street (near what is now Liverpool Street Station), where players on occasion also performed, but their principal theater was a separate structure, enabling the entrepreneurs fully to implement the new idea: the spectators would have to pay at the door, before they saw the show. At the end of the play the actors would only beg for applause and urge return visits. Thus was the box office—originally a locked cash-box—born. The innovation—significantly changing the relationship between the entertainers and their customers—must have been an immediate commercial success, since another theater, the Curtain, soon went up in the same neighborhood, and other theaters soon followed. One penny would get you into the yard where you could stand for the two or three hours with the crowd, milling about, buying apples, oranges, nuts, and bottled ale, or pushing in as close as you could get to the edge of the stage. Another penny would get you out of the rain (or on occasion the hot sun) and onto a seat in one of the covered galleries that ringed the playhouse; a third penny would get you a cushioned seat in one of the "gentlemen's rooms" on the lower level of the galleries, "the pleasantest place," as a theatergoer of the time put it, "where [one] not only sees everything well but can also be seen."

The system of payment was meant in part to ensure some financial transparency: the first penny was supposed to go to the players; the second and third pennies in whole or in part to the "housekeepers." But the partners soon fell out—Burbage, Brayne alleged, had been filching money from the cashbox to which he had a secret key—and they did what Elizabethans with any money at stake constantly did: they went to court. Even after Brayne's death in 1586, the charges and countercharges had not been settled. On the contrary, they grew more tangled and bitter, culminating in a pitched battle on November 16, 1590, when Brayne's widow came with her allies to the Theater to attempt to collect a share of the receipts. Leaning out of a window, James Burbage and his wife shouted that their sister-in-law was a whore and the collectors knaves. Their youngest son, Richard, then about sixteen years old, lay about him with a broomstick and assaulted one of the collectors, "scornfully and dis-dainfully," as the deposition puts it, "playing with this deponent's nose." This rowdy boy with the broomstick is the first recorded glimpse of the celebrated actor who subsequently played Hamlet and most of the other great Shakespearean heroes.

The theatrical world Shakespeare found his way into was volatile, speculative, competitive, and precarious. The stage had vociferous ene-mies: the theaters, preachers and moralists charged, were temples to

Venus and other devilish pagan deities; respectable matrons who went innocently enough to watch the plays were quickly lured into lives of licentiousness; men were sexually aroused by seductive boy actors; the Word of God was mocked and piety held up to ridicule; grave authorities were brought into contempt; seditious ideas were planted in the minds of the multitude. Go to plays, thundered one irate minister, John Northbrooke, "if you will learn how to be false and deceive your husbands, or husbands their wives, how to play the harlots to obtain one's love, how to ravish, how to beguile, how to betray, to flatter, lie, swear, forswear, how to allure to whoredom, how to murder, how to poison, how to disobey and rebel against princes, to consume treasures prodigally, to move to lusts, to ransack and spoil cities and towns, to be idle, to blaspheme, to sing filthy songs of love, to speak filthily, to be proud. . . ." The catalog of vicious lessons continues breathlessly, to be augmented over the years by many other preachers. And as if this were not enough, the wickedness on stage, the theater's enemies complained, was matched by the wickedness of the audience. At our playhouses, wrote Stephen Gosson in 1579, "you shall see such heaving and shoving, such itching and shouldering to sit by the women; such care for their garments, that they be not trod on; such eyes to their laps, that no chips light in them; such pillows to their backs, that they take no hurt; such masking in their ears, I know not what; such giving them pippins, to pass the time; such playing at foot saunt [i.e., footsie] . . . ; such ticking, such toying, such smiling, such winking, and such manning them home, when the sports are ended." It is a terrible thing, moralists sourly observed, that many who sit happily for two hours to watch a play cannot bear to sit for an hour to hear a sermon.

These charges were leveled in the name of closing down the theaters, but apart from leading to a ban on Sunday performances, they principally served, not surprisingly, to intensify the public's interest. "Where shall we go?" wrote John Florio, in an English-Italian phrase book that he published in 1578. "To a play at the Bull, or else to some other place." Florio was born and brought up in London, the son of refugee Italian Protestants. His little language lesson—revealing, as those in modern textbooks are, precisely because it was attempting to be so ordinary and everyday—continued:

Do comedies like you well?

Yea sir, on holy days.

They please me also well, but the preachers will not allow them.

Wherefore? Know you it?

They say, they are not good.

And wherefore are they used?

Because every man delights in them.

"Because every man delights in them": defenders of the stage marshaled many arguments—plays showed virtue rewarded and vice punished, taught good manners, kept minds that might otherwise be plotting mischief occupied with harmless things, and so forth—but the theaters survived and flourished simply because people ranging from lowly apprentices to the queen enjoyed what they saw.

Powerful aristocrats, key government officials, and the queen herself protected the public theaters and the playing companies. If there was a dangerous, subversive force in the realm, they thought, it was not the theaters but the theaters' enemies, the discontented, tirelessly meddlesome Protestant radicals who wanted to sweep away all profane pleasures. But the protection that the queen and her advisers afforded the stage was by no means unconditional; they too were nervous about public assemblies. They behaved, whether from paranoia or from bitter practical experience, as if crowds were inherently dangerous, as if they could easily turn violent, as if, given the chance, they would attack their social superiors and strike at the fundamental institutions of the society. Though official documents always stressed the queen's serene confidence in her loving subjects, many of her less guarded remarks suggest a strong current of suspicion. When Sir Philip Sidney had a shoving match with his social superior, the Earl of Oxford, over a tennis court, Elizabeth gave Sidney a lecture on the difference between an earl and a mere knight, along with a warning: Can you imagine, she asked, what would happen if common people learned that you yourself did not respect rank and title?

Elizabethan officials worried about any public spectacle that they could not control. Even the gathering together of a handful of people could alarm the authorities. Spies were assigned to taverns and inns to listen into conversations and report anything suspicious. Proclamations were issued asking people to be on the watch for anyone speaking "undutiful words." The government issued warnings against people who "lie privily in corners and bad houses, listening after news and stirs, and spreading rumors and tales." Vagabonds lurking in London were subject to harsh punishments. Small wonder that the position of the theaters, even with its powerful friends, was precarious.

Arriving in London in the late 1580s, probably as a hired actor in a troupe of players, Shakespeare entered a relatively new scene, not so new that its basic outlines were unformed but new enough that it was still open and evolving. The playing companies had been accustomed to a nomadic life of almost perpetual touring, with their membership frequently shifting, temporarily splitting apart, and recombining. The rise of the public theaters in a city with a rapidly expanding population hungry for amusement gave at least some of these companies the opportunity to have a lucrative home base where they would do most of their performing. They would still go out on the road from time to time, but the wagon with the costumes and props, the scrambling to find a place to perform, the fraught negotiations with the local authorities would no longer occupy the center of their professional lives.

But even for the most successful companies the transition to a more settled London-centered existence was not easy. Touring was no doubt tiring—after a handful of performances, the troupe would have to pack up and move on—but the actors could get by with a modest repertory. Not so in London. The open amphitheaters were large—they could hold two thousand or more—and the city, though populous by sixteenth-century standards, was only two hundred thousand. This meant that to survive economically it was not enough to mount one or two successful plays a season and keep them up for reasonable runs. The companies had to induce people, large numbers of people, to get in the habit of coming to the theater again and again, and this meant a constantly changing repertoire, as many as five or six plays per week. The sheer magnitude of the enterprise is astonishing: for each company, approximately twenty new plays per year in addition to some twenty plays carried over from previous seasons.

Shakespeare seems to have grasped quickly the special opportunity that the burgeoning public theaters had created. The companies that performed in them had an enormous appetite for new plays. He could help to satisfy this appetite, either on his own or in collaboration with others. His timing could not have been better. There was no writers' guild, no special credentials that he needed to possess, no prerequisites for venturing forth. London would enable him to realize the embryonic ambition to write as well as to act that he may have brought with him from Stratford.

Later in his life it was said that Shakespeare wrote with astonishing facility. "The Players have often mentioned it as an honor to Shakespeare," his friend and rival Ben Jonson wrote, "that in his writing, whatsoever he penned, he never blotted out line." "My answer hath been," Jonson tartly added, "would he had blotted a thousand." Judging from the multiple versions that exist of many of his plays and poems, Shakespeare in fact must have quietly blotted thousands of lines. There is powerful evidence that he extensively revised his work. Yet the impression of a great ease in writing remains and may have extended back even to his early efforts. Words came easily to him, he was a quick study, and he had already absorbed several richly suggestive theatrical models. Though young and untried, he was poised to begin writing for the stage at once. Nonetheless, there are signs that it took a startling aesthetic shock to set Shakespeare's career as a writer fully in motion.

London, the chronicler Stow wrote, "was a mighty arm and instrument to bring any great desire to effect." The great public theaters that went up from the 1570s onward—the Theater, the Curtain, the Rose, the Swan, the Globe, the Red Bull, the Fortune, and the Hope—were in the business of fostering and catering to such great desires. Shakespeare encountered this central principle in its purest form almost immediately upon his arrival, for in 1587, just at the time he was finding his feet in London, crowds were flocking to the Rose to see the Lord Admiral's Men perform Christopher Marlowe's *Tamburlaine*. Shakespeare almost certainly saw the play (along with the sequel that shortly followed), and he probably went back again and again. It may indeed have been one of the first performances he ever saw in a playhouse—perhaps *the* first— and, from its effect upon his early work, it appears to have had upon him an intense, visceral, indeed life-transforming impact.

The dream that Marlowe's startlingly cruel play aroused and brilliantly gratified was the dream of domination. His hero is a poor Scythian shepherd who rises by determination, charismatic energy, and utter ruthlessness to conquer much of the known world. The play, conceived on an epic scale, is full of noise, exotic pageantry, and rivers of stage blood—flags fly, chariots are dragged across the stage, cannons are fired—but the core of its appeal is its incantatory celebration of the will to power:

> Nature, that framed us of four elements,
> Warring within our breasts for regiment,
> Doth teach us all to have aspiring minds.
> Our souls, whose faculties can comprehend
> The wondrous architecture of the world
> And measure every wand'ring planet's course,
> Still climbing after knowledge infinite
> And always moving as the restless spheres,
> Wills us to wear ourselves and never rest
> Until we reach the ripest fruit of all:
> That perfect bliss and sole felicity,
> The sweet fruition of an earthly crown.
>
> (2.7.18–29)

For the space of this play, all of the moral rules inculcated in schools and churches, in homilies and proclamations and sober-minded tracts, are suspended. The highest good—"That perfect bliss and sole felicity"—is not the contemplation of God but the possession of a crown. There is no hierarchy of blood, no divinely sanctioned legitimate authority, no inherited obligation to obey, no moral restraint. Instead, there is a restless, violent striving that can be fully appeased only by grasping (or dreaming of grasping) supreme power.

The part of Tamburlaine was created by an astonishingly gifted young actor in the Lord Admiral's Men, Edward Alleyn, at the time only twenty-one years old. At the sight of the performance, Shakespeare, two years his senior, may have grasped, if he had not already begun to do so, that he was not likely to become one of the leading actors on the London stage. Alleyn was the real thing: a majestic physical presence, with a "well-tuned," clear voice capable of seizing and holding the attention of enormous audiences. Achieving instant and enduring fame for his "stalking and roaring" in the part, Alleyn went on to play Faustus, Barabas, and many other great roles; to marry Henslowe's step-daughter; to become immensely rich from the business side of entertainment; and to found a distinguished educational institution, Dulwich College.

The actor in Shakespeare would have perceived what was powerful in Alleyn's interpretation of Tamburlaine, but the poet in him understood something else: the magic that was drawing audiences did not reside entirely in the actor's fine voice, nor even in the hero's daring vision of the blissful object at which he lunges, the earthy crown. The hushed crowd was already tasting Tamburlaine's power in the unprecedented energy and commanding eloquence of the play's blank verse—the dynamic flow of unrhymed five-stress, ten-syllable lines—that the author, Christopher Marlowe, had mastered for the stage. This verse, like the dream of what ordinary speech would be like were human beings something greater than they are, was by no means only bombast and bragging. Its appeal lay in its own "wondrous architecture": its subtle rhythms, the way in which a succession of monosyllables suddenly flowers into the word "aspiring," the pleasure of hearing "fruit" become "fruition."

Shakespeare had never heard anything quite like this before—certainly not in the morality plays or mystery cycles he had watched back in Warwickshire. He must have said to himself something like, "You are not in Stratford anymore." To someone raised on a diet of moralities and mysteries, it must have seemed as if the figure of Riot had somehow seized control of the stage, and with it an unparalleled power of language. Perhaps, at one of those early performances—before the full extent of Marlowe's recklessness became known—Shakespeare waited, with others in the audience, for the tyrant, soaked with the blood of innocents, to be brought low. That, after all, is what always happened to Riot or to Herod in the religious drama. But what he saw instead was one insanely cruel victory follow another, the rhetoric of triumph becoming ever more intoxicating. "Millions of souls sit on the banks of Styx," exults the murderous conqueror at the play's close,

Waiting the back return of Charon's boat.
Hell and Elysium swarm with ghosts of men
That I have sent. . . .

(5.1.463–66)

Nothing holds Tamburlaine back, no fear, no deference, no respect for the established order of things: "Emperors and kings lie breathless at my feet" (5.1.469). With these words and with the slaughter of the innocent virgins of Damascus, he takes his beautiful bride, the divine Zenocrate, daughter of the conquered sultan of Egypt. Then, shockingly, outrageously, the play was over, and the crowd applauded, cheering the trampling of everything that they had been instructed with numbing repetition to hold dear.

This was a crucial experience for Shakespeare, a challenge to all of his aesthetic and moral and professional assumptions. The challenge must have been intensified when he learned that Marlowe was in effect his double: born in the same year, 1564, in a provincial town; the son not of a wealthy gentleman but of a common artisan, a shoemaker. Had Marlowe not existed, Shakespeare would no doubt have written plays, but those plays would have been decisively different. As it is, he gives the impression that he made the key move in his career—the decision not to make his living as an actor alone but to try also to write for the stage on which he performed—under Marlowe's influence. The fingerprints of *Tamburlaine* (both the initial play and the sequel that soon followed) are all over the plays that are among Shakespeare's earliest known ventures as a playwright, the three parts of *Henry VI*—so much so that earlier textual scholars thought that the *Henry VI* plays must have been collaborative enterprises undertaken with Marlowe himself. The decided unevenness in the style of the plays suggests that Shakespeare may well have been working with others, though few scholars any longer believe that Marlowe was among them. Rather, the neophyte Shakespeare and his collaborators seem to have been looking over their shoulders at Marlowe's achievement.

Marlowe had put together the two parts of *Tamburlaine* out of his strange personal history—spy, double agent, counterfeiter, atheist—but also and as important, out of his voraciously wide reading. Some of the

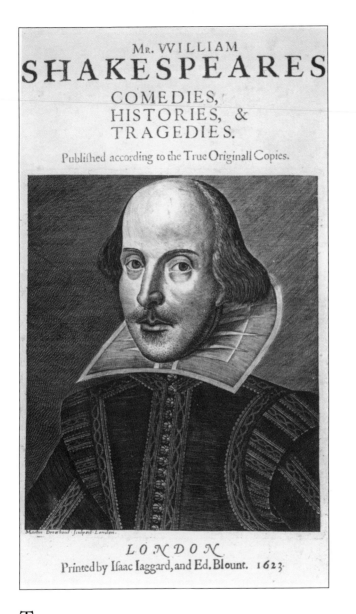

Though Martin Droeshout (c. 1601–c. 1650) was only fifteen when Shakespeare died and thus unlikely to have seen him in person, his engraving on the title page of the First Folio (1623) must have seemed sufficiently accurate to satisfy the editors, who knew Shakespeare well. *By courtesy of W. W. Norton & Company.*

Gloves, of the kind that Shakespeare's father made, were often elaborate luxury items, such as this early seventeenth-century pair made of leather, satin, and gold bobbin lace. *By courtesy of V & A Images / V & A Museum.*

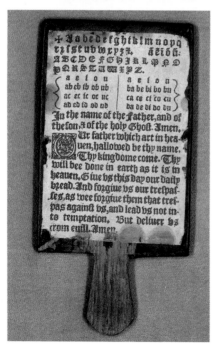

Young Will probably learned his letters from what was known as a hornbook: a printed sheet of parchment or paper mounted on wood and covered with a transparent sheet of animal horn.

By courtesy of the Folger Shakespeare Library.

The nave of Stratford's Guild Chapel, with the remains of the medieval wall painting of Christ and the Last Judgment, whitewashed over in 1563 on instructions from the town chamberlain, John Shakespeare. *By courtesy of Maya Vision International.*

In this copy of a portrait painted shortly after his execution in 1581, Edmund Campion, carrying the palm of martyrdom, is about to be crowned by an angel. Crowning by the Catholic Church took longer: beatified by Pope Leo XIII on December 9, 1886, Campion was canonized by Pope Paul VI in 1970. *By courtesy of Stonyhurst College, Lancashire.*

Record in the Stratford parish register of the christening, on February 2, 1585, of William and Anne Shakespeare's twins, Hamnet and Judith, named after their neighbors Hamnet and Judith Sadler. When, three years later, the Sadlers had a son, they named him William. *By permission of the Shakespeare Birthplace Trust.*

In this painting, attributed to Robert Peake (c. 1551–1626), Queen Elizabeth is carried in procession like a bejeweled idol. *By permission of the Bridgeman Art Library.*

The Shakespeare coat of arms, roughly sketched in 1602 by an official who claimed that "Shakespeare yᵉ Player" should not have been allowed to claim the status of a gentleman. *By courtesy of the Folger Shakespeare Library.*

A detail from Claes Jansz. Visscher's engraving of London Bridge, showing the heads of traitors stuck on pikes. *By courtesy of the Folger Shakespeare Library.*

Panoramic view of early seventeenth-century London by the Amsterdam engraver Claes Jansz. Visscher (1587–1652), showing such sights as St. Paul's Church, the Globe Theater, the bear garden, and London Bridge. *By courtesy of the Folger Shakespeare Library.*

In this miniature, painted by Nicholas Hilliard (c. 1547–1619), the twenty-year-old Henry Wriothesley, third Earl of Southampton, displays the long auburn hair for which he was famous. *By permission of the Bridgeman Art Library.*

No portrait of Christopher Marlowe with a strong claim to authenticity survives, but the dating and provenance of this late sixteenth-century painting, at Corpus Christi College, Cambridge, makes it at least possible that it depicts the playwright as a brooding undergraduate. *By courtesy of Corpus Christi College, Cambridge.*

details of the life of the Scythian conqueror he could have culled from popular English books, but scholars have shown that Marlowe must have followed the leads in these books back to other, less readily available sources in Latin. Some of the details in *Tamburlaine* suggest that Marlowe even picked up information found in Turkish sources not yet translated during the playwright's lifetime into any Western European languages. And crucially, for these plays full of exotic geographical locations, he had access to the recent and very expensive *Theatrum orbis terrarum* by the great Flemish geographer Ortelius. Where could a shoemaker's son find access to this and all the rest? The explanation must lie in the bibliographical and human resources of Cambridge University, where Marlowe enrolled as a student in 1581. In July of that year, for example, a copy of Ortelius's atlas was presented to the university library, and Marlowe's own college, Corpus Christi, already owned a copy.

Shakespeare had no comparable resources upon which he could draw. But he did have a friend in London who probably played a crucial role at this point in his career. Richard Field had come to London in 1578 from Stratford-upon-Avon, where his father and Shakespeare's father were associates, to serve as an apprentice to the printer Thomas Vautrollier, a Protestant refugee from Paris. Vautrollier had a good business: he published schoolbooks, an edition of Calvin's *Institutes of the Christian Religion*, a Latin Book of Common Prayer, works in French, and editions of important classics. Thus described, the list sounds rather dull, but Vautrollier also allowed himself to take certain risks, such as bringing out important works by the heretical theologian and radical Italian philosopher Giordano Bruno (who was later burned at the stake in Naples). And among his best-known publications was a book that turned out to be one of Shakespeare's favorites: Sir Thomas North's translation of Plutarch's *Lives*, a principal source for *Julius Caesar*, *Timon of Athens*, *Coriolanus*, and, above all, *Antony and Cleopatra*.

Richard Field did well for himself in his new calling: after serving for six years as Vautrollier's apprentice and for a seventh year as the apprentice of another printer, in 1587 he obtained admission to the printers' guild, the Stationer's Company. When, in that same year, Vautrollier died, Field married his widow, Jacqueline, and took over the business. By 1589, then, he was established as a master printer, with a busy workshop and an impressive, wide-ranging, and intellectually challenging list of authors. He must also have owned books by his competitors and would have had access to others. He was a hugely valuable resource for his young playwright friend from Stratford.

Even though as a poet Shakespeare dreamed of eternal fame, he does not seem to have associated that fame with the phenomenon of the printed book. And even when he was well established as a playwright, with his plays for sale in the bookstalls in St. Paul's Churchyard, he showed little or no personal interest in seeing his plays on the printed page, let alone assuring the accuracy of the editions. He never, it seems, anticipated what turned out to be the case: that he would live as much on the page as on the stage and that his destiny as a writer was deeply bound up with the technology he must have glimpsed the first time he visited his friend's printing shop in Blackfriars.

When the door opened, Shakespeare would have seen firsthand the beating heart of the London book trade: the compositor bending over the manuscripts, reaching into the trays, pulling out the bits of type and setting them in the rows; the printer inking the completed "formes," or frames in which the printing type was secured, and turning the great screws that pressed the inked formes down onto the mechanical bed on which large sheets of paper were laid; the printing press casting off the sheets which were then folded to make the pages; the proofreader correcting the sheets and going back to the compositor for changes before the pages were taken to the binders to be stitched together. All of this would have been interesting enough in itself as a spectacle (there are many images in Shakespeare's work of the imprinting of marks or signs), but the real excitement for him would have been access to books. Books were expensive, far too expensive for a young actor and untried playwright to buy out of his own pocket, and yet the ambitious Shakespeare needed them if he was to rise to the challenge posed by Marlowe's stupendous work.

How Shakespeare came to the idea of writing his counterthrust to *Tamburlaine*—the three plays about the troubled fifteenth-century reign of Henry VI—is not known. Perhaps the idea was not originally his: there is evidence that the Queen's Men, with which he may have been affiliated at the time, was troubled by Marlowe's success and determined to counter it. Shakespeare may have been invited to join in a project already under way that had bogged down. Plays were often written collaboratively, and the more established writers may have welcomed another hand. Perhaps he began by making a few small suggestions and then found himself increasingly involved and responsible. Alternatively, he may have been in charge from the beginning. But whatever the case, he and any collaborators he had needed books, as Marlowe had needed books. The key books—English chronicles such as Edward Hall's *The Union of the Two Noble and Illustre Families of Lancaster and York*, Geoffrey of Monmouth's *Historia regum Britanniae*, *A Mirror for Magistrates* by Willam Baldwin and others, and, above all, Raphael Holinshed's indispensable and just-published *Chronicles*—were not published by Field or his former master Vautrollier, but it is quite possible that Shakespeare's friend may have owned copies or been able to put him in touch with those who did.

Shakespeare had determined to write a historical epic, like Marlowe's, but to make it an English epic, an account of the bloody time of troubles that preceded the order brought by the Tudors. He wanted to resurrect a whole world, as Marlowe had done, bringing forth astonishing larger-than-life figures engaged in struggles to the death, but it was now not the exotic realms of the East that would be brought to the stage but England's own past. The great idea of the history play—taking the audience back into a time that had dropped away from living memory but that was still eerily familiar and crucially important—was not absolutely new, but Shakespeare gave it an energy, power, and conviction that it had never before possessed. The *Henry VI* plays are still crude, especially in comparison with Shakespeare's later triumphs in the same genre, but they convey a striking picture of the playwright poring over Holinshed's *Chronicles* in search of materials that would enable him to imitate *Tamburlaine*.

The imitation, though real enough, is not exactly an expression of homage; it is a skeptical reply. Marlowe's play concentrated all of the world's driving ambition in a single charismatic superhero; Shakespeare's trilogy is full of Tamburlaine-like grotesques, including one already encountered, the peasant Jack Cade. Cade turns out to be the unwitting puppet of the power-crazed Duke of York, who echoes Tamburlaine's boast:

> I will stir up in England some black storm
> Shall blow ten thousand souls to heaven or hell,
> And this fell tempest shall not cease to rage
> Until the golden circuit on my head
> Like to the glorious sun's transparent beams
> Do calm the fury of this mad-bred flaw.
> 　　　　　　　　(*2 Henry VI*, 3.1.349–54)

The Marlovian accents are still clearer in the speeches of York's evil son, Richard:

> How sweet a thing it is to wear a crown,
> Within whose circuit is Elysium
> And all that poets feign of bliss and joy.
> 　　　　　　　　(*3 Henry VI*, 1.2.29–31)

And the sadistic pleasure is no longer limited to the male world; it extends to the formidable Queen Margaret, triumphing over her enemy York:

> Why art thou patient, man? Thou shouldst be mad,
> And I, to make thee mad, do mock thee thus.
> Stamp, rave, and fret, that I may sing and dance.
> 　　　　　　　　(*3 Henry VI*, 1.4.90–92)

This savage cruelty in a woman astonishes even the fierce York: "O tiger's heart wrapped in a woman's hide!" he exclaims (1.4.138). When order breaks down, everyone wants to be a Tamburlaine.

In Marlowe's vision of the exotic East, vaunting ambition, stopping at nothing, leads to the establishment of a grand world order, cruel but magnificent. That order, as part two of *Tamburlaine* shows, crumbles, but only because everything eventually crumbles: there is no moral other than the brute fact of mortality. In Shakespeare's vision of English history, vaunting ambition leads to chaos, an ungovernable, murderous factionalism and the consequent loss of power at home and abroad. Despite or even because of his ruthlessness, Marlowe's hero bestrides the world like a god, doing whatever it pleases him to do—"This is my mind, and I will have it so" (4.2.91). By contrast, Shakespeare's petty Tamburlaines, even though they are queens and dukes, are like mentally unbalanced small-town criminals: they are capable of incredible nastiness but cannot achieve a hint of grandeur.

In part, this limitation was a consequence of poetic inexperience: Shakespeare was not able, at least at this point in his life, to match the unstoppable, monomaniacal grandiloquence Marlowe commanded. But in part it was a clear choice: Shakespeare refused to give any of his characters, even his stalwart English military hero Talbot, the limitless power Marlowe gleefully conferred on Tamburlaine. Simply to look at Tamburlaine is to see the embodiment of Herculean power; to look on Talbot, by contrast, is to be disappointed. "I see report is fabulous and false," says the Countess of Auvergne, who has lured Talbot to her castle.

> It cannot be this weak and writhled shrimp
> Should strike such terror to his enemies.
> (*1 Henry VI*, 2.3.17, 22–3)

Talbot is an ordinary mortal. When the English forces are routed, he is killed, along with his son, by a French army led by the demonic Joan of Arc. No one in this world is invincible: abandoned by her devils, Joan is soon afterward captured by the resurgent English army, tried for sorcery, and burned at the stake.

Crowds flocked in the late 1580s to see the *Henry VI* plays—this was Shakespeare's first great theatrical success, establishing him as a viable playwright—but they did not come to fantasize about possessing absolute power. On the contrary, they came to shudder at the horrors of popular uprising and civil war. The crowds came too, it seems, to savor heroic sacrifice and to mourn loss. "How it would have joyed brave Tal-

bot," wrote a contemporary playwright, Thomas Nashe, "to think that
after he had lain two hundred years in his Tomb, he should triumph again
on the Stage, and have his bones new embalmed with the tears of ten
thousand spectators at least (at several times) who, in the Tragedian that
represents his person, imagine they behold him fresh bleeding." Nashe,
who may have been one of Shakespeare's collaborators on *1 Henry VI*,
was not an objective witness. But even if he was exaggerating, he was
pointing to a major commercial triumph. Edward Alleyn had found a
rival in the "Tragedian" who played Talbot—in all likelihood, Richard
Burbage; and the visionary poetic genius of Christopher Marlowe had
been challenged from a hitherto unknown talent, a minor actor from
Stratford-upon-Avon.

CHAPTER 7

Shakescene

I F BEFORE HIS SUCCESS with the *Henry VI* plays Shakespeare had not already met Marlowe, he would certainly have met him soon afterward, and along with Marlowe he would have met many of the other playwrights—poets, as they were then called—who were writing for the London stage. They were an extraordinary group, of the kind that emerges all at once in charmed moments, as when a dozen or more brilliant painters all seemed to converge at the same time on Florence or when for years at a time New Orleans or Chicago seemed to have a seemingly limitless supply of stupendous jazz and blues musicians. In all such moments, of course, sheer genetic accident is at work, but there are always institutional and cultural circumstances that help the accident make sense. In late-sixteenth-century London those circumstances included the phenomenal growth of the urban population, the emergence of the public theaters, and the existence of a competitive market for new plays. They included too an impressive, widespread growth in literacy; an educational system that trained its students to be highly sensitive to rhetorical effects; a social and political taste for elaborate display; a religious culture that compelled parishioners to listen to long, complex sermons; and a vibrant, restless intellectual culture. There were very few options for promising intellectuals: the educational system had surged ahead of the existing social system, so that highly educated men who did not want to pursue a career in the church or law had to cast about for something to do with themselves. Disreputable though it was, the theater beckoned.

At some moment in the late 1580s, Shakespeare walked into a room—most likely, in an inn in Shoreditch, Southwark, or the Bankside—and quite possibly found many of the leading writers drinking and eating together: Christopher Marlowe, Thomas Watson, Thomas Lodge, George Peele, Thomas Nashe, and Robert Greene. Other playwrights might have been there as well—Thomas Kyd, for example, or John Lyly, but Lyly, born in 1554, was substantially older than the rest, and Kyd, though he subsequently shared a room with Marlowe, seems to have been held at a distance by the group as a whole. For despite his success as a playwright, Kyd made enough to live on by plodding away as a mere scrivener, a professional penman who copied out texts, and the most stylish writers held such humble occupations in disdain. The group shared a combination of extreme marginality and arrogant snobbishness.

For Marlowe, at least, the marginality of the playhouse may have been part of the pleasure. He led a notoriously risk-taking life. But he had only an extreme case of a restless, risk-taking streak present in many of those who responded to the lure of the theater. One of Marlowe's closest friends, London-born Thomas Watson, had studied at Oxford but left without a degree, at the age of thirteen or fourteen, to travel and study on the Continent, learning, as he put it, "to utter words of diverse sound." He returned to London ostensibly to study law, though he also seems to have been engaged in duplicitous, high-stakes games, somewhere between espionage and extortion. At the same time he threw himself into the literary scene, where he quickly emerged as one of its most learned figures, publishing by the time he was twenty-four years old a Latin translation of Sophocles' *Antigone*, composing original Latin poetry, translating Petrarch and Tasso into Latin hexameters, and experimenting in English for the first time since Wyatt and Surrey with the fashionable Continental form, the sonnet.

Somehow in this hectic life Watson also found time to write plays in

English for the popular stage. Surveying the theater in the late 1590s, Francis Meres ranked Watson with Peele, Marlowe, and Shakespeare as "the best for tragedy"; more sourly, an antagonist, accusing him of fraud, declared that he "could devise twenty fictions and knaveries in a play which was his daily practice and his living." None of these plays survives, and Watson is now best known as the friend who intervened in a street brawl between Marlowe and an innkeeper's son named William Bradley. The brawl, on Hog Lane, near the Theater and the Curtain, ended with Watson's sword stuck six inches into Bradley's chest. Watson and Marlowe were both arrested on suspicion of murder but were eventually released, on grounds of self-defense.

Watson's disturbing combination of impressive learning, literary ambition, duplicity, violence, and rootlessness is a clue to understanding his deep kinship—his blood brotherhood—with Marlowe. It serves as well as an introduction to the group of writers, the so-called university wits, whom the young Shakespeare would have encountered at the outset of his career. Not all of them were quite as sinister as Marlowe and Watson. Thomas Lodge, about six years older than Shakespeare, graduated from Oxford and began to study law. The second son of London's lord mayor, Lodge had a course of respectable prosperity laid out for him, his dying mother having left a bequest to support his studies and to launch him in his legal career. But the prospect of this career evidently disagreed with him, for he forfeited this bequest and his father's goodwill by dropping out and plunging into the literary scene. At about the time Shakespeare was writing or collaborating on the *Henry VI* trilogy, Lodge penned his own play about a country destroyed by factional conflict, *The Wounds of Civil War*, performed by the Lord Admiral's Men. Neither this nor the other plays in which Lodge had a hand showed much talent, and he seems in any case not to have staked all his hopes on a career as a playwright, for in 1588 he embarked on an adventurous voyage to the Canary Islands. He returned with a new literary composition to show for himself, a fine prose romance he titled *Rosalind*: "the fruits of his labors," he wrote of himself, "that he wrought in the ocean when every line was wet with a surge." Like Marlowe and Watson, then, Lodge was a bold risk-taker—in 1591 he sailed with Thomas Cavendish to Brazil and the Straits of

Magellan and returned to tell the tale. But he was a less turbulent spirit: it would have been easier to have a drink with him without fearing for your purse or your life.

Another member of the circle of writers, George Peele, the son of a London salt merchant and accountant, had already as a student at Oxford begun to earn a reputation for wild pranks and riotous living—a book was published chronicling his supposed adventures—but he was also early noted for his gifts as a poet and a translator of Euripides. He seems to have been a sometime actor as well as an energetic writer of lyric poems, pastorals, pageants, and plays for the popular stage. At the time Shakespeare would have first met him, Peele had published verses in praise of his friend Thomas Watson, scripted the lord mayor's pageant, and had a play, *The Arraignment of Paris*, successfully presented to the queen. He was probably at work on *The Battle of Alcazar*, his own response to the immense popularity of Marlowe's *Tamburlaine*. None of this feverish activity brought in much money, and Peele was rapidly running through the dowry brought to him by his wife. But he must have been amusing company: his friend Thomas Nashe called him "the chief supporter of pleasance now living."

Nashe was not normally one to give compliments. Of the university wits, he was the most bitingly satiric, and in the late 1580s, newly arrived in London, he was demonstrating his gift for mockery in a succession of anti-Puritan pamphlets. Three years younger than Shakespeare, the son of the curate of a small Herefordshire parish, Nashe had gone to Cambridge as a "sizar," a scholarship student, and had continued his studies there for a year or more after he took the B.A. degree that enabled him to write "gentleman" by his name. His first publication, an epistle addressed to "the Gentleman Students of both universities," was a harsh review of recent literary efforts—the cruel judgments of a brash young man, leavened with some flattering remarks about his best friends.

Nashe praised Peele, Watson, and a few others for their "deep-witted scholarship," but he had particularly acerbic things to say about upstarts "who (mounted on the stage of arrogance) think to out-brave better pens with the swelling bombast of a bragging blank verse." Nashe's florid style delighted in its own obscurity: "Indeed it may be the engrafted overflow of some kill-cow conceit, that overcloyeth their imagination with a more than drunken resolution, being not extemporal in the invention of any other means to vent their manhood, commits the digestion of their choleric encumbrances to the spacious volubility of a drumming decasyllabon." But through the haze of verbal self-display, the point is sharply clear: certain men with only a grammar school education have had the audacity to write plays in blank verse for the public stage. This type of impudent rustic—a man with little or no Latin, French, or Italian, born to be a servant or small-town lawyer's clerk—busies himself with "the endeavors of Art," imitates the poetic style and favorite meter of his university-trained betters, and thinks he can leap into a new occupation: "if you entreat him fair in a frosty morning, he will afford you whole *Hamlets*, I should say handfuls of tragical speeches." These words were written well before Shakespeare wrote *Hamlet*. Presumably, the specific object of nastiness here was Thomas Kyd, who had no university degree, had served as a lawyer's clerk and a servingman, and had written a play, now lost, about Hamlet. But the general terms of the withering attack also applied perfectly to Shakespeare, as Shakespeare would have understood.

Nashe's epistle was prefixed to a lurid romance, *Menaphon*, penned by the central figure in this circle of writers, Robert Greene. Though he turned out to play an important role in Shakespeare's life, Greene was by no means the most accomplished; Marlowe towered above him, and he would never write anything as good as Nashe's wild picaresque novel, *The Unfortunate Traveler*; Peele's charming play *The Old Wives' Tale*; or even Lodge's elegant Ovidian poem, *Scylla's Metamorphosis*. But Greene was larger than life, a hugely talented, learned, narcissistic, self-dramatizing, self-promoting, shameless, and undisciplined scoundrel. Four years older than Shakespeare, the son of poor parents from Norwich, he managed, like Marlowe and Nashe, to get a scholarship to Cambridge, where he took his M.A. in 1583. He went on to receive another degree from Oxford. With these impressive qualifications and with a marriage to "a gentleman's daughter of good account," Greene seemed set for a prosperous life (he briefly thought he might study medicine), but his desires led him in a different direction. Having squandered his wife's marriage portion, he abandoned her and their small child and headed off to London, uncertain how he would support himself.

Greene, who constantly fictionalized his life, wrote a story of how he was recruited to write for the stage. Since he was an inveterate liar, there is no reason to believe a word of his account, but it must have struck contemporaries as at least plausible, and it served as a kind of literary initiation myth. "Roberto"—for so he calls himself—was sitting by a hedge at the side of the road, complaining about his lot, when he was approached by a man who recognized that he was a gentleman down on his luck. "I suppose you are a scholar," the stranger said, "and pity it is men of learning should live in lack."

Greene then recounted a revelatory moment of social misrecognition. How, he asked the affable stranger, could a scholar possibly be profitably employed? The stranger replied that men of his profession get their whole living by employing scholars.

> "What is your profession?" said Roberto.
> "Truly sir," said he, "I am a player."
> "A player!" quoth Roberto. "I took you rather for a gentleman of great living, for if by outward habit men should be censured [i.e., judged], I tell you, you would be taken for a substantial man."

Here in strikingly pure form is the convincing performance of status, the miming of the "outward habit" of a gentleman, that served to draw Will to the profession of acting. For Greene, however, the performance was a fraud: the actor could pretend to be a substantial man, but in himself he was a thing of nothing.

To succeed in creating his illusion, the actor needed not only expensive costumes but also persuasive words, poetry that he, a mere sham gentleman, could not generate. Hence his need to find a real gentleman like Roberto—educated, cultivated, and in need of cash—whom he could hire. Roberto signs on, in Greene's account, follows the actor to town, and finds himself lodged in "a house of retail," that is, a whorehouse. He is no longer in danger of starving—"Roberto now famozed [sic] for an Arch-playmaking poet, his purse like the sea sometime swelled, anon the like the same sea fell to a low ebb; yet seldom he wanted, his labors were so well esteemed"—but he has prostituted his learning and his talent; his ordinary companions become cardsharps, forgers, and pickpockets; his bones are ravaged by syphilis; and his belly is so puffed up by "immeasurable drinking" that he becomes "the perfect image of the dropsy." He experiences brief bursts of repentance, accompanied by noisy resolutions to change his life, but the resolutions give way at the slightest provocation to renewed dissipation. When the "gentlewoman his wife" begs him to return to her, he ridicules her. With his mistress and their bastard son, he moves from place to place, cheating the innkeepers, running up unpaid tavern scores, eluding his creditors. "So cunning he was in all crafts, as nothing rested in him almost but craftiness."

Such was Greene's self-portrait—"Hereafter suppose me the said Roberto," he wrote halfway through his account, throwing away the thin fictional mask—and for such a notorious liar, it seems surprisingly accurate. He was famous for a life that combined drunken idleness and gluttony with energetic bursts of writing, famous too for his impecuniousness, his duplicity, his intimate knowledge of the underworld, his fleeting attempts at moral reform, and his inevitable backsliding. Back in Norwich once, he wrote, he heard a sermon that moved him to a firm resolution to amend his life, but his profligate friends all laughed at him, and his resolution collapsed. His mistress, Em Ball—with whom he had a short-lived son whom he named Fortunatus—was the sister of the leader of a gang of thieves, one Cutting Ball, who was eventually hanged at Tyburn. Aided no doubt by this accomplished native informant, Greene, setting himself up as a kind of ethnographer, made money turning out pamphlets introducing respectable English readers to London's dense society of cheats, swindlers, and pickpockets: "cozeners," "nips," "foists," "crossbiters," "shifters." Despite his university degrees and his snobbery, he himself had the morals and the manners of a thief: he was particularly proud of the fact that he had sold the same play, *Orlando Furioso*, to two different companies of players, the Queen's Men and the Admiral's Men. His friend Nashe called him "the Monarch of Crossbiters and the very Emperor of shifters." Evidently, Greene regarded actors—by whom he saw himself and other gentleman poets exploited—as particularly appropriate targets for his chicanery. Where the actor's dream was to pass himself off as a gentleman, Greene's dream, realized with perfect success, was to transform himself into a cynical, swaggering London bully.

"Who in London hath not heard of his dissolute and licentious living?" asked one of Greene's bitter enemies, the Cambridge pedagogue Gabriel Harvey. This is a master of arts, Harvey wrote, an educated man, who has chosen to deck himself out "with ruffianly hair, unseemly apparel, and more unseemly company." He has become notorious for his vainglorious boasting, his vulgar clowning, and his trashy imitating of every new fashion. But it is important not to underestimate him: he is sly enough to cheat professional gamesters at their own dirty tricks. An oath breaker and a foulmouthed blasphemer, Greene is a man with no moral compass, and his life is a shambles. Harvey rehearsed as many of the scabrous details as he could muster: Greene's monstrous overeating, his constant shifting of his lodgings, his feasting his friends and then skipping out before paying the bill, his abandonment of his virtuous wife, his pawning of his sword and cloak, his prostitute-mistress and their bastard son Infortunatus, his employment of the mistress's thuggish brother-in-law as a bodyguard, the brother-in-law's execution, his insolence to his superiors, and, when money is short, "his impudent pamphleting, phantastical interluding, and desperate libeling." "Phantastical interluding," Harvey's term for Greene's playwriting, is linked to yet another item in the litany of scandals: "his infamous resorting to the Bankside, Shoreditch, Southwark, and other filthy haunts." Greene could always be found in his true element: the neighborhood of the theaters.

This was the neighborhood to which Shakespeare came in the late 1580s, and this was the figure at the center of the group of playwrights, all in their twenties or very early thirties, whom he encountered. Shakespeare would have had no difficulty recognizing that Marlowe was the great talent, but it was the flamboyant Greene, with his two M.A. degrees, sharp peak of red hair, enormous appetites, and volcanic energy, who was the most striking figure in the fraternity of restless, hungry writers.

Shakespeare's relations to Greene and company might at first have been cordial. The newcomer clearly found much to interest, even fascinate, him in this grotesque figure and his remarkable friends; indeed, he might have sensed immediately what would turn out in fact to be the case: these were people with whom he could get his start as a writer and whom he would remember and imaginatively exploit for the rest of his life. The electrifying effect of *Tamburlaine* upon him was only one facet of this fascination. Shakespeare studied Watson's sonnets and Lodge's *Scylla's Metamorphosis* (whose stanza he borrowed for *Venus and Adonis*); he probably collaborated with Peele in the bloody revenge tragedy *Titus Andronicus*; he repeatedly mined Nashe's satiric wit and probably used him as the model for Mote in *Love's Labour's Lost;* at the height of his powers he took Lodge's prose romance *Rosalind* and turned it into *As You Like It*; and near the end of his career, when he wanted to stage an old-fashioned piece, a "winter's tale," he dramatized Greene's by-now-forgotten story of irrational jealousy, *Pandosto.* In Shakespeare's work there are relatively few signs of the influence of Spenser, Donne, Bacon, or Ralegh, to name a few of his great contemporaries; the living writers who meant the most to him were those he encountered in the seedy inns near the theaters soon after he arrived in London.

For their part, the group of reckless young writers and their leader, Greene, may initially have found Shakespeare an agreeable fellow. He was, by all accounts, pleasant company, affable and witty; and his writing, even at that very early point, doubtless showed that he had real talent. It is possible that he had initially been hired to assist Nashe or Peele in the writing of a play about Henry VI and then displayed his mettle. Alternatively, he undertook to write the history play on his own. In either case, his surprising success as a playwright commanded respect. Not only did Nashe acknowledge in print that something extraordinary had happened—thousands of people wept for the death of an English hero who had been dead for two hundred years—but Marlowe offered the still more impressive tribute of imitation: he sat down to write his own English history play, chronicling the tragic life and death of a king, Edward II, brought down by his consuming love for his handsome favorite. Several of the others also began to mine the chronicles and scribble English history plays, though only Marlowe came close to what Shakespeare had achieved. There are, in any case, enough signs of serious attention to Shakespeare's early work to suggest that the group of writers may at first have actively wanted to cultivate his acquaintance.

The group would probably have been sorely disappointed. First and foremost, of course, Shakespeare lacked the principal qualification of belonging to their charmed circle; he had not attended either Oxford or Cambridge. The little society of writers was, by Tudor standards, quite democratic. Birth and wealth did not greatly matter: Nashe, whose family, as he put it, boasted "longer pedigrees than patrimonies" rubbed shoulders with Marlowe, the cobbler's son; Lodge, the son of the former lord mayor of London, drank with Greene, whose parents in Norwich lived sober, modest lives at a far remove from the glittering guildhall. What mattered was attendance at one or the other of the universities. Even the acerbic Nashe found warm words for his Cambridge college, St. John's, writing years later that he "loved it still, for it ever was and is the sweetest nurse of knowledge in all that university." And long after he had left the university, Greene signed one of his dedicatory epistles "From my Study in Clare Hall."

University education carried a significant social cachet, which these writers were only too happy to vaunt. But, to be fair, it was valued as well for the learning that it signified. Nashe pored over Aretino and Rabelais and gleefully coined words out of Greek, Latin, Spanish, and Italian. Peele joined Nashe in ridiculing an inept hexameter written by Gabriel Harvey. Watson's youthful translation of *Antigone* ended with allegorical exercises in different kinds of Latin verse: iambics, sapphics, anapestic dimeters, and choriambic asclepiadean meter. Shakespeare was by no means without learning—*The Comedy of Errors*, written early in his career, shows how elegantly and lightly he carried his knowledge of Latin comedy—but he was neither capable of nor interested in Watson's type of academic self-display.

Moreover, Shakespeare was by origin a provincial, and, more to the point, he had not completely left the provinces behind. If he had turned away from his father's occupation and left his parents, he had not, like Lodge, incurred a parental curse; if he had left his wife and three small children, he had not, like Greene, burned his bridges. He had none of the dark glamour of the prodigal son. Indeed, even his imagination remained bound up with the local details of country living. And if the young bohemian writers recognized with surprise that the man they deemed a country bumpkin had thought hard about many things; if they grasped that his imagination was far less constrained by convention than theirs; if they were startled by the quickness of his intellect, the breadth of his vocabulary, and his astonishing power to absorb everything he encountered and make it his own, perhaps they also were nettled by something morally conservative in him. The conservatism was already visible in the *Henvy VI* trilogy, with its reaffirmation of the traditional cautionary precepts that Marlowe in *Tamburlaine* had boldly called into question. But it was visible as well in Shakespeare's refusal to throw himself fully into a chaotic, disorderly life. Aubrey did not specify what particular social situation he was referring to when he wrote that Shakespeare "wouldn't be debauched," but a strong candidate would be any invitation from Robert Greene.

Shakespeare may have sensed a snobbish assumption of superiority on the part of the university wits; it would be surprising if they did not look down upon him and surprising if he did not perceive it. He did not contribute commendatory verses to any of the books that they published in the late 1580s and early '90s. No doubt he was not asked to do so. He, in turn, did not likely solicit for himself any commendations of the kind they routinely wrote for one another. None in any case appeared. He did not enter into their literary controversies, just as he seems to have been kept—or kept himself—outside their raucous social circle. This is, after all, a man who soon went on to manage the affairs of his playing company, to write steadily (not to mention brilliantly) for more than two decades, to accumulate and keep a great deal of money, to stay out of prison and to avoid ruinous lawsuits, to invest in agricultural land and in London property, to purchase one of the finest houses in the town where he was born, and to retire to that town in his late forties. This pattern of behavior did not suddenly and belatedly emerge; it established itself early, probably quite soon after the turbulent, confused, painful years that led up to his escape from Stratford and his arrival in London.

Shakespeare looked around at the gentleman poets who were supplying the playing companies with plays. He took in what was exciting about their writing. He made their acquaintance and savored what was startling or amusing about their reckless lives. In the light of his subsequent career, it is possible to imagine his response more fully. He saw that they were proud of their university degrees, their fine Latin and Greek, their scoffing and mockery and carelessness. He saw that they drank for days and nights at a time and then, still half-drunk, threw something together for the printer or the players. He grasped, in all likelihood, that no matter what he wrote, he would remain in their eyes a player, not a poet. Though they may occasionally have exhibited signs of nervousness about the young man from Stratford—they were impressed and troubled, after all, by the success of the *Henry VI* plays—they probably thought that he was rather naive and guileless and that they could easily take advantage of him. Greene in particular, making everyone laugh with his zany stories of coney catching, was confident, in all likelihood, that Shakespeare was a coney to be caught.

One part of this at least is indubitably true: Shakespeare wrote for the theater not as a poet, in the sense that Greene and company understood themselves, but as a player. He was not alone in writing for the stage on which he also performed, but he was the one who was best at it, and the players were quick to recognize how valuable he was. He must also have seemed exceptionally canny and trustworthy about money—the very opposite of the university wits—for a treasury document that mentions him in December 1594, in the company of Burbage and Kempe, suggests that he was already one of those fiscally responsible for the troupe. He knew how to put money in his purse and to keep it there.

Greene's purse, by contrast, was evidently empty when, in August 1592, he fell ill after a dinner, at which Nashe was present, of pickled herring and Rhenish wine. Abandoned by all of his friends, he would have died like a homeless beggar had a poor shoemaker named Isam and his kindly wife not taken him in and cared for him through his final days. Digging for dirt, Greene's inveterate enemy, Gabriel Harvey, went in person to talk with Mrs. Isam. Much of the scene Harvey depicts—the shameless scoundrel, "attended by lice" and begging for a "penny-pot of malmsey," seized by the grip of a terrible fear—may be discounted as the expression of bilious hatred, but some of the melancholy details ring true. The woman told me, Harvey writes, how the dying man "was fain, poor soul, to borrow her husband's shirt, whiles his own was a-washing: and how his doublet and hose and sword were sold for three shillings: and beside the charges of his winding sheet, which was four shillings; and the charges of his burial yesterday, in the New-churchyard near Bedlam, which was six shillings, and four pence, how deeply he was indebted to her poor husband, as appeared by his own bond of ten pounds, which the good woman kindly showed me." She showed him as well a letter Greene left for the wife he had abandoned: "Doll, I charge thee by the love of our youth, and by my soul's rest, that thou wilt see this man paid: for if he and his wife had not succored me, I had died in the streets."

Greene had another dying wish. He asked Mrs. Isam to place "a garland of bayes"—a laurel wreath—on his head: he would go to the grave a poet laureate, even if he had to be crowned by a shoemaker's wife. Harvey takes a predictably sour view of this leave-taking —"vermin to vermin must repair at last"—but he also provides a fuller epitaph:

> Lo, a wild head, full of mad brain and a thousand crotchets: A Scholar, a Discourser, a Courtier, a Ruffian, a Gamester, a Lover, a Soldier, a Traveler, a Merchant, a Broker, an Artificer, a Botcher, a Pettifogger, a Player, a Cozener, a Railer, a Beggar, an Omnigatherum [i.e., miscellaneous assemblage], a Gay Nothing: a Storehouse of bald and baggage stuff, unworth the answering or reading: a trivial and triobular [i.e., worthless] Author for knaves and fools: an Image of Idleness; an Epitome of Fantasticality; a Mirror of Vanity.

Though this catalog suggests a remarkably full life of vice, and though Greene himself often adopted the melancholy voice of an old man looking back upon his prodigal youth, at his death he was only thirty-two years old.

The others in the group quickly followed their leader to the grave. In the same month, September 1592, Thomas Watson, aged about thirty-five, was buried, cause of death unknown—or perhaps in that terrible year of plague, it was not necessary to specify it. Two volumes of his poems were printed posthumously—his friends had no doubt read them already in manuscript—and his name remained for some time in circulation for a less honorable reason: he was invoked in the courts as a scoundrel in two particularly nasty swindles. The following May, Watson's friend Marlowe, who had not yet reached his thirtieth birthday, was killed in a tavern fight, allegedly over the "reckoning," that is, the bill.

George Peele, the great reveler, published a moving verse tribute to his dead friends Watson and Marlowe. Then a few years later, probably in 1596, Peele too was gone. Not quite forty years old, he died, it was said, of a "loathsome disease," possibly syphilis. And in 1601, at thirty-three, the youngest of the original group, Thomas Nashe, died, leaving his grieving father, the minister, to bury him in the country churchyard.

Of the six young university-trained playwrights whom Shakespeare encountered in the late 1580s, only one, Thomas Lodge, managed to survive his thirties and to live what the age would have considered a long life. But not a literary life: abandoning poetry and fiction, Lodge took a degree in medicine and became one of the leading physicians of his day. He died in 1625, at the ripe age of sixty-seven.

After 1593, with Greene, Watson, and Marlowe all dead, Shakespeare, not yet thirty years old, had no serious rivals. He followed up on his major success with the *Henry VI* plays by writing the brilliant *Richard III*. He had experimented, crudely but energetically, with tragedy in the bloody *Titus Andronicus*, and had demonstrated his great strengths as a comic playwright, with *The Two Gentlemen of Verona*, *The Taming of the Shrew*, and *The Comedy of Errors*. He had triumphed. But there was a bitter aftertaste. Greene kept scribbling, or so it was said, even on his deathbed. The claim is not implausible: he was the kind of writer who turned his entire existence into a lurid penny pamphlet. He had left behind him enough material to enable a hack printer and sometime playwright, Henry Chettle, to bring out a posthumous book. *Greene's Groatsworth of Wit, Bought with a Million of Repentance*, rushed into print before the corpse was fully cold, was probably mostly written by Chettle or by someone collaborating with Chettle—perhaps, as some rumors had it, Nashe. But it carried the marks of Greene's own seething resentments. He noisily berated himself. He dangerously accused Marlowe—"thou famous gracer of Tragedians"—of atheism. And then he turned his anger on Shakespeare.

Rehearsing the old rivalry between poets and players, Greene warned his gentlemen friends Marlowe, Nashe, and Peele not to trust those "puppets," the actors, that "speak from our mouths." Actors were mere burrs that cleave to the garments of writers. They would be virtually invisible were they not "garnished in our colors," and yet the ingrates have forsaken him, in his hour of need. Thus far Greene's words might apply to actors like Burbage or Alleyn, but they could hardly fit a player who had also proved himself a successful playwright. To make them fit, Greene (or his ghostwriter) famously shifted ground: "Yes trust them not: for there is an upstart Crow, beautified with our feathers, that with his *Tiger's heart wrapped in a Player's hide*, supposes he is as well able to bombast out a blank verse as the best of you: and being an absolute *Johannes Factotum*, is in his own conceit the only Shakescene in a country." "O tiger's heart wrapped in a woman's hide!" York cries in the third part of *Henry VI*, to describe the ghastly, ruthless woman who waves in his face a handkerchief that she has steeped in the blood of his murdered child.

When he read the line twisted to describe him, Shakespeare might have thought that Greene was accusing him of ruthlessness. Alternatively, he was being charged with poetic excess, the bombastic exaggeration of the style of his betters. The insult is ambiguous, but it would have been clear to Shakespeare that there was an issue of status: an "upstart" is someone who pushes himself in where he does not belong, who dresses himself up as a nightingale though he caws like a crow, who imagines that he is a Johannes Factotum— a "Johnny-do-everything"—when in fact he is merely a second-rate drudge, a "rude groom," who thinks he is an accomplished poet when he is only an "ape" imitating the inventions of others.

These were painful words, particularly in the mouth—as they were said to be—of a dying man; they had something of the finality of a curse, in a world that took such curses with deadly seriousness. And *Greene's Groatsworth* ended with a coda, a retelling of Aesop's fable of the grasshopper and the ant, in which at least one modern interpreter, Ernst Honigmann, detects a further insult. Greene was, of course, himself the wanton grasshopper, carelessly skipping through the meadows in pursuit of pleasure. If Honigmann is right, the miserly ant, a "waspish little worm" who refused to help his "foodless, helpless, and strengthless" acquaintance, was Shakespeare. Greene, in this account, must have asked Shakespeare—who may at this point have already been handling some of the players' finances—for assistance and been refused. The refusal would help to explain the bitterness of the satiric portrait: upstart crow, rude groom, ape, worm.

How Shakespeare responded to the attack tells us a great deal about him. He did not directly answer the charges or, like Harvey, launch a polemical counteroffensive. But he must have quietly done something unusually effective. For, less than three months after publication of the pamphlet, Henry Chettle flatly denied in print having any hand in it: it "was all Greene's." As for himself, Chettle averred, it is well known that he always "in printing hindered the bitter inveighing against scholars." "Scholars"—so Shakespeare was now being treated as if he had, after all, attended university.

There was more: he was not, Chettle wrote, personally acquainted with either of the two playwrights who took offense at Greene's attack, "and with one of them I care not if I never be." This playwright, unnamed, was unquestionably Marlowe, who in December 1592 was evidently not a person whom the hack, his ear to the ground, thought it safe to know. But the other was a different matter. Chettle now understood, as he explained in a twisted and unctuous apology, that he should have blocked the printing of Greene's unwarranted remarks about this second playwright: "That I did not, I am as sorry as if the original fault had been my fault, because myself have seen his demeanor no less civil than he excellent in the quality he professes." This offended figure was also unnamed, but the likeliest candidate is the "upstart Crow." At some point in the past three months, then, Chettle had a "civil" conversation with Shakespeare, or at the very least he had the occasion to observe him in person. He had also, it seems, suddenly acquainted himself with Shakespeare's excellence "in the quality he professes"—an oily periphrasis for writing and acting in plays. And then comes a further motive for this recantation: "Besides, diverse of worship have reported his uprightness of dealing, which argues his honesty, and his facetious grace in writing, that approves his art." "Diverse of worship," that is, socially prominent people, people who have it in their power to make my life miserable, have spoken to me both about the honorableness of Shakespeare's character and about the "facetious grace," the facility and polish, of his writing.

From Shakespeare himself, not a word about Chettle, in the immediate wake of Greene's attack or subsequently, but he got an apology of the kind that poor, impotently sputtering Gabriel Harvey could only dream. Indeed, in the years that followed, relations between Shakespeare and Chettle may well have been cordial. They collaborated, with several other playwrights, on a play, apparently never performed, about Sir Thomas More.

The account was almost settled, but not quite. Greene's phrase "beautified with our feathers" must have stung. For in 1601, when the *Groatsworth of Wit* and the fat scoundrel who penned it had long vanished from view, Shakespeare allowed himself an unusual self-indulgence. Polonius—whose literary pretensions go back to the time when he was "accounted a good actor" "i'th' university" (*Hamlet*, 3.2.91, 90) where, as he tells us, he played Julius Caesar—has put his hands on one of the love letters that Hamlet has sent to his daughter. "Now gather and surmise," he says to Claudius and Gertrude, starting to read: "'To the celestial and my soul's idol, the most beautified Ophelia.'" Then abruptly the old councillor comes to a halt for a piece of literary criticism: "that's an ill phrase, a vile phrase, 'beautified' is a vile phrase" (2.2.109–12).

"Thus," as the clown Feste says in *Twelfth Night*, "the whirligig of time brings in his revenges" (5.1.364). Shakespeare's plays from the 1590s are sprinkled with sly parodies of the words of his erstwhile rivals. Falstaff's overheated sexual excitement in *The Merry Wives of Windsor*— "Let the sky rain potatoes, let it thunder to the tune of 'Greensleeves,' hail kissing-comfits, and snow eringoes" (5.5.16–18)—ridicules Lodge's *Wit's Misery and the World's Madness*. The Moorish king's plaintive words to his starving mother in Peele's *Battle of Alcazar*—"Hold thee, Calipolis. . . . Feed and be fat that we may meet the foe"—returns as a piece of tavern swaggering in *2 Henry IV*: "Then feed and be fat, my fair Calipolis" (2.4.155). And a moment earlier the same drunken swaggerer, Ensign

Pistol, has taken Tamburlaine's famously sadistic taunting of the kings he has yoked to his chariot—"Holla, ye pampered jades of Asia! / What, can ye draw but twenty miles a day?"—and turned it into fustian nonsense:

> Shall pack-horses
> And hollow pampered jades of Asia,
> Which cannot go but thirty mile a day,
> Compare with Caesars and with cannibals,
> And Trojan Greeks?
>
> (2.4.140–44)

There is much more in the same vein, and if all the plays by the university wits had survived, scholars would no doubt have identified still other instances.

These parodies only suggest that Shakespeare was, after all, a human being, who could take some pleasure in returning literary insults and mocking rivals, even dead ones. But something far more remarkable and unpredictable happened in his work with the grotesque figure of Robert Greene. "Thou whoreson little tidy Bartholomew boar-pig," Falstaff's whore, Doll Tearsheet, pouts endearingly, "when wilt thou leave fighting o'days, and foining o'nights, and begin to patch up thine old body for heaven?" To which the fat knight replies, "Peace, good Doll, do not speak like a death's-head, do not bid me remember mine end" (*2 Henry IV*, 2.4.206–10). The deeper we plunge into the tavern world of Falstaff—gross, drunken, irresponsible, self-dramatizing, and astonishingly witty Falstaff—the closer we come to the world of Greene; his wife, Doll; his mistress, Em; her thuggish brother, Cutting Ball; and the whole crew.

Falstaff and his friends have the raffish appeal that the wild crowd of London writers must have exercised on the young Shakespeare. In Falstaff's seedy haunts in Eastcheap, not far from London Bridge, Prince Hal gains access to an urban cast of characters far removed from anything he has known before, and he takes particular delight in having learned their language: "They call drinking deep 'dyeing scarlet,' and when you breathe in your watering they cry 'Hem!' and bid you 'Play it off!' To conclude, I am so good a proficient in one quarter of an hour that I can drink with any tinker in his own language during my life" (*1 Henry IV*, 2.5.13–17). There is, the play suggests, a politics to this language lesson—"when I am King of England I shall command all the good lads in Eastcheap"—but at the same time it seems a thinly disguised depiction of Shakespeare's own linguistic apprenticeship in taverns.

So too the relationship between Falstaff and Hal centers on fantastically inventive, aggressive language games of the kind that several of the university wits specialized in:

> PRINCE HARRY: . . . This sanguine coward, this bed-presser, this horse-back-breaker, this huge hill of flesh—
>
> FALSTAFF: 'Sblood, you starveling, you elf-skin, you dried neat's tongue, you bull's pizzle, you stock-fish—O, for breath to utter what is like thee!—you tailor's yard, you sheath, you bow-case, you vile standing tuck—
>
> (*1 Henry IV*, 2.5.223–29)

This is precisely the trading of comic insults, the public flyting, the madcap linguistic excess for which Greene and Nashe in particular were famous. Perhaps Shakespeare had participated in the games; in any case, he had absorbed the lesson and could outdo their best efforts.

Above all, the prince and his grotesque friend—"that trunk of humours, that bolting-hutch of beastliness, that swollen parcel of dropsies, that huge bombard of sack, that stuffed cloak-bag of guts, that roasted Manningtree ox with the pudding in his belly" (2.5.409–13)— spend their time inventing and playing theatrical games, acting out scenes, and parodying styles of playwriting that had gone out of fashion. The theatrical games make visible other dark thoughts as well: kingship is a theatrical performance by a gifted scoundrel; Hal's father, King Henry IV, has no more legitimacy than Falstaff; Falstaff has taken the place of Hal's father, but the position is precarious; Falstaff, fearing that he will be turned away by Hal, is willing to betray his friends; Hal is planning to throw them all off. "No, my good lord," pleads Falstaff, ostensibly in the role of the prince speaking to his father,

banish Peto, banish Bardolph, banish Poins, but for sweet Jack
Falstaff, kind Jack Falstaff, true Jack Falstaff, valiant Jack Fal-
staff, and therefore more valiant being, as he is, old Jack Falstaff,
Banish not him thy Harry's company,
Banish not him thy Harry's company.
Banish plump Jack, and banish all the world.

(2.5.431–38)

To which Hal, ostensibly in the role of his father, quietly, chillingly
replies, "I do; I will."

While probing the relationships at the center of the plays, the brilliant scenes of improvisatory playacting also probe deeply Shakespeare's
relationship with Greene and company. Or rather, they provide a glimpse
of how Shakespeare looked back upon that relationship years later, when
most of the doomed lot were dead and his own position as England's
reigning playwright was secure. "I know you all," Shakespeare has Hal say
early in *1 Henry IV*, after a scene of jesting and genial wit,

> and will a while uphold
> The unyoked humour of your idleness.
> Yet herein will I imitate the sun,
> Who doth permit the base contagious clouds
> To smother up his beauty from the world,
> That when he please again to be himself,
> Being wanted he may be more wondered at
> By breaking through the foul and ugly mists
> Of vapours that did seem to strangle him.

(1.2.173–81)

To recognize this proximity between Greene and Falstaff is not only
to see how "foul and ugly" were the origins of Shakespeare's golden, capacious, and endlessly fascinating character. To be sure, Greene was tawdry
enough—a drunk, a cheat, and a liar whose actual horizons were pathetically narrow compared to his grandiose projections. That tawdriness is
precisely one of Falstaff's characteristics, quite literally itemized in the

"tavern reckonings, memorandums of bawdy-houses, and one poor pen-nyworth of sugar-candy to make thee long-winded" that Hal finds when he searches his pockets (3.3.146–48). It takes no great detective work on Hal's part to discover how empty Falstaff's claims are—only a fool would take him at his word, and clear-eyed Hal is anything but a fool. It also takes no special gift to see how nasty and common were the actual cir-cumstances of Robert Greene's life. The more demanding and interesting task is to savor the power of the illusions without simply submitting to the cheating and the lies. What Falstaff helps to reveal is that for Shake-speare, Greene was a sleazy parasite, but he was also a grotesque titan, a real-life version of the drunken Silenus in Greek mythology or of Rabelais' irrepressible trickster, Panurge.

Shakespeare seized upon the central paradox of Greene's life—that this graduate of Oxford and Cambridge hung out in low taverns in the company of ruffians—and turned it into Falstaff's supremely ambiguous social position, the knight who is intimate with both the Prince of Wales and a pack of thieves. Falstaff captured Greene's bingeing and whoring, his "dropsical" belly, his prodigal wasting of his impressive talents, his cynical exploitation of friends, his brazenness, his seedy charm. He cap-tured too the noisy, short-lived fits of repentance for which Greene was famous, along with the solemn moralizing that swerved effortlessly into irreverent laughter. "Before I knew thee, Hal, I knew nothing," Falstaff says, adopting the role of the corrupted innocent: "and now am I, if a man should speak truly, little better than one of the wicked. I must give over this life, and I will give it over. By the Lord, an I do not, I am a villain. I'll be damned for never a king's son in Christendom." To which Hal—like the friends who mocked Greene out of his pious resolutions—replies with a simple question: "Where shall we take a purse tomorrow, Jack?" "Zounds, where thou wilt, lad! I'll make one; an I do not, call me villain" (1.2.82–89). So much for moral reform.

Falstaff was not a straightforward portrait of Robert Greene (who was neither a knight nor an old man), any more than the whore Doll Tearsheet was a faithful portrait of the virtuous country wife named Doll whom Greene abandoned or the tavern hostess Mistress Quickly was a portrait of the Mistress Isam from whom he borrowed money and who nursed him through his final illness. Here as elsewhere, Shakespeare's actual world gets into his work, but most often in a distorted, inverted, disguised, or reimagined form. The point is not to strip away the reimaginings, as if the life sources were somehow more interesting than the metamorphoses, but rather to enhance a sense of the wonder of Shakespeare's creation— the immensely bold, generous imaginative work that took elements from the wasted life of Robert Greene and used them to fashion the greatest comic character in English literature.

Greene was by no means the sole source. Like many of Shakespeare's most memorable creations, Falstaff is made out of multiple materials, much of it not from life but from literature. Shakespeare understood his world in the ways that we understand our world—his experiences, like ours, were mediated by whatever stories and images were available to him. When he was in a tavern and encountered a loudmouthed soldier who bragged about his daring adventures, Shakespeare saw that soldier through the lens of characters he had read in fiction, and at that same time he adjusted his image of those fictional characters by means of the actual person standing before him.

In inventing Falstaff, Shakespeare started, as he so often did, from a character in a play by someone else, *The Famous Victories of Henry the Fifth,* which had been performed by the Queen's Men in London and on tour. This crude anonymous play, which chronicled the near-miraculous transformation of Prince Hal from wastrel youth to heroic king, included a dissolute knight, Sir John Oldcastle, as part of the crew of thieves and ruffians in which Hal had become enmeshed. Shakespeare took over this figure (he originally used the same name, only changing it to Falstaff after the descendants of Oldcastle objected) and built upon its spare frame his vast creation. He took the stock figure of the braggart soldier, the blowhard who is always going on about his martial accomplishments but who plays dead when danger comes too close, and combined him with another venerable comic type, the parasite, always hungry and thirsty and always conniving to get his wealthy patron to pick up the tab. To these he added features of the Vice in the morality play—shameless irreverence, the exuberant pursuit of pleasures, and a seductive ability to draw naive youth away from the austere paths of virtue. And he conjoined with these some elements of a newer cultural stereotype, the hypocritical Puritan who noisily trumpets his commitment to virtue while secretly indulging his every sensual vice. But to contemplate these pieces of literary flotsam and jetsam is already to see how complete and unexpected was Shakespeare's transformation of them.

He himself must have been surprised by what began to emerge when he sat down to write *Henry IV*. What would have been predictable, what he may initially have intended, was some version of the lively but largely conventional figure whom in fact he created some years later in *All's Well That Ends Well*. That character, Paroles, has all the appropriately obnoxious traits of the loudmouthed, bragging corrupter of the young, and the audience is invited to delight in his discomfiture. But even here, when his imagination was not operating at the very pinnacle of its power, Shakespeare did something odd, something that casts light back on the infinitely greater Falstaff. Paroles has been utterly humiliated, exposed and disgraced before his friends and fellow officers so devastatingly that the suicide proposed to him is the only honorable course of action. But he is anything but honorable, and, rejecting any thought of putting an end to himself, he takes his leave. "Captain I'll be no more," Paroles ruefully acknowledges, and then his mood shifts:

> But I will eat and drink and sleep as soft
> As captain shall. Simply the thing I am
> Shall make me live.
>
> (4.3.308–11)

This is the life force itself.

This life force is at work to an unparalleled degree in Falstaff. In him too it burns brightest when everything that goes by the word "honor"— name, reputation, dignity, vocation, trustworthiness, truthfulness—is stripped away. "Can honour set-to a leg?" Falstaff asks, at the brink of battle.

No. Or an arm? No. Or take away the grief of a wound? No. Honour hath not skill in surgery, then? No. What is honour? A word. What is in that word "honour"? What is that "honour"? Air. A trim reckoning! Who hath it? He that died o'Wednesday. Doth he feel it? No. Doth he hear it? No. 'Tis insensible then? Yea, to the dead. But will it not live with the living? No. Why? Detraction will not suffer it. Therefore I'll none of it. (*1 Henry IV*, 5.1.130–38)

A few moments later, standing over the corpse of Sir Walter Blunt (killed fighting bravely for the king), Falstaff sharpens the stark opposition between empty words and the only thing that actually matters, at least to him: "I like not such grinning honour as Sir Walter hath. Give me life" (5.3.57–58).

To a degree unparalleled in Shakespeare's work and perhaps in all of English literature, Falstaff seems actually to possess a mysterious inner principle of vitality, as if he could float free not only of Shakespeare's sources in life and in art but also of the play in which he appears. If a theatrical tradition, first recorded in 1702, is correct, Queen Elizabeth herself not only admired Shakespeare's great comic character but also sensed this inner principle: she commanded the author to write a play showing Falstaff in love. In two weeks' time, or so it is said, *The Merry Wives of Windsor* was written, to be first performed on April 23, 1597, at the annual feast to commemorate the founding of the Order of the Garter. Famous already in Shakespeare's lifetime, constantly alluded to throughout the seventeenth century, and the subject of a distinguished book-length study as early as the eighteenth century, the fat knight has for centuries provoked admirers to attempt to pluck out the heart of his mystery: great wit and the ability to provoke wit in others; spectacular resilience; fierce, subversive intelligence; carnivalesque exuberance. Each of these qualities seems true, and yet there is always something else, something elusive that remains to be accounted for, as if the scoundrel had the power in himself to resist all efforts to explain or contain him.

Shakespeare himself evidently struggled to keep his own creation within bounds. The climax of the second of the great history plays in which Falstaff appears is a scene in which Hal, newly crowned as Henry V, brutally dashes his friend's wild expectations of plunder: "I know thee not, old man" (*2 Henry IV*, 5.5.45). It is the most decisive of repudiations. Falstaff is banished from the royal presence on pain of death, and the king's coldly ironic words to the onetime "tutor and feeder of my riots" conjure up the final, literal containment of all that corpulent energy: "know the grave doth gape / For thee thrice wider than for other men" (5.5.60, 51–2). Yet a moment later Falstaff seems already to be slipping free from this noose—"Go with me to dinner. Come, Lieutenant Pistol; come, Bardolph. I shall be sent for soon at night" (5.5.83–85)—and at the play's close Shakespeare announces that he will bring him back once again. "One word more, I beseech you," says the actor who speaks the epilogue. "If you be not too much cloyed with fat meat, our humble author will continue the story with Sir John in it" (lines 22–24). It is as if Falstaff himself refuses to accept the symbolic structure of the play that has just ended.

Yet when he actually sat down to continue the story, by writing a play about Henry V's great triumph over the French at Agincourt, Shakespeare had second thoughts. Falstaff's cynical, antiheroic stance—his ruthless, comic deflation of the idealizing claims of those in power and his steadfast insistence on the primacy of the flesh—proved impossible to incorporate into a celebration of charismatic leadership and martial heroism. That celebration was not without Shakespeare's characteristic skeptical intelligence, but for the play to succeed—for Hal to be something more than a mock king—skepticism had to stop short of the relentless mockery that in two consecutive plays Falstaff so brilliantly articulated. Hence Shakespeare decided to break his promise to the audience and to keep his comic masterpiece out of *Henry V*. Indeed, he decided to get rid of him permanently by providing a detailed narrative of death: "A parted ev'n just between twelve and one, ev'n at the turning o'th' tide," Mistress Quickly memorably recounts,

for after I saw him fumble with the sheets, and play with flowers, and smile upon his finger's end, I knew there was but one way. For his nose was as sharp as a pen, and a babbled of green fields. "How now, Sir John?" quoth I. "What, man! Be o' good cheer." So a cried out, "God, God, God," three or four times. Now I, to comfort him, bid him a should not think of God; I hoped there was no need to trouble himself with any such thoughts yet. So a bade me lay more clothes on his feet. I put my hand into the bed and felt them, and they were as cold as any stone. Then I felt to his knees, and so up'ard and up'ard, and all was as cold as any stone. (*Henry V*, 2.3.11–23)

The drama here is not the death scene itself, which is carefully kept off-stage; the drama, as Shakespeare and his audience understood, is the spectacle of a great playwright killing off the greatest of his comic characters. Of course, given Falstaff's manner of life, the official cause of death must be overindulgence—the equivalent of Greene's fatal feast of pickled herring and Rhenish wine—but the play makes clear that it has staged a symbolic murder: "The King has killed his heart" (2.1.79).

"An upstart Crow, beautified with our feathers": Greene and his crowd, despite their drunken recklessness and bohemian snobbery, saw something frightening in Shakespeare, a usurper's knack for displaying as his own what he had plucked from others, an alarming ability to plunder, appropriate, and absorb. Shakespeare, for his part, understood that he did not belong with these grasshoppers, and he may, as Greene himself seems to imply, have turned down some request for help from the indigent, desperate scoundrel.

In Prince Hal, the author of the *Henry IV* plays saw himself, projecting onto his character a blend of experimental participation and careful, self-protective distance; recognizing the functional utility of his tavern lessons in language games and in role-playing; and unsentimentally accepting the charge of calculated self-interest. Reflecting on the scene he entered into in the late 1580s, Shakespeare acknowledged what he had had to do in order to survive. But the coldness that he attributed to himself—or rather to Hal—was only one aspect of his relationship with Greene, and perhaps not the most important aspect. For if Shakespeare took what he could from Greene—if, as an artist, he took what he could from everyone he encountered—he also performed a miraculous act of imaginative generosity, utterly unsentimental and, if the truth be told, not entirely human. Human generosity would have involved actually giving money to the desperate Greene; it would have been foolish, quixotic, and easily abused. Shakespeare's generosity was aesthetic, rather than pecuniary. He conferred upon Greene an incalculable gift, the gift of transforming him into Falstaff.

CHAPTER 8

Master-Mistress

THE HACK PRINTER Henry Chettle was not the only one
to be squirming in the wake of the attack on Shakespeare as
an "upstart Crow." There were rumors that Thomas Nashe
also had his hand in the attack, that perhaps he had even
ghostwritten the farewell words of his friend Robert Greene. The rumors
make perfect sense: after all, the Cambridge-educated satirist had earlier
heaped comparable scorn in print on poorly educated players, whom he
described as a "rabble of counterfeits" who rashly attempt to imitate their
betters in the writing of blank verse. Nashe might ordinarily have been
pleased thus to be the object of suspicion: in the business of giving
offense, he cultivated the reputation of a reckless wit. But he too must
have had an unusually alarming conversation with someone, for, though
he was not given to backing away from a squabble, he rushed into print
to disclaim any connection to *Greene's Groatsworth of Wit*, which he
called a "trivial lying pamphlet." Nashe did everything he could to ensure
that his vehement disclaimer would be taken seriously: "God never have
care of my soul, but utterly renounce me, if the least word or syllable in it

proceeded from my pen, or if I were any way privy to the writing or print-ing of it." That seems to be the sound of abject panic.

The question is who put Nashe into such a sweat. The answer is not the upstart Shakespeare himself; it must have been someone much more powerful and intimidating. But who? The likeliest candidate by far is someone connected to Henry Wriothesley, third Earl of Southampton. The nineteen-year-old earl is highly unlikely to have gone himself on such a lowly errand, but, like Duke Orsino in *Twelfth Night*, he had many dependent gentlemen eager to do his bidding and serve as his go-between. (A few years later, Southampton mentioned being accompanied somewhere by "only ten or twelve" of his usual attendants.) One candidate for this particular errand would have been his French and Italian tutor, John Florio. Born in London, the son of Protestant refugees from Italy, Florio had already published several language manuals, along with a compendium of six thousand Italian proverbs; he would go on to produce an important Italian-English dictionary and a vigorous translation, much used by Shakespeare, of Montaigne's *Essays*. Florio became a friend of Ben Jonson, and there is evidence that already in the early 1590s he was a man highly familiar with the theater.

But if Southampton, far too grand to meddle in person with a back-stage squabble, would have sent someone like Florio to do his bidding, how would an earl—at the very pinnacle of the status hierarchy—have come to know Shakespeare in the first place? Here, as usual, the precise link is missing, probably irretrievably, but the social ambiguity of the the-ater would certainly have helped to make a meeting possible. Players belonged to an entirely different social universe from noblemen, but playhouses decidedly did not: while whores, pickpockets, and shabby apprentices crowded into the pit, aristocrats, smoking their pipes or sniff-ing pomanders, sat on cushions in the expensive "lords' rooms" to watch the performances and be watched in turn.

Southampton, described in the early 1590s as "young and fantastical" and easily "carried away," was evidently one of these theater lovers. As a contemporary observer once wrote, the young earl and his friend the Earl of Rutland "pass the time in London merely in going to plays every day."

On one of these occasions, struck by Shakespeare's acting in a play or by his gifts as a writer or by his lively good looks, Southampton could easily have gone backstage after the performance to make his acquaintance, or asked a mutual acquaintance to introduce them, or simply and imperiously summoned him to a rendezvous. The likeliest time for their first encounter would have been in 1591 or early 1592, when the earl, having graduated from Cambridge, was attending upon the queen at court and studying law at Gray's Inn.

Courtiers and law students were among the playhouses' most enthusiastic patrons, but Southampton may have taken special pleasure in imaginative escape at this particular moment in his life: he was under enormous pressure to marry. The stakes were not sentimental; they were financial, and they were huge. When Southampton was a young child, his parents had a spectacular breakup. His father accused his mother of adultery, and in the wake of their bitter separation, his mother was forbidden ever to see her son again. Then, just shy of Southampton's eighth birthday, his father died, and the wealthy young heir became the ward of the most powerful man in England, Elizabeth's lord treasurer, Lord Burghley. The elderly Burghley was reasonably attentive to his ward's upbringing—he took the boy into his house, hired distinguished tutors to educate him, and then sent him off to Cambridge University at the tender age of twelve—but the whole wardship system was rotten to the core. Its most sinister feature was the guardian's legal right to negotiate a marriage for his ward. If, upon turning twenty-one, the ward declined the match, he could be liable for substantial damages, to be paid to the family of the rejected party. As it just so happened, Burghley arranged for Southampton to marry his own granddaughter. As it just so happened too, Burghley held the position of Master of the Wards, which meant that he could virtually dictate the fine that would be assessed should Southampton be rash enough to decline. In the event, the young earl did decline, and when he came of age, he was fined the truly staggering sum of five thousand pounds.

Sixteen or seventeen years old when the match was first proposed to him, Southampton refused, declaring that he was averse not to this particular girl but to marriage itself. When it became clear that this was not a passing mood but a fixed resolution, the alarmed kin, foreseeing very clearly the blow to the family fortune, began to increase the pressure. The problem was that the young earl was so enormously rich, and so habitually reckless with his money and land, that the prospect of a substantial loss did not frighten him. He was unaffected too by the displeasure of his guardian and by the urgent pleas of a mother and other more distant relations with whom he had had little or no contact.

In these circumstances, the family, along with Lord Burghley, turned to other tactics. They had to address not Southampton's material interests—that had failed miserably—but his psyche. That is, the task was somehow to enter Southampton's innermost spirit, the hidden place from which his aversion to marriage arose, and refashion it. One of the means they chose was poetry.

The strategy was not entirely foolish: the stubborn, self-willed young nobleman, who had received a fine humanistic education, was steeped in poetry and had been brought up to expect that he would in time be a significant patron of the arts. If he would not take counsel from his sober elders, he might conceivably be reached by more indirect, more artful means. In 1591 he was presented with an elegant Latin poem dedicated to him—the first such dedication that he had received. The poem, *Narcissus*, rehearsed the story of the handsome youth who falls in love with his own reflection in the water and, in a vain attempt to embrace this reflection, drowns. The poem's author, John Clapham, was one of Burghley's secretaries, and the application of the monitory lesson to Southampton seems clear enough.

Clapham may have taken it upon himself to warn his master's ward about the dangers of self-love, but it is more likely that he was charged to do so. The clock was ticking: Southampton was going to turn twenty-one on October 6, 1594. Clapham's poem suggests that already in 1591 the looming deadline was provoking a search for effective methods of persuasion. And this leads us back to Shakespeare. It is possible that someone, either in the circle of Burghley or in the circle of Southampton's mother, had taken note of the fact that the young earl was excited by the talents or by the person of an actor who was also a promising poet. Whoever noticed this excitement—and a wealthy nobleman's slightest inclinations would have been carefully watched—might well have had the clever idea of commissioning the poet to try his hand at persuading the narcissistic, effeminate young earl to marry. Such a commission would help to account for the first 17 of the extraordinary sequence of 154 sonnets that were eventually printed—presumably, though not certainly, with Shakespeare's approval—many years later.

The opening group of Shakespeare's sonnets clearly has a specific person in mind: an exceptionally beautiful, "self-willed" (6.13) young man, who has refused to marry and is thus consuming himself "in single life" (9.2). The poet is careful not to press the specificity too far; a direct, identifiable address to the earl would have been presumptuous and indiscreet. Each of the poems has in effect a built-in principle of deniability. That is, if confronted by an irate reader, the poet could always say, "You have misunderstood me and jumped to a false conclusion. I wasn't referring to *him* at all." But if these poems were in fact written for Southampton, as many believe they were, then Shakespeare fully embraced the analysis of the problem articulated in Clapham's *Narcissus*: the young man is in love with himself, "contracted," as the first sonnet tells him plainly, "to thine own bright eyes" (1.5).

Shakespeare's psychological strategy, however, is the opposite of Clapham's. He does not tell the fair youth that he should tear himself away from his own reflection and beware of self-love. Rather, he tells him that he is insufficiently self-loving:

> Look in thy glass, and tell the face thou viewest
> Now is the time that face should form another.
>
> (3.1–2)

By looking longingly at his reflection, in contemplation of his own beauty, the young man will resolve to do in the flesh what he has done by standing in front of the mirror: produce an image of himself. It is through reproduction—"fresh repair"—that a person can truly love himself by projecting himself into the future; only a fool would "be the tomb / Of his self-love to stop posterity" (3.3, 7–8).

As a subject for sonnets, this procreation theme is wildly unusual, perhaps unprecedented. A sonneteer characteristically woos his beloved or laments her coldness or analyzes his own intense passion. He does not tell a young man that in order to make a precise copy of his own exquisite face, he should resolve to reproduce. Had he written sonnets in praise of the young man's prospective bride, Shakespeare could have held onto at least a semblance of conventionality. He would, in that case, have functioned like one of the painters hired in long-distance marriage negotiations to produce an image of the proposed spouse. But he did nothing of the kind. Though he is urging the youth to eschew masturbation and have sex with a woman—do not "spend / Upon thyself," he writes with striking explicitness, do not have "traffic with thyself alone" (4.1–2, 9)—the identity of the woman, the prospective mother of his child, is apparently a matter of indifference. No woman, he writes, will refuse: "where is she so fair whose uneared womb / Disdains the tillage of thy husbandry?" (3.5–16).

The vision of reproduction Shakespeare is offering his young man is not absolutely female-free, but, within the limits of the flesh, it reduces the role of the woman to the barest minimum: a piece of untilled ground that has not yet brought forth ripe ears of corn. The whole project will be spoiled if the child bears any resemblance to its mother, for the goal is to produce a mirror image of the father alone. In the fertile soil of a nameless, faceless breeder—and, if nameless and faceless, why not simply accept the choice that his guardian has already made for him?—the young man will plant the seed of his own perfect beauty. That beauty itself possesses whatever one might hope to find in a woman's face: "Thou art thy mother's glass," the poet tells the young man, "and she in thee / Calls back the lovely April of her prime" (3.9–10).

A painting has recently been discovered that is thought to be a portrait of Southampton at the time that Shakespeare's procreation sonnets were probably written. The image is a startling one because it transforms what had always seemed hyperbolic in the language of the sonnets into something quite literal. The long ringlets, the rosebud mouth, the consciousness of being "the world's fresh ornament" (1.9), the palpable air of a young man in love with himself, and, above all, the sexual ambiguity make the painting—which had long been mistaken as the image of a woman—serve as a vivid illustration of the qualities Shakespeare was addressing in these exceptionally strange opening sonnets.

The first edition of the entire sequence—a quarto volume bearing the title *Shake-speares Sonnets*—did not appear until 1609. Shakespeare's name, appearing in very large type, clearly was expected to sell copies. But while most printed books in this period eagerly trumpeted, through a dedication, an author's epistle, or some other means, a connection to a powerful patron, this book claimed no clear link and offered no identification of the persons to whom the poems were originally addressed. The publisher's famous dedication in the first edition—"To the only begetter of these ensuing sonnets, Mr. W. H., all happiness and that eternity promised by our ever-living poet, wisheth the well-wishing adventurer in setting forth. T. T."—does not help. It is not clear whether these words reveal something crucial about Shakespeare or merely about the publisher, Thomas Thorpe, whose initials seem to lay claim to the dedication as his own. And if it were somehow established that Shakespeare, rather than Thorpe, wrote the dedication, it would still not be known whether "W. H.," the initials of the "only begetter," slyly reverse those of Henry Wriothesley, the Earl of Southampton, or refer to someone else—perhaps to William Herbert, the Earl of Pembroke, who subsequently showed favor to Shakespeare and to whom (along with his brother Philip) the 1623 folio edition of Shakespeare's works was dedicated. As it happens, in 1597 this wealthy aristocrat, part of a family celebrated for its literary interests, was also being urged to marry. If the opening poems in the sequence seem suited in style to the earlier 1590s, a time for which Southampton is the likeliest candidate, most of the later poems seem on stylistic grounds to date from the late 1590s and the early years of the new century, when Herbert's case is stronger. Could Shakespeare have, as some scholars have proposed, been addressing both young men in succession, cleverly recycling the love tokens? Could some of those same love tokens have originated as poems addressed to other young men or women whom the poet was wooing? There is no way of achieving any certainty. After generations of feverish research, no one has been able to offer more than guesses, careful or wild, which are immediately countered (often with accompanying snorts of derision) by other guesses.

The 154 sonnets are ordered in such a way as to suggest at least the vague outlines of a story, in which the players include, besides the amorous poet and the beautiful young man, one or more rival poets and a dark lady. The reader is positively encouraged to identify Shakespeare with the speaker. Many love poets of the period used a witty alias as a mask: Philip Sidney called himself "Astrophil"; Spenser was the shepherd "Colin Clout"; Walter Ralegh (whose first name was pronounced "water"), "Ocean." But there is no mask here; these are, as the title announces, *Shake-speare's Sonnets*, and the poet puns repeatedly on his own first name:

> Whoever hath her wish, thou hast thy Will,
> And Will to boot, and Will in overplus."
>
> (135.1–2)

One of the startling effects of the best of these poems—a prime reason they have drawn madly fluttering biographical speculations like moths to a flame—is an almost painful intimacy. They seem to offer access to Shakespeare's most private retreat. But the other figures are carefully shrouded. The reader is clearly not meant to grasp, with any assurance, their actual identities.

Enormous effort has been expended to identify the principal rival poet and the "dark lady." Was the rival poet Marlowe or Chapman? Was the dark lady the poet Emilia Lanier, former mistress of the lord chamberlain, or the courtier Mary Fitton, or the prostitute known as Lucy Negro? If even to identify the young man of the first seventeen sonnets as Southampton is rash, to attempt to name these other figures is beyond rashness. In part, the problem is an inability, at this distance in time, to answer key questions: Who constituted Shakespeare's intimate circle in London? Over how long a period of time were these poems written? Did Shakespeare place them in the order in which they were printed? Did he approve their publication? To what degree are the poems directly confessional?

But it is not simply the passage of time that has made the details of the relationship murky. The whole enterprise of writing a sonnet sequence precisely involved drawing a translucent curtain—of one of those gauzy fabrics Elizabethans loved—over the scene, so that only shadowy figures are visible to the public. At the very center of the original title page, beneath *Shake-speare's Sonnets*, there are the words "Never before Imprinted." This prominent announcement (accurate, with two small exceptions, described below) implies that the public has long heard of the existence of these poems but has not until now been able to purchase them. For the writing of sonnets, as contemporary readers well understood, was not normally about getting them into print, where they would simply fall into the hands of anyone who had the money and the interest to buy the book. What mattered was getting the poems at the right moment into the right hands—most obviously, of course, the object of the poet's passion, but also the intimate (and, in the case of Shakespeare and the aristocratic young man, quite distinct) social circles surrounding both the poet and his beloved.

Sonnet writing was in its most prestigious and defining form the sophisticated game of courtiers. Sir Thomas Wyatt and the Earl of Surrey had made it fashionable in the reign of Henry VIII; Sir Philip Sidney had brought it to perfection in the reign of Elizabeth. The challenge of the game was to sound as intimate, self-revealing, and emotionally vulnerable as possible, without actually disclosing anything compromising to anyone outside the innermost circle. In Henry VIII's court the stakes were particularly high—rumors of adultery swirled around the royal household and could lead to the Tower and the scaffold —but even in less alarming social settings sonnets always carried an air of risk. Sonnets that were too cautious were insipid and would only show the poet to be a bore; sonnets that were too transparent could give mortal offense.

There were circles within circles. Presumably, if the first seventeen of Shakespeare's sonnets—the sonnets urging the young man to marry and father a child—were written to Southampton, then Southampton constituted the innermost circle: he was the reader who was privileged to know almost everything. But their closest friends would have known something; those in their wider social circles considerably less; those outside this orbit but still within social range something less again; and so on. The poet's true mastery is most fully displayed if those on the outermost edges still find the poems thrilling and revealing, even though they know absolutely nothing about any of the key players, not so much as their names.

By keeping his poems at some remove from the actual, Shakespeare was able both to share them intimately with the young man, who would have been able easily to fill in the missing personal details, and to circulate them safely among readers who could savor their beauty and admire their maker. "The sweet, witty soul of Ovid lives in mellifluous and honey-tongued Shakespeare," wrote one informed observer of the literary scene in 1598, praising "his sugared Sonnets among his private friends, etc."

Soon the poems started to float free of the group of private friends and take on a life of their own, independent of their immediate circumstances, whatever those circumstances might have been. Versions of two of the sonnets appeared in print in 1599 in an unauthorized collection, *The Passionate Pilgrim. By W. Shakespeare*, whose publisher, William Jaggard, was clearly trying to profit from the poet's celebrity. (Of the twenty poems in the collection, only five are actually by Shakespeare.) It is not only a modern misapprehension to think of such poems as "Shall I compare thee to a summer's day?" as having been written not to a young man but to a woman; already by the 1620s and '30s the sonnets were being copied out as heterosexual rather than homosexual. And this fluidity, this ability to be imaginatively transformed, seems part of the poet's own design, a manifestation of his supreme skill at playing this special game.

Sonnets, then, were at once private and social; that is, they characteristically took the form of a personal, intimate address, and at the same time they circulated within a small group whose values and desires they reflected, articulated, and reinforced. They could eventually reach a wider world—Sir Philip Sidney's sequence of 108 sonnets and eleven songs, *Astrophil and Stella*, written in the early 1580s, came to define courtly elegance for a whole generation of readers—but only a tiny number of readers would know the actual individuals and precise situations to which these intricate poems cunningly allude. Those outside the charmed coterie—and all are now in this category—had to content themselves with admiration for the poet's craft and with groping in the darkness of biographical speculation.

There were reasons in the summer of 1592 why Shakespeare would have been particularly eager to take on a commission to write poems urging a wealthy young man to marry. One of his principal sources of income—the income that supported him and the wife and children he had left behind in Stratford—had vanished. On June 12, 1592, London's lord mayor, Sir William Webbe, had written to Burghley about a riot that had taken place, the night before, in Southwark. A group of felt makers' servants, along with a crowd of "loose and masterless men," had tried to rescue a companion who had been arrested. The unruly mob had assembled, the lord mayor ominously noted, "at a play, which, besides the breach of the Sabbath day, giveth opportunity of committing these and such like disorders." Evidently, Burghley took the threat of further unrest seriously, for on June 23 the Privy Council issued an order suspending all performances in the London theaters. The suspension might not have lasted through the whole summer season—the theater companies, along with other people adversely affected (such as the "poor Watermen of the Bankside," that is, the boatmen who provided transportation across the river), vigorously petitioned for relief—but a far worse disaster struck some six weeks later.

The theater's most dreadful adversary, far worse than puritanical preachers or hostile magistrates, was bubonic plague. Public health regulation in Elizabethan England was haphazard at best, and nothing, or at least nothing accurate, was known about the actual causes of plague. Indeed, one of the official measures routinely taken when plague deaths began to rise—the killing of dogs and cats—undoubtedly made matters worse by destroying the enemies of the rats that in fact, as we now know, carried the fleas that carried the dread bacillus. But people had grasped, through bitter experience, that the isolation of plague victims slowed the spread of the disease—hence the terrible nailing shut of the quarantined houses—and they grasped too that there was a relation between the progress of epidemics and large crowds. Authorities did not cancel church services, but when plague deaths began to rise, they looked askance at any other public assemblies, and when such deaths reached a certain number (above thirty a week in London), they shut the theaters down.

Shakespeare and his fellow actors must have watched nervously as the mortality figures inched up in the warm summer weather and become more and more alarmed as they increased. No doubt the voices of the theater's enemies became more strident, shouting that God had sent the plague to punish London for its sins, above all for whoredom, sodomy, and playacting. Playhouses, bearbaiting arenas, and other places of public assembly—the churches excepted—were ordered to close until further notice. If the playing companies were lucky, the patrons would give them small sums to tide them over. Some of the actors would have packed up some props and costumes in wagons and gone on tour, garnering what income they could, however meager, in the provinces. But that life was a decidedly difficult one, and Shakespeare would doubtless have welcomed an alternative, if one came his way. A proposal to write sonnets to a fabulously wealthy, spoiled young man reluctant to marry would have seemed like a gift from the gods.

Yet even within the first seventeen sonnets, written as if to order, there are signs that the poet's task was complicated by thoughts and feelings that were difficult to reconcile perfectly with the assignment. Perhaps the very relationship that made it plausible for someone to suggest that Shakespeare write these poems stood in the way of their satisfactory accomplishment. "Make thee another self for love of me," the poet urges (10.13), as if he expected his emotional claims to count. But how exactly could they count? And if they did, how exactly could they bear on the plea that the youth father a child? What stake does the poet have in his friend's child? The answer nominally lies in the child's ability to counterbalance the malevolent power of time: when the passing years have irreparably destroyed the exquisite beauty the youth currently possesses, his son will carry that beauty forward into the next generation. But even as he presents this argument, the poet brings forth another, one that manifestly means far more to him and that fulfills the fantasy of perfect, female-free reproduction:

> And all in war with time for love of you,
> As he takes from you, I engraft you new.
> (15.13–14)

"I engraft you new"—the reproductive power in question here is the power of poetry. For a lingering moment the birth of a child still matters: Without a living image of the fair youth to verify all of the poet's claims,

"Who will believe my verse in time to come" (17.1)? But the imagined child here has been reduced to a piece of corroborating evidence, and he soon disappears entirely:

> Shall I compare thee to a summer's day?
> Thou art more lovely and more temperate.
> Rough winds do shake the darling buds of May,
> And summer's lease hath all too short a date.
> Sometime too hot the eye of heaven shines,
> And often is his gold complexion dimmed,
> And every fair from fair sometime declines,
> By chance or nature's changing course untrimmed;
> But thy eternal summer shall not fade
> Nor lose possession of that fair thou ow'st.
> Nor shall death brag thou wander'st in his shade
> When in eternal lines to time thou grow'st.
> > So long as men can breathe or eyes can see,
> > So long lives this, and this gives life to thee.
>
> (sonnet 18)

The dream of the child as mirror image, projected into the future, has been shouldered aside by "this"—*this* love poem, this exquisite mirror made of language, this far more secure way of preserving perfect beauty intact and carrying it forward to succeeding generations. Shakespeare has in effect displaced the woman he was urging the young man to impregnate; the poet's labor, not the woman's, will bring forth the young man's enduring image.

It is, as Shakespeare supremely understood, the stuff of romantic comedy: the go-between becomes romantically entangled. This is the central plot device of *Twelfth Night*. Viola, disguised as a boy and serving Duke Orsino, is assigned the task of helping him woo the countess Olivia: "I'll do my best / To woo your lady," Viola tells her master, adding, in an aside, that her assignment is a painful one: "Whoe'er I woo, myself would be his wife" (1.4.39–41). There is, of course, a striking difference between this situation and the one sketched in the sonnets. Though Viola is dressed like a boy when she sighs longingly for her master, her desire is a woman's desire for a man and thus can be consummated in marriage (as soon as she changes her clothes). But *Twelfth Night* goes out of its way to suggest that gender is not, after all, the crucial issue: Orsino is clearly attracted to the servant he believes to be a sexually ambiguous boy, and Olivia falls madly in love with this same ambiguous go-between. In something of the same spirit, though without the explicit narrative, Shakespeare's sonnets stage the triumph of the poet's own overwhelming love over the initial project of persuading the young man to marry.

Is it the truth or a piece of flattering rhetoric? Impossible to say. But for the vain young recipient of these poems, Shakespeare's narrative—never explicit, but never completely out of view—must have been very gratifying. Something happened to the poet, the sonnets imply, when he undertook to persuade the beautiful youth to marry: he became aware that he was longing for the youth himself. The poet can no longer understand how it will all work out. He knows that the young man regards him as little more than a servant—an aging one at that. But he craves his company, and he feels in his presence something that he never felt with any woman. He wants to charm him, he wants to be with him, he wants to be him; he is his vision of youth, of nobility, of perfect beauty. He is in love with him.

The sonnets express this love in impassioned and extravagant praise: the image of the young man is "like a jewel hung in ghastly night" (27.11); his loveliness exceeds the most idealized accounts of Adonis or Helen (53); he is "as fair in knowledge as in hue" (82.5); his hand is whiter than a lily, and the tint on his cheeks is more delicate than a rose (98); whatever "antique pens" expressed "In praise of ladies dead and lovely knights"—"Of hand, of foot, of lip, of eye, of brow"—was a prophecy of his own beauty (106.4–7). He is the poet's sun, his rose, his dear heart, his "best of dearest" (48.7), his fair flower, his sweet love, his lovely boy.

At the same time, and in comparably impassioned terms, the sonnets elaborate the claims of poetry: "My love shall in my verse ever live young" (19.4); "Not marble nor the gilded monuments / Of princes shall outlive this powerful rhyme" (55.1–2); time's scythe mows everything down and yet "my verse shall stand" (60.13); the remorseless hours will drain the young man's blood and carve wrinkles on his brow, but "His beauty shall in these black lines be seen" (63.13); age's cruel knife may cut "my lover's life" but "never cut from memory / My sweet love's beauty" (63.11–12); "when I in earth am rotten" and you are in your tomb, "Your monument shall be my gentle verse" (81.3, 9). This last phrase casually incorporates the social status that Shakespeare constantly dreamed of, but the dream here is far more ambitious, laying claim to a godlike power: "Your name from hence"—that is, from my gentle verse—"immortal life shall have" (81.5).

The irony, of course, is that the sonnets themselves do not confer any life at all on the *name* of the beloved, for the simple reason that he is never actually named. Shakespeare, it seems, has deliberately kept the beloved's name out of poems that claim to confer upon that name an immortal life.

If it is not unreasonable to speculate that the young man of the opening suite of sonnets is the Earl of Southampton, it is because the earl's personal circumstances perfectly fit the situation that is sketched, because his family had already tried literary persuasion, and, above all, because Shakespeare in the 1590s dedicated to Southampton two long, elaborate nondramatic poems: *Venus and Adonis* and *The Rape of Lucrece*. The dedicatory letters to these long poems are the only such documents from Shakespeare's hand, and, along with the poems they introduce, they tell us a great deal about the man who wrote them—or at least about the side that he wished to present to the earl.

The language of the first of these dedications, to *Venus and Adonis*, is formal, emotionally cautious, and socially defensive: "I know not how I shall offend in dedicating my unpolished lines to your lordship, nor how the world will censure me for choosing so strong a prop to support so weak a burden." Probably written in late 1592, very close to the time he may have written the procreation sonnets, the elegant narrative poem, anything but "unpolished," was clearly a bid for patronage—that is, for protection against renewed "censure" and for any more tangible rewards that the free-spending nobleman might care to offer.

The poet's display of diffidence and anxiety in the dedication may well have been sincere. Published in 1593, *Venus and Adonis* was the first of Shakespeare's works to appear in print. Apparently indifferent to the printing house through most of his career, here for once he showed clear signs of caring. He chose for the printer someone he could trust, his fellow Strat-

This *"Long View" of London from Bankside*, etched in 1647 by Wenceslaus Hollar (1607–1677), provides a strikingly detailed glimpse of a neighborhood with which Shakespeare was intimately familiar. The labels for the bearbaiting arena (also known as the Hope Theater) and the Globe Theater were inadvertently reversed. *By courtesy of the Guildhall Library, London.*

The attack on Shakespeare as an "upstart Crow" in *Greene's Groatsworth of Wit* (1592). Note that the words parodying a line from Shakespeare's Henry VI—"Tygers hart wrapt in a Players hyde"—are marked as a quotation by a different typeface. *By courtesy of the Folger Shakespeare Library.*

pendeſt on ſo meane a ſtay . Baſe minded men all thꝛee of you, if by my miſerie you be not warnd: foꝛ vnto none of you (like mee) ſought thoſe burres to cleaue : thoſe Puppets (I meane) that ſpake from our mouths, thoſe Anticks garniſht in our colours. Is it not ſtrange, that I, to whom they all haue beene beholding: is it not like that you, to whome they all haue beene beholding, ſhall (were yee in that caſe as I am now) bee both at once of them forſaken ? Yes truſt them not : foꝛ there is an vp‑ ſtart Crow, beautified with our feathers, that with his Tygers hart wrapt in a Players hyde, ſuppoſes he is as well able to bombaſt out a blanke verſe as the beſt of you : and beeing an abſolute Iohannes fac totum, is in his owne conceit the onely Shake‑ſcene in a countrey. O that I might intreat your rare wits to be imploied in moꝛe pꝛofitable courſes : & let thoſe Apes imitate your paſt excellence, and neuer moꝛe acquaint them with your admired inuentions . I knowe the beſt huſband of you

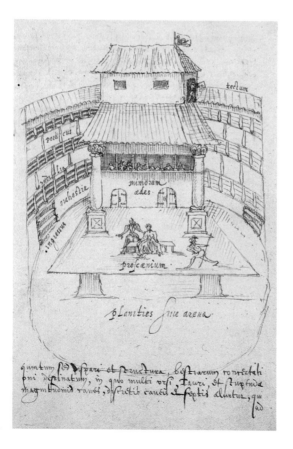

The Dutch traveler Johannes de Witt sketched the Swan Theater in 1596. His lost drawing, preserved in a friend's copy, shows a raised stage on which two women characters (presumably played by boys) are addressed by a chamberlain. *By kind permission of the Univeriteitsbibliotheek, Utrecht.*

"Hand D" in the manuscript of *The Book of Sir Thomas More* (above) is widely believed to be Shakespeare's. As this sample suggests, the claim that he rarely changed or corrected what he wrote down was probably an exaggeration. *By courtesy of the British Library.*

The earliest image of Falstaff and Mistress Quickly, in the frontispiece to *The Wits, or Sport upon Sport* (1662), a collection of short dramatic pieces, one of which featured Falstaff and his exploits. *By courtesy of the Huntington Library.*

This engraving, by the Flemish artist Jan van der Straet (1523–1605), of a sixteenth-century printing shop shows two presses, with compositors and proofreaders. *By courtesy of the Folger Shakespeare Library.*

The dedicatory epistle of
The Rape of Lucrece (1594).
*By courtesy of the Folger
Shakespeare Library.*

TO THE RIGHT
HONOVRABLE, HENRY
VVriothefley, Earle of Southhampton,
and Baron of Titchfield.

HE loue I dedicate to your
Lordfhip is without end:wher-
of this Pamphlet without beginning is but a fuperfluous
Moity. The warrant I haue of
your Honourable difpofition,
not the worth of my vntutord
Lines makes it affured of acceptance. VVhat I haue
done is yours, what I haue to doe is yours, being
part in all I haue, deuoted yours. VVere my worth
greater, my duety would fhew greater, meane time,
as it is, it is bound to your Lordfhip; To whom I wifh
long life ftill lengthned with all happineffe.

Your Lordfhips in all duety.

William Shakefpeare.

A 2

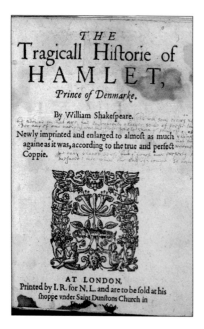

Hamlet exists in three distinct early texts. The second quarto (1604) makes good on the claim, on the title page reproduced here, that it is almost twice as long as the first edition of 1603. The text in the First Folio (1623) is shorter, possibly reflecting cuts made for performance. *By courtesy of the Folger Shakespeare Library.*

In times of plague, as this woodcut suggests, death had dominion over London. *By courtesy of the British Library.*

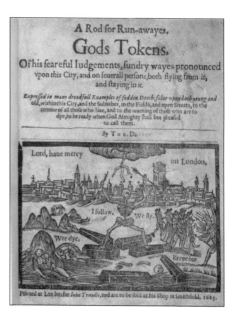

This portrait, widely identified as Shakespeare, was said to have been owned by Sir William Davenant, who claimed to be Shakespeare's godson and hinted that he was his illegitimate child. The simplicity of the dress is set off by the gold earring. *By courtesy of the National Portrait Gallery, England.*

Shakespeare's funeral monument, in Holy Trinity Church, Stratford-upon-Avon, depicts him as he evidently wished in his last years to be seen: the poet as a dignified burgher. *By permission of the Bridgeman Art Library.*

Interior of the new Globe, showing the general dimensions of the yard and the surrounding galleries. *By courtesy of the International Shakespeare Globe Center, Ltd.*

ford-upon-Avon native Richard Field. The choice was a good one: Field produced an unusually handsome small book, suitable for presentation. Shakespeare was attempting, probably for the first and only time in his career, to find a patron, and with the theaters shut down and the plague continuing to rage, he may have thought that a great deal was riding on whether he was successful. Even if Southampton had already manifested his favor, in the wake of *Greene's Groatworth of Wit*, and even if the exalted aristocrat and the lowly player had already had some encouraging personal contact with one another—and, of course, these are merely speculations—Shakespeare could well have been uncertain about the reception of *Venus and Adonis*.

It was as if, in his late twenties, Shakespeare had decided to start afresh in a new profession, as if he had not written anything before. He was attempting to establish himself now not as a popular playwright but as a cultivated poet, someone who could gracefully conjure up the mythological world to which his university-educated rival poets claimed virtually exclusive access. And he was attempting also to address Southampton's particular situation: the poem takes up the theme of the beautiful young man, scarcely more than a boy, who resists the blandishments of the goddess of love. If the poem's "godfather"—the eighteen-year-old nobleman—is pleased with it, Shakespeare writes, then he will attempt "some graver labour. But if the first heir of my invention prove deformed"—like the sonnets, the dedicatory letter metamorphoses poems into children—then the poet will "never after ear so barren a land." Perhaps Shakespeare meant it, for there would be no point in making another effort if Southampton rejected this one out of hand.

The plot of *Venus and Adonis* echoes the sonnets' warning: a beautiful boy's rejection of love—Love herself, in the person of Venus—enables death to triumph over him. For three-quarters of the poem's nearly twelve hundred lines, Venus, feverish with desire, pleads, caresses, lures, harangues, and all but assaults Adonis. Accusing the young man of self-love, she begs him to produce an heir. But all is in vain. Breaking away from the goddess's embrace, Adonis goes off to hunt and is promptly killed by a "foul, grim, and urchin-snouted boar" (line 1105). From the blood that spills from his wound springs a purple flower, the anemone, which grief-stricken Venus plucks and cradles in her bosom.

Taken in the abstract, the argument of *Venus and Adonis* could have appealed to the sober, calculating guardian Burghley. But the experience of the poem is anything but sober. Here too, as in the sonnets, prudential warning cedes place to something else, something seductive that this particular poet, William Shakespeare, is offering the young man. *Venus and Adonis* is a spectacular display of Shakespeare's signature characteristic, his astonishing capacity to be everywhere and nowhere, to assume all positions and to slip free of all constraints. The capacity depends upon a simultaneous, deeply paradoxical achievement of proximity and distance, intimacy and detachment. How otherwise would it be possible to be in so many places at once? Shakespeare offers here in a weirdly concentrated form the sensibility that enabled him to write his plays.

The effect is a tangle of erotic arousal, pain, and cool laughter. At moments, the love goddess seems enormous, a dominatrix towering over her diminutive, unwilling lover:

> Over one arm, the lusty courser's rein;
> Under her other was the tender boy,
> Who blushed and pouted in a dull disdain
> With leaden appetite, unapt to toy.
>   (lines 31–34)

At other moments, she is the fragile heroine of a romance, fainting at a mere disapproving glance, and then, when the remorseful boy tries to revive her, suddenly reduced to a farcical rag doll:

> He wrings her nose, he strikes her on the cheeks,
> He bends her fingers, holds her pulses hard;
> He chafes her lips; a thousand ways he seeks
> To mend the hurt that his unkindness marred.
>   (lines 475–78)

In such passages we seem to be at a great distance from the figures, watching their frantic movements the way the audience of *A Midsummer Night's Dream* watches the crazed lovers in the Athenian woods. But then

without warning—and without ever completely losing the comic detachment—we are unnervingly close. Venus not only sighs for Adonis; she
"locks her lily fingers one in one" (line 228) around the struggling boy
and proposes that he "graze" (line 233) on her body:

> "Within this limit is relief enough,
> Sweet bottom-grass, and high delightful plain,
> Round rising hillocks, brakes obscure and rough,
> To shelter thee from tempest and from rain."
>   (lines 235–38)

Adonis attempts to pull back from her frantic kisses only to submit passively for a few moments out of sheer exhaustion:

> Hot, faint, and weary with her hard embracing,
> Like a wild bird being tamed with too much handling.
>   (lines 559–60)

Metaphors frequently function in poetry as a way of distancing the reader
from a character or situation, but not here. Here they are ways of intensifying physical and emotional proximity, so that we view everything in a
sustained close-up. The dimples in Adonis's cheeks are "round enchant-
ing pits" that "Opened their mouths to swallow Venus' liking" (lines
247–48). The goddess's face "doth reek and smoke" (line 555) with erotic
arousal. And when the two recline—or rather when Venus pulls Adonis
down to the ground—they lie not simply on a bed of flowers, but on
"blue-veined violets" (line 125).

Without once making an appearance in his own person—for, after
all, this is a mythological fantasy—Shakespeare is constantly, inescapably
present in *Venus and Adonis*, as if he wanted Southampton (and perhaps
"the world," at which he glances in his dedication) fully to understand his
extraordinary powers of playful identification. He is manifestly in Venus,
in her physical urgency and her rhetorical inventiveness, and he is in Adonis too, in his impatience and his misogynistic distaste. But he is in
everything else as well. If a mare could write a love poem to a stallion

(and, more precisely, the ecstatic inventory of the beloved's features, known as a blazon), she might write this:

> Round-hoofed, short-jointed, fetlocks shag and long,
> Broad breast, full eye, small head, and nostril wide,
> High crest, short ears, straight legs, and passing strong;
> Thin mane, thick tail, broad buttock, tender hide.
>
> (lines 295–98)

If a hare could write a poem about the misery of being hunted, he might write this:

> Then shalt thou see the dew-bedabbled wretch
> Turn, and return, indenting with the way.
> Each envious brier his weary legs do scratch;
> Each shadow makes him stop, each murmur stay.
>
> (lines 703–6)

The point is not that horses or hares are central to the poem—they are not. The point is that Shakespeare effortlessly enters into their existence.

What do you offer a beautiful, spoiled young aristocrat who has everything? You present him with a universe where everything has an erotic charge, a charge whose urgency confounds the roles of mother and lover. Here is Venus hearing the sound of the hunt and running in panic toward the scene:

> And as she runs, the bushes in the way
> Some catch her by the neck, some kiss her face,
> Some twine about her thigh to make her stay.
> She wildly breaketh from their strict embrace,
> 　Like a milch doe whose swelling dugs do ache,
> 　Hasting to feed her fawn hid in some brake.
>
> (lines 871–76)

How do you awaken and hold a jaded young man's attention? You introduce him to a world of heightened sensitivity to pleasure and to pain. Here is Venus shutting her eyes at the sight of Adonis's fatal wound:

> Or as the snail, whose tender horns being hit
> Shrinks backward in his shelly cave with pain,
> And there, all smothered up, in shade doth sit,
> Long after fearing to creep forth again;
>   So at his bloody view her eyes are fled
>   Into the deep dark cabins of her head.
>   (lines 1033–38)

And if you are begging for the generosity of a noble patron, what stupendous gift can you possibly give in return? You propose symbolically to turn death itself into orgasm. Here is Venus telling herself that the boar intended not to kill Adonis but to kiss him:

> "And, nuzzling in his flank, the loving swine
> Sheathed unaware the tusk in his soft groin."
>   (lines 1115–16)

The "loving swine" has only done what she herself has all along been proposing to do:

> "Had I been toothed like him, I must confess
> With kissing him I should have killed him first."
>   (lines 1117–18)

This is what Shakespeare had to offer.

Evidently, *Venus and Adonis* pleased the earl: judging from the rush of imitations, admiring comments, and reprintings—ten times by 1602!—the poem pleased virtually everyone. (It was particularly popular, it seems, with young men.) Flush with his success, Shakespeare was as good as his word, bringing forth within a year's time the much graver

Lucrece. But this time the tone of the dedicatory letter to Southampton was no longer diffident, tentative, or anxious: "The love I dedicate to your lordship is without end.... What I have done is yours; what I have to do is yours, being part in all I have, devoted yours." Elizabethan dedicatory letters were often quite florid, but what Shakespeare wrote here is not at all typical. This was not, as might have been expected, an exercise in praise or the desire to please or a plea for patronage; this was a public declaration of fervent, boundless love.

Something happened in the course of the year between *Venus and Adonis* and *The Rape of Lucrece*, something led Shakespeare to shift from "I know not how I shall offend" to "love ... without end." There is no direct access to whatever it was, but it is possible that hints may lie in the sonnets. For the sonnets—assuming that most of the first 126 of them were written to the same person—do not merely praise the young man and affirm the power of poetry; they sketch a relationship unfolding over time, in all probability over years. Admiration ripens into adoration; periods of joyful intimacy are followed by absence and desperate longing; the poet finds it tormenting to endure separation from his beloved; he feels in many ways unworthy of so precious a love, but he is also aware that he is able by his art to confer eternity upon the mortal beauty of the young man; he knows that a time will come, perhaps soon, when the young man will see him as decrepit and no longer care for him; he struggles to accept the inevitable loss of a love that has sustained his life; exuberant praise gives way to reproach and self-doubt; the poet is at once excited and tormented by his social inferiority; his passionate devotion slides toward abject subservience, and then this subservience slowly modulates back into a partial critical independence; he insists that the young man is perfect, even as he recognizes deep flaws in his character.

In the midst of this tangle of shifting, obsessive emotions, there are glimpses of what seem to be specific events. The young man succumbs to temptation and sleeps with the poet's mistress. The betrayal is painful less because of her infidelity—"And yet it may be said I loved her dearly" (42.2)—than because of his, for his is the love that truly matters. The poet himself is in some unspecified way unfaithful to the young man but ventures to hope that he will be forgiven for his "transgression" (120.3), just as in comparable circumstances he earlier forgave the young man. The poet has given away a keepsake—a small notebook or writing tablet—that the young man has presented to him, but it does not matter, for the gift is inalienably lodged in his brain and heart. Several rivals—one of them, at least, a writer of considerable distinction—are competing, apparently successfully, for the young man's attention and favor. And the culminating "event": from sonnet 127 onward the poet shifts his obsessive attention away from the fair young man and focuses instead on his feelings—a tangle of desire and revulsion—toward his black-eyed, black-haired, sexually voracious mistress.

Biographers have often succumbed to the temptation to turn these intimations of events into a full-blown romantic plot, but to do so requires pulling against the strong gravitational force of the individual poems. Shakespeare, who had an effortless genius at narrative, made certain that his sonnets would not yield an entirely coherent story. Each of the great poems in the sequence—and there are many—is its own distinct world, a compressed, often fantastically complex fourteen-line rehearsal of an emotional scenario that the playwright could, if he chose, have developed into a scene or an entire play. An example is the justly celebrated sonnet 138, a poem already removed from any narrative context and anthologized during Shakespeare's own lifetime:

> When my love swears that she is made of truth
> I do believe her though I know she lies,
> That she might think me some untutored youth
> Unlearnèd in the world's false subtleties.
> Thus vainly thinking that she thinks me young,
> Although she knows my days are past the best,
> Simply I credit her false-speaking tongue;
> On both sides thus is simple truth suppressed.
> But wherefore says she not she is unjust,
> And wherefore say not I that I am old?
> O, love's best habit is in seeming trust,
> And age in love loves not to have years told.
> > Therefore I lie with her, and she with me,
> > And in our faults by lies we flattered be.

"I do believe her though I know she lies." Since the poet makes clear he knows perfectly well that his mistress is unfaithful, "I do believe her" seems to be short for "I pretend to believe her." The plot, it seems, is one of those cuckoldry stories that fascinated Shakespeare and his contemporaries; the opening lines give voice to the shadowy suspicion that pulls toward farce in *Much Ado About Nothing*, or toward murder in *The Winter's Tale*. The suspicion here has a May-December twist, the anxiety that preys on the mind of Othello, excruciatingly aware that, compared with Desdemona, he is "declined / Into the vale of years—yet that's not much" (3.3.269–70).

The poet goes on, however, to acknowledge that his strategy—pretending to be gullible so as to seem younger than his years—does not actually fool his mistress for a moment, any more than he is fooled by her "false-speaking tongue": "On both sides thus is simple truth suppressed." By now a different plot is in place, neither familiarly farcical nor tragic, something more like the strategic game of mutual lying in which Shakespeare's Antony and Cleopatra (along with almost every other character in that play) indulge. "Simple truth"—the truth of the dark lady's infidelity and the poet's aging—is suppressed by his "simply" crediting her lies, that is, by a deliberate indulgence in a fiction. A way to characterize this indulgence might be Coleridge's phrase for what one does when watching a play: a "willing suspension of disbelief." But the poet is describing his relationship to his lying mistress, not to a work of art.

The game could well lead to an explosion of moral disapproval or self-reproach, conventional ways to banish the deceit and to restore moral order. Indeed, Shakespeare seems to be building toward such an explosion, as he calls the whole pattern of their lives into question:

> But wherefore says she not she is unjust,
> And wherefore say not I that I am old?

But the close of the poem—sliding from "old" to a sighing "O"—surprises us by frankly suspending the impulse to strip away the veil of deception: "O, love's best habit is in seeming trust." Love's "habit," both its habitual behavior and its finest clothing, is a tissue of lies. Instead of moral judgment, there is a candid acceptance of the erotic virtue of mendacity. As the final couplet makes clear, the man and woman who lie to each other lie with each other.

Sonnet writing was a courtly and aristocratic performance, and Shakespeare was decidedly not a courtier or an aristocrat. Yet the challenge of this form proved agreeable to him. To be a very public man—an actor onstage, a successful playwright, a celebrated poet; and at the same time to be a very private man—a man who can be trusted with secrets, a writer who keeps his intimate affairs to himself and subtly encodes all references to others: this was the double life Shakespeare had chosen for himself. If his astonishing verbal skills and his compulsive habit of imaginative identification, coupled with deep ambition, drove him to public performance, his family secrets and his wary intelligence—perhaps reinforced by the sight of the severed heads on London Bridge—counseled absolute discretion.

Such a deliberately chosen double existence helps to explain the paradox that has tantalized centuries of readers: the sonnets are a thrilling, deeply convincing staging of the poet's inner life, an intimate performance of Shakespeare's response to his tangled emotional relationships with a young man, a rival poet, and a dark lady; and the sonnets are a cunning sequence of beautiful locked boxes to which there are no keys, an exquisitely constructed screen behind which it is virtually impossible to venture with any confidence.

A code of discretion and the practice of concealment shape the sonnets, but so do certain shared excitements, recurrent preoccupations, and seductive strategies. It would be folly to take these as a kind of confidential diary, a straightforward record of what actually went on in the relationship between Shakespeare and his deceitful dark lady, whoever she was in real life, or between Shakespeare and the aristocratic young man, whether he was Southampton or someone else, or perhaps an amalgam of multiple lovers. But even a record of fantasies, in part adapted from other poets, in part spun out of the threads of actual relationships, may reveal something about Shakespeare's emotional life.

The sonnets represent the poet and the young man as excited by the immense class and status difference between them. Even while slyly criticizing his beloved—or perhaps because he is slyly criticizing him—Shakespeare plays at utter subservience:

> Being your slave, what should I do but tend
> Upon the hours and times of your desire?
>
>   (571–2)

And he stages too his intense awareness of the social stigma that attaches to his profession:

> Alas, 'tis true, I have gone here and there
> And made myself a motley to the view.
>
>   (110.1–2)

Perhaps this shame, the shame of dressing up like a fool in motley and putting on a show before the gaping public, was something that Shakespeare actually felt, quite apart from the relationship depicted in the sonnets. But here it is part of the erotic dance between himself and the beautiful boy:

> O, for my sake do you with fortune chide,
> The guilty goddess of my harmful deeds,
> That did not better for my life provide
> Than public means which public manners breeds.
> Thence comes it that my name receives a brand,
> And almost thence my nature is subdued
> To what it works in, like the dyer's hand.
> Pity me. . . .
>
>   (111.1–8)

The permanent stain that Shakespeare the performer bears and that indelibly marks his social distance from his aristocratic beloved becomes quite literally part of the appeal: "Pity me."

The age difference between the poet and the young man functions in a similar way, not, that is, as an impediment to desire, but rather as a paradoxical source of excitement, something to be noted, highlighted, and exaggerated:

> As a decrepit father takes delight
> To see his active child do deeds of youth,
> So I, made lame by fortune's dearest spite,
> Take all my comfort of thy worth and truth.
>
> (37.1–4)

Where could the seductive pleasure possibly lie here? Perhaps in a patriarchal society where the young were accustomed to domineering fathers or tyrannical guardians, a weak father figure was thrilling. The excitement of the role reversal must have been intense, intense enough to lead Shakespeare to stage himself as a kind of parasite on the younger man. The poet's performance does not preclude vanity. "Sin of self-love possesseth all mine eye," Shakespeare writes, "And all my soul, and all my every part." But this frank admission of narcissism— "Methinks no face so gracious is as mine"—is only a way of intensifying the beloved's triumph. When he looks into the mirror, Shakespeare writes, he sees that in reality his face is "Beated and chapped with tanned antiquity" (62.1–2, 5, 10) and that whatever pleasure he takes in himself is borrowed from the man he loves: "Painting my age with beauty of thy days" (10.14).

The emotions at play here have something of the blend of adoration and appetite that Shakespeare depicted in Falstaff's feelings toward his sweet boy, Prince Hal. But the roles are reversed: where Shakespeare imagined himself as the young prince in relation to Robert Greene's calculating older man, now he plays the older man to the sweet boy. Perhaps this was one of the inner currents that enabled Shakespeare to transform the character he based on Greene from a mere braggart into the complex, poignant figure of Falstaff, self-loving, calculating, cynical, adoring, abject, and doomed. As Hal sweeps away his memories of Falstaff—"I know thee not, old man"—so the poet urges the young man simply to forget him: "Nay, if you read this line, remember not / The hand that writ it." But the difference is that the poet's request to be forgotten is in reality a declaration of abject love and a thinly disguised appeal to be remembered and loved:

Nay, if you read this line, remember not
The hand that writ it; for I love you so
That I in your sweet thoughts would be forgot
If thinking on me then should make you woe.

                              (71.5–8)

Again and again, the young man is invited to embrace the father he will displace and bury and eventually forget. And the oblivion that lies in the future only serves to intensify the appeal.

One of the most famous of the sonnets (73) sums up the emotional claim that Shakespeare is making on the young man by exaggerating their age difference:

That time of year thou mayst in me behold
When yellow leaves, or none, or few, do hang
Upon those boughs which shake against the cold,
Bare ruined choirs where late the sweet birds sang.
In me thou seest the twilight of such day
As after sunset fadeth in the west,
Which by and by black night doth take away,
Death's second self, that seals up all in rest.
In me thou seest the glowing of such fire
That on the ashes of his youth doth lie
As the death-bed whereon it must expire,
Consumed with that which it was nourished by.
  This thou perceiv'st, which makes thy love more strong,
  To love that well which thou must leave ere long.

Elsewhere in the sonnet sequence there is an emphasis on eternity—the timelessness of the poet's lines, the endless replication of the young man's beauty—but not here. Each of the images—the yellow leaves, the twilight, and the embers—exquisitely conveys transience. It is only a matter of time before it will be irrevocably over: naked branches, darkness, cold ashes lie just ahead. And the transience, the coming-to-an-end that

Shakespeare sees even in the moment of love's flourishing, confers a painful intensity upon the relationship.

For whatever actually happened between Shakespeare and the young man—whether they only stared longingly at one another or embraced, kissed passionately, went to bed together—was almost certainly shaped by an overwhelming sense of transience. This sense did not only, or even principally, derive from the age and class differences that intensified their desires; it derived from the period's understanding of male homosexual love. Elizabethans acknowledged the existence of same-sex desire; indeed, it was in a certain sense easier for them to justify than heterosexual desire. That men were inherently superior to women was widely preached; why then wouldn't men naturally be drawn to love other men? Sodomy was strictly prohibited by religious teaching and the law, but that prohibition aside, it was perfectly understandable that men would love and desire men.

Shakespeare's contemporary Edmund Spenser, a poet celebrated for his moral seriousness, wrote a pastoral poem in which a shepherd declares his passionate love for a youth. Attached to the poem is a commentary by Spenser himself or someone very close to him that notes uneasily that the relationship has some savor of the "disorderly love" that the Greeks called "paederastice." But after all, the commentary continues, from the right perspective "paederastice" is "much to be preferred before gynerastice, that is, the love which enflameth men with lust toward womankind." And then, as if alarmed by what he has just said, the commentator adds a final disclaimer: let no man think that he is defending the "execrable and horrible sins of forbidden and execrable fleshliness."

It is in the context of this seesaw game of acknowledgment and denial that Shakespeare stages his sexual desire for the young man: it is explicitly accepted and ardently expressed as if it were the most natural thing in the world, and at the same time it is deflected, disavowed, or defeated, as if it could never be fully realized. The young man, in sonnet 20, has a woman's face and a woman's gentle heart, but he is better, truer, and more steadfast than any woman. He is, the poet writes, "the master-mistress of my passion." Nature indeed intended to create a woman when she made the young man, but, doting on her own creation, she added something—"she pricked thee out" (20.2, 13)—and therefore defeated the poet of his long-term sexual fulfillment. Shakespeare does not adopt the outraged moralizing tone of Spenser's commentator, but he plays with the same materials—misogyny, intense homosexual desire, disavowal—to which he adds a sense of transience. For even if in the actual relationship half-hidden in the sonnets Shakespeare fulfilled his erotic longings, he knew that this love would never be allowed to stand in the way of the social imperative to marry and produce heirs, precisely that imperative to which Shakespeare gave voice in the opening sonnets.

It was possible for the adolescent Southampton to declare that he was not ready to marry, provided he was prepared to accept the huge financial sacrifice that his refusal entailed. It was possible too for him to have an affair with one or more of the men—and there must have been many—who courted him. It would have been quite another thing for him to abjure marriage altogether. A few men of high rank (though not as high as Southampton's) did indeed refuse to marry—Francis Bacon is a notable example—but quite apart from sexual orientation, most were committed to passing along their name, title, and wealth. In 1598, shortly before his twenty-fifth birthday, Southampton secretly wed one of the queen's maids of honor, Elizabeth Vernon, who was pregnant with his child. The queen was enraged: her maids of honor were meant actually to be maids, and she hated clandestine marriages among her followers. Still, this marriage seems to have been a happy one, sustaining the earl through a long, turbulent, and on occasion extremely dangerous career.

As for the poet, if there is one thing that the sonnets, taken as biographical documents, strongly suggest, it is that he could not find what he craved, emotionally or sexually, within his marriage. Part of the problem may have been the evident mismatch with Anne Hathaway; but perhaps the sonnets suggest too that no single person could ever have satisfied Shakespeare's longings or made him happy. It is not as if he found, outside of his marriage, someone who fulfilled him completely. He focused, it seems, his capacity for ecstatic idealization largely on the young man and his capacity for desire largely on his mistress. And in both cases, there is an obstacle to fulfillment. The poet adores a man whom he cannot possess and desires a woman whom he cannot admire. The beautiful young man, the sonnets ruefully acknowledge, cannot ultimately be his, while the dark lady, even if he could securely possess her, is everything that should arouse revulsion in him. Dishonest, unchaste, and faithless, she has, according to the last sonnets in the sequence, given him something more than revulsion; she has infected him with venereal disease. But still he cannot give her up: "My love is as a fever, longing still / For that which longer nurseth the disease" (147.1–2). That he cannot do so has everything to do with the compulsions of "lust in action" (129.2), the rhythm of tumescence and detumescence that defines for him what it means to be with her: "I call / Her 'love' for whose dear love I rise and fall" (151.13–14). This sexual rhythm, yoking vitality and death, pleasure and disgust, longing and loathing, is not a mere recreation or an escape. As the sonnets insist again and again, the poet's witty, anxious, self-conscious embrace of his own desires defines what it means to be "Will."

There is no room, in the way in which Shakespeare represents himself in the sonnets, for his wife or his children. It does not matter, in this regard, whether the poems were written in the mid-1590s or a decade later: since no one thinks that they were written before Shakespeare married and became a father, all of the sonnets are in effect acts of erasure. There are perhaps a few small exceptions: the possible glimpse of the bygone courtship of his wife in a pun on "hate away" and "Hathaway" in sonnet 145; a very indirect acknowledgment of his infidelity in the opening line of sonnet 152—"In loving thee thou know'st I am forsworn." The sonnet characteristically goes on to berate his mistress for breaking her "bed-vow," but at least for a moment he recognizes that he too has broken his vow. For the most part, he seems to forget. Or rather, the figures of the young man and the dark lady seem to displace and absorb emotions that we might have conventionally expected Shakespeare to feel in and for his family. About Anne Shakespeare he is silent; it is to his beautiful male friend that he writes his most celebrated words about love: "Let me not to the marriage of true minds / Admit impediments" (116.1–2).

CHAPTER 9

Laughter at the Scaffold

HOWEVER GENEROUSLY he may have been rewarded for the sonnets, *Venus and Adonis*, and *The Rape of Lucrece*, Shakespeare did not choose to stake his fortunes, financial or artistic, on his relation to a patron. He chose instead, when the plague abated, to return to the theater, where he rose to preeminence as a playwright remarkably quickly. The playing companies needed to please many different tastes, and they had a huge appetite for new scripts. Hardworking hacks could make good money grinding out dozens of plays: *Three Ladies of London*, *Peddler's Prophecy*, *Fair Em*, *A Sackful of News*, *The Tragical History of the Tartarian Cripple*, *Emperor of Constantinople*. But until the impressive, boisterous arrival on the scene of Ben Jonson in 1597, Shakespeare had only one serious rival, Christopher Marlowe. The two immensely talented young poets, exactly the same age, were evidently locked in mutual emulation and contest. They circled warily, watching with intense attention, imitating, and then attempting to surpass each other. The contest extended beyond the momentous early works, *Tamburlaine* and *Henry VI*, to a brilliant pair of strikingly similar history plays, Shakespeare's *Richard II* and Marlowe's *Edward II*, and an equally brilliant pair of long erotic poems, Shakespeare's *Venus and Adonis* and Marlowe's *Hero and Leander*. Marlowe would not have made the mistake of underestimating Shakespeare. He would have immediately understood that in the words of the hunchback duke of Gloucester, in the third part of *Henry VI* —"I'll make my heaven to dream upon the crown" (3.2.168)—Shakespeare was at once invoking and slyly mocking Tamburlaine's dream of "The sweet fruition of an earthly crown" (2.7.29). Shakespeare, for his part, was in no danger of underestimating Marlowe. Marlowe was the only one of the university wits whose talent Shakespeare might have seriously envied, whose aesthetic judgment he might have feared, whose admiration he might have earnestly wanted to win, and whose achievements he certainly attempted to equal and outdo.

One of Marlowe's achievements might have seemed to Shakespeare, at this early point in his career, beyond his grasp. *Doctor Faustus*, the powerful tragedy of the scholar who sells his soul to the devil, drew deeply on Marlowe's theological education at Cambridge. Though years later, in *Hamlet*, Shakespeare depicted a bookish prince who has been abruptly pulled away from his university studies, and in *The Tempest* he explored the fate of a prince who becomes rapt in his occult reading, he never attempted, early or late, to make the scholar's study the center of the theatrical scene. His fullest answer to Marlowe came on neutral ground, that is, in the depiction of a person whom neither of them is likely ever to have encountered, a Jew.

But how did Marlowe and Shakespeare come to write two of their most memorable plays, *The Jew of Malta* and *The Merchant of Venice*, about Jews? Or rather, in the case of Shakespeare, why did the character of Shylock the Jew take over the comedy in which he appears? For almost everyone thinks that the merchant of Venice of the play's title is Shylock. Even when you realize that the merchant is not the Jew, even when you know that the title is referring to the Christian Antonio, you still instinctively make the mistake. And it is not exactly a mistake: the Jew is at the play's center. *The Merchant of Venice* has a host of characters who compete for the audience's attention: a handsome, impecunious young man in search of a wealthy wife; a melancholy, rich merchant who is hopelessly in love with the young man; women—three of them, no less—who dress themselves as men; a mischievous clown; an irrepressible sidekick; an exotic Moroccan; an absurd Spaniard. The list could be extended. But it is the Jewish villain everyone remembers, and not simply as villain. Shylock seems to have a stronger claim to attention, quite simply more life, than anyone else. The same can be said for Marlowe's Jewish villain, Barabas. Why were the imaginations of Shakespeare and Marlowe set on fire by the figure of the Jew?

The fire glowed against the darkness of almost complete erasure: in 1290, two hundred years before the momentous expulsion from Spain, the entire Jewish community of England had been expelled and forbidden on pain of death to return. The act of expulsion, in the reign of Edward I, was unprecedented; England was the first nation in medieval Christendom to rid itself by law of its entire Jewish population. There was no precipitating crisis, as far as is known, no state of emergency, not even any public explanation. No jurist seems to have thought it necessary to justify the deportations; no chronicler bothered to record the official reasons. Perhaps no one, Jew or Christian, thought reasons needed to be given. For decades the Jewish population in England had been in desperate trouble: accused of Host desecration and the ritual murder of Christian children, hated as moneylenders, reviled as Christ killers, beaten and lynched by mobs whipped into anti-Jewish frenzy by the incendiary sermons of itinerant friars.

By the time of Marlowe and Shakespeare, three centuries later, the Jewish population of England was ancient history. London had a small population of Spanish and Portuguese converts from Judaism, and some of these may have been Marranos, secretly maintaining Jewish practices. But the Jewish community in England had long vanished, and there were no Jews who openly practiced their religion. Yet in fact the Jews left traces far more difficult to eradicate than people, and the English brooded on these traces—stories circulated, reiterated, and elaborated—continually and virtually obsessively. There were Jewish fables and Jewish jokes and Jewish nightmares: Jews lured little children into their clutches, murdered them, and took their blood to make bread for Passover. Jews were immensely wealthy—even when they looked like paupers—and covertly pulled the strings of an enormous international network of capital and goods. Jews poisoned wells and were responsible for spreading the bubonic plague. Jews secretly plotted an apocalyptic war against the Christians. Jews had a peculiar stink. Jewish men menstruated.

Even though almost no one had actually laid eyes on one for generations, the Jews, like wolves in modern children's stories, played a powerful symbolic role in the country's imaginative economy. Not surprisingly, they found their way into the ordinary language that theatrical characters, including Shakespeare's, speak. "If I do not take pity of her I am a villain," says Benedick in *Much Ado About Nothing*, tricked by his friends into declaring a passion for Beatrice. "If I do not love her, I am a Jew" (2.3.231–32). Everyone knew what that meant: Jews were by nature villainous, unnatural, coldhearted. England's royal kings, says the dying John of Gaunt, are renowned for their deeds as far from home "As is the sepulchre, in stubborn Jewry, / Of the world's ransom, blessèd Mary's son" (*Richard II*, 2.1.55–56). Everyone knew what that meant: even in the wake of the Messiah's presence in their midst, Jews stubbornly and perversely clung to their old beliefs, beliefs that could not cleanse and hence ransom them from sin. "No, no, they were not bound," says Peto, contradicting Falstaff's brazen lie that he had bound the men with whom he says he had fought. "You rogue," rejoins Falstaff, "they were bound every man of them, or I am a Jew else, an Hebrew Jew" (*1 Henry IV*, 2.5.163–65). Everyone knew what that meant: a Jew—here, in Falstaff's comic turn, a Jew squared—was a person without valor and without honor, the very antithesis of what the fat braggart is claiming to be.

Shakespeare and his contemporaries found Jews, along with Ethopians, Turks, witches, hunchbacks, and others, useful conceptual tools. These feared and despised figures provided quick, easy orientation, clear boundaries, limit cases. "I think Crab, my dog, be the sourest-natured dog that lives," says the clown Lance in *The Two Gentlemen of Verona*. Everyone in his household weeps at Lance's departure, but the "cruel-hearted cur" does not shed a tear: "He is a stone, a very pebble-stone, and has no more pity in him than a dog. A Jew would have wept to have seen our parting" (2.3.4–5, 8–10). The Jew was a measuring device—here of degrees of heartlessness. He was also an identity marker, as another remark by the merry Lance makes clear: "If thou wilt, go with me to the alehouse. If not, thou art an Hebrew, a Jew, and not worth the name of a Christian" (2.5.44–45). The dog is real, at least in the special sense in which stage animals are real; Lance is real, at least in the special sense in which theatrical characters are real; but the Jew has no comparable reality. Perhaps the most casually devastating sign of the disappearance of real Jews is a quiet joke, rather than an insult: "Signor Costard, adieu," says the diminutive page Mote in *Love's Labour's Lost*, and the clownish Costard replies, "My sweet ounce of man's flesh, my incony Jew!" (3.1.123–24). "Incony," meaning "fine," was a piece of Elizabethan slang. But what is "Jew" doing here? The answer: nothing. Perhaps Costard has simply misheard "adieu" (presumably pronounced "a-Jew"); perhaps in a slangy way he is calling Mote a "jewel" or a "juvenile." Whatever he is saying, he is not referring to actual Jews; Shakespeare calculated, probably correctly, that the accidental reference would make his audience chuckle.

So, some three hundred years after their expulsion from England, the Jews were in circulation as despised figures in stories and in everyday speech, and Shakespeare, particularly early in his career, reflected and furthered this circulation, apparently without moral reservation. For though the audience is meant to feel various degrees of detachment from Benedick, Falstaff, Lance, and Costard, it is not distanced from a casual anti-Semitism that is simply an incidental feature of their comic energy. Jews do not actually appear in these plays, nor do they occupy a significant place in the language the characters speak; on the contrary, they are all but invisible, even in those few minor instances when they are invoked. Shakespeare was being a man of his times. Jews in England in the late sixteenth century had virtually no claim on reality; they had been subject to what the German language so eloquently calls *Vernichtung*, being made nothing.

Yet that is not quite right, for Jews were also constantly and more substantially present to all Christians as "the People of the Book." Without the Hebrew Bible, whose prophesies he fulfills, no Christ. It is possible to be unclear or evasive about whether Jesus was a Jew, but, conceptually at least, it is not possible for Christianity to do without Jews. Every Sunday, in a society in which weekly church attendance was obligatory for everyone, ministers edified their parishioners with passages, in translation, from the sacred Scriptures of the ancient Israelites. A people utterly despised and degraded, a people who had been deported en masse from England in the late thirteenth century and had never been allowed to return, an invisible people who functioned as symbolic tokens of all that was heartless, vicious, rapacious, and unnatural also functioned as the source of the most exalted spiritual poetry in the English language and as the necessary conduit through which the Redeemer came to all Christians.

This conceptual necessity—this historical interlacing of the destiny of Jews and Christians—had, of course, nothing to do with toleration for actual Jews. Certain cities—Venice among them—permitted Jews to reside relatively unmolested for extended periods of time, forbidding them, to be sure, to own land or practice most "honest" trades but allowing, even encouraging, them to lend money at interest. Such fiscal liquidity was highly useful in a society where canon law prohibited Christians from taking interest, but it made the Jews predictable objects of popular loathing and upper-class exploitation. Medieval popes periodically voiced a wish to protect Jews against those more radical Christian voices that called for their complete extinction, man, woman, and child, but the protection was only for the purposes of preserving an object lesson in misery. The papal argument was that an unhappy, impoverished, weak, and insecure remnant was a useful reminder of the consequences of rejecting Christ. Protestants had a somewhat greater interest in exploring the historical reality of ancient Judaism. The drive to return to the practices and beliefs of early Christianity led to a scholarly investigation of Hebrew prayer, the Passover, atonement, general confession, funeral customs, and the like. For a brief time Luther even felt kindly disposed toward contemporary Jews, who had, he thought, refused to convert to a corrupt and magical Catholicism. But when they stubbornly refused to convert to the purified, reformed Christianity he was championing, Luther's muted respect turned to rage, and in terms rivaling those of the most bigoted medieval friar, he called upon Christians to burn the Jews to death in their synagogues.

Luther's *On the Jews and Their Lies* probably had little currency in Elizabethan England. There were, after all, no synagogues left in England to burn, no Jewish community to hate or to protect. Marlowe and

Shakespeare encountered "strangers," vulnerable to attack, but these were men and women belonging to the small communities of Flemish, Dutch, French, and Italian artisans, mostly Protestant exiles, who lived in London. In economic hard times, these aliens were the victims of resentment, targeted by gangs of drunken, loudmouthed, club-wielding idlers baying for blood.

The evidence that Marlowe and Shakespeare personally concerned themselves with this xenophobic violence is, in both cases, suggestive but ambiguous. In 1593 someone nailed up, on the Dutch Church wall in London, an incendiary placard against the resident aliens, one of a series of attacks that the authorities feared would incite violence. The authorities, launching a sweep against the troublemakers, apparently suspected that the author of the placard was Marlowe. Informed that Marlowe had been living with Thomas Kyd, officers went to Kyd's rooms. They did not find Marlowe there, but they searched the rooms and found heretical and blasphemous papers. Kyd, subjected to a brutal interrogation, said that the papers were all Marlowe's. Marlowe was called before the Privy Council, questioned, and released only under orders to report daily in person to the Palace of Westminster.

The suspicion that Marlowe wrote the Dutch Church libel was probably baseless, but it was not motivated by idle paranoia. The author or authors of the toxic words that worried the authorities complained that "like the Jews" the aliens "eat us up as bread"—the image may well have been drawn from a popular play like *The Jew of Malta*—and the nasty placard not only alluded to Marlowe's play *The Massacre at Paris* but was also signed "Tamburlaine." The allusions show that Marlowe's fantasies were current in the minds of some aggrieved people, that his plays had excited them, that his famous eloquence had helped them give their feelings a voice.

Shakespeare's very different response to the xenophobia was signaled in a play that he apparently collaborated in writing with several other playwrights, including Anthony Munday (the probable originator), Henry Chettle, Thomas Heywood, and Thomas Dekker. Before its first performance, the script, *Sir Thomas More,* ran afoul of the censor, Edmund Tilney, Master of the Revels. Tilney did not reject the play outright, but he demanded substantial revisions in several scenes depicting the hatred of "strangers," and he called for the complete elimination of a scene showing the 1517 riots against their presence in England. The reason for this demand seems clear: intensifying tensions culminated in periodic outbursts of rioting. There were particularly ugly episodes in 1592–93 and again in 1595. The authors of *Sir Thomas More* obviously wanted to capitalize on the tensions—everyone in the audience would understand that the scenes from the past were a thinly disguised representation of the world just outside the playhouse walls. The censor evidently was afraid that the play, even if it formally disapproved of the riots it staged, could stir up more trouble.

Though alterations were made and new scenes were written, possibly in response to the censor's demands, the script does not seem to have received official approval, and the play was apparently never performed. But the manuscript, written in multiple hands, somehow survived (it is now in the British Library) and has been pored over for more than a century with extraordinary attention. For though many puzzles about it remain unsolved, including the year the play was first drafted and the year or years when the revisions were made, the manuscript contains what most scholars agree are passages Shakespeare himself penned, the only such autograph manuscript to have been discovered.

One of the passages in Shakespeare's hand—Hand D, as it is more cautiously called—depicts Thomas More, as sheriff of London, successfully persuading the antialien rioters to abandon their rebellious violence and submit themselves to the king. Shakespeare wrote lines that seem exceptionally alert to the human misery and political dangers of forced expulsions. "Grant them removed," Shakespeare's More tells the mob that is demanding that the strangers be driven out of the kingdom,

> and grant that this your noise
> Hath chid down all the majesty of England.
> Imagine that you see the wretched strangers,
> Their babies at their backs, with their poor luggage
> Plodding to th' ports and coasts for transportation,
> And that you sit as kings in your desires,

Authority quite silenced by your brawl
And you in ruff of your opinions clothed:
What had you got? I'll tell you. You had taught
How insolence and strong hand should prevail,
How order should be quelled—and by this pattern
Not one of you should live an agèd man,
For other ruffians as their fancies wrought
With selfsame hand, self reasons, and self right
Would shark on you, and men like ravenous fishes
Would feed on one another.

The overarching point here is a traditional argument for obedience to higher authority, an argument Shakespeare had Ulysses make with even greater eloquence in *Troilus and Cressida*. Once the rabble take matters into their own hands, the warning goes, once the chain of due deference is broken, all civil protections immediately vanish, and the world is given over to the whims of the strong. But it is striking that the point was made through an exercise of sympathetic imagination, and that the scene most vividly conjured up was the moment of collective exile:

Imagine that you see the wretched strangers,
Their babies at their backs, with their poor luggage
Plodding to th' ports and coasts for transportation.

Shakespeare was not writing about the deported Jews of England; it is overwhelmingly unlikely that he was even thinking about Jews. But his lines convey a glimpse of scenes that must have occurred centuries earlier when, as the documentary record shows, at least 1,335 of the Jews expelled from England plodded to the ports and paid for passage to France.

Here is a certain capacity to conjure up the lives of others, an ability to identify even with despised and degraded humanity that sits uncomfortably in Shakespeare's work with "If I do not love her I am a Jew," and other moments of impulsive, unself-conscious Jew-baiting. These latter obviously cannot be taken as the expression of the playwright's considered

"opinion" about Jews or other strangers, nor are they sufficiently individu-
ated or detailed to tell us much about the characters in whose mouths they
appear. They are simply instances of lively or amusing speech, rhetorically
enhanced no doubt, but close enough to ordinary usage to count as realistic representation. Such realism was the medium in which Shakespeare
frequently worked, particularly in the comedies and histories. He seemed
quite comfortable with it; that is, there was little or no sense of strain, no
signal that he wished to rise above and judge the language of the crowd,
no moral revulsion. But there was a different principle at work in the lines
he gave More, a current of feeling that Shakespeare attributed to the
capacity of the imagination. The effect is like a quick sketch by Dürer or
Rembrandt: a few black lines on a blank page and suddenly a whole scene,
charged with pain and loss, surges up. Since the "wretched strangers" in
Sir Thomas More are not Jews, there was no inherent reason for the two
impulses—mockery and identification—to come into tension or to contradict one another. They could have just sat there side by side. But they
did in fact come into conflict for Shakespeare, and the remarkable record
of the conflict is *The Merchant of Venice*.

To understand how this conflict came about, we must return to the
play that Christopher Marlowe had written about a Jew. A black comedy,
brilliant but exceptionally cynical and cruel, *The Jew of Malta* was probably first performed in 1589, near the beginning of Shakespeare's career as
a playwright, and it was an immediate success. Marlowe's antihero, the
Jew Barabas, with his Muslim slave Ithamore, exposes the rottenness of
Malta's Christian world, but in the course of the gleeful exposure, the
play gives voice to a full range of the worst anti-Jewish fantasies. "I walk
abroad a-nights," Barabas declares,

> And kill sick people groaning under walls.
> Sometimes I go about and poison wells;
> And now and then, to cherish Christian thieves,
> I am content to lose some of my crowns,
> That I may, walking in my gallery,
> See 'em go pinioned along by my door.
> (2.3.178–84)

Barabas's love of money is surpassed by his hatred of Christians, his pleasure in contriving and savoring as many of their deaths as he can possibly bring about. The Jew may speak cordially to his Christian neighbors, he may seem to allow his daughter to convert to Christianity, he may even imply his own interest in conversion, but in his heart he is always hatching murder. His homicidal career began, he explains, in the practice of medicine, and he then turned to other professions, always with the same malevolent motive:

> Being young, I studied physic, and began
> To practice first upon the Italian;
> There I enriched the priests with burials,
> And always kept the sexton's arms in ure
> With digging graves and ringing dead men's knells.
> And after that was I an engineer,
> And in the wars 'twixt France and Germany,
> Under pretense of helping Charles the Fifth,
> Slew friend and enemy with my stratagems.
> Then after that was I an usurer,
> And with extorting, cozening, forfeiting,
> And tricks belonging unto brokery,
> I filled the jails with bankrupts in a year,
> And with young orphans planted hospitals,
> And every moon made some or other mad,
> And now and then one hang himself for grief,
> Pinning upon his breast a long great scroll
> How I with interest tormented him.
>
> (2.3.185–202)

Where was Marlowe in all of this? Where was his audience? The spectators were invited to share imaginatively in the homicidal reverie, a reverie built out of the recycled religious hatreds of centuries, but then what? What happened to the poison after it had been vented on the public stage? Perhaps it evaporated; perhaps precisely by venting it, by giving the grotesque libel a full airing, it was exposed as the murderous daydream that it was. No one was ever like Barbaras or Ithamore; no one ever could be, and staging the impossible would have made clear to the audience the absurdity of its fantasy.

The Jew of Malta may indeed have produced such a liberating effect, but probably only among those in the audience already disposed to be liberated. In any case, successful playwrights were in the business of exciting their audiences—the point was to bring crowds of paying customers into the theater—and whatever playing company had the rights to the script must have been pleased to have, in The Jew of Malta, a licensed play they could repeatedly dust off and revive profitably at moments of popular agitation. The group of playwrights who wrote Sir Thomas More also hoped to profit from the excitement of the crowd— the censor who struck the depiction of the popular riot saw very clearly what was going on. But the lines Shakespeare gave to More, in facing down the antialien rioters, pull so sharply against the work of the irresponsible, bloody-minded, cynical Marlowe as to constitute a deliberate reproach. "Imagine that you see the wretched strangers, / Their babies at their backs."

Current scholarly consensus holds that Shakespeare probably wrote his contribution to Sir Thomas More sometime between 1600 and 1605. Like his response to Greene's insults, his response to Marlowe, then, probably came many years after his rival's death. For on May 30, 1593, a few weeks after the posting of the placard on the Dutch Church wall, Marlowe, not yet thirty years old, had gone to Deptford, down by the shipyards east of London, to meet with three men, Ingram Frizer, Nicholas Skeres, and Robert Poley. They spent the day quietly, eating, drinking, and smoking at the house of Eleanor Bull, a bailiff's widow. In the evening after supper, there was a fight, allegedly over the "reckoning," that is, the bill. Frizer claimed that an enraged Marlowe had snatched Frizer's own weapon—a dagger, as the inquest carefully put it, "of the value of twelve pence"—and attacked him. In the ensuing struggle, Marlowe was killed, stabbed through the right eye. Frizer's account was corroborated by the other two men in the room, and the inquest concurred in its report. A month later the queen formally pardoned Frizer, on the grounds of self-defense. Only in the twentieth century did scholarly detective work disclose that the widow Bull's house was not an ordinary tavern but a place with links to the government's spy network, and that Frizer, Skeres, and Poley all had sinister connections to that network, as did Marlowe himself, connections not mentioned, of course, in the inquest. The murder, then, was quite possibly an assassination, though the precise motive has remained obscure.

Already before he left Cambridge, Marlowe had demonstrated not only his power as a poet but also his penchant for risk-taking. Spectacularly ill suited for the life of a country parson or a sober academic, he early became involved in the murky world of conspiracy and spying, the world that Shakespeare may have briefly glimpsed and fled from in Lancashire. The precise circumstances would have been strictly secret at the time and are still more obscure after four hundred years, but it seems that Marlowe was recruited, while still a student, into the intelligence service run by Elizabeth's spymaster, her secretary of state Sir Francis Walsingham. Marlowe was apparently sent to Reims, where he mingled with the English Catholics living in France. Such information as he could ferret out—or provoke—about plots to mount a foreign invasion or assassinate the heretic queen he would have passed along to his superiors. He must have been reasonably good at his nasty work, since the Privy Council wrote to the Cambridge authorities instructing them to award Marlowe his M.A. degree, despite his unexplained absences during term time.

When he came to London to try his hand at playwriting, Marlowe had already begun a move from the artisan class to which his father belonged to the status of a gentleman—he had his university degree in hand—but he was hardly following a conventional life course. His overt sexual interest in men made that course still less conventional, while his opinions—according to the report of the intelligence agent who was assigned to spy on him and the testimony of his roommate Kyd—pushed him to the most dangerous frontiers of freethinking. He used to declare (or so the spy claimed) that Jesus was a bastard and his mother a whore; that Moses was a "juggler," that is, a trickster, who had deceived the ignorant Jews; that the existence of the American Indians disproved Old Testament chronology; that the New Testament was "filthily written" and that he, Marlowe, could do better; that Jesus and St. John were homosexual lovers; and so on. If Marlowe said even a fraction of what was attributed to him, then he could only have survived—and that not for very long—in a social and professional sphere that winked at views that would elsewhere have been instantly and ferociously punished.

At the time of the death, at the age of twenty-nine, of his greatest professional rival, Shakespeare had already shown considerable promise, but his actual achievements could not begin to match the astonishing succession of plays and poems written by Marlowe. They must have known each other personally; the world they inhabited was far too small for anonymity. They may have liked each other, but there were as many grounds for suspicion and dislike as for affection and admiration. Some five years after Marlowe's death, in *As You Like It*, Shakespeare obliquely paid tribute to his rival by quoting one of his most famous lines. A lovesick character, invoking Marlowe as a "dead shepherd," says she now finds his "saw of might" (that is, she finds that his saying is powerful):

> Dead shepherd, now I find thy saw of might:
> "Who ever loved that loved not at first sight?"
> (3.5.82–83)

But elsewhere in the same play there may be a less generous glance at Marlowe. "When a man's verses cannot be understood," complains the clown Touchstone, "nor a man's good wit seconded with the forward child, understanding, it strikes a man more dead than a great reckoning in a little room" (3.3.9–12). These words were not exactly an attack on Marlowe, but insofar as they may have alluded to his murder over a "reckoning," they did so with a complete absence of sentimental feeling.

Beyond the trace of personal competitiveness that had outlasted even the rival's death and beyond the commercial competitiveness of rival playing companies vying for the same audience, there was a disagreement about the nature of the theater, which was also a disagreement about human imagination and human values. Shakespeare saw what was marvelous in Marlowe (there is much more evidence than the passing tribute in *As You Like It*), but he also seems to have disliked quite deeply something in Marlowe's language and imagination. Shakespeare left no programmatic statement of this difference, only his responses in the play-house. And the most sustained of these responses involved the representation of Jews, the marked difference, that is, between Barbaras in *The Jew of Malta* and Shylock in *The Merchant of Venice*.

Marlowe was already dead when Shakespeare began, some time after 1594 and before 1598, to write *The Merchant of Venice*. Though a successful revival of *The Jew of Malta* probably prompted him to try his hand at a play about Jews, Shakespeare was not only glancing over his shoulder at his erstwhile rival. He did not even need Marlowe's play to give him his subject; he may, for example, have seen and remembered an old play entitled *The Jew* that was in vogue when he was still a boy and could well have been performed in the provinces. The play is now lost, but in 1579 a man who generally hated and attacked the theater, Stephen Gosson, went out of his way to praise *The Jew* for exposing "the greediness of worldly choosers" and the "bloody minds of usurers."

But something other than this old play or even Marlowe's newer one must serve to explain why Shakespeare's play turned out to be the peculiarly disturbing achievement that it is. The explanation does not lie in the plot, which is not original to Shakespeare and is highly conventional. At some point in his restless, voluminous reading, Shakespeare came across an Italian story about a Jewish usurer, Ser Giovanni's *Il Pecarone*, which must have struck him as good material for a comedy. (It is worth noting, in passing, that Shakespeare's reading, and indeed the entire Elizabethan book trade, was conspicuously international. The reading public, by modern standards, may have been fairly small, but its interests were strikingly cosmopolitan.) As he often did with texts he liked, Shakespeare lifted the plot wholesale from *Il Pecarone*: the merchant of Venice who borrows money for someone (here, not his friend but his "godson") from a Jewish moneylender; the terrible bond with its forfeit of a pound of the merchant's flesh; the successful wooing of a lady of "Belmonte" who comes to Venice disguised as a lawyer; her clever solution to the threat of the bond by pointing out that the legal right to take a pound of flesh does not include the legal right to take a drop of blood; the slightly nervous comic business of the rings. There was nothing original, then, in the shape of Shakespeare's play; even the Belmont plot of the caskets and the suitors, which did not come from Ser Giovanni, was lifted from elsewhere and thoroughly shopworn. There is exquisite poetry in the scene of Bassanio's successful wooing and, still more so, in the throwaway scene near the end of the play between Jessica and Lorenzo, sitting on the moonlit bank; there is a memorable depiction in Antonio of a state of depression, an unshakable melancholy that seems linked to his frustrated love for Bassanio. But the play would not count for much—it would seem roughly comparable to, say, *The Two Gentlemen of Verona* and other lesser efforts—were it not for the stupendous power of Shylock.

Shakespeare may have long had it in mind that he would write a play about a usurer. He may not have known any Jews, but he would certainly have known usurers, beginning with his own father, who had twice been accused of violating the law by charging usurious interest. The regulations against moneylending had been eased in 1591, and after he grew wealthy from the theater, Shakespeare himself seems to have been involved in at least one such transaction, either on his own or as a middleman. A letter has survived by chance, in the archives of the Stratford Corporation, to Shakespeare from Richard Quiney, a prominent Stratford tradesman. Quiney's letter, dated October 25, 1598, was written from his inn in London, where he had evidently come in the hope of borrowing money for himself and another Stratford citizen, Abraham Sturley, from their "Loveing good ffrend & contreymann m^r w^m Shackespere." On the same day, Quiney wrote to Sturley with the terms of the proposed loan— a rate of thirty or forty shillings on a loan of thrity or forty pounds—and ten days later Sturley replied. He was pleased to hear "that our countryman Mr. Wm. Shak. would procure us money."

It is only the fact that Shakespeare wrote *The Merchant of Venice* that makes these transactions surprising. For though officially the English declared by statute that usury was illegal under the law of God and had driven out the only people who were exempt, by reason of being Jews, from this prohibition, the realm's mercantile economy could not function without the possibility of moneylending. In the absence of a banking system, in our sense of the term, the English tried at least to hold lending rates down to 10 percent, and many individuals devised clever means, legal and illegal, to get around the official constraints. Even John Shakespeare's robustly illegal dealings—interest rates of 20 and 25 percent—were fairly standard.

Christian usurers, even when they were not directly called by that name, occupied a position roughly comparable to the one held by the Jews: officially, they were despised, harassed, condemned from the pulpit and the stage, but they also played a key role, a role that could not be conveniently eliminated. It was possible for usurers to live more or less respectable lives, as Shakespeare's father did, but the deep contradiction between stigma and esteem, contempt and centrality, was probably always there in the shadows, ready to emerge. Shakespeare loved contradictions of this kind; his art greedily pounced upon them and played with them. But there is still the question of how he got to Shylock.

Something set Shakespeare's imagination on fire, something enabled him to discover in his stock villain a certain music—the sounds of a tense psychological inwardness, a soul under siege—that no one, not even Marlowe, had been able to call forth from the despised figure of the Jew. Very little is understood about the life experiences, either then or now, that make such creative leaps possible, but one can at least imagine a set of plausible triggering events in the everyday world Shakespeare inhabited.

Shakespeare was in London for at least part of 1594. In that year the bubonic plague, which had caused the theaters to be shut down for much of the season, abated enough to allow the players to perform once again in the city. The closing of the theaters had taken a severe toll on the playing companies. The Queen's Men were tottering; the Earl of Hertford's Men called it quits; the Earl of Pembroke's Men went bankrupt and had to sell their costumes; the Earl of Sussex's Men were forced to disband when their patron died; and the same fate befell the Earl of Derby's Men upon the mysterious death—by poison, it was rumored—of their patron, Ferdinando, Lord Strange. Out of this ruinous situation, two companies, absorbing the best talent, emerged to dominate the London theater scene: the Lord Admiral's Men, under the protection of Charles Howard, Lord Howard of Effingham, and the Lord Chamberlain's Men, under the protection of Howard's father-in-law, Henry Carey, Lord Hunsdon. The Lord Admiral's Men had, above all, the celebrated actor

Edward Alleyn and the great impresario Philip Henslowe; they performed south of the river, in the handsome Rose playhouse. The Lord Chamberlain's Men performed at Shoreditch, in Burbage's Theater. Their leading actor was Richard Burbage, and they picked up, from the ruins of the Earl of Derby's Men, the celebrated clown Will Kempe, along with John Heminges, Augustine Phillips, George Bryan, and Thomas Pope. All of these men, and one more besides, were "sharers"— that is, shareholders in the enterprise, managing affairs, bearing the costs, and splitting the profits. The additional sharer was William Shakespeare.

Shakespeare's company was poised to take advantage of the renewed opportunities, provided that the plague deaths did not once again soar. Mercifully, the death rates remained relatively low, and the populace could once again begin to look for amusements. London, however, was by no means completely calm: though the famous "Protestant wind" had scuttled the Spanish Armada in 1588, there were recurrent fears of invasion and constant rumors of plots against the life of Queen Elizabeth. The threat was real enough to be taken seriously by sober people; government spies, penetrating swirling, murky intrigues in embassies and at court, found ample reason to be jittery. One group, the fiercely anti-Spanish, militantly Protestant faction around the queen's ambitious favorite, the Earl of Essex, was particularly exercised about actual or potential plots. On January 21, 1594, the Essex faction got what it wanted: the queen's personal physician, Portuguese-born Roderigo (or Ruy) Lopez, was arrested on the charge that he was intriguing with the king of Spain, who had, according to intercepted letters, agreed to send him an enormous sum of money—50,000 crowns, equal to 18,800 pounds—to do some important service.

Essex had tried some years before to recruit Lopez as a secret agent. Lopez's refusal—he chose instead directly to inform the queen—may have been prudent, but it created in the powerful earl a very dangerous enemy. After his arrest, he was initially imprisoned at Essex House and interrogated by the earl himself. But Lopez had powerful allies in the rival faction of the queen's senior adviser William Cecil, Lord Burghley, and his son, Robert Cecil, who also participated in the interrogation and reported to the queen that the charges against her physician were base-less. According to court observers, Elizabeth gave Essex a tongue-lashing, "calling him *rash and temerarious youth*, to enter into a matter against the poor man, which he could not prove, and whose innocence she knew well enough; but malice against him, and no other, hatch'd all this matter, which displeas'd her much, and the more, for that, she said, her honor was interested herein." Now, of course, Essex's own honor was at stake, and he and his allies moved quickly to find evidence to substantiate their charges. The complex tangle of spies and sleazy informers and the labo-rious sifting of documents—what the rival Cecils grudgingly describe as "all the Confessions, Examinations, Depositions, Declarations, Mes-sages, Letters, Tickets, Tokens, Conferences, Plots and Practices"—need not detain us. Suffice it to say that at the trial that opened in London on February 28, 1594, Dr. Lopez was charged and promptly convicted of conspiring to poison his royal patient. According to informers, Lopez had agreed to undertake the poisoning in exchange for 50,000 crowns to be paid by Philip II of Spain. Strangely enough, the supposed agent of this Catholic conspiracy, Lopez, was not a secret Catholic. He was—or rather, since he now professed to be a good Protestant, he had once been—a Jew. Many suspected, as Essex's ally Francis Bacon wrote, that he was still "in sect secretly a Jew (though here he conformed himself to the rites of Christian religion)."

It is difficult to say whether Lopez was actually guilty of high treason. Once the case came to trial, the result was almost a foregone conclusion, so there is no certainty to be drawn from the conviction. That it came to trial is testimony to the power of Essex, whose prestige was on the line, but it is also testimony to Lopez's taste for international and domestic intrigue, to his unsavory acquaintances, and to his venality—he was evi-dently taking bribes from many different sources. These qualities, how-ever, only bear witness to the fact that the royal physician was a man of the court, with privileged access to the queen herself and therefore in a posi-tion to profit. He may have gone still further: after maintaining his inno-cence, he confessed, perhaps in earnest or perhaps only to avoid being tortured, that he had indeed entered into a treasonous-sounding negotiation with the king of Spain, but he insisted that he had done so only in order to cozen the king out of his money. Whatever else he was—scoundrel, confidence man, or traitor—Lopez was a pawn in tense factional rivalries of the kind that Elizabeth manipulated adroitly. As long as the Cecils saw fit to support him, in the hope that Essex would be embarrassed, the physician was safe; as soon as that support vanished—as soon as his dubious associations made him a liability—he was as good as dead.

In the prosecutor's summary, Roderigo Lopez was not only a greedy villain; he was, like the sly Jesuits he so much resembled, the sinister agent of wicked Catholic powers determined to destroy the Protestant queen. At the same time, he was a Jewish villain:

> Lopez, a perjured murdering traitor, and Jewish doctor, worse than Judas himself, undertook to poison her, which was a plot more wicked, dangerous, and detestable than all the former. He was Her Majesty's sworn servant, graced and advanced with many princely favors, used in special places of credit, permitted often access to her person, and so not suspected, especially by her, who never fears her enemies nor suspects her servants. The bargain was made, and the price agreed upon, and the fact only deferred until payment of the money was assured; the letters of credit for his assurance were sent, but before they came into his hands, God most wonderfully and miraculously revealed and prevented it.

Lopez was, by all accounts, a practicing Christian, an observant Protestant, thoroughly assimilated into high society, and the English generally contented themselves with outward religious conformity. But the particular profile of his wickedness—the greed, perfidiousness, secret malice, ingratitude, and murderousness—seemed to call for a special explanation, one that would also reinforce the sense that the queen had been miraculously saved by divine intervention. Traditional hatred of Jews and the particular topicality of Marlowe's *Jew of Malta* (whose antihero, one might recall, began his career as a doctor who poisoned his patients) gave Lopez's Jewish origins an important place in the narrative of his conspiracy.

Lopez and the two Portuguese agents who allegedly were his inter-mediaries were quickly convicted, but the queen unaccountably delayed the approval needed to carry out the death sentence, a delay that pro-voked what government officials described as "the general discontent of the people, who much expected this execution." Finally, on June 7, 1594, the people—or, in any case, the factions who were pressing for execu-tion—got what they wanted. Lopez and the others were taken from the Tower of London, where they had been held. Asked if he could declare any reason why the sentence should not be carried out, Lopez replied that he appealed to the queen's own knowledge and goodness. After legal formalities were concluded, the three prisoners were carried on a hurdle past jeering spectators to the execution ground at Tyburn, where a crowd was awaiting them.

Was William Shakespeare in this crowd? The trial of Lopez, with its factional infighting and lurid charges, had generated intense interest. Shakespeare, in any case, was interested in executions: his early farce, *The Comedy of Errors*, is structured around the countdown to an execution, and the executioner's ax casts a grim shadow across *Richard III* and other histories. He was fascinated professionally by the behavior of mobs and fascinated too by the comportment of men and women facing the end. His most famous lines on the subject come in *Macbeth*, in the description of the last moments in the life of a thane who had betrayed the king:

> Nothing in his life
> Became him like the leaving it. He died
> As one that had been studied in his death
> To throw away the dearest thing he owed
> As 'twere a careless trifle.
>
> (1.4.7–11)

It is reasonable to suppose that the dramatist who wrote those lines had wit-nessed executions for himself, events that occurred in the capital city with horrifying frequency. Indeed, the lines betray a certain connoisseurship.

The execution of Dr. Lopez was a public event. If Shakespeare did personally witness it, he would have seen and heard something beyond the ordinary, ghastly display of fear and ferocious cruelty. In the wake of his conviction, Lopez evidently had sunk into a deep depression, but on the scaffold he roused himself and declared, according to the Elizabethan historian William Camden, that "he loved the Queen as well as he loved Jesus Christ." "Which coming from a man of the Jewish profession," Camden adds, "moved no small Laughter in the Standers-by."

This laughter, welling up from the crowd at the foot of the scaffold, could well have triggered Shakespeare's achievement in *The Merchant of Venice*. It was, for a start, exceptionally cruel: in a matter of moments, a living man would be hanged and his body torn into pieces. The crowd's laughter denied the solemnity of the event and treated violent death as an occasion for amusement. More specifically, it denied Lopez the end he was attempting to make, an end in which he hoped to reassert his faith as the queen's loyal subject and as a Christian soul. The last words a person spoke were ordinarily charged with the presumption of absolute honesty: there was no longer any room for equivocation, no longer any hope of deferral, no longer any distance between the self and whatever judgment lies beyond the grave. This was, in the most literal sense, the moment of truth. Those who stood and laughed made it clear—clear to one another and clear to Lopez himself—that they did not believe him. "Coming from a man of the Jewish profession": Lopez did *not* profess Judaism; he publicly adhered to Protestantism and invoked Jesus Christ. The laughter turned Lopez's last words from a profession of faith into a sly joke, a carefully crafted double entendre: "he loved the Queen as well as he loved Jesus Christ." Precisely: since, in the eyes of the crowd, Lopez was a Jew and a Jew does not in fact love Jesus Christ, his real meaning was that he tried to do to the queen what his accursed race did to Jesus. His words took the form of a declaration of innocence, but the crowd's response turned them into an ambiguous admission of guilt. Some in the crowd could have thought that the admission was inadvertent, a hypocritical overreaching that had toppled unwittingly into confession. Others, still more amused, could have concluded that the ambiguity was deliberate. Lopez the Jew was practicing an art perfected, it was said, by the Jesuits: equivocation. He was trying to protect his family and reputation by fraudulently insisting on his innocence while at the same time subtly telling the truth.

These laughing spectators, in other words, thought they were watching a real-life version of *The Jew of Malta*.

Early in Marlowe's play, the villainous Jew persuades his daughter to pretend that she wishes to convert to Christianity and enter a nunnery. He tells her that "A counterfeit profession," that is, a falsely pretended belief, a mendacious performance, "is better / Than unseen hypocrisy" (1.2.292–93). On this dubious moral principle—that it is better deliberately to dissemble than to be an unconscious hypocrite—Barabas fashions his own performance, crafting a string of double entendres delivered with a wink or a sly aside to the audience. Plotting murder, he lures the governor's lovesick son Lodowick to his house by offering him a precious "diamond"—his daughter Abigail. When Lodowick, continuing the metaphor, asks, "And what's the price?" Barabas mutters as an aside, "Your life." "Come to my house," he adds aloud, "And I will giv't Your Honor"; then again, the murderous aside, "with a vengeance." To reassure his intended Christian victim, Barabas speaks of his "burning zeal" for the nunnery, and then adds, for the audience's amusement, "Hoping ere long to set the house afire!" (2.3.65–68, 88–89). That is precisely the kind of joke that the crowd thought it heard when Lopez made his last speech.

Lopez's execution was the last act of a comedy, or so the crowd's laughter, conditioned by *The Jew of Malta*, suggested. If it was cruel, it was also perfectly reasonable to laugh. A wicked plot to murder the queen—a plot that combined the hated figure of the Catholic king of Spain and the hated figure of the Jew—had been providentially thwarted. Was Shakespeare attracted or repelled by what went on at the foot of the scaffold? Did he admire the way Marlowe's dark comedy had helped to shape the crowd's response, or was he sickened by it? The only evidence is the play that Shakespeare wrote in the wake of Lopez's death, and the answer it suggests is that he was both intrigued and nauseated. He borrowed heavily from Marlowe—Shakespeare was always a great borrower—but he created a set of characters and a range of emotions utterly alien to Marlowe's art. He wanted, it seems, to excite laughter at a wicked Jew's discomfiture—not, to be sure, in a play about international intrigue, but in a play about money and love—and he wanted at the same time to call the laughter into question, to make the amusement excruciatingly uncomfortable.

The Merchant of Venice is full of amused mockery: "I never heard a passion so confused," chuckles one of the Venetian Christians, Solanio,

> So strange, outrageous, and so variable
> As the dog Jew did utter in the streets. .
> "My daughter! O, my ducats! O, my daughter!
> Fled with a Christian! O, my Christian ducats!"
> (2.8.12–16)

"Why, all the boys in Venice follow him," laughs his friend Salerio, giving us a glimpse of the crowd's raucous amusement, "Crying, 'His stones, his daughter, and his ducats!'" (2.8.23–24). And when Shylock's fiendish plot to avenge himself by cutting out a pound of good Antonio's flesh is defeated in court, the Jew's discomfiture, as he is forced to convert, is accompanied by a chorus of triumphant mockery from Graziano:

> Beg that thou mayst have leave to hang thyself—
>
> . . . .
>
> A halter, gratis. Nothing else, for God's sake.
>
> . . . .
>
> In christ'ning shalt thou have two godfathers.
> Had I been judge thou should have had ten more,
> To bring thee to the gallows, not the font.
> (4.1.359–96)

Shakespeare chose not to bring his Jew to the gallows—in all of his comedies, he carefully avoided killing off his villains, at least onstage—but the mocking voices of Salerio, Solanio, and Graziano are very close to what the playwright would have heard at the foot of the scaffold on which Lopez was hanged. *The Merchant of Venice* found a way to give the spectators something of what the crowd at the execution enjoyed, but without the blood and gore. Shylock is the traditional killjoy of romantic comedy: deaf to music, the enemy of pleasure, he stands in the way of young love. But he is something worse than the conventional tyrannical, possessive father who must be defeated by budding youth. "Shylock the

Jew" is, as the title page of the first quarto puts it, a figure of "extreme cruelty," the rigid, inflexible representative of the Old Law, an unforgiving, remorseless, embittered, and murderous alien who threatens the happiness of the entire community. Defeated in court—not as a Jew but as a non-Venetian, an "alien"—Shylock is forcibly drawn into that community, but Graziano's mockery makes it clear that the newly christened convert will always be, as Camden said of the convert Lopez, "a man of the Jewish profession"; that is, Shylock's conversion is just comedy's kinder, gentler way of killing him off.

Yet the fact is that the mockers Salerio, Solanio, and Graziano are probably the least likable characters in *The Merchant of Venice*. They are not depicted as villainous, and their laughter echoes through the play, but their grating words are repeatedly registered as embarrassing, coarse, and unpleasant. "Thou art," as Bassanio tells Graziano, "too wild, too rude and bold of voice" (2.2.162). Shakespeare did not repudiate their raucous voices—the voices that he may have heard laughing at the Jew Lopez; on the contrary, he wanted his comedy to draw them into the celebration of Shylock's undoing. But the spirit of the play is not their spirit.

A comic playwright thrives on laughter, but it is as if Shakespeare had looked too closely at the faces of the crowd, as if he were repelled as well as fascinated by the mockery of the vanquished alien, as if he understood the mass appeal of the ancient game he was playing but suddenly felt queasy about the rules. "Imagine that you see the wretched strangers": When he had such strangers—Lopez or Shylock—fixed in his imagination, Shakespeare was uneasy with what he saw. Shylock's forced conversion—a plot device not found in Shakespeare's source—is an attempt to evade the nastier historical alternatives: the grisly execution Shakespeare may have personally witnessed; the mass expulsion of the Jews he could have read about in the chronicles of England. But as the laughter in the courtroom plainly demonstrates, conversion does not actually work to settle the issue of the stranger. Even Shylock's daughter Jessica, who has eloped and become a Christian of her own volition, is not exempt: the clown Lancelot grumbles that as a Jew's daughter she is damned, and, besides, "This making of Christians will raise the price of hogs" (3.5.19).

But rising pork prices are the least of the problems that the play explores. Shakespeare chose not to do to Shylock what the Elizabethan state did to Lopez, but he opted for anatomy of a different kind. Unsettling the whole comic structure that he borrowed from his Italian source, he took the risk of dissecting the interior of his villain and probing more deeply than he had ever done before. To be sure, Shylock at moments is something of a puppet, but, even jerked upon his strings, he reveals what Shakespeare has achieved. In one of the more rigidly mechanistic moments in the play, Shylock is pulled in radically different directions: he tries to track down his daughter Jessica, who has robbed him and eloped with the Christian Lorenzo; at the same time Shylock learns that the merchant Antonio, whom he hates and would like to destroy, is suffering serious business reverses. Salerio and Solanio have already mocked the Jew's frantic outcries—"'My daughter! O, my ducats! O, my daughter!'"—and now the comic spectacle itself takes place. The scene begins with Shylock asking for news—of all of Shakespeare's characters, he is the most obsessed with news—from the fellow Jew he has sent to find his daughter.

> SHYLOCK: How now, Tubal? What news from Genoa? Hast thou
>   found my daughter?
> TUBAL: I often came where I did hear of her, but cannot find her.
> SHYLOCK: Why, there, there, there, there.
>
> (3.1.67–71)

Repetition is one of the keys to Shylock's music. In sound and sense both, "there" seems to spring from Tubal's "where," yet it is not really about place, Genoa or anywhere else. It is the register of Shylock's disappointment, and it is an attempt at consolation, the "there, there" spoken by a friend. But a friend does not speak the words; they are spoken by Shylock himself, and their numb repetition moves beyond frustrated hope and failed consolation to something else. Repeated words of this kind are drained of whatever meaning they may have started with; they become instead placeholders for silent thinking.

How do characters in a play—who are, after all, only jumbles of words upon a page—convey that they have something going on inside them? How do spectators get the impression of depths comparable to those they can barely fathom and understand within themselves? Shakespeare, unrivaled at conveying this impression, in the course of his career developed many means for doing so, including most famously the soliloquy. But his mastery of the soliloquy was gradual, and, along the way, he explored other devices, including repetition. Shylock does not articulate a coherent response to the news that his daughter has not been found; he only mumbles the same, meaningless word. But some emotional and thought process is occurring beneath the surface—the repeated word functions precisely to create such a surface—and we begin to glimpse whatever it is in his next words: "A diamond gone." The diamond seems for an instant to refer to Jessica (Barabas refers to his daughter Abigail as a diamond), but the completion of the sentence wrenches us in a different direction: "A diamond gone cost me two thousand ducats in Frankfurt" (3.1.71–72).

At such a moment the audience has in effect seen something invisible: the grieving mind's queasy, unconscious shift from emotional to monetary loss. Or rather, it has glimpsed the secret passage that links the Jew's daughter and the Jew's ducats. For as the next lines make clear, Shakespeare implies that there is something Jewish, something specific to the Jewish "nation," in this confounding of the familial and the financial: "The curse never fell upon our nation till now—I never felt it till now. Two thousand ducats in that and other precious, precious jewels." What curse? For a moment, Shylock seems to accede fully to the Christian belief that the Jews are accursed, a terrible fate he has now for the first time directly experienced. And in his pain and rage he attempts to turn the curse upon his daughter:

I would my daughter were dead at my foot and the jewels in her ear! I would she were hearsed at my foot and the ducats in her coffin! No news of them? Why, so. And I know not what's spent in the search. Why thou, loss upon loss: the thief gone with so much, and so much to find the thief, and no satisfaction, no revenge, nor

no ill luck stirring but what lights o' my shoulders, no sighs but o'
my breathing, no tears but o' my shedding. (3.1.72–81)

Did Shakespeare know that Orthodox Jews customarily mourn, as if dead,
children who have abandoned the faith? Perhaps. He surely believed that
moneylenders, Jewish or not, treated money as if it were alive and could
breed, and hence could treat lost money as if it were dead. Perhaps Shylock
means to say that he would wish his daughter dead if only he could recover
his money; perhaps that he wishes both the death of his daughter and the
recovery of his money. But his words also express a morbid fantasy of giving daughter and money together a proper burial, "loss upon loss."

When Tubal contradicts Shylock's claim that he alone is suffering—
"Yes, other men have ill luck too. Antonio, as I heard in Genoa"—Shylock interrupts excitedly, his manic, repetitive phrases now signaling not
secret thoughts but excitement, surprise, and stabs of pain:

SHYLOCK: What, what, what? Ill luck, ill luck?
TUBAL: Hath an argosy cast away coming from Tripolis.
SHYLOCK: I thank God, I thank God! Is it true, is it true?
TUBAL: I spoke with some of the sailors that escaped the wreck.
SHYLOCK: I thank thee, good Tubal. Good news, good news! Ha,
    ha—heard in Genoa?
TUBAL: Your daughter spent in Genoa, as I heard, one night four-
    score ducats.
SHYLOCK: Thou stick'st a dagger in me. I shall never see my gold
    again. Fourscore ducats at a sitting? Fourscore ducats?
TUBAL: There came divers of Antonio's creditors in my company to
    Venice that swear he cannot choose but break.
SHYLOCK: I am very glad of it. I'll plague him, I'll torture him. I am
    glad of it.

(3.1.82–97)

This is the stuff of comedy, and it is certainly possible to play the scene
for laughs, but the rising tide of anguish stifles the laughter, even as it

forms. The audience is brought in too close for psychological comfort to the suffering figure. Spattered by Shylock's exclamations, it cannot get to the distance appropriate for detached amusement.

It is possible that Shakespeare lost control of his own imagination here. Apart from "Hand D" of *Sir Thomas More,* no manuscript record of his writing process survives, but in an anecdote that circulated in the seventeenth century, he is said to have remarked of *Romeo and Juliet* that he had in the third act to kill Mercutio—the wildly anarchic mocker of romantic love—before Mercutio killed him. Perhaps something of the same kind began to happen with *The Merchant of Venice*; perhaps Shylock refused to keep his place in the imaginative scheme that had consigned him to the role of comic villain. But Shylock is more central than Mercutio, and there is too much evidence of authorial craft to be comfortable with the notion that the character simply escaped the playwright's control. Shakespeare could easily have ended the scene between Shylock and Tubal at the point at which the comic spirit makes a strong bid to reassert itself. But instead Tubal continues his report:

> TUBAL: One of them showed me a ring that he had of your daughter for a monkey.
> SHYLOCK: Out upon her! Thou torturest me, Tubal. It was my turquoise. I had it of Leah when I was a bachelor. I would not have given it for a wilderness of monkeys.
> TUBAL: But Antonio is certainly undone.
> SHYLOCK: Nay, that's true, that's very true. Go, Tubal, fee me an officer. Bespeak him a fortnight before. I will have the heart of him if he forfeit, for were he out of Venice I can make what merchandise I will. Go, Tubal, and meet me at our synagogue. Go, good Tubal; at our synagogue, Tubal.
>
> (3.1.98–108)

The words about Jessica's extravagance seem for a moment simply to continue Shylock's fretting about his lost jewels, but suddenly the pain deepens and the laughter dries up. It is as if the ring were something more than a piece of the Jew's wealth, as if it were a piece of his heart.

The Merchant of Venice is a play in which material objects are strangely charged or animated. There is the "Jewish gaberdine" on which Antonio spits (1.3.108); the "vile squealing of the wry-necked fife" that Shylock cannot abide and against which he hopes to "stop my house's ears—I mean my casements" (2.5.29, 33); the "merry bond" whose physical existence directly threatens Antonio's life (1.3.169). At first glance this animation might seem solely the malign effect of the Jewish moneylender, who makes barren metal "breed" (1.3.92, 129), but the Christians turn out to be equally involved. Salerio and Solanio imagine

> dangerous rocks
> Which, touching but my gentle vessel's side,
> Would scatter all her spices on the stream.
>   (1.1.31–33)

The suitors who seek Portia's hand in marriage discover their fate by unlocking one of three metal "caskets" that contain emblematic pictures, while the whole last act plays with the symbolic power of rings. But no object has greater power than that turquoise, linked to the name of Shylock's dead wife and glimpsed for a brief moment of anguish. Shylock immediately turns to plotting against Antonio—"I will have the heart of him if he forfeit, for were he out of Venice I can make what merchandise I will"—but what he has just said about the ring anticipates what the courtroom scene definitively discloses: revenge, not money, is what Shylock is after.

Does this mean that Shakespeare thought that Dr. Lopez—who received a valuable ring, sent to him by the king of Spain, that figured in his trial and that the queen kept after his execution—was after something other than money when he allegedly plotted to kill the queen for 50,000 crowns? There is no way to know. *The Merchant of Venice* is not a commentary on a case of treason; it is a romantic comedy with a villainous usurer whose principal resemblances to Lopez are his alien status and the

Jewishness that Lopez himself denied. The key link, apart from a general public excitement that may have helped box-office receipts, is the crowd's laughter, laughter that Shakespeare at once sought to capture and to unsettle. The crowd laughed because it thought it was in on a sly, Marlovian joke: "he loved the Queen as well as he loved Jesus Christ." This was, or so they understood, the confession of a would-be murderer, a man for whom the word "love" actually meant "hate."

Though he was in the business of amusing a popular audience, Shakespeare was clearly not altogether comfortable with this laughter. The play that he wrote at once borrows from *The Jew of Malta* and repudiates its corrosive, merciless irony. Whatever else I am, the playwright seems to be saying, I am not laughing at the foot of the scaffold, and I am not Marlowe. What sprang up in place of Marlovian irony was not tolerance—the play, after all, stages a forced conversion as the price of a pardon—but rather shoots of a strange, irrepressible imaginative generosity. This generosity makes theatrical trouble; it prevents any straightforward amusement at Shylock's confusion of his daughter and his ducats, and, what is more disturbing, it undermines the climactic trial scene. That scene is the comedy's equivalent of the real-world execution: it is meant to reach satisfying legal and moral closure, to punish villainy, and to affirm central values of the dominant culture. All of the elements seem to be in place: a wise duke, an implacable Jewish villain sharpening his knife for slaughter, a supremely eloquent appeal for mercy, a thrilling resolution. Yet this scene, as the experience of both the page and the stage repeatedly demonstrates, is deeply unsettled and unsettling. The resolution depends upon the manipulation of a legal technicality, the appeal for mercy gives way to the staccato imposition of punishments, and the affirmation of values is swamped by a flood of mingled self-righteousness and vindictiveness. Above all, without mitigating Shylock's vicious nature, without denying the need to thwart his murderous intentions, the play has given us too much insight into his inner life, too much of a stake in his identity and his fate, to enable us to laugh freely and without pain. For Shakespeare did something that Marlowe never chose to do and that the mocking crowd at Lopez's execution could not do; he wrote out what he imagined such a twisted man, about to be destroyed, would inwardly say:

I am a Jew. Hath not a Jew eyes? Hath not a Jew hands, organs, dimensions, senses, affections, passions; fed with the same food, hurt with the same weapons, subject to the same diseases, healed by the same means, warmed and cooled by the same winter and summer as a Christian is? If you prick us do we not bleed? If you tickle us do we not laugh? If you poison us do we not die? And if you wrong us shall we not revenge? (3.1.49–56)

CHAPTER 10

Speaking with the Dead

SOMETIME IN THE SPRING or summer of 1596 Shakespeare
may have received word that his only son, Hamnet, eleven years
old, was ill. It is possible he understood and responded at once,
or he may have been distracted by affairs in London. There was
much to preoccupy him. On July 22 the lord chamberlain, Henry Carey,
the queen's powerful cousin and the patron of Shakespeare's company, died.
The lord chamberlainship went to Lord Cobham, but the players were
kept by Carey's son George, Lord Hunsdon. (When Cobham died within
less than a year, the post of lord chamberlain went to George Carey, so that
the company, after only a brief interval of being known as the Lord Hunsdon's Men, once again became the Lord Chamberlain's Men.) The death
of their patron and the flurry of uncertainty must have been disconcerting
for the players, and their disquiet was no doubt intensified by renewed calls
by preachers and civic officials for the closing of the theaters in order to
protect London's moral and physical health. Performances were banned in
all city inns, and it is possible that during the summer of 1596 the city
authorities managed to obtain an order temporarily closing down all the
playhouses. Such a closure—known as an inhibition—would help to explain

why some members of Shakespeare's company were on the road that summer, performing at Faversham (in Kent) and other places.

Shakespeare may have accompanied his fellow actors on tour, or he may well have stayed back in London to work on one or another of the plays he must have been writing for the company at this time: *King John*, *1 Henry IV*, or *The Merchant of Venice*. Whether in London or on tour he would at best have only been able to receive news intermittently from Stratford, but at some point in the summer he must have learned that Hamnet's condition had worsened and that it was necessary to drop everything and hurry home. By the time he reached Stratford the eleven-year-old boy—whom, apart from brief returns, Shakespeare had in effect abandoned in his infancy—may already have died. On August 11, the father presumably saw his son buried at Holy Trinity Church: the clerk duly noted in the burial register, "Hamnet filius William Shakspere."

Unlike Ben Jonson and others who wrote grief-stricken poems about the loss of beloved children, Shakespeare published no elegies and left no direct record of his paternal feelings. The whole enterprise of acquiring the coat of arms must at one point have had something to do with his expectations for his son and heir, and Shakespeare's last will and testament displays a strong interest in passing along his property to his male descendants; but these are signs too formal and conventional perhaps to tell us about his inward state. It is sometimes said that parents in Shakespeare's time could not afford to invest too much love and hope in any one child. One out of three children died by the age of ten, and overall mortality rates were by our standards exceedingly high.

Death was a familiar spectacle; it took place at home, not out of sight. When Shakespeare was fifteen, his nine-year-old sister Anne died, and there must have been many other occasions for him to witness the death of children. But did familiarity breed detachment? The private diary of a contemporary doctor, recently deciphered, shows that desperate spouses and parents, inconsolable with grief, were constantly coming to him for treatment. Human emotions are not rationally coordinated with actuarial figures. Some Elizabethan parents may have learned to withhold affection or to protect themselves from misery, but by no means all did.

In the four years following Hamnet's death, the playwright, as many have pointed out, wrote some of his sunniest comedies: *The Merry Wives of Windsor, Much Ado About Nothing, As You Like It*. But the plays of these years were by no means uniformly cheerful, and at moments they seem to reflect an experience of deep personal loss. In *King John*, probably written in 1596, just after the boy was laid to rest, Shakespeare depicted a mother so frantic at the loss of her son that she is driven to thoughts of suicide. Observing her, a clerical bystander remarks that she is mad, but she insists that she is perfectly sane: "I am not mad; I would to God I were" (3.4.48). Reason, she says, and not madness, has put the thoughts of suicide in her head, for it is her reason that tenaciously keeps hold of the image of her child. When she is accused of perversely insisting on her grief, she replies with an eloquent simplicity that breaks free from the tangled plot:

> Grief fills the room up of my absent child,
> Lies in his bed, walks up and down with me,
> Puts on his pretty looks, repeats his words,
> Remembers me of all his gracious parts,
> Stuffs out his vacant garments with his form.
> (3.4.93–97)

If there is no secure link between these lines and the death of Hamnet, there is, at the very least, no reason to think that Shakespeare simply buried his son and moved on unscathed. He might have brooded inwardly and obsessively, even as he was making audiences laugh at Falstaff in love or at the wit contests of Beatrice and Benedick. Nor is it implausible that it took years for the trauma of his son's death fully to erupt in Shakespeare's work.

In a very late play, there may be a trace of Shakespeare's periodic visits to Stratford at the time when his son was still alive. "Are you so fond of your young prince as we / Do seem to be of ours?" one friend asks another. "If at home, sir," is the reply,

> He's all my exercise, my mirth, my matter;
> Now my sword friend, and then mine enemy;
> My parasite, my soldier, statesman, all.

He makes a July's day short as December,
And with his varying childness cures in me
Thoughts that would thick my blood.

(1.2.165–72)

"If at home, sir": the words fit the play, but they also fit the playwright. Perhaps, reflecting upon what might have kept thick blood, that is, melancholy, at bay, Shakespeare found himself thinking back to his son. The play in which these lines appear, *The Winter's Tale*, features a precocious little boy who languishes and dies when his madly jealous father turns against his mother.

Whether in the wake of Hamnet's death Shakespeare was suicidal or serene, he threw himself into his work. The later 1590s was an amazingly busy and productive period in his life, with a succession of brilliant plays, frequent performances at court and in the public theaters, and growing celebrity and wealth. As a sharer in his company, Shakespeare was probably directly involved in all aspects of its daily affairs, including the increasingly acrimonious conflict with Giles Allen, the owner of the land in Shoreditch on which the Theater, where the Lord Chamberlain's Men chiefly performed, had been built. The lease that James Burbage and his partner had taken back in 1576 was about to expire, and Allen refused to renew it, at least on terms that Burbage's sons, who had taken over the protracted negotiation upon the death of their father, could accept.

Finally, the talks broke off, and the Theater was closed. In some desperation, the company began to perform at the nearby Curtain, but the venue was not nearly so successful, and revenues evidently began to fall off. To raise money, they did something that playing companies generally resisted: they sold off four of their most popular playbooks, *Richard III, Richard II, 1 Henry IV,* and *Love's Labour's Lost*, to an enterprising publisher who brought them out in quarto editions. No doubt the ready cash was of some help, but it must have seemed less like a solution than an ominous step in a direction that would eventually lead to selling off their costumes and disbanding altogether.

The real solution was a daring one. On the snowy night of December 28, 1598, in a season cold enough to make the Thames freeze over, the players came together in Shoreditch. They carried lanterns and bore arms—in the words of one deposition, "swords, daggers, bills, axes and such like." The small company, aided perhaps by a few hired thugs, may not immediately strike one as a formidable force, but as actors were all trained in wielding weapons and as London had no regular police force, they were adequate for the enterprise. They posted guards around the perimeter, and then together with a dozen workmen, they proceeded to dismantle the Theater. In the morning light they loaded the heavy timbers on wagons and began the work of carting them across the river to a site they had secured not far from the Rose Theatre, in Southwark. The landlord, Allen, was apoplectic and sued for trespass, but the legal situation was a complex one, for the Burbages' lease stipulated a right to retrieve any structures they had built on Allen's land. The deed, in any event, was done, though it is difficult to understand how it was accomplished in a single night in the darkness.

Over the next months the gifted carpenter Peter Streete cleverly recycled the pieces of the old playhouse and fashioned a splendid new theater. A many-sided wooden polygon, roughly one hundred feet across, with a huge platform stage jutting into the pit and three galleries, it could hold over three thousand spectators, an astonishing figure for a city London's size and a tribute to the actors' immense power to project complex words and emotions. (Today's Globe, on the Bankside, has about half the capacity.) A small group of investors, Shakespeare among them, had financed the ambitious enterprise. For their motto they chose the phrase *Totus mundus agit histroniem*, roughly, "The whole world plays the actor," and for their sign they apparently had an image of Hercules bearing the world on his shoulders. They called their new playhouse the Globe.

By virtue of his investment, Shakespeare was now more than a sharer in the playing company. By the terms of the contract signed on February 21, 1599, he owned a tenth of the Globe, as did four of his fellow actors, John Heminges, Thomas Pope, Augustine Phillips, and Will Kempe. Kempe, the company's popular clown, famous for his antic dancing and his obscene songs, had an immediate falling-out with his partners; he sold his share and went off, making a sour joke about those he called

"Shakerags." The company was temporarily without a clown—it took some time to find the subtle, dwarfish Robert Armin—and Shakespeare's next play, *Julius Caesar*, was notably without a juicy part for a fool.

Shakespeare moved to Southwark, to be near the Globe, which was ready by June, a stunningly rapid turnaround. One might have expected them to open with a light crowd-pleaser, but the Lord Chamberlain's Men chose to inaugurate their new theater with *Julius Caesar*, a tragedy apt for a public still intensely anxious about the threat of an assassination attempt against their queen. A Swiss tourist to London, Thomas Platter, went to see it and wrote home one of the few contemporary eyewitness accounts of a Shakespeare performance: "On the 21st of September after lunch, about two o'clock, I crossed the water with my party, and we saw the tragedy of the first emperor Julius Caesar acted very prettily in the house with the thatched roof, with about fifteen characters." At the play's end, Platter notes, "according to their custom, they danced with exceeding elegance, two each in men's and two in women's clothes, wonderfully together." With *Julius Caesar* and the other strong plays in the company's repertoire, the Globe was launched, so successfully indeed that in six months' time their rivals at the nearby Rose Theatre packed up and headed across the river, to a new theater in Cripplegate, called the Fortune.

Driving the competition out of the immediate neighborhood did not mean an end to commercial competition altogether. On the contrary, by the end of 1599, the Lord Chamberlain's Men were engaged in an increasingly intense theatrical struggle with a newly revived private company, the Children of Paul's, followed the next year by another repertory company, the Children of the Chapel at Blackfriars. The fact that the players were boys did not lessen the seriousness of their challenge: these were sophisticated, sharp-witted, highly accomplished companies with a very strong audience appeal. In his next play Shakespeare provided a glimpse of the competition. Why has the company of players come all the way to Elsinore, Hamlet asks; surely their reputation and profit were both greater in the city. Rosencrantz explains that their audience has drastically fallen off: "there is, sir, an eyrie of children, little eyases," that is, young hawks; "These are now the fashion" (2.2.326, 328). When he sat down to write *Hamlet,* Shakespeare was looking over his shoulder at the children's companies and pretending to worry—not altogether comically—that they would put his troupe out of business.

Writing a play about Hamlet, in or around 1600, may not have been Shakespeare's own idea. At least one play, now lost, about the Danish prince who avenges his father's murder had already been performed on the English stage, successfully enough to be casually alluded to by contemporary writers, as if everyone had seen it or at least knew about it. Back in 1589 it was a play on Hamlet that figured in Nashe's ridicule of the rude upstart (probably Thomas Kyd) who never attended university but still had the impudence to set himself up as a playwright: "if you entreat him fair in a frosty morning, he will afford you whole *Hamlets,* I should say handfuls of tragical speeches." And seven years later another one of the university wits, Thomas Lodge, echoed the mocking tone when he referred to a devil who looked "as pale as the Vizard of the ghost which cried so miserably at the Theatre, like an oyster-wife, 'Hamlet, revenge!'" Either the play was still onstage—an exceptionally long run in the Elizabethan theater—or it had been recently revived, or it had simply become proverbial for somewhat vulgar theatrical intensity. Lodge and Nashe thought that their readers would effortlessly conjure up the story.

Someone in the Lord Chamberlain's Men, with an eye on revenues, may simply have suggested to Shakespeare that the time might be ripe for a new, improved version of Hamlet. For that matter, with his high stakes in the company's profits, Shakespeare was singularly alert to whatever attracted London crowds, and he had by now long experience in dusting off old plays and making them startlingly new. The likely author of the earlier play, Thomas Kyd, was no obstacle: possibly broken by the torture inflicted upon him when he was interrogated about his roommate Marlowe, he had died back in 1594, at the age of thirty-six. In any case, neither Shakespeare nor his contemporaries were squeamish about stealing from one another.

Shakespeare had certainly seen the earlier Hamlet play, probably on several occasions. He may well have acted in it, in which case he would have had in his possession the roll of paper strips, glued together, on which his part and the cues for his entries and exits were written. Elizabethan actors generally had access only to their particular roll—from whence we get the term "role"—and not to the script as a whole; it was too expensive to copy it out in its entirety, and the playing companies were wary about allowing their scripts to circulate widely. They might on special occasions make copies for favored patrons, and in times of financial necessity they would sometimes sell plays to printers. But they wanted the public principally to encounter plays in the playhouse, not in the study. (Of course, keeping the scripts out of print greatly increased the likelihood that they would eventually be lost—as the early version of Hamlet and many others were—but that was no concern of the companies.)

Whether or not he had access to the script of the Hamlet play, Shakespeare had to an astounding degree something that virtually every actor at the time had to possess: an acute memory. Everything he encountered, even tangentially and in passing, seems to have stayed with him and remained available to him years later. Scraps of conversation, official proclamations, long-winded sermons, remarks overheard in the tavern or on the street, insults exchanged by carters and fishwives, a few pages that he could only have glanced at idly in a bookseller's shop—all was somehow stored away in his brain, in files that his imagination could open up at will. His memory was not perfect—he made mistakes, confused one place for another, transposed names, and the like—but the imperfections only demonstrate that there was nothing compulsive or mechanical about his remarkable gift. His memory was an immense creative resource.

When he set to work on his new tragedy, then, Shakespeare likely had the old play about Hamlet by heart, or as much of it as he chose to remember. It is impossible to determine, in this case, whether he sat down with books open before him—as he clearly did, for example, when writing *Antony and Cleopatra*—or relied on his memory, but he had also certainly read one and probably more than one version of the old Danish tale of murder and revenge. At the very least, judging from the play he wrote, he carefully read the story as narrated in French by François de Belleforest, whose collection of tragic tales was a publishing phenomenon in the late sixteenth century. (It went through at least ten editions.) Belleforest had taken the Hamlet story from a chronicle of Denmark compiled in Latin in the late twelfth century by a Dane known as Saxo the Grammarian. And Saxo in turn was recycling written and oral legends that reached back for centuries before him. Here then, as so often throughout his career, Shakespeare was working with known materials—a well-established story, a familiar cast of characters, a set of predictable excitements.

Shakespeare was himself a known quantity. It would have been reasonable for anyone who had followed his career to conclude by 1600 that he had already fully mapped the capacious boundaries of his imaginative kingdom. It must have seemed likely that he would continue as a professional playwright to repeat in imaginative ways what he had already brilliantly accomplished, but it would have seemed scarcely probable that he could find new continents to explore. No one, probably not Shakespeare himself, could have predicted that something astonishing was about to happen.

Though he was still young (only thirty-six years old), he had in the course of a decade achieved extraordinary things in three major genres—comedy, history, and tragedy—with plays that are each in their way so perfect that it would have been difficult to imagine going beyond them. Indeed, in the years that followed he made no attempt to surpass the two parts of *Henry IV* and *Henry V*, as if he understood that he had done what he was capable of doing in the history play. And though he shortly was to write the stupendous *Twelfth Night*, he did not in the genre of comedy actually go beyond what he had created in *A Midsummer Night's Dream, Much Ado About Nothing*, and *As You Like It. Hamlet* turned out to inaugurate a creative frenzy that also brought forth *Othello, King Lear, Macbeth, Antony and Cleopatra*, and *Coriolanus*, but a well-informed contemporary theatergoer in 1600 had no reason to expect that Shakespeare had not already demonstrated what he could do in tragedy as well. Among the more than twenty plays he had written were *Titus Andronicus, Romeo and Juliet*, and *Julius Caesar*. Indeed, these were not his only tragedies; three of the plays that modern editors (following the editors of the first folio) now classify as histories—the third part of *Henry VI, Richard III*, and *Richard II*—were published during his lifetime as tragedies.

The distinction between tragedy and history was not an important one for Shakespeare, or indeed for many of his playwriting contemporaries: the underlying structure of most of human history, with its endless pattern of rise and fall, seemed to him tragic, and conversely tragedy as he conceived it was rooted in history. For that matter, as *The Merchant of Venice* amply shows, his sense of comedy was laced through with pain, loss, and the threat of death, and his sense of tragedy had room for clowning and laughter. Literary theorists of the time urged strict adherence to the rules of decorum that derived from Aristotle: they vehemently opposed what Sir Philip Sidney called the mingling of kings and clowns. Writing in 1579, when Shakespeare was still a schoolboy, Sidney wrote a mocking description of a typical English play, with its loose, wildly free-form plot. The description, meant to make readers groan, turns out to anticipate precisely what Shakespeare would do brilliantly throughout his career. At one moment, Sidney snorted in derision, three ladies walk across the stage, and you are supposed to imagine them gathering flowers; by and by four actors appear with swords and bucklers, and you are expected to see the clash of two great armies; then comes news of a shipwreck, and you are to blame if you do not take the stage for a perilous rock. "You shall have Asia of one side, and Afric of the other, and so many other under-kingdoms, that the player, when he cometh in, must ever begin with telling where he is, or else the tale will not be conceived."

What Sidney and others wanted was something altogether more orderly. The stage, they argued, should always represent but one place; the time represented should at most be a single day; and exalted emotions aroused by tragedy should never be tainted with the "scornful tickling" and lewd laughter of comedy. These are strictures, derived from Aristotle, that Shakespeare, along with his fellow professional playwrights, routinely violated.

The indifference to the boundaries that obsessed learned critics in England and on the Continent helps to explain something baffling about Shakespeare's whole career, and particularly about its first decade: the absence of any clear or logical pattern of artistic development. Editions of the collected works that organize them neatly into groups—first the comedies one after another, followed by the histories, the tragedies, and finally the romances—completely misrepresent what actually happened. Attempts to organize the works according to an orderly progression of Shakespeare's soul—from lighthearted youth to a serious engagement with power to a melancholy brooding about mortality and finally to the wise serenity of old age—are similarly misleading. This is someone who had *A Midsummer Night's Dream* and *Romeo and Juliet* on his desk (and in his imagination) at the same moment, and who perceived that the joyous laughter of the one could be almost effortlessly transformed into the tears of the other. This is someone who climaxes his witty, lighthearted comedy of upper-class courtship, *Love's Labour's Lost*, with news that the princess's father has suddenly died, so that all the impending marriages must be put on hold. This is someone who gets his audience to laugh at the ghastly Richard III assessing the team of murderers he has hired to kill his brother:

> Your eyes drop millstones when fools' eyes fall tears.
> I like you, lads.

> (1.3.351–2)

And finally, this is someone who in successive plays written in the years directly before *Hamlet* shifted ground from the civil wars of late medieval England to the Sicilian courtship of Beatrice and Benedick to the battle of Agincourt to the assassination of Julius Caesar to a pastoral romance in the Forest of Arden. Each of these plays has its own distinct vision, and yet, strangely, each also has room for what it would at first glance seem to exclude.

IF SHAKESPEARE HAD DIED in 1600, it would have been difficult to think that anything was missing from his achievement and still more difficult to think that anything yet unrealized was brewing in his work. But *Hamlet* makes clear that Shakespeare had been quietly, steadily developing a special technical skill. This development may have been entirely deliberate, the consequence of a clear, ongoing professional design, or it may have been more haphazard and opportunistic. The achievement was, in any case, gradual: not a sudden, definitive discovery or a grandiose invention, but the subtle refinement of a particular set of representational techniques. By the turn of the century Shakespeare was poised to make an epochal breakthrough. He had perfected the means to represent inwardness.

What the audience sees and hears is always in some sense or other public utterance—the words that the characters say to one another or, in occasional asides and soliloquies, directly to the onlookers. Playwrights can pretend, of course, that the audience is overhearing a kind of internal monologue, but it is difficult to keep such monologues from sounding stagy. *Richard III*, written around 1592, is hugely energetic and powerful, with a marvelous, unforgettable main character, but when that character, alone at night, reveals what is going on inside of him, he sounds oddly wooden and artificial:

> It is now dead midnight.
> Cold fearful drops stand on my trembling flesh.
> What do I fear? Myself? There's none else by.
> Richard loves Richard; that is, I am I.
> Is there a murderer here? No. Yes, I am.
> Then fly! What, from myself? Great reason. Why?
> Lest I revenge. Myself upon myself?
> Alack, I love myself. Wherefore? For any good
> That I myself have done unto myself?
> O no, alas, I rather hate myself
> For hateful deeds committed by myself.
> I am a villain. Yet I lie: I am not.
>
> (5.5.134–45)

Shakespeare is following his chronicle source, which states that Richard could not sleep on the eve of his death, because he felt unwonted pricks of conscience. But though it has a staccato vigor, the soliloquy, as a way of sketching inner conflict, is schematic and mechanical, as if within the character onstage there was simply another tiny stage on which puppets were performing a Punch-and-Judy show.

In *Richard II*, written some three years later, there is a comparable moment that marks Shakespeare's burgeoning skills. Deposed and imprisoned by his cousin Bolingbroke, the ruined king, shortly before his murder, looks within himself:

> I have been studying how I may compare
> This prison where I live unto the world;
> And for because the world is populous,
> And here is not a creature but myself,
> I cannot do it. Yet I'll hammer it out.
> My brain I'll prove the female to my soul,
> My soul the father, and these two beget
> A generation of still-breeding thoughts.
>
> (5.5.1–8)

Much of the difference between the two passages has to do with the very different characters: the one a murderous tyrant full of manic energy, the other a spoiled, narcissistic, self-destructive poet. But the turn from one character to the other is itself significant; it signals Shakespeare's growing interest in the hidden processes of interiority. Locked in a windowless room, Richard II watches himself think, struggling to forge a metaphoric link between his prison and the world, reaching a dead end, and then forcing his imagination to renew the effort: "Yet I'll hammer it out." The world, crowded with people, is not, as he himself recognizes, remotely comparable to the solitude of his prison cell, but Richard wills himself to generate—out of what he pictures as the intercourse of his brain and soul—an imaginary populace. What he hammers out is a kind of inner theater, akin to that already found in Richard III's soliloquy but with a vastly increased complexity, subtlety, and, above all, self-consciousness. Now the character himself is fully aware that he has constructed such a theater, and he teases out the bleak implications of the imaginary world he has struggled to create:

> Thus play I in one person many people,
> And none contented. Sometimes am I king;

Then treason makes me wish myself a beggar,
And so I am. Then crushing penury
Persuades me I was better when a king.
Then am I kinged again, and by and by
Think that I am unkinged by Bolingbroke,
And straight am nothing. But whate'er I be,
Nor I, nor any man that but man is,
With nothing shall be pleased till he be eased
With being nothing.

(5.5.31–41)

Richard II characteristically rehearses the drama of his fall from kingship as a fall into nothingness and then fashions his experience of lost identity—"whate'er I be"—into an intricate poem of despair.

Written in 1595, *Richard II* marked a major advance in the playwright's ability to represent inwardness, but *Julius Caesar*, written four years later, shows that, not content with what he had mastered, Shakespeare subtly experimented with new techniques. Alone, pacing in his orchard in the middle of night, Brutus begins to speak:

It must be by his death. And for my part
I know no personal cause to spurn at him,
But for the general. He would be crowned.
How that might change his nature, there's the question.
It is the bright day that brings forth the adder,
And that craves wary walking. Crown him: that!

(2.1.10–15)

This soliloquy is far less fluid, less an elegant and self-conscious poetic meditation, than the prison soliloquy of Richard II. But it has something new: the unmistakable marks of actual thinking. Richard speaks of hammering it out, but the words he utters are already highly polished. Brutus's words by contrast seem to flow immediately from the still inchoate to-ing and fro-ing of his wavering mind, as he grapples with a set of momentous questions: How should he respond to the crowd's desire to crown the ambitious Caesar? How can he balance his own personal friendship with Caesar against what he construes to be the general good? How might Caesar, who has thus far served that general good, change his nature and turn dangerous if he is crowned? "It must be by his death"—without prelude, the audience is launched into the midst of Brutus's obsessive brooding. It is impossible to know if he is weighing a proposition, trying out a decision, reiterating words that someone else has spoken. He does not need to mention whose death he is contemplating, nor does he need to make clear—for it is already part of his thought—that it will be by assassination.

Brutus is speaking to himself, and his words have the peculiar shorthand of the brain at work. "Crown him: that!"—the exclamation is barely comprehensible, except as a burst of anger provoked by a phantasmic image passing at that instant through the speaker's mind. The spectators are pulled in eerily close, watching firsthand the forming of a fatal resolution—a determination to assassinate Caesar—that will change the world. A few moments later, Brutus, intensely self-aware, describes for himself the molten state of consciousness in which he finds himself:

> Between the acting of a dreadful thing
> And the first motion, all the interim is
> Like a phantasma or a hideous dream.
> The genius and the mortal instruments
> Are then in counsel, and the state of man,
> Like to a little kingdom, suffers then
> The nature of an insurrection.
>
> (2.1.63–69)

Was it at this moment, in 1599, that Shakespeare first conceived of the possibility of writing about a character suspended, for virtually the whole length of a play, in this strange interim? Brutus himself is not such a character; by the middle of *Julius Caesar*, he has done the dreadful thing, the killing of his mentor and friend—possibly his own father—and the remainder of the play teases out the fatal consequences of his act.

If Shakespeare did not grasp it at once, then certainly by the follow-

ing year he understood perfectly that there was a character, already popular on the Elizabethan stage, whose life he could depict as one long
phantasma or hideous dream. That character, the prince of the inward
insurrection, was Hamlet.

Even in its earliest known medieval telling, Hamlet's saga was the
story of the long interval between the first motion—the initial impulse or
design—and the acting of the dreadful thing. In Saxo the Grammarian's
account, King Horwendil (the equivalent of Shakespeare's old King
Hamlet) is killed by his envious brother Feng (the equivalent of
Claudius) not secretly but in plain view. The brother has a thin cover
story—he says that Horwendil had been brutally abusing his gentle wife,
Gerutha—but the reality is that the ruthless Feng is powerful enough to
seize his brother's crown, his realm, and his wife and get away with it.
The only potential obstacle is Horwendil's young son Amleth, for everyone in this pre-Christian world of treachery and vengeance understood
that a son must avenge his father's murder. Amleth is still a child and no
danger to anyone, but when he grows up, his obligation will be clear. The
murderous Feng understands this strict social code as well, of course, and,
if the boy does not quickly come up with a stratagem, his life is worth
nothing. In order to survive long enough to take his just revenge, Amleth
feigns madness, persuading his uncle that he cannot ever pose a threat.
Flinging dirt and slime on himself, he sits by the fire, listlessly whittling
away at small sticks and turning them into barbed hooks. Though the
wary Feng repeatedly sets traps to try to discern some hidden sparks of
intelligence behind his nephew's apparent idiocy, Amleth cunningly
avoids detection. He bides his time and makes plans. Mocked as a fool,
treated with contempt and derision, he eventually succeeds in burning to
death Feng's entire retinue and in running his uncle through with a
sword. He summons an assembly of nobles, explains why he has done
what he has done, and is enthusiastically acclaimed as the new king.
"Many could have been seen marvelling how he had concealed so subtle
a plan over so long a space of time."

Amleth thus spends years in the interim state that Brutus can barely
endure for a few days. Shakespeare had developed the means to represent
the psychological reality of such a condition—something that neither

Saxo nor his followers even dreamed of being able to do. He saw that the Hamlet story, ripe for revision, would enable him to make a play about what it is like to live inwardly in the queasy interval between a murderous design and its fulfillment. The problem, however, is that the theater is not particularly tolerant of long gestation periods: to represent the child Hamlet feigning idiocy for years in order to reach the age at which he could act would be exceedingly difficult to render dramatically compelling. The obvious solution, probably already reached in the lost play, is to start the action at the point at which Hamlet has come of age and is ready to undertake his act of revenge.

Thomas Lodge's allusion to the ghost that cried so miserably, like an oyster-wife, "Hamlet, revenge!" suggests that this lost play also added a key character to the story: the spirit of Hamlet's murdered father. Perhaps that ghost only appeared to give the audience a shiver of fear—that is how Thomas Kyd had used a ghost in his greatest success, *The Spanish Tragedy*—but it is equally possible that Kyd (or whoever wrote the lost *Hamlet*), rather than Shakespeare, first introduced a crucial change in the plot that made the ghost's appearance much more than decorative. In Saxo the Grammarian's Hamlet story, as in the popular tale by Belleforest, no ghost appears. There is no need for a ghost, for the murder is public knowledge, as is the son's obligation to take revenge. But when he set out to write his version of the Hamlet story, either following Kyd's lead or on his own, Shakespeare made the murder a secret. Everyone in Denmark believes that old Hamlet was fatally stung by a serpent. The ghost appears in order to tell the terrible truth:

> The serpent that did sting thy father's life
> Now wears his crown.
>
> (1.5.39–40)

Shakespeare's play begins just before the ghost reveals the murder to Hamlet and ends just after Hamlet exacts his revenge. Hence the decisive change in the plot—from a public killing known to everyone to a secret murder revealed to Hamlet alone by the ghost of the murdered man— enabled the playwright to focus almost the entire tragedy on the con-

sciousness of the hero suspended between his "first motion" and "the acting of a dreadful thing." But something in the plot has to account for this
suspension. After all, Hamlet is no longer, in this revised version, a child
who needs to play for time, and the murderer has no reason to suspect that
Hamlet has or can ever acquire any inkling of his crime. Far from keeping
his distance from his nephew (or setting subtle tests for him), Claudius
refuses to let Hamlet return to university, calls him "Our chiefest courtier,
cousin, and son" (1.2.117), and declares that he is next in succession to the
throne. Once the ghost of his father has disclosed the actual cause of
death—"Murder most foul, as in the best it is, / But this most foul,
strange, and unnatural"—Hamlet, who has full access to the unguarded
Claudius, is in the perfect position to act immediately. And such an
instantaneous response is precisely what Hamlet himself anticipates:

> Haste, haste me to know it, that with wings as swift
> As meditation or the thoughts of love
> May sweep to my revenge.
>
> (1.5.27–31)

The play should be over by the end of the first act. But Hamlet
emphatically does not sweep to his revenge. As soon as the ghost vanishes, he tells the sentries and his friend Horatio that he intends "To put
an antic disposition on" (1.5.173), that is, to pretend to be mad. The
behavior makes perfect sense in the old version of the story, where it is a
ruse to deflect suspicion and to buy time. The emblem of that time, and
the proof of the avenger's brilliant, long-term planning, are the wooden
hooks that the boy Amleth, apparently deranged, endlessly whittles away
on with his little knife. These are the means that, at the tale's climax,
Amleth uses to secure a net over the sleeping courtiers, before he sets the
hall on fire. What had looked like mere distraction turns out to be brilliantly strategic. But in Shakespeare's version, Hamlet's feigned madness
is no longer coherently tactical. Shakespeare in effect wrecked the compelling and coherent plot with which his sources conveniently provided
him. And out of the wreckage he constructed what most modern audiences would regard as the best play he had ever written.

Far from offering a cover, the antic disposition leads the murderer to set close watch upon Hamlet, to turn to his counselor Polonius for advice, to discuss the problem with Gertrude, to observe Ophelia carefully, to send for Rosencrantz and Guildenstern to spy upon their friend. Instead of leading the court to ignore him, Hamlet's madness becomes the object of everyone's endless speculation. And strangely enough, the speculation sweeps Hamlet along with it:

> I have of late—but wherefore I know not—lost all my mirth, forgone all custom of exercise; and indeed it goes so heavily with my disposition that this goodly frame, the earth, seems to me a sterile promontory. This most excellent canopy the air, look you, this brave o'erhanging, this majestical roof fretted with golden fire—why, it appears no other thing to me than a foul and pestilent congregation of vapours. What a piece of work is a man! How noble in reason, how infinite in faculty, in form and moving how express and admirable, in action how like an angel, in apprehension how like a god—the beauty of the world, the paragon of animals! And yet to me what is this quintessence of dust? (2.2.287–98)

"But wherefore I know not"—Hamlet, entirely aware that he is speaking to court spies, does not breathe a word of his father's ghost, but then it is not at all clear that the ghost is actually responsible for his profound depression. Already in the first scene in which he appears, before he has encountered the ghost, he is voicing to himself, as the innermost secret of his heart, virtually the identical disillusionment he discloses to the oily Rosencrantz and Guildenstern:

>   O God, O God,
> How weary, stale, flat, and unprofitable
> Seem to me all the uses of this world!
> Fie on't, ah fie, fie! 'Tis an unweeded garden
> That grows to seed; things rank and gross in nature
> Possess it merely.
>   (1.2.132–37)

His father's death and his mother's hasty remarriage, public events and not secret revelations, have driven him to thoughts of "self-slaughter."

Hamlet's show of madness, then, seems a cover for something like madness. Indeed, he never seems more genuinely insane than at the moment, in his mother's closet, in which he insists that he is perfectly sane and warns his mother not to disclose his strategy. "What shall I do?" cries the frightened queen. "Not this, by no means, that I bid you do," answers Hamlet, jumbling together his injunction with his obsessive fantasies:

> Let the bloat King tempt you again to bed,
> Pinch wanton on your cheek, call you his mouse,
> And let him for a pair of reechy kisses,
> Or paddling in your neck with his damned fingers,
> Make you to ravel all this matter out,
> That I essentially am not in madness,
> But mad in craft.
>
> (3.4.164–72)

Gertrude may be saying exactly what she believes when she tells Claudius a few moments later that Hamlet is "Mad as the sea and wind when both contend / Which is the mightier" (4.1.6–7).

By excising the rationale for Hamlet's madness, Shakespeare made it the central focus of the entire tragedy. The play's key moment of psychological revelation—the moment that virtually everyone remembers—is not the hero's plotting of revenge, not even his repeated, passionate self-reproach for inaction, but rather his contemplation of suicide: "To be, or not to be; that is the question." This suicidal urge has nothing to do with the ghost—indeed, Hamlet has so far forgotten the apparition as to speak of death as "The undiscovered country from whose bourn / No traveller returns" (3.1.58, 81–82)—but rather has to do with a soul sickness brought on by one of "the thousand natural shocks / That flesh is heir to."

Hamlet marks a sufficient enough break in Shakespeare's career as to suggest some more personal cause for his daring transformation both of his sources and of his whole way of writing. A simple index of this transformation is the astonishing rush of new words, words that he had never used before in some twenty-one plays and in two long poems. There are, scholars have calculated, more than six hundred of these words, many of them not only new to Shakespeare but also new to the written record of the English language. This linguistic explosion seems to come not from a broadened vision of the world but from some shock or series of shocks to his whole life. If *Hamlet* was written not in 1600 but in early 1601, then, as some scholars believe, one shock might have been the insurrection—to use Brutus's word, in *Julius Caesar*—that led to the execution of the Earl of Essex and, more important, to the imprisonment of Shakespeare's patron, friend, and possible lover, the Earl of Southampton. Accompanied by Southampton, Essex, who had long been the queen's cosseted favorite, had gone off to Ireland in 1599 as the general of an expeditionary force designed to crush a rebellion led by the Earl of Tyrone. The enterprise, like so many others in Ireland, had failed miserably in the face of staunch Irish resistance, and in late 1600, suddenly and without the queen's permission, Essex returned to London. Placed under house arrest and enraged by the queen's refusal to readmit him to favor, the proud and impetuous earl assembled his friends and attempted to stage an armed putsch—the official purpose was to defend his life and save the queen from her evil counselors, Cecil and Ralegh. The London crowd refused to back the rising, and it was quickly over. The outcome of the trial was a foregone conclusion. On February 25, 1601, three strokes of the ax separated Essex's head from his shoulders. The execution of several of his principal supporters and friends followed in short order.

Shakespeare had every reason to be shaken by the upheaval. It was not only a matter of the possible loss of Southampton, who, though ultimately spared, seemed in early 1601 likely to be executed along with Essex. For the playwright personally and for his company, a set of decisions that they had made in the years leading up to the insurrection could have led to disaster. In late 1596 or early 1597, Shakespeare had elected, by using the name Oldcastle for the fat knight in *Henry IV*, whom he eventually and under pressure renamed Falstaff, to risk offending William Brook, the seventh Lord Cobham, who traced his descent from the historical Oldcastle. Brook was not the wisest choice of an antagonist, for at the time or very soon after, he was appointed lord chamberlain, the post ultimately responsible for overseeing the licensing of plays. But he was the known enemy of Essex and Southampton, and it was presumably for this reason that Shakespeare felt licensed, like the fool in one of his plays, to take a jibe at him.

Then in 1599, quite uncharacteristically, Shakespeare introduced a direct topical reference into one of his plays. Near the close of *Henry V*, the Chorus, conjuring up the scene of the king's triumphal return to London after the battle of Agincourt, abruptly turns to contemporary events. "How London doth pour out her citizens," the Chorus exclaims.

> As, by a lower but high-loving likelihood,
> Were now the General of our gracious Empress—
> Bringing rebellion broachèd on his sword,
> How many would the peaceful city quit
> To welcome him!
>
> (5.0.24, 29–34)

"A lower but high-loving likelihood": even with the note of prudential caution and calculation, the Chorus's lines were a gesture of support for Essex, a gesture soon followed by something much more dangerous. Several days before the rising, a few of the conspirators called on Shakespeare's company, the Lord Chamberlain's Men, and asked to "have the play of the deposing and killing of King Richard II to be played the Saturday next." The representatives of the company—and it seems likely that Shakespeare, along with Augustine Phillips and a few other veteran players, was among them—protested that the play was too old to make a profit. The conspirators offered to subsidize the performance with an extra payment of forty shillings, a substantial sum, and the play was accordingly performed.

The strategy, it seems, was to plant the idea of a successful rebellion in the minds of the London crowd and perhaps also to shore up the plotters' own courage. This at least is how, in the wake of the arrests, the authorities regarded the special performance, and this is how the queen herself seems to have understood it. "I am Richard II," she fumed. "Know ye not that?" The Lord Chamberlain's Men had ventured onto exceedingly dangerous ground—two of the key conspirators were questioned about the performance, as if it might have been an integral part of the plot—but somehow Augustine Phillips, who spoke on behalf of the company, managed to persuade the magistrates that the players knew nothing about the intended rising. "They had their forty shillings more than their ordinary for it," he testified, "and so played it accordingly."

These events, which took place in February 1601, would certainly have alarmed Shakespeare. The brush with disaster might have led a more timid playwright to be cautious: he could have set aside the tragedy and quickly turned to another, more innocuous project. Instead, with the same eye for box-office receipts that governed the negotiation over *Richard II*, his company performed *Hamlet*, a highly political play about betrayal and assassination, a play that includes a remarkable scene of an armed popular insurrection breaking into the royal sanctuary past the guards and threatening the life of the king. Of course, the insurrection, led by Laertes, does not succeed, and Claudius's exquisite piece of hypocrisy eerily mimes the official line about Queen Elizabeth:

> There's such a divinity doth hedge a king
> That treason can but peep to what it would,
> Acts little of his will.
>
> (4.5.120–22)

These scenes would have been enough to excite a London audience shaken by the events of 1601, but they do not actually constitute a direct reference to them, and they could be easily explained away. After all, political upheaval, betrayal, and assassination were Shakespeare's theatrical stock-in-trade—witness *Richard III*, *Julius Caesar*, *Richard II*, *Henry V*, and so on. Essex and the imprisonment of Southampton must have preyed on Shakespeare's mind, but it is difficult to attribute anything in *Hamlet* specifically to these events, and it is particularly difficult to attribute what is startling and innovative about the play to them. Though the links to the insurrection are intriguing, some version of Shakespeare's *Hamlet* was, in all likelihood, being performed before Essex took his fateful steps. Shakespeare may have ventured to add some lines or scenes to heighten the connection between the play and contemporary events, but the key elements of the play must already have been in place, as suggested by a marginal note that Gabriel Harvey (the Cambridge academic entangled in disputes with Nashe and Greene) jotted down in his copy of Chaucer. "The Earl of Essex much commends *Albion's England*," Harvey writes, in an account of contemporary literary fashions, and then continues, "The younger sort takes much delight in Shakespeare's *Venus and Adonis*; but his *Lucrece* and his *Tragedy of Hamlet, Prince of Denmark* have it in them to please the wiser sort." The present tense suggests that Essex was alive when Harvey penned the first clear reference to Shakespeare's tragedy.

Something deeper must have been at work in Shakespeare, then, something powerful enough to call forth the unprecedented representation of tormented inwardness. "To be, or not to be": as audiences and readers have long instinctively understood, these suicidal thoughts, provoked by the death of a loved one, lie at the heart of Shakespeare's tragedy. They may well have been the core of the playwright's own inward disturbance. The Shakespeares had named their twins, Judith and Hamnet, after their Stratford neighbors Judith and Hamnet Sadler. The latter appears in Stratford records as both Hamnet and Hamlet Sadler; in the loose orthography of the time, the names were virtually interchangeable. Even if the decision to redo the old tragedy were a strictly commercial one, the coincidence of the names—the act of writing his own son's name again and again—may well have reopened a deep wound, a wound that had never properly healed.

But, of course, in *Hamlet*, it is the death not of a son but of a father that provokes the hero's spiritual crisis. If the tragedy swelled up from Shakespeare's own life—if it can be traced back to the death of Hamnet—something must have made the playwright link the loss of his child to the imagined loss of his father. I say "imagined" because Shakespeare's father was buried in Holy Trinity Churchyard on September 8, 1601: the handwriting may have been on the wall, but he was almost certainly still alive when the tragedy was written and first performed. How did the father's death become bound up so closely in Shakespeare's imagination with the son's?

Shakespeare undoubtedly returned to Stratford in 1596 for his son's funeral. The minister, as the regulations required, would have met the corpse at the entry to the churchyard and accompanied it to the grave. Shakespeare must have stood there and listened to the words of the prescribed Protestant burial service. While the earth was thrown onto the body—perhaps by the father himself, perhaps by friends—the minister intoned the words, "Forasmuch as it hath pleased Almighty God of his great mercy to take unto himself the soul of our dear brother here departed, we therefore commit his body to the ground, earth to earth, ashes to ashes, dust to dust; in sure and certain hope of the Resurrection to eternal life."

Did Shakespeare find this simple, eloquent service adequate, or was he tormented with a sense that something was missing? "What ceremony else?" cries Laertes, by the grave of his sister Ophelia; "What ceremony else?" (5.1.205, 207). Ophelia's funeral rites have been curtailed because she is suspected of the sin of suicide, and Laertes is both shallow and rash. But the question he repeatedly asks echoes throughout *Hamlet*, and it articulates a concern that extends beyond the boundaries of the play. Within living memory, the whole relationship between the living and the dead had been changed. In Lancashire, if not closer to home, Shakespeare could have seen the remnants of the old Catholic practice: candles burning night and day, crosses everywhere, bells tolling constantly, close relatives wailing and crossing themselves, neighbors visiting the corpse and saying over it a Paternoster or a De Profundis, alms and food distributed in memory of the dead, priests paid to say Masses to ease the soul's perilous passage through purgatory. All of this had come under attack; everything had been scaled back or eliminated outright. Above all, it was now illegal to pray for the dead.

The first Protestant prayer books had retained the old formula: "I commend thy soul to God the father almighty, and thy body to the ground, earth to earth, ashes to ashes, dust to dust." But vigilant reformers felt that these words had too much of the old Catholic faith hidden within them, and so a simple change was made: "We therefore commit his body to the ground. . . ." The dead person is no longer directly addressed, as if he retained some contact with the living. The small revision makes a large point: the dead are completely dead. No prayers can help them; no messages can be sent to them or received from them. Hamnet was beyond reach.

Catholics believed that after death, while wicked souls went directly to hell and saintly souls to heaven, the great majority of the faithful, neither completely good nor completely bad, went to purgatory. Purgatory was a vast prison house under the earth where souls would suffer torments until they had paid for the sins they had committed during life. (Some thought there was an entry to it in Ireland, through a cave in the county of Donegal discovered by Saint Patrick.) These sins were not so wicked as to entail an eternity of woe, but they had left a stain that needed to be burned away before the soul could enter heaven. All of the souls in purgatory, without exception, were saved and would eventually ascend to bliss. That was the good news. The bad news was that purgatorial sufferings, painted on church walls and described in hallucinatory detail by preachers, were horrible. One instant of fiery pain in the afterlife was worse, churchmen taught, than the worst pain a person could suffer in life. Indeed, the torments of souls imprisoned in purgatory were identical, except in their duration, to the torments of the damned in hell. And this duration, though limited, was not inconsiderable. One Spanish theologian calculated that an average Christian would have to spend approximately one to two thousand years in purgatory.

Fortunately, the Catholic Church taught, there was a way to help your loved ones and yourself. Certain good works—prayers, alms, and above all special Masses—could significantly ease the suffering, reduce the purgatorial prison term, and hasten the soul's passage to heaven. You could prudently arrange for these good works on your own behalf, during your lifetime, and you could bestow them on those who had passed away. The wealthy and powerful endowed chantries where priests would say prayers in perpetuity for the dead, and they founded civic institutions— almshouses, hospitals, schools—designed to generate an abundant supply of prayers for the founder. Poorer people saved their pennies to pay for sets of Masses, available in different packages. The most effective was said to be the trental, a sequence of thirty Masses, but even one or two could help.

What evidence was there for the efficacy of these measures? In addition to church doctrine, there was the testimony of the dead themselves. Many stories were told of ghosts who had returned to earth from purgatory, desperately pleading for help. And after the help was given, these same ghosts would often return to thank the giver and bear witness to the immense comfort that their charitable donations had provided. The ghostly apparitions that people actually encountered were almost always terrifying. They could be harbingers of catastrophe, signs of madness, or manifestations of evil, for the devil could assume the shape of a dead person and sow wicked ideas in the minds of the unsuspecting. But the church's teachings helped make sense of what was happening when people were haunted by the spirits of those whom they had loved: the dead in their purgatorial suffering were simply pleading to be remembered. "Remember our thirst while ye sit and drink," the Catholic Thomas More heard the voices of the dead crying; remember "our hunger while ye be feasting; our restless watch while ye be sleeping; our sore and grievous pain while ye be playing; our hot, burning fire while ye be in pleasure and sporting. So might God make your offspring after remember you." And with remembrance, in the form of the appropriate rituals, would come relief.

Zealous Protestants regarded this whole set of beliefs and institutional practices as an enormous confidence game, a racket designed to extract money from the credulous. Purgatory, they said, was "a poet's fable," an elaborate fantasy that had been imposed upon the whole society, top to bottom, so that king and fishwife alike were being ruthlessly exploited. Persuaded by these arguments or, more plausibly, simply eager to seize church wealth, Henry VIII dissolved the monasteries and chantries that had been the ritual centers of the Catholic cult of the dead. Under his Protestant successors, Edward VI and Elizabeth I, reformers in Parliament abolished the whole system of intercessory foundations created to offer prayers for souls in purgatory. The authorities kept many of the hospitals, almshouses, and schools, of course, but stripped them of their ritual functions. And through sermons and homilies and the church service itself, the clergy made a systematic effort to reeducate the populace, urging their flock to reimagine the whole relationship between this life and the beyond.

This was not an easy task. Belief in purgatory may well have been abused—plenty of pious Catholics thought it was—but it addressed fears and longings that did not simply vanish when people were told by the officials of the church and the state that the dead were beyond all earthly contact. Ceremony was not the only or even the principal issue. What mattered was whether the dead could continue to speak to the living, at least for a short time, whether the living could help the dead, whether a reciprocal bond remained. When Shakespeare stood in the churchyard, watching the dirt fall on the body of his son, did he think that his relationship with Hamnet was gone without a trace?

Perhaps. But it is also possible that he found the service, with its deliberate refusal to address the dead child as "thou," its reduction of ritual, its narrowing of ceremony, its denial of any possibility of communication, painfully inadequate. And if he could make his peace with the Protestant understanding of these things, others close to him assuredly could not. Nothing is known of his wife Anne's beliefs about death, though there may be a very small hint in the strange inscription that was placed on her grave in 1623 by her daughter Susanna. "A mother's bosom you gave, and milk and life," the inscription begins; "for such bounty, alas! I can only render stones!" The lines that follow imply the radical idea that the dead woman's soul, as well as her body, is imprisoned in the grave: "Rather would I pray the good angel to roll away the stone from the mouth of the tomb, that thy spirit, even as the body of Christ, should go forth." But these may be Susanna's heterodox views and not at all those of Anne Hathaway Shakespeare, let alone ones she might have held back in 1596, the year of Hamnet's death.

Shakespeare's parents, John and Mary, also presumably stood by Hamnet's grave. Indeed, they had spent far more time with the boy than his father had, for while Shakespeare was in London, they were all living together in the same house with their daughter-in-law and the three grandchildren. They had helped to raise Hamnet, and they tended Hamnet through his last illness. And about his parents' beliefs with regard to the afterlife, specifically about his father's beliefs, there is some evidence. This evidence strongly suggests that John Shakespeare would have wanted something done for Hamnet's soul, something that he perhaps appealed urgently to his son to do or that he undertook to do on his own. The arguments, or pleading, or tears that may have accompanied such appeals are irrevocably lost. But at least there is a trace of what Shakespeare's father (and, presumably, his mother as well) would have thought necessary, proper, charitable, loving, and, in a single word, Christian.

Back in the 1580s, while Thomas Lucy was combing the neighborhood of Stratford for Catholic subversives and Catholics were said to be hiding the evidence of their dangerous loyalties, John Shakespeare (if the papers discovered in the eighteenth century were authentic) put his name to something seriously incriminating: the "spiritual last will and testament" that the Jesuits had circulated among the faithful. At the time William may have known nothing about this—his father probably slipped the papers between the rafters and roof tiles of the Henley Street house in secrecy—but the faith and anxiety that led to the signing of the document would probably have come up at the funeral of Hamnet. For what John Shakespeare had hidden away had specifically to do with death.

The "spiritual testament" was a kind of insurance policy for the Catholic soul, and it must have seemed particularly important to those who could not practice their faith openly or who were under pressure to collaborate with the Protestants. The signer declares that he is a Catholic, but he adds that if at any time he should chance "by suggestion of the devil to do, say, or think" anything contrary to his faith, he formally revokes his sin and wills "that it be held for neither spoken or done by me." So too if he should happen not to receive the proper Catholic last rites—confession, anointing, and communion—he wishes that they be performed "spiritually." He knows that he "is born to die, without knowing the hour, where, when, or how" and fears that he could be "surprised on a sudden." Hence he is grateful, he declares, for the opportunity to experience penance now, for he knows that he could be taken out of this life "when I least thought thereof: yea even then, when I was plunged in the dirty puddle of my sins."

Catholics were taught in this period to be particularly fearful of a sudden death, a death that would prevent the ritual opportunity to settle the sinner's accounts with God and to show the appropriate contrition. Any stains that had not been removed in this life would have to be burned away in the afterlife. The "spiritual testament" was an attempt to address this fear, and it went on to enlist family and friends as allies:

> I John Shakespeare do . . . beseech all my dear friends, parents, and kinsfolk, by the bowels of our Savior Jesus Christ, that since it is uncertain what lot will befall me, for fear notwithstanding lest by reason of my sins I be to pass and stay a long while in Purgatory, they will vouchsafe to assist and succor me with their holy prayers and satisfactory works, especially with the holy Sacrifice of the Mass, as being the most effectual means to deliver souls from their torments and pains.

Those who set their name to such a document (and it is at least plausible that John Shakespeare was among them, and probable that he shared their concerns) were not speaking solely for themselves; they were asking those who loved them to do something crucially important for them, something that the state had declared illegal.

In 1596, at the funeral of Hamnet, the issue would almost certainly have surfaced. The boy's soul needed the help of those who loved and cared for him. John Shakespeare, who had virtually raised his grandson, may well have urged his prosperous son William to pay for masses for the dead child, just as he likely wanted masses to be said for his own soul. For he was getting old and would soon be in need of the "satisfactory works" that could shorten the duration of his agony in the afterlife.

If this delicate subject was broached, did William angrily shake his head or instead quietly pay for clandestine Masses for Hamnet's soul? Did he tell his father that he could not give his son—or, looking ahead, that he would not give him—what he craved? Did he say that he no longer believed in the whole story of the terrible prison house, poised between heaven and hell, where the sins done in life were burned and purged away?

Whatever he determined at the time, Shakespeare must have still been brooding over it in late 1600 and early 1601, when he sat down to write a tragedy whose doomed hero bore the name of his dead son. His thoughts may have been intensified by news that his elderly father was seriously ill back in Stratford, for the thought of his father's death is deeply woven into the play. And the death of his son and the impending death of his father—a crisis of mourning and memory—constitute a psychic disturbance that may help to explain the explosive power and inwardness of *Hamlet*.

A ghost comes back to earth to demand revenge: this is the thrilling theatrical device that everyone remembered from the earlier Elizabethan play about Hamlet, and Shakespeare invests the scene with incomparable power. "If thou didst ever thy dear father love . . . ," the ghost says to his groaning son, "Revenge his foul and most unnatural murder" (1.5.23–25). But, strangely enough, the spectral injunction that Shakespeare's Hamlet dwells upon is not this stirring call to action but something quite different: "Adieu, adieu, Hamlet. Remember me." "Remember thee?" Hamlet echoes, clutching his head.

> Ay, thou poor ghost, while memory holds a seat
> In this distracted globe. Remember thee?
>
> (1.5.91, 95–97)

On the face of things, as Hamlet's tone of incredulity suggests, the request is absurd: the son is hardly likely to forget the return of his father from the grave. But in fact Hamlet does not sweep to his revenge, and it turns out that remembering his father—remembering him in the right way, remembering him at all—is far more difficult to do than he imagined. Something interferes with the straightforward plan, an interference whose emblem is the feigned madness that makes no sense in the plot. And it turns out that this interference springs from the same sources that may have led Shakespeare's own father to sign the Catholic "spiritual testament," with its desperate plea to his family and friends: Remember me.

"I am thy father's spirit," the ghost tells his son,

> Doomed for a certain term to walk the night,
> And for the day confined to fast in fires

Till the foul crimes done in my days of nature
Are burnt and purged away. But that I am forbid
To tell the secrets of my prison-house
I could a tale unfold whose lightest word
Would harrow up thy soul.

(1.5.9–16)

Shakespeare had to be careful: plays were censored, and it would not have been permissible to refer to purgatory as a place that actually existed. There is thus a sly literalness in the ghost's remark that he is forbidden "To tell the secrets of my prison-house." But virtually everyone in Shakespeare's audience would have understood what this prison-house was, a location Hamlet himself signals when he swears, a few moments later, "by Saint Patrick" (1.5.140), the patron saint of purgatory.

The ghost has suffered the fate so deeply feared by pious Catholics. He has been taken suddenly from this life, with no time to prepare ritually for his end. "Cut off even in the blossoms of my sin," he tells his son, adding in one of the play's strangest lines, "Unhouseled, dis-appointed, unaneled" (1.5.76–77). "Unhouseled"—he did not receive last communion; "dis-appointed"—he did not undertake deathbed confession or appointment; "unaneled"—he did not receive extreme unction, the anointing (or aneling) of his body with holy oil. He went into the afterlife without having undertaken any preparatory penance, and now he is paying the full price: "O horrible, O horrible, most horrible!" (1.5.80).

What does it mean that a ghost from purgatory erupts into the world of *Hamlet* pleading to be remembered? Even setting aside for a moment the fact that purgatory, according to the Protestant church, did not exist, the allusions to it here are an enigma, for spirits in God's great penitentiary could not by definition ask anyone to commit a crime. After all, they are being purged of their sins in order to ascend to heaven. Yet this ghost is not asking for Masses and alms; he is preempting God's monopoly on revenge by demanding that his son kill the man who murdered him, seized his crown, and married his widow. Audiences then as now would not necessarily worry about this—the play is not, after all, a theology lesson. But Hamlet worries about it, and his paralyzing doubts and anxieties displace revenge as the center of the play's interest.

The official Protestant line in Shakespeare's time was that there were no ghosts at all. The apparitions that men and women encountered from time to time—apparitions that uncannily bore the appearance of loved ones or friends—were mere delusions, or, still worse, they were devils in disguise, come to tempt their victims to sin. Hamlet at first declares that he has seen an "honest ghost" (1.5.142), but his initial confidence gives way to uncertainty:

> The spirit that I have seen
> May be the devil, and the devil hath power
> T'assume a pleasing shape; yea, and perhaps,
> Out of my weakness and my melancholy—
> As he is very potent with such spirits—
> Abuses me to damn me.
>
> (2.2.575–80)

Such thoughts lead to a cycle of delay, self-reproach, continued failure to act, and renewed self-reproach. They account for the play-within-the-play—Hamlet's device to get some independent confirmation of the ghost's claims—and for the hero's queasy sense of groping in the dark. And they are linked to a broader sense of doubt and disorientation in a play where the whole ritual structure that helped men and women deal with loss has been fatally damaged.

Shakespeare would have experienced the consequences of this damage as he stood by the grave of his son or tried to cope with his father's pleas for help in the afterlife. The Protestant authorities had attacked the beliefs and outlawed the practices that the Catholic Church had offered as a way to negotiate with the dead. They said that the whole concept of purgatory was a lie and that all one needed was robust faith in the saving power of Christ's sacrifice. There were those who firmly possessed such faith, but nothing in Shakespeare's works suggests that he was among them. He was instead part of a very large group, probably the bulk of the population, who found themselves still grappling with longings and fears that the old resources of the Catholic Church had served to address. It was because of those longings and fears that people like John Shakespeare secretly signed "spiritual testaments."

All funerals invite those who stand by the grave to think about what, if anything, they believe in. But the funeral of one's own child does more than this: it compels parents to ask questions of God and to interrogate their own faith. Shakespeare must have attended the regular services in his Protestant parish; otherwise his name would have turned up on lists of recusants. But did he believe what he heard and recited? His works suggest that he did have faith, of a sort, but it was not a faith securely bound either by the Catholic Church or by the Church of England. By the late 1590s, insofar as his faith could be situated in any institution at all, that institution was the theater, and not only in the sense that his profoundest energies and expectations were all focused there.

Shakespeare grasped that crucial death rituals in his culture had been gutted. He may have felt this with enormous pain at his son's graveside. But he also believed that the theater—and his theatrical art in particular—could tap into the great reservoir of passionate feelings that, for him and for thousands of his contemporaries, no longer had a satisfactory outlet.

The Reformation was in effect offering him an extraordinary gift— the broken fragments of what had been a rich, complex edifice—and he knew exactly how to accept and use this gift. He was hardly indifferent to the success he could achieve, but it was not a matter of profit alone. Shakespeare drew upon the pity, confusion, and dread of death in a world of damaged rituals (the world in which most of us continue to live) because he himself experienced those same emotions at the core of his being. He experienced them in 1596, at the funeral of his child, and he experienced them with redoubled force in anticipation of his father's death. He responded not with prayers but with the deepest expression of his being: *Hamlet*.

In the early eighteenth century, the editor and biographer Nicholas Rowe, trying to find out something about Shakespeare's career as an actor, made inquiries, but memories had faded. "I could never meet with any further account of him this way," Rowe noted, "than that the top of his performance was the Ghost in his own *Hamlet*." Enacting the purgatorial spirit who demands that the living listen carefully to his words—"lend thy serious hearing / To what I shall unfold" (1.5.5–6)—Shakespeare must have conjured up within himself the voice of his dead son, the voice of his dying father, and perhaps too his own voice, as it would sound when it came from the grave. Small wonder that it would have been his best role.

CHAPTER 11

Bewitching the King

HAMLET MARKED AN EPOCH for Shakespeare as a writer as well as an actor. With this play, he made a discovery by means of which he relaunched his entire career. Already, prior to 1600, he had amassed considerable experience as a writer of tragedy. In *Titus Andronicus, Richard III, Romeo and Juliet, Richard II*, and *Julius Caesar*, he had explored the lust for revenge, the pathological ambition and fatal irresponsibility of monarchs, the murderous enmity of households, and the fatal consequences of political assassination. The crucial breakthrough in *Hamlet* did not involve developing new themes or learning how to construct a shapelier, tighter plot; it had to do rather with an intense representation of inwardness called forth by a new technique of radical excision. He had rethought how to put a tragedy together—specifically, he had rethought the amount of causal explanation a tragic plot needed to function effectively and the amount of explicit psychological rationale a character needed to be compelling. Shakespeare found that he could immeasurably deepen the effect of his plays, that he could provoke in the audience and in himself a peculiarly passionate intensity of response, if he took out a key explanatory element, thereby occluding the rationale, motivation, or ethical principle that accounted for the action that was to unfold. The principle was not the making of a riddle to be solved, but the creation of a strategic opacity. This opacity, Shakespeare found, released an enormous energy that had been at least partially blocked or contained by familiar, reassuring explanations.

Shakespeare's work had long been wryly skeptical of official explanations and excuses—the accounts, whether psychological or theological, of why people behave the way they do. His plays had suggested that the choices people make in love are almost entirely inexplicable and irrational, which is the conviction that generates the comedy in *A Midsummer Night's Dream* and the tragedy in *Romeo and Juliet*. But at least love was the clearly identifiable motive. With *Hamlet,* Shakespeare found that if he refused to provide himself or his audience with a familiar, comforting rationale that seems to make it all make sense, he could get to something immeasurably deeper. The key is not simply the creation of opacity, for by itself that would only create a baffling or incoherent play. Rather, Shakespeare came increasingly to rely on the inward logic, the poetic coherence that his genius and his immensely hard work had long enabled him to confer on his plays. Tearing away the structure of superficial meanings, he fashioned an inner structure through the resonant echoing of key terms, the subtle development of images, the brilliant orchestration of scenes, the complex unfolding of ideas, the intertwining of parallel plots, the uncovering of psychological obsessions.

This conceptual breakthrough in *Hamlet* was technical; that is, it affected the practical choices Shakespeare made when he put plays together, starting with the enigma of the prince's suicidal melancholy and assumed madness. But it was not only a new aesthetic strategy. The excision of motive must have arisen from something more than technical experimentation; coming in the wake of Hamnet's death, it expressed Shakespeare's root perception of existence, his understanding of what could be said and what should remain unspoken, his preference for things untidy, damaged, and unresolved over things neatly arranged, well made, and settled. The opacity was shaped by his experience of the world and of his own inner life: his skepticism, his pain, his sense of broken rituals, his refusal of easy consolations.

In the years after *Hamlet*, Shakespeare wrote a succession of astonishing tragedies—*Othello* in 1603 or 1604, *King Lear* in 1604 or 1605, and *Macbeth* in 1606—that drew upon his discovery. Repeatedly, he took his source and deftly sliced away what would seem indispensable to a coherent, well-made play. Thus though *Othello* is constructed around the remorseless desire of the ensign Iago to destroy his general, the Moor, Shakespeare refused to provide the villain with a clear and convincing explanation for his behavior. That explanation would not have been difficult to find: it was already there, fully articulated, in Shakespeare's source for his play, a short story by the Italian university teacher and writer Giambattista Giraldi (known to contemporaries as "Cinthio.") "The wicked Ensign," Cinthio writes of Iago, "taking no account of the faith he had pledged to his wife, and of the friendship, loyalty, and obligations he owed the Moor, fell ardently in love with Desdemona, and bent all his thoughts to see if he could manage to enjoy her." Afraid to show his love openly, the ensign does everything he can to hint to the lady that he desires her, but Desdemona's thoughts are entirely focused upon her husband. She does not merely reject the ensign's advances; she does not even notice them. Incapable of conceiving such purity of love, Cinthio's ensign concludes that Desdemona must be in love with someone else. The likeliest candidate, he concludes, is the Moor's handsome corporal, and he plots to get rid of him. But that is not all, Cinthio explains: "Not only did he turn his mind to this, but the love which he had felt for the Lady now changed to the bitterest hate, and he gave himself up to studying how to bring it about that, once the Corporal were killed, if he himself could not enjoy the Lady, then the Moor should not have her either." Everything neatly follows.

But not in Shakespeare's play. His villain does not dream of possessing Desdemona, nor is she the particular object of his hatred. To be sure, there is a moment in which he seems about to rehearse the motive that Cinthio had provided:

> That Cassio loves her, I do well believe it,
> That she loves him, 'tis apt and of great credit.
> The Moor—howbe't that I endure him not—
> Is of a constant, loving, noble nature,

> And I dare think he'll prove to Desdemona
> A more dear husband. Now I do love her too.
>   (2.1.273–78)

Since Shakespeare's Iago thinks only that his slander will be a plausible one—"'tis apt and of great credit"—this is not quite Cinthio's Iago, who genuinely believes that Desdemona must be in love with the handsome corporal. But the two versions of the villain seem to converge in those last words: "Now I do love her too." Yet it is precisely here that Shakespeare can be caught in the act of creating his special effect:

>   Now I do love her too,
> Not out of absolute lust—though peradventure
> I stand accountant for as great a sin—
> But partly led to diet my revenge
> For that I do suspect the lusty Moor
> Hath leapt into my seat, the thought whereof
> Doth, like a poisonous mineral, gnaw my inwards.
>   (2.1.278–84)

What in Cinthio was simple and clear, in Shakespeare becomes opaque: "Not out of absolute lust." A further motivation—Iago's fear that he has been cuckolded by Othello—displaces the first, but neither is convincing, and the addition of further layers only weakens the explanatory force of all of them, leaving intact the terrible inner torment. Iago's murky attempt to account for his obsessive, unappeasable hatred—in Coleridge's memorable phrase, "the motive-hunting of motiveless malignity"—is famously inadequate. And, crucially, this inadequacy becomes an issue in the tragedy itself. Near the play's end, when Othello has finally understood that he has been tricked into believing that his wife was unfaithful, that he has murdered the innocent woman who loved him, and that his reputation and whole life have been destroyed, he turns to Iago and demands an explanation. Exposed as a moral monster, caught, and pinioned, Iago's terrible reply—his last utterance in the play—is a blank refusal to supply the missing motive:

Demand me nothing. What you know, you know.
From this time forth I never will speak word.
                                    (5.2.309–10)

The words are specific to *Othello* and to the fathomless cruelty of its villain, but the opacity extends to crucial elements in each of Shakespeare's great tragedies.

Perhaps the greatest instance of strategic opacity comes in the play Shakespeare wrote shortly after *Othello*, *King Lear*. Lear's story—his misguided anger at the one daughter who truly loves him; his betrayal by the two wicked daughters upon whom he has bestowed all of his wealth and power—had often been told before. Shakespeare could have heard it recounted from the pulpit or seen it mentioned briefly in Spenser's *Faerie Queene* or read a fuller account in the chronicles to which he was addicted. He had almost certainly seen a version of it performed onstage. He could have been struck by its resemblance to one or more of the old folktales he clearly loved as a child: to "Cinderella," perhaps, with its one sweet daughter set against her wicked sisters, and, still more, to the story of the virtuous daughter who falls into disfavor for telling her splenetic father she loves him as much as salt. But the fate of Lear was principally rehearsed in Shakespeare's time both as a piece of authentic British history from the very ancient past (c. 800 B.C.E.) and as a warning to contemporary fathers not to put too much trust in the flattery of their children. Lear foolishly sets a love test: "Which of you," he asks his three daughters, "shall we say doth love us most?" (1.1.49). In some versions of the story, including Shakespeare's, this test occurs at the moment when the father feels he can no longer manage his affairs and decides to retire.

But why does Lear, who has, as the play begins, already drawn up the map equitably dividing the kingdom among his three daughters, stage the love test at all? In Shakespeare's principal source, an old Queen's Men play called *The True Chronicle History of King Leir* (eventually published in 1605 but dating from 1594 or earlier), there is a gratifyingly clear answer. Leir's strong-willed daughter Cordella has vowed that she will only marry a man whom she herself loves; Leir wishes her to marry the man he chooses for his own dynastic purposes. He stages the love test, anticipating that in competing with her sisters, Cordella will declare that she loves her father best, at which point Leir will demand that she prove her love by marrying the suitor of his choice. The stratagem backfires, but its purpose is clear.

Once again, as he did in *Hamlet* and *Othello*, Shakespeare simply cut out the motive that makes the initiating action of the story make sense. Lear says he wants an answer to his question so that he can divide the kingdom according to the level of each daughter's love, but the play opens with characters discussing the map of the division—it has already been drawn up—and noting that the portions are exactly equal. And Lear makes matters still stranger by proceeding to test Cordelia, as if there were something still at stake, after he has already given away, with a great show of precision, the first two-thirds of his realm.

By stripping his character of a coherent rationale for the behavior that sets in motion the whole ghastly train of events, Shakespeare makes Lear's act seem at once more arbitrary and more rooted in deep psychological needs. His Lear is a man who has determined to retire from power but who cannot endure dependence. Unwilling to lose his identity as absolute authority both in the state and in the family, he arranges a public ritual—"Which of you shall we say doth love us most?"—whose aim seems to be to allay his own anxiety by arousing it in his children. But Cordelia refuses to perform: "What shall Cordelia speak? Love and be silent" (1.1.60). Lear demands an answer: "Speak." When she says "Nothing" (1.1.85–86), a word that echoes darkly throughout the play, Lear hears what he most dreads: emptiness, loss of respect, the extinction of identity.

At the end of the play, extinction comes to Lear in a more terrible form than he had imagined. The old Queen's Men play and all the other versions of the story concluded with Lear's reconciliation with Cordelia and with his restoration to the throne. Shakespeare's original audience must have expected some version of this upbeat ending, though perhaps they anticipated that the play's final moments would show the death of the aged Lear and the ascent to the throne of his virtuous daughter. What they would not have foreseen was that Shakespeare would cut out the triumph of Cordelia—the vindication that made moral sense of the whole narrative— and instead depict the ruined king holding his murdered daughter in his arms and howling with grief. "Is this the promised end?" asks one of the bystanders, voicing what must have been the audience's incredulity. In this unprecedented climax, the theatrical effect we have been calling opacity seems to be made literal—"All's cheerless, dark, and deadly"—as the dying Lear swings wildly from the delusive hope that Cordelia is still alive to the impossibly bleak recognition that she is dead:

> No, no, no life!
> Why should a dog, a horse, a rat, have life,
> And thou no breath at all? Thou'lt come no more,
> Never, never, never, never, never!
> (5.3.262, 289, 304–7)

These words, the tragedy's climactic imagining of what it feels like to lose a child, are the most painful that Shakespeare ever wrote.

They were written, however, not about Hamnet but about Cordelia, and not in the immediate wake of the playwright's loss but almost a decade later, at a time of prosperity and success. Shakespeare's career was flourishing. Queen Elizabeth's death in 1603, bringing to an end a remarkable forty-five-year reign, had not harmed him or his company. Quite the contrary: within a matter of weeks the new ruler, James VI of Scotland, who became James I of England, acted to make the Lord Chamberlain's Men his own theater company, the King's Men.

The king and his family evidently found his new troupe marvelously entertaining. The troupe performed eight plays at court in the winter of 1603–4. The next season, they had eleven court performances, including *The Spanish Maze* (now lost), two satiric comedies by Ben Jonson (*Every Man in His Humour* and *Every Man out of His Humour*), and fully seven plays by Shakespeare: *Othello, The Merry Wives of Windsor, Measure for Measure, The Comedy of Errors, Henry V, Love's Labour's Lost,* and *The Merchant of Venice*. Indeed, the king enjoyed *The Merchant of Venice* enough to order it performed twice in three days, on February 10 and 12, 1605. The late queen had taken pleasure in the theater, but this new royal patronage represented an unprecedented level of success, both for the company and for its principal playwright.

Shakespeare not only had a share in the profits from all the company's court and public performances, but as part owner of the Globe, he also received a portion of the rent that all of the sharers paid (that is, he was in effect in the happy position of paying rent to himself). Imagination, entrepreneurial skill, and unremitting labor had made him a wealthy man; he had, as Juliet's nurse says, thinking of the sound of coins in money sacks, "the chinks" (*Romeo and Juliet*, 1.5.114). There is no evidence—as there is, for example, with Ben Jonson or John Donne—that Shakespeare laid out his money for books (let alone for paintings, or antique coins, or small bronzes, or indeed for any other object of learning or art). What interested him was real estate in and around Stratford.

He could easily have afforded a place for his wife and children to live in London, but they—or he—evidently preferred that they remain in the country. In late 1597, about a year after Hamnet's death, Shakespeare settled Anne and the two girls, fourteen-year-old Susanna and twelve-year-old Judith, at New Place, the large, three-story brick and timber house he had purchased in Stratford. The house had been built late in the fifteenth century by the town's leading citizen, and though it was demolished in the eighteenth century, surviving sketches and other records suggest that it bore witness to the playwright's remarkable success in the world. With five gables, ten rooms heated by fireplaces, gardens and orchards on three sides, two barns and other outbuildings, New Place was a residence fit for a gentleman of means. In May 1602 and again in July 1605, Shakespeare made very substantial investments in "yardlands" and leases of tithes in the Stratford area. He was now, in addition to a successful playwright and actor, a significant local rentier and one of Stratford's leading citizens.

Transactions of this size would have required one or more visits home, in addition to those he customarily made—once a year, the seventeenth-century biographer John Aubrey noted—to see his family. The obvious place to break the long journey by horseback was in Oxford, where Shakespeare customarily frequented, according to early gossips, a winehouse called the Taverne. The Taverne was owned by a vintner named John Davenant, who lived there with his wife, Jane, and a growing family, including the son William who later became the distinguished Restoration playwright. John Davenant was said to be an intensely serious fellow—no one ever saw him smile—but he was prosperous and highly respected, so much so that he was elected mayor of Oxford. Jane Davenant was said to be "a very beautiful woman, and of a very good wit and of conversation extremely agreeable."

Shakespeare seems to have been close to the family. William Davenant's older brother Robert, a parson, recalled that when he was a child Shakespeare "gave him a hundred kisses." William claimed that he was named after Shakespeare, and among his intimate friends he hinted that Shakespeare was something more than his godfather. It seemed to him, he would say over a glass of wine, that he wrote "with the very spirit" of Shakespeare. Then as now, ambitious playwrights in their most exuberant bursts of narcissistic self-confidence may have been tempted to make this extravagant claim, but Davenant's drinking friends believed him "contented enough to be thought" Shakespeare's son. It is perhaps the most striking tribute to Shakespeare's exalted reputation in the late seventeenth century that a distinguished gentleman—William was an ardent royalist who was imprisoned during the Interregnum for his adherence to the monarchy and later knighted—would boast that he was a humbly born playwright's illegitimate child. Certainly, some contemporaries were shocked: it seemed to them a bit much for Davenant to enhance his artistic reputation by making his mother, as they put it, a whore.

William Davenant was christened on March 3, 1606, so if there is any truth to his heavy hints, Shakespeare would have been in Oxford at various times in the late spring and summer of 1605, perhaps in connection with the substantial real estate purchase he finalized in July. The possibility that Shakespeare was making visits to Oxford during this period is intriguing for reasons other than speculation about his secret love life. From August 27 to 31, 1605, King James, accompanied by his queen, Anne of Denmark, and his son Henry, paid Oxford his first official visit. During these four days, the university mounted four plays, three in Latin and the fourth, for the sake of the ladies (and for those gentlemen whose Latin was shakier than they were inclined to admit), in English. These were hardly casual or impromptu affairs: theatrical costumes were hired from the King's Revels company in London, and the great stage designer Inigo Jones was employed to construct special machinery to change the scenes. If he were anywhere near Oxford at the time, Shakespeare would have had the strongest professional reason to see how the performances were received.

Things apparently did not go well. The queen and the ladies took offense at an almost naked man who performed in the first of the plays, *Alba* (written in part by the great scholar Robert Burton). The king was apparently bored by this play and the next; actually fell asleep during the third, *Vertumnus*; and did not even bother to attend the fourth. The one play of the four to survive, *Vertumnus*, tends to bear out the king's critical judgment, but its failure must have been a particular disappointment. The officials had turned to Matthew Gwinn, a former fellow of St. John's College who had in 1603 published a Latin tragedy on the life of Nero and, more important, had been one of the overseers for the plays performed at the visit of Queen Elizabeth to Oxford in 1592. In the early seventeenth century Gwinn was practicing as a physician in London (he was, among other things, the physician of the prisoners in the Tower), but, as a person of distinction and experience, he was brought back to write a play for the scholarly king. He was also commissioned to stage a welcoming event, one that seems to have particularly interested Shakespeare.

As the king, arriving with his entourage, reached St. John's College, he was greeted with a "device"—a kind of pageant or miniature play— written by Gwinn. Three "sibyls," that is, three boys dressed to look like ancient prophetesses, greeted James. They approached him, the text says, "as if from a wood"; carrying branches in their hands, perhaps, they emerged, in one observer's account, from "a castle made all of ivy." The first sibyl's words recalled a legendary event that had befallen Banquo, an eleventh-century Scot from whom James traced his descent: Banquo encountered the "fatal Sisters," who foretold "power without end" not to him but to his descendants. "We three same Fates so chant to thee and thine," the speaker went on to tell James, launching into a series of antiphonal salutations:

Hail, whom Scotland serves!
Whom England, hail!
Whom Ireland serves, all hail!
Whom France gives titles, lands besides, all hail!
Hail, whom divided Britain join'st in one!
Hail, mighty Lord of Britain, Ireland, France!

From this distance, the greeting ceremony seems an unpromising bit of fluff, but it was carefully calculated to please the king. The invocation of the distant ancestor Banquo reached comfortably back before the terrible awkwardness of his more recent forbears. James was, after all, the son of Mary, Queen of Scots, the restless intriguer whom Elizabeth had imprisoned and then, under intense pressure from incensed members of Parliament shouting "Kill the witch," reluctantly executed. It assured James that his loyal English subjects regarded him not as a Scottish interloper, son of the scarlet whore of Babylon, but as the destined ruler of the united realm. And it extended the vision of fame and grandeur and stability to James's children, Henry and Charles: "We set no times nor limits to the fates."

James was nervous, deeply nervous. He could relax, toy with abstruse scholarly questions, get drunk, fondle his handsome male favorites, lose himself in the peculiar joy of killing animals. He could, in the right mood, laugh at himself and be teased, even quite coarsely. But he could never entirely escape the terror that haunted him. Attempts to delight him with fireworks displays or surprises tended to go awry; chance events could conjure up horrible memories of his past; and though he was an ardent hunter, he could never learn to fence, because the sight of a drawn sword would suddenly send him into a panic.

He had good reason for fear. Not only had his mother been executed by the queen on whose throne he now sat, but his father had died at an assassin's hand. He himself had narrowly escaped assassination on at least one and perhaps more than one occasion. He believed that his enemies would stop at nothing in their attempts to harm him and his children: he feared not sharp steel alone but also wax figurines stuck with pins and the mumbled charms of toothless old women. Like Elizabeth and Henry

VIII, he was made intensely anxious by prognostications: attempts to predict the future by sorcery or other magical means were felonies. Hence even Matthew Gwinn's innocuous little ceremony of greeting had a slight element of daring. Still, it must have been deeply reassuring for James to be told that his rule and the rule of his descendents had been prophesied centuries before—the boys of St. John's were a kind of theatrical charm to ward off the sick fear at the pit of his stomach. The king's pleasure must have been evident, for the little ceremony of greeting—whether Shakespeare stood in the crowd watching it or heard about it from one of the bystanders—seems to have stuck in the playwright's imagination.

A year later, in the summer of 1606, the king of Denmark came to England to visit his daughter, Queen Anne. "There is nothing to be heard at court," writes one observer of the visit, "but sounding of trumpets, hautboys, music, revelings, and comedies." It was probably on one of these festive occasions that James sat down with his guests to see *Macbeth,* a new tragedy performed by his company, the King's Men. When the three weird sisters appeared onstage, did the king recall the pleasant little pageant outside of St. John's College? Probably not. He had, after all, seen many extravagant shows since his accession to the English throne, and there were other things to occupy his mind.

But Shakespeare must have seen, or heard about, those three boys dressed up as ancient sibyls, and he had not forgotten them. He conjured them up in *Macbeth* to restage the reassuring vision of unbroken dynastic succession. Midway through the play, Macbeth goes out to talk with the "secret, black, and midnight hags." "My heart / Throbs to know one thing," Macbeth says to them,

> Tell me, if your art
> Can tell so much, shall Banquo's issue ever
> Reign in this kingdom?
>
> (4.1.64, 116–19)

The witches urge him to content himself with what he already knows, but Macbeth insists on an answer. He cannot endure the uncertainty—"I will be satisified," he shouts (4.1.120)—and he gets in response a strange spectacle, a pageant that resembles the entertainments mounted to reassure kings.

It is the general pattern of Shakespeare's tragedies that when the hero gets what he wants, the result is devastating. Macbeth wins a great battle for his king, Duncan, and is handsomely honored, but the honor only whets his restless discontent. He kills Duncan and seizes the crown, but the treason initiates an unending nightmare of suspicion and anxiety. He orders the assassination of his friend Banquo, but the ghost of the murdered man haunts him, and he is dismayed by the escape of Banquo's son. He longs to feel secure, unconstrained, and "perfect," as he puts it, "Whole as the marble, founded as the rock." Instead he feels "cabined, cribbed, confined, bound in / To saucy doubts and fears" (3.4.20–21, 23–24). It is to relieve these doubts and fears that he turns to the witches and demands that they show him what lies ahead. But the answer Macbeth sees is for him a singularly bitter one, since it is not his own line of succession that is on display in the witches' pageant but the heirs of a man he has murdered, Banquo. Eight kings pass before him, the last bearing a glass that shows many more to follow. The magic mirror is a familiar device from witch lore, and it may in the court production in 1606 have served a further purpose: the actor could have approached the throne and held the glass so that Banquo's heir James would see his own reflection. Here, as in the Oxford device, the fatal sisters prophesy "power without end." "What," asks the despairing Macbeth, "will the line stretch out to th' crack of doom?" (4.1.133).

Shakespeare constructed *Macbeth* around, or perhaps as, a piece of flattery. The flattery is not direct and personal, the fulsome praise characteristic of many other royal entertainments in the period, but indirect and dynastic. That is, James is honored not for his wisdom or learning or statecraft but for his place in a line of legitimate descent that leads all the way from his noble ancestor in the distant past to the sons that promise an unbroken succession. In order to enhance this point Shakespeare had to twist the historical record. Gwinn's pageant probably took Banquo from Raphael Holinshed's *Chronicle*, a book Shakespeare had used heavily in his English histories. But when, following Gwinn's lead, Shakespeare opened to the Scottish section of Holinshed, he would have found that Banquo figures as one of the murderous Macbeth's chief allies, not as his moral alternative. ("At length therefore, communicating his purposed intent with his trusty friends, amongst whom Banquo was the chiefest, upon confidence of their promised aid, he slew the king.") Shakespeare's Banquo, by contrast, is a figure of probity and decency. When Macbeth cautiously asks for his assistance, without specifying what action he has in mind, the upright thane delicately but firmly declares his allegiance to the reigning king. Shakespeare transforms James's ancestor, then, from a collaborator into a resister. It must have been agreeable to James—whose immediate past was a sickening tangle of conspiracy and betrayal—to be told that his line was founded on a rock of rectitude.

The vision of stable rule and secure dynastic succession would have appealed to more than the king alone. A few months earlier, the whole country had been deeply shaken by the discovery—at the last possible minute—of a plot to destroy James, his entire family and court, and virtually all the political leaders of the realm. On November 4, 1605, the night before King James I was due to appear in person to open a new session of Parliament, officers of the Crown, alerted some days before by a hint in an anonymous letter, apprehended Guy Fawkes in a cellar that extended beneath the Parliament House. The cellar was loaded with barrels of gunpowder and iron bars, concealed by a load of lumber and coal. Carrying a watch, a fuse, and tinder, Fawkes intended to put into execution a desperate plot devised by a small group of conspirators, embittered by what they perceived as James's unwillingness to extend toleration to Roman Catholics. Under ferocious torture, Fawkes revealed the names of those who had conspired with him to blow up the entire government. The conspirators were hunted down. Those who resisted were killed on the spot; others were arrested and, after a trial that the king watched in secret, were hanged, cut down while they were still alive, slit open, and hewed in quarters.

Among those arrested and brought to trial for the Gunpowder Plot was Father Henry Garnet, the head of the clandestine Jesuit mission in England. Garnet, against whom there was very little hard evidence, pleaded innocent, but the government prosecutors made much of the fact that he was the author of *A Treatise of Equivocation*, a book defending the morality of giving misleading or ambiguous answers under oath. Once again James watched the trial from a secret vantage point. Convicted of treason, Garnet was dragged on a hurdle to Saint Paul's Churchyard for execution, his severed head then joining the others displayed on pikes on London Bridge.

"The King is in terror," wrote the Venetian ambassador; "he does not appear nor does he take his meals in public as usual. . . . The Lords of the Council also are alarmed and confused by the plot itself and (by) the King's suspicions; the city is in great uncertainty; Catholics fear heretics, and vice-versa; both are armed, foreigners live in terror of their houses being sacked by the mob." If the bloody denouement of what the prosecutor, Sir Edward Coke, called a "heavy and doleful tragedy" was meant to bring calm to the nation, it did not entirely succeed. On March 22, a rumor quickly spread that the king had been stabbed with an envenomed knife, some said by English Jesuits, some by Scots in women's apparel, some by Spaniards and Frenchmen. Gates were locked, soldiers were levied, courtiers looked pale, women began to wail—until the king issued a proclamation insisting that he was alive. The country had experienced a nightmare from which it had not yet completely awakened.

The King's Men, like the other theater companies, would have had to think hard about what would best suit this moment, both for the general London audience and for the court. In *Macbeth*, Shakespeare seems to have set out to write a play that would function as a collective ritual of reassurance. Everyone had been deeply shaken: the whole of the ruling elite, along with the king and his family, could have been blown to bits, the kingdom ripped apart and plunged into the chaos of internecine religious warfare. The staging of the events of eleventh-century Scotland— the treacherous murder of the king, the collapse of order and decency, the long struggle to wrest the realm from the bloody hands of traitors— allowed its seventeenth-century audience to face a symbolic version of this disaster and to witness the triumphant restoration of order.

The plot of *Macbeth*, to be sure, is very far from the Gunpowder Plot: there is no Catholic conspiracy, no threatened explosion, no last-minute reprieve for the kingdom. But Shakespeare plants subtle allusions of which the most famous is a joke that must have provoked a ripple of shuddering laughter through its original audiences. The strangely comic moment comes in the immediate wake of one of the most harrowing scenes of dread and soul sickness that Shakespeare ever wrote. Macbeth has just treacherously murdered the sleeping king Duncan, a guest in his castle. Deeply shaken by the deed and gripped by fear and remorse, he and his ambitious wife are exchanging anxious words when they hear a loud knocking at the castle gate. The knocking is a simple device, but in performance it almost always has a thrilling effect, an effect subtly antic- ipated by Macbeth's horrified sense before the murder that the very image of what he is about to do makes "my seated heart knock at my ribs" (1.3.135). As the insistent knocking continues, the conspirators exit to wash the blood off their hands and to change into their nightgowns. Lady Macbeth is—or strives to seem—icily calm, calculating, and confi- dent: "A little water clears us of this deed" (2.2.65). Not so the appalled Macbeth: "Wake Duncan with thy knocking. I would thou couldst," he declares in horror or despair, longing or bitter irony (2.2.72). At this point, a porter, roused by the noise but half-drunk from the evening's rev- elry, appears. As he grumblingly goes to unlock the gate, he seems to be still in a dream state. He imagines that he is the gatekeeper in hell, open- ing the door to new arrivals. "Here's an equivocator," he says of one of these imaginary sinners, "that could swear in both the scales against either scale, who committed treason enough for God's sake, yet could not equivocate to heaven. O, come in, equivocator" (2.3.8–11). This treason- ous equivocator knocking on hell's gate is almost certainly an allusion to the recently executed Jesuit Henry Garnet.

Why didn't Shakespeare, or any other playwright, represent more directly the supremely dramatic events of November 1605? After all, those events not only formed a perfect story of national danger and sal- vation but even—as carefully stage-managed by James's principal adviser, the Earl of Salisbury—gave the king himself a crucial role in uncovering the diabolical plot. The anonymous letter of warning said only that "they shall receive a terrible blow this Parliament, and yet they shall not see who hurts them." Salisbury claimed that he and the Privy Council were not sure what to make of these opaque phrases until the king brilliantly deciphered them and sent them searching the cellar. The statute making

November 5 a day of national thanksgiving proclaimed that the ruinous plot would have succeeded "had it not pleased Almighty God, by inspiring the King's most excellent Majesty with a divine spirit, to interpret some dark phrases of a letter showed his Majesty, above and beyond all ordinary construction." This melodramatic account seems like a gift specially prepared for a theater company; why couldn't the King's Men accept it?

The answer lies in part in a long-term history of official wariness, a history that extends back before the public theaters in London were even built. In 1559, the first year of Elizabeth's reign, the queen instructed her officers not to permit any "interlude" to be "played wherein either matters of religion or of the governance of the estate of the commonweal shall be handled or treated." While it would have been almost impossible to enforce such a prohibition in the broadest sense, without simply banning the theater, the censors were alert to anything that came too close to contemporary controversies. Moreover, the monarch and the ruling elite were uneasy about being represented onstage, no matter how flattering the portrayal. By allowing such representations, they would in effect be ceding control of their own persons, and they feared that the theater would only succeed, as the queen put it, in "making greatness familiar."

Nonetheless, in the wake of the national near catastrophe and the last-minute redemption, it is surprising that the text of *Macbeth* does not contain so much as a prologue, written to the king, celebrating the recent escape; or a complimentary allusion to James's role as the special enemy of Satan and the beloved of God; or a grateful acknowledgment of the happiness of being ruled by Banquo's wise heir. That Shakespeare limited himself to dark hints about an equivocator who belongs in hell may be linked to a disturbing experience that his company had had the previous winter. The King's Men were by all measures a great success: between November 1, 1604, and February 12, 1605, they gave no fewer than eleven performances at court, all but three of them plays by Shakespeare. But one of these performances ran into the kind of trouble that could have had disastrous consequences. Buoyed by the monarch's patronage and secure in their place as the premier company, they evidently decided to test the conventional limits of representation. They thought they might interest the king and please their larger audience with a play based on a dramatic event in James's life: his narrow escape from assassination, or so he claimed, in August 1600 at the hands of the Earl of Gowrie and his brother Alexander.

As with the Gunpowder Plot, the official account of the event reads like a melodrama: out hunting in Scotland with his retinue, the king was induced by a strange story of a pot of gold coins to ride off to Gowrie House. There he was lured by Alexander Gowrie to ascend without attendants into the turret. Left behind in the hall and increasingly anxious, the king's followers were led to believe that their master had slipped away and ridden off, but just as they were about to go in search of him, they were startled by the sight of James leaning from a window of the turret and shouting, "I am murdered! Treason!" The door of the turret was locked, but John Ramsay, one of the king's men, managed to ascend by a different stair and break into the chamber, where he found James struggling with Alexander. Ramsay stabbed the king's assailant in the face and neck, while downstairs other followers of the king dispatched the assailant's brother, the Earl of Gowrie.

It is probably no accident that the story seems too good to be true. Many disinterested observers must have smelled a rat—a treacherous political killing of two powerful nobles whom the king distrusted and to whom he was in debt to the tune of eighty thousand pounds. The state evidently felt it had to shore up the story of a treasonous attempt on the king's life. Not only did the Earl of Gowrie betray a subject's obligation of loyalty to his sovereign, according to the official account, not only did he trample on a host's obligation to his guest, but he also violated the worship of God: a "little close parchment bag, full of magical characters and words of enchantment" was found on the earl's body at his death. It was only when the bag was removed from him that his body began to bleed. The Hebrew characters proved that its bearer was a "cabbalist," the magistrates declared, "a studier of magic, and a conjuror of devils." The torture of several witnesses with the "boot"—a device that crushed the bones of the feet—produced the full array of evidence that the state required, and a flurry of executions, along with the king's seizure of the Gowrie property, brought the episode to a close. Scottish ministers were instructed "to praise God for the King's miraculous delivery from that vile treason." Several refused, whether because they doubted the story or thought the instruction idolatrous, and were promptly dismissed from their posts. Most grudgingly complied.

Some playwright affiliated with the King's Men—perhaps Shakespeare himself—grasped that this story would make an exciting play. The company knew, of course, that they would be violating the Elizabethan taboo on representing living magnates and contemporary or near-contemporary events, since someone (and here too Shakespeare is a possibility) would have had to play the part of James. But they may have wanted to test whether the restriction would be continued into the new regime. Moreover, they may have noted that the king had gone out of his way to reward anyone who actively supported his version of the bloody events at Gowrie House, and they calculated that an English audience would find these events fascinating. They were at least partly right: in December 1604 *The Tragedy of Gowrie* was twice performed before large crowds. But, as a court spy noted, the play did not please everyone: "whether the matter or manner be not well handled, or that it be thought unfit that Princes should be played on the Stage in their Life-time, I hear that some great Councilors are much displeased with it, and so 'tis thought shall be forbidden." The company did not fall from favor as a consequence of their miscalculation, but the play was evidently banned. There is no record of other performances, and the text did not survive.

A year later, in the wake of the Gunpowder Plot, the King's Men thought once again about doing a Scottish play, but they knew that they had to be more careful this time. If they wanted to stage a Scottish tale of treason—the story of a noble host who, corrupted by black magic, attempts to murder his royal guest—they would have to push it far back in time. And if they wanted to perform something that would capture the king's imagination, they had to study his mind more attentively. That mind, as James's English subjects were discovering, was extremely strange.

Queen Elizabeth's godson, a celebrated wit named John Harington, recounted an audience with the king in 1604. James began in a pedantic vein—he showed off his learning, Harington wrote, "in such sort as made me remember my examiner at Cambridge"—and went on to literature, with a discussion of the Italian epic poet Ariosto. Then the conversation took a strange turn: "His Majesty did much press for my opinion touching the power of Satan in matter of witchcraft, and . . . why the Devil did work more with ancient [i.e., old] women than others." Harington tried to deflect the odd urgency of the king's question with an off-color joke: he reminded the king that Scripture says the devil has a preference for "walking in dry places." But James did not simply laugh and move on to other matters. There was, he said, a weird apparition in the heavens in Scotland before his mother's death, "a bloody head dancing in the air." The English courtier restrained himself and made no further attempt at comedy.

James's anxiety about witches and apparitions was no laughing matter, and it obviously behooved anyone interested in the king's favor—a playwright as much as a courtier—to take its full measure. There may have been an understanding among the King's Men that their principal playwright would undertake to do some research into James's fantasy life, with a view toward writing a play specifically designed to please him. No formal agreement would have been necessary, for the desirability of understanding James in order to please him—particularly after the debacle of *The Tragedy of Gowrie*—was obvious enough. Shakespeare may not have been merely passing through Oxford by chance in August 1605; he may have been there on assignment, watching James's reactions the way Horatio in *Hamlet* watches the king.

Observing how the king responded to the shows put on for him would have been useful (it would in this case have given a clear indication of the sort of thing that put him to sleep), but it did not answer the key questions: What would keep the king awake? What would catch his attention without triggering his fear? What would excite his interest, gratify his curiosity, arouse his generosity, make him long for more? The King's Men needed to enter the king's head. Staring at James from the midst of the cheering crowd was no substitute for the kind of conversational insight that Harington had, a privilege from which a mere player would have been excluded. There were, however, other means of access into the king's interests and imagination. James had taken the unusual step of publishing a learned dialogue on witchcraft in 1597, the *Dae-*

monologie. This work, which went through two London editions in 1603 and which Shakespeare could easily have encountered, acknowledges the existence of skepticism—"many can scarcely believe that there is such a thing as witchcraft"—but argues that disbelief is a step toward atheism and damnation. Witches do indeed exist and are a significant danger to the whole realm.

Shakespeare knew about witches long before the Scottish king lectured his subjects on them. He would have heard of the ecclesiastical commissions that traveled through the country seeking out necromancers, conjurers, and magical healers; the parliamentary statutes repeatedly passed making "witchcrafts, enchantments, and sorceries" punishable by death; the laws forbidding anyone from attempting through charms or other illicit means to know "how long her Majesty shall live or continue, or who shall reign as King or Queen of this Realm of England after her Highness's decease." He may well have read the act passed in 1604 against anyone who

> shall consult, covenant with, entertain, employ, feed, or reward any evil and wicked Spirit to or for any intent or purpose; or take up any dead man, woman, or child out of his, her, or their grave, or any other place where the dead body resteth, or the skin, bone, or any other part of any dead person, to be employed or used in any manner of witchcraft, sorcery, charm, or enchantment; or shall use, practice, or exercise any witchcraft, enchantment, charm, or sorcery, whereby any person shall be killed, destroyed, wasted, consumed, pined, or lamed in his or her body.

As a person with deep roots in country life, Shakespeare would have heard of and perhaps directly known cases where sick cattle or damaged crops or children dying of lingering illnesses were blamed upon the malevolent magic of neighbors. People could attribute such catastrophes to natural causes as well, but an unexpected blow—a violent storm; a mysterious, wasting sickness; an inexplicable case of impotence—set them grumbling menacingly at the poor, ugly, defenseless old woman in the hovel at the end of the lane. "Many witches are found there," a German visitor to England noted in 1592, "who frequently do much mischief by means of hail and tempests."

An ambitious, self-aggrandizing justice of the peace named Brian Darcy published an account of the pretrial examinations of accused witches that he conducted in Essex in 1582. His account provides a close-up, eerily detailed glimpse of a rural community grappling with everyday concerns, and in this case a community being prodded by its magistrate toward violent persecution. Using the testimony of small children and quarreling neighbors to ferret out the occult crimes he knew he would discover, the zealous magistrate identified a whole network of witches who conspired with demonic spirits—"familiars" in the form of dogs, cats, and toads, with names like Tiffin, Titty, and Suckin—to wreak havoc. After she had a falling-out with Mrs. Thurlow, Ursula Kemp sent her spirit Tiffin ("like a white lamb") to rock Thurlow's infant's cradle, until the infant almost fell onto the ground. "Mother Mansfield" came to Joan Cheston's house and asked for some curds. Joan said she had none, "and within a while after some of her cattle were taken lame." "Lynd's wife" reported that Mother Mansfield came to her and asked for a "mess of milk"; she refused, explaining that "she had but a little, not so much as would suckle her calf." That night her calf died. It is all at a similarly local level: a small uncharitable act, a few harsh words—and then the nasty consequences. A farmer's wife churns and churns but can get no butter; thread breaks in the spindle, even though the spindle was perfectly smooth; a child who has been robust begins to languish. This was the everyday world of places like Snitterfield and Wilmcote and Shottery, the villages near Stratford that Shakespeare knew from the inside. What was missing, if they were lucky, was a Brian Darcy to transform the ordinary tension, frustration, and grief of early modern village life into judicial murder.

From James's *Daemonologie*, Shakespeare would have learned that though the king was struck by the fact that so many of the people accused of witchcraft were old women from small villages, he was not at all interested in the local hatreds and heartbreaks that generated most of the accusations. Unlike Brian Darcy's, the king's mind soared away from the familiar rancors of rural life. As befitted a monarch of wide reading,

James had grand metaphysical theories, complex political strategies, the subtle ideas of an intellectual and a statesman. He was, moreover, well aware that many of the charges of witchcraft were mere fantasies and lies, and he was proud of his perspicacity.

By themselves, James thought, witches have no magical powers. But they have made a pact with the devil, a pact solemnized in the nightmarish assemblies known as sabbats. In order to lure Christians away from the true faith, the devil deludes his followers into thinking that they have been granted special gifts and that they possess the ability to harm their neighbors. Hence what appear to be the effects of magic are for the most part counterfeits, illusions cunningly crafted to deceive "men's outward senses." These illusions are often startlingly impressive, to be sure, but their effectiveness is not surprising, "since we see by common proof that a simple juggler will make a hundred things seem both to our eyes and ears otherwise than they are." The devil's power has limits, set down before the foundations of the world were laid—he cannot create actual miracles, he cannot destroy godly magistrates, he cannot read thoughts— but he is more accomplished than the greatest mountebank. Indeed, the devil teaches his disciples "many jugglery tricks at cards, dice, and such like, to deceive men's senses" with false miracles; he is an exceptionally subtle corrupter of anyone with moral weaknesses; and if he cannot read thoughts, he is learned enough in physiognomy to guess at men's thoughts by studying their faces.

The devil's goal is the ruin not of a tiny hamlet but of a whole kingdom, and hence his principal target is not this or that local villager but God's own representative on earth, the king. It is to ensnare princes that the devil teaches his disciples, his "scholars," as the owlish James calls them, his tricks. And, as one might expect of a malevolent being who has lived for centuries, closely observed men and beasts and the natural world, and thoroughly mastered the arts of deception, the devil's tricks are impressive. "He will make his scholars to creep in credit with Princes," James writes, "by fore-telling them many great things"—the outcome of battles, the fate of commonwealths, and the like—"part true, part false." If Satan's scholars only spoke lies, their master would soon lose credit, and if they straightforwardly told the truth, they could scarcely do the devil's work. So their prognostications are "always doubtsome, as his Oracles were." Through his astonishing agility Satan provides other means for witches to please princes, "by fair banquets and dainty dishes, carried in short space from the farthest part of the world." And he seems to confer upon his agents spectral forces, "which all are but impressions in the air, easily gathered by a spirit," in order to delude men's senses.

Ambiguous and deceptive prophecies; seductive pleasures; airy, insubstantial illusions—these are among the devices witches employ, James thought, when they set out to destroy someone. Shakespeare, as *Macbeth* shows, took careful note. He may also have gone out of his way to acquaint himself with the king's actual dealings with witches. He could have inquired about these dealings from anyone who had been in Scotland during James's reign there, and there were many potential informants, since a great number of his compatriots followed James to London. He could also have read about them in a sensational pamphlet, *News from Scotland*, published in 1591. Two years before, a storm had disrupted James's marriage arrangements; his bride-to-be, Anne of Denmark, was supposed to sail from Denmark to Scotland in 1589, but thunder, lightning, and rain forced the ship to take refuge in Oslo. James impetuously sailed there and married her. When he returned some months later to Scotland, he became convinced that the tempest had been the result of diabolical intervention. He became directly involved in an unprecedented series of witchcraft investigations, investigations that claimed to discover a network of witches in North Berwick—about twenty miles from Edinburgh, on the Firth of Forth—involved in communal devil worship.

One of the accused, Agnes Thompson, confessed to the king and his council that on Halloween 1590 some two hundred witches had sailed to the town in sieves. Then, while one of the coven, Geillis Duncane, played a tune on a small instrument, a "Jew's trump," they sang and danced their way into the kirk (church) where Satan impatiently awaited them. The devil put his buttocks over the pulpit railing for the witches to kiss, as a sign of fealty, and then made his "ungodly exhortations," focusing his malice against "the greatest enemy he hath in the world," namely, the king of Scotland. James thus found himself the direct object of attack in the satanic sermon, no doubt a satisfying confirmation of the sanctity of his royal person, but also unnerving. For during interrogation—and James was an enthusiastic user of torture to obtain confessions—Agnes Thompson disclosed some of the devices that had been used against him: "She confessed that she took a black toad, and did hang the same up by the heels three days, and collected and gathered the venom as it dropped and fell from it in an oyster shell, and kept the same venom close covered, until she should obtain any part or piece of foul linen cloth that had appertained to the King's Majesty." If she had been able to get hold of a fragment of his shirt or handkerchief, she told the king, and had anointed it with the venom, then she would have "bewitched him to death." And though this plot was frustrated, she and her companions had succeeded in causing at least some harm. They had christened a cat, tied body parts from a dead man to its limbs, and then thrown it into the sea. The effect was to raise "such a tempest in the sea as a greater hath not been seen" and to provoke a contrary wind against the king's ship, coming from Denmark. "His Majesty had never come safely from the sea, if his faith had not prevailed above their intentions."

Disposed though he was to believe every one of these absurd charges, James was eager not to seem naive, and he declared that the miserable women he was interrogating, stripping, prodding obscenely, and torturing were all "extreme liars." But one of them, Agnes Sampson, took him aside and told him "the very words" that he had exchanged with his bride on their wedding night in Norway. James was astonished "and swore by the living God that he believed that all the devils in hell could not have discovered the same, acknowledging her words to be most true." The king was then convinced that the witches were present not only on the tempest-tossed sea and in the graveyard where they dug up corpses and performed their obscene rites, but also in the bedroom, where they somehow overheard the most intimate moments of marital conversation.

These beliefs, and both the political pretensions and the deep fears they bespoke, were not hidden away in some dark place where only James's intimates knew of them; they were matters of public record.

Shakespeare seems to have noted them carefully, and he may have observed something still more germane to his purpose. When James heard that the witches had danced into the North Berwick kirk to the sound of a reel played on a small trumpet by Geillis Duncane, he was struck with "a wonderful admiration." He sent for the witch and commanded her to play the same dance before him.

Poor Geillis Duncane: a maidservant, she had originally aroused her master's suspicions because she had proved all too successful in her efforts "to help all such as were troubled or grieved with any kind of sickness." Though she first protested that she was innocent, a series of brutal body searches and tortures—"the Pilliwinks upon her fingers, which is a grievous torture, and binding or wrenching her head with a cord or rope"—had elicited from her the desired confession. Now she found herself performing the fatal role that had been violently imposed upon her before the fascinated, horrified, and pleased king. "In respect of the strangeness of these matters," *News from Scotland* reports, James "took great delight to be present at their examinations." Witchcraft was not only a frightening danger; it was also a wonderful show.

As Shakespeare grasped, the king was aroused by witches to "a wonderful admiration"—precisely the effect that the King's Men were hoping to achieve. Hence the astonishing spectacle with which Shakespeare opened his new Scottish show:

> When shall we three meet again?
> In thunder, lightning, or in rain?
> (*Macbeth*, 1.1.1–2)

Taking over Gwinn's device—three sibyls stepping forward as if from a wood and prophesying the future—Shakespeare recapitulates the promise to Banquo's heirs of stable dynastic rule. Yet the pretty civilities of St. John's College are altogether swept away. Once again Shakespeare radically altered his source, literally introducing opacity—"fog and filthy air"—where there was once simple transparency. The play begins with three strange creatures all right:

> What are these,
> So withered, and so wild in their attire,
> That look not like th'inhabitants o'th' earth
> And yet are on't?...
>
> . . . .
>
> You should be women,
> And yet your beards forbid me to interpret
> That you are so—
>
> (1.3.37–44)

But the scene is a wild heath. When Macbeth enters, the "weird sisters" greet him in terms that startlingly recall, virtually as a quotation, Gwinn's entertainment:

> FIRST WITCH: All hail, Macbeth! Hail to thee, Thane of Glamis
> SECOND WITCH: All hail, Macbeth! Hail to thee, Thane of Cawdor.
> THIRD WITCH: All hail, Macbeth, that shalt be king hereafter!
>
> (1.3.46–48)

But what was reassuring is now turned inside out, what was warmly welcoming is made chilling. Even within the world of the play, Macbeth, to whom the ostensibly happy prophecy is made, registers the disturbance. "Good sir," asks his friend Banquo, "why do you start and seem to fear / Things that do sound so fair?" (1.3.49–50).

Shakespeare was burrowing deep into the dark fantasies that swirled about in the king's brain. It is all here: the ambiguous prophecies designed to lure men to their destruction, the "Shipwrecking storms and direful thunders" (1.2.26) that once threatened Anne of Denmark, the murderous hatred of anointed kings, the illusory apparitions, the fiendish equivocations, the loathsome concoction of body parts, even the witches' sailing in a sieve to do their diabolical mischief—

> But in a sieve I'll thither sail,
> And like a rat without a tail

I'll do, I'll do, and I'll do.
(1.3.7–9)

If James had been fascinated by a command performance of diabolical music, the King's Men would give him that and more:

> Come, sisters, cheer we up his sprites,
> And show the best of our delights.
> I'll charm the air to give a sound
> While you perform your antic round,
> That this great king may kindly say
> Our duties did his welcome pay.
>   (4.1.143–48)

"This great king"—the witches are referring to Macbeth, but it is not the imagined usurper who craved demonic entertainment; it is the living king of England and Scotland.

Why should Shakespeare have risked the irony of this transformation? Why, for that matter, did he risk the transformation of Gwinn's reassuring compliment into a nightmarish tragedy of betrayal and destruction? *Macbeth* does not represent disaster miraculously averted; it does not confirm the belief that a divinity hedges an anointed king; it does not support James's fantasy that a truly good man is invulnerable to the malice of witchcraft. Trust is violated, families are destroyed, nature itself is poisoned. To a king who paled at the sight of sharp steel, it offered the insistent spectacle of a bloody dagger, both a real dagger and what Macbeth calls a dagger of the mind. True, the pageant promises the throne to an endless succession of Banquo's heirs. True as well, the restoration of order in the tragedy's final moments could be seen as a representation of the order that had been restored to the realm after the Gunpowder Plot: the severed head of Macbeth, carried onstage at the concluding moment by the victorious Macduff, was a reminder of the conspirators' heads that members of the audience could see every time they walked across London Bridge. Yet *Macbeth* hardly sits comfortably with the functions of prince-pleasing or popular reassurance. The materials Shakespeare worked with touched off something extremely peculiar in him, something that does not fit the overarching scheme.

Shakespeare was a professional risk-taker. He wrote under pressure—judging from its unusual brevity, *Macbeth* was composed in a very short time—and he went where his imagination took him. If the cheerful sibyls of St. John's became the weird sisters dancing around a cauldron bubbling with hideous contents—

> Scale of dragon, tooth of wolf,
> Witches' mummy, maw and gulf
> Of the ravined salt-sea shark,
> Root of hemlock digged i'th' dark,
> Liver of blaspheming Jew,
> Gall of goat, and slips of yew
> Slivered in the moon's eclipse,
> Nose of Turk, and Tartar's lips,
> Finger of birth-strangled babe
> Ditch-delivered by a drab
>   (4.1.22–31)

—then Shakespeare was obliged to pursue the course. The alternative was to write the kind of play that would put James to sleep and send the thrill-seeking crowds to rival theaters. But this explanation still leaves open the question of why Shakespeare's imagination took the peculiar turn that it did.

Something comparable to the potent blend of opportunism and imaginative generosity, appropriation and moral revulsion aroused in Shakespeare by the crowd's laughter at Lopez's execution may have been at work. When Shakespeare learned about the king's wonder and delight at Geillis Duncane's performance, he grasped what could be done to gratify the king's fantasies, and at the same instant his imagination began to enter into the figure of the condemned. He and his company would perform in the place, as it were, of the witch and her coven. They would sing the songs and chant the charms and provide the fascination that James desired. And they would complicate that fascination, moving through the figures of the weird sisters to the larger, more familiar world of domestic intimacy and court intrigue.

It is the general gift of the imagination to enter into the lives of others, but in the case of witches there is a special and particular bond: witches are the progeny of the imagination. The witchmongers of the Middle Ages and the Renaissance—the men who thought that there should be more denunciations of neighbors, more body searches, tortures, trials, and, above all, executions—believed that witches trafficked in fantasy. According to the famous witchcraft manual, the *Malleus maleficarum*, devils provoke and shape fantasies by direct corporeal intervention in the mind. Demonic spirits can incite what the authors, the Dominican inquisitors Heinrich Kramer and James Sprenger, call a "local motion" in the minds of those awake as well as asleep, stirring up and exciting the inner perceptions, "so that ideas retained in the repositories of their minds are drawn out and made apparent to the faculties of fancy and imagination, so that such men imagine these things to be true." This process of making a stir in the mind and moving images from one part of the brain to another is, they write, called "interior temptation." It can lead men to see objects before their eyes—daggers, for example— that are not in fact there; conversely, it can lead men *not* to see other objects—their own penises, for example—that are still there, though concealed from view by what the inquisitors term a "glamour." Hence, Kramer and Sprenger write, "a certain man tells that, when he had lost his member, he approached a known witch to ask her to restore it to him. She told the afflicted man to climb a certain tree, and that he might take which he liked out of a nest in which there were several members. And when he tried to take a big one, the witch said: You must not take that one; adding because it belonged to a parish priest."

Reading this and other passages in the *Malleus maleficarum*, an older contemporary of Shakespeare's, an English country gentleman named Reginald Scot, said that he was tempted to regard the whole work as a "bawdy discourse," a kind of obscene joke book. But he checked the impulse: "these are no jests," he writes, "for they be written by them that were and are judges upon the lives and deaths of those persons." Scot's response in 1584 was to publish *The Discovery of Witchcraft*, the greatest

English contribution to the skeptical critique of witchcraft. On his accession to the English throne, James ordered all copies of Scot's book to be burned. But it seems, from allusions that he made to it, that Shakespeare got hold of a copy and read it when he wrote *Macbeth*.

Scot argues that it is the masters of language, the poets, who have been the principal sources of the murderous fantasies that lead to witch hunts. The poet Ovid affirms, writes Scot, that witches

> can raise and suppress lightening and thunder, rain and hail, clouds and winds, tempests and earthquakes. Others do write, that they can pull down the moon and the stars. Some write that with wishing they can send needles into the livers of their enemies. Some that they can transfer corn in the blade from one place to another. Some, that they can cure diseases supernaturally, fly in the air, and dance with devils. . . . They can raise spirits (as others affirm) dry up springs, turn the course of running waters, inhibit the sun, and stay both day and night, changing the one into the other. They can go in and out at auger holes, and sail in an egg shell, a cockle or muscle shell, through and under the tempestuous seas. They can go invisible, and deprive men of their privities, and otherwise of the act and use of venery. They can bring souls out of the graves.

Such are the visions that poets have given us, and they have led people to torture and kill their innocent neighbors. But, Scot concludes, there is a defense against this ghastly mistake: do not believe the songs that poets sing.

The King's Men did not preach anything of the kind: dressing themselves up as witches, they were determined to profit from those obsessions. The weird sisters in Shakespeare's play apparently traffic in bad weather: "When shall we three meet again? / In thunder, lightning, or in rain?" (1.1.1–2). They seem to cause unnatural darkness: "By th' clock 'tis day, / And yet dark night strangles the travelling lamp" (2.4.6–7). They make themselves invisible, fly in the air, dance with devils, sail in a sieve, cast spells, and drain men dry. But, though many of the demonic powers listed by Scot as the inventions of poets are alluded to in *Macbeth*, it is oddly difficult to determine what, if anything, the witches actually do in the play.

The opacity in *Macbeth* is not produced by the same radical excision of motivation Shakespeare so strikingly employed in *Hamlet*, *Othello*, and *King Lear*. If the audience does not know exactly why Hamlet assumes his madness or Iago hates Othello or Lear puts the love test to his daughters, it most assuredly knows why Macbeth plots to assassinate King Duncan: spurred on by his wife, he wishes to seize the crown for himself. But in a tortured soliloquy, Macbeth reveals that he is deeply baffled by his own murderous fantasies:

> My thought, whose murder yet is but fantastical,
> Shakes so my single state of man that function
> Is smothered in surmise, and nothing is
> But what is not.
>
> (1.3.138–41)

At the center of the familiar and conventional motive there is a dark hole— "nothing is / But what is not." And this hole that is inside Macbeth is linked to the dark presence, within his consciousness and within the play's world, of the witches. Do they actually arouse the thought of murdering Duncan in Macbeth's mind, or is that thought already present before he encounters them? Do they have some affinity with Lady Macbeth—who calls upon the spirits that attend on mortal thoughts to "unsex" her (1.5.38–39)—or is their evil completely independent of hers? Does the witches' warning—"beware Macduff" (4.1.87)—actually induce Macbeth to kill Macduff's family, or has he already waded too deep in bloodshed to turn back? Do their ambiguous prophecies lead him to a final, fatal over-confidence, or is his end the result of his loss of popular support and the superior power of Malcolm's army? None of the questions are answered. At the end of the play the weird sisters are left unmentioned, their role unresolved. Shakespeare refuses to allow the play to localize and contain the threat in the bodies of witches.

Macbeth leaves the weird sisters unpunished but manages to implicate them in a monstrous threat to the fabric of civilized life. The genius of the play is bound up with this power of implication, by means of which the audience can never quite be done with them, for they are most suggestively present when they cannot be seen, when they are absorbed in the ordinary relations of everyday life. If you are worried about losing your manhood and are afraid of the power of women, it is not enough to look to the bearded hags on the heath, look to your wife. If you are worried about temptation, fear your own dreams. If you are anxious about your future, scrutinize your best friends. And if you fear spiritual desolation, turn your eyes on the contents not of the hideous cauldron but of your skull: "O, full of scorpions is my mind, dear wife!" (3.2.37).

The witches—eerie, indefinable, impossible to locate securely or to understand—are the embodiment of the principle of opacity that Shakespeare embraced in his great tragedies. Shakespeare's theater is the equivocal space where conventional explanations fall away, where one person can enter another person's mind, and where the fantastic and the bodily touch. This conception of his art is what it meant for him to take the place of Geillis Duncane and perform his theatrical witchcraft before the wondering gaze of the king. There is no record of the king's response, but Shakespeare's company never fell from its position as the King's Men.

CHAPTER 12

The Triumph of
the Everyday

S HAKESPEARE SEEMS TO HAVE begun contemplating the possibility of retirement—not so much planning for it as brooding about its perils—as early as 1604, when he sat down to write *King Lear*. The tragedy is his greatest meditation on extreme old age; on the painful necessity of renouncing power; on the loss of house, land, authority, love, eyesight, and sanity itself. This vision of devastating loss surged up not in an eccentric recluse and not in a man facing the onset of his own decay, but in a hugely energetic and successful playwright who had just turned forty. Even at a time when life expectancy was short, forty years old was not regarded as ancient. It was the middle of the passage, not the moment of reckoning. Shakespeare was in age closer to the play's young people— Goneril, Regan, and Cordelia; Edgar and Edmund—than he was to the two old men, Lear and Gloucester, whose terrible fates he depicts.

Once again, there is no easy, obvious link between what Shakespeare wrote—here a tremendous explosion of rage, madness, and grief—and the known circumstances of his own life. His father had died in 1601, probably in his sixties. In 1604 his mother was still alive and not, as far as we know, either mad or tyrannical. He had two daughters, but he could hardly claim that he had given them everything or that they had attempted to turn him out of his own house. He had, it is true, a younger brother named Edmund, the name of the villainous plotter in *King Lear*, but Edmund Shakespeare—an aspiring actor in London—was obviously no match for the bastard son of Gloucester, any more than Shakespeare's brother Richard could conjure up, in anything but name, England's homicidal hunchback king.

Shakespeare might well have been set to thinking about the story of Lear by a widely discussed lawsuit that had occurred in late 1603. The two elder daughters of a doddering gentleman named Sir Brian Annesley attempted to get their father legally certified as insane, thereby enabling themselves to take over his estate, while his youngest daughter vehemently protested on her father's behalf. The youngest daughter's name happened to be Cordell, a name almost identical to Cordella, the name of the daughter in the venerable legend of King Leir who tried to save her father from the malevolent designs of her two older sisters. The uncanny coincidence of the names and the stories must have been hard to resist.

Whether or not the Annesley case actually triggered the writing of the tragedy, Shakespeare was singularly alert to the way in which the Leir legend was in touch with ordinary family tensions and familiar fears associated with old age. For his play's central concerns, Shakespeare simply looked around him at the everyday world. This seems at first an odd claim: of all of his tragedies, *King Lear* seems the wildest and the strangest. The old king swears by Apollo and Hecate and calls upon the thunder to "Smite flat the thick rotundity o' the world!" (3.2.7). His friend, the Earl of Gloucester, thinks he is the victim of divine malevolence: "As flies to wanton boys are we to the gods; / They kill us for their sport" (4.1.37–38). The Bedlam beggar Poor Tom screams that he is possessed by a legion of exotic devils: Modo, Mahu, and Flibbertigibbet. But despite the constant invocation of a grand metaphysical frame, the play's events, terrible and trivial alike, occur in a universe in which there seems to be no overarching design at all. The devils are altogether fictional, and the gods on whom Lear and Gloucester call are conspicuously, devastatingly silent. What surrounds the characters with their loves and hatreds and torments is the most ordinary of worlds—"low farms, / Poor pelting villages, sheep-cotes, and mills" (2.3.17–18)—and the action that triggers the whole hideous train of events is among the most ordinary of decisions: a retirement.

In the culture of Tudor and Stuart England, where the old demanded the public deference of the young, retirement was the focus of particular anxiety. It put a severe strain on the politics and psychology of deference by driving a wedge between status—what Lear at society's pinnacle calls "The name, and all the additions to a king" (1.1.136)—and power. In both the state and the family, the strain could be somewhat eased by transferring power to the eldest legitimate male successor, but as the families of both the legendary Lear and the real Brian Annesley show, such a successor did not always exist. In the absence of a male heir, the aged Lear, determined to "shake all cares and business" from himself and confer them on "younger strengths," attempts to divide his kingdom among his daughters so that, as he puts it, "future strife / May be prevented now" (1.1.37–38, 42–43). But this attempt, centered on a public love test, is a disastrous failure, since it leads him to banish the one child who truly loves him.

Shakespeare contrives to show that the problem with which his characters are grappling does not simply result from the absence of a son and heir. In his most brilliant and complex use of a double plot, he intertwines the story of Lear and his three daughters with the story of Gloucester and his two sons, a story he adapted from an episode he read in Philip Sidney's prose romance, *Arcadia*. Gloucester has a legitimate heir, his elder son, Edgar, as well as an illegitimate son, Edmund, and in this family the tragic conflict originates not in an unusual manner of transferring property from one generation to another, such as Lear is attempting, but rather in the reverse: Edmund seethes with murderous resentment at the disadvantage entirely customary for someone in his position, both as a younger son and as what was called a base or natural child.

In the strange universe of *King Lear*, nothing but precipitous ruin lies on the other side of retirement, just as nothing but a bleak, featureless heath lies on the other side of the castle gate. In Shakespeare's imagination, the decision to withdraw from work—"To shake all cares and business from our age," as Lear says, "Conferring them on younger strengths" (1.1.37–38)—is a catastrophe. To be sure, the work in question here is ruling a kingdom, and Shakespeare's age had every reason to fear the crisis in authority that inevitably accompanied the debility of the ruler and the transfer of power. But the play is not only a warning to monarchs. It taps into a far more pervasive fear in this period, a period that had very few of the means that our society (itself hardly a model of virtue) now routinely employs to ease the anxieties and relieve the needs of the old.

Shakespeare's world constantly told itself that authority naturally inhered in the elderly. At stake, they said, was not simply a convenient social arrangement—convenient, in any case, for the old and for anyone who hoped someday to become old—but rather the moral structure of the universe, the sanctified, immemorial order of things. But at the same time, they nervously acknowledged that this order of things was unstable and that age's claim to authority was pathetically vulnerable to the ruthless ambitions of the young. Once a father had turned over his property to his children, once he had lost his ability to enforce his will, his authority would begin to crumble away. Even in the house that had once been his own, he would become what was called a sojourner. There could even be a ritualized acknowledgment of this drastic change in status, as testimony in a contemporary lawsuit suggests: having agreed to give his daughter in marriage to Hugh, with half of his land, the widower Anseline and the married couple were to live together in one house. "And the same Anseline went out of the house and handed over to them the door by the hasp, and at once begged lodging out of charity."

Retelling the Leir story was one way that Shakespeare and his contemporaries articulated their anxiety, but they had other, more practical ways to deal with the fragility of custom. Parents facing retirement frequently hired a lawyer to draw up what were called maintenance agreements, contracts by which, in return for the transfer of family property, children undertook to provide food, clothing, and shelter. The extent of parental anxiety may be gauged by the great specificity of many of these requirements—so many yards of woolen cloth, pounds of coal, or bushels of grain—and by the pervasive fear of being turned out of the house in the wake of a quarrel. Maintenance agreements stipulated that the children were only legal guardians of their parents' well-being, "depositaries" of the parental property. The parents could "reserve" some rights over this property, and, theoretically at least, if their "reservation" was not honored, they could move to reclaim what they had given away.

King Lear, set in a pagan Britain roughly contemporary with the prophet Isaiah, is very far from the Renaissance world of customary arrangements and legal protections—the world of the yeomen, artisans, and tradesmen from whose midst Shakespeare had emerged. But, notwithstanding the play's archaic setting, at the core of the tragedy is the great fear that haunted the playwright's own class: the fear of humiliation, abandonment, and a loss of identity in the wake of retirement. Lear's maddened rage is a response not only to his daughters' vicious ingratitude but also to the horror of being turned into an ordinary old man, a sojourner begging his children for charity:

> Ask her forgiveness?
> Do you but mark how this becomes the house:
> "Dear daughter, I confess that I am old;
> Age is unnecessary. On my knees I beg
> That you'll vouchsafe me raiment, bed, and food."
> (2.4.145–49)

His cruel daughter, in response, unbendingly proposes that he "return and sojourn with my sister" (2.4.198).

Near the climax of this terrible scene in which the wicked Goneril and Regan, by relentlessly diminishing his retinue, in effect strip away his social identity, Lear speaks as if he had actually drawn up a maintenance agreement with his daughters:

> LEAR: I gave you all—
> REGAN: And in good time you gave it.
> LEAR: Made you my guardians, my depositaries;
>   But kept a reservation to be followed
>   With such a number.
> (2.4.245–48)

But there is no maintenance agreement between Lear and his daughters; there could be none in the world of absolute power—of all or nothing—that he inhabits.

Shakespeare had no intention of someday going to the door of New Place, stepping across the threshold, and then asking his daughters to take him back in as a sojourner. It was not a matter of mistrust—he seems to have loved and trusted one of his daughters at least. It was a matter of identity. If *King Lear* is any indication, he shared with his contemporaries a fear of retirement and dread of dependence upon children. And from the surviving evidence, he could scarcely be expected to find comfort in the enduring bond with his wife. His way of dealing with this fear was work—the enormous labors that enabled him to accumulate a small fortune—and then the investment of his capital in land and tithes (an agricultural commodities investment), so that he could assure himself a steady annual income. He could not count on acting and touring and turning out two plays a year forever; someday it would have to come to a stop. What then? From 1602 to 1613, in the midst of astonishingly creative years, Shakespeare carefully accumulated and laid out his money so that in his old age he would never have to depend upon his daughters—or upon the theater.

Shakespeare had made his fortune virtually entirely on his own. His mother's inheritance, such as it was, had been first mortgaged and then forfeited through his father's incompetence or improvidence; his father's standing in Stratford had been compromised by debt and possibly by recusancy; his brothers amounted to little or nothing, his sister, Joan, married a poor hatter; and he himself had married a woman of very modest means. No convenient bequests had come his way; no wealthy relations had provided assistance at key moments; and no local magnate had spotted his brilliant promise when he was still a boy and helped him to a start in life. New Place was the tangible fruit of his own imagination and his hard work.

To acquire such a house meant that Shakespeare had had to save his money. The limited evidence that survives suggests that in London he lived frugally. He rented rooms in relatively modest surroundings: records from a minor lawsuit show that in 1604—the year he wrote part or all of

Measure for Measure, All's Well That Ends Well, and *King Lear*—he lived above a French wig-maker's shop on the corner of Mugwell and Silver Streets in Cripplegate, at the northwest corner of the city walls. He seems to have had an affinity for neighborhoods—Shoreditch, Bishopsgate, Cripplegate, and the Clink in Surrey—inhabited by artisans, many of whom were émigrés from France or the Low Countries. These were not disreputable haunts, but they were modest, and the rents were low. How many rooms he rented, or how spacious they were, is unknown, but he seems to have furnished them sparsely. His personal property in London, assessed for tax purposes, was only five pounds. (The property of the most affluent inhabitant of the parish was assessed at three hundred pounds.) Of course, Shakespeare could have hidden things away—books, paintings, plate—to reduce his liability, but the assessors at least saw very few signs of wealth.

Generations of scholars have combed the archives for more details, but the principal records are a succession of notices for the nonpayment of taxes. In 1597, the year Shakespeare bought the handsome New Place, the tax collectors for Bishopsgate ward affirmed that William Shakespeare, assessed the sum of thirteen shillings fourpence on his personal property, had not paid. The next year he was again delinquent, and a further notice, in 1600, when he was living on the Surrey side of the river, suggests that he was still in arrears. He may in the end have paid his taxes—the records are incomplete—but it does not seem likely. Shakespeare was someone who not only lived a modest London life but also hated to let even small sums of money slip through his fingers.

Perhaps he was worrying about the financial security of his wife and daughters back in Stratford, perhaps he hated the example of his father's embarrassments, perhaps he told himself that he would do anything not to end up like the wretched Greene. For whatever the reason, Shakespeare seems to have treated money—his money at least—with considerable seriousness. No one refers to him as a skinflint, but he did not like to waste his substance, and he was clearly determined not to be an easy mark for anyone. In 1604 he was storing more malt in his barn in Stratford than he (or, more to the point, his wife) needed for domestic consumption. He sold twenty bushels of it to a neighboring apothecary, Philip Rogers, who had a sideline brewing ale. Rogers's debt, including another two shillings he borrowed from Shakespeare, amounted to a little over two pounds. When the debtor returned only six shillings, Shakespeare hired a lawyer and took his neighbor to court to recover the remaining thirty-five shillings tenpence and damages. Thirty-five shillings tenpence was not a trivial sum at the time, but neither was it a king's ransom. It took energy to pursue the matter, just as it took energy a few years later when Shakespeare once again went to court to recover the six pounds, plus damages, that he said was owed to him by John Addenbrooke.

Shakespeare was hardly alone in pursuing such small sums; he lived in a litigious age, and the courts were flooded with suits of this kind. But no one forced him to go through the process, made all the more time-consuming by the fact that in some of these cases he probably had to travel to Stratford to do so. No, the odd pounds and shillings and pence must have mattered to him, and not, strictly speaking, because the owner of New Place needed them to live on.

Standing in the graveyard at Elsinore, Hamlet contemplates a skull that the gravedigger has dislodged with his dirty shovel: "This fellow might be in 's time a great buyer of land," he remarks to Horatio,

> with his statutes, his recognizances, his fines, his double vouchers, his recoveries. Is this the fine of his fines and the recovery of his recoveries, to have his fine pate full of fine dirt? Will his vouchers vouch him no more of his purchases, and double ones too, than the length and breadth of a pair of indentures? The very conveyances of his lands will hardly lie in this box; and must th'inheritor himself have no more, ha? (5.1.94–102)

It is altogether fitting that Hamlet should speak with such wry disdain. For on the one hand, he is the prince of Denmark, far above mere moneygrubbing, and on the other hand, as he has made overwhelmingly clear, he is indifferent to all worldly ambition. But where did Prince Hamlet, we might wonder, get his technical knowledge of the property law he despises—recognizances, double vouchers, recoveries, and the like? From someone who had a lively interest in land purchases: the playwright him-self. Is this hypocrisy? Not at all. Shakespeare could imagine what it would feel like to be a melancholy prince and conjure up his brooding laughter at the vanity of human striving, but he himself could not afford to be indifferent to the everyday enterprise of making a living.

At the time he was writing Hamlet's lines about the "great buyer of land," Shakespeare's interest in real estate investments was apparently becoming known to his fellow townsmen, who must, in any event, have been struck by his worldly success. In 1598 Abraham Sturley of Stratford wrote to a friend, then in London, that according to information he had received, "our countryman Mr. Shaksper is willing to disburse some money upon some odd yardland or other at Shottery or near about us." These are Stratford businessmen consulting with each other about the best way to get their "countryman" to invest in some scheme of theirs—the playwright was evidently regarded as both wealthy enough and canny enough to make a careful, coordinated approach to him worthwhile.

In May 1602 Shakespeare paid £320 for four "yardlands"—well over one hundred acres—of arable land in Old Stratford, north of Stratford-upon-Avon. A few months later he acquired title to a quarter-acre parcel, comprising a garden and a cottage, just opposite his garden at New Place. And in July 1605, a year after he took Rogers to court for thirty-five shillings, Shakespeare paid the very substantial sum of £440 for a half interest in a lease of "tithes of corn, grain, blade, and hay" in and around Stratford. The lease—in effect an annuity—brought him £60 per annum. He was planning for his future: the profit from the tithes would continue through his lifetime and into the lives of his heirs.

An investment of this size reflected the exceptionally large income that Shakespeare was earning in the early years of the reign of James I. The suppression of *The Tragedy of Gowrie* could have harmed both Shakespeare's company and his career, but it did not. James displayed a peculiar quality that contemporaries would repeatedly note: he was nerv-ous, sensitive, and on occasion dangerously paranoid, but then unexpect-edly he could ignore or even laugh uproariously at what others—and not only absolute monarchs—could have taken as gross insults. In the case of the premier theater company of his new kingdom, he may simply have regarded the players as too insignificant to care about, for good or ill. Or perhaps he regarded the players as a collective version of the court jester, whom Shakespeare depicts with such wry sympathy in *Twelfth Night*, *King Lear*, and elsewhere: the master can on occasion be annoyed with or even threaten his clown—"Take heed, sirrah; the whip" (*King Lear*, 1.4.94)—but it would be vulgar to get more seriously nettled.

The King's Men were exceptionally busy, both at court and at the Globe, and Shakespeare must have been heavily involved as writer, director, and actor, as well as principal business partner. His workload must have been staggering. He would have had to keep track of the receipts and expenditures; rewrite some of the scenes; help with the casting; decide on cuts; weigh in on interpretive decisions; consult on the properties, costumes, and music; and of course memorize his own parts. We have no idea in how many of the plays he actually appeared in the frenetic 1604–5 season, but it must have been more than a few. In such circumstances, the companies were not large enough to exempt one of its named actors from the stage, even if that particular actor was busy with a dozen other things. His name appears as one of the ten "principal comedians" in a 1598 performance of *Every Man In his Humour*. Presumably, he appeared in this play again at its court revival, and he probably made appearances in at least some of his own plays, many of which, notwithstanding the doubling of parts, require large casts.

Even for actors extraordinarily well trained in the arts of memory—and even for the playwright who wrote the plays—it must have been exhausting to mount so many complex productions in such a short time. But, of course, the invitation to perform before the king and the court was a signal honor, as well as a rich source of income: receiving a handsome £10 per performance, the company made £100 in the Christmas and New Year's season of 1605–6, £90 in that of 1606–7, £130 in 1608–9 and again in 1609–10, and £150 in 1610–11. These are very large sums of money, earned in the short holiday season. Meanwhile, the company continued to perform a full repertoire of plays at the Globe, and they still on many occasions packed their gear and went on tour: Oxford in May and June 1604; Barnstaple and Oxford again in 1605; Oxford, Leicester, Dover, Saffron Walden, Maidstone, and Marlborough in 1606. We do not know if Shakespeare went on all of these trips; by the early fall it was already time for him to think hard about the coming season, when the company would introduce new plays, revive still others, perform again at court, keep their public audience happy at the Globe.

As always, Shakespeare had a special, grim reason to throw himself into a frenzy of work: one morning someone—it could be a lackey in an attic room or a great lady in her curtained bed—would wake up with the telltale buboes in the groin or the armpits. The plague would have announced its return, and in a matter of days or weeks the theaters would be shut down. It must have seemed crucially important to all of the company members always to be putting money in their purses, while there was money to be had. They could not afford to miss any occasion for profit, and, plague permitting, the regime of James I provided many occasions.

Shakespeare and his company had not been forced to choose one venue or another and let the others slip away: they had not been frozen out of the new Scottish-dominated court; they had not alienated their London popular audience; they had not lost touch with the cities and towns where they would perform on tour. On the contrary, they had consolidated their grip on each of these key constituencies and were busily trying to add yet another venue. The plan did not originate with Shakespeare, but it must have become part of his long-term strategy. The strategy was to dominate the market—the market here being the performance of plays to the court and to the public at large, in London and in the provinces—or to come as close to doing so as possible.

During the reign of Elizabeth, in 1596, the entrepreneur James Burbage (the father of the famous actor) paid six hundred pounds for property that had, until the dissolution of the monasteries, been part of a large friary, belonging to the order known as the Friars Preachers or Black Friars. The location was a desirable one: though it was within the city walls, it was a "liberty" and hence outside the jurisdiction of the city fathers. A theater had already been established twenty years earlier in one of the Blackfriars halls, where a succession of children's companies had performed. But this enterprise had collapsed after eight financially troubled years, and the indoor theater had gone silent. The enterprising

Burbage smelled a profit, if he could reopen it for performances by what was then the Lord Chamberlain's Men. He had built the Theater, one of England's first outdoor playhouses; now, by reconstructing the hall where the children's companies had played, he would open England's first indoor playhouse for adult actors. The location was prestigious—not in the suburbs, hard by the bearbaiting arenas and execution grounds, but right in the heart of the city. The Blackfriars hall was much smaller than the Globe, but it had the great advantage, given the vagaries of the English weather, of being roofed and enclosed. It was, at least by comparison with the open amphitheaters, a place of decorum and even luxury. Disorderly crowds would not stand restlessly around the stage; instead, everyone would be seated. Hence admission prices could be greatly increased—from the mere pennies at the Globe to as high as two shillings in Blackfriars—and, as it was possible to illuminate the hall by candlelight, there could be evening as well as afternoon performances.

Everything to do with the theater was a high-risk speculation, but given the popularity of the Lord Chamberlain's Men, the scheme would probably have begun to pay off at once, had it not been for an unexpected complication: the neighbors found out about Burbage's plan and vehemently objected. A petition was signed by thirty-one residents of the precinct, including Shakespeare's printer friend, Richard Field, and the company's own noble patron, the lord chamberlain himself, who happened to live in the same complex of buildings. They argued that the theater would be a traffic nightmare, that it would attract "all manner of vagrant and lewd persons," that the crowds would increase the risk of plague, and, an all-but-irresistible clincher, that the players' drums and trumpets would disrupt services and drown out sermons in nearby churches. The government blocked the reopening of the theater, and James Burbage soon after died. His death was probably not caused, as some have said, by a broken heart—in his late sixties, he had weathered many similar crises, and nothing in his career suggests that he had a sensitive heart. Still, anxiety about the huge investment must have clouded his last days and would certainly have preoccupied his heirs. The hall was rented out for forty pounds per year to the Children of the Chapel Royal—one of the companies of boy actors—so at least there was some income. But it was not until 1608, twelve years after the original investment, that the company, now the King's Men, finally succeeded in performing in the Blackfriars Theater. The fact that they managed to do so, against deep-seated opposition, is a sign of how powerful they had become.

It was James Burbage's son, Richard, who brought his father's plan to fruition. The brilliant actor, who created many of the great Shakespearean roles, proved to be a canny, resourceful, and tenacious businessman as well. Following the model of the Globe Theater, Burbage organized a syndicate to hold and administer the new playhouse. Its seven equal partners each held a one-seventh share in the Blackfriars playhouse for a term of twenty-one years. Shakespeare, already a sharer in the Globe, was one of the partners in the new venture, the culmination of an elaborate entrepreneurial strategy.

The King's Men were firmly established as the court's favorite entertainers; they carried the royal stamp of favor upon them when they traveled; they attracted huge London audiences to their Bankside amphitheater, the Globe; and they would now cater as well to a more exclusive clientele at the Blackfriars, which could accommodate some five hundred higher-paying spectators. Gallants eager to show off their clothes could even pay to sit on the Blackfriars stage and become part of the spectacle. The practice— not permitted at the Globe—must have annoyed the actor in Shakespeare: later in the century a riot broke out during a performance of *Macbeth* when a nobleman slapped an actor who had remonstrated with him for crossing directly in front of the action in order to greet a friend on the other side of the stage. And it must have annoyed the playwright in him as well, since the stage-sitters could conspicuously get up and walk out during the play. But the businessman in Shakespeare must have found the extra profit irresistible.

Somehow, in the midst of this frenzy of activity—the relocation of the Globe; the adjustment to the new Scottish regime; the recruitment of new actors; the rush of court performances; the learning of new roles; the exhausting provincial tours; the harried negotiations over the reopening of Blackfriars; and the hurried trips back to Stratford to see his wife and children, bury his mother, celebrate the marriage of his daughter, purchase real estate, and conduct petty lawsuits—Shakespeare also found the time to write. Small wonder that as early as 1604 he had begun to brood about retirement.

To make retirement a viable option, it was not only a matter of accumulation and investment; the author of *King Lear* had to rethink his relation to the world. To judge from the plays, his mind was fantastically restless—"an extravagant and wheeling stranger," as Othello is described (1.1.137). His imagination swooped from archaic Britain to contemporary Vienna, from ancient Troy to France's Roussillon, from medieval Scotland to Timon's Athens and Coriolanus's Rome. The scene in the sprawling *Antony and Cleopatra* moves back and forth from the queen's palace in Alexandria to Rome, with detours to Sicily, Syria, Athens, Actium, and assorted military camps, battlefields, and monuments. The strange play *Pericles*, which he co-authored with the very minor writer George Wilkins, is even more unmoored, shifting from Antioch to Tyre to Tarsus to Pentapolis (in what is now Libya) to Ephesus to Mytilene (on the island of Lesbos). It is as if, more than anything else, Shakespeare's mind feared—or defied—enclosure.

But the problem posed by retirement was not enclosure. "I could be bounded in a nutshell," Hamlet says, "and count myself a king of infinite space, were it not that I have bad dreams" (2.2.248–50). Shakespeare's bad dream, or so at least *King Lear* suggests, had to do with a loss of power and the threat of dependency posed by age. As his career progressed, he shifted the principal focus of his plays away from ardent young men and women, impatient to get on with their lives, to the older generation. This shift is obvious in *King Lear*, with its tormented old men, but it can also be seen, though more subtly, in the character of Othello, who worries about his age, and in Macbeth, whose vitality ebbs away before our eyes:

> My way of life
> Is fall'n into the sere, the yellow leaf,
> And that which should accompany old age,
> As honour, love, obedience, troops of friends,
> I must not look to have.
>
> (5.3.23–27)

And instead of Romeo and Juliet or Rosalind and Orlando, as Shake-speare's quintessential vision of what it means to be in love, he gives us "grizzled" Antony and his wily Cleopatra, "wrinkled deep in time" (3.13.16, 1.5.29).

It will not do to force the point: Shakespeare's last play, *The Two Noble Kinsmen*, which he probably wrote in 1613–14 with the playwright John Fletcher, fifteen years his junior, is a tragicomic story of young lovers. Another product of this collaboration, the lost *Cardenio* (based on a source in *Don Quixote*), was probably also about the perils and pleasures of youthful passion. But it is striking that *The Two Noble Kinsmen* contains a grotesque description of a very old man, as if Shakespeare were contemplating with a shudder what he feared might lie ahead:

> The agèd cramp
> Had screwed his square foot round,
> That gout had knit his fingers into knots,
> Torturing convulsions from his globy eyes
> Had almost drawn their spheres, that what was life
> In him seemed torture.
>
> (5.2.42–47)

And, more significant, the greatest of these late plays, *The Winter's Tale* and *The Tempest*, both have a distinctly autumnal, retrospective tone. Shakespeare seems to be self-consciously reflecting upon what he has accomplished in his professional life and coming to terms with what it might mean to leave it behind.

From very early in his career, Shakespeare recycled and transformed what he had already tried out, but the ghosts of his past accomplishments haunt the late plays to an exceptional degree. *The Winter's Tale* is a reworking in particular of *Othello*, as if Shakespeare had set himself the task once again of staging a story of male friendship and homicidal jealousy, but this time without any tempter at all. The effect is the most extreme version in his work of the radical excision of motive: there is no reason at all why King Leontes should suspect his beautiful wife, nine months pregnant, of adultery with his best friend; no reason why he should cause the death of his only son, order his newborn daughter to be abandoned, and destroy his own happiness; and there is no reason why he should, after sixteen years, recover the daughter and the wife whom he has believed long dead. The fatal madness comes upon him suddenly and without provocation; and the restoration takes the conspicuously irrational and dangerous form of magic: a statue brought to life.

Where is Shakespeare in this strange story, a story lifted from his old rival Robert Greene? In part, he seems playfully to peer out at us behind the mask of a character he added to Greene's story, the rogue Autolycus, the trickster and peddler and "snapper-up of unconsidered trifles" (4.3.25–26). As a fragment of wry authorial self-representation, Autolycus is the player stripped of the protection of a powerful patron and hence revealed for what he is: a shape-changing vagabond and thief. He embodies the playwright's own sly consciousness of the absurdity of his trade: extracting pennies from the pockets of naive spectators gaping at the old statue trick stolen from a rival. And if the spectacular finale is not simply a trick, akin to a cardsharp's sleight of hand, if the playwright manages to give it an eerie power, then Shakespeare is somewhere else onstage, peering out from behind a different mask—that of the old woman who arranges the whole scene of the statue's coming-to-life. There is something deliberately witchlike about the dead queen's friend Paulina, for there is something potentially illicit about this resurrection, something akin to the black art of necromancy: "those that think it is unlawful business / I am about, let them depart" (5.3.96–97).

A peculiar queasiness comes over the play's end. It is as if not this one play alone but the whole of Shakespeare's enterprise—the bringing of the dead to life, the conjuring up of the passions, the effacement of rational motives, and the exploration of secret places in the soul and in the state—were being called into question. Either it is a fraud, set up to extract money from the gullible, or it is witchcraft. If the audience stays in the theater, it is because of the wonder of the spectacle and because of the reassuring hope, articulated by Leontes, that its causes and effects are simply those of the ordinary world:

> O, she's warm!
> If this be magic, let it be an art
> Lawful as eating.
>
> (5.3.109–11)

And with this, the play moves quickly to its end, running just ahead of the mockery it knows is close behind: "That she is living," says Paulina,

> Were it but told you, should be hooted at
> Like an old tale. But it appears she lives.
>
> (5.3.116–18)

The Winter's Tale hints, for those in the audience listening carefully enough to pick up the suggestion, that Leontes' queen was not dead but that she lived hidden for sixteen years in a house that Paulina has visited "privately twice or thrice a day" (5.2.95). Nothing is made of the hint; it may be there to reassure spectators who might have been otherwise reluctant to applaud necromancy, but it is so brief that it is difficult to see how it could have worked in performance. Perhaps instead it was a personal reassurance, the playwright's tiny superstitious note to himself, as if he were warding off the intimation that what he did was a form of magic.

Shakespeare had revealed this intimation before, in *A Midsummer Night's Dream* and *Macbeth*. Now, at the end of his career, he returned to it, at first playing with it obliquely in *The Winter's Tale* and then finally facing it directly and embracing it. The protagonist of *The Tempest* is a prince and a powerful magician, but he is also unmistakably a great playwright—manipulating characters, contriving to set them up in relation to one another, forging memorable scenes. Indeed, his princely power is precisely the playwright's power to determine the fate of his creations, and his magical power is precisely the playwright's power to alter space and time, create vivid illusions, cast a spell. Shakespeare's plays are rarely overtly self-reflexive: he wrote as if he thought that there were more interesting (or at least more dramatic) things in life to do than write plays. Though from time to time he seems to peer out, somewhere within Richard III or Iago or Autolycus or Paulina, for the most part he keeps himself hidden. But at last in *The Tempest*, he comes if not directly to the surface, then at least so close that his shadowy outline can be discerned.

The Tempest is not, strictly speaking, Shakespeare's last play. Written probably in 1611, it was followed by *All Is True* (now more often called *Henry VIII*), *The Two Noble Kinsmen*, and the lost *Cardenio*. But none of these latter plays is a wholly personal vision; each was written in collaboration with John Fletcher, whom Shakespeare seems to have handpicked as his successor as principal playwright for the King's Men. *The Tempest* is the last play Shakespeare wrote more or less completely on his own—no collaborator and, as far as is known, no direct literary source—and it has the air of a farewell, a valediction to theatrical magic, a retirement.

Though in exile, the magician Prospero has the kind of power that an absolute monarch could never actually possess, the power that only a great artist has over his characters. The power, as Shakespeare represents it, is hard-won—the result of deep learning and of a trauma in the distant past, "the dark backward and abyss of time" (1.2.50). Prospero had been the Duke of Milan, but, absorbed in his occult studies and inattentive to practical affairs, he was overthrown by his usurping brother. Cast adrift and shipwrecked with his daughter on an ocean island, he has used his secret arts to enslave the deformed and brutish Caliban and to take under his command the spirit Ariel. Then, as the play opens, fate and his own magical powers bring onto the island his enemies. His brother and his brother's principal ally, along with their dependents, are in his hands. Audiences accustomed to walking by gibbets on their way to the theater had a very good idea of their likely fate. Prospero does not even have the nominal restraints imposed upon Renaissance rulers by institutions; on the island he rules there are none. If Shakespeare's principal model for the magician's realm is the theater, with its bare stage and its experimental openness—a world where anything is possible—another model invoked by the play is one of the islands encountered by European voyagers to the New World. On such islands, as many contemporary reports made clear, restraint tended to melt away, and, for those in command, anything was possible. With years of isolation to brood on his injuries and plan his revenge, Prospero is free to do with his hated enemies entirely as he chooses.

What he chooses to do—at least by the standards of Renaissance princes and playwrights alike—is next to nothing. For *The Tempest* is a play not about possessing absolute power but about giving it up. Lear also gives up his power, of course, but that renunciation is a disaster. Prospero reclaims what was his by birthright—the dukedom of Milan, that is, his social authority and wealth in an ordinary, familiar world. But he abandons everything that has enabled him to bring his enemies under his control, to force them to submit to his designs, to manipulate them and the world into which he has introduced them. In short, he abandons the secret wisdom that has made him godlike.

> I have bedimmed
> The noontide sun, called forth the mutinous winds,
> And 'twixt the green sea and the azured vault
> Set roaring war—to the dread rattling thunder
> Have I given fire, and rifted Jove's stout oak
> With his own bolt; the strong-based promontory
> Have I made shake, and by the spurs plucked up
> The pine and cedar; graves at my command
> Have waked their sleepers, oped, and let 'em forth
> By my so potent art. But this rough magic
> I here abjure.
>
> (5.1.41–51)

If these words belong not only to Prospero but also to Prospero's creator, if they reflect what Shakespeare felt in contemplating retirement, then they mark a sense both of personal loss and of personal evolution. In *King Lear* retirement had seemed an unmitigated catastrophe; in *The Tempest* it seems a viable and proper action. In both cases, to be sure, the action is understood as an acknowledgment of mortality: Lear says that he will "Unburthened crawl toward death" (1.1.39); Prospero says that when he returns to Milan, "Every third thought shall be my grave" (5.1.315). Although, as his investment in long-term annuities suggests, Shakespeare himself expected that he would live much longer than in fact he did, he was clear-eyed about what lay on the far side of his decision. Yet in *The Tempest*, Prospero's decision to give up his "potent art" and return to the place of his origin is not only or even principally about exhaustion and the anticipation of death. The magician in fact knows that he is at the height of his powers: "My high charms work" (3.3.88). His choice—the breaking of the staff, the drowning of the book "deeper than did ever plummet sound" (5.1.56), and the voyage home—is represented not as weakness but as a moral triumph.

It is a triumph in part because it marks Prospero's decision not to exact vengeance against those who have injured him—"The rarer action is / In virtue than in vengeance" (5.1.27–28)—and in part because something about the power that Prospero wields, though wielded in the name of justice and legitimacy, order and restoration, is dangerous. In what does the power consist? Creating and destroying worlds. Bringing men and women into an experimental space and arousing their passions. Awakening intense anxiety in all the creatures he encounters and forcing them to confront what is hidden within them. Bending people to serve him. Prospero's charms do not work on everyone—his brother Antonio seems singularly unaffected—but for those on whom it does work, it is potentially destructive as well as redemptive. In any case, it is an excess of power, more than an ordinary mortal should have.

The clearest sign of that excess comes in the tremendous speech abjuring his "rough magic." Since the play opens with Prospero arousing an enormous storm, his specific allusion to that particular magical power makes theatrical sense, but he goes on at once to claim and to renounce something else:

> graves at my command
> Have waked their sleepers, oped, and let 'em forth
> By my so potent art.
>
>   (5.1.48–50)

This was for Shakespeare's culture the most feared and dangerous form of magic, the sign of diabolical powers. It is not something Prospero, the benign magus, has actually done in the course of *The Tempest*, nor it is something that his own account of his life would lead us to imagine him doing. But as a description of the work of the playwright, rather than the magician, it is unnervingly accurate. It is not Prospero but Shakespeare who has commanded old Hamlet to burst from the grave and who has brought back to life the unjustly accused Hermione. Shakespeare's business throughout his career had been to awaken the dead.

At the end of *The Tempest*, in an epilogue rare in Shakespeare's work, Prospero steps forward, still in character, but stripped of his magical powers:

> Now my charms are all o'erthrown,
> And what strength I have's mine own,
> Which is most faint.
>
> (lines 1–3)

He has become an ordinary man, and he needs help. He is asking for applause and cheers—the theatrical premise, still tied by a thread to the plot, is that the audience's hands and breath will fill his sails and enable him to return home—but the terms in which he does so are peculiarly intense. The appeal for applause turns into an appeal for prayer:

> Now I want
> Spirits to enforce, art to enchant;
> And my ending is despair
> Unless I be relieved by prayer,
> Which pierces so, that it assaults
> Mercy itself, and frees all faults.
> As you from crimes would pardoned be,
> Let your indulgence set me free.
>
> (lines 13–20)

For Prospero, whose morality and legitimacy are repeatedly insisted upon, this guilt does not make entire sense, but it might have made sense for the playwright who peers out from behind the mask of the prince. What did it mean to do what Shakespeare had done? Why, if he is implicated in the figure of his magician hero, might he feel compelled to plead for indulgence, as if he were asking to be pardoned for a crime he had committed? The whiff of criminality is just a fantasy, of course, but it is a peculiar fantasy, of a piece with the hint of necromancy—"Th'expense of spirit," to use a phrase from the sonnets, "in a waste of shame" (129.1).

Against a background of personal caution, prudential calculation, and parsimoniousness, Shakespeare had built his career on acts of compulsive identification, the achievement of petty thefts coupled with an immense imaginative generosity. Though he had in his own affairs kept himself from the fate of Marlowe or Greene, he had in the playhouse trafficked in reckless passion and in subversive ideas. He had turned everything life had dealt him—painful crises of social standing, sexuality, and religion—into the uses of art and had turned that art into profit. He had managed even to transform his grief and perplexity at the death of his son into an aesthetic resource, the brilliant practice of strategic opacity. Is it surprising that his pride in what he had accomplished—he comes before us not as one of what *A Midsummer Night's Dream* calls "rude mechanicals" (3.2.9) but as prince and a learned magician—was mingled at the end with guilt?

Perhaps too he had slowly wearied of his own popular success or had come to question its worth. He had, as a performer and a playwright, appealed again and again for applause, and he must have been gratified that he generally received it. But if he fully knew who he was—and the figure of the princely magician suggests that Shakespeare understood what it meant to be Shakespeare—then he may have decided that he had had enough. He would finally be able to turn away from the crowd.

To judge from the pattern of Shakespeare's investments, the thought that he would leave the theater someday must have been with him for a long time. And because virtually all of these investments, apart from those in the playhouse, were in and around Stratford, he must have long harbored the dream that he eventually attempted to realize: he would leave London and return home. He had gone back again and again over the years, of course, but this return would be decisively different. He would give up his rented rooms, pack up his belongings, and actually take possession of the fine house and the barns and the arable lands he had purchased. He would pull back from the peddling of fantasies, or, rather, such playwriting as he might continue to do would now become a sideline, as the real estate had once been a sideline. Living with his aging wife and unmarried daughter, Judith; spending time with his beloved daughter Susanna, her husband, John Hall, and his granddaughter, Elizabeth; watching over his property, participating in local quarrels; visiting with old friends, he would be a respected Stratford gentleman, no more nor less.

But the closer he came to making this decision, the more his whole lifework seemed to flood back over him. The central preoccupations of almost all his plays are there in *The Tempest*: the story of brother betraying brother; the corrosive power of envy; the toppling of a legitimate ruler; the dangerous passage from civility to the wilderness; the dream of restoration; the wooing of a beautiful young heiress in ignorance of her social position; the strategy of manipulating people by means of art, especially through the staging of miniature plays-within-plays; the cunning deployment of magical powers; the tension between nature and nurture; the father's pain at giving his daughter to her suitor; the threat of social death and the collapse of identity; the overwhelming, transformative experience of wonder. The startling revelation of this very late play is that nothing of Shakespeare's immense imaginative life was actually lost. There is a famous song in *The Tempest* about the body of a drowned man:

> Full fathom five thy father lies.
>   Of his bones are coral made;
> Those are pearls that were his eyes;
>   Nothing of him that doth fade
> But doth suffer a sea-change
> Into something rich and strange.
>   (1.2.400–405)

The same is true of Shakespeare's poetic imagination: nothing had faded—all that had happened over the decades was that the bones of his works had suffered a sea change into something rich and strange.

How could Shakespeare give all of this up? The answer is that he couldn't, at least not entirely. When he actually left London is not known. He may have moved back to Stratford as early as 1611, just after he finished *The Tempest*, but he did not cut all of his ties. He was no longer over-whelmingly present, but he collaborated with John Fletcher on at least three plays. And in March 1613 he made the last of his real estate invest-ments, not this time in Stratford, but in London. For the large sum of £140 (£80 of which was in cash), he purchased a "dwelling house or tene-ment" built over one of the great gatehouses of the old Blackfriars priory. This was precisely the kind of dwelling that he could have bought, had he wished his wife and children to live with him in London, during the long years of his professional life there. But it was only now that he had returned to Stratford that he decided he wanted to own something in the city. Though his Blackfriars house was in hailing distance of the Blackfri-ars Theater and close too to Puddle Wharf, where boats could take him quickly across the river to the Globe, Shakespeare does not seem to have bought it to live in. He may have arranged to stay there during his trips back to London—to see the plays on which he had collaborated or to conduct business—but he rented it to someone named John Robinson. Still, he owned something in the place where he had wielded his magical powers.

The transaction by which Shakespeare acquired title to the Blackfri-ars property was an odd and very complex one, involving three official co-purchasers who put up no money—it was Shakespeare alone who did so—but who were appointed as trustees. The only plausible explanation that has ever been offered is that the arrangement was an elaborate con-trivance designed to keep his wife, Anne, from having any dower rights to the property should she outlive him. Did Anne know that her husband had set up the purchase in this way, or was it to be an unpleasant surprise, along with the second-best bed? We do not know, but all signs indicate that Shakespeare's return to Stratford, his decision to embrace the ordi-nary, was not an easy one.

At the very beginning of July 1613, only a few months after he com-pleted the expensive Blackfriars purchase, news would have reached Shakespeare of a disaster that must have had a powerful impact upon him: on June 29, during a performance of the new play he had co-authored with Fletcher, the Globe Theater—the structure he himself had helped to build back in the winter of 1599—had burned to the ground.

Here, in a letter written three days after the event, is a version of the account that would have quickly been brought to Stratford:

> The King's players had a new play, called *All is true*, representing some principal pieces of the reign of Henry VIII, which was set forth with many extraordinary circumstances of pomp and majesty, even to the matting of the stage; the Knights of the Order with their Georges and garters, the Guards with their embroidered coats, and the like: sufficient in truth within a while to make greatness very familiar, if not ridiculous. Now, King Henry making a masque at the Cardinal Wolsey's house, and certain chambers [i.e., small cannons] being shot off at his entry, some of the paper, or other stuff, wherewith one of them was stopped, did light on the thatch, where being thought at first an idle smoke, and their eyes more attentive to the show, it kindled inwardly, and ran round like a train, consuming within less than an hour the whole house to the very grounds.
>
> This was the fatal period of that virtuous fabric, wherein yet nothing did perish but wood and straw, and a few forsaken cloaks; only one man had his breeches set on fire, that would perhaps have broiled him, if he had not by the benefit of a provident wit put it out with bottle ale.

No injuries or deaths, then, but a severe financial blow to the sharers in the King's Men and to the "housekeepers" of the playhouse, a blow that fell with particular force upon Shakespeare himself, who was both a sharer and a housekeeper. It could have been much worse: the company's costumes and its jealously guarded playbooks were saved. If these had not been quickly carried out of harm's way, the King's Men might well have been ruined, for the costumes represented a huge investment and many of the playbooks may well have been the sole complete copies. A more rapidly moving fire could have meant that half of Shakespeare's plays—those that had not already appeared in quartos—would never have found their way into print.

Still, it was bad enough. This was a world without disaster insurance, and the cost of rebuilding the playhouse would have to be shouldered by

Shakespeare and the other owners. Even though he was a relatively wealthy man, this was precisely the kind of outlay of capital that Shakespeare, having left London and distanced himself from the daily operation of the King's Men, would not have wished to make, and he may well have decided to get out there and then. As there is no mention in his last will and testament of the valuable shares he held in the playing company and the Globe, he must have liquidated those assets earlier, though the record of the transaction, and hence the precise date, is lost. If, as seems likely, he sold the shares in the wake of the fire, Shakespeare would have made still more decisive his act of retirement.

Near the end of *The Tempest*, Prospero, declaring that "Our revels now are ended," abruptly breaks off the wedding masque he has, through his magical powers, created for his daughter and son-in-law. The actors, he explains,

> were all spirits, and
> Are melted into air, into thin air;
> And like the baseless fabric of this vision,
> The cloud-capped towers, the gorgeous palaces,
> The solemn temples, the great globe itself,
> Yea, all which it inherit, shall dissolve;
> And, like this insubstantial pageant faded,
> Leave not a rack behind.
>
> (4.1.148–56)

In the summer of 1613, these lines must have seemed in retrospect eerily prophetic: the great Globe itself had indeed dissolved. Shakespeare had been haunted all his life by a sense of the insubstantiality of things—it is the almost inescapable burden of the actor's profession—and the fire only made literal what he already knew and what his magician hero had declared:

> We are such stuff
> As dreams are made on, and our little life
> Is rounded with a sleep.
>
> (4.1.56–58)

The building itself, of course, could always be rebuilt—the Globe was up and running again in a year's time—but its fragility was one sign among many that Shakespeare, reaching his fiftieth birthday in 1614, could read in himself and in his world. His brother Gilbert died in 1612, at the age of forty-five; a year later his brother Richard died just shy of his fortieth birthday. Shakespeare's mother, Mary, had brought eight children into the world; only two of them, Will and his younger sister Joan, were still alive. For us, fifty is an age of undiminished vigor, and even then it was hardly ancient, but Shakespeare seems to have thought of himself as well struck in years and may have drawn from his own inner life Prospero's strange remark: "Every third thought shall be my grave."

Perhaps it was precisely this acknowledgment of evanescence that made Shakespeare hold on all the more tenaciously to the very substantial assets he had accumulated in the course of his life. Three wealthy landowners, Arthur Mainwaring, William Replingham, and William Combe, came up with a scheme to enclose substantial acreage near Stratford, including some of the land in which Shakespeare was a titheholder. Enclosure—rationalizing the jumble of small holdings and common fields, concentrating holdings, building fences, taking some of the land out of tillage to allow systematic, profitable sheep grazing—was a popular economic strategy for the very rich, but it was generally hated by those less wealthy. It tended to make grain prices rise, overturn customary rights, reduce employment, take away alms for the poor, and create social unrest. To its credit, the Stratford Corporation vigorously opposed the enclosure scheme. Since Shakespeare's tithes were potentially at risk, he could have been expected to join the opposition, which was led by his cousin Thomas Greene, the town clerk.

A memo Greene jotted down of a conversation held on November 17, 1614, provides a vivid glimpse of the ordinary world, in its grainy detail, in which Shakespeare was fully immersed. He had imagined kings and princes carving up huge territories:

> Of all these bounds, even from this line to this,
> With shadowy forests and with champains riched,

> With plenteous rivers and wide-skirted meads,
> We make thee lady.
>
> > (*King Lear*, 1.1.61–64)

But it was now on a far different scale and for different stakes that he was operating.

> At my cousin Shakespeare, coming yesterday to town, I went to see him how he did. He told me that they assured him they meant to enclose no further than to Gospel Bush and so up straight (leaving out part of the dingles to the field) to the gate in Clopton hedge, and take in Salisbury's piece. And that they mean in April to survey the land and then to give satisfaction, and not before. And he and Mr. Hall say they think there will be nothing done at all.

Seconded by his son-in-law John Hall, Shakespeare told Greene that he was not going to back the corporation in protesting the proposed enclosure; indeed, he thought, or claimed to think, that "there will be nothing done at all." Either Shakespeare was lied to ("they assured him . . .") or he was lying, for less than two months later, in early January, the work began. The encloser Combe, who seems to have been a nasty and pugnacious fellow, ordered a ditch to be dug; there were arguments, harsh words, and blows. Women and children from Stratford and nearby Bishopton organized themselves, went out, and filled in the ditch; and a long court fight began. Shakespeare stayed out of it, indifferent to its outcome perhaps. For already back in October, he had reached an agreement with the enclosers that if his tithe interests were at all compromised, he would have "reasonable satisfaction . . . in yearly rent or a sum of money." He did not stand to lose anything, and he did not choose to join his cousin Greene in a campaign on behalf of others who might be less fortunate. Perhaps, as some have said, Shakespeare believed in modernizing agriculture and thought that in the long run everyone would prosper; more likely, he simply did not care. It is not a terrible story, but it is not uplifting either. It is merely and disagreeably ordinary.

The same can be said perhaps about the difficulties surrounding the marriage of his daughter Judith, the ill-fated twin sister of Hamnet. His elder daughter, Susanna, had wed someone Shakespeare liked, but Judith's proposed match, Thomas Quiney, was designed to make any father of the bride wince. At least he would not have come as a complete surprise. The Shakespeares and the Quineys had been acquainted for many years—as one of the rare surviving letters to the playwright shows, the groom's father had once asked Will for a loan. Young Quiney was twenty-seven years old, a vintner by trade; Judith was thirty-one: not quite the age difference between William and Anne, but enough perhaps to trigger a twinge of uneasiness if Shakespeare had come to feel that a husband should be older than his wife. The initial problem, in any case, was not the age difference; it was a matter of the marriage license. The couple wanted to marry in 1616 during the Lenten season, when weddings were officially prohibited without special permission. Failing to obtain this permission, they were married anyway and then got caught. When Thomas failed to show up on the appointed day at the consistorial court in Worcester, where he would have faced a fine, he was promptly excommunicated. Judith may have shared in this punishment. Shakespeare was hardly a paragon of piety, but he had always been rather careful to avoid trouble—it was a strategy that went back a long way in his life—and this unpleasantness may have upset him.

He was in for something far more upsetting. A month after the wedding between Judith and Thomas, an unmarried Stratford woman named Margaret Wheeler died in childbirth, and her child died with her. Sexual transgressions—"whoredom, fornication, and uncleanness," in the words of the official homily—were routinely investigated and punished in this period, and the death of the unwed mother and child did not close the case. It would in any event have been difficult, in a town the size of Stratford, to keep such secrets for long. On March 26, 1616, the newlywed Thomas Quiney confessed in the vicar's court that he was responsible and was sentenced to a humiliating public penance, which he evaded by donating five shillings to the poor.

Shakespeare may have had very limited physical and psychological strength to deal with the crisis: in less than a month's time, he would be dead. The public disgrace of his son-in-law no doubt came at the worst possible moment for him. Indeed, some biographers have gone so far as to attribute Shakespeare's decline to the shock of Quiney's confession and the public humiliation. This seems highly implausible: Shakespeare was hardly a rigid Victorian moralist. In *The Tempest*, he had Prospero urge strict chastity before marriage, but he had also written *Measure for Measure* and other plays that depict sexual appetite with compassion or wry amusement. For that matter, Anne Hathaway had been pregnant when he stood with her at the altar. Shakespeare may have felt some version of the sentiments of the old shepherd in *The Winter's Tale*—"I would there were no age between ten and three-and-twenty, or that youth would sleep out the rest; for there is nothing in the between but getting wenches with child, wronging the ancientry, stealing, fighting. . . ." (3.3.58–61)—but he is unlikely to have fallen apart at the revelation of his son-in-law's behavior. Still, this was an ugly story, and it was his own daughter, not some imaginary Audrey or Jaquenetta, who must have felt the full force of the humiliation.

Shakespeare had probably been feeling unwell for some months, for already in January, just at the time he must have learned of the proposed wedding, he had called for his attorney, Francis Collins, and asked him to draft his last will and testament. The document, for reasons unknown, was not completed at that time, but on March 25, the day before Thomas Quiney's sentencing in the ecclesiastical court, Collins returned, and Shakespeare finished his will, signing the pages with a very shaky hand. The will was both cursory and sour in relation to his wife, Anne, the recipient of the famous second-best bed. But in relation to his daughter Judith it was much more careful and canny. The great bulk of the estate would go to Susanna and her husband, but Judith would not be excluded entirely. She would be given immediately the reasonably handsome marriage portion of a hundred pounds and could, under highly restrictive conditions, receive more money. Collins, or the clerk who was writing down the words dictated by the dying man, made a telling correction. "I give and bequeath unto my son-in-law," Shakespeare evidently began and then, at the thought of Thomas Quiney, abruptly changed course: "son-in-law" is crossed out and replaced with "daughter Judith." There would, the will stipulates, be another £50 in the marriage portion, but only if Judith renounced her claim to one of the properties she might have expected to inherit. And if she or any children she might bear should still be alive after three years, another £150 would be theirs; if Judith were dead and there were no children, then £100 would go to Susanna's daughter, Elizabeth Hall, and £50 to Shakespeare's surviving sister, Joan. Not a penny then to Judith's husband, Thomas Quiney. Indeed, Judith herself, should she live (as in fact she did), would only get the annual interest from the £150, not the principal, and Quiney could claim the sum only if he came up with the equivalent amount in land. In other words, his daughter Judith was not getting much of her father's wealth, and her husband—not mentioned by name—would not get his hands on any of it.

That is not quite all. Among the numerous small bequests—his sword to Thomas Combe; five pounds to Thomas Russell; money to buy rings for "my fellows" John Heminges, Richard Burbage, and Henry Condell; and so forth—there was a token of remembrance for his younger daughter: Judith was to receive "my broad silver-gilt bowl." But virtually everything else of value—money, New Place, the Blackfriars gatehouse, and "all my barns, stables, orchards, gardens, lands, tenements," etc., etc.—went to Susanna and her husband and to their children and children's children. To the poor of Stratford, this very wealthy man left the modest sum of ten pounds. Nothing for the church; nothing for the local school; no scholarship for a deserving child; no bequest to a worthy servant or apprentice. Beyond the family and a very small circle of friends, there was no extended world of concern. And even within the family, almost everything had contracted to the single line Shakespeare hoped to establish and maintain. Anne and Judith would have understood exactly what it all meant for them.

The contraction of his world helps perhaps to explain how quietly he passed from it. His burial on April 25, 1616, is noted in the Stratford register, but there are no contemporary accounts of his last hours. He was not at all slighted: he was buried, as befitted such an important person, in the chancel of Holy Trinity Church, and already by the 1630s, the painted funerary monument, familiar to innumerable tourists to Stratford, had been erected. But no one at the time thought to record the details of his illness or his passing, or at least no documents doing so have survived. The earliest known account of Shakespeare's death was jotted down in the early 1660s by John Ward, vicar of Stratford from 1662 to 1681. Ward dutifully reminded himself to read the works of Stratford's most famous writer—"Remember to peruse Shakespeare's plays, and be versed in them, that I may not be ignorant in that matter"—and then noted what he had heard about the great man's end: "Shakespeare, Drayton, and Ben Jonson had a merry meeting, and it seems drank too hard, for Shakespeare died of a fever there contracted."

That such a merry meeting could have taken place is not inconceivable: Michael Drayton, an accomplished poet, was from Warwickshire, and perhaps, as some have thought, he and Jonson came to Stratford to celebrate Judith's wedding. But there are certainly no corroborating signs of paternal joy in Judith's marriage, and fevers are not ordinarily contracted from hard drinking. Ward's brief note is probably not to be trusted, any more than is the still briefer comment from the late seventeenth century about Shakespeare's end: "He died a papist." This comment, penned by a chaplain of Corpus Christi College, Oxford, named Richard Davies, is intriguing, given Shakespeare's complex relationship to Catholicism, but, as Davies provides no further evidence, it may only reflect a sense that he had returned at the end of his life to the point from which he had begun.

Even if we strip away the machinations over the enclosures, the probable sense of disappointment in his younger daughter, the disgrace of Thomas Quiney, the sour anger toward his wife; even if we imagine his Stratford life as a sweet idyll—the great poet watching the peaches ripen on the espaliered trees or playing with his granddaughter—it is difficult to escape a sense of constriction and loss. The magician abjures his astonishing, visionary gift; retires to his provincial domain; and submits himself to the crushing, glacial weight of the everyday.

He who had imagined the lives of kings and rebels, Roman emperors and black warriors, he who had fashioned a place for himself in the wild world of the London stage, would embrace ordinariness. Shakespeare would enact a final, fantastic theatrical experiment: the everyday life of a country gentleman, the role he had been slowly constructing for years through the purchase of the coat of arms, the investments, the decision to keep his family in Stratford, the careful maintenance of old social networks. Why would he have done such a thing? In part, perhaps, because of a lingering sense of lack. Shakespeare began his life with questions about his faith, his love, and his social role. He had never found anything equivalent to the faith on which some of his contemporaries had staked their lives. If he himself had once been drawn toward such a commitment, he had turned away from it many years before. To be sure, he had infused his theatrical vision with the vital remnants of that faith, but he never lost sight of the unreality of the stage and never pretended that his literary visions could simply substitute for the beliefs that led someone like Campion to his death. And though he may have had brief glimpses of bliss, he had never found or could never realize the love of which he wrote and dreamed so powerfully. From the perspective of this sense of lack—a skeptical intimation of hollowness in faith and in love—his performance of the role of the ordinary gentleman might be seen as a crucial achievement.

But the embrace of the everyday is surely not only a question of lack and compensation; it is a question of the nature of his whole magnificent imaginative achievement. Throughout his career Shakespeare was fascinated by exotic locations, archaic cultures, and larger-than-life figures, but his imagination was closely bound to the familiar and the intimate. Or rather, he loved to reveal the presence of ordinariness in the midst of the extraordinary. Shakespeare has been criticized from time to time for this quality: pedants have sourly observed that his toga-wearing Romans throw up their hats in the air, as if they are London workmen; critics concerned with decorum have complained that a handkerchief—something you blow your nose in—is too vulgar an object to be mentioned, let alone to serve at the center of a tragedy; and at least one great writer—Tolstoy—thought that an aged Lear who walks about raving wildly was an appropriate object not of awe but of moral revulsion and aesthetic contempt.

It is true: Shakespeare's imagination never soared altogether above the quotidian, never entered the august halls of the metaphysical and shut the door to the everyday. In *Venus and Adonis*, we see the sweat on the face of the goddess of love. In *Romeo and Juliet*, while the grieving parents weep over Juliet's lifeless body, the musicians who have been hired for the wedding quietly joke with each other while they put away their instruments—and then decide to linger for the funeral dinner. In *Antony and Cleopatra*, the same observer who describes sultry Cleopatra on her gorgeous barge also paints a very different picture: "I saw her once / Hop forty paces through the public street" (2.2.234–35).

He made a decision early in his life, or perhaps a decision was made for him: he had something amazing in him, but it would not be the gift of the Demiurge; rather, it would be something that would never altogether lose its local roots. There is a letter that was written by Machiavelli shortly after he had lost his position in Florence and had been forcibly rusticated. He writes with disgust of the vulgar arguments and stupid games he was forced to watch at the local taverns. His only relief came in the evenings, when he could put off the clothes sullied by the banalities of the daylight hours. Dressed in a rich gown, he would take down from his shelves his beloved authors—Cicero, Livy, Tacitus—and feel that at last he had companions fit for his intellect. Nothing could be further from Shakespeare's sensibility. He never showed signs of boredom at the small talk, trivial pursuits, and foolish games of ordinary people. The highest act of his magician Prospero is to give up his magical powers and return to the place from which he had come.

Perhaps Shakespeare was drawn home by something else, a motive that—unlike all the others in his very private life—seems to lie in plain sight. Everyone has noticed the slight in his will to his wife, Anne, along with the slights to his daughter Judith and to her scapegrace of a husband. But that will is also, in its quiet way, a remarkable declaration of love, a declaration that may help to explain what drew him back to Stratford. The woman who most intensely appealed to Shakespeare in his life was twenty years younger than he: his daughter Susanna. It cannot be an accident that three of his last plays—*Pericles*, *The Winter's Tale*, and *The Tempest*—are centered on the father-daughter relationship and are so deeply anxious about incestuous desires. What Shakespeare wanted was only what he could have in the most ordinary and natural way: the pleasure of living near his daughter and her husband and their child. He understood that this pleasure had a strange, slightly melancholy dimension, a joy intimately braided together with renunciation—that is the burden of those last plays. But it is a strangeness that hides within the boundaries of the everyday. And that is where he was determined to end his days.

Bibliographical Notes

■ALL BIOGRAPHICAL STUDIES of Shakespeare necessarily build on the assiduous, sometimes obsessive archival research and speculation of many generations of scholars and writers. The long history of this enterprise is the subject of Samuel Schoenbaum's *Shakespeare's Lives* (New York: Oxford University Press, 1970) and Gary Taylor's *Reinventing Shakespeare: A Cultural History from the Restoration to the Present* (New York: Weidenfeld and Nicolson, 1989). Schoenbaum delights in chronicling the mythmaking extravagances and absurdities of Shakespeare biography, but there is at least as much to admire as to ridicule.

I have profited greatly not only from recent research, which has painstakingly winkled out some intriguing new details about the playwright's life and times, but also from nineteenth- and early-twentieth-century studies. These studies came under fierce attack from C. J. Sisson in 1934 in an influential essay, "The Mythical Sorrows of Shakespeare" (in *Studies in Shakespeare: British Academy Lectures*, ed. Peter Alexander [London: Oxford University Press, 1964], 9–32), but recent scholarship, including Marjorie Garber's *Shakespeare's Ghost Writers: Literature as Uncanny Causality* (New York: Methuen, 1987), Leah Marcus's *Puzzling Shakespeare: Local Reading and Its Discontents* (Berkeley: University of California Press, 1988), and Richard Wilson's *Will Power: Essays on Shakespearean Authority* (Detroit: Wayne State University Press,

1993), has reassessed their significance and usefulness. Foremost among them is J. O. Halliwell-Phillipps's two-volume *Outlines of the Life of Shakespeare*, 10th ed. (London: Longmans, 1898). Also useful and suggestive are Edward Dowden, S*hakspere: A Critical Study of His Mind and Art* (London: Henry King, 1876); Frederick Fleay, *A Chronicle History of the Life and Work of William Shakespeare, Player, Poet, and Playmaker* (London: Nimmo, 1886); Sidney Lee, *A Life of William Shakespeare* (New York: Macmillan, 1898); George Brandes, *William Shakespeare: A Critical Study* (New York: Frederick Unger, 1898); Charles Elton, *William Shakespeare, His Family and Friends* (London: John Murray, 1904); Charlotte Stopes, *Shakespeare's Warwickshire Contemporaries* (Stratford-upon-Avon: Shakespeare Head Press, 1907); and David Masson, *Shakespeare Personally* (London: Smith, Elder, 1914). Edgar Fripp's two-volume *Shakespeare, Man and Artist* (London: Oxford University Press, 1938) is a chaotic treasure trove of valuable information, which I have repeatedly mined.

Among more recent biographies, the most thorough, informative, and steadily thoughtful is Park Honan's *Shakespeare: A Life* (Oxford: Oxford University Press, 1998), which I have frequently consulted. Jonathan Bate's fine collection of essays, *The Genius of Shakespeare* (London: Picador, 1997), contains important biographical insights, as does Katherine Duncan-Jones's *Ungentle Shakespeare: Scenes from His Life* (London: Arden Shakespeare, 2001). Among the other biographical studies upon which I have drawn are Marchette Chute's lively *Shakespeare of London* (New York: Dutton, 1949); M. M. Reese's *Shakespeare: His World and His Work* (London: Edward Arnold, 1953); Stanley Wells's *Shakespeare: A Dramatic Life* (London: Sinclair-Stevenson, 1994); Eric Sams's *The Real Shakespeare: Retrieving the Early Years, 1564–1594* (New Haven: Yale University Press, 1995); I. L. Matus's *Shakespeare, In Fact* (New York: Continuum, 1999); Anthony Holden's *William Shakespeare* (Boston: Little, Brown, 1999); and Michael Wood's *In Search of Shakespeare* (London: BBC, 2003), written to accompany a BBC television series.

Though by definition unreliable and often wildly inaccurate, some of the most searching reflections on Shakespeare's life have come in the form of fiction: *Nothing Like the Sun: A Story of Shakespeare's Love-Life* (London: Heinemann, 1964), by Anthony Burgess, who also wrote a lively straightforward biography (*Shakespeare* [Hammondsworth: Penguin, 1972]); Edward Bond's play *Bingo* (London: Methuen, 1974); Marc Norman and Tom Stoppard's screenplay for the film *Shakespeare in Love* (New York: Hyperion, 1998); and, above all, the brilliant "Scylla and Charybdis" chapter of James Joyce's *Ulysses*.

At the other end of the spectrum from fiction, several important volumes make available the crucial historical documents upon which all Shakespeare biographies are based. These volumes, upon which I have drawn heavily throughout this book, include B. R. Lewis, *The Shakespeare Documents: Facsimiles, Transliterations, and Commentary*, 2 vols. (Stanford: Stanford University Press, 1940); Samuel Schoenbaum, *William Shakespeare: Records and Images* (New York: Oxford University Press, 1981); David Thomas, *Shakespeare in the Public Records* (London: HMSO, 1985); Robert Bearman, *Shakespeare in the Stratford Records* (Phoenix Mill, UK: Alan Sutton, 1994); and, above all, Schoenbaum, *William Shakespeare: A Documentary Life* (New York: Oxford University Press, 1975; also available in a 1977 compact edition).

Equally indispensable is the scholarship of the indefatigable E. K. Chambers: the two-volume *William Shakespeare: A Study of Facts and Problems* (Oxford: Clarendon, 1930), rich in significant details often buried in footnotes, asides, and appendices; the two-volume *Medieval Stage* (London: Oxford University Press, 1903); and the monumental four-volume *Elizabethan Stage* (Oxford: Clarendon, 1923). Geoffrey Bullough's eight-volume *Narrative and Dramatic Sources of Shakespeare* (New York: Columbia University Press, 1957–75) usefully brings together almost all of the known sources of Shakespeare's plays and thereby provides a suggestive guide to Shakespeare's wide and restless reading.

The evidence painstakingly gathered, edited, and appraised in Schoenbaum, Chambers, and Bullough is present throughout every chapter of this book. In the bibliographical notes below, I have listed the other principal sources, both primary and secondary, upon which I have drawn. I have, wherever possible, grouped these sources together by topic, in the order in which the particular topic appears in each chapter, so that readers eager to pursue one or another aspect of Shakespeare and his age can find their way through the immense forest of critical resources.

Convenient orientation to contemporary Shakespeare scholarship can be found in two valuable collections of essays, upon which I have repeatedly drawn: *A Companion to Shakespeare*, ed. David Scott Kastan (Oxford: Blackwell, 1999), and *New History of Early English Drama*, ed. John D. Cox and David Scott Kastan (New York: Columbia University Press, 1997). Many individual essays in these volumes bear on the topics I have treated.

All quotations from Shakespeare's works in *Will in the World* are from *The Norton Shakespeare*, ed. Stephen Greenblatt, Walter Cohen, Jean E. Howard, and Katharine Eisaman Maus (New York: W. W. Norton, 1997). (Citations to *King Lear* are from the conflated text version.) The Oxford edition of Shakespeare's plays, upon which *The Norton Shakespeare* is based, has an extraordinarily detailed *Textual Companion*, ed. Stanley Wells and Gary Taylor, which I have found valuable, as I have the individual volumes of the Arden Shakespeare series.

CHAPTER 1: PRIMAL SCENES

On Shakespeare's schooling, William Baldwin's bulky two-volume *William Shakspere's Small Latine and Lesse Greeke* (Urbana: University of Illinois Press, 1944) is comprehensive but dull and daunting. C. R. Thompson's *School in Tudor England* (Ithaca: Cornell University Press, 1958) is a helpful introduction. Joel Altman's *The Tudor Play of Mind* (Berkeley: University of California Press, 1978) suggestively links school exercises and the writing of plays. Roger Ascham's *The Schoolmaster* (1570), a key Elizabethan educational text in which the teaching of Latin plays a central role, is available in a modern edition, ed. Lawrence Ryan (Ithaca: Cornell University Press, 1967).

On the love of verbal display in Elizabethan culture, a classic work is Rosemond Tuve, *Elizabethan and Metaphysical Imagery* (Chicago: University of Chicago Press, 1947). On the whole scope of literary production in this period, C. S. Lewis's brilliant and opinionated *English Literature in the Sixteenth Century, Excluding Drama* (Oxford: Clarendon, 1954) remains indispensable. Among the immense number of critical studies of Shakespeare's relation to language, Frank Kermode's *Shakespeare's Language* (New York: Farrar, Straus and Giroux, 2000) is an illuminating place to begin.

On the mystery plays, see V. A. Kolve, *The Play Called Corpus Christi* (Stanford: Stanford University Press, 1966); Rosemary Woolf, *The English Mystery Plays* (Berkeley: University of California Press, 1972); and Glynne Wickham, *Early English Stages: 1300 to 1660*, 2nd ed. (New York: Routledge, 1980). Two earlier books, Willard Farnham, *The Medieval Heritage of Elizabethan Tragedy* (Berkeley: University of California Press, 1935), and H. C. Gardiner, *Mysteries' End: An Investigation of the Last Days of the Medieval Religious Stage* (New Haven: Yale University Press, 1946), remain particularly valuable. Bernard Spivack, *Shakespeare and the Allegory of Evil* (New York: Columbia University Press, 1958), and Robert Weimann, *Shakespeare and the Popular Tradition in the Theater: Studies in the Social Dimension of Dramatic Form and Function* (Baltimore:

Johns Hopkins University Press, 1978), are useful guides to the "morality" backgrounds of Shakespeare's plays. Andrew Gurr, "The Authority of the Globe and the Fortune," in *Material London, ca. 1600*, ed. Lena Cowan Orlin (Philadelphia: University of Pennsylvania Press, 2000), 250–67, is illuminating on the magistrate's power to license plays. On seasonal rituals, see C. L. Barber, *Shakespeare's Festive Comedy: A Study of Dramatic Form and Its Relation to Social Custom* (Princeton: Princeton University Press, 1959), and François Laroque, *Shakespeare's Festive World: Elizabethan Seasonal Entertainment and the Professional Stage* (Cambridge: Cambridge University Press, 1993).

Hostility to performances of plays, whether by schoolboys or professionals, is explored in Jonas Barish, *The Antitheatrical Prejudice* (Berkeley: University of California Press, 1981). For a close look at the important traveling company with which Shakespeare may have been associated, see Scott McMillan and Sally-Beth MacLean, *The Queen's Men and Their Plays* (Cambridge: Cambridge University Press, 1998).

The principal accounts of Elizabeth's royal progresses are found in John Nichols, ed., *The Progresses and Public Processions of Queen Elizabeth*, 3 vols. (London, 1823). Robert Langham's letter describing the Kenilworth festivities is available in a modern edition by R. J. P. Kuin, *Robert Langham: A Letter* (Leiden: Brill, 1983).

CHAPTER 2: THE DREAM OF RESTORATION

On Shakespeare's provincial environment, Mark Eccles, *Shakespeare in Warwickshire* (Madison: University of Wisconsin Press, 1961), provides a brief, yet surprisingly rich initiation. C. L. Barber and Richard Wheeler have suggestive psychoanalytic reflections on Shakespeare's relation to his father in *The Whole Journey: Shakespeare's Power of Development* (Berkeley: University of California Press, 1986) and in "Shakespeare in the Rising Middle Class," in *Shakespeare's Personality*, ed. Norman Holland, Sidney Homan, and Bernard Paris (Berkeley: University of California Press, 1989). On the presence of technical vocabularies in Shakespeare, see David Crystal and Ben Crystal, *Shakespeare's Words: A Glossary and Language Companion* (London: Penguin, 2002). On the pattern of loss and recovery in Shakespeare's late plays, see Northrop Frye, *A Natural Perspective: The Development of Shakespearean Comedy and Romance* (New York: Harcourt, Brace and World, 1965).

L. B. Wright's *Middle-Class Culture in Elizabethan England* (Ithaca: Cornell University Press, 1935) is a classic, if contested, guide to Elizabethan social structures, as is Lawrence Stone's *The Crisis of the Aristocracy: 1558–1641* (London: Oxford University Press, 1986). See also Felicity Heal and Clive Holmes, *The Gentry in England and Wales, 1500–1700* (Basingstoke, UK: Macmillan, 1994), and Joyce Youings, *Sixteenth Century England: The Penguin Social History of Britain* (London: Penguin, 1984). On yeomen, the social class from which Shakespeare descended, see Mildred Campbell, *The English Yeoman under Elizabeth and the Early Stuarts* (New Haven: Yale University Press, 1942). On the wool trade, see Peter J. Bowden, *The Wool Trade in Tudor and Stuart England* (London: Macmillan, 1962). On Stratford, see *Minutes and Accounts of the Corporation of Stratford-upon-Avon and Other Records, 1553–1620*, ed. Richard Savage and Edgar Fripp (Dugdale Society, 1921–30), supplemented by a volume of the same title edited by Levi Fox (Dugdale Society, 1990).

Prices and wages in Shakespeare's time are difficult to weigh in relation to the modern world, but for an initial glimpse, see the royal proclamation governing London wages, reprinted in Ann Jennalie Cooke, *The Privileged Playgoers of Shakespeare's London: 1576–1642* (Princeton: Princeton University Press, 1981). E. A. J. Honigmann and Susan Brock produced an edition of wills by Shakespeare and his contemporaries in the London theater, *Playhouse Wills, 1558–1642* (Manchester: Manchester University Press, 1993).

CHAPTER 3: THE GREAT FEAR

On the struggle between Catholics and Protestants in the sixteenth century, see Patrick Collinson, *The Birthpangs of Protestant England* (Houndmills, UK: Macmillan, 1988); Debora Shuger, *Habits of Thought in the English Renaissance* (Berkeley: University of California Press, 1990); and Eamon Duffy, *The Stripping of the Altars: Traditional Religion in England c. 1400–c. 1580* (New Haven: Yale University Press, 1992); all provide useful and usefully different points of orientation.

On the religion of Shakespeare and his family, there continues to be lively debate. Against the claim by Fripp, in *Shakespeare, Man and Artist*, that Shakespeare's father was a Puritan, Peter Milward's *Shakespeare's Religious Background* (London: Sidgwick and Jackson, 1973) summarizes arguments for his Catholicism. That John Shakespeare was a Catholic would seem to be confirmed by his "spiritual last will and testament," but the original is lost and its authenticity has been challenged. There are useful articles by James McManaway, "John Shakespeare's 'Spiritual Testament'" in *Shakespeare Survey* 18 (1967): 197–205, and F. W. Brownlow, "John Shakespeare's Recusancy: New Light on an Old Document," in *Shakespeare Quarterly* 40 (1989): 186–91. The case against authenticity is summarized in J. O. Halliwell-Phillips, *Outlines of the Life of Shakespeare* (1898), 2:399–404 and has been vigorously resumed by Robert Bearman in "John Shakespeare's 'Spiritual Testament': a Reappraisal" in *Shakespeare Survey* 56 (2003): 184–203, but more recent scholarship has cautiously tended to confirm its authenticity.

E. A. J. Honigmann's important *Shakespeare: The Lost Years* (Manchester: Manchester University Press, 1985) focused attention on the young Shakespeare's possible Lancashire connection, which continues to be intensely investigated and debated. Christopher Haigh's *Reformation and Resistance in Tudor Lancashire* (London: Cambridge University Press, 1975) provides a useful account of the religious stuggle in that region. Some of the most tantalizing findings for Shakespeare studies are reported in Richard Wilson's "Shakespeare and the Jesuits," in *The Times Literary Supplement* (December 19, 1997): 11–13, and explored in *Shakespeare and the Culture of Christianity in Early Modern England*, ed. Dennis Taylor and David N. Beauregard (New York: Fordham University Press, 2003). Here too there are dissenting views, including those presented by Robert Bearman in "'Was William Shakespeare William Shakeshafte?' Revisited," *Shakespeare Quarterly* 53 (2002): 83–94. Bearman's arguments are countered by Honigmann in "The Shakespeare/Shakeshafte Question, Continued," *Shakespeare Quarterly* 54 (2003): 83–86. Jeffrey Knapp, in *Shakespeare's Tribe* (Chicago: University of Chicago Press, 2002), strenuously argues that the adult Shakespeare was committed to a broad-based Erasmian Christianity, carefully limited in its central doctrinal tenets, tolerant of the range of beliefs and practices that lay outside those tenets, and steadfastly communitarian. I have also had the benefit of reading in manuscript Wilson's book *Secret Shakespeare: Studies in Theatre, Religion, and Resistance* (Manchester: Manchester University Press, 2004). In Wilson's view, the young Shakespeare was linked in some way to the Jesuits' "terrorist cells" in Lancashire. Though he became wary of fanaticism, Wilson argues, Shakespeare remained a Catholic throughout his life and coded many cryptic Catholic messages in his plays.

On Campion, Richard Simpson's 1867 biography, *Edmund Campion*

(London: Williams and Norgate), remains authoritative; Evelyn Waugh's *Edmund Campion* (Boston: Little, Brown, 1935) is eloquent and highly partisan. See also E. E. Reynolds, *Campion and Parsons: The Jesuit Missions of 1580–1* (London: Sheed and Ward, 1980); Malcolm South, *The Jesuits and the Joint Mission to England during 1580–1581* (Lewiston, NY: Mellen, 1999); and James Holleran, *A Jesuit Challenge: Edmund Campion's Debates at the Tower of London in 1581* (New York: Fordham University Press, 1999).

CHAPTER 4: WOOING, WEDDING, AND REPENTING

On Shakespeare's marriage, the principal source remains J. W. Gray, *Shakespeare's Marriage* (London: Chapman and Hall, 1905). David Cressy's *Birth, Marriage, and Death: Ritual, Religion, and the Life-Cycle in Tudor and Stuart England* (New York: Oxford University Press, 1997) is an illuminating guide to the contemporary conduct of the major life-cycle events. For the demographic estimates, I have relied on E. A. Wrigley and R. S. Schofield, *The Population History of England, 1541–1871* (Cambridge, MA: Harvard University Press, 1981). Anthony Burgess's amusing novel, *Nothing Like the Sun*, is built around the presumption that Anne Whatley of Temple Grafton was a real person, Shakespeare's lost love, rather than the trace of a clerical error.

For the sentimental picture of Shakespeare in the bosom of his family, see the nineteenth-century lithograph, by an unknown artist, reproduced in Schoenbaum, *William Shakespeare: Records and Images*, 199. The idea that sonnet 145 might be an early poem to Anne Hathaway is discussed in Andrew Gurr, "Shakespeare's First Poem: Sonnet 145," *Essays in Criticism* 21 (1971): 221–26.

The second-best bed is interpreted as a "tender remembrance" in Lewis, *The Shakespeare Documents*, 2:491, who cites Joseph Quincy Adams. For a more realistic reading of Shakespeare's last will and testament, see E. A. J. Honigmann, "Shakespeare's Will and Testamentary Traditions," in *Shakespeare and Cultural Traditions: The Selected Proceedings of the International Shakespeare Association World Congress, Tokyo, 1991*, ed. Tetsuo Kishi, Roger Pringle, and Stanley Wells (Newark: University of Delaware, 1994), 127–37. Frank Harris, in *The Man Shakespeare and His Tragic Life-Story* (New York: Michael Kennerley, 1909), depicts a Shakespeare consumed with loathing for his wife; it is from Harris that I take the suggestion that the curse on the person who moves his bones was

Shakespeare's way of keeping his wife from being laid, at her death, by his side. On the late seventeenth-century visitor to the grave who was told that the curse was Shakespeare's last poem, see Chambers, *William Shakespeare*, 2:259.

CHAPTER 5: CROSSING THE BRIDGE

On hunting (and its illegal cousin, poaching), see Edward Berry, *Shakespeare and the Hunt: A Cultural and Social Study* (Cambridge: Cambridge University Press, 2001). Samuel Schoenbaum's irenic view of Thomas Lucy's character is found in *William Shakespeare: A Documentary Life*, 107. There is a suggestive chapter on Somerville in Stopes, *Shakespeare's Warwickshire Contemporaries*. In *Secret Shakespeare* Richard Wilson revives the theory, first advanced by the Victorian critic Richard Simpson, that Somerville was not an isolated lunatic but rather a participant in a serious conspiracy. He did not commit suicide in the Tower, the theory goes, but was murdered by fellow conspirators in order to prevent his revealing incriminating evidence at the moment of his execution. (Why he should have waited until that moment is not readily apparent.) At some point before he wrote *Hamlet* (1600–1601), Shakespeare probably read Luis de Granada's *Of Prayer and Meditation* (1582), but the link to Somerville should not be exaggerated: there was another edition of Luis's work, published in 1599, without the incendiary dedicatory letter by Richard Harris that led Somerville to his fatal resolution.

On touring, the ongoing volumes of the *Records of Early English Drama* (Toronto: University of Toronto Press, 1979–) are invaluable. Peter Greenfield, "Touring," in *New History of Early English Drama*, ed. John D. Cox and David Scott Kastan (New York: Columbia University Press, 1997), 251–68; and Sally-Beth MacLean," The Players on Tour," in *Elizabethan Theatre*, vol. 10, ed. C. E. McGee (Port Credit, Ontario: P. D. Meany, 1988), 55–72, are useful and suggestive. On the possible connection of Shakespeare to the Queen's Men, see McMillan and MacLean, *The Queen's Men and Their Plays*.

For the impression London made upon first-time visitors, the place to begin is William Rye, *England as Seen by Foreigners* (London: John Russell Smith, 1865). See also A. L. Beier and Roger Finlay, eds., *London 1500–1700: The Making of a Metropolis* (London: Longman, 1986); N. L. Williams, *Tudor London Visited* (London: Cassell, 1991); Lawrence Manley, *Literature and Culture in Early Modern London* (Cambridge: Cambridge University Press, 1995);

and David Harris Sacks, "London's Dominion: The Metropolis, the Market Economy, and the State," in *Material London, ca. 1600*, 20–54. The characterization of London as "the Fair that lasts all year" is cited in Sacks.

A crucial primary source for this and the following chapter is John Stow's 1598 *Survey of London*, available in a modern edition, ed. C. L. Kingsford (Oxford: Clarendon, 1971).

On the legal concept of benefit of clergy, see my "What Is the History of Literature?" *Critical Inquiry* 23 (1997): 460–81. On the concept of "moral luck," see Bernard Williams, *Moral Luck: Philosophical Papers, 1973–1980* (Cambridge: Cambridge University Press, 1981).

CHAPTER 6 : LIFE IN THE SUBURBS

Ian Archer has a useful account of "Shakespeare's London," in *A Companion to Shakespeare*, ed. David Scott Kastan (Oxford: Blackwell, 1999), 43–56. On London's "entertainment zone," see Steven Mullaney, *The Place of the Stage: License, Play, and Power in Renaissance England* (Chicago: University of Chicago Press, 1987). On bearbaiting, see S. P. Cerasano, "The Master of the Bears in Art and Enterprise," *Medieval and Renaissance Drama in England* 5 (1991): 195–209; and Jason Scott-Warren, "When Theaters Were Bear-Gardens; or, What's at Stake in the Comedy of Manners," *Shakespeare Quarterly* 54 (2003): 63–82. The contemporary amused by the spectacle of the ape on the pony was the Spanish secretary to the Duke of Najera, who visited Henry VIII in 1544 (cited in Chambers, *Elizabethan Stage*, from whence the Dekker quotation and the account of the Southwark spectacle also come).

A mid-sixteenth-century undertaker kept a gruesome contemporary record of London's "theater of punishments": *The Diary of Henry Machyn, Citizen and Merchant-Taylor of London, from A.D. 1550 to A.D. 1563*, ed. John Gough Nichols (London: Camden Society, 1848). Machyn's diary stops before Shakespeare's birth, but there is no sign in the later sixteenth century of a substantial reduction in the punishments he so assiduously notes.

On the design and operation of the principal London playhouses in Shakespeare's time, see, in addition to Chambers's *Elizabethan Stage*, Herbert Berry, *Shakespeare's Playhouses* (New York: AMS Press, 1987); Andrew Gurr, *The Shakespearean Stage, 1574–1642*, 3rd ed. (Cambridge: Cambridge University Press,

1992); William Ingram, *The Business of Playing: The Beginnings of Adult Professional Theater in Elizabethan London* (Ithaca: Cornell University Press, 1992); and Arthur Kinney, *Shakespeare by Stages* (Oxford: Blackwell, 2003). Many of the finer details of theatrical architecture and finance remain in dispute.

A famous resource for Elizabethan theater studies is the detailed account book kept by the impresario Philip Henslowe. The book, *Henslowe's Diary*, has been edited by R. A. Foakes (2nd ed.; Cambridge: Cambridge University Press, 2002). One problem, even with this remarkably detailed record, is to understand the contemporary significance of the charges and payments. Helpful guidance may be found in Roslyn L. Knutson, *Playing Companies and Commerce in Shakespeare's Time* (Cambridge: Cambridge University Press, 2001); G. E. Bentley, *The Profession of Dramatist in Shakespeare's Time, 1590–1642* (Princeton: Princeton University Press, 1971); and Peter Davison, "Commerce and Patronage: The Lord Chamberlain's Men's Tour of 1597," in *Shakespeare Performed*, ed. Grace Ioppolo (London: Associated University Presses, 2000), 58–59.

The attacks on the stage by Northbrooke and Gosson, along with the ironic dialogue by Florio, are conveniently assembled in Chambers, *Elizabethan Stage*. There is an excellent account of the anxieties of Elizabethan officials in Lacey Baldwin Smith, *Treason in Tudor England: Politics and Paranoia* (Princeton: Princeton University Press, 1986). On the government's attempts to regulate the theater, see Richard Dutton, *Mastering the Revels* (London: Macmillan, 1991), and Janet Clare, *"Art Made Tongue-Tied by Authority": Elizabethan and Jacobean Dramatic Censorship* (New York: St. Martin's, 1990).

All citations of the plays of Christopher Marlowe, with the exception of *2 Tamburlaine*, are from *English Renaissance Drama*, ed. David Bevington, Lars Engle, Katharine Eisaman Maus, and Eric Rasmussen (New York: W. W. Norton, 2002). *2 Tamburlaine* is cited from Christopher Marlowe, *Plays*, ed. David Bevington and Eric Rasmussen (Oxford: Oxford University Press, 1998). The large critical literature on the impact of Marlowe on Shakespeare includes an illuminating article by Nicholas Brooke, "Marlowe as Provocative Agent in Shakespeare's Early Plays," in *Shakespeare Survey* 14 (1961): 34–44.

On Edward Alleyne, see S. P. Cerasano, "Edward Alleyn: 1566-1626," in *Edward Alleyn: Elizabethan Actor, Jacobean Gentleman*, ed. Aileen Reid and Robert Maniura (London: Dulwich Picture Gallery, 1994), 11–31. There is no proof that Edward Alleyne was the first Tamburlaine, but he was famous for the part, and Nashe's reference to him in 1589 as the Roscius of the contemporary players suggests that Alleyne created the role.

On Shakespeare's relation to the printing press, see David Scott Kastan, *Shakespeare and the Book* (Cambridge: Cambridge University Press, 2001), and Peter W. M. Blayney, *The First Folio of Shakespeare*, 2nd ed. (New York: W. W. Norton, 1996). On Shakespeare's reading, in addition to Bullough's eight-volume *Narrative and Dramatic Sources of Shakespeare*, I have found useful Henry Anders, *Shakespeare's Books: A Dissertation on Shakespeare's Reading and the Immediate Sources of His Works* (Berlin: Reimer, 1904); Kenneth Muir, *The Sources of Shakespeare's Plays* (London: Methuen, 1977); Robert S. Miola, *Shakespeare's Reading* (Oxford: Oxford University Press, 2000); and Leonard Barkan, "What Did Shakespeare Read?" in *Cambridge Companion to Shakespeare*, ed. Margareta de Grazia and Stanley Wells (Cambridge: Cambridge University Press, 2001), 31–47.

CHAPTER 7: SHAKESCENE

On the competitive world in which Shakespeare worked, see James Shapiro, *Rival Playwrights: Marlowe, Jonson, Shakespeare* (New York: Columbia University Press, 1991), and James Bednarz, *Shakespeare and the Poets' War* (New York: Columbia University Press, 2001). On the collaborations that coexisted with the rivalries, see Jeffrey Masten, *Textual Intercourse: Collaboration, Authorship, and Sexualities in Renaissance Drama* (Cambridge: Cambridge University Press, 1997), Jonathan Hope, *The Authorship of Shakespeare's Plays: A Socio-Linguistic Study* (Cambridge: Cambridge University Press, 1994), and Brian Vickers, *Shakespeare, Co-Author: A Historical Study of Five Collaborative Plays* (Oxford: Oxford University Press, 2002). It is striking that the five plays to which Vickers devotes his lengthy study—*Titus Andronicus, Timon of Athens, Pericles, Henry VIII*, and *The Two Noble Kinsmen*—are, by a wide consensus, among the weakest to bear Shakespeare's name. The odd effect, then, of the most recent account of collaboration is to reinforce a highly traditional account of Shakespeare's singular creative genius.

Helpful and informative on the way in which Shakespeare and his contemporaries organized and conducted their professional lives are Bentley, *The Profession of Dramatist in Shakespeare's Time, 1590–1642*; Peter Thomson, *Shakespeare's Professional Career* (Cambridge: Cambridge University Press, 1992); Andrew Gurr, *The Shakespearian Playing Companies* (Oxford:

Clarendon, 1996); and Knutson, *Playing Companies and Commerce in Shakespeare's Time*. Though not always reliable, T. W. Baldwin, *The Organization and Personnel of the Shakespearean Company* (Princeton: Princeton University Press, 1927), lays out most of the key information. T. J. King, *Casting Shakespeare's Plays: London Actors and Their Roles, 1590–1642* (Cambridge: Cambridge University Press, 1992); Tiffany Stern, *Rehearsal from Shakespeare to Sheridan* (Oxford: Oxford University Press, 2000); and David Bradley, *From Text to Performance in the Elizabethan Theatre: Preparing the Play for the Stage* (Cambridge: Cambridge University Press, 1992), are illuminating, along with G. E. Bentley, *The Profession of Player in Shakespeare's Time, 1590–1642* (Princeton: Princeton University Press, 1984). In *Shakespeare as Literary Dramatist* (Cambridge: Cambridge University Press, 2003), Lukas Erne argues that Shakespeare was more interested than scholars have usually recognized in the printed as well as the performance aspect of his plays.

On Shakespeare as performer, see Meredith Skura, *Shakespeare the Actor and the Purposes of Playing* (Chicago: University of Chicago Press, 1993). David Wiles, *Shakespeare's Clown: Actor and Text in the Elizabethan Playhouse* (Cambridge: Cambridge University Press, 1987), and David Mann, *The Elizabethan Player: Contemporary Stage Representation* (London: Routledge, 1991), are useful, as is Jean Howard, *The Stage and Social Struggle in Early Modern England* (London: Routledge, 1994).

Shakespeare's extraordinary talent was not ignored by his contemporaries and rivals. For some of their responses, see E. A. J. Honigmann, *Shakespeare's Impact on His Contemporaries* (London: Macmillan, 1982), and the two-volume *Shakspere Allusion-Book: A Collection of Allusions to Shakspere from 1591 to 1700*, ed. John Munro (London: Oxford University Press, 1932). Emrys Jones, *The Origins of Shakespeare* (Oxford: Clarendon, 1977), is illuminating on the first flowering of this talent.

Marlowe's strange and violent life has been the subject of many biographies, including Charles Nicholl's engagingly speculative *The Reckoning: The Murder of Christopher Marlowe* (London: Jonathan Cape, 1992), Constance Kuriyama's *Christoper Marlowe: A Renaissance Life* (Ithaca: Cornell University Press, 2002), and David Riggs, *The World of Christopher Marlowe* (London: Faber, 2004). *Greene's Groatsworth of Wit, Bought with a Million of Repentance* (1592) is available in an informative edition by D. Allen Carroll (Binghamton: Center for Medieval and Early Renaissance Studies, 1994).

CHAPTER 8: MASTER-MISTRESS

On Southampton's claim to be the fair young man of the sonnets, see, especially, G. P. V. Akrigg, *Shakespeare and the Earl of Southampton* (Cambridge, MA: Harvard University Press, 1968). On the career of the possible go-between, see Frances Yates, *John Florio: The Life of an Italian in Shakespeare's England* (Cambridge: Cambridge University Press, 1934).

Joel Fineman, who had little or no interest in Shakespeare's biography, has, in my view, written the most psychologically acute study of the sonnets, *Shakespeare's Perjured Eye* (Berkeley: University of California Press, 1986). The editions of the sonnets by Stephen Booth (New Haven: Yale University Press, 1977), Katherine Duncan-Jones (Arden Shakespeare, 1997), and Colin Burrow (Oxford Shakespeare, 2002) each provide abundant commentaries, as does Helen Vendler's *The Art of Shakespeare's Sonnets* (Cambridge, MA: Harvard University Press, 1997); and Duncan-Jones rehearses in detail the competing identifications of the principal figures in the sequence. In *Shakespeare and the Goddess of Complete Being* (London: Faber and Faber, 1992), Ted Hughes has brilliant pages on *Venus and Adonis*, which he views as the key to unlocking Shakespeare's whole poetic achievement. Leeds Barroll's *Politics, Plague, and Shakespeare's Theater: The Stuart Years* (Ithaca: Cornell University Press, 1991) describes the circumstances that led to the periodic closing of the theaters on public health grounds. In "Elizabethan Protest, Plague, and Plays: Rereading the 'Documents of Control,'" *English Literary Renaissance* 26 (1996): 17–45, Barbara Freedman argues against the view that plague closures were always enforced.

The homoeroticism of Shakespeare's sonnet sequence was registered with shock at least as early as the eighteenth century, when the editor George Steevens remarked, "It is impossible to read [it] without an equal mixture of disgust and indignation." On the complex erotic environment in which Shakespeare lived, worked, and (presumably) loved, see Stephen Orgel, *Impersonations: The Performance of Gender in Shakespeare's England* (Cambridge: Cambridge University Press, 1996); Alan Bray, *Homosexuality in Renaissance England*, 2nd ed. (New York: Columbia University Press, 1995); and Bruce R. Smith, *Homosexual Desire in Shakespeare's England: A Cultural Poetics* (Chicago: University of Chicago Press, 1991), as well as his *Shakespeare and Masculinity* (New York: Oxford University Press, 2000). Eve Kosofsky Sedgwick's chapter on the sonnets in her book *Between Men: English Literature and Male Homosocial Desire* (New York: Columbia University Press, 1985) is also extremely interesting.

CHAPTER 9: LAUGHER AT THE SCAFFOLD

In *Shakespeare and the Jews* (New York: Columbia University Press, 1996), James Shapiro argues that there was a significant, if clandestine, Jewish community in London in Shakespeare's time. Though this claim is debatable, Shapiro provides ample evidence for a widespread Elizabethan and Jacobean interest in Jews. See also David S. Katz, *The Jews in the History of England, 1485–1850* (New York: Oxford University Press, 1994), and Laura H. Yungblut, *Strangers Settled Here Amongst Us: Policies, Perceptions, and the Presence of Aliens in Elizabethan England* (London: Routledge, 1996).

In " 'There Is a World Elsewhere': William Shakespeare, Businessman," in *Images of Shakespeare: Proceedings of the Third Congress of the International Shakespeare Association, 1986*, ed. Werner Habich, D. J. Palmer, and Roger Pringle (Newark: University of Delaware Press, 1988), 40–46, E. A. J. Honigmann analyzes Shakespeare's own involvement in moneylending and other mercantile enterprises, as does William Ingram, "The Economics of Playing," in *A Companion to Shakespeare*, ed. David Scott Kastan (Oxford: Blackwell, 1999) 313–27.

On the single surviving manuscript play that may contain scenes in Shakespeare's handwriting, see Scott McMillin, *The Elizabethan Theatre and "The Book of Sir Thomas More"* (Ithaca: Cornell University Press, 1987), and T. H. Howard-Hill, ed., *Shakespeare and* Sir Thomas More: *Essays on the Play and Its Shakespearian Interest* (Cambridge: Cambridge University Press, 1989). The dating of *Sir Thomas More* and of Shakespeare's own participation in the project is uncertain. The script may have been drafted by Anthony Munday and others in 1592–93 or 1595, at the time of the agitation against "strangers"; Shakespeare could have been involved from the beginning or could, as seems more likely, have made his additions as late as 1603 or 1604 during a further attempt to have it approved for performance.

Direct evidence of Shakespeare's personal involvement with the community of "strangers" living in London dates from the early seventeenth century. In 1604, and probably for some time before, he was living in rented rooms on the corner of Mugwell and Silver Streets. His neighbors in the tenement were Christopher Mountjoy, a French Protestant, and his wife, Marie. Mountjoy had fled to England in the wake of the St. Bartholomew's Day massacre in 1572 and had prospered as a manufacturer of ladies' wigs and other headgear. In 1612 Shakespeare was deposed as a witness in a lawsuit between Mountjoy and his son-in-law Stephen Belott. The latter claimed that his father-in-law had pledged to give him sixty pounds on marrying and to leave him a legacy of two hundred pounds. Both parties to the suit agreed that in 1604 Shakespeare had helped, at the parents' request, to persuade the young man to marry Mountjoy's daughter and therefore knew the terms that had to be agreed upon. In his testimony Shakespeare spoke well both of the Mountjoys and of Belott, whom he had known, he said, "for the space of ten years or thereabouts," but he declared under oath that he did not remember the precise financial terms of the marriage settlement. The documents from the lawsuit were unearthed in 1909; there is a good account of them in Samuel Scheonbaum's *Records and Images* and in Park Honan's *Shakespeare: A Life.*

CHAPTER 10: SPEAKING WITH THE DEAD

For the development of the Shakespearean soliloquy, see Wolfgang Clemen, *Shakespeare's Soliloquies*, trans. C. S. Stokes (London: Methuen, 1987). On Shakespeare's working and reworking of *Hamlet* and other plays, see John Jones, *Shakespeare at Work* (Oxford: Clarendon, 1995). On the impact on Shakespeare of the death of Hamnet, see the sensitive psychoanalytic account by Richard P. Wheeler, "Death in the Family: The Loss of a Son and the Rise of Shakespearean Comedy," in *Shakespeare Quarterly* 51 (2000): 127–53. In *Hamlet in Purgatory* (Princeton: Princeton University Press, 2001), I have written at length on the consequences for Shakespeare of the change in the relationship between the living and the dead. See also Roland M. Frye, *The Renaissance Hamlet: Issues and Responses in 1600* (Princeton: Princeton University Press, 1984). On the larger historical, cultural, and theological issues, see Theo Brown, *The Fate of the Dead: A Study of Folk-Eschatology in the West Country after the Reformation* (Ipswich, UK: D. S. Brewer, 1979); Clare Gittings, *Death, Burial, and the Individual in Early Modern England* (London: Croom Helm, 1984); Julian Litten, *The English Way of Death: The Common Funeral since 1450* (London: R. Hale, 1991); Cressy, *Birth, Marriage, and Death;* and Duffy, *The Stripping of the Altars.*

CHAPTER 11: BEWITCHING THE KING

Alvin Kernan's *Shakespeare, the King's Playwright: Theater in the Stuart Court, 1603–1613* (New Haven: Yale University Press, 1995) discusses Shakespeare's relation to James.

On the relation of *Macbeth* to the Gunpowder Plot, see Henry Paul, *The Royal Play of Macbeth* (New York: Macmillan, 1950), and Garry Wills, *Witches and Jesuits: Shakesepare's Macbeth* (New York: Oxford University Press, 1995). On the Gowrie conspiracy, see Louis Barbé, *The Tragedy of Gowrie House* (London: Alexander Gardner, 1887). Kramer and Sprenger's *Malleus maleficarum* is available in an English translation and edition (1928; repr., New York: Dover, 1971) by Montague Summers, who also edited Reginald Scot's *Discoverie of Witchcraft* (1930; repr., New York: Dover, 1972). Keith Thomas, *Religion and the Decline of Magic* (London: Weidenfeld and Nicolson, 1971), and Stuart Clark, *Thinking with Demons: The Idea of Witchcraft in Early Modern Europe* (Oxford: Clarendon, 1997), are particularly helpful on the place of the occult in the mentality of the period. In "Shakespeare Bewitched," in *New Historical Literary Study: Essays on Reproducing Texts, Representing History*, ed. Jeffrey N. Cox and Larry J. Reynolds (Princeton: Princeton University Press, 1993), 108–35, I discuss at greater length Shakespeare's relation to witch hunting.

CHAPTER 12: THE TRIUMPH OF THE EVERYDAY

Bernard Beckerman, *Shakespeare at the Globe* (New York: Macmillan, 1962), and Irwin Smith, *Shakespeare's Blackfriars Playhouse: Its History and Its Design* (New York: New York Universitiy Press, 1964), are both extremely useful introductions to Shakespeare's principal theaters in the latter part of his career. On staging, Alan Dessen and Leslie Thomson's *A Dictionary of Stage Directions in English Drama, 1580–1642* (Cambridge: Cambridge University Press, 1999) is illuminating, as is Dessen's *Elizabethan Stage Conventions and Modern Interpreters* (Cambridge: Cambridge University Press, 1984). The account of the burning of the Globe, from a letter, dated July 2, 1613, written by Sir Henry Wotton to his nephew Sir Edmund Bacon, is cited in Chambers, *Elizabethan Stage*, 4:419–20.

Index